LIFE CRISES AND EXPERIENCES OF LOSS IN ADULTHOOD

LIFE CRISES AND EXPERIENCES OF LOSS IN ADULTHOOD

Edited by

Leo Montada
Sigrun-Heide Filipp
University of Trier
Melvin J. Lerner
University of Waterloo, Canada

Routledge
Taylor & Francis Group
LONDON AND NEW YORK

First published 1992 by Routledge

Published 2013 by Routledge
2 Park Square, Milton Park, Abingdon, Oxfordshire OX14 4RN
711 Third Avenue, New York, NY 10017

First issued in paperback 2016

Routledge is an imprint of the Taylor & Francis Group, an informa business

Library of Congress Cataloging-in-Publication Data

Life crises and experiences of loss in adulthood / Leo Montada, Sigrun
-Heide Filipp & Melvin J. Lerner (eds.).
p. cm.
Based on a conference held at the University of Trier in July 1989.
Includes bibliographical references and index.
ISBN 0-8058-1001-3
1. Life change events—Congresses. 2. Loss (Psychology)-
-Congresses. 3. Stress (Psychology)—Congresses. 4. Adjustment (Psychology)—Congresses. I. Montada, Leo. II. Filipp, Sigrun
-Heide. III. Lerner, Melvin J., 1929– .
[DNLM: 1. Adaptation, Psychological—congresses. 2. Bereavement-
-congresses. 3. Life Change Events—congresses. 4. Stress, Psychological—congresses. WM 172 L721 1989]
RC455.4.L53L52 1992
155.9'3—dc20
DNLM/DLC
for Library of Congress 91-38257
CIP

ISBN 13 : 978-1-1389-9541-3 (pbk)
ISBN 13 : 978-0-8058-1001-1 (hbk)

Contents

Part IV Developmental Perspectives on Coping with Loss

Part V Searching for Protective Factors

Contributors

Nancy E. Adler, Center for Social and Behavioral Sciences, University of California, 1350 Seventh Avenue, San Francisco, CA 94143

Tracy L. Bennett Herbert, Dept. of Psychology, University of California, Los Angeles, 1283 Franz Hall, CA 90024

Hans Werner Bierhoff, Fachbereich Psychologie, Philipps-Universität Marburg, Gutenbergstr. 18, D-3550 Marburg/Lahn

Jochen Brandtstädter, Fachbereich I Psychologie, Universität Trier, Postfach 3825, D-5500 Trier

Bram P. Buunk, Psychologisch Instituut Heymans, Social and Organisational Psychology, University of Groningen, Grote Kruisstraat 2/1, 9712 Groningen, The Netherlands

David A. Chiriboga, Dept. of Graduate Studies, School of Allied Health Sciences, The University of Texas Medical Branch, Galveston, TX 77550

Rebecca L. Collins, Dept. of Psychology, University of British Columbia, 2136 West Mall, Vancouver V6T 1Y7, British Columbia, Canada

Robyn M. Dawes, Dept. of Social and Decision Sciences, College of Humanities and Social Sciences, Carnegie Mellon University, Pittsburgh, PA 15213

Richard A. Dienstbier, Dept. of Psychology, University of Nebraska, 209 Burnett Hall, Lincoln, NE 68588

Christine Dunkel-Schetter, Dept. of Psychology, University of California, 1283 Franz Hall, Los Angeles, CA 90024

Seymour Epstein, Dept. of Psychology, University of Massachusetts at Amherst, Tobin Hall, Amherst, MA 01003

Sigrun-Heide Filipp, Fachbereich I Psychologie, Universität Trier, Postfach 3825, D-5500 Trier

Friedrich Försterling, Fakultät für Psychologie und Sportwissenschaft, Universität Bielefeld, Postfach 8640, D-4800 Bielefeld 1

Michael Frese, Fachbereich 06 Psychologie, Justus-Liebig Universität Gießen, Otto-Behaghel-Str. 10, D-6300 Gießen

Dieter Frey, Institut für Psychologie, Christian-Albrechts-Universität Kiel, Olshausenstr. 40/60, D-2300 Kiel

Monique A.M. Gignac, Dept. of Psychology, University of Waterloo, Ontario, Canada N2L 3G1

Sharon Holleran, Psychological Clinic, University of Kansas, 315 Fraser Hall, Lawrence, KS 66045

Lori M. Irving, Psychological Clinic, University of Kansas, 315 Fraser Hall, Lawrence, KS 66045

Barbara Krahé, Institut für Psychologie, Freie Universität Berlin, Habelschwerdter Allee 45, D-1000 Berlin 33

Anja Leppin, Institut für Psychologie, Freie Universität Berlin, Habelschwerdter Allee 45, D-1000 Berlin 33

Melvin J. Lerner, Dept. of Psychology, University of Waterloo, Ontario, Canada N2L 3G1

John Lydon, Dept. of Psychology, McGill University, 1205 Dr. Penfield Avenue, Montreal, Quebec, Canada H3A 1B1

Dale T. Miller, Dept. of Psychology, Princeton University, Green Hall, Princeton, NJ 08544

Suzanne M. Miller, Dept. of Psychology, Temple University, Philadelphia, PA 19122

Leo Montada, Fachbereich I Psychologie, Universität Trier, Postfach 3825, D-5500 Trier

Geoffrey M. Reed, Dept. of Psychiatry and Biobehavioral Sciences, 760 Westwood Plaza, Los Angeles, CA 90024

Gerolf Renner, Fachbereich I Psychologie, Universität Trier, Postfach 3825, D-5500 Trier

Ralf Schwarzer, Institut für Psychologie, Freie Universität Berlin, Habelschwerdter Allee 45, D-1000 Berlin 33

Kelly G. Shaver, Dept. of Psychology, College of William and Mary, Williamsburg, VA 23185

Sandra T. Sigmon, Psychological Clinic, University of Kansas, 315 Fraser Hall, Lawrence, KS 66045

Roxane C. Silver, Dept. of Psychology, University of California, 1283 Franz Hall, Los Angeles, CA 90402

Charles R. Snyder, Psychological Clinic, University of Kansas, 315 Fraser Hall, Lawrence, KS 66045

Darryl G. Somers, Dept. of Communications, Government of Canada, Ottawa, Ontario, Canada K1T 0C8

Margaret S. Stroebe, Psychologisches Institut, Universität Tübingen, Friedrichstr. 21, D-7400 Tübingen 1

Wolfgang Stroebe, Psychologisches Institut, Universität Tübingen, Friedrichstr. 21, D-7400 Tübingen 1

Shelley E. Taylor, Dept. of Psychology, University of California, 1283 Franz Hall, Los Angeles, CA 90024

William Turnbull, Dept. of Psychology, Simon Fraser University, Burnaby, B.C., Canada V5A 1S6

Thomas Ashby Wills, Ferkauf Graduate School of Psychology and Albert Einstein College of Medicine, Yeshiva University, 1300 Morris Park Avenue, Bronx, NY 10461

Philip G. Weiler, Dept. of Community Health, University of California, Davis, CA

Camille B. Wortman, Institute for Social Research, Survey Research Center, University of Michigan, 426 Thompson Street, Ann Arbor, MI 48106

Barbara W.K. Yee, Dept. of Graduate Studies, School of Allied Health Sciences, The University of Texas Medical Branch, Galveston, TX 77550

Mark P. Zanna, Dept. of Psychology, University of Waterloo, Ontario N2L 3G1, Canada

Preface: Perspectives on the Experience of Loss

This volume is a result of a conference at the University of Trier, Germany, in July 1989. The goals of the conference were (a) to provide an overview of recent advances in research on critical life events and losses associated with them, (b) to stimulate new approaches to the analysis of these events, and (c) to compare the psychology of victims' experiences of stress and losses with the psychology of observers' reactions to those victims. Papers presented were thoroughly discussed by a panel that represented a good deal of expertise in this field of research. The volume is organized into six interrelated parts. It ends with some methodological comments.

PART I
THE IMPACT OF SPECIFIC LIFE CRISES AND LOSS EXPERIENCES

In the first part, the focus is on the various and individually varying kinds of impact which specific stressful experiences and losses have on those who are confronted with them.

Wolfgang and Margaret Stroebe deal with the impact of ***bereavement.*** They provide an overview of theoretical and research literature, revealing a shift from focusing on the risks of morbidity and mortality by bereavement to the risks for psychological health. They first discuss theories of grief and, subsequently, develop their own model, the "deficit model of partner loss" which covers not only the role of the relationship to the deceased, but also the role of situational demands and individual coping resources. Covering many classical issues in research, their own longitudinal study, the Tübingen Study, enables the authors to distinguish vulnerability factors (e.g., emotional instability) and recovery factors (e.g., social support, internal control beliefs). While losing the partner by death certainly bears the risk of impaired psychological and somatic health, the recovery for most bereaved is substantial within the period of one to two years. The authors also identify predictors of high levels of long-term depression following bereavement, in particular low internal control belief and the fact of having experienced a sudden, unpredictable death which confirms their fears of living in an uncontrollable world.

Based on the rich results of her longitudinal study with ***cancer*** patients, ***Sigrun-Heide Filipp*** warns against creating *psychological myths* by premature generalizations from empirical evidence, in particular with regard to the role of time in coping with threat. The three data sets selected give evidence that stage models of coping with losses are to be questioned, that temporal consistencies in coping behaviors are impressively high and that the psychological impact of cancer proves to be rather independent of the patient's age. In addition, the study clearly shows the *limitations of illusions and of positive thinking* in coping with a life-threatening disease: Increases in hopelessness were found to be a definite function of the temporal distance from death, thus contradicting the notion of acceptance and resolution in the terminally ill.

In summarizing the results from three studies examining the ***recovery from severe accidents, Dieter Frey*** points to the importance of *causal attributions, control beliefs*, and *perceptions of injustice*. Patients who perceived their accident as unavoidable, who did not ask "Why me?", who did not blame themselves, and who had a sense of control over the process of recovery, proved to recuperate at a faster rate (as indicated by time spent in the hospital and time passed until work was resumed). Since longitudinal data were available, some cause-effect relationships could be identified: To withdraw from asking the "Why me?" question was found to antecede recovery. In addition, the author was able to cross-validate these findings in studies with HIV-patients, patients with CHD as well as with recently bereaved widowers.

Nancy Adler's chapter deals with the *societal myths* about the psychological and emotional consequences of ***abortion***: Her conclusion is that abortion, in general, is not a traumatic event. Rather, it frequently helps to reduce stress associated with the crisis of an unwanted pregnancy. Nevertheless, *guilt, grief, and other negative emotions* can be observed in some women as an aftermath of abortion. Results from several studies were used to describe the *risk factors* of this group, e.g., self-blame for having become pregnant, marital status, social pressure before and after the decision to have an abortion, and reasons for terminating the pregnancy.

Michael Frese deals with the impact of ***unemployment*** and ***work stress***, questioning the frequently assumed efficacy of positive illusions and other ways of coping with crisis and stress. Based on data from several studies, he corroborates his thesis that *positive illusions* might be *functional only in a short-time perspective* if, in the long run, they are likely to be destroyed by reality. Hope to find employment that proves to be illusionary might be worse than "*realistic pessimism.*" His studies suggest that a sour grapes theory will not help to overcome the psychological stress at work, nor will blunting and other strategies of emotional coping effectively overcome it. It might, therefore, be considered a myth that adverse features of reality can be ignored or compensated for over time by wishful thinking or other coping mechanisms.

David Chiriboga, Barbara Yee, and Philip Weiler deal with the stress of caring. This chapter could have been placed in Part VI, too, where social reactions to victims are focused. It was placed in Part I, however, since its focus is on stress responses and ways of coping with the stress among those caring for a parent suffering from Alzheimer's Disease. ***Providing care for a dependent parent*** may indeed mean high levels of stress and various losses. In the study reported, various criteria of well-being, the perceived stress associated with caregiving, and the amount of care provided were predicted from various data sets, e.g., from parent variables (including their functional capacities), from attributes of the caregiver, the availability of social support, from further concomitant stressful experiences and daily hassles. The table of results is extensive giving evidence of large differences between respondents with respect to how they cope with the stress of caring. The authors' findings suggest that an accumulation of stress in various domains of life will frequently be detrimental to health and well-being. Therefore, the *situational context of caregiving* should be investigated carefully same as the *specific demands posed on caregivers* by their dependent parent. In addition, retrospective reports about the parent (e.g., as demanding, upset, responsible, kind, happy, pleasant) also proved to be related to the caregiver's level of distress as well as to specific affective states (anxiety, depression, guilt); overall this clearly suggests that the quality of parent-child transactions prior to the disease influences adult children's attempts to cope with the stress of caring.

PART II
THE IMPACT OF VIEWS ABOUT RESPONSIBILITIES AND AVOIDABILITY

The chapters of the second part focus on the impact of views about causation, responsibility, avoidability, and justice, views - that proved to be extremely important for how victims experience, appraise, and deal with their lot.

Friedrich Försterling discusses research on ***attribution*** at the interface of basic and applied science. When people face stress and loss, their answers to the question "Why?" are considered to be important. Reactions to critical life events are mediated by causal attributions drawn from informations or beliefs about the covariation between possible causes and the effects to be explained (i.e., the events). These attributions can be more or less veridical, often biased and they may provide self-enhancing motives. Försterling asks whether the *degree of veridicality* *in victims' attributions* might influence observers' evaluations of these victims. He reports findings supporting the view that victims who attribute more veridically are also judged more positively. In addition, he advises that researchers consider the veridicality dimension also when studying the effects of attributions on victims' well-being and adjustment. In a second part of his chapter, Försterling points out that in basic laboratory experiments on attribution information is typically delivered to the subjects in an incomplete way, and that "biases" as, for instance, the "fundamental attribution error" are due to this incompleteness. Based on own findings he argues that by providing a complete table of informations according to Kelley's dimensions "consensus," "consistency," and "distinctiveness," major errors and biases that are frequently reported in research on attribution can easily be eluded. Thus, when observing *biased attributions*, made by both the victims and the observers, one usually does not explore the body of informations on which they are based. In any case, Försterling's work could give important hints to anybody who attempts to change attributions.

Leo Montada concentrates on the role of ***responsibility attributions*** and ***perceived injustice*** in dealing with losses by distinguishing between the *victim perspective* and the *observer perspective*. For victims, perceiving injustice is assumed to be an additional risk factor interferring with adjustment and recuperation. In few studies so far victims' perceptions of injustice have been explicitly assessed. Indirect evidence is found in studies suggesting that events which are perceived as uncontrollable and nonnormative views that are associated with perceived injustice are particularly risky. Indirect evidence is also found in studies on coping: Some coping strategies, such as downward comparisons and search for meaning, do yield positive effects since they allow for reducing feelings of unjust victimization. Positive *functions of "self-blame"* may be explained similarily, i.e., in avoiding subjective injustice which is implied in blaming others. However, self-blame may have both positive and negative effects on adjustment, mediated by the *various emotional reactions* that are *compatible with self-responsibility*, such as anger about an avoidable mistake, guilt because of a fault, hope to be able to avoid a similar loss in the future, and a lack of outrage against others. Hypotheses on the different effects of self-blame are corroborated in a study with paraplegic accident victims. Moreover, *perceived injustice* proved to be a *powerful negative predictor of adjustment*. From the observer perspective, attribution of responsibility to the victim is, instead, generally functional: It is associated with feelings of one's own invulnerability, perceptions of control and optimism, as well as with a lack of doubts about whether the world is a just place. These hypotheses, too, are supported by empirical data. A further set of findings suggests that attributing responsibility to victims interferes with prosocial emotions, such as sympathy and the readiness to support the victims. Taking some responsibility for the disadvantages of others will, instead, dispose subjects to prosocial commitments towards them.

Kelly Shaver starts his discussion with the impact of ***attributions of responsibility and blame*** on victims' stress experiences. He criticizes the undifferentiated use of the concept of "blame" in the literature—"blame" being used both for *attributions of causality, or of responsibility, or of blameworthiness* which definitely have different meanings. He voices doubts about the assumption that self-blame should generally have proadaptive functions and he argues that in most cases self-blame as well as being blamed by others will add to the stress imposed on victims. Therefore, he developed a "*blame inoculation program*" in order to enable victims to better avoid or manage the stress resulting from self-blame or from being blamed by others. This training program focuses on a clarification of the concepts of causality, responsibility, and blame, and aims at the insight that responsiblity and blameworthiness should be applied only to intentional actions which cannot be justified by adequate reasons.

Dale Miller and William Turnbull apply a ***judgmental heuristic approach*** to issues of ***observing and experiencing victimization***: They raise the question of how available are *counterfactual thoughts* about the possibility of another and better outcome. This is very important both for victims and observers. According to their analysis, the answer may depend on *knowledge about the mutability of the course of events and victims' actions* that led to the bad outcome. For instance, conscious decisions made by the victim to change the usual or planned course of his or her actions or thinking of the ease with which the actual sequence of events or actions could have been altered by the victim, make counterfactual thoughts of a better outcome highly available. On the other hand, to act according to duties and obligations as well and to perceive a high probability of being confronted with a similar threat in the future, will reduce the probability of counterfactual thinking. Based on experimental studies, the authors argue that the intensity of observers' and victims' affective responses to victimization depends on the fact how easily another course of events can be imagined, whereas the quality of affective responses (pity, resentment, guilt, helplessness) also depends on the content of imaginable alternatives. Moreover, the studies revealed *characteristical differences between victims and observers* in their affective responses to imagined alternative courses of events. It seems to be most important to keep in mind that affective responses represent appraisals of reality which frequently are viewed in contrast to imagined alternative realities that might have been.

PART III
WAYS OF DEALING WITH CRISES AND LOSS

The third part is devoted to the analysis of specific ways to deal with losses: downward comparison, upward affiliation, holding positive illusions, blunting or monitoring in the face of threat, and "reality negotiations."

Tom Wills' chapter, the first one in this part thoroughly reviews basic theory and research on the role of ***similarity in downward comparisons*** in coping with stress. According to Festinger, comparisons with similar others are aimed at gaining information about the self. In cases of distress, however, self-enhancement often is the primary goal which may be easiest achieved by comparing oneself to even more unfortunate others. This is supported by various experimental studies showing that subjects who experience fear, threat, feelings of incompetence, the ascription of negative traits, and so on, tend to compare themselves with others who are less well off. This assumption is further supported by results from field studies with subjects suffering various kinds of physical illness and stigmatization. The major part of Wills' chapter is devoted to the advancement of a more differentiated model of *the role of similarity in social comparisons*. Addressing the question, whether comparisons with others who suffer a worse fate regularly prove to be self-enhancing, or whether they may be embarrassing, instead, if these others are in fact similar to oneself, Wills distinguishes *four relevant dimensions of similarity*: similarity in fate, similarity in future, similarity in personality, and similarity in perceived causes of distress and disorder. His proposed hypotheses about main and interaction effects of these similarity types require future basic as well as applied research, yet they offer useful heuristics to enrich the repertoire for interpreting empirical findings.

Shelley Taylor, Bram Buunk, Rebecca Collins, and ***Geoffrey Reed*** analyze the various functions of social comparisons prevalent among people experiencing crises, threats, or losses. They suggest that people tend to engage in downward ***social comparisons*** whereas they seek upward ***social affiliations***. The guiding hypothesis is that *downward comparisons serve self-enhancing purposes* and the regulation of negative emotions, whereas *upward contacts meet divergent needs*, e.g., to gain useful information about how to overcome threat and to gain hope and inspiration. The authors review several of their own studies with cancer and AIDS patients and with people experiencing marital problems. Their findings prove that people in the face of threat do indeed tend to upwardly affiliate, but prefer downward comparisons. When asked for the affective consequences of downward as well as upward comparisons, subjects reported more frequently positive emotions, e.g., feeling happy and pleased, as a result of both upward and downward comparisons. Negative affect was less frequent under both conditions but more frequent for downward comparisons. Results are discussed with regard to the theory of downward comparison and its limitations in predicting an overall beneficial effect. Instead, engaging in social comparisons under threat is seen as a double-edged sword.

Melvin Lerner and ***Darryl Somers*** report a complex study on employees expecting a ***loss of job*** by plant closure. The study was designed to explore the prevalence of control beliefs, beliefs to get another job, beliefs about the severity of the situation, and further *possibly illusionary beliefs*. In accordance with evidence from other studies the authors found that the majority of respondents had a good morale and rated their own situation more favorably than the one of comparable others. *Effects of these beliefs on well-being, on the way of coping* (emotion-focused versus problem-focused), *and on job seeking activities were explored*. Moreover, expert-rated employability as a measure of objective employability was assessed so that illusionary beliefs could be distinguished from realistic ones. The effects of positive beliefs proved to be neither general across subjects nor across criteria nor stable over two points in time. Instead, *complex interactions were observed*, objective employability moderating the effect of positive beliefs on the level of job-seeking activities. Whether illusions have to be seen as functional or dysfunctional seems to depend on the criteria used, the temporal distance from threat, and the individual's abilities and resources. Sometimes, positive thinking represents a resource in terms of engaging in adequate reality-based activities, sometimes it may interfere with such activities. The authors' findings are a strong argument for having a closer look on factors that moderate the effect of positive illusions.

Suzanne Miller advances her concept of ***blunting versus monitoring*** as a personal disposition to either tune into or tune out of threats. She asks when and for whom cognitive avoidance will have favorable effects and when and for whom the opposite might be true. She reviews empirical findings on the differences between monitors and bluntors with respect to the best method to prepare them for diagnostic or surgical procedures, with respect to side-effects of medication, and with respect to number and variety of reported symptoms. Monitors tune into threats, they seek information about them, they need relaxation in order to endure them, they pay attention to all symptoms, and they seem to suffer more symptoms and side-effects. The main part of the chapter is reserved to a discussion of several forms of anxiety disorders—generalized anxiety, panic disorder, agoraphobia, obsessive-compulsive disorder, posttraumatic stress disorder—the symptomatology of which suggests that the monitoring processes have gone awry. It is, however, not suggested that blunting would generally be a better strategy or a protective personality factor. Blunting is, for instance, not the best "choice" in situations when a prolonged attention to symptoms is important. Since *the functional value of blunting or monitoring depends on the particular case*, flexibility in the use of avoidant and attentional strategies is considered a goal in educating patients.

Charles Snyder, Lori Irving, Sandra Sigmon, and Sharon Holleran outline ways of motivated or biased ***"reality negotiations"*** starting from a self-theory with the components of ***linkage to and valence of outcomes***. Various strategies aimed at protecting or fostering a positive self-image are derived from their model: lessening the linkage to negative outcomes (using one of several forms of excuses), minimizing their negative valence, increasing the linkage to positive outcomes, or minimizing positiveness of outcomes one is not linked to. The model is applicable to people who have a negative self-image which is maintained or even worsened by opposite strategies of reality negotiations: decreasing the linkage to positive outcomes, decreasing positiveness of outcomes to which one is not linked to, and so forth. The model is very useful to understand a wide variety of phenomena in the study of experiences with loss.

PART IV
DEVELOPMENTAL PERSPECTIVES ON COPING WITH LOSS

In the fourth part modes of coping with developmental decline are the central issue.

Jochen Brandtstädter and Gerolf Renner deal with the puzzling phenomenon that elderly people in the face uncontrollable events and irreversible losses (which are not compensated by comparable gains) will not necessarily become and stay depressed. The authors argue that current models of depression such as the learned helplessness theory cannot explain how people recover from depression after a permanent loss. The authors differentiate between two styles of coping with such experiences: ***tenacious goal pursuit*** representing the tendency to pursue goals in the face of obstacles and high risks of failure, and ***flexible goal adjustment*** representing the tendency to disengage easily from commitments to accommodate one's goals and evaluative standards. In a large cross-sequential study on changes in subjective developmental perspectives and control orientations during adulthood including five age cohorts an age-related increase in flexible goal adjustment and decrease in tenacious goal pursuit were revealed. The positive relationship between subjective developmental deficits and depression proved to be buffered by the level of flexible goal adjustment. The authors conclude that such a coping strategy contributes to a positive life perspective in the face of irreversible losses which are typical for the later phases of life.

Melvin Lerner's ***and Monique Gignac***'s chapter is dealing with the issue of ***why elderly people maintain high levels of contentment and self-esteem when facing adversities***. They advance the thesis that elderly people may learn to take various perspectives toward their losses. This process is reconstructed in analogy to the development of social role taking and introduced as ***self-role taking*** which allows people to recognize how their views about their experiences determine their own emotional reactions. In doing so, they gain better control over their emotional lives and their experiences allowing them more freedom to choose the perspectives that do express their personal identity best. This, in turn, will help them to integrate these experiences into their knowledge of their whole lives and their value orientations without distorting or denying the adversive nature of theses experiences. In an *interview study*, two groups of elderly people were identified, who were similar with respect to well-being, health status, and their life situations, but who differed with respect to the ways they dealt with adverse experiences: one group of people who had acquired a self-reflective perspective taking allowing them to take a relativistic position in terms of tolerating differences between people, and a second group characterized by a more defensive strategy of coping with threat, i.e., by engaging more often in avoidance of, resistance toward and denial of adverse events. The interview transcripts that were obtained from these elderly people nicely illustrate the distinctive features of self-role taking.

PART V
PERSONAL RESOURCES AND RECOVERY FROM LOSS

The search for *personal resources* and *protective factors* is represented in Part V, comprising the *physiological level* with the concept of toughness, the *personality level* with the concept of constructive thinking, the *social level* with the concept of interpersonal trust and trustworthiness, and the various notions of social support. The part is introduced by a chapter discussing the shortcomings of traditional models which focus exclusively on risk factors in dealing with life crises.

Camille Wortman and ***Roxane Silver*** start their chapter with an overview of their current research program on how people cope with irrevocable ***losses due to*** serious ***physical injuries***, or the ***death of a spouse or a child***. According to the empirical findings presented, the authors argue that irrevocable losses, in general, are neither powerfully predicting mental or physical health problems nor are they usually experienced as devastating as traditional beliefs of laymen and professionals might suggest. This, for example, is also proven by the prevalence of positive emotions following losses which is rapidly growing as time since the loss event increases. The authors are tracing some theoretical ideas frequently presented in studies on loss events: the helplessness model, stage models of grief and loss, and the stress and coping model. They claim not to find adequate explanations for an individual's *positive development* in these theories, and they argue that a theory of helplessness and depression is less needed than a model of how victims overcome these states. Stage models are considered useful for the description of the course of coping with adversity, yet not for explaining *victims' adaption and recovery*. In addition, some of the more specific predictions derived from stage models proved not to fit the data, e.g., a lack of immediate grief does not predict later problems, but, instead, long-term adjustment. To adhere to the stage model may even have detrimental effects if, for instance, health providers expect that people must go through a period of distress and push victims into such a reaction. The authors give a prospect of their future work in which they intend to investigate *protective factors* against devastation and health problems. In particular, they will focus on *the role of world views* that might possibly account for differences between victims experiencing the same kind of loss. They argue convincingly that prospective longitudinal designs are needed to identify cause-effect relationships as well as antecedents of initial adjustment which cannot be discovered in studies that are started after the loss event happened.

Richard Dienstbier's chapter is the only one written from a psychobiological perspective. The concepts of ***toughness and toughening up*** are explained and applied to the issue of coping and adjustment to stress, crisis, and loss. Two arousal systems are distinguished, the peripheral "SNS-adrenal-medullary-system" regulating the release of peripheral catecholamines, and the "pituitary-adrenal-cortical-system" stimulating the release of cortisol. The author's main theses are that the first system is working with less side-effects than the second one, that it can be trained or toughened (e.g., by aerobic training and other challenging efforts and experiences), and that toughened individuals are better equipped to meet stressors. *On the physiological level*, tough organisms show a reduced pituitary-adrenal-cortisol response to stress situations, their arousal declines faster upon the end of stress, and facing continuous strain or threat, sufficient catecholamine levels are maintained for longer periods enabling them to deal with the challenges or threats. *On the personality and performance level*, tough individuals are emotionally more stable, have less psychosomatic symptoms, higher levels of ego strength, lower levels of neuroticism, they reach better scores in achievement tests, and so forth. The neurophysiology of these effects is explained in detail, and the arguments are thoroughly founded by empirical findings. Implications of the theory for dealing with life crises and losses and their impact on to health are outlined in detail, as well: Tough individuals should be able to appraise more situations as challenging rather than threatening. In the face of loss, tough individuals should sustain less depletion of central catecholamine and have a lower increase in cortisol. The suppression of the *immune system* by high cortisol levels and the depletion of central catecholamine is an explanation for the fact that toughening reduces the probability of health problems caused by stress. Finally, life-event research is reviewed under the perspective of this theory, yielding explanations for the observation that not every major change in life does increase the probability of illness as was originally hypothesized by Holmes and Rahe. Rather, since positive events are challenging, they may even contribute to toughness same as all the daily hassles do that people are able to manage.

Seymour Epstein developed the concept of ***constructive thinking*** out of his cognitive-experiential self-theory, and he outlines the structure of a *Constructive Thinking Inventory* comprised of scales to assess emotional coping, behavioral coping, categorical thinking, superstitious thinking, naive optimism, esoterical thinking, and a global scale to measure constructive thinking. He presents *results from four studies* with nonclinical samples in which the relationship between constructive thinking and mental and physical well-being was examined. Good constructive thinkers are reported to experience less stress and to be able to carry a heavier productive load, while poor constructive thinkers are reported to react to a laboratory stress situation with a greater increase in negative thoughts and affect arousal and physiological arousal. Epstein's findings allow the conclusion that poor constructive thinking has the status of a trait variable that promotes negative thinking in general and about potential stressors, thus resulting in negative affect and heightened arousal. Of special interest are hints to see convergent validity in relation to other frequently used measures that are considered to reflect *protective factors* (Seligman's ASQ, Rutter's E-A-scales, Kobasa & Maddi's hardiness scale, and Sarason's SSQ).

Hans Werner Bierhoff discusses ***trust and trustworthiness*** as potentially protecting factors in coping with adverse life events. The effects of trust on coping with stress are hypothesized within a heuristic model which is structured in analogy to Kobasa's hardiness model. He starts with a review of conceptualizations and research on trust aimed at identifying its precursors as well as situational and personal conditions. Thereafter, *effects of trust* are evidenced: social disclosure, social support, cooperation, and veridical communication. Distinctions are made between trust as a generalized expectancy and the trustworthiness of specific persons. Assessment scales for these constructs, their psychometric qualities, and validity correlates are reported. The impact of trust and trustworthiness attributions on self-disclosure, approaching others for help and advice, on compliance with the advice of professionals, and on the tendency to drop out of the therapy, is demonstrated by referring to own and other authors' results. Attributes of professional and nonprofessional helpers as well as of the communication between clients and helpers that evoke trust are outlined and strategies to gain trustworthiness are discussed. Finally, Bierhoff advances the *role of trust in social systems* pointing to the reciprocity of attributed trustworthiness and to self-disclosure making trust an essential feature of close relationships.

PART VI
UNDERSTANDING SOCIAL RESPONSES TO VICTIMS

The four chapters of Part VI analyze social responses to victims both supportive ones and negative ones such as derogation and blame. The chapters by Ralf Schwarzer and Anja Leppin and by John Lydon and Mark Zanna both deal with social support. The first one focusing on the effects, the second one on conditions of granting social support. The chapters by Barbara Krahé and by Tracy Bennett Herbert and Christine Dunkel-Schetter are dealing with explanations of negative social reactions.

Ralf Schwarzer and ***Anja Leppin*** review the conceptualizations and empirical evidence on ***the effects of social support***. They propose a model entailing the components of social integration (social network structure, relational content), "cognitive" social support (expected availability of support and its evaluation), "behavioral" social support (mobilization, receipt, and evaluation) and relate these components to personality variables (self-esteem and social competence), stress appraisal, and coping behavior in order to predict mental health with the aspects of well-being and negative affect as indicators of mental health.

In a *meta-analysis of seventy studies on the support-depression relationship* they reveal a large variation in correlation coefficients from substantially negative ($r = -.66$) to moderately positive ones ($r = +.39$). The overall rated average ($r = -.22$) may be interpreted as the protective effect of social support. Detailed comparisons revealed that social support has a stronger negative impact on depression than social integration, and that "cognitive" social support has a greater impact than "behavioral" social support. The authors discuss *methodological caveats* why cause-effect interpretations of these relationships might be premature, why the effects of social support might be underestimated, and why the analysis of more complex interactions (as suggested by the model) will be needed in further research.

Typically, social support is expected from and provided by people in close relationship to the victims. ***John Lydon*** and ***Mark Zanna*** explore the conditions of granting support. They derive hypotheses from the ***psychology of commitment***—arguing that commitment is validly evidenced only ***in cases of adversity***—as well as from dissonance theory stating that behavior which is inconsistent with one's self-concept is arousing or even aversive. From various experiments with student samples the authors report that *value relevance and adversity interact in predicting commitments* to a variety of personal projects, i.e., in cases of high adversity, the strength of a commitment depends on the value relevance. The causal direction of this relationship was explored in a longitudinal study with students doing volunteer work with various groups of people needing support. The results impressively corroborated the hypothesis that, in cases of high value relevance, commitments became stronger with growing adversity (stress, costs, or strain). Applying the theory of commitment to granting of social support to needy members in close relationships, several *implications of the theory* are discussed: the experience of guilt or shame, respectively, the need for justification, in cases of lacking commitment, and the vulnerability and grief of highly committed caregivers in cases of failing attempts to support. Finally, commitment is distinguished from control in that it creates meaning and value, sometimes despite a lack of control.

Barbara Krahé's chapter deals with ***reactions to rape victims***, especially the negative attitudes and stereotypical beliefs about rape that frequently imply a secondary victimization after the primary one. The focus of her chapter is on factors that influence people's attributions of responsibility to victims of rape. The author offers a brief review of the relevant literature followed by a report of own studies that reveal the importance of "rape myth acceptance" in shaping observers' reactions. However, rape myth acceptance proved to interact with victims' prerape behavior (role-conforming versus role-discrepant): People with high rape myth acceptance tend to attribute the more responsibility to the victim (and less to the assailant), the more role-discrepant her prerape behavior was. In a second study, police officers' conceptions of the prototypical rape situation (as contrasted to dubious situations and false rape complaints) were identified revealing the subjective definitions of rape they held. These probably influence the credibility police officers attribute to the victim's report about having been raped. The chapter thus offers important information on preconditions of negative social reactions toward rape victims.

Tracy Bennett Herbert and Christine Dunkel-Schetter give a rich overview of ***negative social reactions to victims*** and the circumstances under which they are likely to be observed. They compiled *evidence from various research traditions* including research on victims (e.g., rape victims, cancer patients, bereaved persons), research on social reactions toward depressed people, the interdisciplinary social support literature, and the social psychology of helping behavior. After having distinguished negative reactions and ineffective attempts of support, they propose six categories of negative social reactions: rude or insensitive remarks, negative effective reactions, negative evaluations, victim blame and derogation, physical avoidance and rejection, and discrimination. Illustrative examples for all six categories are provided from several lines of research. Special attention is given to inconsistencies in social reactions by referring to mixed positive and negative reactions, to alterations between support and absence of support and to a combination of effective and ineffective attempts of support. Such inconsistencies are likely to be observed in family members or intimates, and might be highly irritating to people in distress.

Turning to the *determinants of negative social reactions*, factors of the victim as well as the social network members are outlined. Two kinds of victim factors are identified by empirical research: victim's level of distress or depression and victim's poor coping behavior. As factors of social network members the need for control and the need to preserve a belief in a just world were identified as disposing to negative reactions toward victims which, in turn, may be mediated by particular causal attributions for the event. Feelings of helplessness and frustration vis à vis victims were also suggested as possible dispositions to avoid contact. In this respect it is also of interest to have a look on the dimensions of events which may be associated with differential emotional arousal.

METHODOLOGICAL COMMENTS

The volume ends with some ***methodological quandaries*** that ***Robyn Dawes*** advances by pointing to the fact that the effects of any particular factor are ususally studied within but one population and within one single context, both characterized by many specific features which are as a rule not observed or might even be unobservable. *Any generalization of the results from one population or context to another is highly risky*. The strength of the observed effects will depend highly on the heterogeneity of populations and contexts which are systematically included in the studies. It will also highly depend on controlling for other factors that are able to produce the effects under study or to interfere with them. Therefore, statistics of effect strength have to be put in relation to the sampling of subjects, occasions, and contexts. Since the goal of research frequently is to make cross-situational generalizations, the sampling of contexts and populations is recommended as a strategy of research. This strategy alone will allow to discover interaction effects in addition to main effects across contexts. Dawes's comments contain a warning against a premature explanation of lacking main effects by speculatively assuming interaction effects which must be of a cross nature in that case (not merely enhancing or diminishing main effects). To assume moderator effects—how plausible they might be—has to be proven empirically by reliable evidence. It will be up to the reader to qualify the empirical evidence reported in this volume in the light of Robyn Dawes' quandaries.

ACKNOWLEDGMENTS

The conference, on which this volume is based, was supported by a grant from Volkswagen Foundation (Hannover, Germany). The editors wish to express their thankfulness to the Foundation.

Katharina Schmidt read all chapters carefully for errors, omissions, and discrepancies and worked on the subject index together with Sigrid Kühberger and Herbert Fliege; Marie-France Haupt typed the manuscript and worked on the author index; Dieter Ferring and Thomas Klauer managed to layout the camera-ready version of the book. The editors highly appreciate their help.

Leo Montada, University of Trier, Germany
Sigrun-Heide Filipp, University of Trier, Germany
Melvin J. Lerner, University of Waterloo, Ontario, Canada

I The Impact of Specific Life Crises and Loss Experiences

1 Bereavement and Health: Processes of Adjusting to the Loss of a Partner

Wolfgang Stroebe
Margaret S. Stroebe
University of Tübingen

THE HEALTH CONSEQUENCES OF BEREAVEMENT

To underline the severity of loss experiences, scientific publications on the Health Consequences of Bereavement (e.g., McCrae & Costa, 1988) frequently point out that loss of a spouse is listed as the most stressful life event on the Social Readjustment Rating Scale of Holmes and Rahe (1967). However, the study of the health consequences of bereavement has a much longer history. The first scientific treatment of bereavement was probably published in 1621 by Robert Burton, whose Anatomy of Melancholy relies on evidence from poetic accounts and from physicians' reports to argue that bereavement leads to depression, physical illness, suicide, and even death from natural causes. That Burton's view about the deleterious nature of bereavement was shared by the medical science of his day can be seen from the fact that "griefe" was made responsible for ten deaths in one of the early death statistics of London for the year 1657 (Dr. Heberden's Bill, cited in Parkes, 1986).

Two centuries later, the first Surgeon General of the United States, Benjamin Rush (1835), described the results of autopsies of individuals who had died of grief as clearly showing that there had been heart congestion and inflammation, accompanied by rupturing of the auricles and ventricles. Rupture of the heart is, of course, a rare condition, but when it does occur it is usually caused by coronary thrombosis. Thus, these early physicians may not have been as far from the truth as it seems.

The first evidence of a significant health deterioration following bereavement which could still be accepted by today's scientific standards has been provided by

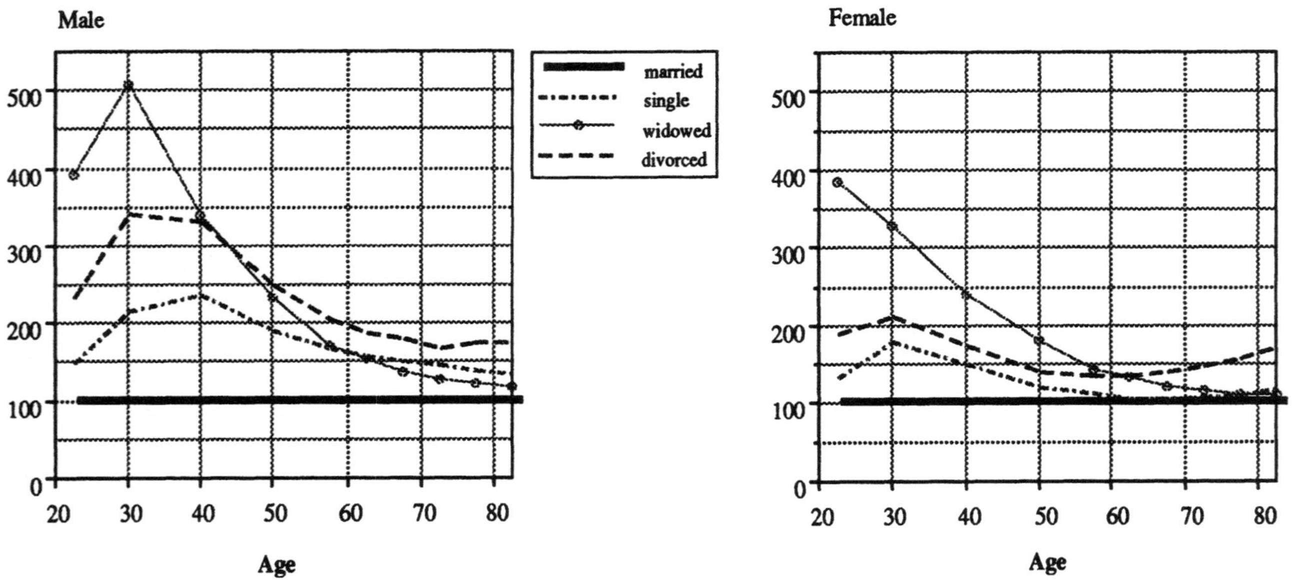

FIG. 1.1. Age-specific death rates for each marital-sex class as percentages of death rates for unmarried persons of corresponding sex and age; United States 3-year average, 1949-1951 (from Shurtleff, 1956).

the British epidemiologist William Farr in 1858, more than forty years before Durkheim's famous monograph on suicide. Farr, who compared the mortality of the bereaved to that of married individuals of the same sex and age, concluded that the "single individual is more likely to be wrecked on his voyage than the lives joined together in matrimony." But, he went on, "if the single suffer greatly from disease and high death risk, the have-been married suffer still more" (Farr, 1975, p. 440).

Farr's analysis of the relationship between bereavement and mortality marks the beginning of systematic empirical investigation in this area that today has grown into a substantial body of evidence. The pattern of marital status differences in mortality found by Farr over a century ago has been replicated in many studies (e.g., Kraus & Lilienfeld, 1959; Shurtleff, 1955). Apart from the higher mortality rate of

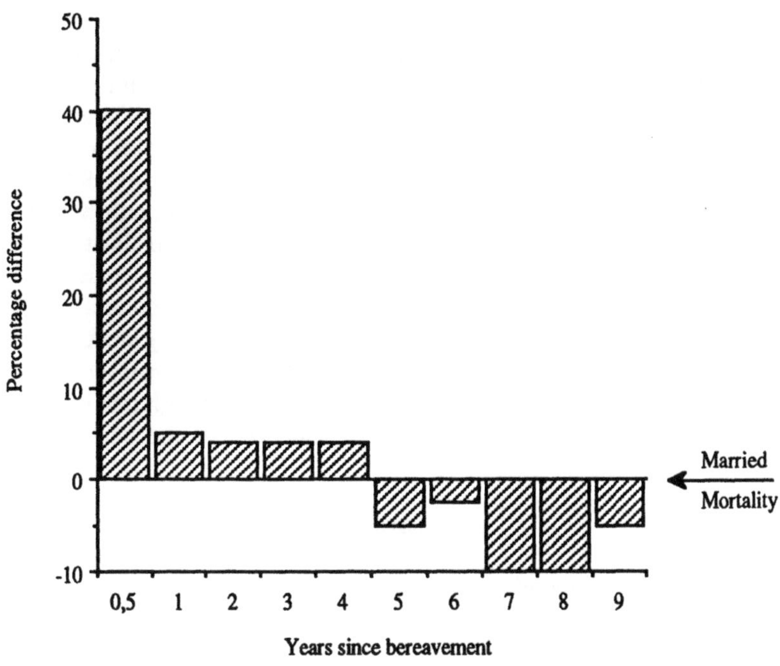

FIG.1.2. Percentage between mortality rate of widows over 54 and that of married men of the same age, by year since bereavement (from Parkes et al., 1969).

the widowed, these data also indicated that widowers are more vulnerable than widows and that the younger widowed are at greater risk than the older (Figure 1.1).

As convincing as these cross-sectional data seem to be, they are open to a great number of alternative interpretations, such as selection, homogamy, or joint unfavorable environment (cf. Stroebe, Stroebe, Gergen, & Gergen, 1981). However, when these alternative influences are controlled for in longitudinal studies such as the classic study by Parkes, Benjamin, and Fitzgerald (1969), the higher mortality risk of the bereaved can still be demonstrated (Figure 1.2).

Studies of the impact of partner loss on *psychological health* have had a much shorter tradition. The theoretical basis for this research was laid in Freud's (1917) classic paper on "Mourning and Melancholia." The first larger scale empirical study was conducted by Erich Lindemann (1944) and published in his landmark paper on "Symptomatology and Management of Acute Grief." Twenty years later, Parkes (1964) analyzed the frequency of loss experiences in the cases of over 3000 psychiatric patients admitted to the Bethlehem Royal and Maudsley Hospital in London during the years 1949 to 1951. He concluded that the number of patients whose illness followed the loss of a spouse was six times greater than expected. This study stimulated further research in Britain (e.g., Robertson, 1974; Stein & Susser, 1969) and in the United States of America (e.g., Gove, 1972).

Although most of the earlier studies of the health consequences of bereavement were methodologically flawed (cf. Stroebe & Stroebe, 1987), the accumulation of confirming findings from more recent large-scale longitudinal studies eliminated our doubts that the experience of partner loss increases the risk of morbidity and mortality (e.g., Helsing & Szklo, 1981; Kaprio & Koskenvuo, 1983). However, while most people suffer greatly from the loss experience, only very few suffer lasting health impairment. Thus, instead of continuing to illustrate the health consequences, we should begin to identify this risk group. Identification of the people who are at risk of permanent health impairment is important for practical as well as theoretical reasons. The practical reason is that early identification would make preventive intervention feasible. The theoretical reason is that knowledge of the personal and situational characteristics involved in high risk is important for evaluating the validity of theoretical explanations of the bereavement-health relationship.

THEORIES OF GRIEF

The two dominant theories of grief are Freud's psychoanalytic and Bowlby's attachment theory. Despite significant differences in assumed processes, both approaches show a convergence in their assumptions about the causes of "pathological grief" and in recommendations for its resolution.

According to the psychoanalytic perspective (e.g., Freud, 1917), when a loved one dies, the bereaved person is faced with the struggle to sever the ties and detach the energy invested in the deceased person. The *psychological function* of grief is, then, to free the individual of his or her bond to the deceased, achieving a gradual detachment by means of reviewing the past and dwelling on memories of the deceased. Grief is completed when most of the libido is withdrawn from the lost object and transferred to the new one. Thus, in Freud's view the bereaved need to *"work through"* their loss, grief cannot otherwise be overcome. The main cause of pathological grief according to Freud is the existence of *ambivalence* in the relationship with the lost object. By preventing the normal transference of the libido from the lost person to a new object, ambivalence is said to be the cause of the pathological development of clinical depression.

Bowlby's theory of attachment (Bowlby, 1971, 1975, 1981) emphasizes the biological rather than the psychological function of grieving. The *biological function* of grief is to regain proximity to the attachment figure, separation from which has caused anxiety. In the case of permanent loss this is not possible, and such a response is dysfunctional. However, Bowlby also argues for an active working through of loss, referring to the cognitive act of redefining self and situation, and to the process of realization and of reshaping internal representational models to align them with changes that have occurred.

Like Freud, Bowlby sees the proximal cause of pathological grief in the relationship with the lost person. However, the distal cause is childhood experiences with attachment figures. These experiences are assumed to have a lasting influence on later relationships. For example, frequent separation from attachment figures in childhood can lead to *anxious attachment* in later relationships which then results in chronic grief, a pathological reaction consisting of an indefinite prolongation of grief over the death of a partner. Alternatively, anxious attachment can cause a person to become *compulsively self-reliant* in his or her later relationships. This is assumed to be the cause of *delayed grief*, a pathological reaction by which the onset of grief is delayed. Finally, a child who is prematurely forced into a caregiver role (e.g., because the mother is depressive or has alcohol problems) may become *compulsively care-giving* in later relationships, a condition that is also a risk factor for *chronic grief.*

Even though it seems plausible that the quality of the marital relationship is an important determinant of grief resulting from partner loss, these theories do not allow one to derive predictions about other known determinants of grief reactions such as the circumstances of the loss or the extent of social support following a loss. Dissatisfaction with these theories led us to develop our own theoretical framework which we based on cognitive stress theory and called it the *Deficit Model of Partner Loss* (Stroebe et al., 1981; Stroebe & Stroebe, 1987).

The Deficit Model is an adaptation of interactionist cognitive stress models (e.g., French & Kahn, 1962; Lazarus, 1966; Lazarus & Folkman, 1984) to bereavement. According to these models, stress results from the perceived imbalance between situational demands and individual coping resources. A situation is experienced as stressful when the perceived demands tax or exceed an individual's coping resources and when failure to cope leads to important negative consequences for the individual. To predict the intensity of the stress resulting from a loss, the Deficit Model assesses both the situational demands and the coping resources available to the grieving individual.

Situational Demands. A marital couple can be considered a social group with a differentiated system of roles regulating the division of labor as well as the distribution of rewards. However, marital couples typically far exceed other social groups in the extent of mutual social support. As a rule their attachment is stronger to each other than toward other adults and they are likely to fulfill a wider range of functions for each other than is normal for social groups. Since bereavement marks the end of this close mutual relationship, the loss is likely to result in a number of deficits in areas in which the spouse had previously been able to rely on the partner. More specifically, the loss of the partner leads to deficits in areas which can broadly be characterized as loss of instrumental support (support in task functions, such as raising children, earning income), loss of validational support (support in validating one's beliefs about "reality"), and loss of emotional support (expressions of caring and love). Since the role of "spouse" is likely to be central for an individual's self-concept, the death of the partner will also be associated with a loss of social identity.

Coping Resources. According to the interactionist definition of stress, individual differences in coping resources are as important as variations in situational demands in determining bereavement outcome. In an analysis of the resources which are likely to affect the individual's ability to cope with bereavement, we distinguished between intrapersonal and interpersonal resources. Intrapersonal resources consist of the personality traits, abilities, and skills which enable a person to cope with the loss. All external resources, regardless of whether they are owned by the person (e.g., financial resources) or contributed by others (e.g., social support), are categorized as interpersonal (for a more extensive review, see Stroebe & Stroebe, 1987).

Thus, the Deficit Model differs from the depression theories of Freud and Bowlby in the following points:

1. It incorporates an interpersonal perspective by conceiving of social support as an important coping resource.
2. Risk is not seen only as a function of the relationship to the deceased, other (intra- and interpersonal) factors are relevant.
3. Outcome is not seen only in terms of normal and pathological grief (usually clinical depression). Since it accepts that the stress of bereavement is likely, for example, to affect the immune system, it accounts for a range of physical health consequences as well.
4. The stress framework enables an examination of cognitive strategies of coping as well as direct actions.

THE TÜBINGEN LONGITUDINAL STUDY OF BEREAVEMENT

The Tübingen Longitudinal Study was designed to test some of the predictions of this theory. A further aim of the Tübingen study was to assess a bias inherent in the design of in-depth studies, which seriously threatens the validity of their conclusions, namely attrition. Understandably, the recently bereaved are not very willing to participate in interviews that probe into their loss experience. Since participation and health status are likely to be related in bereavement studies, low acceptance rates could seriously bias findings about health consequences of bereavement (for a detailed presentation of the findings of this study, see Stroebe & Stroebe, 1989; Stroebe, Stroebe, & Domittner, 1988).

Sample and Procedure

In the Tübingen study a sample of 30 widows and 30 widowers was interviewed three times during the first two years following their loss. Measures of their health and well-being were compared to those of a matched sample of married individuals. Data were also collected on the health status of some of the widowed who *refused* participation. The sample consisted of all the widowed and married individuals under the age of 60, drawn from five towns in Southern Germany, who agreed to participate in the study. Thus, our sample was drawn from the total population rather than recruited through hospitals, churches, or widow-to-widow programs, sources which are likely to introduce a systematic selection bias.

Addresses of all recently bereaved individuals in the area were supplied through the local registrars' offices. The bereaved individuals were sent a letter outlining the study and asking for their cooperation. Out of respect for their bereaved condition, no pressure was put on persons to participate if they expressed lack of interest. Those who did not decline participation by mail or telephone were then phoned a few days afterwards to arrange an interview. The interview participants consisted of a sample of 30 widows and 30 widowers (mean age of the widowed sample: 53.05 years). Widowed individuals who refused interview participation by phone were asked whether they were willing to complete a short questionnaire.

The 30 married women and 30 married men (mean age of the married sample: 53.75 years) who participated in the comparison group were individually matched to the widowed by sex, age, socioeconomic status, number of children, and town of residence. They were recruited from addresses of a larger number of matched individuals supplied by the registration offices of the five towns. Letters were sent to these married persons, explaining that we were interested in the relationship between marital status and the quality of life.

Times of Measurement

The participants were interviewed three times. For the bereaved, the first interview took place between four to seven months (median: 5.5) after the loss. The second interview was conducted seven to eleven months (median: 8.0) after the first one, that is, approximately 14 months after the loss. The third and final interview took place approximately one year after the second interview (median: 11.9), i.e., just over two years after the loss.

Structured interviews as well as self-report scales were used for data collection. The first two interviews were extensive sessions held at the homes of the participants. The third interview was a shorter one conducted by telephone. With the exception of questions about the circumstances of the loss, the interviews of the widowed and married groups were fairly similar. At the end of each interview, participants were given (or at Time 3, sent) a questionnaire containing the personality and health measures. They were asked to fill out this questionnaire within the next few days and return it to the interviewers by mail. All participants returned the questionnaire, but a few failed to complete all the items. If more than 20% of the items of a given scale had not been completed, the scale was eliminated from the analysis.

Health Measures

Since the major focus of this study was on the health impact of bereavement, a great number of self-report measures of psychological and physical health were included. For reasons of space limitations, this report will be restricted to only two of the health measures: depression and somatic complaints. This limitation will not bias the report, since the pattern of health findings is very consistent across measures. Depression was assessed by the German version of the Beck Depression Inventory (BDI; Beck, 1967; Kammer, 1983). Somatic complaints were assessed by a symptoms checklist (Beschwerdenliste, BL) developed by Zerssen (1976). The BL lists 24 somatic complaints (e.g., dizziness, difficulty in swallowing, indigestion, excessive sweating, restlessness, neck and shoulder pain). Respondents had to indicate the extent to which they suffered from each symptom on a 4-point scale (0 = *not at all* to 3 = *very much*); the total score being the sum of these points.

Acceptance Rates

To achieve a sample size of 60 widowed for the interviews, 217 persons were approached. Of those who refused to participate in an interview, 24 were willing to fill out the mailed questionnaire. The overall acceptance rate for interview or questionnaire was therefore 39%, while the acceptance rate for interview was 28%. For the married sample, the acceptance rate was 34%. Although the general level of acceptance was rather low, these rates are not atypical in this area. However, since some of the bereaved who were unwilling to participate in the interviews were willing to respond to a written questionnaire, we were able to assess the bias due to attrition (Stroebe & Stroebe, 1989).

Drop-Out Rates

Of the individuals who agreed to be interviewed, 82% of the widowed and 90% of the married participated in all three interviews. This is a very low drop-out rate. There was no significant health difference between those who dropped out after the first or second interview and those who completed all three sessions.

Recovery From Bereavement

The health impact of bereavement was examined by comparing the health differences between the bereaved and married participants at the three interview time points. Figures 1.3 and 1.4 present the BDI and BL scores of the widowed and married samples (for all three points in time). As expected, three factor (marital status, sex, time) analyses of variance conducted on these health measures resulted in significant Marital Status × Time interactions. Compared to the married, widowed individuals had a much higher level of depressive and somatic complaints at four to seven months after the loss, but improved considerably over the 18-month period. In addition, there were the usual "sex main effects", with women having more complaints than men.

The fact that, at least during the first year of bereavement, the bereaved have higher scores on the BDI and BL than the married controls says very little about the *severity* of the health consequences of bereavement. Therefore, an attempt was made to evaluate the magnitude of these health effects. Since the cut-off points suggested by Beck (1967) for the BDI are frequently used in screening for psychiatric interviews, the percentage of married and widowed participants who were classified as mild to severe (a score of 11 and above) and as moderate to severe (a score of 19 and above) were computed.

A comparison of the percentage of widowed and married with severe symptoms at Times 1 and 3 confirmed the impression that whereas the widowed had serious problems six months after the loss, there was a great deal of improvement over the two-year period. Thus, at six months after their loss, 42% of the widowed as compared to 10% of the married had scores on the BDI which fell within the range of mild to severe depression according to the Beck criteria. The more stringent criteria for moderate to severe depression were fulfilled by 14% of the widowed but only by 5% of the married, a difference which does not reach an acceptable level of significance. Two years after the loss, the percentage widowed with BDI scores in the range of mild to severe depression had dropped considerably, but at 27% was still significantly higher than that for the married.

The findings of this study offer support for the prediction that the experience of losing a spouse through death is associated with poor mental and physical health.

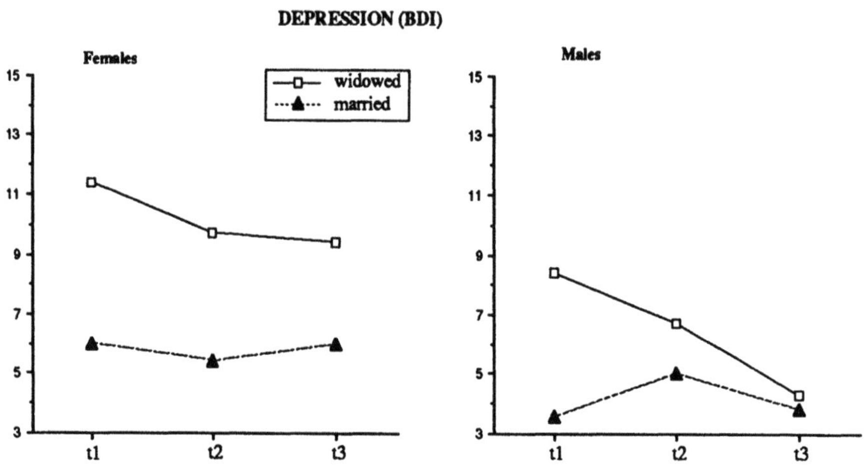

FIG.1.3. Mean BDI scores of widowed and married respondents who participated in all three interviews.

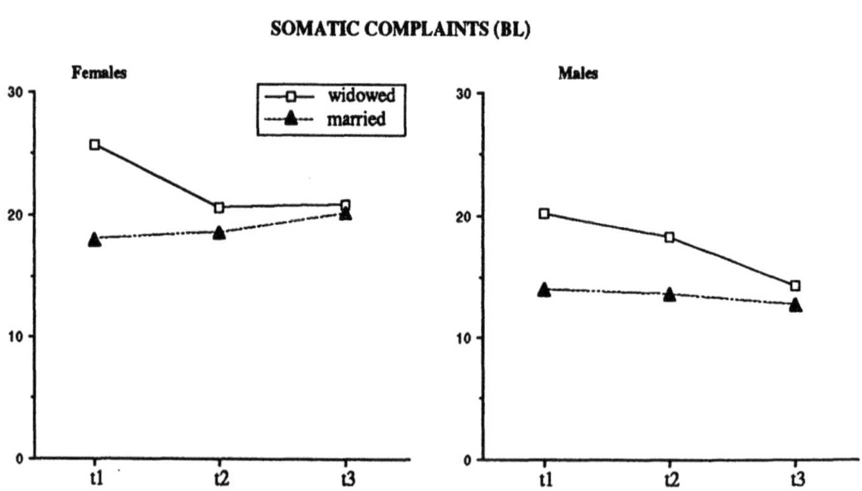

FIG.1.4. Mean BL scores of widowed and married respondents who participated in all three interviews.

The widows and widowers interviewed at four to seven months after the loss of their partners indicated significantly higher levels of depression and listed more somatic complaints. We also have additional data which indicate that 13 of the 60 bereaved reported an increase in the use of psychotropic medication, whereas none of the married did. Similarly, 19 of the bereaved but only 4 of the married reported instances of new illnesses for the months after bereavement (or a comparable time period in the case of the married controls).

The health and well-being of the widowed improved significantly over the two-year period of our study. However, although the difference between married and widowed was no longer significant when average levels of depression or somatic complaints were considered, two years after bereavement nearly a third of the widowed (17% more than the married) still had depression scores which fell within the range of mild to severe. Thus, while most of them recovered over the two-year period, there seemed to be a small minority of bereaved who did not conform to this recovery process. In the next section an attempt will be made to identify this group of high risk individuals.

Risk Factors in Bereavement Outcome

Risk factors in bereavement are variables which increase the individual's vulnerability to the loss experience (vulnerability factors) or slow down adjustment to widowhood (recovery factors). Variables which are associated with the same level of health impairment in widowed and nonwidowed individuals cannot be considered risk factors. For example, widows have frequently been reported to have higher depression rates than widowers. However, this does not mean that widows are more depressed at losing their spouses than widowers are, for the reason that females, in general, have higher depression rates than males. There are two strategies to control for the main effect of a variable on health: One can either include non-bereaved controls, so that between group comparisons can be made, and/or one can rely on longitudinal comparisons where relative recovery can be plotted. Thus, risk factors are variables which show a statistical interaction with marital status on health in cross-sectional designs or with time on health in longitudinal designs.

Because the design of the Tübingen study was cross-sectional and longitudinal, it enabled us to distinguish between vulnerability and recovery factors. Since vulnerability factors (e.g., emotional instability) intensify the initial health impact of bereavement, their effect should have been strongest at Time 1 decreasing over time, while the effect of recovery factors that facilitate adjustment and coping (e.g., social support) should have increased over time. However, although this is a useful analytic distinction, it is likely that most risk variables will affect vulnerability as well as recovery.

Social Support

According to our Deficit Model, the availability of social support is one of the important resources which should allow the bereaved to cope with deficits resulting from the loss. Thus, we expected a buffering effect (i.e., an interaction of marital status and social support on health measures). Our study included two measures of social support:

1. *Perceived social support* was measured with a scale that assessed functions of social support (cf. Cohen & Wills, 1985). However, the subscales that assessed emotional, instrumental, appraisal, and contact support were so highly intercorrelated that we used the total support score in all of our analyses.
2. In addition, the interview assessed *received social support* by the number of social contacts an individual had experienced during the month before *and* the satisfaction with these contacts. While there was no relationship between perceived social support and number of contacts, there was a moderate correlation ($r = .54$) when the number of contacts was weighted by satisfaction.

Even though there was a significantly positive relationship between social support and our health measures, there was neither evidence of a buffering effect for perceived support nor for received social support (weighted with satisfaction): The availability of supportive individuals had similarly positive effects on married and on widowed individuals.

Expectedness of Loss

The death of a partner dramatically changes the life of the surviving spouse. Adjustment to such changes takes time. Sudden, unexpected, untimely deaths are therefore believed to result in poorer adjustment and higher risk of mental and physical debilities during bereavement than bereavements that had been anticipated. Empirical evidence for this hypothesis is, however, not very consistent (cf., Stroebe & Stroebe, 1987). Some studies found that unexpectedness of loss had a negative effect on health outcome (Ball, 1977; Lundin, 1984; Parkes, 1975; Sanders, 1983), but other studies did not (Bornstein, Clayton, Halikas, Maurice, & Robbins, 1973; Breckenridge, Gallagher, Thompson, & Peterson, 1986; Maddison & Walker, 1967).

In view of these inconsistencies, it was important to see whether an expectedness effect could be demonstrated for the participants of the Tübingen study. On the basis of their reports on how long in advance they had known about the impending death of their spouse, our widowed participants were divided into an "unexpected loss group" (less than one day warning) and an "expected loss group" (one day and more). Although unexpected loss was associated with a higher level of depressive symptoms (13.61 vs. 9.06) and somatic complaints (27.00 vs. 20.47) six months after the loss, this difference was only marginally significant for the BDI and not significant at all for the BL in two factor (expectedness, sex) analyses of variance. Furthermore, there were no significant effects of expectedness at Times 2 and 3. Thus, expectedness seemed to have only a weak effect on health reactions and only during the first six months after the loss. This pattern of findings suggests that expectedness increases vulnerability, but does not affect recovery. However, as we will see later, this conclusion must be modified in the light of the analysis of individual differences in reactions.

Internal-External Control Beliefs

According to the learned-helplessness theory (Abramson, Seligman, & Teasdale, 1978), control beliefs play an important role as stress moderators. Some researchers (e.g., Ganellen & Blaney, 1984; Johnson & Sarason, 1978) argue that since the state of learned helplessness is characterized by a belief in the inability to control important aspects of life, people who already believe that they have little control should be more likely to react to stress with depression than those who have high control beliefs. Research on critical life events has typically supported this prediction (e.g., Ganellen & Blaney, 1984; Johnson & Sarason, 1978). In contrast, Pittman and Pittman (1979) argued that individuals who expect control will be more severely affected by uncontrollable situations once they realize that they truly have no control. Using an experimental induction of learned helplessness, they were able to support this prediction.

In our study, locus of control was measured at four to seven months after the loss with the German version of the Interpersonal Control Scale of Levenson (1973; Mielke, 1979). The Interpersonal Control Scale (IPC) provides three fairly independent scores indicating the extent to which individuals believe that what happens to them is either under their own internal control (IPC-I), or externally controlled by chance (IPC-C) or by powerful others (IPC-P).

Implicit in the learned helplessness interpretation of reactions to bereavement is the assumption that the loss experience invalidates expectations of control for those individuals who believe that they have control over their outcomes. To test this hypothesis, the impact of bereavement on control beliefs was assessed by two factor (marital status, sex) analyses of variance on IPC scores: Marital status did not affect IPC-I and IPC-P scores but had a main effect on IPC-C. Thus, consistent with the hypothesis derived from the learned-helplessness theory, the widowed believed more than the married that the consequences of their actions were controlled by chance. To check whether the unexpectedness of loss led to a further shift in external control beliefs, two factor (expectedness, sex) analyses of variance were conducted on the IPC scores. These analyses did not result in any significant effects. Thus, whether a loss happened suddenly or after a period of forewarning, it did not

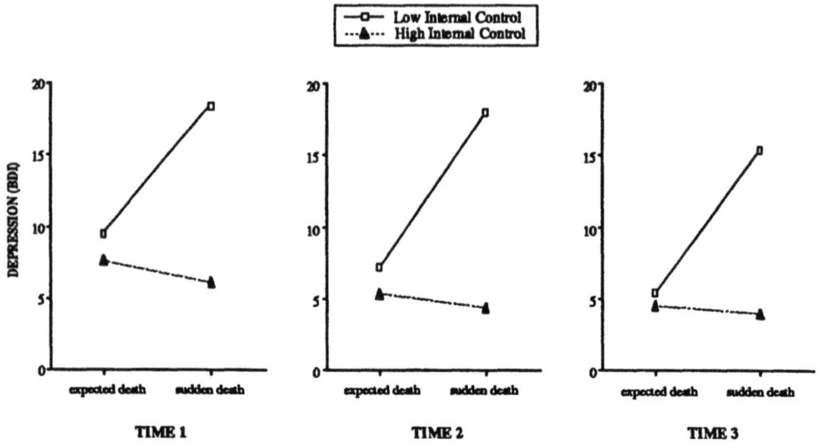

FIG. 1.5. Mean BDI scores of widowed respondents by internal control beliefs and expectedness of loss, for individuals who participated in all three interviews (from Stroebe et al., 1988).

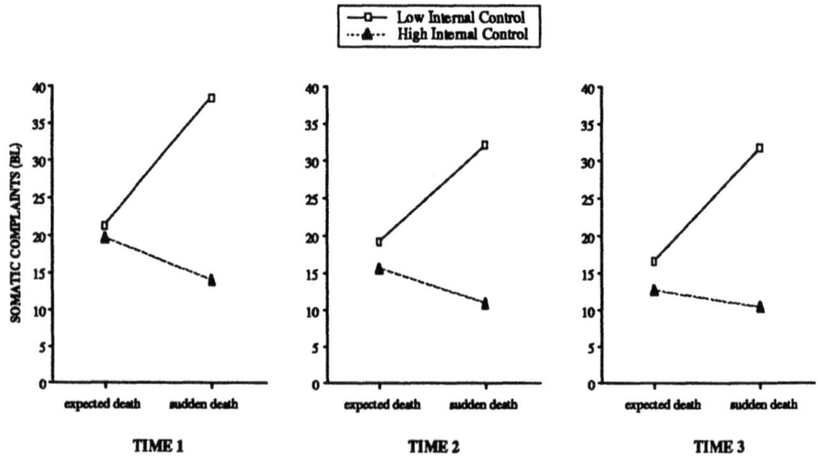

FIG. 1.6. Mean BL scores of widowed respondents by internal control beliefs and expectedness of loss, for individuals who participated in all three interviews (Stroebe et al., 1988).

significantly affect the individuals' beliefs in internal or chance control of their outcomes.

To assess the potential role of control beliefs as moderators of the bereavement-health relationship, the sample was then divided by median split into groups with high or low beliefs in chance (IPC-C) and internal control (IPC-I). (The powerful other scale was considered less relevant in the context of bereavement.) Four factor (locus of control, marital status, sex, time) analyses of variance conducted on the BDI and BL did not result in significant interactions of either chance or internal control beliefs and marital status on health. However, when expectedness was used as a factor instead of marital status, a highly significant interaction emerged between expectedness and internal control beliefs on the BDI and BL scores. Thus, while unexpected loss resulted in high depression and somatic complaints scores for individuals who believed that they had little internal control over their outcomes, it had little impact on individuals with low scores on the IPC-I scale (see Figures 1.5 & 1.6). The interaction between chance beliefs and expectedness did not even approach significance.

In summary, the bereavement experience seemed to have increased individuals' beliefs that their outcomes are controlled by chance. Furthermore, unexpectedness of loss interacted with internal control beliefs to moderate bereavement outcome: Individuals with low internal control beliefs who suffered an unexpected loss appeared to react with severe depressive symptoms and somatic complaints and improved very little over the two-year period.

Why should this subgroup be at high risk? The following explanation seems plausible: Those bereaved from sudden death had been exposed to an unpredictable life event over which they had no control (due to the suddenness of death). This brings with it a high risk of depression. There are alternative strategies available for coping with and coming to terms with this circumstance. On the one hand, an effort can be made to retain a belief in control, despite "evidence" to the contrary. This option would seem more likely to be followed by people who believe in internal control. They would feel that it was up to them to come to terms with the unexpected change in their lives. As a consequence, they are likely to make an effort to recover from depression. On the other hand, if they do not believe in internal control, if the sudden death confirmed their belief that they have no control over their outcomes, they will respond with resignation, make no effort, and remain depressed. Circumstances are different following an expected death: There was opportunity to exercise some control over the course of events before death (medical treatment intervention; nurturing the personal relationship with the terminally ill person; shared anticipatory grief). Control beliefs would not, then, be so called into question by the death.

Grief Work

According to Freud and Bowlby, one would expect the high risk group (low internal control beliefs; sudden death) to differ from the other bereaved in the way they conduct their grief work. To examine this question we had to develop our own measures, since the concept of grief work had not been operationalized in a way that excluded confounding with depression, and had not previously been put to an empirical test (for a consideration of the grief work hypothesis see Stroebe & Stroebe, in press). We reasoned that people who work through their grief confront their loss, while those who do not engage in grief work distract themselves and avoid anything which would remind them of the deceased. We included a 6-item grief work scale in our Grief Symptoms Questionnaire, which assessed the extent to which individuals avoid or confront the loss. In addition, we asked a number of questions in the interview which assessed the extent of grief work (avoidance of reminders of the loss; distraction; control of emotionality; nondisclosure of feelings about the loss). These measures showed low, but positive intercorrelations (Stroebe & Stroebe, in press).

To check whether our high risk group differed from the other groups in terms of grief work, we conducted the Sex × Time × Expectedness × Control Beliefs analyses of variance using our grief work scale and the various interview items as dependent measures. These analyses did not result in a significant Expectedness × Control Beliefs interaction on any of these measures. This seems to suggest that the coping strategies people followed in dealing with their loss were not strongly related to health outcome.

Since this result could have been due to the low reliability of our grief work measures, we decided to conduct further analyses. We reasoned that if any of these coping strategies should affect health outcome, the bereaved who engaged in this strategy should improve more over time than those who did not engage in it. To test this hypothesis, we conducted hierarchical regression analyses with the coping variables at Time 1 as predictors and the health measures at Time 3 as criteria. Since we were interested in improvements in health due to engaging in a given coping strategy, we entered the particular health measure at Time 1, before we entered the set of coping measures. This type of analysis also controls for the possibility that differences in coping are due to differences in health measures (i.e., individuals who are depressed may talk less and use avoiding rather than confronting strategies). Separate analyses were conducted for widows and widowers (cf. Stroebe & Stroebe, in press).

For widows, the findings from this analysis seemed to support the conclusions drawn from the analyses reported earlier. When we entered the BDI at Time 1 in the first step with BDI at Time 3 as the criterion, the BDI scores of widows at Time 1 accounted for nearly 80% of the variance of their BDI scores at Time 3. Not surprisingly, entering the five coping variables into the equation in a second step did not result in a significant increase in the explained variance. For widowers, however, a different pattern emerged. For them the BDI score at Time 1 accounted for only 35% of the variance of the BDI scores at Time 3. Furthermore, entering the grief work measures in a second step increased the explained variance to more than 50%.

The analysis of the BL scores led to similar differences. Again, Time 1 scores accounted for 74% of the variance of the Time 3 measure for widows, but for only 56% for widowers. Furthermore, entering the grief work measures in Step 2 increased the amount of explained variance for widowers but not for widows.

These findings suggest that grief work is effective (at least to some extent) for widowers but not for widows. For widows, the presence or absence of grief work appeared to be unrelated to psychological distress. Those of the widows who were most depressed six months after the loss were also most depressed 18 months later, regardless of whether they had engaged in grief work or not. For widowers, on the other hand, there is some indication that grief work is related to improvement in depressive and somatic symptoms. Widowers who seek distraction in order to avoid confronting the loss or who control their feelings of grief rather than let themselves go, show less improvement in their adjustment to loss than widowers who do not engage in these coping strategies.

How can we explain the gender difference in the impact of grief work on depression? Although there do not seem to be any clearcut gender differences in the preference for avoiding versus confrontational styles of grief work (Stroebe & Stroebe, in press), we would argue that there are gender differences in the effectiveness with which each of these strategies is used. Two reasons seem plausible. First, there are far more opportunities for widowers than for widows to avoid constant reminders of their loss. Our southern German sample was largely drawn from traditional family backgrounds, where the men go to work and the women are the homemakers. Given these role differences, men are more frequently outside the home and away from memories of their deceased spouse. Women, on the other hand, are constantly surrounded by the environment that they had shared with their late partner. Second, sex differences in role norms may reinforce this difference. There are strong social norms for men to avoid showing an emotion such as grief, whereas women are encouraged to disclose their feelings (Belle, 1987). It seems likely, then, that men are able to block confrontation more completely than women are. Following this argument, widowers would be more effective in using avoidant strategies than widows would.

CONCLUSION

Historical changes in the kinds of research questions that have been topical in bereavement research were illustrated in the first part of this paper. Following the early concern to establish whether bereavement will lead to an excess risk of mortality, came the related interest in the mental and physical health consequences of loss. Once it was established that bereavement could have deleterious consequences, the interest turned to understanding the nature of the vulnerability of some bereaved or groups of bereaved persons: What puts some, but not others, at risk of poor mental and physical health outcome following bereavement? Our research attempted to provide a theoretical framework, the Deficit Model, to explain these health effects, and the Tübingen Longitudinal Study of Bereavement was designed to test some of the assumptions of this model and to establish risk factors for poor bereavement recovery.

Recently, many research interests were directed toward identifying cognitive variables underlying the mental and physical health risks (Hansson, Stroebe, & Stroebe, 1988). Our own work has moved in this direction, too. One cognitive mechanism that came out strongly as a predictor of poor recovery in our investigation was personal control beliefs in situations of sudden, unexpected bereavements. Having identified a subgroup of poor recoverers, the next question was how these high risk individuals would cope with loss: Will they differ from those who cope better in the way they deal with their grief? On the basis of earlier theoretical formulations, one would expect differences in "grief work" between these and other bereaved persons, for working through grief had been identified as an essential coping strategy. As our results showed, this assumption did not hold for our sample. A revision of the grief work hypothesis, to take gender differences in coping with bereavement into account, was suggested.

REFERENCES

Abramson, L. Y., Seligman, M. E. P., & Teasdale, J. D. (1978). Learned helplessness in humans: Critique and reformulation. *Journal of Abnormal Psychology, 87*, 49-74.

Ball, J. F. (1977). Widow's grief: The impact of age and mode of death. *Omega, 7*, 307-333.

Beck, A. T. (1967). *Depression: Clinical, experimental, and theoretical aspects*. New York: Hoeber.

Belle, D. (1987). Gender differences in the social moderators of stress. In R. Barret, L. Biener, & G. Baruch (Eds.), *Gender and stress* (pp. 257-277). New York: Free Press.

Bornstein, P., Clayton, P. J., Halikas, J. A., Maurice, W. L., & Robbins, E. (1973). The depression of widowhood after 13 months. *British Journal of Psychiatry, 122*, 562-566.

Bowlby, J. (1971). *Attachment and loss (Vol. 1): Attachment*. Harmondsworth: Pelican Books.

Bowlby, J. (1975). *Attachment and loss (Vol. 2): Separation*. Harmondsworth: Pelican Books.

Bowlby, J. (1981). *Attachment and loss (Vol. 3): Loss: Sadness and depression*. Harmondsworth: Pelican Books.

Breckenridge, J., Gallagher, D., Thompson, L., & Peterson, J. (1986). Characteristic depressive symptoms of bereaved elders. *Journal of Gerontology, 41*, 163-168.

Burton, R. (1977). *The anatomy of melancholy*. New York: Random House. (Originally published 1621.)

Cohen, S., & Wills, T. A. (1985). Stress, social support, and the buffering hypothesis. *Psychological Bulletin, 98*, 310-357.

Farr, W. (1975). Influence of marriage on the mortality of the French People. In N. Humphreys (Ed.), *Vital statistics: A memorial volume of selections from reports and writings of William Farr* (pp. 438-441). Methuen, NY: The Scarecrow Press. (Originally published 1858.)

French, J. R. P., Jr., & Kahn, R. L. (1962). A programmatic approach to studying the industrial environment and mental health. *Journal of Social Issues, 18*(3), 1-47.

Freud, S. (1917). Trauer und Melancholie. *Internationale Zeitschrift für ärztliche Psychoanalyse, 4,* 288-301.

Ganellen, R. J., & Blaney, P. H. (1984). Stress, externality, and depression. *Journal of Personality and Social Psychology, 52,* 326-337.

Gove, W. R. (1972). The relationship between sex roles, marital roles, and mental illness. *Social Forces, 51,* 34-44.

Hansson, R. O., Stroebe, M. S., & Stroebe, W. (1988). Current research in bereavement and widowhood research. *Journal of Social Issues, 44*(3), 207-216.

Helsing, K. J., & Szklo, M. (1981). Mortality after bereavement. *American Journal of Epidemiology, 114,* 41-52.

Holmes, T. H., & Rahe, R. H. (1967). The Social Readjustment Rating Scale. *Journal of Psychosomatic Research, 11,* 213-218.

Johnson, J. H., & Sarason, I. G. (1978). Life stress, depression, and anxiety: Internal-external control as a moderator variable. *Psychosomatic Research, 22,* 205-208.

Kammer, D. (1983). Eine Untersuchung der psychometrischen Eigenschaften des deutschen Beck-Depressionsinventars (BDI). *Diagnostica, 28,* 48-60.

Kaprio, J., & Koskenvuo, M. (1983). *Mortality after bereavement: A prospective study.* Unpublished manuscript, Department of Public Health Science, University of Helsinki, Finland.

Kraus, A. S., & Lilienfeld, A. M. (1959). Some epidemiological aspects of the high mortality rate in the young widowed group. *Journal of Chronic Diseases, 10,* 207-217.

Lazarus, R. S. (1966). *Psychological stress and the coping process.* New York: McGraw-Hill.

Lazarus, R. S., & Folkman, S. (1984). *Stress, appraisal, and coping.* New York: Springer.

Levenson, H. (1973). Multidimensional locus of control in psychiatric patients. *Journal of Consulting and Clinical Psychology, 41,* 397-404.

Lindemann, E. (1944). Symptomatology and management of acute grief. *American Journal of Psychiatry, 101,* 141-148.

Lundin, T. (1984). Morbidity following sudden and unexpected bereavement. *British Journal of Psychiatry, 144,* 84-88.

Maddison, D. C., & Walker, W. L. (1967). Factors effecting the outcome of conjugal bereavement. *Britih Journal of Psychiatry, 113,* 1057-1067.

McCrae, R. R., & Costa, P. T., Jr. (1988). Psychological resilience among widowed men and women: A 10-year follow-up of a national sample. *Journal of Social Issues, 44*(3), 129-142.

Mielke, R. (1979). *Entwicklung einer deutschen Form des Fragebogens zur Erfassung interner vs. externer Kontrolle von Levenson (IPC).* (Bielefelder Arbeiten zur Sozialpsychologie, Bd. 46) .Bielefeld: Universität Bielefeld.

Parkes, C. M. (1964). Recent bereavement as a cause of mental illness. *British Journal of Psychiatry, 110,* 198-204.

Parkes, C. M. (1975). Unexpected and untimely bereavement: A statistical study of young Boston widows and widowers. In B. Schoenberg, I. Gerber, A. Wiener, D. Kutscher, D. Peretz, & A. Cam (Eds.), *Bereavement: Its psychosocial aspects* (pp. 119-138). New York: Columbia University Press.

Parkes, C. M. (1986). *Bereavement: Studies of grief in adult life.* London: Penguin. (Originally published 1972.)

Parkes, C. M., Benjamin, B., & Fitzgerald, R. G. (1969). Broken heart: A statistical study of increased mortality among widowers. *British Medical Journal, 1,* 740-743.

Pittman, N. L., & Pittman, T. S. (1979). Effects of amount of helplessness training and internal-external locus of control on mood and performance. *Journal of Personality and Social Psychology, 37,* 39-47.

Robertson, N. C. (1974). The relationship between marital status and risk of psychiatric referral. *British Journal of Psychiatry, 124,* 191-202.

Rush, B. (1835). *Medical inquiries and observations upon the diseases of the mind.* Philadelphia: Grigg and Elliot.

Sanders, C. (1983). Effects of sudden versus chronic illness death on bereavement outcome. *Omega, 13*, 227-241.
Shurtleff, D. (1955). Mortality and marital status. *Public Health Reports, 70*, 248-252.
Stein, Z., & Susser, M. W. (1969). Widowhood and mental illness. *British Journal of Preventive and Social Medicine, 23*, 106-110.
Stroebe, M. S., & Stroebe, W. (1989). Who participates in bereavement research? A review and empirical study. *Omega, 20*, 1-29.
Stroebe, M. S., & Stroebe, W. (in press). Does "grief work" work? *Journal of Consulting and Clinical Psychology*.
Stroebe, M. S., Stroebe, W., Gergen, K. J., & Gergen, M. (1981). The broken heart: Reality or myth? *Omega, 12*, 87-105.
Stroebe, W., & Stroebe, M. S. (1987). *Bereavement and health*. New York: Cambridge University Press.
Stroebe, W., Stroebe, M. S., & Domittner, G. (1988). Individual and situational differences in recovery from bereavement: A risk group identified. *Journal of Social Issues, 44*(3), 143-158.
Zerssen, D., von (1976). *Die Beschwerdenliste (BL)*. Weinheim: Beltz.

2 Could it be Worse? The Diagnosis of Cancer as a Prototype of Traumatic Life Events

Sigrun-Heide Filipp
University of Trier

Researchers interested in crisis and loss have often investigated their topics with a particular focus on the impact of these experiences on physical health and well-being. To understand the extent to which critical life events are of pathogenetic significance presumably has been a major impetus guiding the various research endeavors, and the search for decrements in health status following exposure to critical life events accordingly appears to be a common element in these studies, (for an overview, see Creed, 1985). Despite some critical comments with regard to the methodological flaws of many studies (e.g., Rahe, 1988; Schroeder & Costa, 1984), such an approach unfortunately has neglected the fact that deterioration in health status is in itself one of the most critical experiences people might have to cope with in their lives.

When, several years ago, we first started to investigate the impact of critical life events in a male community sample, primarily focusing on subsequent changes in adults' belief systems within a longitudinal design (see Filipp, Ahammer, Angleitner, & Olbrich, 1980), we were impressed by the observation that health-related events—as compared to many other events in various life domains—had been rated by our subjects as the most threatening ones; and this, in addition, held true for all age groups under investigation (35 to 75 years). In our next studies, rather than considering the diversity of critical life events that might occur within a certain time span of observation, we preferred a single-event approach by selecting the onset of chronic and severe physical illness, in particular, cancer as a sample case. First, this helped to circumvent the problem of how to "count" and classify events in order to measure the "stress of life." Second, it presumably is not in need of further justification to investigate the diagnosis of cancer as a well-selected example of traumatic life events that deserves an in-depth analysis of the coping process and its contextual embeddedness. Accordingly, in 1983 we started the Trier Longitudinal Study on Coping with Chronic Disease in which the course of coping with and adapting to cancer was to be observed. Before we turn to this study in more detail, we shall briefly comment on life-threatening disease as a special case of dealing with loss and crisis.

LOSS AND CRISIS: THE SPECIAL CASE OF LIFE-THREATENING DISEASE

Within the tradition of life-event research, the issue of what constitutes "critical" life events and of how their impact should be measured has been extensively discussed (for an overview, e.g., Cohen, 1988; Thoits, 1983). Various suggestions have been made, ranging from the disruptiveness or amount of change in people's lives considered to be the crucial element up to multidimensional conceptions of what makes life experiences particularly "critical" ones (see Reese & Smyer, 1983). Whatever perspectives one is willing to adopt in defining "critical," virtually all attributes listed in the various definitions are easily applicable to the description of the diagnosis of cancer. In that regard, the diagnosis of cancer can be conceived of as a prototype of experiences of loss and crisis in general.

First of all, this might have to do with the fact that people in our cultures normally are not "educated" to deal with disease and death. Neither are they taught respective lessons at school, nor do they usually learn from"models" how to handle threats to life. Even if models are available in their social worlds, people rather prefer to look at the sunnier sides of life. According to the widely held belief in one's invulnerability and "unrealistic optimism" (Weinstein, 1980), people usually do not consider the onset of chronic disease as one of the possible experiences and realities in their lives. Thus, neither does anticipatory socialization—in whatsoever setting—with regard to such traumatic experiences take place, nor do people, in general, voluntarily engage in ways of anticipatory coping with potential threats to their healths or even lives. In that respect, one could borrow another term from cognitive psychology here and characterize the diagnosis of cancer as a "weakly scripted situation" (Abelson, 1981), for which ways of acting (let aside "behavioral routines") are not readily at hand. Whereas other negative life experiences (e.g., loss of a loved one), at least partially, are embedded into culturally shaped ways of responding (e.g., by public rituals or mourning customs; see Averill, 1979; Stroebe & Stroebe, 1987), thus, often facilitating the coping process, the initial diagnosis of cancer, presumably is accompanied much more often by behavioral disorganization.

When we look at more "popular" notions of what turns life experiences into "critical" ones, all of them are equally descriptive of the diagnosis of cancer: Threats to health and life, by definition, represent existential plights (Weisman, 1979) and arouse extremely strong negative emotions—may be even in a more or less universal manner and presumably due to the myths and metaphors surrounding cancer (Sontag, 1977). In addition, cancer is far beyond the (primary) control of those suffering from it and—at least in many cases—even beyond physicians' control. Patients often are exposed to their diagnosis in a completely unpredictable way, taking into consideration that the detection of cancer in many cases simply occurs "by chance." Furthermore, to suffer from cancer in most cases interferes with a large spectrum of action goals people have set for themselves, thus, necessitating disengagement from commitments and their replacement with new options and goals—"coping tasks" that are particularly painful to accomplish and often exceed people's capabilities (Klinger, 1975; see also Brandtstädter & Renner, this volume). Finally, to be diagnosed a cancer patient in almost all cases means a threat to fundamental beliefs about the self (e.g., being a strong, powerful, effective, or "functioning" person) that have guided individual courses of action in the past. The necessity to often dramatically alter the self-system may add to the diagnosis of cancer as being one of the most negative life experiences in general.

In sum, there are quite a few arguments for conceiving the diagnosis of cancer in terms of a particularly traumatic event, and one is tempted to quickly answer the question as to whether something "could be worse" in people's lives simply by saying "no." Yet, simple questions usually do not allow for simple and premature answers. It is trivial to state that interindividual variations in emotional reactions to cancer—as well as to any other event—are of crucial importance. Thus, we will need to know more about the conditions that might shape our answers. In this chapter, we would like to highlight the *role of time* in coping with and adapting to cancer in that respect: Does time make a difference in experiencing cancer, and is it related to which answers should be given to our question "Could it be worse?". Before we turn to the various aspects of time and their presumed role in coping with cancer, we will first give a brief description of our study.

THE TRIER LONGITUDINAL STUDY ON COPING WITH CHRONIC DISEASE[1]

General Aims, Design, and Sample

A variety of investigations of how people cope with chronic disease in general or with cancer in particular have been conducted within the last decades (for overviews, see Burish & Bradley, 1983; Moos, 1984; Watson & Greer, 1986). Many of these studies have been guided by the assumption that basic research is urgently needed in order to gain insights into the dynamics and mechanisms of coping and ultimately to help patients to cope effectively with their lot. Despite the empirical evidence one can rely on so far, various desiderata still characterize this domain of research. In

[1]The research reported here was supported by a grant from the Deutsche Forschungsgemeinschaft (German Research Foundation; Fi 346/1-3).

particular, when we planned our study we realized that there was a considerable lack of longitudinal observations of the process of coping with and adapting to cancer. In addition, many studies suffer from not having recruited a sufficiently large sample, which also prevents the consideration of larger sets of theoretically interesting variables! We tried to circumvent these shortcomings, and the general aims of our study are accordingly at least threefold.

First, we were interested in observing the course of coping with cancer over time, that is in temporal consistencies with regard to the various coping behaviors. Therefore, we constructed a longitudinal design with repeated measurements and, additionally, recruited patients differing in time elapsed since their diagnosis. Second, we searched for determinants of coping with cancer by including various sets of predictors and for determinants of *temporal variations* in the course of coping over time. Medical variables had been obtained from the patient's physician at the time of study onset, based on the assumption that clinical status may shape the course of coping with cancer. Yet, personality variables and indicators of the patient's social integration have been regarded as equally important, in particular those constructs that allow for the derivation of meaningful hypotheses (e.g., dispositional self-consciousness, self-efficacy, and generalized outcome expectancies). Social network variables as well as measures of perceived family support were also included.

A third aim, finally, was to identify "adaptive" coping behaviors, both in a short-term and in a long-term perspective. For that purpose, a set of multiple criteria of coping effectiveness was once more considered. This is described below.

The study extended over two years with a total of five measurement waves. Within the first year, coping behaviors (as well as perceived coping tasks) were assessed four times at intervals of three to four months. Two years after the first wave, a follow-up assessment (Time 5) was made. All variables presumed to be either "predictors" or "adaptational outcomes" were assessed on at least two occasions in order also to allow for strategies of causal modeling (e.g., Jøreskog & Sørbom, 1988).

Patient sampling was conducted in cooperation with several hospitals and institutions for cancer care and rehabilitation in West Germany, all patients being recruited within these medical settings. At the first time of measurement, our sample consisted of $N = 332$ patients (178 females, 154 males) with a mean age of 51 years (age span: 20 to 74 years). Since we were aware of the fact that "cancer" stands for a host of diseases differing in symptomatology, etiology, prognosis, and so forth, while our recruiting procedure did not allow for a homogeneous sample from the very beginning, we subsequently—based on the fairly large number of patients—subdivided the sample according to medical variables or used these variables as covariates in a series of analyses. With regard to site of tumor, the largest subgroup was comprised of patients with carcinoma of the breast ($n = 83$), malignancies in the digestive system ($n = 63$), in the area of the mouth, the throat, and the larynx ($n = 47$), and patients with cancers of the blood or lymphatic system

($n = 43$). At the initial interview, 50% of the sample had been diagnosed within the previous year and time elapsed since diagnosis varied between 1 and 840 weeks ($M = 112$ weeks). A subsample of $n = 128$ patients (38.5%) had already had a cancer recurrence before participating in the study. The most common types of medical treatment applied were surgery (79.9% of the sample), radiation therapy (48.9%), and chemotherapy (27.3%). A few patients had undergone psychotherapy and were excluded from the sample due to uncontrollable effects on our measures. At Time 4, that is after one year, $n = 202$ patients were still participating in the study; at Time 5 (after two years), the sample still consisted of $n = 145$ patients. Of course, we have been controlling for systematic dropout effects, and will in the latter part of this chapter come back particularly to this issue.

The Assessment of Coping in Cancer Patients

Within the last two decades, so much has been said and written about "coping" that one even hesitates to add a few more statements to the field. Even years later, Taylor's (1984) critique of the scientific status of coping research ("... it is hard to think of a literature that is in worse shape," p. 2313) still seems to be justified. It is not our intention to make any effort to clear up the field; rather, we would like to start by presenting a few general arguments that should help to understand our own approach to the study of coping with cancer.

Problems in Studying Coping

There may be many reasons why coping research still considerably lacks conceptual clarity. To understand some of them, it may be helpful to consider the distinction between various scientific strategies proposed by Herrmann (1979). He differentiates psychological domain programs from quasi-paradigmatic research programs underscoring that psychological theories have divergent functions within both. Whereas the latter are characterized by theory construction in itself and by attempts to test a theory's applicability to various fields, the former are related to a particular domain (like anxiety, speech disorders, or whatsoever); this is taken as the explicandum to which adequate theoretical tools are to be applied. Coping research certainly presents an instance of psychological domain programs, being in search of theories that might offer means of *reconstructing* what constitutes that domain.

There are some good examples in the literature of how theories serve such an instrumental function, that is, theories that have proven their usefulness in other domains and are now applied to the study of coping (e.g., social comparison theory, see Wills, this volume; or attribution theory; see the various chapters in this volume by Försterling, Montada, and Shaver). To adopt a certain theoretical perspective, of course, implies that the (potential) variety of coping responses is reduced to a single concept instead of considering the "totality" of behaviors to be observed in people coping with loss and crisis. Many researchers obviously decided not to confine themselves to a particular theoretical perspective, though at the price of facing quite a few problems in their further study of coping with loss and crisis.

One fundamental problem is related to the observation that what is considered as "coping" behavior must not be *phenomenally distinct* from other behaviors. For example, to visit good friends can be considered as an item in a coping checklist while, at the same time, it may be nothing else than a behavioral act motivated by the desire to see good friends. Earlier, we have referred to this as the "first-order distinction problem" in coping research (Braukmann & Filipp, 1984). Obviously, behaviors should only be subsumed under "coping" if they are observed under particularly "stressful" circumstances; it is interesting to note that a similar problem has also been addressed in the study of social support in which the duality of many social behaviors (i.e., "supportive" behaviors as opposed to „regular" social exchanges) has also become apparent (Thoits, 1985).

However, to define "coping" only by referring to a particular situational context does not enhance conceptual clarification either; rather, it confronts us with the "second-order distinction problem:" If "coping" behaviors are conceptually related to stressful circumstances, should all behaviors in the face of crisis and loss then be subsumed under "coping"? Most researchers probably would deny this and would argue that one should conceive of coping only in terms of behaviors that serve a *protective* function. The German word for "coping" (Bewältigung) does have exactly such a connotation and is etymologically rooted primarily in the concept of *mastery*—thus, equating coping with "successful"coping. Yet, if we are to speak of coping only in terms of behaviors that serve protective functions, which one should we select on an a priori basis? We know of no theoretical proposition (or law) based on which we could relate a particular behavior (e.g., information seeking) to a particular positive outcome, thus, qualifying it almost universally as a "protective" response. Whether certain (coping) behaviors prove to be beneficial or not, depends not only on the nature of the "stressor" itself but also certainly varies across people, and it will finally also depend on how coping effectiveness is measured as well as on the time perspective that is adopted in evaluating it (see Suls & Fletcher, 1985).

In short, a given coping strategy is not intrinsically adaptive or maladaptive, rather, it may be beneficial for some people in some situations at some times. In addition, as we have argued elsewhere (Filipp & Klauer, 1991), the nature of success is elusive in the domain of coping as well and can, by no means, be defined unambiguously. Hence, to confound coping with good adaptational outcomes does not help in conceptually clarifying it. Obviously, coping is a *relational* concept (or an at least two-valued predicate) comprised of behaviors through which whatsoever (perceived) situational demands are transformed into whatsoever (subjectively) desired end-states. Given the potential variety of situational demands, of desired outcomes, and of the heterogeneity of behaviors that might serve the various instrumental functions in relating "is" to "ought," it is not surprising that the term "coping," rather than being a theoretical construct, is much more like an umbrella term for an only seemingly unified body of research. Thus, coping research, in general, might even not constitute what Herrmann (1979) called a domain program.

Although we have been much aware of these and quite a number of other problems in defining and measuring coping, we did feel that the study of how cancer patients "cope" with their disease can, by no means, be postponed. Rather, the development of an appropriate measure deserved some time.

Measuring Coping Responses to Cancer

Since it was our intention to observe coping behaviors longitudinally, we first decided to describe them on a rather micro-analytic level rather than using broad categories of coping (e.g., monitoring vs. blunting; see Miller, this volume). In addition, we did not want to conceptually reduce coping to a single theoretical construct, as outlined above, but preferred to look at a variety of coping modes that might also differ in their variability over time. In order to circumvent a more or less arbitrary selection of coping responses, we first classified them with respect to an

		Attentional focus			
		Centered on disease		Distracted from disease	
		Sociability		Sociability	
		High	Low	High	Low
Level of response	Covert	"I worried whether physicians can really help me" (27)	"I tried to find out whether I did something wrong" (25)	"I said to myself that there are many people who are worse off compared to me" (47)	"I imagined that things will get better sometimes" (52)
	Overt	"I shared experiences in managing the illness with other patients" (01)	"I looked for information on my illness in books and journals" (22)	"I encouraged other people and tried to cheer them up" (08)	"I kept busy with things that filled me out" (06)

FIG. 2.1. A three-dimensional system for the classification of coping responses and selected item examples (from Filipp & Klauer, 1988)

a priori model comprised of three basic behavioral dimensions (see Figure 2.1): (a) attentional focus (i.e., behaviors indicating distraction from vs. focus upon the disease), (b) level of coping response (i.e., overt vs. intrapsychic), and (c) degree of sociability (i.e., behaviors reflecting withdrawal from others vs. integrating others into one's coping efforts).

These dimensions were then cross-classified yielding eight mutually exclusive groups of coping responses, each group being represented by eight items describing a particular response. This total of 64 items was then included in a questionnaire for the patient to answer on 6-point scales how *often* within the last weeks he or she had exhibited each response (Trierer Skalen zur Krankheitsbewältigung; TSK; see Klauer, Filipp, & Ferring, 1989). According to our interest in temporal variations in coping behaviors, frequency ratings were preferred to ratings of „typicalness“ (see also the isue of "episodic" vs. "dispositional" measures in coping research: Cohen, 1987).

This a priori pattern of coping responses, however, was not confirmed in dimensional analyses of our data. Exploratory and subsequently performed confirmatory factor analyses yielded a structural pattern of five factors that were, then, used for the construction of the scales measuring the five coping modes: (I) *Rumination (RU)*, comprised of items describing intrapsychic responses focusing on the disease and implying social withdrawal (e.g., engagement in temporal comparisons and causal reasoning); (II) *Search for Affiliation (SA)*, reflective of highly sociable coping behaviors implying diversion and attentional distraction from the disease; (III) *Threat Minimization (TM)*, describing intrapsychic, presumably emotion-focused coping responses, like self-instructions toward positive thinking and maintaining trust in the medical regimen; (IV) *Information Seeking (IS)*, describing overt reactions aimed at gaining knowledge of the disease and its treatment, preferrably by joining the company of other cancer patients; (V) *Search for Meaning in Religion (SR)*, comprising attempts to find meaning in the illness experience with special reference to religious issues. Because we used unit weighting instead of factor scores in the calculation of scale values, the coping scales *RU* and *SI* as well as *TM* and *SA* are moderately, though significantly, intercorrelated at each of the four measurement waves. Without being exhaustive, of course, these scales cover a wide range of coping responses, some of which can also be found in other studies using a different rationale (e.g., Felton, Revenson, & Hinrichsen, 1984; Ray, Lindop, & Gibson, 1982; Taylor, 1983; Weisman, 1979). All scales were shown to be sufficiently reliable and consistent; split-half coefficients ranging between .74 (*SA*) and .90 (*SR*), Cronbach's *alpha* between .74 (*RU*) and .88 (*IS*). The TSK scales, thus, obviously allow for the description of individual differences that can then can be related to various predictor variables as well as to various outcome criteria in order to investigate their effectiveness.

The Assessment of Coping Effectiveness in Cancer Patients

Current literature on coping with crisis and loss seems to be dominated by an ideal that is most commonly reflected in homeostatic models of functioning, that is, victims of life crises are expected to return to a precrisis baseline within an adequate period of time (see Caplan, 1964). Thus, the issue of "coping effectiveness," at first glance, seems to be rather easy to resolve. From a developmental perspective, however, the idea also has been proffered that personal gains and benefits can equally result from being exposed to crisis and loss, which means that coping effectiveness is rather to be equated with "growth" than with homeostasis (see Lerner & Gignac, this volume). Obviously, to speak of successful or effective coping is a question of the metatheoretical perspectives one is willing to adopt (and a question of values, as well). To borrow a similar notion given by Baltes and Baltes (1990) with regard to the definition of "successful aging," one could find a solution in the direction of an "all-encompassing definition of successful coping" by looking at *multiple* criteria. The study of coping effectiveness in cancer patients particularly is in need of such an approach, since it can probably be assumed that certain coping behaviors might reveal divergent effects on various criteria and/or at various times. This can already be concluded from the intense discussion on whether measures of "quality of life" should be preferred to "length of survival time" as indicators of adaptation in patients suffering from chronic or incurable disease (see Filipp & Klauer, 1991). For example, *dysphoric* mood (as measured by the Bradburn Affect Balance Scale) has been shown to predict 1-year survival in a sample of breast cancer patients (see Derogatis, Abeloff, & Melisaratos, 1979), indicating that even low levels of subjective well-being, *per se*, cannot unanimously be used as indicators of maladjustment, since other adaptational outcomes (i.e., length of survival) may be attainable only at the price of negative affect.

Accordingly, we included a set of multiple criteria in our study, in order to measure coping effectiveness, namely clinical status at Time 5, as well as various indicators of emotional adjustment and the patient's social and occupational (re)integration. We will only refer to a few of the various measures: Hopelessness was assessed by a German version (Krampen, 1979) of the scale developed by Beck, Weissman, Lester, and Trexler (1974). In their conception, hopelessness is comprised of negative generalized expectancies about oneself and future outcomes, at the same time emphasizing a loss of motivation in the sense of a "giving-up" response, and the emotional state associated with it. In addition, an instrument to measure subjective well-being was administered at all measurement points (BfS; von Zerssen, 1976), from which—based on self-ratings on 28 bipolar scales describing positive versus negative affective states—a single score is computed for level of well-being. Self-esteem was measured with a German version of the instrument developed by Rosenberg (1965). In addition, a series of ratings made by the patient with regard to his or her subjective coping efficacy (also in comparison to others) had been obtained. Of course, it was of crucial importance not to confound measures of coping behaviors with measures of coping effectiveness (as is, for example, the case when "hopelessness/helplessness" is considered a coping dimension; see Greer, 1991). We will now turn to a selection of results from our study, confining ourselves to the role of temporal factors in coping with and adapting to cancer.

THE ROLE OF TIME AS A FACTOR IN COPING WITH CANCER

One of the fundamental attributes of our lives and our environment is its dependence upon time, and some authors argue that virtually no other concept is so central to human life and behavior as time (Zakay, 1989): Astronomical phenomena, for example, produce recurrent cycles of light and dark as well as seasonal changes in day length and temperature. Superimposed on our biological adaptation to these periodicities are cultural adaptations in the form of conventional time representations (e.g., clocks, calendars) that provide frameworks for individual and collective action. In particular, adults are able to use hours, days, weeks, or years flexibly to remember the time of past events, to orient to the present, and to plan for the future (Friedman, 1989).

It is well known among psychologists that time can be viewed from quite a number of different angles—not only with regard to the length of the scales used (seconds to years or centuries) but also with regard to whether we speak of experienced or spontaneously estimated time versus time measured by conventional clocks or calendars. In addition, developmental psychologists are familiar with the concept of historical time, proposing that different birth cohorts might differ in their development and behavior as a result of when people are born and the various cirumstances associated with growing up within a certain historical context (Elder, 1979).

There are many good reasons to assume that time also plays a prominent role in coping with cancer, although empirical evidence is scarce in many respects. We will now turn our interest to the various ways in which one can look at time as a factor in coping with cancer, namely by focusing on (a) life time, normally indicated by chronological age; (b) exposure time, as indicated by time that has elapsed since the diagnosis of cancer (observed either longitudinally or cross-sectionally); and (c) time as distance from death or survival time. These various temporal factors have been addressed in research with a different impetus, and the body of knowledge varies considerably in size and conclusiveness, as will be shown in the next sections. Of course, a fourth aspect of time, psychological time, should also be mentioned briefly. We all know from introspection that there are moments of experience that seem to last forever and others that seem to fly by almost unnoticed. Unfortunately, however, studies on the psychology of time have primarily dealt with temporal judgments in experimental settings (for an overview, see Levin &

Zakay, 1989) rather than with experiences of the passage of time in people living under stressful conditions. Although there is experimental evidence on how the affective quality of situations might influence the experience of duration (see Galinat & Borg, 1987), we know of no research in which psychological time has been investigated in patients suffering from chronic disease or in other victims of life crisis. We did not address this issue, either, but have some anecdotical evidence that the passage of time is a salient aspect in patients' illness representations (for a report on this issue, see Filipp, 1990).

Coping With Cancer at Various Ages

Developmental psychologists have sharpened our understanding of the significance of whether certain life experiences occur "in time" or "off time" with regard to socially or biologically prescribed time tables of the life span (see Baltes, 1979; Filipp, 1981; Neugarten, 1968)—"off-time" events generally being considered the more "serious" ones. Related to this is the idea that *when* certain events occur in people's lives is often a much more important issue than *whether* these events occur at all. Although chronological age (or any other variable indicating the individual's position in the life cycle) is so easy and reliable to assess, its significance in research on coping with cancer, however, has often been overlooked. Yet, there are quite a few arguments in support of the assumption that the diagnosis of cancer does have different meanings and vary in impact at different stages of the life span.

First, it is argued within psychodynamic theories of coping that ways of coping with loss and crisis themselves undergo a "maturation" process that should be observable in age differences in coping (Haan, 1977; Vaillant, 1977). Similarly, one could interpret the age-related increase in "accomodative coping strategies" reported by Brandtstädter and Renner (this volume) as a reflection of older people's growing insight into the limitations of their own controlling responses. Second, besides such a developmental interpretation of changes in coping, it has been argued that "off-time" life events are more difficult to cope with because victims cannot as easily rely on *social support* as in the case of normative events (see Brim & Ryff, 1980). Third, as Montada (this volume) has proposed, "off-time" events are more difficult to deal with since in these cases the question "Why me?" is much faster at hand than in the case of "in-time" events, and painful feelings of injustice are much more likely to be experienced. Fourth, by referring to the life span as a sequence of developmental tasks to be accomplished, one could argue that chronic disease, when diagnosed in earlier rather than later years, has a much higher impact. . In younger patients, cancer should interfere with many more long-ranging life goals and options (e.g., with regard to occupational attainments or social integration) and thus affect more life domains than when diagnosed later in the life span.

There are some studies in which coping with physical illness had been related to the age variable. For example, Viney and Westbrook (1982) investigated coping behaviors in patients suffering from various diseases and found a positive correlation between age and the use of "fatalistic" coping strategies. Felton and Revenson (1987) reported "expression of emotion" and "information seeking" to be used less often in older patients than in younger ones, and this effect proved to be independent of the severity of the various diseases from which their patients suffered.

When we now turn to our results from the Trier Longitudinal Study on Coping with Chronic Disease, it becomes obvious that chronological age does play a less significant role in how patients cope with and adapt to cancer than one would expect from the various lines of reasoning presented above. First of all, no age differences could be observed with regard to measures indicating emotional adjustment to illness, that is, hopelessness, self-esteem, and subjective well-being at any measurement occasion. In addition, four of the five coping modes under study, that is, Rumination, Search for Affiliation, Information Seeking, and Search for Meaning in Religion, also proved to be unaffected by chronological age at each of the four measurement waves. Only with regard to Threat Minimization a positive linear relation between chronological age and coping was consistently found across all measurement waves.

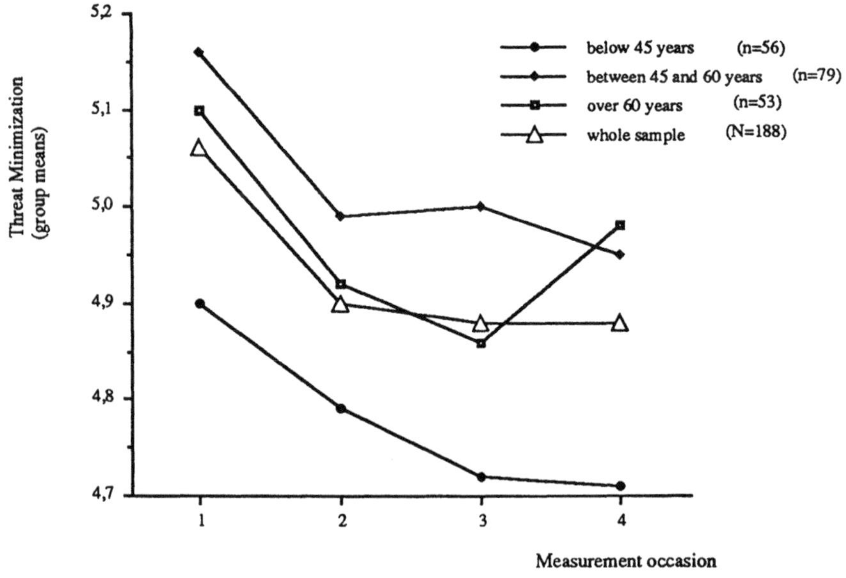

FIG. 2.2 Temporal variations in Threat Minimization in various age groups.

As can be seen in Figure 2.2, this effect is primarily due to a much less frequent use of threat minimization within the younger group (below 45 years of age), whereas differences between the two other age groups as well as nonlinear effect components were nonsignificant. Analysis of variance revealed that the effect of age was nonoverlapping with a linear decreasing trend across measurement waves being observed in the whole sample ($F_{(3;573)} = 10.07, p < .001$, averaged effect of age group: $F_{(2;191)} = 4.93, p < .01$). If one is willing to conceive of Threat Minimization as a special case of accommodation to loss and threat, the consistent positive association between age and Threat Minimization nicely parallels the findings reported by Brandtstädter and Renner (this volume) on an age-related increase of accomodative coping modes.

That chronological age proved not to be a rather important temporal dimension in how cancer patients cope with and adapt to their disease, may, of course, be partially due to the status of the age variable itself. One cannot take for granted, of course, that patients differing in age do, accordingly, live under different circumstances (in terms of family cycle, occupational carreer, etc.) that might account for variations in the impact of cancer. On the other hand, one might also conclude from these data that the diagnosis of cancer is a traumatic experience at all ages; thus, individual differences in coping with cancer should rather be due to psychosocial variables than to age per se.

The Passage of Time in the Course of Coping With Cancer

Perspectives in Studying the Passage of Time

Researchers who focus on the passage of time in coping with crisis mainly do so with respect to two different, yet interrelated, issues: (a) They either look for temporal variations in *coping behaviors* guided by the assumption that coping unfolds as a process over time and refuting the idea of trait-like dispositions to handle stress (in particular, Lazarus & Folkman, 1984), or (b) they focus on variations in *emotional adjustment* since the traumatic event occurred. This latter, primarily "outcome-oriented," approach aims at the identification of certain stages that victims of crisis have to undergo in order to attain an ultimate stage of recovery and resolution (on this issue, see Silver & Wortman, 1980; Wortman & Silver, this volume). Although some studies have used cross-sectional designs by comparing samples differing in time elapsed since the traumatic event (e.g., Mattlin, Wethington, & Kessler, 1990), such questions obviously call for longitudinal designs with repeated measurements. In particular, if one is interested in the role that time may play in coping with cancer, cross-sectional comparisons may suffer from considerable methodological flaws, since the various samples are not necessarily drawn from the same population—the "older" samples, by definition, being comprised of survivors.[2]

Why should time make a difference in how cancer patients cope with and adapt to their illness? It is a widely accepted notion that stressful situations, in general, unfold over time as is, for example, implied in the concept of "stressor sequences" proposed by Elliot and Eisdorfer (1982). Even when the traumatic event under consideration itself is a more or less time-bound experience, it continues to have impact on the individual due to a variety of subsequent event-related changes in various life domains. This is even more pronounced in the case of cancer: Cancer as a disease itself may change (for the worse or better) over time and confront the patient with the imposition of changing demands—presumably accompanied by and resulting in changes in ways of perceiving and coping with one's illness. Even in the case of nonrecurrent cancer or otherwise "stable" circumstances, it can probably be assumed that coping with cancer is a process that involves different types of task and demands at different times; this may often be reflected by a continuous change in hopes and fears as well as in the patient's appraisals of his or her situation.

Changing demands imposed on cancer patients, and hence changes in coping, may also be caused by changes in reactions from the patient's social environment (see Dunkel-Schetter, 1984; Peters-Golden, 1982). In particular, a significant decrease in availability and/or adequacy of social support observed over time has been reported from various studies. For example, Neuling and Winefield (1988) found from their longitudinal study of recovery after surgery for breast cancer that emotional support and reassurance, particularly from family members, showed a clear decrease over time. Similarily, Aymanns (in press) could show that time elapsed since diagnosis in his sample of $N = 169$ cancer patients did have a significant effect on patients' satisfaction with family support; higher temporal distances from diagnosis being associated with less satisfaction.

Finally, for most cancer patients, life will never be the same as it was before their diagnosis—even for those who perceive themselves as cured. If one is willing to accept this as a general proposition, the value of simplistic homeostatic models that favor "return to precrisis level of functioning" as the ultimate outcome of coping has to be heavily drawn into question (see above). Rather, it is helpful to conceive of coping with cancer in terms of a *transition* process that, by definition, has to be described on the temporal dimension.

---

[2] Nevertheless, one could create another analogy to developmental research and speak of time here in terms of "event cohorts." Such an approach would highlight the distinction as to whether event cohorts might differ in coping behaviors as a function of length of experience with their disease and/or as a function of "historical" events associated with the cohort variable (e.g., changes in medical care; cancer deaths of prominent people). Although we can only speculate at that point, we think that ideas borrowed from developmental psychology could widen our perspective on how temporal factors influence the way in which patients cope with their disease.

There are various ways to conceive of transitions and to highlight different processes implied in transitions. Janoff-Bulman and Schwartzberg (1991) have recently proposed a general model of personal change following traumatic events. They argue that changes take place primarily at the level of victims' basic assumptions about their selves and their world. Transitions, then, are equated with processes by which victims of life crisis, step by step, have to replace one set of ideas, beliefs, and values with another within their assumptive worlds. Jacobson (1986), taking a slightly different perspective, argues that transitions are reflective of a change in time orientation: Whereas individuals in the beginning of a transition (usually marked by a crisis) typically look backwards, for example, by evaluating their past lives and by ruminating about the causes of what has happened, they later begin to look forward to the reorganization of their lives. In some cases, patients may later create a situation for themselves in which their resources are equal to or even exceed the demand imposed on them; in other cases, the transition process may end in a "deficit state" in which resources are inadequate to cope with a (dramatically) altered life situation. Thus, to speak of transitions does not intrinsically imply "happy endings"—quite contrary to the propositions advocated within the so-called "stage models." Finally, one can also think of transitions primarily in terms of a process in which self-images are to be revised and new "possible selves" to be created for the future (Filipp, 1983; Horowitz, 1979; Markus & Nurius, 1986). Whatever particular perspective is adopted, to speak of phases, stages, or transitions has widened our understanding of the temporal variations that might characterize coping with cancer.

Empirical Evidence on Temporal Variations in Coping With Cancer

When we look for investigations of temporal variations in coping with cancer, the literature reveals that this has not been of central interest to researchers. Longitudinal studies are still rather scarce, and researchers who used longer time spans of observation in their studies with cancer patients did so primarily in the sense of *prediction* studies in which, for example, reactions to the diagnosis of cancer at an earlier point in time were assessed and related to indicators of successful adaptation (e.g., Sobel & Worden, 1979) or to the course of the disease itself (e.g., DiClemente & Temoshok, 1985) assessed at a later point in time. The issue as to whether coping behaviors remain rather stable over time clearly has been of comparably minor interest. If related empirical evidence is reported at all, it mostly stems from studies that have investigated coping in the context of less serious events than cancer.

The study by Folkman and Lazarus (1985) may serve here as an example. Their data obtained from a sample of college students at three stages of a mid-term examination support their notion of coping as a process unfolding over time in that all coping behaviors under study (with the exception of "self-blame") proved to either increase or decrease depending on their presumed functions in dealing with achievement stress at various points in time. The study by McCrae (1989) presents another example. Based on earlier cross-sectional data on age differences in coping drawn from a community sample, the author was able to retest almost one half of his original sample seven years later. Whereas cross-sectional analyses had shown evidence of age (or cohort) differences in the use of several of these coping mechanisms, none of these effects was consistently paralleled by changes in repeated measures and cross-sequential analyses. The author concludes that aging per se has little effect on coping behavior, rather, coping is seen mainly as a function of enduring characteristics of the individual rather than as a reflection of maturation processes.

As outlined above, a central aim of the Trier Longitudinal Study of Coping with Chronic Disease was to investigate change or stability in coping with cancer over time and to identify correlates of temporal consistencies in coping. Of course, some criteria must be fulfilled in order to study coping as a *process* and to avoid methodological pitfalls (see also Folkman & Lazarus, 1985). Our study certainly met these criteria (e.g., multiple measurements occasions, frequency ratings of responses). What do our findings tell us about the passage of time in coping with cancer? First, we have to briefly comment on the concept of stability, which—as is well-known—has to be conceived of as a multifaceted phenomenon, including structural invariance, positional stability, level stability, as well as ipsative stability.

Structural invariance is the prerequisite for testing all other facets of stability, since to administer the same instrument does not guarantee measurement equivalence over time or across different populations (see Baltes & Nesselroade, 1973). We tested structural invariance with structural equation modeling (Jøreskog & Sørbom, 1988), since this methodological approach allows for the specification and test of models that imply successively restrictive assumptions concerning the observed factor structure. Goodness-of-fit criteria for four models showed that one model that tested the invariance of factor loadings and factor covariances over time fitted our data best, χ^2 (170, N = 202) = 185.67, $p < .20$, $GFI = .97$. Thus, measurement equivalence can be taken as guaranteed, and comparisons across time can be performed reliably.

As a next facet of stability, we tested *level stability,* referring to the frequency in use of the various coping modes and observable from group means comparisons across various measurement occasions. Various MANOVAs with a repeated-measurement factor were performed accordingly. Results showed that the frequency of Rumination ($F(3;579) = 3.38, p < .05$), Threat Minimization ($F(3; 582) = 11.82, p < .01$), and Information Seeking ($F(3;585) = 2.89, p < .05$) significantly decreased over time—the effect of repeated measurement being especially pronounced for Threat Minimization. On the other hand, Search for Affiliation and Search for Meaning in Religion proved to be quite stable on the level of means.

We then considered the temporal stability of interindividual differences in coping behaviors—often referred to as *positional stability.* Based on propositions from Generalized Classical Test Theory (Steyer, 1987; Tack, 1980), we, once more, specified models within the framework of structural equation modeling that allowed for the estimation of coefficients of *consistency* and *specificity* for each coping mode (for a more detailed description, see Ferring, Klauer, Filipp, & Steyer, 1990). These coefficients describe the amount of variance in coping behaviors that is either explained by person factors (e.g., coping styles) or by characteristics of the situation (and/or their interaction). In order to illustrate these results, they are proportionally expressed (percentage of variance explained by person factors) as depicted in Figure 2.3.

As can be seen from Figure 2.3, a considerable amount of consistency can be observed for each of the five coping modes over time; specificity, although being accordingly low, still provides systematic variance due to situational factors (i.e., measurement occasions). Obviously, then, our measures of coping with cancer, though not completely insensitive to change, seem to reflect primarily person-specific modes of coping with cancer rather than highlighting the role of time.

Thus, we can conclude from these results that—again contrary to our expectations and to the various arguments outlined above—temporal consistencies in coping with cancer are impressively high; in particular, interindividual differences in the use of the various coping strategies remain fairly stable. This is clearly in support of propositions made by those researchers who underline the role of personality in coping with loss and crisis (e.g., McCrae, 1989; Miller, this volume). At the same time, our results draw into question whether coping indeed unfolds as

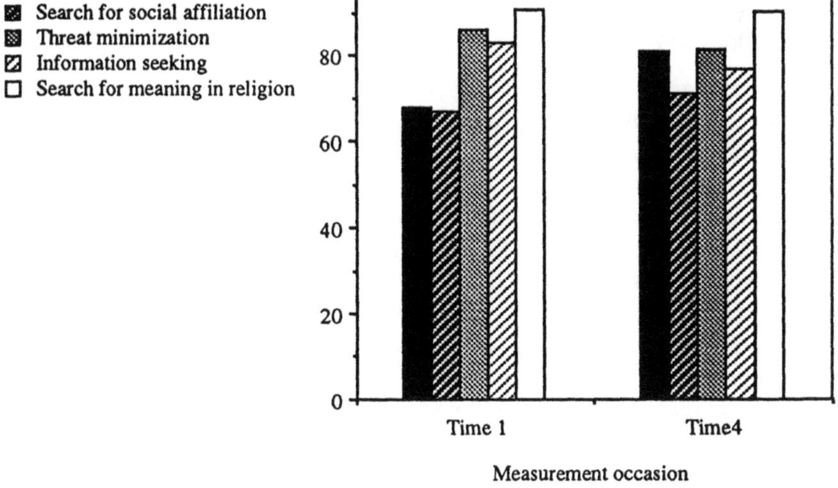

FIG. 2.3 Relative proportions of consistency in five modes of coping at two occasions of measurement.

a process over time, as has been repeatedly stated by the Lazarus group (e.g., Folkman & Lazarus, 1985).

Of course, the significant decrease in Rumination, Information Seeking, and Threat Minimization (observed on the level of means) seems to reflect that some ways of dealing with cancer become less important over time. It is interesting to state that in our case, this is primarily true for those coping responses in which the common element is that attention is focused upon rather than distracted from one's disease. On the other hand, this result based on the longitudinal observation of coping behaviors could not be replicated in cross-sectional comparisons in which time elapsed since diagnosis served as an indicator of the passage of time—although we are aware that such a "pseudolongitudinal" research strategy (see Watson & Kendall, 1983) must not necessarily yield identical results. It should be briefly mentioned here that, in addition, interaction effects of time since diagnosis and measurement occasion could also not be found from various MANOVAs. Obviously—as one must conclude from these results—we will have to continue by analyzing *differential patterns* of coping over time carefully and, paying particularly attention to ipsative stabilities (see Ferring & Filipp, 1991).

The observation that temporal consistencies in coping behaviors are rather high may be seen as important both from the perspective of basic research as well as from a practical point of view; since it is related to the issue of what determines coping and to the issue of how easily coping behaviors can be altered by systematic intervention. On the other hand, many researchers may be much more interested in how adjustment to cancer unfolds over time rather than in temporal variations in coping behaviors alone—an issue to which we will turn next.

Empirical Evidence on Temporal Variations in Adjustment to Cancer

Implicitly inherent in the thinking of laymen and elaborated in stage models of the coping process as well, is the expectation that victims of life crisis gradually "come to terms" with their lot. Accordingly, one would expect that with the passage of time cancer patients learn to emotionally adjust to their disease and to accept it as a reality of their lives! We know from the work of Wortman and her colleagues (see Wortman & Silver, this volume) that this, however, is by no means to be observed universally, neither in parents who have lost an infant due to Sudden Infant Death Syndrome nor in victims of father-daughter incest (Silver, Boon, & Stones, 1983). Similarly, Gottesman and Lewis (1982), based on observations of cancer patients over an interval of 15 weeks, reported that crisis (as measured by the Halpern Crisis Scale) was not resolved within that time span. On the other hand, Weisman (1979) concludes from his studies with cancer patients that the first two to three months after diagnosis are the "most distressing" ones and that afterwards "problems tend to settle down" (p. 80). McIvor, Riklan, and Reznikoff (1984) report from their study with patients suffering from multiple sclerosis that the longer a patient is suffering from this disease the more likely it is that he or she will be severely depressed.

Since time itself is not a very meaningful variable, in particular in studying adjustment to potentially recurrent disease or to ongoing harm, some researchers have subdivided their samples into patients who had one remission versus patients who had stayed recurrence-free. Interestingly enough, as Weisman and Worden (1986) reported, many patients experienced recurrence as less traumatic than their initial diagnosis. Recurrence, accordingly, proved to be unrelated to deteriorations in psychological well-being. Similarly, McIvor et al. (1984) report that patients suffering from multiple sclerosis who already had one remission proved to be less depressed than those without remission.

When we refer to our own results again, they, at first glance, prove to be clearly in contradiction to popular notions of recovery and adjustment as well. A series of MANOVAs yielded that the variables meant to indicate emotional adjustment (hopelessness, emotional well-being, subjective coping efficacy, and self-esteem) did not change "for the better" across the time span under observation. This picture is also reflected in results from cross-sectional comparisons in which the effect of time elapsed since diagnosis on these various outcome variables also proved to be nonsignificant.[3]

However, to expect improvements in emotional adjustment over time presupposes that cancer patients, at least in the beginning, indeed did suffer from hopelessness, negative affect, lowered self-esteem, or feelings of being overwhelmed by their disease. When we compare the means of some of these variables with those obtained from a community-dwelling sample of $N = 202$ (male) adults, however, we were quite surprised: With regard to *hopelessness*, the group of cancer patients proved not to score higher than the healthy "control" group! Obviously, even at the earlier points in time, our sample of cancer patients had already achieved comparatively low levels of hopelessness, thus presumably creating a "floor effect," which does not allow for considerable improvement over time. Contrary to this finding, a similar conclusion cannot be drawn with regard to *subjective well-being*. With regard to this measure, cancer patients as compared to the general population ($t\,(327) = 7.42, p < .001$), proved to have significantly lower scores, that is to suffer more from negative affect. However, emotional well-being did not change across time either; thus, in this case, stability has to be equated with unaltered negative affect rather than with the maintenance of hope as in the other case.

Of course, our presentation would be incomplete if we did not at least briefly investigate the role of time in moderating the relationship between coping behaviors

---

[3] When time elapsed since diagnosis is substituted by the patients' medical status, a slightly different picture emerged: We subdivided the sample according to whether patients were (a) in primary treatment, (b) remained recurrence-free, or (c) have had a relapse, and we found quite striking differences between these groups in ways of coping, yet, less pronounced differences in indicators of adjustment.

and indicators of emotional adjustment. Do coping behaviors change with regard to their presumed effectiveness over time?

Empirical Evidence on Temporal Variations in Coping Effectiveness

To study this issue, a third set of analyses was performed, in which we tested whether the *relationship* between coping behaviors and indicators of adjustment varies across the occasions of measurement, that is, we looked for time as a moderator of the coping-distress relationship.

Based on the observation that Rumination, Search for Affiliation, and Threat Minimization were significantly associated with emotional well-being and hopelessness synchronously, we, in a next step, investigated the diachronous effects of coping on these outcomes using cross-lagged structural equation models (Ferring, 1989; Rogosa, 1979). In brief, these analyses revealed that, after partialling out the variance due to the autoregression in coping and distress, four different patterns of results emerged: (a) Threat Minimization had significant synchronous as well as diachronous effects on hopelessness—frequent use of that coping mode resulting in lowered levels of hopelessness; (b) Rumination showed a significant positive

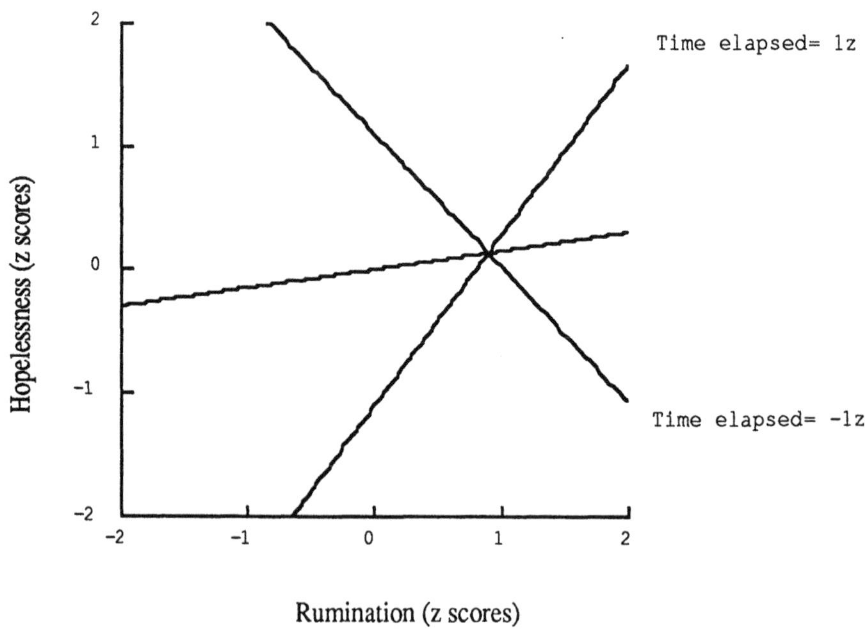

FIG. 2.4. Interaction effect of time elapsed since diagnosis and Rumination (Time 2) on Hopelessness.

synchronous association with hopelessness, yet had no effect over time; rather, Rumination itself proved to be significantly predicted by prior levels of hopelessness. (c) Search for Affiliation proved to be synchronously related to low levels of hopelessness, and, in turn, to be enhanced by low levels of hopelessness; Information Seeking and Search for Meaning in Religion proved to be completely unrelated to hopelessness at all points of observation (for further details, see Filipp, Klauer, Freudenberg, & Ferring, 1990).

With respect to the issue as to whether time elapsed since diagnosis might be moderating the coping-distress relationship, interaction effects of time and coping on hopelessness were tested in a series of regression analyses. A clear pattern of results emerged from these analyses only for the relationship between rumination and hopelessness (see Figure 2.4):

When predicting Hopelesseness at Time 2 from Rumination at Time 1 and Rumination at Time 2, low levels of Hopelessness proved to be associated with frequent ruminations only within the group of patients with a longer time span since diagnosis. Within the group of patients for whom time elapsed since diagnosis was longer, Rumination was related to *higher* levels of Hopelessness. This finding, at first glance, supports the notion of Silver et al. (1983) according to which rumination may be adaptive in earlier stages yet become increasingly maladaptive at later points in time, indicating, for example, a failure to find meaning in what has happened. Unfortunately, however, the interaction effect just reported proved to be no longer significant after Hopelessness at Time 2 was introduced as autoregressor in predicting Hopelessness at Time 4, which again points to the high stability in this variable.

Taking these results together, we can conclude as follows: First, interindividual differences in coping behaviors are characterized by considerably high degrees of stability over time. It would certainly be premature to refer to this result as supporting the notion of "coping styles," since up to 35% of the variance still observed were explained by situational factors (measurement occasion). On the other hand, as we know from analyses reported elsewhere (see Filipp, Klauer, & Ferring, in press), interindividual differences in coping behaviors clearly proved to be related to rather enduring personality characteristics (e.g., dispositional self-consciousness), which might contribute to the positional stabilities in the coping behaviors under study.

Second, when we look at the mean level, it becomes clear that some modes of coping are used less frequently with the passage of time, in particular, rumination, threat minimization, and information seeking; whereas search for affiliation and search for meaning in religion do not show such a decrease and tend to remain stable over time. Speaking of coping in terms of a *process*, thus may be appropriate with respect to some, yet by no means to all, ways of coping.

Third, when we look for changes in patients' emotional adjustment to their disease, as indicated by the various criteria of coping effectiveness at all measurement occasions, the stabilities to be observed are quite strikingly high: Hopelessness, already being at a comparatively low level at the first measurement wave, proves to be unaltered by the passage of time both in a longitudinal and cross-sectional perspective. Subjective well-being does not change over time either, yet, in this case, pointing to rather chronic negative affect in cancer patients. Anyhow, there is much less temporal variation in emotional responses to cancer than one would expect on the basis of the various lines of reasoning presented in the literature.

Fourth, with regard to the question as to whether certain ways of coping change with regard to their effectiveness over time, we found a rather differentiated pattern of results. When taking hopelessness as an outcome criterion, synchronous effects as well as diachronous effects of coping modes could be found. Two ways of coping with cancer, namely information seeking and search for meaning in religion proved to be neither adaptive nor maladaptive—they are simply unrelated to adjustment. In addition, time (in this case, time elapsed since diagnosis) did not prove to be a powerful moderator of the relationship between coping and adaptational outcomes.

Obviously, our results reported here highlight the necessity of longitudinal designs in studying coping with physical illness. Not only do they allow for the observation of temporal consistencies at various levels; in addition, by using strategies of causal modeling they allow for a better insight into the coping-distress relationship. Differential patterns of result emerge depending on which mode of coping and which adaptational outcome is considered. Due to the stabilities of these variables, effects of coping on distress and vice versa may be observed or may even disappear over time. In sum, if one wants to look at the complexity of the life situation within which patients coping with life-threatening disease find themselves, longitudinal research certainly is the via regia.

So far, we have looked at our sample as a whole rather than observe the course of coping with and adapting to cancer in various subsamples (e.g., in male vs. female patients) or in groups with different types of malignancy. We are also still in the process of analyzing our data on the level of ipsative stabilities (Ferring & Filipp, 1991); yet, we are already able to adopt a more differential perspective on length of survival to which we turn in the last section.

Time as Distance From Death

Predicting Length of Survival in Cancer Patients

Another aspect of time often referred to in research with cancer patients is *survival time*. For many decades, researchers have tried to predict length of survival not only from medical but also from psychological variables (e.g., Weisman & Worden, 1975). This research tradition traces back to psychoanalytic theories of somatic disorders (see Engel & Schmale, 1967) and is now receiving renewed attention from researchers interested in the relationship between behavior and affect, on the one hand, and responses of the immune system, on the other (for an overview, see Dorian & Garfinkel, 1987). For example, Levy and her colleagues (see Levy & Wise, 1988) found higher natural killer cell activity in women who were more distressed and maladjusted following surgery for breast cancer. Based on follow-up observations (time interval up to 2 years), Jensen (1987) reported neoplastic spread in breast cancer patients to be associated with repressive personality style and reduced expression of negative affect (among a few other psychological variables), after disease stage at original diagnosis and a variety of medical variables at study onset had been controlled for. On the other hand, Cassileth et al. (1985) were less successful in predicting length of survival or time to relapse, respectively, in a sample of patients suffering from melanoma and breast carcinoma; according to their results, social and psychological factors were unrelated to length of survival or time to relapse (as well as to medical variables themselves, e.g., extent of disease, performance status).

Studies on survival time in cancer patients may sometimes have been suffering from an "optimistic bias" in overestimating the role of psychosocial factors; presumably, they more often suffered from methodological shortcomings with regard to the issue of causality, and, in particular, as to whether initial medical status had been carefully controlled for. On the other hand, if cancer itself is already at an advanced stage (as seems to be true in the sample of Cassileth et al., 1985), biological factors certainly will override and predominate psychological ones; the potential influence of the latter being limited in these cases though not necessarily in others. Accordingly, as Greer (1991) concluded from a recent overview of his own work as well as from replication and other relevant studies a convincingly high number of studies, in which medical status (indicated by, e.g., lymph node invasion or physician's prognosis) was indeed carefully controlled for, appeared to underline the independent role of psychological factors in predicting length of survival or risk of recurrence.

The issue of survival time, however, has been addressed in those studies from a somewhat different perspective than the one adopted in the Trier Longitudinal Study on Coping with Chronic Disease. The research strategy typically employed by other researchers is to recruit a sample of patients that is fairly homogeneous with regard to medical parameters, to assess psychosocial variables at a rather early point in the course of the disease (e.g., in newly diagnosed patients), and to relate these variables to medical status observed at a follow-up measurement.

Comparing Decedents and Survivors in Coping and Adaptation

Quite contrary to the work referred to, so far, the primary focus in our study was upon a two-year longitudinal *follow-through* observation of the coping process in cancer patients rather than on predicting the *follow-up* status of these patients at a later point in time. As is true for any longitudinal investigation, attempts to control for systematic dropout effects in the data were of crucial importance to us; thus, we tried to identify whether patients who had dropped out during the study—either due to death or due to "experimental mortality"—prove *post hoc* to differ systematically from those patients still enrolled in the study. In part, we also have been inspired by gerontological work and by observations stemming from elderly people in which "distance from death" proved to be a better predictor of cognitive functioning than chronological age—indicated by the so called "terminal drop" in the various measures of cognitive functioning (e.g., Jarvik & Bank, 1983). Accordingly, one can adopt a *follow-back* perspective by tracing back the course of coping with and adapting to cancer in those patients who had died and compare it to the course of coping in those still alive. In particular, we were interested as to what point in time differences between both samples might become observable. This, of course, necessitated a control, if at all possible, of differences in initial medical status between both samples. We will now turn to the various comparisons we performed and discuss the results obtained.

Matching Procedure. During the first year of our study $n = 56$ patients ($n = 30$ men, $n = 26$ women) had died from their cancer. In order to allow for comparisons with patients who were still alive after Time 4, the sample of decedents was matched with survivors with respect to age, sex, and medical variables (as obtained from their physicians at the time of study onset). In particular, tumor site and size, lymph node invasion, metastases, and multimorbidity were used as variables in the matching procedure. In addition, physicians' ratings of their patients' prognosis, compliance, and coping effectiveness were considered. After having matched the patients with regard to these criteria, the sample size of the deceased patients was reduced to $n = 23$, and the matching group of survivors comprised of $n = 20$ patients. This is due to the fact that $n = 33$ patients had died too early in order to allow for longitudinal observations as well as due to missing values in the set of medical variables.

Subsequent analyses with t tests and χ^2 tests proved that both groups did not differ with respect to age and gender, as well as various medical variables (tumor site, lymph node invasion, metastases, and multimorbidity). Yet, matching efforts were less successful with respect to three important indicators of clinical status: Tumor size proved to be larger, more patients have had a relapse, and physicians' ratings with regard to prognosis were less favorable within the sample of deceased patients as compared to the sample of survivors. Thus, both samples were not appropriately matched with respect to *all* medical variables. As we mentioned before, however, unlike other studies on survival time, we did not attempt to predict length of survival from the various psychological measures, which certainly would have necessitated complete matching. Rather, we tried to trace back longitudinally the course of coping in terminal cancer patients as compared to patients not facing death and to gain additional empirical evidence with respect to the prominent thesis of "acceptance" and "resolution" observed in the last stages of coping.

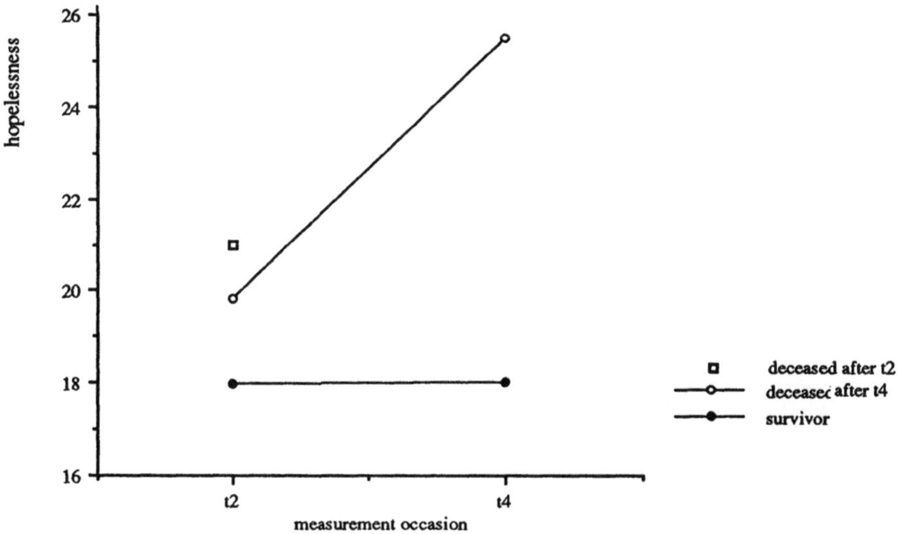

FIG. 2.5. Levels of hopelessness in decedents and survivors at two times of measurement.

Hopelessness in decedents and survivors. When we now look at various indicators of coping effectiveness, in particular at level of hopelessness, striking differences are revealed: Hopelessness yields a highly significant increase between Time 2 and Time 4 in those patients who had died after Time 4, whereas no such change can be observed in the sample of survivors (see Figure 2.5).

This difference is particularly remarkable since both groups, though already differing in some indicators of clinical status already at the time of study onset, were *equal* in level of hopelessness at Time 2. At that time, obviously, hopelessness proved to be unrelated to, for example, poor prognosis or to having had a relapse, whereas subsequent increase in hopelessness became reflective of distance from death. The role of hopelessness is even more pronounced when testing its discrimination power compared to the medical variables mentioned above. Results from a stepwise discriminant analysis, first of all, allowed for the correct classification of 84% of all cases. Despite physicians' prognosis at study onset, Hopelessness at Time 4 was the most important variable in discriminating both groups.

Obviously, the dramatic increase in hopelessness in patients who subsequently died reflects the breakdown of all coping mechanisms that might have, up to then, helped these patients to maintain well-being and hope in the face of even advanced cancer. If the idea that such a breakdown indeed has occurred at a certain point in time offers a plausible interpretation, it should then be reflected in the course of coping over time in the group of decedents, as well.

Coping Behaviors of Decedents and Survivors. When we look at temporal variations in coping in both groups, significant differences for two of the five coping strategies emerge. Whereas Threat Minimization showed a continuous decrease over time in both groups and Information Seeking proved to be rather unaffected by the passage of time, significant interaction effects (measurement time by group) could be observed for Search for Affiliation as well as for Search for Meaning in Religion.

As can be seen from Figure 2.6, the group of decedents did use search for meaning in religion as a coping strategy much more often than the group of survivors, the difference between the two becoming increasingly pronounced at later points in time. Since, as already reported above (and presumably quite contrary to what one might expect), Search for Meaning in Religion proved not to be a beneficial strategy in emotionally adjusting to cancer—being completely unrelated to hope, subjective well-being, and self-esteem—coping by turning to religion in the face of death did not protect those patients from becoming increasingly hopeless.

With regard to Search for Affiliation, both groups proved to have a fairly similar increase in this coping mode between Time 1 and Time 2, while apparently responding differently thereafter. Whereas frequency in turning to others in the group of survivors remains rather stable, a significant drop between Time 3 and Time 4 is to be observed in the group of decedents—presumably even forced by progressive exacerbations of functional status. It should be remembered here that

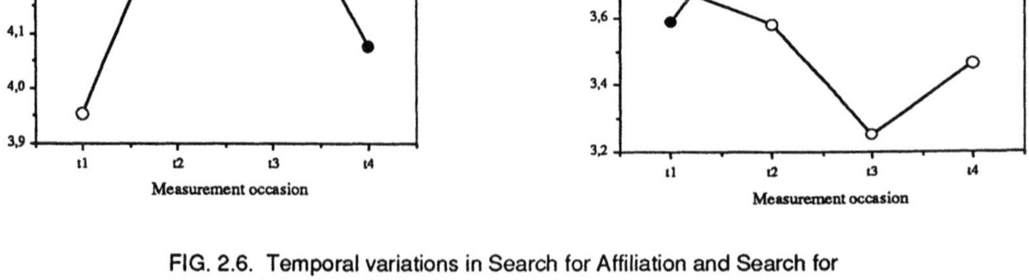

FIG. 2.6. Temporal variations in Search for Affiliation and Search for Meaning in Religion in decedents and survivors.

search for affiliation proved to be negatively related to hopelessness (and to the various other adaptational outcomes), not only synchronously but also diachrononously, and proved also to be predictive of *changes* in these variables. Thus, it can probably be assumed that increase in hopelessness in patients deceased after Time 4 is, at least partially, due to an increase in withdrawal from others who, up to then, might have helped them to maintain hope. In addition, we also found an increase (though just missing statistical significance) in ruminative thoughts and temporal comparisons in the group of decedents that obviously accompanied feelings of hopelessness as well.

Hopelessness and the Acceptance of Death

Of course, the observed increase in hopelessness in the face of death may be a not too surprising result from our study. It is certainly reflective of the fact that most patients in that subsample no longer adhered to "false hopes." How does this finding fit into the discussion of stage models? Does it support the "myth" (Wortman & Silver, 1989) that the terminally ill patient will also enter a stage of acceptance and resolution? We believe that answers to these questions are ultimately related to and dependent on the *value* we attach to hopelessness as a condition of human existence. The loss of hope in terminally ill patients certainly reflects that they obviously are in close touch with reality, thus hopelessness is simply to be equated with what Frese (this volume) has called "realistic pessimism." If one wishes to emphasize the cognitive component of hope, accordingly, one could speak of hopelessness in terms of *acceptance* of death. In that sense, hopelessness might have "positive" connotations and might even be associated with wisdom and tranquility. On the other hand, one could emphasize the emotional component of hopelessness, which—according to all conceptions—is related to negative affect that accompanies the process of "giving up" wishes, strivings, and expectations (see Snyder, 1989). From that point of view, the observed increase in hopelessness in the face of death should be seen to be more reflective of *despair* rather than calm acceptance, and may come close to what Alloy and Abramson (1988) have called "*depressive* realism" (our italics). In that sense, hopelessness clearly loses the above mentioned "positive" connotations. Without any doubt, hopelessness is a complex construct—a mixture of cognitions, emotions, and motivations—to which we attach maybe quite different, even culturally shaped values (see Frese, this volume). It seems that our measures may be not fine-graded enough to disentangle this complexity, thus, being rather ambiguous with respect to affective quality of "hopelessnes" in the terminally ill.

It might be helpful in this respect to also look at changes in subjective well-being over time and to relate these to changes in hopelessness.

As can be seen from Figure 2.7, the group of decedents is again quite different from the group of survivors. Whereas subjective well-being became increasingly positive over time in the group of survivors, a significant decrease in well-being was

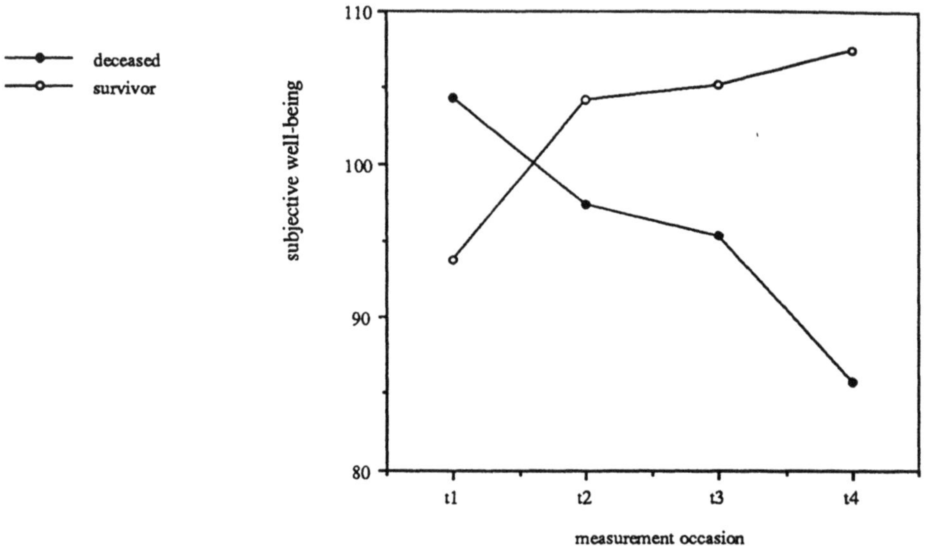

FIG. 2.7. Temporal variations in subjective well-being in decedents and survivors.

characteristic of the group of patients deceased after Time 4. If one looks at these results together with those obtained for hopelessness, one might conclude that hopelessness in terminally ill patients is indeed much more related to negative affect and despair rather than to tranquillity and "acceptance."

Our results thus imply a twofold message: First and technically speaking, the various measures used in our study prove to be highly sensitive for distance from death as a temporal factor. Second, they have to been seen in support of the notion that many popular (and elsewhere highly appropriate) conceptions of coping in terms of, for example, constructive thinking (Epstein, this volume), holding positive illusions (Taylor, 1989), maintaining a fighting spirit (Greer, 1991), or engaging in downward comparisons (Wills, 1987) may be of rather limited value if one wants to describe how terminally ill patients deal with their approaching death. Whether our results are also to be seen in contradiction to the notion that "acceptance of death" is likely to occur in the last stages largely depends on what we really mean by "acceptance" and "hopelessness."

CONCLUDING REMARKS

In this very last part of our chapter, it is appropriate to reconsider the question that was posed in the title of this paper: Could something be worse than being diagnosed a cancer patient? Although it is often argued that this type of question is more a concern to patients or other victims of life crises themselves (i.e., as a means of dealing with their lot by construing hypothetical worse worlds; cf. Taylor & Brown, 1988), researchers, as well, have assumptions as to which life experiences are the particularly critical and traumatic ones. As we tried to argue throughout this chapter, the answer to the question whether or not something could be worse should be ultimately related to *time* and *timing*.

First, from a developmental point of view we offered some arguments for the assumption that being diagnosed a cancer patient in the *younger years* of the life span should aggravate its impact due to a variety of reasons. Thus, especially with regard to young patients it seemed to be hard to think of other life experiences that could be worse. However, the age variable proved to be rather "insensitive," and our results on hopelessness and other indicators of (mal)adjustment, in sum, show that it is not chronological age that might worsen the experience of cancer.

Second, according to assumptions widely held in theory and research, we expected that the *earlier stages* within the process of coping with cancer are the crucial ones as reflected in symptoms of crisis and heightened anxiety and depression. Quite contrary to these expectations, time elapsed since diagnosis, both in a cross-sectional as well as in a longitudinal perspective, proved to be completely unrelated to variations in coping with and adjusting to cancer. Even more surprisingly, mean level of hopelessness in our sample of cancer patients proved to be almost equal to mean level of hopelessness in a community sample despite their enormously different life circumstances! Obviously—again speaking on the level of group means—ways of coping with cancer in our sample proved to be rather effective in terms of maintaining hope and creating a rather optimistic outlook.

Thus, by looking at hopelessness as an indicator of "whether something could be worse" in our patients' lives, we must conclude that this obviously is not the case: In general, the diagnosis of cancer did not exceed our patients' coping resources and did not leave them in deep and/or prolonged depression. Whatever factors may explain inter- and/or intraindividual variations in hopelesseness, chronological age as well as time elapsed since diagnosis certainly play a far minor role than was expected. Accordingly, two prominent myths about the importance of time and timing in answers to whether something could be worse than being a cancer patient had to be refuted.

However, we did gain insight in some conditions under which individual coping resources seem to collapse and to be ineffective in protecting cancer patients from becoming increasingly hopeless. *Distance from death* —a temporal dimension so far mainly used in gerontological work—proved to be *the* crucial variable. The breakdown of all coping efforts that had helped to maintain hope even in the face of severe and life-threatening disease at earlier points in time seemed to characterize the very last stages before patients are going to die—resulting in tremendous increases in hopelessness. Despite the widely held belief in people's ability to accept their nearing death, our data clearly are in contradiction to such a myth. Yet, we are aware of and briefly commented on the ambiguities inherent in how researchers (including ourselves) conceive of and measure „hopelessness"—is is to be equated with "calm acceptance" or "despair"? We only know that our patients in the face of death obviously have learned not to adhere to "false hopes" anymore. But as long as we are not able to disentangle the various connotations of hopelessness, we, as researchers, are left behind with quite a few unanswered questions.

REFERENCES

Abelson, R. P. (1981). Psychological status of the script concept. *American Psychologist, 36*, 715-729.

Alloy, L. B., & Abramson, L. Y. (1988). Depressive realism: Four theoretical perspectives. In L. B. Alloy (Ed.), *Cognitive processes in depression* (pp. 223-265). New York: Guilford Press.

Averill, J. (1979). The functions of grief. In C. E. Izard (Ed.), *Emotions in personality and psychopathology*. (pp. 337-368). New York: Plenum.

Aymanns, P. (in press). *Familiale Unterstützung bei Krebserkrankungen*. Bern: Huber.

Baltes, P. B. (1979). Life-span developmental psychology: Some converging observations on history and theory. In P. B. Baltes & O. G. Brim, Jr. (Eds.), *Life-span development and behavior*, (Vol. 2, pp. 256-281). New York: Academic Press.

Baltes, P. B., & Baltes, M. M. (Eds.). (1990). *Successful aging. Perspectives from the behavioral sciences*. Cambridge: Cambridge University Press.

Baltes, P.B., & Nesselroade, J. (1973). The developmental analysis of individual differences on multiple measures. In J. Nesselroade & H.W. Reese (Eds.), *Life-span developmental psychology: Methodological issues* (pp. 219-251). New York: Academic Press.

Beck, A. T., Weissman, A., Lester, D., & Trexler, L. (1974). The measurement of pessimism: The hopelessness scale. *Journal of Clinical and Consulting Psychology, 42*, 861-865.

Braukmann, W., & Filipp, S.-H. (1984). Strategien und Techniken der Lebensbewältigung. In U. Baumann, H. Berbalk, & G. Seidenstücker (Hrsg.), *Klinische Psychologie. Trends in Forschung und Praxis* (Vol. 6, S. 52-87). Bern: Huber.

Brim, O. G., Jr., & Ryff, C. D. (1980). On the properties of life events. In P. B. Baltes & O. G. Brim, Jr. (Eds.), *Life-span development and behavior* (Vol. 3, pp. 368-388). New York: Academic Press.

Burish, T. G., & Bradley, L. A. (Eds.). (1983). *Coping with chronic disease. Research and applications.* New York: Academic Press.

Caplan, G. (1964). *Principles of preventive psychiatry*. New York: Basic Books.

Cassileth, B. R., Lusk, E. J., Miller, D. S., Brown, L. L., & Miller, C. (1985). Psychological correlates of survival in advanced malignant disease. *New England Journal of Medicine, 312*, 1551-1555.

Cohen, F. (1987). Measurement of coping. In S. V. Kasl & C. L. Cooper (Eds.), *Stress and health: Issues in research methodology* (pp. 283-306). Chichester/New York: Wiley.

Cohen, L. H. (1988). *Life events and psychological functioning. Theoretical and methodological issues.* London: Sage.

Creed, F. (1985). Life events and physical illness. A review. *Journal of Psychosomatic Research, 29*, 113-124.

Derogatis, L. R., Abeloff, M. D., & Melisaratos, N. (1979). Psychological coping mechanisms and survival time in metastatic breast cancer. *Journal of the American Medical Association, 242*, 1504-1508.

DiClemente, R. J., & Temoshok, L. (1985). Psychological adjustment to having citaneous malignant melanoma as a predictor of follow-up clinic status. *Psychosomatic Medicine, 47*, 81.

Dorian, B., & Garfinkel, P. E. (1987). Stress, immunity and illness - a review. *Psychological Medicine, 17*, 393-407.

Dunkel-Schetter, C. (1984). Social support and cancer: Findings based on patient interviews and their implications. *Journal of Social Issues, 40*(4), 77-98.

Elder, G. H. (1979). Historical change in life patterns and personality. In P. B. Baltes & O. G. Brim (Eds.), *Life-span development and behavior* (Vol. 2, pp. 118-159). New York: Academic Press.

Elliott, G. R., & Eisdorfer, C. (1982). *Stress and human health.* New York: Springer.

Engel, G. L., & Schmale, A. H. (1967). Psychoanalytic theory of somatic disorder. *Journal of the American Psychoanalytic Association, 15*, 344-365.

Felton, B. J., & Revenson, T. A. (1987). Age differences in coping with chronic illness. *Psychology and Aging, 2*, 164-170.

Felton, B. J., Revenson, T. A., & Hinrichsen, G. A. (1984). Stress and coping in the explanation of psychological adjustment among chronically ill adults. *Social Science and Medicine, 18*, 889-898.

Ferring, D. (1989). Krankheitsbewältigung und Hoffnungslosigkeit bei Krebspatienten: Spezifikation und Testung konkurrierender Kausalmodelle. In J.-U. Sandberger & G. Seidel (Hrsg.), *Herbsttagung der AG Strukturgleichungsmodelle* (pp. 99-109). Frankfurt: Deutsches Institut für Internationale Pädagogische Forschung.

Ferring, D. & Filipp, S.-H. (1991). *The analysis of stability and change in coping behavior via structural equation modeling: Structural invariance, level stability, positional stability, and growth curves.* Poster, presented at the European Science Foundation's Longitudinal Network's summing-up conference, March 21-23, 1991, Budapest.

Ferring, D., Klauer, T., Filipp, S.-H., & Steyer, R. (1990). Psychometrische Modelle zur Bestimmung von Konsistenz und Spezifität im Bewältigungsverhalten. *Zeitschrift für Differentielle und Diagnostische Psychologie, 11*, 37-51.

Filipp, S.-H. (1981). Ein allgemeines Modell für die Analyse kritischer Lebensereignisse. In S.-H. Filipp (Hrsg.), *Kritische Lebensereignisse* (S. 3-52). München: Urban & Schwarzenberg.

Filipp, S.-H. (1983). Die Rolle von Selbstkonzepten im Prozeß der Auseinandersetzung mit und Bewältigung von kritischen Lebensereignissen. *Zeitschrift für personenzentrierte Psychologie und Psychotherapie, 2*, 39-47.

Filipp, S.-H. (1990). Subjektive Krankheitstheorien. In R. Schwarzer (Hrsg.), *Gesundheitspsychologie. Ein Lehrbuch* (S. 247-262). Göttingen: Hogrefe.

Filipp, S.-H., Ahammer, I., Angleitner, A., & Olbrich, E. (1980). *Eine Untersuchung zu inter- und intraindividuellen Differenzen in der Wahrnehmung und Verarbeitung von subjektiv erlebten Persönlichkeitsveränderungen* (Forschungsberichte aus dem Projekt „Entwicklungspsychologie des Erwachsenenalters“ Nr. 11). Trier: Universität, Fachbereich I, Psychologie.

Filipp, S.-H., & Klauer, T. (1988). Ein dreidimensionales Modell zur Klassifikation von Formen der Krankheitsbewältigung. In H. Kächele & W. Steffens (Hrsg.), *Bewältigung und Abwehr. Beiträge zur Psychologie und Psychotherapie schwerer körperlicher Krankheiten* (S. 51-69). Heidelberg: Springer.

Filipp, S.-H., & Klauer, T. (1991). Subjective well-being in the face of critical life events: The case of successful copers. In F. Strack, M. Argyle, & N. Schwarz (Eds.), *Subjective well-being. An interdisciplinary perspective* (pp. 213-235). Oxford: Pergamon.

Filipp, S.-H., Klauer, T., & Ferring, D. (in press). Self-focused attention in the face of adversity and threat. In H. W. Krohne (Ed.), *Attention and avoidance.* New York: Springer.

Filipp, S.-H., Klauer, T., Freudenberg, E., & Ferring, D. (1990). The regulation of subjective well-being in cancer patients: An analysis of coping effectiveness. *Psychology and Health, 4*, 305-317.

Folkman, S., & Lazarus, R. S. (1985). If it changes it must be a process: Study of emotion and coping during three stages of a college examination. *Journal of Personality and Social Psychology, 48*, 150-170.

Friedman, W. J. (1989). The representation of temporal structure in children, adolescents and adults. In I. Levin & D. Zakay (Eds.), *Time and human cognition. A life-span perspective* (pp. 259-305). Amsterdam, NL: Elsevier/North Holland.

Galinat, W. H., & Borg, I. (1987). On symbolic temporal information: Beliefs about the experience of duration. *Memory and Cognition, 15*, 308-317.

Gottesman, D., & Lewis, M. S. (1982). Differences in crisis reactions among cancer and surgery patients. *Journal of Consulting and Clinical Psychology, 50*(3), 381-388.

Greer, S. (1991). Psychological response to cancer and survival. *Psychological Medicine, 21*, 43-49.

Haan, N. (Ed.). (1977). *Coping and defending: Processes of self-environment organization.* New York: Academic Press.

Herrmann, T. (1979). *Psychologie als Problem: Herausforderungen der psychologischen Wissenschaft.* Stuttgart: Klett-Cotta.

Horowitz, M. (1979). Psychological responses to serious life events. In V. Hamilton & D.M. Warburton (Eds.), Human stress and cognition (pp. 235-264). Chichester: Wiley.

Jacobson, D. E. (1986). Types and timing of social support. *Journal of Health and Social Behavior, 27*, 250-264.

Janoff-Bulman, R., & Schwartzberg, S. S. (1991). Toward a general model of personal change. In C. R. Snyder & D. R. Forsyth (Eds.), *Handbook of social and clinical psychology. The health perspective* (pp. 488-509). New York: Pergamon.

Jarvik, L. F., & Bank, L. (1983). Aging twins: Longitudinal psychometric data. In K. W. Schaie (Ed.), *Longitudinal studies of adult psychological development* (pp. 40-63). New York: The Guilford Press.

Jensen, M. R. (1987). Psychobiological factors predicting the course of breast cancer. *Journal of Personality, 55*, 317-342.

Jøreskog, K. G., & Sørbom, D. (1988). *LISREL VII. A guide to the program and apllications.* Chicago, Il.: SPSS. INC.

Klauer, T., Filipp, S.-H., & Ferring, D. (1989). Zur Spezifität der Bewältigung schwerer körperlicher Erkrankungen: Eine vergleichende Analyse dreier diagnostischer Gruppen. *Zeitschrift für Klinische Psychologie, 18*, 144-159.

Klauer, T., Filipp, S.-H., & Ferring, D. (1989). Der "Fragebogen zur Erfassung von Formen der Krankheitsbewältigung" (FEKB): Skalenkonstruktion und erste Befunde zu Reliabilität, Validität und Stabilität. *Diagnostica, 35*, 316-335.

Klinger, E. (1975). Consequences of commitment to and disengagement from incentives. *Psychological Review, 82*, 1-25.

Krampen, G. (1979). Hoffnungslosigkeit bei stationären Patienten. *Medizinische Psychologie, 5*, 39-49.

Lazarus, R., & Folkman, S. (1984). *Stress, appraisal, and coping*. New York: Springer.

Levin, I., & Zakay, D. (Eds.). (1989). *Time and human cognition. A life-span perspective.* Amsterdam, NL: Elsevier/North Holland.

Levy, S. M., & Wise, B. D. (1988). Psychosocial risk factors and cancer progression. In C. L. Cooper (Ed.), *Stress and breast cancer* (pp. 77-96). Chichester: Wiley.

Markus, H., & Nurius, P. (1986). Possible selves. *American Psychologist, 41*, 954-969.

Mattlin, J. A., Wethington, E., & Kessler, R. C. (1990). Situational determinants of coping and coping effectiveness. *Journal of Health and Social Behavior, 31*, 103-122.

McCrae, R. R. (1989). Age differences and changes in the use of coping mechanisms. *Journal of Gerontology, 44*, 161-169.

McIvor, G. P., Riklan, M., & Reznikoff, M. (1984). Depression in multiple sclerosis as a function of length and severity of illness, age, remissions, and perceived social support. *Journal of Clinical Psychology, 40*, 1028-1033.

Moos, R. H. (Ed.). (1984). *Coping with physical illness*. New York: Plenum.

Neugarten, B. L. (Ed.). (1968). *Middle age and aging: A reader in social psychology*. Chicago: University of Chicago Press.

Neuling, S. J., & Winefield, H. R. (1988). Social support and recovery after surgery for breast cancer: Frequency and correlates of supportive behaviors by family, friends, and surgeon. *Social Science and Medicine, 27*, 385-392.

Peters-Golden, H. (1982). Breast cancer: Varied perceptions of social support in the illness experience. *Social Science in Medicine, 16*, 483-491.

Rahe, R. (1988). Recent life changes and coronary heart disease: 10 years' research. In S. Fisher & J. Reason (Eds.), *Handbook of life stress, cognition, and health* (pp. 317-335). Chichester: Wiley.
Ray, C., Lindop, J., & Gibson, S.(1982). The concept of coping. *Psychological Medicine, 12*, 385-395.
Reese, H. W., & Smyer, M. A. (1983). The dimensionalization of life events. In E. J. Callahan & K. A. McCluskey (Eds.), *Life-span developmental psychology. Nonnormative life events* (pp. 1-35). New York: Academic Press.
Rogosa, D. (1979). Causal models in longitudinal research: Rationale, formulation, and interpretation. In J. R. Nesselroade, & P. B. Baltes (Eds.), *Longitudinal research in the study of behavior and development* (pp. 263-302). New York: Academic Press.
Rosenberg, M. (1965). *Society and the adolescent self-image*. Princeton, NJ: Princeton University Press.
Schroeder, D. H., & Costa, P. T., Jr. (1984). Influence of life event stress on physical illness: Substantive effects or methodological flaws? *Journal of Personality and Social Psychology, 46*, 853-863.
Silver, R. L., Boon, C., & Stones, M. H. (1983). Searching for meaning in misfortune: Making sense of incest. *Journal of Social Issues, 39*(2), 81-102.
Silver, R. L., & Wortman, C. B. (1980). Coping with undesirable life events. In J. Garber & M. E. P. Seligman (Eds.), *Human helplessness. Theory and applications* (pp. 279-340). New York: Academic Press.
Snyder, C. R. (1989). Reality negotiation: From excuses to hope and beyond. *Journal of Social and Clinical Psychology, 8*, 130-157.
Sobel, H. J., & Worden, J. W. (1979). The MMPI as a predictor of psychosocial adaptation to cancer. *Journal of Consulting and Clinical Psychology, 47*, 716-724.
Sontag, S. (1977). *Illness as a metaphor*. New York: Random House.
Steyer, R. (1987). Konsistenz und Spezifität: Definition zweier zentraler Begriffe der Differentiellen Psychologie und ein einfaches Modell zu ihrer Identifikation. Zeitschrift für Differentielle und Diagnostische Psychologie, 8, 245-258.
Stroebe, W., & Stroebe, M. S. (1987). *Bereavement and health. The psychological and physical consequences of partner loss*. Cambridge: Cambridge University Press.
Suls, J., & Fletcher, B. (1985). The relative efficacy of avoidant and nonavoidant coping strategies: A meta-analysis. *Health Psychology, 4*, 249-288.
Tack, W. (1980). Zur Theorie psychometrischer Verfahren. Formalisierung der Erfassung von Situationsabhängigkeit. *Zeitschrift für Differentielle und Diagnostische Psychologie, 1*, 87-106.
Taylor, S. E. (1983). Adjustment to threatening events: A theory of cognitive adaptation. *American Psychologist, 41*, 1161-1173.
Taylor, S. E. (1984). Issues in the study of coping: A commentary. *Cancer, 53*, 2313-2315.
Taylor, S. E. (1989). *Positive illusions. Creative self-deceptions and the healthy mind.* New York: Basic Books.
Taylor, S. E., & Brown, J. (1988). Illusion and well-being: A social psychological perspective on mental health. *Psychological Bulletin, 103*, 193-210.
Thoits, P. A. (1983). Dimensions of life events that influence psychological distress: An evaluation and synthesis of the literature. In H. B. Kaplan (Ed.), *Psychosocial stress. Trends in theory and research* (pp. 33-103) New York: Academic Press.
Thoits, P. A. (1985). Social support and psychological well-being: Theoretical possibilities. In J. G. Sarason & B. R. Sarason (Eds.), Social support: Theory, research, and application (pp. 51-70). Dordrecht: Nijhoff.
Vaillant, G. E. (1977). *Adaptation to life*. Boston, MS: Little Brown.
Viney, L. L., & Westbrook, M. T. (1982). Patterns of anxiety in the chronically ill. *British Journal of Medical Psychology, 55*, 87-95.
Watson, D., & Kendall, P.C. (1983). Methodological issues in research on coping with chronic disease. In T. G. Burish & L. A. Bradley (Eds.), *Coping with chronic disease. Research and applications* (pp. 39-85). New York: Academic Press.
Watson, M., & Greer, S. (Eds.). (1986). *Psychosocial issues in malignant disease*. Oxford: Pergamon.
Weinstein, N. D. (1980). Unrealistic optimism about future life events. *Journal of Personality and Social Psychology, 39*, 806-820.

Weisman, A. D. (1979). *Coping with cancer*. New York: McGraw-Hill.

Weisman, A. D., & Worden, J. W. (1975). Psychosocial analysis of cancer deaths. *Omega, 6*, 61-75.

Weisman, A. D., & Worden, J. W. (1986). The emotional impact of recurrent cancer. *Journal of Psychosocial Oncology, 3*(4), 5-16.

Wills, T.A. (1987). Downward comparison as a coping mechanism. In C.R. Snyder & C.E. Ford (Eds.), Coping with negative life events: Clinical and social-psychological perspectives (pp. 243-268). New York: Plenum.

Wortman, C.B. & Silver, R.C. (1989). The myths of coping with loss. Journal of Consulting and Clinical Psychology, 57, 349-357.

Zakay, D. (1989). Subjective time and attentional resource allocation: An integrated model of time estimation. In I. Levin & D. Zakay (Eds.), *Time and human cognition. A life-span perspective* (pp. 365-399). Amsterdam, NL: Elsevier/North Holland.

Zerssen, D., von (1976). *Die Befindlichkeitsskala*. Weinheim: Beltz.

3 Psychological Factors Related to the Recuperation of Accident Victims

Dieter Frey
University of Kiel

This chapter provides an overview of our research concerning the recuperation process after severe accidents. Special attention is given to the effect of psychological variables on the duration of stay in hospital as well as the posthospital recovery process until the return to work. It was found that psychological factors concerning the cause of the accident (past) as well as the consequences of the accident (future) play a more important role than medical factors (e.g., the severity of the injury) in predicting the length of a patient's stay in hospital and the length of absence from work.

RELEVANT PSYCHOLOGICAL FACTORS

How far does the recuperation process of accident patients depend on psychological factors? Is it just a matter of chance whether a person who has had an accident recovers very quickly or relatively slowly from the injuries caused by this accident? If this is not just a matter of chance, is it then possible to identify some regularities in the recovering process? From everyday observation we know that some people recover very quickly from an injury, whereas others recover relatively slowly, even in cases of similar injuries. It can be supposed that, in addition to physical aspects, psychological factors play a role in the recuperation process. What roles do the psychological factors play in recuperation? In this article we present research from some studies that tried to discover which psychological factors are important for the recuperation process. We were especially interested in psychological factors concerning the past, the cause of the accident (e.g., perceived avoidability, causal attribution, the "Why me?" question) as well as the future (perceived control over convalescence, predictability of recuperation, etc.).

An accident injury can be experienced not only as a physical lesion but also as an extreme psychological stressor (life event; see Dohrenwend & Dohrenwend, 1974). When experiencing accidents persons are deprived of their basic need of having control over an event and thus, they experience a "loss of control" (Taylor, 1983). Several authors (e.g., Abramson, Seligman, & Teasdale, 1978; Fisher, 1984; Lazarus, 1981) consider the degree of experienced loss of control or the perceived controllability of a situation as being an essential factor in reacting during a stress situation.

Field experiments dealing with aspects of control over an aversive event have shown that persons who believed that they had some sort of control over a situation had a more favorable psychological and physical well-being than those who did not believe this (Langer & Rodin, 1976; Rodin & Langer, 1977; Schulz, 1976; Schulz & Hanusa, 1978).

In contrast to the consistent research results on the effects of control over a present (or future) situation, research investigating causal attributions concerning physical illness or injury is ambiguous. For example, some studies have shown self-blame to have a positive effect (e.g., Bulman & Wortman, 1977), while others have proven the opposite to be true (e.g., Taylor et al., 1984). This inconsistency may be due to the fact that few longitudinal studies were made and that the measurement of adaptation among these studies was performed at different points in time. Therefore, we have designed our studies to have two, respectively three different measurement times.

The following section presents an overview of three studies. Their goal was to investigate which psychological factors have an influence upon the length of stay in hospital and the duration of the posthospital recuperation process until returning to work. Considering this goal, we interviewed our patients for the first time two or three days after their accident about cognitions concerning both their accident as well as convalescence.

METHOD

Subjects

Our groups of subjects were patients in the Department of Accident Surgery at the University Hospital in Kiel. All patients were under treatment in the hospital ward outside the intensive care unit and received their first interview two to three days after their accident. The patient's accidents included recreational and sport accidents, traffic accidents, accidents at work, and accidents that had happened within the home.

Design and Procedure

The questioning itself was conducted as a structured interview. The patients were provided with response scales for each question, and the questions were read out loud, word for word. The interview lasted about 20 to 30 minutes.

In the first interview, patients answered questions on five-point scales concerning causal attributions for the accident, avoidability of the accident, whether the patient asked him/herself the "Why me?" question, perceived control over convalescence, the predictability of convalescence, the extent to which they expressed their fears and worries to physicians and family, pleasantness of the activity during which the accident had happened, and so forth.

From a medical standpoint, the *severity of an injury* is an important determinant in the recuperation process. To take this factor into account, we evaluated patients according to an "Injury Severity Scale" (ISS; see Baker & O'Neill, 1976; Baker, O'Neill, Haddon, & Long, 1974;).[1] The ISS assesses the overall degree of severity of the multiple injuries a person has suffered, ranging from (1) *minor injuries* to (75) *fatal injuries*. In the present studies, ISS ratings were made by a trained physician, who was unaware of the aim of the studies. This score varied between 4 and 32 ($M = 10.9$; $SD = 6.7$).

The number of days of hospitalization was used as one *index for the recuperation process*. A second index for the recuperation process was the number of days until the patient recommenced to work. Both variables represent the length of the entire recuperation process. The first, however, reflects more upon the duration of the need for constant medical care (according to the ward physician's opinion), while the second reflects more upon the patient's own view of his or her ability to return to work. The length of time before returning to work was assessed by a questionnaire sent to the patient about 3 to 4 months after discharge from the hospital, and again, if the patient had not resumed work up to that time, about 6 to 8 months later.

RESULTS

Analyses of covariance (covariant: ISS) were carried out to determine the relationship between the cognitions measured and the length of hospitalization as well as the length of the entire recovery process.

In the following, we have summarized the results of all three studies (for more details, see Frey & Rogner, 1987; Frey, Rogner, & Havemann, in press; Frey, Rogner, Schüler, Körte, & Havemann, 1985).

---

[1]The ISS is based on the 'Abbreviated Injury Scale' (AIS) of the American Association of Automotive Medicine (1980). The AIS is a scale with which each single injury (for example, specific wounds, burns, fractures, etc.) can be clearly classified according to its severity.

Findings with respect to length of stay in the hospital:

1. Patients who considered that their accident was unavoidable stayed longer in hospital and suffered more medical complications than those who considered their accident avoidable.
2. Considering causal attributions, self-blame tended to be associated with a longer stay in hospital and more medical complications.
3. Patients asking themselves the "Why me?" question stayed longer in hospital and had more medical complications than those patients who did not ask themselves why the accident had to happen to them.
4. Patients supporting their recuperation process through their own efforts stayed fewer days in hospital and had fewer medical complications than those patients who believed they had no control over their recuperation.
5. Patients who showed a high degree of self-cure treatment in previous illnesses stayed a shorter length of time in hospital than those with a low degree of self-cure treatment.
6. Patients who subjectively believed after the accident (two or three days) that they could well predict the course of their recuperation process stayed fewer days in hospital than those who did not believe that.
7. Patients expecting serious personal problems at home stayed more days in hospital than those who were not expecting such problems.

Findings with respect to length of absence from work:

1. Patients who believed (two or three days after the accident) that they had control over their convalescence, returned to work much earlier than those patients who believed they could not control their convalescence.
2. Patients who subjectively believed in a high predictability of the course of their recuperation process went back to work earlier than patients who did not believe that.
3. Patients who found the activity interesting in which they were engaged when the accident happened, went back to work significantly earlier than those who did not find the activity interesting.

The above results are based on analyses of covariance with the severity of injury due to the accident serving as covariate. Regression analyses were also applied in the studies. The objective severity of the injury alone did not account for more than 20% of the variance concerning length of stay in hospital in our studies; however, when added to the psychological variables, about 45% of the variance could be accounted for. As far as returning to work is concerned, the severity of the injury explained in all studies nearly 0% of the variance, whereas the psychological variables explained between 60% and 70% in our three studies.

DISCUSSION

First, the results clearly show that psychological variables have an influence on the length of stay in hospital as well as on the delay in returning to work. Second, they reveal that the psychological variables responsible for length of hospitalization are not always the same as those responsible for the delay in returning to work. Third, our results clearly show that psychological variables play a much greater role in the recovery process than the actual severity of injury.

That severity of injury accounts for little of the variance in length of hospital stay seems at first glance very surprising. It shows that the medical evaluation two or three days after the accident is a poorer predictor than the psychological factors. The fact that a person thinks the accident was unavoidable, does not blame him or herself, and does not ask the "Why me?-question but perceives future control demonstrates that these psychological factors may override the severity of injury and may have an important influence on the healing process.

That the severity of injury has no influence on the delay in returning to work is not surprising. The indication to return to work, especially in a country with socialized medicine, is more dependent on psychological factors like how much a person enjoys his or her work. Also it seems plausible that the attractiveness of the activity during which the accident happened has no influence on the length of hospital stay but on the length of absence from work.

There is evidence from research on further life events we have recently finished, that the same variables are relevant in the adaption process in these cases, too. We studied samples of (a) HIV-patients, (b) coronary patients, and (c) widowed persons.

In a longitudinal study of HIV-patients, we found that similar factors are relevant concerning the immune status (T4/T8 ratio). We found, for example, that those HIV-patients had a better immunological state who did not ask the "Why me?" question, who thought that the development of the disease was under their own control, and who found their disease to be a challenge (see Bliemeister, Frey, Aschenbach, & Köller, in press).

With coronary patients, we also found in longitudinal studies that those subjects who did not ask the "Why me?" question, as well as those who thought that they could control their recuperation, had a better physical and psychological well-being.

Finally, with people who suffered from the death of their partner, we found in a longitudinal study higher levels of physical and psychological well-being half a year after the death among respondents who no longer asked "Why me?", who believed themselves to be optimistic concerning the future, and who thought that they had control over their own life.

So, it seems to be that similar cognitive affective variables concerning the past and the future are relevant in explaining and predicting the adaptation process after having experienced various severe stressors. These studies clearly emphasize the relevance of psychological factors on the adaption process.

In further research on the recuperation or adaptation process of severe stressors, it would probably be feasible to take the following points into consideration:

First, it is not clear that a specific psychological variable, such as avoidability, is indeed causal for producing the effect. It cannot be excluded that another variable (or a synthesis of variables), which is connected with avoidability, and which we have not measured, produces the effect. In further research, therefore, broader individual coping styles, such as the degree to which a patient reveals depressive characteristics, should be measured and the relationship to our measured variables tested.

Second, given the fact that our psychological variables are indeed causal for the effect, it is unclear what the physiological, endocrinological, and immunological mediators are. Future research, therefore, should put more emphasis on this relationship.

Third, in future research, intervention programs should also be created in which cognitions are encouraged that are beneficial for the recuperation process. However, before such theories or intervention programs are created, more research is necessary to clarify the causality as well as the relationship between psychological and physiological variables.

REFERENCES

Abramson, L. Y., Seligman, M. E. P., & Teasdale, J. D. (1978). Learned helplessness in humans: Critique and reformulation. *Journal of Abnormal Psychology, 87*, 49-74.

American Association of Automotive Medicine (Ed.). (1980). *Die abgekürzte Verletzungsskala (AIS)*. (Revidierte Fassung). Morton Grove: American Association of Automotive Medicine.

Baker, S. P., & O'Neill, B. (1976). The injury severity score: An update. *Journal of Trauma, 16*, 882-885.

Baker, S. P., O'Neill, B., Haddon, W., & Long, W. (1974). The injury severity score. *Journal of Trauma, 14*, 187-196.

Bliemeister, J., Frey, D., Aschenbach, G., & Köller, O. (in press). Zum Zusammenhang zwischen psychosozialen Merkmalen und dem Gesundheitszustand HIV-Infizierter. Eine interdisziplinäre Querschnittstudie. *Zeitschrift für Klinische Psychologie.*

Bulman, R. J., & Wortman, C. B. (1977). Attributions of blame and coping in the "real world": Severe accident victims react to their lot. *Journal of Personality and Social Psychology, 35*, 351-363.

Dohrenwend, B. S., & Dohrenwend, B. P. (Eds.). (1974). *Stressful life events: Their nature and effects.* New York: Wiley.

Fisher, S. (1984). *Stress and the perception of control.* London: Erlbaum.

Frey, D., & Rogner, O. (1987). The relevance of psychological factors in the convalescence of accident patients. In G. R. Semin & B. Krahé (Eds.), *Issues in contemporary German social psychology* (pp. 241-257). London: Sage.

Frey, D., Rogner, O., & Havemann, D. (in press). Psychological factors in the convalescence of accident patients. *Journal of Basic and Applied Social Psychology.*

Frey, D., Rogner, O., Schüler, M., Körte, C., & Havemann, D. (1985). Psychological determinants in the convalescence of accident patients. *Journal of Basic and Applied Social Psychology, 6*, 317-328.

Langer, E. J., & Rodin, J. (1976). The effects of choice and enhanced personal responsibility for the aged. *Journal of Personality and Social Psychology, 34*, 191-198.

Lazarus, R. S. (1981). The stress and coping paradigm. In C. Eisdorfer, D. Cohen, A. Kleinmann, & P. Maxim (Eds.), *Models for clinical psychopathology* (pp. 177-214). New York: Spectrum.

Rodin, J., & Langer, E. J. (1977). Long-term effects of a control-relevant intervention with the institutionalized aged. *Journal of Personality and Social Psychology, 35*, 897-902.

Schulz, R. (1976). Some life and death consequences of perceived control. In J. S. Caroll & J. W. Payne (Eds.), *Cognition and social behavior* (pp. 135-153). Hillsdale, NJ: Erlbaum.

Schulz, R., & Hanusa, B. (1978). Long-term effects of control and predictability-enhancing interventions: Findings and theoretical issues. *Journal of Personality and Social Psychology, 36*, 401-411.

Taylor, S. E. (1983). Adjustment to threatening events: A theory of cognitive adaptation. *American Psychologist, 38*, 1161-1173.

Taylor, S. E., Lichtman, R. R., Wood, J. V., Bluming, A. Z., Dosik, G. M., & Leibowitz, R. L. (1984). Breast self-examination among diagnosed breast cancer patients. *Cancer, 54*, 2528-2532.

4 Abortion: A Case of Crisis and Loss? An Examination of Empirical Evidence

Nancy E. Adler
University of California, San Francisco

Political controversy surrounding the legal status of abortion has generated a great deal of interest in research on the psychological effects of abortion. A number of researchers, however, have studied abortion less out of an interest in the effects of the procedure itself than as a model of stress and loss. This chapter will present a brief overview of the research on psychological responses of women following abortion and then examine the utility of using abortion as a model for studying coping and loss.

PSYCHOLOGICAL RESPONSES FOLLOWING ABORTION

There are many studies dealing with psychological and emotional responses of women following induced abortion. These studies have varied in the quality and rigor of the research design and have often come to contradictory conclusions (Adler et al., 1990). One reason for the mixed findings may be that personal conviction and ideological and theoretical assumptions about the nature of the abortion experience have colored research more in this area than in others.

Early research, done in an era in which abortion was not legal, tended to consist of clinical case studies. Therapists who were treating women in their practice who had experienced difficulties following abortion would not only write about the individual case, but would often conclude that such responses were typical of all women following abortion. These conclusions would then be cited without regard to the original basis for the conclusion (Simon & Senturia, 1966). In the 1950s and early 60s it was frequently asserted that abortion was a major contributor to psychopathology (Ebaugh & Heuser, 1947; Simon & Senturia, 1966), which Kummer (1963) attributed to enforcement of a taboo against abortion.

Another reason that this conclusion was readily accepted may have been that it was consistent with assumptions regarding the psychology of women (Deutsch, 1945). Belief in the strength of the "maternal instinct" led many to assume that any woman who violated this instinct by terminating a pregnancy would be traumatized. This view is now being propounded by some members of anti-abortion organizations who claim that abortion is not a normal stressor, but a trauma similar to the trauma endured by soldiers in Vietnam. Claims are being made for the existence of "post-abortion trauma syndrome" parallel to "post-traumatic stress disorder" noted in Vietnam War veterans (Speckhard, 1987).

Psychodynamic theories also encouraged a focus on psychopathological responses and an overemphasis of severe negative reactions. Fingerer (1973) examined whether predictions that would be drawn from psychoanalytic theory regarding negative psychological effects of abortion were actually shown by women experiencing abortion. She gave a set of standardized tests, including the Spielberger State-Trait Anxiety Inventory, the Affective Adjective Checklist, and a measure of depressive symptomatology (the SDS) to a group of 324 women who were coming to a clinic for an abortion. The women completed the scales prior to undergoing the procedure. Another group of women completed the questionnaires within days after the procedure. The same measures were given to a sample of men and women who accompanied patients to the clinic; they were asked to complete it in terms of how they thought the women who were having abortions would feel the day after the procedure. The same task of predicting how women would respond to abortion was given to a set of postdoctoral students in two psychoanalytic training programs.

Fingerer compared the actual responses of women prior to and following their abortion with those predicted by the people accompanying them and by the psychoanalytically oriented therapists. The most negative responses were given by the psychoanalytic postdoctoral students predicting how women would respond following abortion. These were significantly more negative than responses given by abortion patients themselves either before or after abortion; predicted responses by the therapists were also significantly more negative than the responses predicted by the friends and relatives accompanying the abortion patients. Responses predicted by the accompanying friends and relatives, in turn, were more negative than those actually expressed by the women themselves either prior to the abortion or afterwards. In brief, responses of the women after abortion were more positive than predicted by their friends and relatives and *far* more positive than predicted by postdoctoral therapists. Fingerer concludes that "the psychological aftereffects of abortion seem to reside in psychoanalytic theory and societal myths" (p. 225).

On the one hand, then, are assertions and case studies suggesting that abortion is a crisis which can be associated with psychopathology. On the other, the study by Fingerer suggests that these effects are due to myths and bias. A careful reading of the literature suggests that the latter may be closer to the actual situation.

A REVIEW OF THE LITERATURE

Recently, the American Psychological Association convened a panel of experts to review the literature on psychological responses of women following abortion. The panel was charged with examining this literature and determining what, if any, conclusions could be drawn from it.[1]

Members of the panel were aware of the substantial methodological problems in many of the studies (Public Interest Directorate, 1987) and set minimum criteria for including a study in its review. Three criteria were set for a study to be included. First, in order to generalize to current conditions in the United States, the sample had to be of women in the United States. The experience of abortion may vary in different cultures in which it holds different meaning and where the actual experience of terminating a pregnancy may differ. Second, the procedure had to be done under legal conditions in which there were no institutional barriers (such as approval by a panel of physicians) for obtaining the abortion. Finally, the study had to be of a definable sample and involve standard data collection techniques allowing for statistical analysis. Although these are not stringent criteria and allow for reasonable confidence in the generalizability of findings, very few studies met these criteria. Out of an initial pool of over 200 studies, we identified only 20 that qualified for the review. The overview that follows below is based on those twenty studies.

Descriptive Statistics

Findings regarding the frequency of various negative and positive responses following abortion are consistent with the hypothesis that abortion is not a traumatic event. In fact, abortion may serve to reduce distress associated with the crisis of an unwanted pregnancy more than it does to create a new crisis.

In studying responses following abortion one is inevitably picking up on reactions to the entire experience of having had an unwanted pregnancy that is subsequently terminated. The extent to which abortion creates additional distress or reduces distress can be indirectly assessed by examining responses before and after the procedure. Some studies obtained measures of emotional responses and/or psychological functioning both prior to the abortion and afterwards. "Before" measures were generally taken on the day of the procedure and may have been heightened by the anticipation of the procedure. "After" measures varied in the times of their assessment, with some taken in the recovery room or clinic within hours after the procedure and others days, weeks, or months after the procedure. Over time (both from before the procedure to afterwards and from immediately afterwards to several weeks later), there appears to be a drop in negative affect. For

[1] A brief summary of the findings of the panel has been published (Adler et al., 1990) and a more extended paper is being prepared. Portions of this chapter may overlap some sections of these two reports.

example, Cohen and Roth (1984) studied women prior to the abortion as they came to the clinic, and again in the recovery room. As shown in Table 4.1, the women showed significant decreases on measures reflecting stress and distress: the Impact of Event Scale, and the depression and anxiety subscales of the Symptom Checklist. Major, Mueller, and Hildebrandt (1985) found significantly lower scores on the short form of the Beck Depression Inventory among women three weeks after undergoing an abortion compared to their responses immediately following the procedure. Freeman, Rickels, Huggings, Garcia, and Pollin (1980) also found declines in scores in the SCL-90 from before the abortion to after. Unfortunately, none of these studies included controls for the effects taking these measures twice.

In addition to drops in levels of negative affect, the absolute levels of distress tend to be low. For example, Lazarus (1985) obtained ratings of whether or not women had experienced a number of different emotions during the two weeks following abortion. The most common feeling, reported by 76% of women, was relief. Only 49 women out of the 228 studied (17%) reported feeling guilt, which was the most commonly reported negative emotion.

Emotional responses following abortion do not necessarily fall on a single positive-negative dimension. Some early studies asked women to make such ratings. For example, in a study by Osofsky and Osofsky (1972) women were asked to report their feelings about the abortion of a five-point scale running from "negative: much guilt" to "positive: much relief." However, women may feel *both* relief and guilt. A factor analysis of responses reporting the intensity with which a range of emotions was experienced in the three months following abortion revealed

TABLE 4.1

Correlated t-Tests between Time 1 and Time 2 of Impact of Event Subscales (Intrusion and Avoidance) and Symptom Checklist Subscales (Depression and Anxiety)

	Time 1		*Time 2*		
Symptom	*Mean*	*SD*	*Mean*	*SD*	*t*
Intrusion	17.5	(9.1)	15.3	(9.0)	3.02**
Avoidance	16.7	(9.0)	14.6	(9.7)	2.05*
Depression	24.1	(11.8)	18.4	(12.2)	4.90*
Anxiety	17.3	(11.4)	13.9	(11.8)	2.73**

**$p < .01$ *$p < .05$

three different factors (Adler, 1975). As predicted, the positive emotions formed a separate factor. Scores on this factor, which included relief and happiness, were the highest, indicating the strongest intensity: On a scale ranging from 1, not at all, to 5, extremely, mean ratings were 3.96. Interestingly, the negative emotions formed two separate factors. One factor consisted of guilt, shame, and fear of disapproval and appeared to be affective responses to norm violation. The second factor consisted of regret, anxiety, depression, doubt, and anger and appeared to reflect responses to loss and more internally based concerns. The mean levels of intensity of these two sets of emotional responses were relatively low: 2.26 for the internally-based emotions and 1.81 for the socially based emotions.

The pattern of correlations between the factor scores on each of the three emotion factors and other variables was consistent with the interpretation given above of the two kinds of negative emotions (Adler, 1975). These are presented in Table 4.2. Women indicated before the abortion how difficult it was for them to decide whether or not to have an abortion. The degree of difficulty in deciding beforehand was significantly correlated with the extent to which the internally -based negative emotions were experienced afterwards, but was unrelated to either socially based negative emotions or positive emotions experienced after the procedure. In contrast, the socially based negative emotions correlated with two variables that may be associated with greater social disapproval of abortion. Controlling for the effects of age, women who were unmarried and those who attended church more often experienced the socially based emotions more strongly in the months following abortion; these variables were not related to the experience of either the internally based negative emotions or the positive emotions.

In a longer term follow-up, Athanasiou and colleagues (1973) compared responses of women undergoing first-trimester abortion, second-trimester abortion, and term delivery. They started with a large sample, and carefully matched women in each of the groups to make them comparable on ethnicity, age, parity, marital status, and socioeconomic status. Thirty-eight women in each group were studied. Thirteen to sixteen months after their abortion or delivery, the women completed the MMPI and the Symptom Checklist. The researchers found that the groups were "startlingly similar." Only two differences emerged in the follow-up: The women in the term birth groups scored higher on the paranoia subscale of the MMPI than did either abortion group, and women who had a first-trimester abortion reported fewer somatic symptoms on the SCL than did either the delivery group or those who had undergone a second-trimester abortion. It is also noteworthy that none of the groups was beyond normal bounds on any of the subscales of the MMPI: On none of the subscales was the average score for the group two standard deviations or more above the standardized norm.

These studies all suggest a rather benign course following abortion. However, we have very few studies with strong clinical measures following the procedure. Probably the best study regarding risk of psychopathology following abortion is not from the United States but from Denmark. David, Rasmussen, and Holst (1981)

TABLE 4.2

Relationship Between Background Variables and Emotion Response Factors
(Correlation and Partial Correlation Controlling for Age)

	Emotion Response Factors		
	Socially Based Negative Emotions	*Positive Emotions*	*Internally Based Negative Emotions*
Age	-.30*	.06	-.24*
Marital Status	-.35**	.11	-.26*
	(-.26*)	(.10)	(-.17)
Religion	.10	.09	.01
	(.11)	(.09)	(.02)
Religious Attendance	.28*	.17	-.07
	(.29*)	(.17)	(-.08)
Education	-.17	-.10	.22
	(-.18)	(-.09)	(.21)
Decision Difficulty	.22	-.13	.37**
	(.19)	(-.13)	(.35**)

Note. The correlation coefficients, presented in parentheses, are those that result when the effects of age controlled for; from Adler, N. E. (1975).
*p < .05
**p < .01

took advantage of the fact that Denmark maintains population registries that cover both birth and abortion, as well as admission to psychiatric hospitals. They examined rates of admission to psychiatric hospitals for all women in the population age fifteen to 49 years and compared these to rates for women who had given birth during the year, and for women who had undergone an abortion during the year. They excluded all women who had been admitted to a psychiatric hospital within fifteen months prior to their admission to rule out pre-existing pathology. Admission rates to psychiatric hospitals were charted for the three months following birth or abortion. As Table 4.3 shows, the rate of admissions is somewhat but not dramatically higher for women who delivered and who had an abortion compared to the population as a whole, and is affected by age.

The differences in rates for abortion versus delivery depends on the marital status of the women. Rates of hospital admission for women who were currently married or never married and who delivered or aborted were comparable (11.9 for women who delivered versus 12.6 for women who aborted). However, among women who were separated, divorced or widowed, the rate of psychiatric admissions was far greater for the women who underwent abortion than for those who delivered (16.9 for those giving birth versus 63.8 for those who aborted). This difference may have to do with the extent of loss associated with the abortion for the women who were separated, divorced, or widowed. This must remain speculative since there are no data on the reasons for the abortion. It seems likely that a number of these pregnancies were initially wanted, and the abortion may have been associated with a change in the relationship with the partner. In addition, these women may have been in more difficult life situations, compounding the stresses involved in the unwanted pregnancy and its termination. It should be noted, however, that the risks associated with childbearing in this study may be underestimated. There may be a bias against hospitalizing a new mother, particularly if she is nursing, out of a desire not to separate the child from its mother.

Predictor Variables

While absolute levels of distress following abortion are low on average, women vary in the extent to which they experience negative emotions and psychological states following abortion. Understanding the factors associated with a more positive or negative response will increase our insight into the nature of the abortion experience, as well as help identify women who may be at higher risk for negative responses and in need of intervention.

Although by definition a pregnancy is unwanted at the time of an abortion, women may vary in the extent to which their pregnancy is unwanted and the reasons for which termination is sought. Some earlier studies of abortion were done in states in which abortion was granted only if there was specific justification for it. In these states, abortions were generally granted on medical grounds (i.e., a threat to the physical health of the mother or abnormalities of the fetus such as those resulting from exposure to rubella), or on psychiatric grounds (i.e., a threat to the mental

TABLE 4.3

Total Number of Women, Number of First Admissions to Psychiatric Hospitals, and Rate of Admissions per 10,000 Women Under Age 50 Within Three Months After Delivering Babies or Obtaining Abortions in Denmark During 1975; and Total Number of Women, Number of First Admissions and First-Admission Rate for all Danish Women Aged 15-49 in 1974-1975; by Age-group

Age-group	*Women who delivered*			*Women who had abortions*			*All women aged 15-49*		
	Total no.	*Psychiatric admissions*	*Rate*[a]	*Total no.*	*Psychiatric admissions*	*Rate*[a]	*Total no.*[b]	*Psychiatric admissions*	*Rate*[c]
Total	71,378	86	12.0	27,234	50	18.4	1,169,819	3,493	7.5
< 19	4,812	3	6.2	4,375	5	11.4	180,465[d]	354	4.9
20-24	24,808	26	10.5	5,820	11	18.9	184,911	503	6.8
25-29	27,150	31	11.4	6,303	13	20.6	207,885	585	7.0
30-34	11,452	19	16.6	5,504	14	25.4	166,970	601	9.0
35-49[e]	3,156	7	22.2	5,232	7	13.4	429,588	1,450	8.4

Note. From David et al. (1981).
[a]Total annual admissions adjusted for three-month period by dividing annual rate by four.
[b]By January 1, 1975.
[c]Adjusted to three-month rate to conform to rates for women who delivered and who obtained abortions.
[d]None under age 15.
[e]All women aged 35-49 aggregated because of small number of these women in abortion and delivery groups.

health of the mother). The most negative psychological responses were shown among women who were granted abortions on medical grounds rather than for social or psychiatric reasons (Niswander & Patterson, 1967; Peck & Marcus, 1966; Simon, Senturia, & Rothman, 1967). Women terminating pregnancies on medical grounds are likely to have been carrying pregnancies that would have been wanted were it not for the particular problem. In contrast, women terminating their pregnancies on psychiatric grounds are far more likely to have experienced the pregnancy as unwanted and aversive.

There has been no research on nonrestricted abortion which has specifically examined the association of postabortion responses with the reasons for which termination was sought. However, some related research suggests that the more a pregnancy is initially wanted, the greater the sense of loss and the more likely it may be that a woman will experience a negative reaction. For example, (although not meeting the criteria for inclusion the review because a lack of statistical reporting) a study of women who had abortions because diagnostic genetic testing during pregnancy indicated a problem with the fetus suggests that both the woman and her male partner may be at risk for depression and marital conflict (Blumberg, Golbus, & Hanson, 1975). Pregnancies terminated after genetic testing are almost always pregnancies that are wanted but which become problematic because of the results of the tests.

Several studies have examined satisfaction with the decision to undergo abortion. These studies find that women who report relatively little difficulty deciding to have an abortion and relatively greater satisfaction with the decision before the abortion are more likely to show positive responses following the abortion (Adler, 1975; Osofsky & Osofsky, 1972; Shusterman, 1979). In contrast, women who report social pressure or who are coerced into having an abortion are at higher risk for negative reponses afterwards. Finally, Major et al. (1985) found that women who reported before an abortion that their pregnancy was personally meaningful had more physical complaints afterwards and anticipated more negative consequences than did women who reported finding less meaning in the pregnancy.

Research findings on factors associated with more positive or negative responses to abortion are in line with research on other stressful life events. These studies point to the importance of social support, attribution process, and coping processes in adapting to the event.

Social support for the decision to have an abortion has been found to contribute to adjustment afterwards, but in complex ways. As we know, social support is not a unitary variable and the complexity of it is reflected in the research on its influence in postabortion response. One study found that for younger women (under age 23), anticipated or actual support from parents was significantly associated with better adjustment, while for relatively older women (over 23), it was the partner's response that was critical (Bracken, Hachamovitch, & Grossman, 1974). Other studies have shown that having a more positive relationship with the partner, feeling she can depend on her partner, having informed the partner of the decision, and perceiving support for the decision to terminate are each associated with more positive responses following abortion (Moseley, Follingstad, Harley, & Heckel, 1981; Shusterman, 1979).

As in other research, studies of abortion show that it's not always the case that the more the social support the better. Major et al. (1985) recorded whether a male partner accompanied a woman to the abortion clinic or the day of the procedure; partners were present for about one-third of the women. Those who were accompanied showed more symptoms of depression immediately following the procedure and had more physical complaints than those whose partners did not accompany them. Since it could be that women who were more upset and anxious about the abortion beforehand were more likely to get their mates to accompany them, the researchers looked at the characteristics of women who were accompanied or not. They found that those whose partners came with them to the clinic were younger and also expected beforehand to cope less well with the abortion. However, even when controlling for these differences, the accompanied women still scored higher on depression immediately after the procedure than did the unaccompanied.

In another study, Robbins (1984) examined regret a year after either abortion or delivery in a group of unmarried women. Among the women who had terminated their pregnancies, regret was greater among those who had maintained a strong relationship with their partner than among those relationships that had grown weaker or ended. Among women who delivered no relationship between strength of the relationship and regret was found.

There have been surprisingly few studies on attribution and coping in relation to abortion. Those that have been done suggest that these are useful variables in studying short-term reactions, but have not yet been clearly linked to longer-term responses.

Major and her colleagues have conducted two studies on the effects of differing attributions for the cause of the pregnancy or responses to its termination. In one study (Major et al., 1985) women who were seeking abortions indicated the extent to which they thought the pregnancy had occurred because of their character, their behavior, the situation, another person, or chance. Women who blamed the pregnancy on their own character showed higher levels of depression and anticipated more negative consequences after the abortion than did those low in self-blame; no other attributions were linked to negative outcomes.

In addition to examining the role of attributions, Major et al. (1985) looked at the expectations held by the women regarding how well they expected before the abortion to cope with its effects. Women who expected before the procedure to cope better with the abortion did, in fact, show more positive responses afterwards. In a second study Mueller and Major (1989) measured women's attributions for pregnancy and expectations for coping and then randomly assigned them to a control group or to one of two interventions. One intervention was designed to reduce self-blame for the pregnancy and one was designed to improve expectations for coping. Both the naturally occurring levels and the experimental intervention showed the expected relationships, with more positive coping expectancies and lower self-blame being associated with more positive adjustment.

The type of coping strategies used by women during the procedure may also influence responses afterwards. Cohen and Roth (1984) asked women to complete the Impact of Event Scale, two subscales of the Symptom Checklist (anxiety and depression) and a measure of "Active Approach" both before undergoing a first-trimester abortion and again in the recovery room afterwards. The Active Approach scale was designed for the study and measured the extent to which the woman used an active strategy for coping with the abortion and her feelings about it. Two sample items were, "I thought about what my options were" and "I tried to deal with my feelings about it" (p. 141). While, as noted earlier, psychological distress dropped overall from beforehand to afterwards, the use of an active coping strategy was associated with a relatively greater decrease in distress, with women scoring higher on the Active Approach scale showing a significantly greater drop in distress than those showing less use of active approach.

The results just presented deal with the immediate aftermath of abortion. In the study by Major et al. (1985) there was a follow-up three weeks later which showed weaker and less consistent results. Thus, we cannot say much about long-term effects. The longest follow-up is two years (Zabin, Hirsch, & Emerson, 1989). However, data presented by Wortman and Silver (1989) regarding patterns of responses following stressful life events document that the emergence of psychological symptomatology in the long-term is unlikely if such symptoms have not emerged within a short time after the event. Given this, it seems unlikely that the patterns of results will change dramatically with longer-term follow-up.

ABORTION AS A MODEL OF CRISIS AND LOSS

Using abortion as a model of crisis and/or loss has both advantages and disadvantages. It is an excellent model for studying the function of meaning in determining responses to a life event. Abortion, particularly early abortion, is an ambiguous event in terms of the loss. In the context of religious differences, changing scientific evidence, and current discussions about when life begins, just what is lost is open to a good deal of interpretation. There is likely to be wide variation in what meaning is attributed to the pregnancy that is terminated. What one woman may experience as the loss of an infant, another may conceptualize as removal of unwanted, inert tissue.

Abortion also provides a good instance for studying the role of attribution and blame. The occurrence of an unwanted pregnancy and the necessity of terminating it are likely to provoke a search for cause and blame. Unwanted pregnancy and abortion are both stigmatized events. The causes that the woman perceives for the occurrence of the pregnancy and for its termination may affect the meaning associated with the abortion and, in turn, influence her response to the abortion. In studying attributional processes, we must also examine the actual circumstances under which the pregnancy occurred. The actual circumstances of the pregnancy as well as the woman's perception of causes, may affect the woman's responses following its termination.

Finally, abortion can provide a good model for studying the interplay of social and psychological forces. Moré than most events of loss, abortion is enmeshed in a social context. The rights and wrongs of the action are a matter of public discussion (Baird & Rosenbaum, 1989). Other people, both those close to the woman, and those who may not even know her, are likely to have strong feelings about what she is doing. In the United States now, a woman going in for an abortion may have to walk through an angry crowd screaming at her that she is a murderer. The private meaning of the event may be changed or reinforced by the social surroundings and responses to it. Since we are now entering an era in the United States where the legal status of abortion is in question and where the legality and availability of abortion may differ from one state to another, there may be emerging opportunities to study the effects of abortion under different social conditions. Similarly, cultural beliefs and values associated with abortion vary in different countries and in different subcultures. Cross-cultural research on psychological responses may shed light on some of these processes.

The turmoil and controversy about abortion make it difficult to study, however. One set of difficulties arises from the fact that the social environment is changing so rapidly and on so many levels that it may be difficult to identify the factors contributing to how abortion is experienced. Another set of difficulties arises from the fact that abortion is stigmatized. Women may not want to admit that they have had an abortion or participate in research which is identified as abortion research. Thus, volunteer effects, which are a potential problem for any research, may be even greater in studies of abortion.

Finally, interpreting responses following abortion is complicated by the fact that one cannot disentangle responses to abortion from those relating to the experience of unwanted pregnancy. Just as abortion holds different meanings for individual women, so does pregnancy. A given pregnancy can represent a woman's hopes for healing a rift in a problematic relatinship or it can reflect a teenager's hopes for achieving adult status and independence from parents. In contrast, another pregnancy may be the result of contraceptive failure and symbolize only a dreaded event. Or it may result from the woman's failure to use contraception and may symbolize one more situation in which she has failed. Although we speak of reactions to abortion, we cannot separate out the effects of experiencing an unwanted pregnancy. Responses to having become pregnant and the events that are triggered by its occurrence may have a greater effect on later psychological functioning than will the termination of the pregnancy.

Better prospective studies are needed to examine psychological responses to abortion. Ideally, one would obtain baseline measures of women prior to their becoming pregnant, and follow them through the occurrence of the pregnancy, decision-making regarding resolution, and its aftermath. This approach would require a large initial population, but the frequency of occurrence of unwanted pregnancy in some groups is sufficiently high that such an approach is feasible. A more efficient approach, but one that does not give a true baseline, is to study women coming in for pregnancy tests as was done by Zabin et al. (1989). This approach is well-suited for making comparisons between women who are not pregnant versus those who are, and between those who carry to term versus those who terminate.

In conducting prospective longitudinal studies, it will be important to ascertain reproductive and other events that occur after the initial interview. A woman who terminates a pregnancy may become pregnant again and then carry to term; responses several years later will reflect both occurrences as well as other events. There may be critical experiences that will influence later responses to abortion. Reproductive events, particularly problems of infertility or complications of a subsequent pregnancy, may cause a woman to reflect back on a prior abortion, though we do not know to what effect.

All studies of responses to abortion should include assessments of several domains of functioning. Positive functioning and well-being should be measured as well as distress and dysfunction. In addressing concerns about the effects of abortion on mental health, it would be particularly helpful to have clinically based measures for which norms exist indicating whether or not responses fall within a pathological range.

Finally, studies that aim to determine responses to abortion, as distinct from the whole experience of having an unwanted pregnancy that is terminated by abortion, should include appropriate control groups. The best comparison would be women who carry an unwanted pregnancy to term and relinquish the child for adoption. Unter conditions where abortion is available, such samples are difficult to find; some women are ideologically opposed to abortion and may carry to term and relinquish their infants, but the numbers of such women have been relatively small. However, if abortion laws become more restrictive, there may be increasing numbers of women who will have to carry unwanted pregnancies to term and may relinquish the infant. Longitudinal studies following women who terminate and who deliver and relinquish the infant would be particularly important in determining the effects of abortion versus the alternative of carrying a truly unwanted pregnancy to term.

CONCLUSIONS

To recap, the best available studies on psychological responses following legal, nonrestrictive abortion in the United States suggest that severe negative reactions are infrequent in the immediate and short-term aftermath. This is particularly true for the first-trimester abortions. While overall reactions are likely to be mild, some women will be at relatively greater risk for experiencing negative emotions or responses afterwards. As the APA panel concluded, "Women who are terminating pregnancies that are wanted and meaningful; who lack support from their partner or parents for the abortion; or who have more conflicting feelings or are less sure of their decision beforehand may be at relatively higher risk for negative consequences" (Adler et al., 1990, p. 43).

The patterns of responses found after abortion are consistent with results from studies examining samples of people who have experienced other types of life stresses. These results point to the importance of social and cognitive processes in shaping responses to the event. The meaning associated with the event, the attributions made for why it occurred, the type and degree of social support, and the actual experience can all influence outcome. Abortion provides a good model for studying these processes, but is subject to a complex variety of factors affecting both the women themselves and researchers studying them. Studies of abortion thus need to be designed with particular sensitivity to the social setting and to the researcher's own assumptions and biases.

REFERENCES

Adler, N. E. (1975). Emotional responses of women following therapeutic abortion. *American Journal of Orthopsychiatry, 45,* 446-454.

Adler, N. E., David, H. P., Major, B. N., Roth, S. H., Russo, N. F., & Wyatt, G. E. (1990). Psychological responses after abortion. *Science, 248,* 41-44.

Athanasiou, R., Oppel, W., Michelson, L., Unger, T., & Yager, M. (1973). Psychiatric sequelae to term birth and induced early and late abortion: A longitudinal study. *Family Planning Perspectives, 5,* 227-231.

Baird, R. M., & Rosenbaum, S. E. (Eds.). (1989). *The ethics of abortion.* Buffalo: Prometheus Books.

Blumberg, B. D., Golbus, M. S., & Hanson, K. H. (1975). The psychological sequelae of abortion performed for a genetic indication. *American Journal of Obstetrics and Gynecology, 122,* 799-808.

Bracken, M. B., Hachamovitch, M., & Grossman, G. (1974). The decision to abort and psychological sequelae. *The Journal of Nervous and Mental Disease, 158,* 154-162.

Cohen, L., & Roth, S. (1984). Coping with abortion. *Journal of Human Stress, 10,* 140-145.

David, H., Rasmussen, N., & Holst, E. (1981). Postpartum and postabortion psychotic reaction. *Family Planning Perspectives, 13,* 88-93.

Deutsch, H. (1945). *The psychology of women: A psychoanalytic interpretation.* New York: Grune & Stratton.

Ebaugh, F., & Heuser, K. (1947). Psychiatric aspects of therapeutic abortion. *Postgraduate Medicine,* 2, 325-332.

Fingerer, M. (1973). Psychological sequelae of abortion: Anxiety and depression. Journal of *Community Psychology, 1,* 221-225.

Freeman, E. W., Rickels, R., Huggings, G. R., Garcia, C. R., & Pollin, J. (1980). Emotional distress patterns among women having first or repeat abortions. *Obstetrics and Gynecology, 55,* 630-636.

Kummer, J. M. (1963). Post-abortion psychiatric illness—a myth? *American Journal of Psychiatry, 119,* 980-983.

Lazarus, A. (1985). Psychiatric sequelae of legalized first trimester abortion. *Journal of Psychosomatic Obstetrics and Gynecology, 4,* 141-150.

Major, B., Mueller, P., & Hildebrandt, K. (1985). Attributions, expectations, and coping with abortion. *Journal of Personality and Social Psychology, 48,* 585-599.

Moseley, D. T., Follingstad, D. R., Harley, H., & Heckel, R. V. (1981). Psychological factors that predict reaction to abortion. *Journal of Clinical Psychology, 37*, 276-279.

Mueller, P., & Major, B. (1989). Self-blame, self-efficacy, and adjustment to abortion. *Journal of Personality and Social Psychology, 57*, 1059-1068.

Niswander, K., & Patterson, R. (1967). Psychological reaction to therapeutic abortion. *Obstetrics and Gynecology, 29*, 702-706.

Osofsky, J., & Osofsky, H. (1972). The psychological reaction of patients to legalized abortion. *American Journal of Orthopsychiatry, 42*, 48-59.

Peck, A., & Marcus, H. (1966). Psychiatric sequelae of therapeutic interruption of pregnancy. *Journal of Nervous and Mental Disease, 143*, 417-425.

Public Interest Directorate (1987). *Psychological sequelae of abortion*. Presented to the Office of the U.S. Surgeon General as follow-up report to oral presentation, December 2, 1987. Washington, DC: American Psychological Association.

Robbins, J. M. (1984). Out of wedlock abortion and delivery: The importance of the male partner. *Social Problems, 31*, 334-350.

Shusterman, L. R. (1979). Predicting the psychological consequences of abortion. *Social Science and Medicine, 13A*, 683-689.

Simon, N. M., & Senturia, A. G. (1966). Psychiatric sequelae of abortion. *Archives of General Psychiatry, 15*, 378-389.

Simon, N. M., Senturia, A. G., & Rothman, D. (1967). Psychiatric illness following therapeutic abortion. *American Journal of Psychiatry, 124*, 59-65.

Speckhard, A. C. (1987). *The psycho-social aspects of stress following abortion*. Kansas City, MO: Sheed & Ward.

Wortman, C. B., & Silver, R. C. (1989). The myths of coping with loss. *Journal of Consulting and Clinical Psychology, 57*, 349-357.

Zabin, L. S., Hirsch, M. B., & Emerson, M. R. (1989). When urban adolescents choose abortion: Effects on education, psychological status, and subsequent pregnancy. *Family Planning Perspectives, 21*, 248-255.

5 A Plea for Realistic Pessimism: On Objective Reality, Coping with Stress, and Psychological Dysfunction

Michael Frese
University of Giessen

It behooves us to start an article for a German-American conference volume with a few words on cultural differences between the U.S.A. and Germany. There is a general optimism in the U.S.A. that is also reflected in the coping literature: An attempt to cope is usually seen as a way out (sometimes, I have even observed something like a pressure to be optimistic). Not so in Germany: Germans are usually much more pessimistic with regard to the possibilities of coping with stress. Interestingly, this difference is also reflected in the respective constitutions. While the major psychological variable in the American constitution is the optimistic "pursuit of happiness," the equivalent in the German constitution is the development and expansion of personality (Entfaltung der Persönlichkeit). Note, that going through depression may be part of the development of personality, while it certainly would contradict the pursuit of happiness.

In this article I shall take a more Germanic point of view: I shall argue for the bleak and pessimistic side of the possibilities of coping (similarly, Schönpflug, 1986). In fact, given certain circumstances, I shall argue for realistic pessimism.

To argue my point, I shall shortly discuss the circumstances that speak for realistic pessimism. Then I shall back up claims with four sets of empirical data: (1) A longitudinal study on unemployment demonstrating that optimism leads to more depression for the unemployed in the long run. (2) A study on control at work showing that adjusting one's aspiration level to noncontrol situations does not do away with the objective consequences of noncontrol. (3) A study on stress at work indicating that low monitoring does not imply positive consequences as suggested by Miller, Brody, and Summerton (1988). (4) Two longitudinal studies on stress at work assessing various coping strategies with a questionnaire that show no evidence for a long-term positive function of coping strategies. At best, the results are inconclusive; at worst, they suggest that coping strategies increase the negative effects of stressors on psychosomatic complaints.

THE ARGUMENT OF POSITIVE ILLUSIONS

There is now a large body of research, ably summarized by Taylor and Brown (1988) and Taylor (1989), that argues for the health-enhancing effect of positive illusions. Their main argument is that people view themselves in an unrealistically positive light, and that illusions of control and unrealistic optimism have positive consequences for mental health because they help to uphold happiness and an active approach to life as well as a stronger social orientation. Taylor (1989) is quite careful to point out that positive illusions do not imply that one completely loses contact with reality.

I do not want to quarrel with most of the empirical data and the arguments given by Taylor. For most conditions, her arguments are right. This is particularly true for illusions about one's own capacities (maybe in comparison to others) or for past events that are redrawn in memory to foster a positive self-image (Greenwald, 1980). However, there is a set of conditions, in which an opposite hypothesis might hold: If the situation is perceived to be important by the individual, if there is "objective" feedback, and, most importantly, if the situation demands actions, unfounded optimism (illusions) about the realities of life may turn out to be destructive *in the long run*. Illusions destroyed are worse than realistic pessimism.

If the situation is of no particular importance (because it does not affect long-term and important goals), as in many experimental settings, illusions can be upheld without problems and there are no long-term negative effects. Furthermore, if the situation does not provide feedback on one's actions, illusions can have positive consequences. Again, this happens in many experimental settings in which the person does not develop his or her own goals and, therefore, does not really act in the proper sense of the term (for the concept of action, see Frese & Sabini, 1985). Furthermore, the experiment is short-term and does not produce long-term consequences. Moreover, if the situation has occurred in the past (e.g., having finished school, a class, or a relationship, etc.), illusions about past behaviors may be an indication of high self-esteem; they do not have negative consequences because one cannot affect the past situations anyhow.

Taylor (1989) describes the usefulness of illusions in situations of high importance that exist currently—for example, having cancer. However, cancer does not *afford actions* (except medical actions that are usually under tight control and supervision from the medical setting and do not have to be initiated and maintained by the person), and feedback is not regularly related to actions (cancer has its own course, often distinct from what a person does or does not do).

Thus, it is useful to find situations that permit the study of *long-term consequences* in which the person has to *initiate actions* and in which there is *feedback* by the environment that is strong enough not to be overlooked and objective enough not to be disregarded. Two situations (among others) have such qualities: unemployment and stress at work. In unemployment, there is high pressure to do something about it and to search for a job (as a matter of fact, German law, for example, stipulates that only people actively searching for jobs will receive unemployment compensation). Similarly, the work area does not allow idle contemplation but requires that one actively deals with the situation at hand (the reason why managers are less affected by stressors at work may be the fact that they are able to turn away from the situation and can at least delegate certain stressors, while the normal blue-collar worker cannot do this). Thus, in these two situations, there should be no advantage to a strategy of developing illusions. This will be shown in the following studies.

STUDY 1: HOPE AND UNEMPLOYMENT

In a study on unemployment (Frese, 1987; Frese & Mohr, 1987), we developed a scale called "hope for control." Items on this scale were, for example, "If one applies for a job often enough, then one will get a job again." The study was longitudinal and started out with unemployed, older, blue-collar workers who were already unemployed in Berlin (time t_1). Eighteen months later, they were asked to fill out a questionnaire again (time t_2). Some of them were still unemployed, while others had found a job but had lost it again in the meantime. A third group had found a job and was now employed. A fourth group was able to retire prematurely.

If illusions help a person to deal with the situation of unemployment, then hope should help to reduce depression. This was indeed the case. The correlations between hope for control and depression were -.11 (n.s. for t_1) and -.55 ($N = 51$, $p < .01$ in t_2). Since one of the negative correlations was significant, this speaks for the hypothesis that hope helps one to deal with the problems of unemployment—backing the concept that optimism has positive effects even if illusory. But note, this is only true concurrently. What about the long-term effect? Here, there were quite different relationships. The two unemployed groups showed a predictive correlation of hope for control$_{t1}$ on depression$_{t2}$ (i.e., depression 18 months later) of $r = .39$ ($p < .05$, $N = 26$). Thus, in the case of people whose hopes were disappointed, earlier high (illusory) hope was predictive of later depression. In contrast, for those people whose hopes had become true because they were now either employed or retired, the respective correlation was negative ($r = -.27$, $p = .098$, $N = 25$).

A somewhat different way to present the data is to calculate the correlations between the current state of unemploment at time t_2 and depression at the same time for two subgroups: those whose hopes had been high at time t_1 and those who already had low hopes at this time (the retired were excluded in this analysis). For the low-hope-for-control subgroup at t_1, the correlation was .12 ($N = 21$, n.s.), while the high hope for control subgroup showed a correlation of .73 ($p < .001, N = 20$) between unemployment and depression at t_2. Thus, it was the group with a high degree of hope that suffered most from prolonged unemployment. (By the way, hope also decreased significantly for the prolonged unemployed across time.[1])

In summary, this study shows that illusions do help to uphold (or, at least, do not impair) health in the short run. But this is not the case in the long run. Disappointments because of illusions produce depression to a much larger extent in the case of prolonged unemployment than in the group that started out with few illusions. I am aware, of course, that such a result has to be replicated, and that the sample on which the study is based is rather small. However, these kinds of results may suggest that it is unwise to produce hope in the unemployed when there is little objective evidence that they will find a job in the near future.

STUDY 2: SELF-DECEPTION ABOUT THE OBJECTIVE SITUATION OF CONTROL AT WORK: DOES IT HELP?

This is another variant of the theme of this paper: It does not help to kid oneself about reality. According to the optimistic view, one way to increase happiness is to blend out real problems in the work situation. Two ways of doing this are to trivialize the negative situation or to adjust one's aspiration level ("I really do not want this kind of job!"). In the following, I want to show that self-deception with regard to control aspirations and nonchalance vis-à-vis reality is not a useful device to improve health (although in this cross-sectional study it does not impair health).

One aspect of the field of stress at work that has attracted research has been control at work (Frese, 1989; Johnson & Hall, 1988; Karasek, Baker, Marxer, Ahlbom, & Theorell, 1981; Sauter, Hurrell, & Cooper, 1989). It has been shown that noncontrol at work interacts with stressors, jointly producing more psychosomatic complaints than either noncontrol or stressors alone (Semmer & Frese, 1990). It is possible, of course, to adjust one's aspiration level: One does not really like to have control in the first place. A clinician who wants the client to be happy in spite of objective hindrances might suggest such a strategy (see Lazarus, 1982).

According to the optimistic variant of self-deception, people with a low craving for control at work or people who actually reject control should not be negatively affected by the issue of noncontrol. To test this assumption, I developed a scale on control rejection in the work situation. Since most people would simply say that they would want to have more control at work if there were no stipulations associated with it, items were constructed that also gave negative implications of

[1] Another result of this study was that depression was not predictive of later prolonged unemployment but that unemployment was predictive of depression even when earlier depression was held constant.

control. Two sample items are: "I would rather be told exactly what I have to do. Then I make fewer errors." "I only do what I am told to do. Then nobody can reproach me for anything."

This scale on control rejection was given to a sample of German, male, blue-collar workers from several companies in the metal industry ($N = 206$). Additionally, psychological stressors and control were measured by having trained observers rate each work place and having the subjects fill out a respective questionnaire (more information on this study can be found in Frese, 1985; Semmer, 1984; Semmer & Frese, 1990). Thus, we obtained both data: the "objective" observers' ratings and the subjects' responses. The dependent variable was a well-validated questionnaire on psychosomatic complaints (Mohr, 1986).

Noncontrol per se does not have any relationship with psychosomatic complaints. Only the interaction of noncontrol and stressors is significantly associated with psychosomatic complaints. Thus, control rejection should moderate this particular effect.

Since moderation is the important concept, we divided control into high- and low-control groups and further subdivided each group into high and low control rejection. The dependent variable was the correlation between psychological stressors at the work place and psychosomatic complaints. Figure 5.1 gives the results. For our purposes, the most important number is the correlation for the low-control and high-control-rejection cell. If the optimistic concept is correct that people can trivialize control and adjust to the noncontrol situation, then the correlation should be lower in this cell than in the low-control, low-control-rejection cell. If this means that they kid themselves on the objective importance of control to deal with the stress situation, control rejection should not help. As one can see in Figure 5.1, there was no support for the optimistic view on coping. Rather, the correlation was highest in the low-control and high-control-rejection cell—and most pronounced when control and stressors were measured with observers' ratings.

Thus, the results support a view that I have called the sour-grape effect (Frese, 1984), like the fox in the fable who turns away from the sweet looking grapes that he cannot reach, pronouncing them to be too sour. Again, there is evidence for the more pessimistic view on coping with the world. One actually would have to change the objective control situation at work in order to have an impact on health rather than just suggesting to the workers that their work situation is not really that bad and that they should just forget about obtaining control in the work situation. Purely cognitive adjustments and adaptations that do not change the real world clearly have limits.

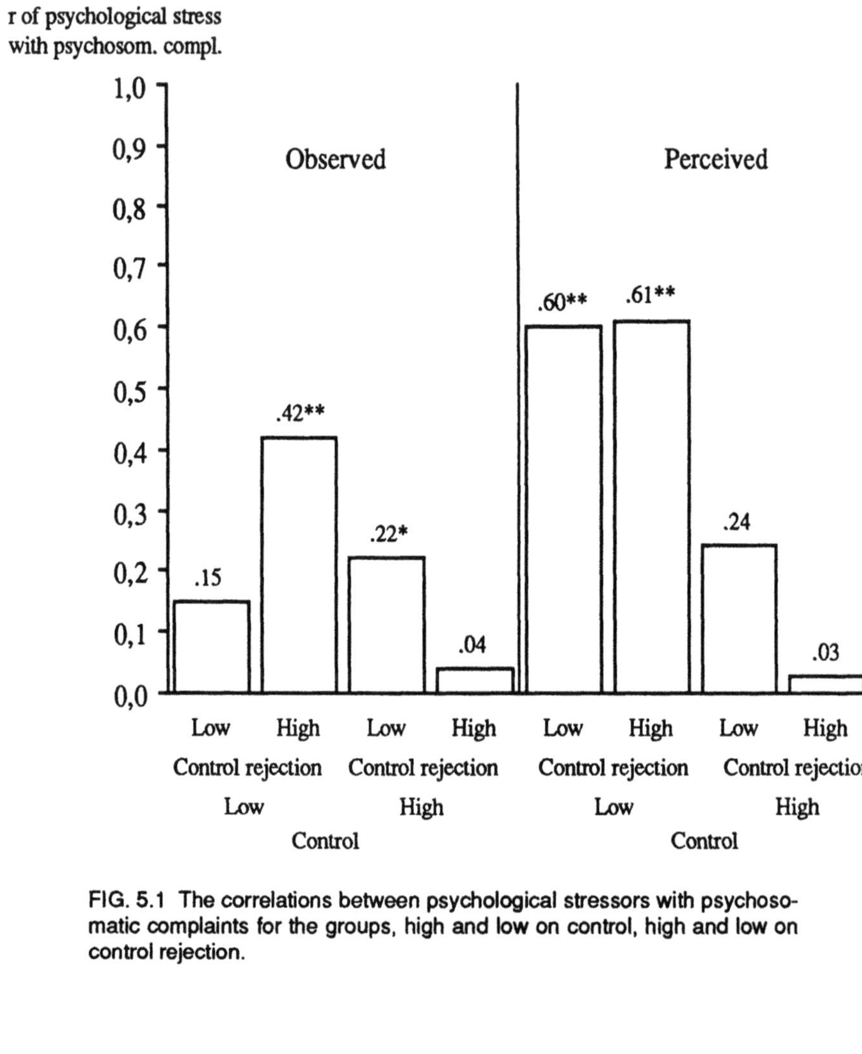

FIG. 5.1 The correlations between psychological stressors with psychosomatic complaints for the groups, high and low on control, high and low on control rejection.

STUDY 3: KEEPING STRESSFUL REALITY OUT OF YOUR MIND: BLUNTING VERSUS MONITORING

Miller (1987; Miller et al., 1988; see also her article in this book) has developed a scale on monitoring and blunting. This scale measures whether people turn toward reality when they are under threat (monitoring) or whether they keep reality out (blunting). The monitoring scale seems to be a better predictor for health-related issues, and it is therefore used more often than the blunting scale (Miller et al.,

1988). Miller et al. have suggested that the low monitors do better in health-related areas. Similarly, high-blunting/low-monitoring subjects were less aroused and anxious in various experimental settings involving threats (Miller, 1987).

It can once more be asked, whether results of studies on short-term threats can be generalized to long-term problems like stress at work. Again, 170 German, male, blue-collar workers in the metal industry received the monitoring and blunting questionnaire (Miller, 1987) as well as a questionnaire on stressors and resources at work. In this study, only the perceived stressors and resources were ascertained. (Actually, the study was a third wave of the longitudinal Study 2. Experimental mortality was very low: Of the 193 subjects who had given us their addresses in Study 2, 10 had moved and could not be traced, an additional 2 had died, and 2 were too sick to answer the questionnaire.) Since monitoring is supposed to be a moderator (Frese, 1986), the question is, again, how it influences the relationship between stressors and psychosomatic complaints. As Miller et al. (1988) have suggested, only the monitoring scale was used and it was divided on the median. This produced 95 low monitors and 70 high monitors (there were some missing data on the monitoring scale).

Table 5.1 shows that both groups had more or less the same arithmetic means for stressors, thus they were exposed to the same intensity of the stressors. The correlations are, of course, more important. The correlations between stressors (as well as resources) and psychosomatic complaints are shown for the two groups—the high and the low monitors. For stressors, the correlations were nearly all positive—this is not surprising because stressors should have a relationship with psychosomatic complaints. Additionally, in six out of eight cases, the correlations were higher for the low monitoring group and in six out of eight cases they were only significant for this group. The differences were not clearly significant, except in one case (in an additional case, the z-score showed a marginal significance between the two subgroups). While the results were not absolutely clear, there was little support for Miller et al.'s findings in this particular setting. Apparently, in a field study on long-term stressors at work, the low monitors have larger correlations between stressors and psychosomatic complaints than the high monitors, suggesting that the low monitors may suffer more from stressors.

Surprisingly the results were more pronounced for resources at work and they took the same direction. Both complexity and variability usually have a positive function (Karasek, 1989). But in this study, the positive function only held for high monitors but not for low monitors. Thus, it pays to monitor one's environment closely in a persistent stress situation that affords action.

TABLE 5.1

Monitoring as a Moderator

Work variables (Stressors and resources)	*Arithmetic means for stressors*		*Correlations with psychosomatic complaints*		*r to z for significance of differences for r s*
	Low monitors	*High monitors*	*Low monitors*	*High monitors*	
Uncertainty	2.7	2.8	.32**	.06	z = 1.58 §
Intensity/ Concentration	3.3	3.4	.26**	-.04	z = 1.82*
Danger of accidents	2.4	2.8	.24*	.12	n.s.
Organizational problems	2.7	2.7	.32**	.17	n.s.
Environmental stress	2.6	2.6	.17	.34**	n.s.
Social stressors	2.0	2.0	.38**	.20	n.s.
Job insecurity	3.1	3.2	.27**	.29*	n.s.
One-sided physical stressors	1.7	1.8	.20*	.17	n.s.
Control	5.2	5.2	.03	-.13	n.s.
Complexity	5.5	5.8	.12	-.30**	z = -2.52**
Variability	6.5	6.8	.03	-.25*	z = -1.70*

§ = $p < .10$
* = $p < .05$
** = $p < .01$

STUDIES 4 AND 5: COPING IN GENERAL

The last two longitudinal studies support the ultimate in pessimism: With one exception, we have found no coping strategy that can unequivocally be called positive. Similarly to the Lazarus group (Aldwin, Folkman, Schaefer, Coyne, & Lazarus, 1980), we have developed several coping scales with regard to (work) stressors. After pretesting, we used four different stressors that most German, male, blue-collar workers had found to be stressful („When something bothers me in my work...," "When I am under pressure in my work...," "When I have an argument with my colleague...," "When I have an argument with my wife..."). Various potential coping strategies were listed after each of these four situations. A principal component analysis revealed six clear and stable factors, all but one of which cut across the different stress situations („socially focused positive outlook" only referred to two situations). They are displayed in Table 5.2.

Two additional coping scales did not have the same format: Denial (alpha = .73) and Avoidance (alpha = .63). They only referred to work pressure per se and were of a Likert-type format.

Coping is supposed to moderate the influence of stressors on ill health. This was directly tested in two longitudinal studies. One longitudinal study had two waves across 16 months (N = 90; again, this study was based on the subjects in Study 2). The second longitudinal study had two waves across 66 months (N = 170; again, this study was based on the subjects in Study 2).

The moderator effect was tested with the help of hierarchical regression analyses with an interaction term (Cohen & Cohen, 1975; Zedeck, 1971). This procedure implies that an interaction term "Stressor × Coping" is introduced into a hierarchical regression equation as the last term. If this interaction term proves to be significant

TABLE 5.2
Coping Factors

IF SOMETHING BOTHERS ME IN MY WORK, THEN
(Pressure, argument with colleague, argument with spouse)

1. Positive outlook (5 items; Alpha = .68)
   "...I say consciously to myself: 'Now be calm'"

2. Socially focussed positive outlook (9 items; Alpha = .78)
   "...I think that there are better sides to him/her"

3. Brooding (6 items; Alpha = .81)
   "...I think about it for some days"

4. Socially oriented coping (6 items; Alpha = .70)
   "...I ask other colleagues for help"

5. Attention diverting (5 items; Alpha = .72)
   "...I try to divert my attention from this"

6. Repression
   "...I swallow down my anger"

after coping and stressors and the dependent variable measured at t_1 have been included into the regression equation, then a change of the dependent variable at t_2 can be said to be due to the moderator effect of coping. If the beta of this interaction term is positive, it means that the particular coping strategy turns out to reduce the effect of stressors on ill health. Thus, coping works as a buffer, as most theorists of coping would have it (e.g., Lazarus & Folkman, 1984). In contrast, if the interaction term is negative, it means that coping actually enhances the negative effects of stressors on ill health.

Table 5.3 presents the significant betas for the interaction terms in both longitudinal studies. Since moderated regressions are rather conservative, a significance criterion of .10 was used throughout. Only the two stressors psychological stressors and social stressors were included into the regressions. In contrast to the other analyses described so far in this article, four ill health variables were used as dependent variables: psychosomatic complaints, anxiety, irritation/strain, and

TABLE 5.3

Coping Strategies and the Effects of Stressors on Ill-Health

	Longitudinal studies			
	16 months (t2)		*5 1/2 years (t3)*	
	Function of coping		*Function of coping*	
Coping strategy	*Negative betas*	*Positive betas*	*Negative betas*	*Positive betas*
Socially focused positive outlook		3	4	
Positive outlook	2		2	
Socially oriented coping	1	1	3	1
Repression		1	2	1
Brooding	1		1	
Attention diverting		2		2
Denial	1		1	
Avoidance	1	1	1	1

Note. Moderated regression: Number of significant betas of psychological and social stressors $_{t1}$ × coping $_{t1}$; dependent variables: Psychosomatic complaints $_{t2/t3}$, anxiety $_{t2/t3}$, irritation $_{t2/t3}$, and depression $_{t2/t3}$.

depression (the t_1 of these variables was always partialled out within the hierarchical regression procedure, so that actual change of ill health was measured).

There are at least three possible interpretations of the results presented in Table 5.3. First, the results just show a random pattern. Since there were two stressors, eight coping strategies, and four dependent variables, a total of 64 regression analyses were computed. The 14 significant interaction terms of the first longitudinal study might just be random. The same would apply for the 19 significant interaction terms in the second longitudinal study. The divergent patterns of the two studies would just be due to noise in the data.

The second interpretation can be placed in a different methodological framework. Frese (1986) has analyzed the coping data of the 16-month study with a different method (cross-lagged panel correlations). He has suggested that questionnaire studies on coping can only tap conscious thoughts (of course, this is also true of interview studies). Since most coping strategies are not consciously reflected but used automatically (as most action strategies are), only a certain part of the coping strategies are ascertained within these studies. Automaticity is usually interrupted if something goes wrong, and then the person turns toward conscious strategies. Thus, the more things do not work out (e.g., a set of coping strategies), the more they are consciously represented or reconstructed. Therefore, a higher score on coping in questionnaires may actually imply that more things went wrong. Therefore, there are positive correlations between coping strategies and ill health.

The third interpretation is one of content. According to this interpretation, the data show that some coping strategies, like "socially focused positive outlook", may actually be positive over the shorter run (across the 16 months of the first longitudinal study), but in the longer run, the same strategies turn out to have a negative effect (an enhancing effect of stressors on ill health). It is interesting to see that there were more significant negative betas in the longer longitudinal study. While, the negative betas in the first longitudinal study usually remained negative in the second one, the positive betas turned into negative ones in the second study. There was only one exception: attention diverting.

I think that the first interpretation is probably wrong. A pure random result is unlikely because our 19 significances with the criterion $p < .10$ represent about 30% of all the computations. Thus, the second and the third interpretations are more interesting. It is difficult to decide between them. My recent thinking has shifted in the direction of the third interpretation because the data seem to show a difference between the two longitudinal studies.

Whatever the preferred interpretation: There is no evidence whatsoever that coping has a consistent positive effect. The coping strategies researched in these studies were of the emotion-focused type (Lazarus & Folkman, 1984) with the exception of "socially oriented coping." As a matter of fact, we would assume with Carver, Scheier, and Weintraub (1989) that problem-oriented coping strategies may actually produce positive results on health. This would be so, we assume, because problem-oriented strategies have an impact on objective reality.

Others have observed similar findings. Carver et al. (1989) have found negative relations between their emotion-focused coping strategies and anxiety (unfortunately, this was not a longitudinal study). Aldwin and Revenson (1987) have shown that nearly all of their coping strategies had negative effects on health. Only one problem-solving strategy, namely instrumental action, which presumably is most directly related to actually changing objective conditions, showed a positive buffer effect.

GENERAL DISCUSSION

Thus, a pessimistic point of view on coping prevails. As long as the objective conditions are not changed, or the prerequisites for changing these conditions do not exist (namely monitoring the stressors), negative effects are to be seen. They may not appear immediately but they show up over the long run.

As a matter of fact, even coping strategies that initially have a positive impact, like optimism, turn out to be negative when the objective situation stays negative (i.e., unemployment prevails or reappears). Attempting to reduce one's aspirations may work but again it does not override objective reality (as in the case of control rejection). Monitoring may be negative in a short-term threat situation or when the actual threat does not really turn out to be existent (as in some experiments). But with continuing stressors, like those at work, it is more useful to attend to them closely. In the last two longitudinal studies, the general picture occurs again: Even those few coping strategies that have positive buffer effects in the 16-month study become negative enhancer effects in the 66-month longitudinal study. With one exception, emotion-oriented coping does not seem to work very well.

Of course, this is not true of all coping strategies at all times. As suggested in the introduction, the situation of work and its stressors, as well as unemployment are special situations. They are long-term, they afford action, they are obtrusive and salient, and they are difficult to talk away or to blank out of one's mind.

The question is now, what should one do. Is my position possibly quite inhumane because it leaves people with their doubts and pessimism? In my view, a way out is a sort of existentialist approach. Just as the physician in Camus' *Black Plague* did his work in spite of his knowledge of futility, people can approach stressors in a similar way. I was recently asked by a popular journal what I would suggest to the unemployed. My answer took the same direction: Just continue to apply, even though you should know that there is very little chance that the application will have any positive consequences. Just continue to be active because it is part of being unemployed. It belongs to unemployment to attempt to find a job—even if this is futile. Attempt to deal with life, knowing full well that there is little chance that you are able to, because it is part of life to be active in spite of everything that we correctly perceive in a pessimistic light.

I am not arguing for unrealistic pessimism, of course. Those things that can be influenced and can be accomplished should be seen within an optimistic perspective. But when there is reason for pessimism, the approach of taking the bitter pill of dealing with the objective reality now can contribute to being able to feel better later because it may lead to better action strategies. In this light, Germanic pessimism may have optimistic consequences after all.

REFERENCES

Aldwin, C., Folkman, S., Schaefer, C., Coyne, J. C., & Lazarus, R. S. (1980). *Ways of coping: A process measure*. Paper presented at the 88th annual meeting of the American Psychological Association, Montreal, Quebec.

Aldwin, C. M., & Revenson, T. A. (1987). Does coping help? A reexamination of the relation between coping and mental health. *Journal of Personality and Social Psychology, 53*, 337-348.

Carver, C. S., Scheier, M., & Weintraub, J. K. (1989). Assessing coping strategies: A theoretically based approach. *Journal of Personality and Social Psychology, 56*, 267-283.

Cohen, J., & Cohen, P. (1975). *Applied multiple regression/correlational analysis for the behavioral sciences*. Hillsdale, NJ: Erlbaum.

Frese, M. (1984). *Do workers want control at work or don't they: Some results on denial and adjustment*. Berlin: Institut für Humanwissenschaft in Arbeit und Ausbildung der Technischen Universität Berlin (available from the author).

Frese, M. (1985). Stress at work and psychosomatic complaints: A causal interpretation. *Journal of Applied Psychology, 70*, 314-328.

Frese, M. (1986). Coping as a moderator and mediator between stress at work and psychosomatic complaints. In M. H. Appley & R. Trumbull (Eds.), *Dynamics of stress. Physiological, psychological, and social perspectives* (pp. 183-206). New York: Plenum.

Frese, M. (1987). Alleviating depression in the unemployed: Adequate financial support, hope, and early retirement. *Social Science and Medicine, 25*, 213-215.

Frese, M. (1989). Theoretical models of control and health. In S. L. Sauter, J. J. Hurrell, Jr., & C. L. Cooper (Eds.), *Job control and worker health* (pp. 107-128). Chichester: Wiley.

Frese, M., & Mohr, G. (1987). Prolonged unemployment and depression in older workers: A longitudinal study of intervening variables. *Social Science and Medicine, 25*, 173-178.

Frese, M., & Sabini, J. (1985). Action theory: An introduction. In M. Frese & J. Sabini (Eds.), *Goal directed behavior: The concept of action in psychology* (pp. 17-25). Hillsdale, NJ: Erlbaum.

Greenwald, A. G. (1980). The totalitarian ego: Fabrication and revision of personal history. *American Psychologist, 35*, 603-618.

Johnson, J. V., & Hall, E. M. (1988). Job strain, workplace, social support, and cardiovascular disease: A cross-sectional study of random sample of the Swedish working population. *American Journal of Public Health, 78*, 1336-1342.

Karasek, R. (1989). Control in the workplace and its health-related aspects. In S. L. Sauter, J. J. Hurrell, Jr., & C. L. Cooper (Eds.), *Job control and worker health* (pp. 129-159). Chichester: Wiley.

Karasek, R. A., Baker, D., Marxer, F., Ahlbom, A., & Theorell, T. (1981). Job decision latitude, job demands, and cardiovascular disease: A prospective study of Swedish men. *American Journal of Public Health, 71*, 694-705.

Lazarus, R. S. (1982). The costs and benefits of denial. In S. Breznitz (Ed.), *Denial of stress* (pp. 1-30). New York: International Universities Press.

Lazarus, R. S., & Folkman, S. (1984). *Stress, appraisal, and coping*. New York: Springer.

Miller, S. M. (1987). Monitoring and blunting: Validation of a questionnaire to assess styles of information seeking under threat. *Journal of Personality and Social Psychology, 52*, 345-353.

Miller, S. M., Brody, D. S., & Summerton, J. (1988). Styles of coping with threat: Implications for health.

Miller, S. M., Brody, D. S., & Summerton, J. (1988). Styles of coping with threat: Implications for health. *Journal of Personality and Social Psychology, 54*, 142-148.
Mohr, G. (1986). *Die Erfassung psychischer Befindensbeeinträchtigungen bei Industriearbeitern.* Frankfurt: Peter Lang.
Sauter, S. L., Hurrell, J. J., Jr., & Cooper, C. L. (Eds.). (1989). *Job control and worker health.* Chichester: Wiley.
Schönpflug, W. (1986). Behavior economics as an approach to stress theory. In M. H. Appley & R. Trumbull (Eds.), *Dynamics of stress. Physiological, psychological, and social perspectives* (pp. 81-98). New York: Plenum.
Semmer, N. (1984). *Streßbezogene Tätigkeitsanalyse: Psychologische Untersuchungen zur Analyse von Streß am Arbeitsplatz.* Weinheim: Beltz.
Semmer, N., & Frese, M. (1990). *Control as a moderator of the effect of stress at work on psychosomatic complaints: A longitudinal study with different measures.* Unpublished manuscript, University of Munich or University of Bern.
Taylor, S. E. (1989). *Positive illusions. Self-deception and the healthy mind.* New York: Basic Books.
Taylor, S. E., & Brown, J. D. (1988). Illusion and well-being: A social psychological perspective on mental health. *Psychological Bulletin, 103*, 193-210.
Zedeck, S. (1971). Problems with the use of "moderator" variables. *Psychological Bulletin, 76*, 295-310.

6 Stress and Coping in the Context of Caring[1]

David A. Chiriboga
Barbara W. K. Yee
University of Texas Medical Branch, Galveston

Philip G. Weiler
University of California, Davis

This chapter examines the multiple domains of stressors that may affect the lives of caregivers. We will draw extensively from a research project, conducted in the United States of America but with Canadian ties, that applied a basic stress paradigm to a study of caregivers with dependent elderly parents suffering from Alzheimer's Disease. The first section deals with stress as a general topic, and considers why it is applicable to the caregiving context. The following sections review the literature on caregiving as a personally and socially significant issue and then present findings from our own research. The central theme is that a more comprehensive understanding of caregiver stress can be obtained when those stressors specific to the context of caregiving, as well as those derived from other areas of the caregiver's life, are considered.

STRESS AS A MULTIFACETED CONDITION

Although the stress of caregiving is well documented (e.g., Brody, 1985; Ory et al., 1985; Pearlin, Turner, & Semple, 1989; Zarit, Orr, & Zarit, 1985), the range of stressors that potentially affect caregivers has received only minimal attention. This lack of attention may stem from the fact that the source of distress is often viewed as self-evident: Obviously, it would seem, caregiver distress arises from issues surrounding the dependency condition and the need to provide care.

[1]The investigations reported in this paper were supported in part by National Institute on Aging grants R01 AG05150 and AG00002, in part by National Institute of Mental Health grant No. MH33713, and in part by an award from the John Sealy Memorial Endowment Fund.

A contrasting perspective emphasizes the utility of recognizing the multiple stressors that affect the lives of individuals. At issue is whether caregivers are being influenced primarily by a single and specific stress context or by a potentially infinite range of stressors, some directly linked to the caregiver role, some indirectly linked, and some that might occur independently of the caregiver role. Middle-aged caregivers, especially women, may be facing loss of social status, loss of leisure time, economic loss resulting from caregiving expenses, loss of friends who are made uncomfortable by presence of the dementing parent, and the loss of the parent's selfhood and companionship (Brody, 1990). They may also be facing a host of other stressors related to their own particular life stage: the departure of children, death of friends due to heart attacks, loss of physical vigor and youthful attractiveness, and all the other "exit events" that begin to accrue in the second half of life and that serve as portends of increased risk (e.g., Brown & Harris, 1989; Chiriboga, 1989a; Paykel, 1982).

As implied in the preceding paragraph, it may also be helpful to consider caregiving from a life-course perspective. A number of researchers (e.g., Elder, 1982; Fiske & Chiriboga, 1990; Gergen, 1977) have argued that place along the life course influences how an individual will react to a particular kind of stress condition. Their findings also suggest the importance of the historical period in shaping the impact of a stress condition such as caregiving. For example, a distinguishing characteristic of Alzheimer's Disease in 1991 is the absence of any curative agent or efficacious means of symptomatic relief. The potential impact on caregivers of effective techniques of secondary or tertiary prevention for Alzheimer's Disease would be enormous, if only because it would provide a modicum of hope.

Stress: A Few Definitional Issues

In applying a stress perspective to issues [and ideas] concerning loss and the family caregiver, one source of possible confusion is that the term stress encompasses many different concepts, and is used in many different ways. For many people "stress" actually refers to the distress people experience after facing a critical and challenging experience. For others the term refers either to the critical and challenging experience, or, more frequently, to an underlying paradigm that includes three components: stressors, mediators, and responses.

Integral to the aforementioned stress paradigm is the notion that the relationship between stress exposure and response is not a mechanical and pre-ordained relationship but one orchestrated by a variety of mediators, such as social support, self-esteem, and coping strategies. The stressors are impinging agents, including life events as well as chronic situations and daily hassles. Responses are the consequences of stress exposure, and again can be broad in range. Most investigators consider either some physical health response such as hypertension or even the common cold, or psychological responses such as anxiety or depression. As argued in this chapter, variations in the amount of help provided by the caregivers can also be considered as variations in possible stress responses.

Stressors: What are they? Stressors come in many sizes and shapes. Some researchers draw a distinction between stressors that represent acute and time-limited situations and those that may persist for longer periods of time. Acute stressors have probably received more attention than the more durable or chronic stressors. The longstanding life-event genre of research (e.g., Holmes & Rahe, 1967) falls into this acute stress category. Life events have been found to predict all sorts of physical mental and social dysfunction—everything, in fact, from coronary heart disease (e.g., Lynch, 1977) to general psychiatric symptomatology (e.g., Chiriboga, 1984; Dohrenwend, 1986) to depression (e.g., Brown & Harris, 1989; Paykel, 1982; Pearlin, 1982).

While acute and major stressors have received the bulk of attention, some interesting and exciting research is found at the level of minor or day-to-day situations. Lazarus and Folkman (1984), for example, have examined the impact of day-to-day hassles on the physical and emotional well-being of middle-aged men and women. They conclude that hassles exert a stronger influence on our mental health and well-being than does exposure to the more well-known life events. Similarly, Pearlin (1985) reports a greater significance of what he calls "durable" events over those that reflect acute or time-limited conditions.

At the current stage in the evolution of stress research, it would seem that conceptualization has gained the edge on stress measurement. During the 1960s and 1970s, there was an accepted and seemingly well-validated "tool" with which to assess stressors. This consensus has given way to what often seems a bewildering array of possible instruments, many of them with unclear psychometric properties and unproven applicability (Chiriboga, 1989b). This, at least, was what seemed to be the situation four years ago when a team of researchers including the authors and Dr. Melvin Lerner set out to study stress experiences of people who provided care to parents afflicted with Alzheimer's Disease.

Caregiving to Patients with Alzheimer's Disease: A Potential Stressor

Alzheimer's Disease (AD) is a crippling disease that affects over 5% of the elderly, with most recent estimates indicating the proportion may rise to roughly 48% of the oldest old (Evans et al., 1989). The slow and insidious course of AD imposes a tremendous and continuing strain on loved ones. The economic and emotional costs to families are uncountable, and the costs to society run into billions of dollars annually (e.g., Huang, Cartwright, & Hu, 1988). To add to this already grim picture, current projections suggest at least an 11% increase in prevalence by the year 2000 (Mortimer, 1988; see also Evans et al., 1989), with the costs in nursing care alone expected to equal approximately 50 billion dollars in 2000 and up to $149 billion (Schneider & Guralnik, 1990).

Despite increasing government involvement, it is generally recognized that families continue to provide the bulk of support for AD patients and their families (Brody, 1990; see also Light & Lebowitz, 1989). The spouse is generally the major provider when available and capable, but adult children are a major source of support and often are the preferred provider (Wan, 1982). Typically, these children are responsive to parental needs (Brody, 1985, 1990). One review concludes that "family members provide an extraordinary amount of assistance to their older family members" (Springer & Brubaker, 1984, p.16). This is especially true in the case of AD.

Attention to parental need can exert a heavy burden: An increasing number of middle-aged and older people, especially women, are caught between competing obligations to their parents, to their children and spouses, and to their own plans for the remaining years (Brody, 1990). The stress engendered by these competing demands may lead to physical and mental dysfunction, no matter how much care is actually provided to the parents (e.g., Kiecolt-Glaser & Glaser, 1989; Ory et al., 1985; Zarit et al., 1985). Responsibilities to the older generation can also impair performance at work (Moeller & Shuell, 1988) and keep family members, again primarily women, out of the labor force (Nissel, 1984).

Due to the central role spouse and children play in the care and well-being of older family members, there has been growing concern in the ability of the family to provide care, and in the identification of those factors that debilitate caregivers, increase the risk of institutionalization for the dependent member, or generally reduce the quality of life (Colerick & George, 1986; Kane & Kane, 1987; Ory et al., 1985; Zarit et al., 1985). One critical factor is assumed to be stress exposure (e.g., Chiriboga, Weiler, & Nielsen, 1989; Pearlin et al., 1989), as will be outlined in the next section.

CAREGIVER STRESS: AN EMPIRICAL STUDY

Caregiving in the context of Alzheimer's Disease is an area of research that can readily be studied from the perspective of stress theory and its associated methodologies. In the remainder of this chapter the focus will shift to an empirical consideration of how stress exposure affects the lives of one understudied group of caregivers: adult children who provide care to a parent afflicted with AD. The research represents an effort to address some of the criticisms leveled against caregiver research by including repeated measurements, male as well as female caregivers, objective assessments by health professionals of the care recipient, and multiple approaches to measuring stressors, mediators, and responses.

The Design

We chose to employ a two-wave panel design for the study, with the two waves separated by approximately ten months. This time interval is clearly not sufficient to plot trends in either the trajectory of Alzheimer's Disease, or of social stress and adaptation among caregivers. Rather, it was selected primarily to allow us to examine the psychometric properties of some of the more innovative instruments and questions designed specifically for the study, and to set the stage for any more extended follow-ups that might become possible.

The Sample

One problem we had to resolve for the pending investigation concerned identification of the study population. Since caregivers to AD patients represent an extremely heterogeneous group, we opted for a sampling strategy that drew on a variety of sources. The 385 adult children we finally interviewed all had parents with a diagnosis of probable Alzheimer's Disease. These parents ($N = 201$) were the target source, and were drawn from four basic populations; they were (a) geriatric clients who had sought services in two hospitals, two clinics, three community health centers, and six home health care agencies; (b) residents of board and care facilities; (c) residents of skilled and intermediate care facilities; or (d) clients whose child belonged to either of two ADRDA (Alzheimer's Disease and Related Disorders) groups serving the catchment area.

The Caregivers. The sample of adult children were all residents of the Central Valley area of Northern California; they ranged in age from 27 to 67, with 50 representing the average age. Reflecting the fact that caregiving is most often performed by women, 30% were men and 70% were women. This was not an elite sample: over 50% had not completed their college education. However, reflecting the affluence of the agricultural area from which the sample was drawn, only 21% had family incomes of less than $20,000, and 27% reported incomes of $45,000 and over; 9% felt they did not have enough money to make ends meet, and one third had just enough to get by.

The overwhelming majority, approximately 90%, represented whites of European descent. The remainder included African Americans (4%), Hispanic Americans (3%), and Asian Americans (1%). Seventeen percent had no children, while 29% had already launched their children. The mean age of their children was 25. Most of the subjects were either Catholic (20%) or Protestant (53%), but two thirds either never attended services or did so only on religious holidays.

Whenever possible, we interviewed two adult children in the family. Our sample includes 142 sibling pairs, which means that approximately 75% of the adult child respondents were included in pairs. By and large, these caregivers were not isolated from other family members; most, for example, saw siblings more than once a month. About 60% felt they were the primary caregiver, with 33% saying it was a sibling. Perhaps because the majority lived less than one hour's drive away from their parent, contact was frequent: 33% saw their afflicted parent daily, and another 38% saw their parent on a weekly basis.

In addition to family contact, 21% of the adult children belonged to some kind of self-help group for families with a member afflicted with AD, and 86% reported that they had turned to someone for help and advice about the problems associated with their parent. The resource most commonly accessed was a medical doctor:

over 64% sought advice from a doctor. The second most frequently accessed resource was a sibling (35%), while friends came in third (29%). Despite the use of social resources, 39% currently felt themselves to be "very much" to "extremely" troubled by the situation they found themselves in. At the other extreme, 24% were either "only a little" or "not at all" troubled.

The Parents. Nearly all of the 201 parents had already received a diagnosis of probable AD prior to participating in the study, but this diagnosis was confirmed by a physician on the basis of medical histories, assessments by a geriatric nurse practitioner or third year medical student, and structured instruments and tests. The median length of time since patients had initially been diagnosed was 24 months, with a range of 0 to 156 months. The majority, 85%, had been born within the United States of America, about 21% were currently married, and 76% were women; 36% of the parents lived alone, 11% lived with an interviewed caregiver, and another 13% lived either in board and care facilities or skilled nursing facilities. They ranged in age from 50 to 95, with 41% being in their 80s.

The Data Pool on Caregivers

The assessment of caregivers was based on a battery of structured as well as unstructured questions. Much of the battery represented accepted and more or less standardized instruments, but approximately half represented new measurement approaches that were developed in cooperation with Dr. Melvin Lerner, who led a Canadian-based research effort focused on how adult children conceptualize issues related to caring for a dependent parent. The battery was administered during interviews that averaged about three hours in length, and in a questionnaire that was also given to the adult children. Here only a brief description will be provided of the measures addressed in the present chapter. Besides basic demographic information and data on social resources (see above), stressors and stress responses as well as parent characteristics (as viewed by the caregiver) have been assessed.

Stressors

Given that a major goal of the investigation was to assess not only stressors that were directly related to caregiving, but also stressors of everyday life, a variety of stress indices was included. These tapped life events, hassles, and perceived burden of care; additional structured questions were also included to expand on content. Selection of all instruments was based on the need for relatively brief measurement tools, as well as on their psychometric properties and established validity. It should be noted that a rather extensive selection of stress inventories for older populations exists (Chiriboga, 1989b), but that none has as yet achieved the status of being the standard of choice.

Life-Event Inventory. This 37-item inventory is based on a larger inventory (Chiriboga, 1977; Fiske & Chiriboga, 1990) applicable to persons at all stages of adult life. The shorter version is more focused on the kinds of life events faced by persons in middle and later life, and on negative events rather than positive events. Although the instrument includes data on perceptions of events, the measures referred to in this paper consider the frequency of events in various life domains (work, marital, family, nonfamily, social life, financial, and miscellaneous) experienced during the past year. For the purpose of this presentation, a simple summary of all reported life events was used.

Hassles Inventory. A 13-item Hassles Inventory (Chiriboga & Cutler, 1980; see also Chiriboga, 1984) was administered that assesses hassles in the areas of work, marital, family, nonfamily, financial, and caregiving (two items). Frequency ratings were made on a 5-point scale for items such as "Hassled by my helping responsibilities." Subscales based on factor analyses and item content have been developed in each of the six areas, although in this presentation summary measures were included for General Hassles (alpha = .72) and Caregiver Hassles (alpha = .74).

Structured Questions. For the present analyses, two structured questions were included: "How stressful has taking care of your parent been for you?" and "How stressful do you think it will be in the future to take care of your parent?," with responses on 4-point scales ranging from "not stressful" to "very stressful."

Stress Response

While the response component of the stress paradigm is inherently multidimensional, it is often assessed by means of a single measure such as depression (Elliott & Eisdorfer, 1982). Since the association of stressors with caregiver functioning was a major concern, such functioning was considered in several different ways. One indicator, caregiver burden, is probably the most common outcome measure in caregiver research. Another, depression, is not only the most commonly employed indicator of stress response (Elliott & Eisdorfer, 1982) but one with demonstrated sensitivity to stress conditions involving the loss of a relationship (e.g., Brown & Harris, 1989). Also included were measures of the amount of help provided to the parents.

The Caregiver Burden Scale, a 22-item instrument assessing both emotional and behavioral-relational strain imposed upon caregivers (Zarit et al., 1985), was administered. Its items are similar to those in other instruments (e.g., Montgomery, Gonyea, & Hooyman, 1985), but have better content validity. Internal reliability for the total score has been reported at .79 (Zarit et al., 1985); our own calculations yielded an alpha of .90. Higher scores for the summary score indicate greater burden.

Depression was measured by the 13-item Depression subscale, drawn from the Hopkins Symptoms Checklist-90 (Derogatis & Cleary, 1977). The measure of depression represented a summation of scores for all 13 items (alpha = .89); higher scores indicate greater depression.

The Provision of Care. Caregiving behavior may be considered in part a response to the objective circumstances and in part a response to the stress context surrounding caregiving. Our measure of caregiving behavior represents a modification of an instrument, included in the OARS Multidimensional Functional Assessment Questionnaire (Duke University Center, 1978) that is designed to assess the ability to perform what are called "activities of daily life" (ADLs). Rather than assessing the ability of the parent, the instrument was modified to ask how often caregivers assisted their parent with each of 14 ADLs (e.g., how often did they make phone calls for the parent, take them to the doctor, help in the preparation of meals). Frequency rating for each activity had been made on an 8-point rating scale ranging from "never" to "more than once a day." The Care Provision Scale was designed to provide a more objective indicator of caregiver burden than the Zarit Burden Scale described above. In a factor analysis with oblique factor rotation, two factors were obtained that together accounted for 67% of the original variance: I. Basic Caring (alpha = .95) with 10 items referring to help for the parent with basic activities such as dressing, toileting, and grooming; II. Instrumental Caring (alpha = .65) with 4 items dealing with more complex activities, e.g., taking the parent someplace for social reasons, taking the parent someplace for medical or therapeutic reasons, assisting in financial matters, and making phone calls for the parent.

It should be emphasized that caregiver burden and amount of care provision can be considered not only as stress responses but as potential stressors or stress modifiers, as well. The amount of care provided, for example, may affect a caregivers' perception of burden, while the latter may increase the risk of depression. In the analytic models to be discussed below, burden and care provision are first considered as responses, but are then entered into the analyses as potential predictors of other responses.

Parent Characteristics

Finally, measures, based on interviews with the adult child, included descriptors of parent with AD: how long it had been since the first symptoms were noticed by the caregiver, frequency of contact with parent, parent's present residence etc. We also asked caregivers to rate their parent on 12 bipolar adjectives, both for the period prior to the onset of AD and for the present. The adjectives included: rich—poor, strong—weak, grateful—ungrateful, upset—calm, happy—sad, kind—cruel, fair—unfair, cooperative—uncooperative, responsible—irresponsible, generous—frugal. This instrument was based on a semantic differential approach to scaling (Chiriboga, Catron, & Associates, in press; Osgood, Suci, & Tannenbaum, 1957);

correlations over the 10-month test-retest interval averaged .62 for the premorbid ratings and .50 for the ratings of the parent at the time of the interviews.

The Data Pool on Parents

In addition to interviews with the adult children, their AD-afflicted parents were assessed by a geriatric nurse practitioner. The latter prepared a medical history based on existing records and interviews with family and health providers, and performed a number of tests and ratings such as the Dementia Rating of Reisberg, Ferris, de Leon, and Crook (1982), the Depression Rating Scale (Sheikh & Yesavage, 1986), and the Hachinski (1983) Ischematic Rating. Relevant to this chapter are two additional instruments that were administered, measuring functional independence and cognitive status.

Functional Independence was measured by the Blessed-Roth IADL (Blessed, Tomlinson, & Roth, 1968), an 11-item inventory that taps both activities of daily life (ADLs) and instrumental activities of daily life (IADLs). A principal components factor analysis with orthogonal rotation yielded a five-item ADL scale (ability to eat, dress, exercise bladder control, find their way inside their own dwelling, and recognize familiar people and surroundings; alpha = .95) and a five-item IADL scale (ability to recall recent events, remember short lists, manage money, find their way on familiar streets, and perform household tasks; alpha = .65).

Cognitive Status, considered a key mediating variable, was measured by two separate but overlapping instruments based on the geriatric nurse practitioner's assessment: the Mini-Mental State examination (MMS; Folstein, Folstein, & McHugh, 1975) and the Blessed Orientation Test (Blessed et al., 1968). Scores on the two instruments are highly intercorrelated (Black, 1990); only the MMS summary score (alpha = .93) will be used here.

Patient Functioning and the Prediction of Caregiving

Of concern to many health professionals are the conditions associated with levels of caregiving. The literature provides little in the way of definitive information on care provision, although a number of studies suggests that caregiving behavior may not be directly and closely associated with type and level of functional impairment. In the following series of analyses, we look first at measures associated with the actual functional impairments of the patient, and then consider the caregiver's response to these impairments.

Predicting Patients' Activities of Daily Life

The related concepts of "(instrumental) activities of daily life" (ADLs and IADLs) are basic to the study of caregiving, since they serve as indices of functional adequacy in both simple and more complex tasks of living. To examine functional adequacy, a simple hierarchical model was developed as a predictive tool. The model considers several basic characteristics of the parent (age, gender, how long they have displayed symptoms), cognitive status (as measured by the MMS), and caregiver characteristics (marital status, financial status, gender, age, whether the respondent is the primary caregiver) as predictive sets. As is true of all hierarchical models, there is an underlying assumption that sets can be ordered along a continuum: characteristics of the patient are assumed to precede the present situation and therefore were entered into the predictive equation first; the patient's current cognitive status is seen as more relevant and antecedent than any particular characteristic of the caregiver and therefore was entered after the basic character-

TABLE 6.1
Results from Hierarchical Regression Analyses Predicting Parent's Ability to Perform Activities of Daily Life (ADLs) and Instrumental Activities of Daily Life (IADLs)

Predictors		*ADLs*			*IADLs*	
	R^2	R^2*-Change*	*Beta*	R^2	R^2*-Change*	*Beta*
Parent Variables	.04	.04**		.04	.04**	
Age			.13*			.12*
Gender						
Duration of Illness			.17**			.18***
Parent's Mental State	.45	.40***	.64***	.18	.14***	.37***
Carer Variables	.46	.02		.19	.02	
Married			.10*			
Adequate Finances						
Income						
Gender						
Age						
Primary Provider						

Note. Variables with Beta weights below .10 are eliminated.
*p <.10; **p <.05; **p <.01

istics; finally, characteristics of the caregiver are assumed to play a minor but potentially relevant role in the patient's ability to function and therefore were entered last.

As we consider the results, it is important to bear in mind that functional adequacy, the characteristic being predicted, was assessed by a geriatric nurse practitioner and therefore represents a fairly objective measure of the parents' capabilities. For both ADL and IADL scores, longer durations of the illness (as noticed by caregiver, at least) were associated with greater levels of functional impairment, and there was a tendency for greater age to be associated with more evidence of impairment (Table 6.1). Severity of cognitive deficits, as measured by the MMS, was also significantly associated with greater impairment, especially in the ADL scores. None of the characteristics of the caregiver did contribute significantly to the patient's ability to perform the various activities of daily life.

While these results are hardly surprising, they do underscore the risk factors associated with the functional dependencies of dementing persons. These risk factors arise from the circumstances of the patient and seem to have little if anything to do with characteristics of the caregiver. Cognitive status was strongly associated with both types of functioning. However, functional dependency was also associated at significant levels with duration of the illness condition. Finally, there was a suggestion that older patients were more impaired in their ADLs and IADLs. This last finding would be expectable for any sample of older adults, regardless of whether they were demented or not.

Predicting the Provision of Help

When attention turned to the prediction of care provided by the caregiver with regard to both types of daily activities (ADLs and IADLs), the hierarchical model was expanded into a rudimentary caregiver-stress model. There was a reordering of the initial three predictive sets that have already been described; since the focus was now on the caregiver, characteristics of the caregiver were now the first entered into the analyses. ADL and IADL assessments of parental functioning were added to the MMS score found in the third set, while a fourth set consisted of stress experiences of the caregiver, with these experiences including both stressors specific to caregiving (summary score for the two caregiver hassles, ratings on present and anticipated stresses related to the parent), and stressors of everyday life (summary scores for general hassles and life events).

The results were not as straightforward as the results described before: Looking first at how much time the caregivers spent providing help with ADLs, we find (with entry of the caregiver characteristic set) that more help with ADLs was provided by primary caregivers and by those who earn less money (Table 6.2). Demographic characteristics of the parent were not associated with care provision, but the set dealing with adequacy of parental functioning did make a difference, ADL functioning being the key variable: Parents with greater ADL dependencies received more help with ADLs. Finally, the set dealing with caregiver's stress experiences did not contribute significantly, although there was a tendency for caregivers who reported fewer overall hassles to provide their parent with more ADL help.

With regard to help with instrumental activities of daily life, the results were somewhat similar. Once again we find that being the primary caregiver is linked to greater provision of care, and that demographic characteristics of the parent did not

TABLE 6.2
Results from Hierarchical Regression Analyses Predicting Caregiver's Help with Activities of Daily Life (ADLs) and Instrumental Activities of Daily Life (IADLs)

Predictors		*ADLs Help*			*IADLs Help*	
	R^2	R^2-*Change*	*Beta*	R^2	R^2-*Change*	*Beta*
Carer Variables	.10	.10***		.07	.07**	
Married						
Adequate Finances						
Income			-.18**			
Gender						
Age						
Primary caregiver			.20***			.27***
Parent Variables	.12	.02			.10	.03
Age						
Gender						
Duration of Illness						
Parent's Mental State	.14	.02	-.19**	.16	.06***	.22**
Carer Stress	.16	.02		.22	.06***	
General Hassles			-.14*			-.16*
Life events						.12*
Caregiver hassles						.20**
Rated stress						

Note. Variables with Beta weights below .10 are eliminated.
*p <.10; **p <.05; **p <.01

make a difference in the amount of care. However, the functional adequacy of the parent does play a role: Caregivers were more likely to provide IADL support to parents who manifested less cognitive impairment. This finding makes a great deal of sense: It would be expected that parents who were more intact mentally would still be making an effort to perform IADLs, and therefore would need more help in performing them.

The final set, dealing with caregiver's stress, made a significant contribution. As was found in the prediction of help with ADLs, people with fewer general hassles were more likely to provide help with IADLs. In addition, those who experienced more hassles in their role as caregivers also provided more care; here the direction of causality may very well be that those who provided more help felt more hassled by caregiving, rather than the reverse. There was also a suggestion that caregivers who experienced more life events provided more help—a relationship that makes little intuitive sense.

Predicting Stress Responses

In another series of analyses, we have considered the question of how well caregiver functioning, in general, is predicted by the measures included in our caregiver-stress model. Here the focus was on factors contributing to the prediction of a potential stress response, caregiver burden, that is specific to the context of caregiving, as well as on factors contributing to the prediction of the more general condition of depression. Rationale for the comparative analyses is that while depression is one of the most commonly-used outcome criteria in the broad field of stress, researchers interested in caregiver stress most frequently employ a measure of burden as the preferred outcome variable. In the following analyses we will consider whether the same, or different, factors predict both measures.

The analytic model for the two regressions was very similar to that used in predicting patient functioning as well as caregiver provision of help. The order of variable-set entry was as follows: (1) basic characteristics of the caregiver; (2) basic characteristics of the parent with AD; (3) functional status of the parent, including cognitive status; (4) events and hassles reported by the caregiver; (5) caregiver's provision of help with ADLs and IADLs; and (6) burden (used when predicting depression).

In the analysis *predicting caregiver burden*, entry of the basic demographic set yielded that being the primary caregiver was strongly associated with greater burden (Table 6.3)—a certainly neither new, nor surprising finding. With the entry of the next set, that dealing with parent characteristics, the importance of the context within which caregiving takes place continues to expand. The longer the parent had been recognized to have the disease, the less the burden; this finding suggests that either caregivers accommodate to the obligations or that the burden of care lessens as the patient reaches the later stages of the disease, or both.

Perhaps of greater interest is that providing care to a mother tended to be associated with greater burden. This finding expands on another surprising finding

TABLE 6.3

Results from Hierarchical Regression Analyses Predicting Caregiver Burden and Depression

Predictors	Burden			Depression		
	R^2	R^2-Change	Beta	R^2	R^2-Change	Beta
Carer Variables	.07	.07**		.07	.07**	
Married						
Adequate Finances						-.14*
Income (dollars)						
Gender						.14**
Age						
Primary Caregiver			.23***			
Parent Variables	.11	.04**		.09	.02	
Age						
Gender			.12*			
Duration of Illness			-.16**			.14*
Parent's Mental State	.17	.06***	-.21**	.10	.01	
Carer Stress	.36	.19***		.33	.23***	
General Hassles						.30***
Life events						
Carer hassles		.23***				
Rated stress		.23***			.20***	
Future stress		.17**				
Help Provision	.47	.11***		.34	.00	
With ADLs			.22***			
With IADLs			.19***			
Carer Burden				.35	.02**	
Total burden						.17**

Note. Variables with Beta weights below .10 are eliminated.
*p <.10; **p <.05; **p <.01

from the study: When matching gender of child and parent, daughters providing care to a mother reported the greatest burden, while daughters providing care to a father reported the least (Nielsen, 1990). Both findings seemed to be explained by the fact that fathers are more likely to have a living spouse. Even though the amount of caregiving was not diminished when another parent was available, case studies suggested that having a nondement parent lessened the perceived burden (Nielsen, 1990). In other words, the adult child caregiver may be less likely to feel that he or she bears the ultimate responsibility as long as the other parent survives.

Functional capacities of the patient made an overall contribution to burden. Again, the results seem counter-intuitive at first glance: Parents with fewer ADL dependencies created more of a burden for their caregivers. What we have found in several years of operating both a geriatric service and an Alzheimer's Disease Diagnostic and Treatment Center, however, is that demented patients in the earlier stages of the disease impose the greatest demands on caregivers, e.g., by being generally highly mobile and thus more likely to get into trouble.

With entry of the measures of life events and hassles, the fourth set, the greatest contribution to the predictive equation was found. Stressors that were most strongly associated with burden were those that were specific to the caregiving context: hassles arising from the caregiver role, and ratings on amount of present and anticipated stress. In each case, greater exposure to stressors was associated with greater burden. Similarly, with the two last sets of predictors we find that the greater the amount of help provided with ADLs and IADLs, the more likely the caregiver was to report feeling burdened.

Overall, then, we have found that the caregiver-stress model accounts for substantial portions of the variance in the reported burden of caring. Of particular interest is the important role of factors specific to the caregiving context, such as being the primary caregiver, functional levels of the patient, amount of stressors, and care provision.

We now turn to the *prediction of depression*, a phenomenon that certainly is not unique to caregiving, but which also may be exacerbated by it. As was the case for all preceding analyses, the regression of depression on variables of the caregiver-stress model produced a highly significant predictive equation with, in this case, a respectable 59% of the variance in caregiver depression being accounted for.

We began by examining the contribution of caregivers' basic demographic characteristics. This set of variables was significantly associated with depression (Table 3). The variables making a significant contribution included income and gender: those in poorer financial circumstances and women as caregivers were more likely to report depressive symptoms. Such findings are hardly surprising, and are in accord with the literature both on depression and psychological symptomatology in general (e.g., Chiriboga, 1984; Derogatis & Cleary, 1977; Pearlin, 1982), and for caregivers (e.g., Pruchno & Resch, 1989).

Characteristics of the parent were not associated with depression, although there was a tendency for greater depression if the parent had been sick for longer periods of time. On the other hand, the set of measures dealing with stressors again made the greatest contribution to explained variance: a highly significant 23%. In contrast to the prediction of burden, the strongest association was for the measure of general hassles: The more hassled the caregivers were in areas other than caregiving, the more likely they were to be depressed. There was, however, a significant association with caregivers' ratings of stress induced by the caregiving role: those with more stress were more depressed. And finally, when levels of reported caregiver burden were entered into the predictive model, the result was a significant, although minor, contribution. As would be anticipated, caregivers who reported greater burden were also more likely to be depressed.

The findings just presented underline the importance of overall levels of stress. One striking finding in the prediction of depression is the contribution of a stress measure, day-to-day hassles, that draws on experiences outside of the caregiver role. This finding emphasizes the fact that caregivers have other roles to play, other lives to lead; stressors involved in caregiving represent only one area of importance in their lives. When researchers step in, and prepare their armamentarium of measurement tools, they often are so focused on the topic of their own interest that a wide range of highly relevant variables may be excluded. The implication of our findings is that such researchers need both comprehensive or global inventories of stress conditions and inventories that are specific to the condition under study.

Expanding the Basic Stress Model

Up to this point the analyses have focused on conditions affecting the well-being of both patient and caregiver, using components of a basic model of caregiver stress. The last topic to be addressed deals with an area rarely considered in caregiver research: whether personal characteristics of the patient prior to becoming ill can influence how the patient is subsequently treated. The study of historical information is problematic since the investigator must commonly rely on memories of the past. Although such information is highly susceptible to bias in recall, our past research (e.g., Chiriboga et al., in press; Fiske & Chiriboga, 1990) has indicated that structured approaches can yield retrospective data that are reliable and seemingly valid. Here we examine information obtained from one such structured instrument: the semantic differential.

As mentioned above, the focus of attention was on ratings by caregivers of their parent for a period prior to the onset of the signs and symptoms of Alzheimer's Disease. Test-retest reliability for the 12 bipolar adjectives in the semantic differential ranged from the low .50s to the mid .70s over a 10-month period. In contrast, ratings of the parent's present characteristics, at Waves I and II, correlated at substantially lower levels, from the low .30s to high .50s. While both sets of correlations fall within the range of those generally reported for personality tests (e.g., Fiske & Chiriboga, 1990), the greater stability of the retrospective data is especially supportive of the argument that caregivers were rating the same characteristics at two points in time. The lower stability of ratings referring to parent's present characteristics may reflect the progressive mental deterioration that is the hallmark of their disease.

One issue that can be addressed with this data set concerns whether perceptions of the parent's pre-onset personality characteristics are associated with caregiver behavior and status in the present. The analyses followed an empirical model based on earlier studies of stress-inducing experiences (e.g., Chiriboga et al., in press). In each regression seven sets of variables were entered sequentially. The first set described characteristics of the caregiver and included age, gender, marital status, and income. The second set described characteristics of the parent and included age, gender, and residential status prior to the onset of dementia. The third set described parental personality rated on the 12-item semantic differential by the caregiver. The fourth set consisted of a single item that represented time elapsed since the symptoms of dementia first became evident. The fifth set described level of cognitive impairment of the parent, as assessed by total score from the MMS. The sixth set consisted of a single variable that noted whether the respondent was the primary caregiver or not. Finally, the seventh set assessed the extent to which life—according to the caregiver's view—had become better or worse since onset of the parent's dementia.

Results of all regression analyses indicated that the basic model was effective in predicting the dependent variables, namely caregiver depression, amount of care provided, ratings of present stress, and ratings of anticipated stress. However, at the same time it was clear that many of single predictors contributed little to the final equation and in fact increased error variance. For this reason a second series of analyses was performed in which only predictors that reached at least trend ($p = .10$) levels of significance were included. It is this second set of regressions that will be described next. Please bear in mind that this second set of equations predicted significant levels of variance for all four dependent variables considered.

Predicting Caregiver Depression. The nine variables included in the predictive equation together accounted for an adjusted 12% of the variance in caregiver depression (Table 6.4). Looking just at those that made a contribution at the trend level or better, we find that female caregivers, those of lower income, those with parents who had not lived with caregiver prior to onset of the illness, those whose parents prior to onset could be characterized as happy and/or uncooperative, and caregivers whose life had worsened since onset of the parent's illness all were more depressed.

Predicting Amount of Care Provided. The seven variables included in the regression analysis together accounted for an adjusted 12% of the variance in the amount of care provided. We found that caregivers who provided higher levels of care had lower incomes, were the primary caregiver and/or felt life had become worse since the parental illness, had parents who had not lived with either a sibling

TABLE 6.4

Results from Hierarchical Regression Analyses Predicting Various Aspects of Caregiver Well-being

Predictors	*Depression*			*Care provided*			*Anticipated Stress*			*Present Stress*		
	R^2	R^2*-Change*	*Beta*	R^2	R^2*-Change*	*Beta*	R^2	R^2*-Change*	*Beta*	R^2	R^2*-Change*	*Beta*
Carer Variables	.08	.08***		.02	.02**					.10	.10***	
Gender			.16**									.19***
Income			-.22***			-.16**						-.26***
Parent Variables	.10	.02**		.04	.02*		.12*	.01	.02*			
Age			.10									
Lives w/subject			-.12*						-.12*			
Lives w/family						-.13*						
Parent rated as ...	.14	.04*		.07	.03		.07	.06**		.11	.01*	
Happy			.11*									.12*
Fair			.04			-.05						
Cooperative			-.20**			.16*						
Irresponsible						.10*			.17**			
Poor									.16**			
Strong									.08*			
Generous			.11									
Perceived Change												
Parent's Mental State							.09	.02*	.13*			
Primary Caregiver				.13***	.06***	-.25***						
Quality of Life	.16***	.02*	-.13*	.16***	.03**	-.17***				.14***	.03**	-.18**

Note. Variables with Beta weights below .10 are eliminated. *p <.10; **p <.05; **p <.01

or relative prior to the illness and who had been characterized as cooperative and/ or irresponsible.

Predicting Present Stress. The four variables included in the predictive equation together accounted for an adjusted 13% of the variance in caregiver stress. Daughters as caregivers as opposed to sons, those with lower incomes, those with parents who prior to illness onset could be characterized as unhappy, and those who felt life had become worse since onset of parental problems, all felt that dealing with their parent had been more stressful.

Predicting Anticipated Stress. With the five variables included in the predictive equation, a total of 6% adjusted variance was accounted for. If the parent had not lived with caregiver prior to onset of symptoms, if the parent prior to illness had been characterized as irresponsible, poor, and weak, and if the parent showed at present relatively less cognitive impairment, then the future stress was expected to be higher than present stress.

SOME FINAL COMMENTS

This chapter began with a presentation of a theoretical rationale for studying the stressors of caregiving from a broadened perspective, and then proceeded to examine empirical support for this perspective. The data represent a sampling of findings from an ongoing study that includes a physician, psychologists, anthropologists, and specialists in health education and promotion. These researchers, moreover, are based in two states of the United States as well as in Canada, and we are in the process of replicating and cross-replicating each other's research.

The Prediction of Functional Dependency and Care Provision

The first analyses that was presented had to do with the nuts and bolts, as it were of caregiving: predicting functional dependencies in the patient and predicting the amount of care provided. There are two basic findings that stem from our ongoing studies of functional dependencies. The first is that inability to perform all sorts of daily activities is predicted very strongly by factors that seem quite reasonable and logical: the parent's higher age, higher duration of illness, and higher levels of impairment in cognitive functioning.

The second finding is that the amount of care provided in daily activities (ADLs, IADLs) is not linked very strongly with expectable and plausible factors such as cognitive status and functional dependency. Instead, a variety of stressors, representing both life events and hassles, made strong contributions to the prediction of caregiving behavior.

The Prediction of Caregiver Well-Being

When attention turned to the prediction of stress response, the goal was to identify factors that make a difference in how well the caregivers dealt with the stressors to which they were exposed. Analyses with two criteria of stress response strongly suggested that stressors play an important role in the well-being of caregivers, and that these stressors are not restricted to those that pertain directly to the caregiving role. The results demonstrated that general kinds of stressors, especially those of the hassles type, were most strongly associated with indices of well-being. The findings also suggest that chronic problems arising from the caregiver role may provide the context for stress overload. In other words, under conditions of chronic strain in one area of life, the individual may begin to fall apart in other areas, which in turn may exacerbate the basic problem.

To expand on this last point, there seem to be at least two ways in which stress build-up may lead to crisis (Chiriboga, 1989a). In one we experience a sudden piling up of stressor events that leads to a feeling of overload or crisis. Another, perhaps more insidious way may involve the individual experiencing stressors that begin to cross over from a particular role, such as caregiving, to work, family, hobbies, etc. At a certain point the individual may be experiencing just about as much stress as he or she can tolerate, in all sectors. At that point, any additional stressor may lead to a condition we might refer to as the "Camel's Back Syndrome." Little stressors have built up, and their cumulative load may not even be recognized at the conscious level. The last stressor, perhaps one that seems actually to be relatively minor, such as the care recipient refusing to eat, then acts to trigger all the pent-up emotion. It is in fact the proverbial "straw that broke the camel's back."

The stressors of caregiving, of course, do not necessarily lead to crisis conditions. In our research we have encountered individuals heavily stressed in the caregiver part of life but with normal loads in all others. Such people seem to be doing extremely well from a phenomenological point of view. Whether by accident, fate, or skill, they have managed to "contain" the crisis of caregiving. We also encounter on occasion individuals who react to the conditions imposed by a dependent parent with a sense of challenge, and who in fact seem to thrive in the situation.

Whether the reaction is one of crisis or challenge, the literature and our own results suggest the importance of a careful and comprehensive assessment of the stress context faced by caregivers. Given the relevance of both general and caregiver-specific stressors in predicting burden and depression, one conclusion that may be drawn is that health professionals concerned with adult child caregivers might wish to consider the use of a multiple instrument approach to assessment of the stress in their subjects and clients. While to date most instruments designed to assess the stress loads of caregivers have focused almost exclusively on caregiving itself, a number of well-constructed and psychometrically sound measures of hassles and other minor events (e.g., Chiriboga & Cutler, 1980; Lazarus &

Folkman, 1984; Zautra, Guarnaccia, Reich, & Dohrenwend, 1988;), life events (e.g., Lewinsohn, Mermelstein, Alexander, & MacPhillamy, 1985; Murrell, Norris, & Grote, 1988), and chronic strains (e.g., Pearlin, 1982) are readily available (see also Chiriboga, 1989b).

Knowing only the individual's level of stress exposure, however, will not by itself reveal the whole story of how well the caregiver is faring. For example, consistent with the general literature on their role as a stress mediator (e.g., Pearlin, 1982), measures of social support were directly associated with well-being on all three indicators of stress response: The more support available, the better off the caregiver was.

The findings also suggested the importance of time and context. For example, in predicting caregiver's burden, length of time the parent had shown obvious signs and symptoms of Alzheimer's Disease was a significant variable. That longer durations of illness were related to lower levels of depression, might appear almost contra-intuitive. That is, it might seem more plausible that the longer the illness had been manifested, the greater would be the cumulative burden imposed on the caregiver. And in fact, a frequent comment by adult children who attend a geriatric clinic directed by one of my colleagues, for example, concerns how terrible it is to see valued and loved parents gradually lose their individuality and vitality.

Of the many possible reasons for the illness-burden association that we did find, one that was brought up by subjects themselves, in their anecdotal comments and in response to questions about the stresses of caregiving, is that in the later stages of the disease the parent makes fewer demands on the caregiver, either because the patient was already institutionalized or because the patient was essentially bedfast and therefore relatively more easy to manage. This interpretation parallels a conclusion of Haley and Pardo (1987), who report evidence that the stresses imposed upon caregivers may peak during the intermediate phases of Alzheimer's Disease, when the patient is still active and possibly more agitated or belligerent.

The role of illness duration highlights once again the fact that caregiving is not a single event or condition but a long and complex process in which many problems, both temporary and lasting, may arise. At any given moment, not that many will be incapacitated or in crisis. Overall, our findings emphasize the utility of employing more generalized models of stress in studying or attempting to understand the situations in which caregivers find themselves. In particular, a broad predictive net must be cast in order to best understand the conditions affecting the well-being of caregivers. Perhaps the overall conclusion that can be reached on the basis of the data presented is that caregivers are individuals in their own right, not simply caregivers, and that the factors that govern their lives are multiple. Some are unique to the caregiver context, others transcend that context.

Ghosts of the Past

In the last series of analyses, we examined the extent to which patients' personality characteristics in the past were associated with present levels of care provision. This venture into the somewhat taboo area of historical ratings was spurred by past work that had yielded measures with reasonable psychometric properties (e.g., Chiriboga et al., in press). Since the ratings, made by caregivers, did seem to generate useful information, we considered how the parents' characteristics prior to onset of Alzheimer's Disease were related not only with a caregiver's current level of well-being, but with his or her caregiving behavior as well. Our results suggested that the way parents are viewed is associated with the well-being of caregivers and the kind of care provided.

The direction of the relationships between parent characteristics and caregiver status was of particular interest. Results indicated that having a parent who in the past displayed negative characteristics generally was associated with caregiver distress, but having a happy and pleasant pre-onset parent was not necessarily associated with reduced caregiver distress. For example, having an uncooperative parent was associated with greater caregiver depression and less care being provided to the parent. Having a parent who used to be a happy individual was associated with greater depression and perceptions of greater stress in the caregiver role.

These findings do make intuitive sense, although on an admittedly post-hoc basis. It may be that more uncooperative, upset, and irresponsible parents continue to create problems and greater demands on their caregivers as they progress through their disease. A parent who was kind and happy prior to illness may create special difficulties for the caregiver, in the sense that the loss of this very special and giving person may evoke a greater sense of loss. One interpretation is that a demanding parent may create what is viewed as an unwarranted intrusion on the caregiver's quest for personal autonomy and self-fulfillment, a "good" parent may underscore for the child caregiver the importance of filial obligations.

REFERENCES

Black, S. (1990). *Dimensional structure of standard tests of cognitive deficit.* Unpublished masters' thesis, University of Texas Medical Branch, Galveston.

Blessed, G., Tomlinson, B. E., & Roth, M. (1968). The association between quantitative measures of dementia and of senile change in the cerebral gray matter of elderly subjects. *British Journal of Psychiatry, 114,* 797-811.

Brody, E. M. (1985). Parent care as a normative family stress. *The Gerontologist, 25,* 19-29.

Brody, E. M. (1990). *Women in the middle: Their parent-care years.* New York: Springer.

Brown, G. W., & Harris, T. (1989). Depression. In G. W. B. Brown & T. O. Harris (Eds.), *Life events and illness* (pp. 49-93). New York: Guilford Press.

Chiriboga, D. A. (1977). Life-event weighting systems: A comparative analysis. *Journal of Psychosomatic Research, 21,* 415-422.

Chiriboga, D. A. (1984). Social stressors as antecedents of change. *Journal of Gerontology, 39,* 468-477.

Chiriboga, D. A. (1989a). Stress and loss in middle age. In R. Kalish (Ed.), *Midlife loss: Coping strategies* (pp. 42-88). Newbury Park, CA: Sage.
Chiriboga, D. A. (1989b). The measurement of stress exposure in later life. In K. Markides (Ed.), *Aging, stress, and health* (pp. 13-41). London: Wiley.
Chiriboga, D. A., Catron, L. S., & Associates (in press). *Divorce: Crisis, challenge, or relief?* New York: New York University Press.
Chiriboga, D. A., & Cutler, L. (1980). Stress and adaptation: Life-span perspectives. In L. Poon (Ed.), *Aging in the 1980s: Psychological issues* (pp. 347-362). Washington, DC: American Psychological Association.
Chiriboga, D. A., Weiler, P. G., & Nielsen, K. (1989). The stress of caregivers. *Journal of Applied Social Sciences, 13*(1), 118-141.
Colerick, E. J., & George, L. K. (1986). Predictors of institutionalization among caregivers of patients with Alzheimer's Disease. *Journal of the American Geriatric Society, 34*, 493-498.
Derogatis, L. R., & Cleary, P. A. (1977). Confirmation of the dimensional structure of the Symptoms Checklist-90: A study in construct validation. *Journal of Clinical Psychology, 33*, 981-989.
Dohrenwend, B. P. (1986). Note on a program of research on alternative social psychological models of relationships between life stress and psychopathology. In M. H. Appley & R. Trumbull (Eds.), *Dynamics of stress: Physiological, psychological, and social perspectives* (pp. 283-293). New York: Plenum.
Duke University Center for the Study of Aging and Human Development (1978). *Multidimensional functional assessment: The OARS methodology*. Durham, NC: Duke University Press.
Elder, G. H., Jr. (1982). Historical experience in the later years. In T. K. Hareven & K. J. Adams (Eds.), *Aging and life course transitions: An interdisciplinary perspective* (pp. 75-107). New York: Guilford Press.
Elliott, G. R., & Eisdorfer, C. (Eds.). (1982). *Stress and human health: Analysis and implications of research*. New York: Springer.
Evans, D. A., Funkenstein, H. H., Albert, M. S., Scherr, P. A., Chown, M. J., Hebert, L. E., Hennekens, C. H., & Taylor, J. O. (1989). Prevalence of Alzheimer's Disease in community population of older persons. *Journal of the American Medical Association, 262*, 2551-2556.
Fiske, M., & Chiriboga, D. A. (1990). *Continuity and change in adult life*. San Francisco: Jossey-Bass.
Folstein, M. F., Folstein, S. E., & McHugh, P. R. (1975). Mini-Mental State: A practical method for grading the cognitive state of patients for the clinician. *Journal of Psychiatric Research, 34*, 139-198.
Gergen, K. J. (1977). Stability, change, and chance in understanding human development. In N. Datan & H. W. Reese (Eds.), *Life-span development psychology: Dialectical perspectives on experimental research* (pp. 136-158). New York: Academic Press.
Hachinski, V. C. (1983). Differential diagnosis of Alzheimer's Disease: Multi-infarct dementia. In B. Reisberg (Ed.), *Alzheimer's Disease* (pp. 188-192). New York: Free Press.
Haley, W. E., & Pardo, K. M. (1987). *Relationship of stage of dementia to caregiver stress and coping*. Paper presented at 95th annual convention of the American Psychological Association, New York.
Holmes, T., & Rahe, R. (1967). The Social Readjustment Rating Scale. *Journal of Psychosomatic Research, 11*, 213-218.
Huang, L., Cartwright, W. S., & Hu, T. (1988). The economic cost of senile dementia in the United States, 1985. *Public Health Reports, 103*(1), 3-7.
Kane, R. A., & Kane, R. L. (1987). *Long-term care: Principles, programs, and policies*. New York: Springer.
Kiecolt-Glaser, J. K., & Glaser, R. (1989). Caregiving, mental health, and immune function. In E. Light & B. D. Lebowitz (Eds.), *Alzheimer's Disease treatment and family stress: Directions for research* (pp. 245-266). Washington, DC: US Government Printing Office.
Lazarus, R. S., & Folkman, S. (1984). *Stress, appraisal, and coping*. New York: Springer.
Lewinsohn, P. M., Mermelstein, R. M., Alexander, C., & MacPhillamy, D. J. (1985). The Unpleasant Events Scale: A scale for the measurement of aversive events. *Journal of Clinical Psychology, 41*, 483-498.

Light, E., & Lebowitz, B. D. (1989). Issues in Alzheimer's Disease and family research. In E. Light & B. D. Lebowitz (Eds.), *Alzheimer's Disease treatment and family stress: Directions for research* (p. 1). Washington, DC: US Government Printing Office.

Lynch, J. J. (1977). *The broken heart: The medical consequences of loneliness*. New York: Basic Books.

Moeller, J. W., & Shuell, H. (1988). *Elder care: Caregiving in the workplace*. Berkeley, CA: Summer Series on Aging, American Society on Aging.

Montgomery, R. J. V., Gonyea, J. G., & Hooyman, N. R. (1985). Caregiving and the experience of subjective and objective burden. *Family Relations, 34*(1), 19-26.

Mortimer, J. A. (1988). Epidemiology and aging. In J. A. Brody & G. L. Maddox (Eds.), *Epidemiology and aging* (pp. 150-164). New York: Springer.

Murrell, S. A., Norris, F. H., & Grote, C. (1988). Life events in older adults. In L. H. Cohen (Ed.), *Life events and psychological functioning: Theories and methodological issues* (pp. 96-122). Newbury Park, CA: Sage.

Nielsen, K. E. (1990). *Caregiver stress*. Unpublished doctoral thesis, The Fielding Institute, Santa Barbara, CA.

Nissel, M. (1984). The family costs of looking after handicapped elderly relatives. *Aging and Society, 4*(2), 185-204.

Ory, M. G., Williams, T. F., Emer, M., Lebowitz, B., Rabins, P., Salloway, J., Sluss-Radbaugh, T., Wolff, E., & Zarit, S. (1985). Families, informal supports, and Alzheimer's Disease: Current research and future agendas. *Research on Aging, 7*, 623-644.

Osgood, C. E., Suci, G. J., & Tannenbaum, P. H. (1957). *The measurement of meaning*. Urbana: University of Illinois Press.

Paykel, E. S. (1982). Life events and early environment. In E. S. Paykel (Ed.), *Handbook of affective disorders* (pp. 146-161). New York: Guilford.

Pearlin, L. I. (1982). The social contexts of stress. In L. Goldberger & S. Breznitz (Eds.), *Handbook of stress: Theoretical and clinical aspects* (pp. 367-279). New York: The Free Press.

Pearlin, L. I. (1985). Life strains and psychological distress among adults. In A. Monat & R. S. Lazarus (Eds.), *Stress and coping: An anthology* (2nd ed., pp. 192-207). New York: Columbia University Press.

Pearlin, L. I., Turner, H., & Semple, S. (1989). Coping and the mediation of caregiver stress. In E. Light & B. D. Lebowitz (Eds.), *Alzheimer's Disease treatment and family stress: Directions for research* (pp. 198-217). Washington, DC: US Government Printing Office.

Pruchno, R. A., & Resch, N. L. (1989). Husbands and wives as caregivers: Antecedents of depression and burden. *The Gerontologist, 29*, 159-165.

Reisberg, B., Ferris, S. H., de Leon, M. J., & Crook, T. (1982). The global deterioration scale for the assessment of primary degenerative dementia. *American Journal of Psychiatry, 139*, 1136-1139.

Schneider, E. L., & Guralnik, J. M. (1990). The aging of America: Impact on health care costs. *Journal of the American Medical Association, 263*, 2335-2340.

Sheikh, J. I., & Yesavage, J. A. (1986). Geriatric Depression Scale (GDS): Recent evidence and development of a shorter version. In T. L. Brink (Ed.), *Clinical gerontology: A guide to assessment and intervention* (pp. 165-173). New York: Haworth Press.

Springer, D., & Brubaker, T. H. (1984). *Family caregivers and dependent elderly: Managing stress and maximizing independence*. Beverly Hills, CA: Sage.

Wan, T. T. H. (1982). *Stressful life events, social-support networks, and gerontological health.* Toronto: Lexington Books.

Zarit, S. H., Orr, N. K., & Zarit, J. M. (1985). *The hidden victims of Alzheimer's Disease: Families under stress*. New York: New York University Press.

Zautra, A. J., Guarnaccia, C. A., Reich, J. W., & Dohrenwend, B. P. (1988). The contribution of small events to stress and distress. In L. H. Cohen (Ed.), *Life events and psychological functioning: Theories and methodological issues* (pp. 123-148). Newbury Park, CA: Sage.

II The Impact of Views About Responsibilities and Avoidability

7 Antecedents and Consequences of Causal Attributions for Critical Life Events

Friedrich Försterling
University of Bielefeld

The present article discusses attribution research that was guided by the belief that basic social psychology and applied (e.g., clinical) psychology can benefit from each other. It is outlined how clinical questions can be cast in an attribution framework and then shown that the same framework can be used to view theory, research, and practice dealing with coping and critical life events. Secondly, I will point out that reactions to stressful and critical life events and questions of behavior change are an interesting area for basic researchers in social psychology to test and elaborate their theories. Some theoretical developments in the attribution area will be reported that have occurred when attribution conceptions were applied to clinical questions.

BASIC ATTRIBUTION RESEARCH

Attribution research is concerned with the antecedents and consequences of the causal ascriptions of events. Theories and research on the antecedents of attributions (attribution research) address the question as to how individuals come to judge certain causes such as their own person or the stimuli they interact with as responsible for an outcome.

According to Heider (1958), information about the presence and absence of possible causes in conjunction with the event that is in need of explanation is the most fundamental mechanism that guides the attribution process. The most important theoretical conception that has addressed this mechanism is Kelley's (1967,

1973) covariation principle. It states that "an effect will be attributed to the cause with which it covaries" (p. 108) and has been convincingly demonstrated empirically (see, for a summary, Hewstone & Jaspars, 1987). For instance, when an effect (e.g., person P loses his job) only covaries with the person (nobody else lost the job; there is "low consensus") and not with the entity (he lost all his other jobs before; there is low distinctiveness), the effect (job loss) will be attributed to the person. On the other hand, when the effect only covaries with the entity (e.g., he only lost this job but no other jobs; high distinctiveness) and not with the person (everybody lost this particular job; high consensus), the effect will be attributed to the entity (aspects of the particular job).

Attributional theories, on the other hand, are concerned with the behavioral and emotional consequences of these ascriptions. Weiner's attributional approach to achievement behavior (see, for a summary, Weiner, 1986) and the attributional model of learned helplessness (Abramson, Seligman, & Teasdale, 1978) are the most influential attributional models. Attributional research has demonstrated that our reactions (behaviors and emotions) to a particular event are determined by the way in which we explain the event. For instance, when we explain a job loss (or failure in general) through factors that are internal, stable, global, and uncontrollable (such as our lack of general ability), we might feel depressed and give up; whereas attributions to external, variable, specific, and controllable causes (e.g., mismanagement of the firm) may lead to anger and protest.

CRITICAL LIFE EVENTS FROM AN ATTRIBUTIONAL VIEWPOINT

From the perspective of an attribution theorist, crises and critical life events share many similarities with the events that elicit causal attributions. Critical life events are by definition important, mostly negative, and they are often unexpected. These characteristics will almost guarantee (see Weiner, 1985) that the person experiencing these events will ask *why* they have happened (i.e., search for an attribution for the event). In addition, it can be expected that the cause or the causes that are perceived to be responsible for the event will be among the determinants of the reactions to and the coping behavior with the event.

Attributionally oriented research within the area of critical life events and coping has adopted many of the basic premises and methodological tools of basic attribution research. Like most applied areas of attribution theory, research about coping and critical life events has concentrated on the consequences of attributions. It has been asked how individuals who cope well with accidents (e.g., Brewin, 1982; Bulman & Wortman, 1977), losses or rape (Janoff-Bulman, 1979), or diseases such as cancer (Michela & Wood, 1986; Taylor, 1983) attribute the causes for these negative events, and how these causal attributions differ from those of individuals who do not cope as well.

For instance, Michela and Wood (1986), have summarized studies indicating that heart attack patients who feel that they were responsible for their heart attack will comply better with medical recommendations than individuals who do not accept responsibility. The idea that the attribution for a serious illness affects the individual's adaptation and coping and, as a result, the further course of the illness has received support in a study by Affleck, Tennen, Croog, and Levine (1987). These authors have reported significant (albeit small) correlations between the tendency to blame other individuals or "stress" (probably external uncontrollable causes) for the (own) heart attack and the occurrence of a second heart attack within the subsequent eight years.

A further relevant line of research is concerned with how individuals cope with and adapt to difficult and/or tragic life events such as accidents, cancer surgery, or rape. In a frequently cited study, Bulman and Wortman (1977) investigated the coping behavior of individuals who had become paralyzed following accidents that resulted in spinal cord injuries. The authors found that individuals who blamed other persons or other external factors for the accident adapted comparatively less well to their handicaps than individuals who "blamed themselves" for the accident. (The degree of adaptation was measured through ratings made by the hospital staff.)

Similarly, Taylor (1983) has reported that breast cancer patients who believed that their cancer was caused by controllable factors (many of them did!) such as "dieting" or "negative attitudes" coped better with their misfortune than those who attributed the illness to uncontrollable causes. Brewin (1982) has reported a similar finding: His subjects were industrial workers who had received minor injuries during accidents at work (fractures and bone damages). As a measure of adaptation, he used the length of time (weighted with the prognosis of medical doctors) that the workers stayed away from their job. It was found that workers who perceived themselves to be responsible (culpable) for the accidents coped better with their injuries (stayed away from work for a shorter time) than those individuals who explained the accident with factors external to themselves. (Naturally, the operationalization of "coping behavior" was limited to a very narrow aspect of this phenomenon.)

Furthermore, Janoff-Bulman (1979) has suggested that coping reactions of rape victims are in part determined by their causal explanations as to "why" they have been raped. The author found that rape victims who attributed their experience to characterological (stable) factors (e.g., "I have been raped because I have certain personality traits") had more difficulty coping with this negative event than persons who blamed their behavior (e.g., "I was raped because I walked alone in dangerous part of town"). It is quite conceivable that persons with characterological attributions had harder time searching for ways to avoid being raped again, whereas for those who used behavioral attributions, some relatively minor changes in their own behavior appeared to be sufficient to provide future protection.

Hence, there seems to be suggestive evidence indicating that the maintenance of a concept of "control" has a positive influence on how individuals cope with the consequences of stressful life events.

Limitations and Shortcomings in Attributional Coping Research

As already indicated above, attributional coping research is primarily concerned with the consequences of attributions (C —> R) and not so much with the antecedents of causal cognitions (S —> C). In this respect, they resemble the attributional models within the achievement and helplessness domain. I will now describe an attempt to integrate attribution (antecedent) models with attributional (consequence) models within the achievement and helplessness domain. Furthermore, I shall illustrate how such an integration can also be attempted within the field of coping and critical life events.

To do so, I will outline how research on "therapeutic" attributional change has developed in the achievement and helplessness domain to then show that a comprehensive application of attributional theories for clinical questions such as behavior modification necessitates an integration of attributional and attribution theory. Then I will introduce empirical research that tests hypotheses resulting from this theoretical integration and will furthermore show how such research could also be conducted in the field of critical life events and coping.

Attributional Change and an Integration of Attribution and Attributional Models

The history of attributional change research started with the finding that attributions of negative events such as failures or uncontrollability influence individuals' reactions toward these events. For instance, Weiner (see Weiner, 1986, for a summary) found that internal, stable attributions for failure (as opposed to, e.g., external, variable ones; i.e., to lack of ability) led individuals to decreased expectancies of future success and reduced persistence and performance. In the same way, researchers in the area of helplessness and depression have shown that internal, stable, and global attributions of failure may lead to helplessness and feelings of depression.

Based on these findings, attributional intervention programs have been designed (see, e.g., Dweck, 1975; Wilson & Linville, 1982; and Försterling, 1985, for a summary). In these studies, subjects with certain "undesirable" reactions such as low persistence and performance or negative achievement affects are identified. Secondly, in a therapeutic stage, attributions that are assumed to lead to the undesirable consequences are substituted by ones that lead to desirable consequences. And third, it is assessed whether this intervention has led to the intended behavioral changes. These programs are effective in that they change cognitions and behaviors in the expected direction. For instance, Wilson and Linville (1982) have reported that subjects who were trained to make variable attributions for their failures at college had a lower college drop-out rate compared to (untrained) controls.

With regard to the findings on the attributional determinants of reactions to critical life events, one might proceed in the same way and design attribution change programs. Researchers could try to teach subjects (patients) to make "good" or desirable attributions, that is, those that have been found to be used by "good copers." For instance, it appears possible that coping researchers will find that subjects need little time in the hospital or will rapidly look for a job following job loss when they make attributions for the critical event to controllable factors. One might then decide to train "bad copers" to make the same attributions that "good copers" use.

However, when using these attributional conceptions for purposes of behavioral and cognitive change, one difficulty immediately becomes apparent. That is, the research on the consequences of attributions and on the resulting therapeutic suggestions has neglected the antecedents of attributions. In these studies, a certain behavioral or emotional reaction (e.g., lack of persistence or feelings of resignation) is a priori defined as undesirable and worthy of therapeutic change. Moreover, the attribution that leads to the respective ("bad") reaction is considered as worthy of change and should be—according to attributional training programs—substituted with a causal cognition that leads to more "desirable" consequences. However, it is typically not asked under which situational antecedents the respective attribution was formed and the reaction was exhibited.

This line of thought, however, violates two of the guiding ideas of attribution research, that is (1) that individuals strive to gain a realistic understanding of the causes of events, and (2) that this realistic causal understanding enables individuals to functionally adapt to their environment (see Heider, 1958; Kelley, 1967, 1973). This assumed relationship between the veridicality of the attribution and the functionality of the reaction is depicted schematically in Figure 7.1.

According to these basic assumptions (and Figure 7.1), attributional change seems only advisable when individuals make unrealistic attributions, but not when the attribution reflects situational antecedents. For instance, when failure at a task "objectively" is caused by lack of ability, it might be quite functional in the long run to feel resigned and to quit attempting task solution. Under such circumstances it might be quite maladaptive to persist. Only if failure is truly due to lack of effort and falsely perceived as due to lack of ability (or vice versa) should reattribution be attempted.

But how can one decide which attribution is realistic and which one is unrealistic? Naturally, one needs to look at the antecedent attribution variables. We have chosen to define the veridicality of a causal perception using Kelley's covariation principle (Försterling, 1986, 1988; Försterling & Rudolph, 1988): An attribution can be considered as realistic—and should lead to functional results—when it is consistent with the antecedent covariation informations and unrealistic when it violates them.

For instance, if a factory worker has been laid off several times (high consistency), he was the only one to be fired (low consensus), and he got layed off from different jobs before (low distinctiveness), then it would seem realistic that he attributes the job loss to something about himself and subsequently changes aspects of his behavior. However, if he would "unrealistically" maintain that his job losses are caused by a bad economic situation in his geographic area, he might decide to move, and he will not be able to eliminate the cause of his prior failures.

To test whether realistic attributions (i.e., those consistent with the Kelley model) are perceived as leading to functional reactions, we conducted several simulation studies in which both, antecedent information as well as the attributions were manipulated. We then assessed whether subjects considered the attribution and the resulting behavior as functional or not (see Försterling & Rudolph, 1988).

For instance, we provided subjects with antecedent information designed to lead to person attributions in one condition: for example, Peter failed (effect), he had always failed in the past (high consistency), he was the only one who failed the task (low consensus), and he failed at several other tasks (low distinctiveness). In another condition, we provided subjects with information that would suggest a circumstance attribution for the same effect: low consistency (he only failed this time), high consensus (everybody failed at this task), and low distinctiveness (he succeeds at other tasks). Cross-cutting these two antecedent conditions, the stimulus person was either described as attributing the event to the person (his own

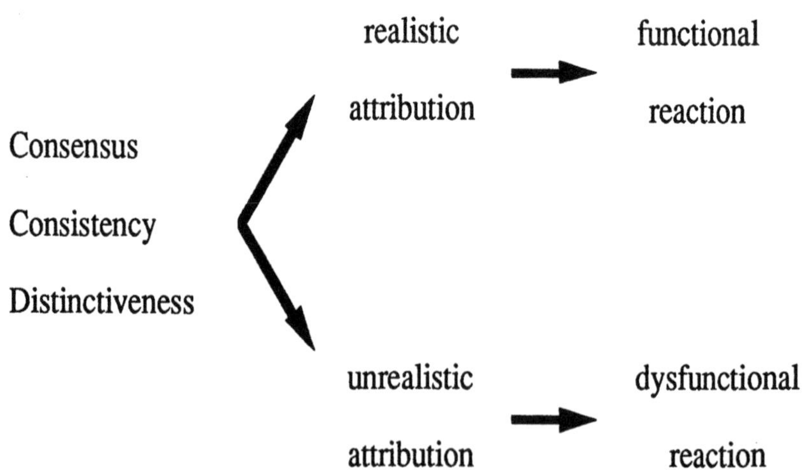

FIG. 7.1. The assumed relationship between the veridicality of the attribution and the functionality of the reaction.

inability) or to the circumstances (the teacher selected tasks that were too difficult). Naturally, each attribution was realistic in one condition and unrealistic in the other condition. Table 7.1 shows (consistent with the predictions derived from Figure7.1) that the stimulus person who made realistic attributions was generally evaluated more positively on a number of variables (e.g., his attribution was perceived as more appropriate, he was expected to be more successful in the long run, and he was perceived as more likable than the stimulus person who made unrealistic attributions). Hence, under certain conditions, even attributions to lack of ability appear to have positive consequences in the long run, and making realistic attributions appears to lead to favorable peer evaluation. Or, in more statistical terms, stimulus person evaluation was primarily a function of the interaction of the independent variables (antecedents and attributions) rather than of main effect of the attribution.

We have tested the hypothesis that attributions consistent with the covariation principle are perceived as leading to functional results, whereas unrealistic attributions are perceived as leading to inappropriate results, with different subject groups and in different content areas, and we feel confident that these findings are quite replicable (Bartus, 1989; Wind, 1988).

Nevertheless, due to the simulative nature of (most of) the reported studies, it is not yet clear whether realistic attributions "actually" lead to more favorable attributions than unrealistic ones; they are merely perceived as doing so. More laboratory or possibly field research is needed to answer these questions more satisfactorily.

In addition, there may well be some "exceptions to the rule" that realistic attributions lead to functional reactions. It is conceivable that sometimes non-

TABLE 7.1

Mean Judgements on Perceived (1) Justification of an Attribution; (2) Appropriateness of the Resulting Action; (3) Likeability of the Stimulus Person; and (4) Expected Success in the Long Run

	Antecedent Information leading to Person Attributions		*Antecedent Information leading to Circumstance Attributions*	
	Circumstance Attribution	*Person Attribution*	*Circumstance Attribution*	*Person Attribution*
1.	3.40	4.93	7.33	1.87
2.	4.40	6.27	7.20	2.40
3.	4.85	6.67	6.47	5.21
4.	2.93	3.73	7.93	6.33

veridical attributions serve the goal of protecting the individual from debilitating emotional reactions. For instance, when a person is diagnosed as fatally ill, an (unrealistic) belief about the controllability of the causes of the illness might protect the individual from despair or depression about the illness, at least in the short run. However, it can be anticipated that the individual will be confronted with the true nature of the cause of the illness at some point in time and will then have to adapt to the possibly anxiety-provoking causal explanation. Hence, as a working hypothesis, it seems quite reasonable that realistic attributions lead to functional reactions. in that they enable the individual to maximize chances of survival and to attain happiness in the long run.

Moreover, the findings on how observers perceive the consequences of and react to unrealistic attributions are a question of interest in their own right. For instance, coping researchers are also interested in predicting social reactions to a victim in addition to the victim's own reactions. The present analysis suggests that social reactions toward a victim of a critical life event are a function of both the situation (as captured by attribution antecedent variables) as well as the subjective interpretation of the victim (and not only of the latter).

To summarize, whether individuals who make realistic attributions for critical life events will actually exhibit more functional emotional and behavioral reactions following such events (as suggested by Figure 7.1) than individuals who make unrealistic attributions is still a question that is in need of empirical testing. To answer it, life-event research would need to use designs that not only assess attributions but, in addition, attributionally relevant situational information.

Elaborations of the Kelley Model and Implications for Attributions About Critical Life Events

As I suggest that the Kelley model is an appropriate tool to capture some of the attributionally relevant aspects of a situation, I would like to report on some of our recent research on this model (e.g., Försterling, 1989). I will then demonstrate how findings from such research can be applied to questions of coping research and address the question of "distorted" or erroneous attribution.

In connection with attempts to conduct attributional retraining and to create situations that should unequivocally lead to certain attributions, we took Kelley's suggestion that the attribution process can be conceptualized as an ANOVA analogy quite literally. In that analogy, the possible causes (persons, entities, and circumstances, i.e., time) are the independent variables and the effects the dependent ones. In the simplest case, an individual who carries out an ANOVA with these three independent variables would need to group his or her observation within a $2 \times 2 \times 2$ design as depicted in Table 7.2. Then, the effect should be attributed to the cause that is present when the effect is present and absent when the effect is absent. For instance, when the effect only occurs for one person at all times and entities, then the effect should be attributed to the person and not to entities and times

(Example 1). If, however, the effect is only present for certain entities and not for others, and this is so for all persons at all times (Example 2), then it should be attributed to the entity. We found, however, that verbal information about consensus, consistency, and distinctiveness, which has been used in research designed to test the Kelley model thus far (e.g., McArthur, 1972, and the subsequent studies that have used her paradigm), does not provide individuals with complete information with regard to these cells. Most importantly, consensus, consistency, and distinctiveness are silent with regard to Cells 7 and 8.

More specifically, subjects in a McArthur-type study typically receive the description of an effect (e.g., person 1 succeeds at an exam (Entity 1) at Time 1; this information corresponds to Cell 1 in Table 2), and then receive information about the three informational dimensions. Consensus informs the subject about whether the effect also occurred for other persons, for example, "most others failed at the task" (low consensus) or "most others also succeeded" (high consensus). Hence, subjects get information about Cells 5 or 6 in Table 7.2, but it is not clear about which of these two cells. In addition, distinctiveness information (e.g., high distinctiveness: "Tom failed at most other tasks;" low distinctiveness: "Tom succeeds at most other tasks as well") informs the subject about Cells 3 or 4 in Table 7.2, but, again, it is unclear about which of these two cells. Finally, consistency information (high consistency: "Tom also succeeded at this task in the past;" low consistency: "Tom did not succeed at this task in the past") provides us with information about Cell 2 in Table 7.2.

In a recent study (Försterling, 1989), I investigated subjects' attributions when they were provided with all (eight pieces of) information relevant to the naive ANOVA (see Table7. 2). The data revealed that person, entity, and time attributions

TABLE 7. 2

The Kelley Model as an Analogy to a 2 x 2 x 2 ANOVA Design

	Person 1				*Person 2*			
	Entity 1		*Entity 2*		*Entity 1*		*Entity 2*	
	Time 1	*Time 2*	*Time 1*	*Time 2*	*Time 1*	*Time 2*	*Time 1*	*Time 2*
	1	*2*	*3*	*4*	*5*	*6*	*7*	*8*
Example 1	E	E	E	E	-	-	-	-
Example 2	E	E	-	-	E	E	-	-

were rated most responsible when the effect only covaried with the respective cause and not with the remaining two causes. Subjects even rated interactions of causes such as "an interaction of the person and the entity" or "the entity and time" as most important when the effect, in fact, only occurred in the presence of the respective two causes.

Hence, the data were remarkably consistent with the ANOVA predictions. In addition, two of the major errors and biases reported in the attribution literature, that is, the often reported underuse of consensus information (see Kassin, 1979) and the fundamental attribution error (see Ross, 1977), disappeared as soon as subjects received complete ANOVA-relevant information. Hence, when scientists look at the same data subjects use for their inferences, they do not find the subjects' errors anymore (see Cheng & Novick, 1990).

Therefore, I would like to urge clinical attribution researchers to reassess whether one can truly report on attribution errors or biases in good versus bad copers: For instance, Taylor and Brown (1988) have reported that misperceptions of reality (illusions) lead to well-being. This may well apply to a diversity of cognitions. However, when looking at the preceding arguments with regard to causal attributions, the question whether good or bad copers are more veridical in their causal judgments cannot be answered: Not one single study exists in which subjects (say depressed or nondepressed or good and bad copers) are confronted with all the information required for a complete ANOVA analogy. The ANOVA analogy, however, would be the logical choice for a normative model of causal attributions.

In line with the above arguments, it would seem reasonable if attributionally oriented coping research were to investigate not only the role of causal attributions for coping but also the role of causal attributions for coping in different "causal environments." I think that the $2 \times 2 \times 2$ ANOVA analogy could be a helpful conceptual tool to analyze and classify the attributionally relevant antecedents of different critical life events. One could ask whether different critical life events are characterized by different data patterns in this $2 \times 2 \times 2$ matrix. For instance, totally different data patterns can be assumed when an older woman loses her husband than when a young man loses his job. The "data pattern" in the $2 \times 2 \times 2$ table for the loss of the husband would probably be characterized by the following facts (see Table 7.2): The loss (the event that is in need of explanation) can be located in Cell 1 of Table 7.2: She lost her husband (Entity 1) at a specific point of time). However, the same event did (naturally) not happen before (i.e., did not occur in Cell 2 of Table 7.2), and it does occur for other persons of comparable age at this point in time (i.e., the effect is present in Cell 7 but not at earlier times (i.e., the effect is not present in Cell 8). In this example we do not have observations with regard to Cells 3 to 6, as we assume that the lady is only married to one husband and that no other person is married to her husband in the meantime.

The data pattern described in the preceding example should—according to the covariation principle—give rise to an attribution to the causal factor "time" (more specifically the husband's age) as a cause for the loss. In addition, we would therefore predict that this attribution would be helpful for coping. However, if the widow would choose characteristics of her own person or her husband's behavior to explain his death, she might react with guilt or anger, and this could inhibit effective coping.

When looking at the hypothesized data pattern of the young man who lost his job (this event constitutes the effect in Cell 1 of Table 7.2), different reactions would seem appropriate for good coping. Assume, that this man has lost this very same job already in the past (the effect is present in Cell 2) and that he was successful in maintaining other jobs (the effect is not present in Cells 3 and 4). In addition, other persons do not lose other jobs (the effect does not occur in Cells 7 and 8), and other individuals also do not lose the job that our hypothetical person just lost (the effect is not present in Cells 5 and 6). Under these circumstances, an attribution to an interaction of the person and the job (entity) would be the appropriate attribution according to the covariation principle. Hence, different reactions than in the first example (loss of a husband) would seem appropriate: It might be quite adaptive to feel guilt or anger in this situation about the job loss.

These examples illustrate that under different circumstances that are characterized by different covariational patterns in the $2 \times 2 \times 2$ table, different attributions will prove to be helpful for effective coping.

REFERENCES

Abramson, L. Y., Seligman, M. E. P., & Teasdale, J. D. (1978). Learned helplessness in humans. *Journal of Abnormal Psychology, 87*, 49-74.

Affleck, G., Tennen, H., Croog, S., & Levine, S. (1987). Causal attribution, perceived benefits, and morbidity after a heart attack: An 8-year study. *Journal of Consulting and Clinical Psychology, 55*, 29-35.

Bartus, B. (1989). *Situation, Attribution und die Evaluation von Lehrerreaktionen auf Schulleistungen.* Unpublished master's thesis, Universität Bielefeld.

Brewin, C. R. (1982). Adaptive aspects of self-blame in coping with accidental injury. In C. Antaki & C. R. Brewin (Eds.), *Attributions and psychological change. Applications of attributional theories to clinical and educational practice* (pp. 119-133). London: Academic Press.

Bulman, R. J., & Wortman, C. B. (1977). Attributions of blame and coping in the "real world": Severe accident victims react to their lot. *Journal of Personality and Social Psychology, 35*, 351-363.

Cheng, P. W., & Novick, L. R. (1990). A qualitative contrast model of causal induction. *Journal of Personality and Social Psychology, 58*, 545-567.

Dweck, C. S. (1975). The role of expectations and attributions on the alleviation of learned helplessness. *Journal of Personality and Social Psychology, 36*, 451-462.

Försterling, F. (1985). Attributional retraining: A review. *Psychological Bulletin, 98*, 495-512.

Försterling, F. (1986). Attributional conceptions in clinical psychology. *American Psychologist, 41*, 275-285.

Försterling, F. (1988). *Attribution theory in clinical psychology.* Chichester: Wiley .

Försterling, F. (1989). Models of covariation and causal attribution: How do they relate to the analogy of analysis of variance? *Journal of Personality and Social Psychology, 57*, 615-625.

Försterling, F., & Rudolph, U. (1988). Situations, attributions, and the evaluation of behavior. *Journal of Personality and Social Psychology, 54*, 225-232.

Heider, F. (1958). *The psychology of interpersonal relations*. New York: Wiley.

Hewstone, M., & Jaspars, J. (1987). Covariation and causal attribution: A logical model of the intuitive analysis of variance. *Journal of Personality and Social Psychology, 53*, 663-672.

Janoff-Bulman, R. (1979). Characterological versus behavioral self-blame: Inquiries into depression and rape. *Journal of Personality and Social Psychology, 37*, 1798-1809.

Kassin, S. M. (1979). Consensus information, prediction, and causal attribution: A review of the literature and issues. *Journal of Personality and Social Psychology, 37*, 1966-1988.

Kelley, H. H. (1967). Attribution theory in social psychology. In D. Levine (Ed.), *Nebraska Symposium on Motivation* (pp. 192-238). Lincoln: University of Nebraska Press.

Kelley, H. H. (1973). The process of causal attributions. *American Psychologist, 28*, 107-128.

McArthur, L. A. (1972). The how and what of why: Some determinants and consequences of causal attributions. *Journal of Personality and Social Psychology, 22*, 171-193.

Michela, J. L., & Wood, J. V. (1986). Causal attributions in health and illness. In P. C. Kendall (Ed.), *Advances in cognitive-behavioral research* (Vol. 5, pp. 179-235). New York: Academic Press.

Ross, L. (1977). The intuitive psychologist and his shortcomings: Distortions in the attribution process. In L. Berkowitz (Ed.), *Advances in experimental social psychology* (Vol. 10, pp. 173-220). Orlando: Academic Press.

Taylor, S. E. (1983). Adjustment to threatening events: A theory of cognitive adaptation. *American Psychologist, 38*, 1161-1173.

Taylor, S. E., & Brown, J. (1988). Illusion and well-being. A social-psychological perspective on mental health. *Psychological Bulletin, 103*, 193-210.

Weiner, B. (1985). "Spontaneous" causal search. *Psychological Bulletin, 79*, 74-84.

Weiner, B. (1986). *An attributional theory of motivation and emotion*. New York: Springer.

Wilson, T. D., & Linville, P. W. (1982). Improving the academic performance of college freshmen with attributional techniques. *Journal of Personality and Social Psychology, 49*, 287-293.

Wind, U. (1988). *Situation, Attribution und einige Aspekte von Führungsverhalten und Führungserfolg*. Unpublished master's thesis, Universität Bielefeld.

8 Attribution of Responsibility for Losses and Perceived Injustice

Leo Montada
University of Trier

THE ISSUE OF INJUSTICE IN CRITICAL LIFE EVENTS

Suffering the death of a loved one, the loss of health through illness or an accident, the loss of wealth, social status, personal security, or self-confidence through unemployment, through economic, political, natural, or technical catastrophes or through criminal offenses: Are all these losses just "bad fate"; is a deity punishing us; are the victims themselves, other people, or institutions responsible? Questions like these are asked by victims, bystanders, and others who learn about the event and raise the issue of justice whether the losses are deserved or not (Lerner, 1980; Lerner & Simmons, 1966; Steil & Slochover, 1985).

Questions of justice are rarely answered unanimously. People have different information, views, attitudes, prejudices, motives, and so forth that lead to different answers. A great deal depends on the answers. Victims' own answers determine to a large extent how successfully they will cope with stressful events and their consequences (e.g., Affleck, Tennen, Croog, & Levine, 1987; Bulman & Wortman, 1977; Jaspars, Fincham, & Hewstone, 1983; Taylor, 1983): If they consider themselves treated unjustly, it could confront them with additional stress. Depending on the answers of others, victims and their fates will be judged differently: They will either receive empathy and support, or they will be blamed and derogated (e.g., Lerner, 1980; Meyer & Mulherin, 1980; Ross & DiTecco, 1975; Shaver, 1970, 1985; Walster, 1966). If the case is brought to trial, victims' claims for expiation or compensation might be accepted, or else they might be rejected, adding a loss of belief in justice to the primary loss caused by the event itself.

While the issue of justice is rarely addressed explicitly in empirical studies, there is considerable indirect evidence suggesting that it is frequently raised by victims as well as by others who learn about the misfortune. The issue of justice is implied, for instance, in the victims' question "Why me?" as well as in their blaming those whom they consider to be responsible for their losses. It might also be implied when victims are blaming themselves, since this may help them to avoid the feelings of injustice that would be aroused if they would hold others responsible. Issues of justice are also implied in many cognitive, emotional, and behavioral responses by others who are observing or who come to know of the victims' hardships and losses. If they consider the losses to be undeserved, they might feel outraged and blame those whom they consider responsible; they might feel sympathetic distress with the victims which might be motivating to help and support them. If they consider themselves responsible for the victims' undeserved hardships, they might feel guilty. The issue of justice is also touched when observers are blaming the victim, e.g., for having behaved carelessly (Ryan, 1971); this might be a "defensive attribution of responsibility" that is functional to avoid feelings of own vulnerability (Shaver, 1970; Walster, 1966) or to preserve the belief in a just world (Lerner, 1977, 1980).

To state injustice presupposes answers to questions such as "Are anybody's entitlements violated?", "Is anybody responsible for this?", "Is anybody to blame for this?", or "Who is responsible for restitution or compensation?". Perceiving injustice presupposes the view that another person or institution has violated justified entitlements of the victim either by action or by inaction. If losses have been incurred through the victim's own behavior and decisions, if, in other words, they have been self-inflicted, injustice is not an issue: The racing driver who suffered an accident through his own fault, the gambler who lost his money in Monte Carlo or on the stock market, the AIDS-patient who was not willing to use safe sex practices, or the heavy smoker with lung cancer, they all may not perceive their losses as unjust. Losses resulting from freely chosen risky enterprises are not conceived of as unjust, especially when the risks were anticipated and accepted in view of possible gains or pleasant experiences. At the core of injustice is the perception of a responsible agent or agency neglecting or violating the entitlements of others who, consequently, become victims.

It makes a difference, whether those who suffer losses perceive themselves as victims of blind fate, as victims of actions and decisions of others, as losers in a game, or as "victims" of their own risky actions, wrong decisions, or negligent behavior: Whenever victims perceive themselves being responsible for bad events and the subsequent outcomes, we expect feelings of guilt, shame, or self-directed anger, not, however, feelings of injustice.

To feel victimized or to perceive others being unjustly victimized, one needs (a) to identify a person, an institution, or a deity as the responsible agent; if (b) the losses are perceived as undeserved, as unfair, this agent should be blamed. Not every loss is an unjust one: Losses may also be conceived as a punishment for offences or negligence or as just compensation for undeserved advantages (in postwar Germany, for instance, an additional tax had to be paid by those owners whose property had not been destroyed during the war; these taxes were used to compensate the less fortunate who lost their property). It might also be that losses are not considered unfair when they are generally incurred or caused by legitimate legal norms that are obligatory for all similar members of society (e.g., the tax system). In the following section, the issue of injustice will first be discussed from the perspective of the victim, thereafter from the perspective of the observer.

THE PERSPECTIVE OF THE VICTIM

Risk Factors in Critical Life Events: A Reinterpretation in Terms of Injustice

Experiencing losses as unjust is an aspect that is not regularly assessed in research on critical life events. It is, however, assumed to be an important risk factor that complicates the task of coping since feelings of injustice imply additional stress. To my knowledge, there is little empirical research explicitly investigating the impact of perceived injustice on the success of coping with losses. Indirect evidence may be derived from studies which demonstrate that blaming others for having caused their losses proved to be detrimental (cf. Affleck et al., 1987; Bulman & Wortman, 1977; Rogner, Frey, & Havemann, 1987). Moreover, some well-known dimensions related to the riskiness of events may be reinterpreted in terms of justice, namely foreseeability, normativeness, and controllability of events (Montada, 1988, in press): There is empirical evidence that unexpected as well as nonnormative and uncontrollable (externally determined) events and their associated losses are more stressing and risky in terms of psychic and somatic health problems they cause (cf. Filipp & Gräser, 1982). Yet, some studies produced inconsistent results which suggest the existence of interacting and moderating factors (e.g., Stroebe & Stroebe, 1987, on the expectedness of loss of a spouse). One approach to deal with inconsistent data consists in clarifying theoretical assumptions. It is in this line that I would like to reinterpret the three aforementioned dimensions in terms of perceived injustice.

Foreseeability

Why should it be easier to avoid feelings of injustice if losses had not been unforeseeable? To give a general answer, I would like to refer to Moore (1984), who asked the old question why is there social peace during long lasting historical periods in many nations despite enormous inequalities in wealth or power. He argued that people tend to avoid feelings of injustice by justifying given life circumstances, including given inequalities, and that they tend to do this even if they are not living on the sunny side of life. They justify what they and others have and, consequently, consider themselves to be entitled to have it. However, when things are changing for the worse, especially when changes occur suddenly and unexpectedly, these entitlements are often perceived as being violated by society or by those in power, and feelings of injustice (such as moral outrage) will result as well as a readiness for protest and rebellion. Moore (1984) describes numerous historical cases where protest movements and rebellions were preceded by a rapid drop in living standards for parts of the population. Critical life events frequently imply unexpected losses and, consequently, are perceived as violations of subjectively justified entitlements.

There are further justice-related interpretations which seem appropriate in specific cases such as the following: (1) The foreseeable death of a loved one after a long-term severe illness may often be considered less unjust by the bereaved than a sudden death because it might be considered a relief from long-term pain and anxiety for the deceased, and it may take the burden of work and helplessness from the bereaved person vis-à-vis the suffering of the dying. In this case, death may not only be a loss, it might also mean some gains, which implies that there is less reason given to perceive the death as unjust. (2) In some cases, foreseeability means the awareness of risks, like in cases of dangerous sports, risky economic endeavors, dangerous surgery, or poor preparation for examinations. Whether losses or fiascos are considered undeserved depends on their perceived avoidability: The more the subject was free to avoid the risks the less unjust they will be considered. In these cases foreseeability means controllability. (3) In some cases, foreseeability means "normality." Mandatory retirement at 65 years of age may, of course, be perceived as inequitable with respect to competence and level of performance, but at least it is the social norm and insofar it is normal for all people of that age, and many others of the same age will also have to retire and lose their professional role.

Normativeness

Aside from age-graded events that imply some losses—which does not exclude the chance of gains at the same time—such as starting school, becoming a parent, taking on professional responsibilities, the empty nest situation, or retirement, there are "historically graded" events like natural or economic catastrophes, wars, and so forth that affect large parts of the population more or less, including one's own reference groups. In such cases, the experience of injustice is less likely than in cases of nonnormative events (like, for instance, crimes, accidents, diseases) that happen to single individuals or only a few persons. In these latter cases, the question "Why me?" is obvious, and perceived injustice will be more likely since there are no others similar in nature suffering the same or an even worse fate that would offer opportunities for downward comparisons. (Of course, shared fate as compared to individual fate does not always prevent every feeling of injustice: e.g., if unemployment is unequally and inequitably frequent within one group of the population, this group may—as a group—experience the allocation of jobs as unjust.)

Moreover, when a bad fate is shared by many people it is not likely that it will be explained by referring to negative attributes or false behavior of an individual victim (cf. Kelley, 1973). Derogative internal attributions ("blaming" the victim) that represent secondary unjust victimizations are more frequently expected in case of individual "nonnormal" fate.

Controllability

Losses through critical life events are not per se just or unjust. As stated above, injustice implies that another person or institution is held responsible. A person who suffers disadvantages caused by own decisions does not have a target for complaints about unjust victimization. Racing drivers who survive an accident but are left physically handicapped will not complain about injustice if they consider the accident to be their own fault or a natural risk of this sport. Kidney donors will presumably not perceive themselves as victims but rather as moral heroes as long as they were free to decide whether or not to donate one of their kidneys (and the surgeon did not make a mistake in transplanting the organ): Feelings of injustice are unlikely when losses result from voluntary engagements; one's own decisional control implies responsibility for the consequences.

Coping Strategies That Help to Avoid Feelings of Injustice

The need for justice can be satisfied by asserting and carrying through an entitlement up to a trial in court with the intention of obtaining adequate compensation for disadvantages and/or with the goal of punishing the violator. The need for justice can also be satisfied by the violator's true apologies, meaning that he/she acknowledges (a) the entitlements of the victim, (b) his/her responsibility for having violated them, and (c) his/her liability for blame (Goffman, 1971).

Moreover, there are some coping strategies that can be understood as strategies to reduce or to avoid feelings of injustice. By denying the weight of losses through attributing some responsibility to oneself, victims are able to avoid perceiving themselves as victims. Strategies such as downward comparisons, imagining that things could still be worse, looking for gains in the victimizing event, which will compensate the losses to some extent (e.g., gaining freedom by getting divorced, gaining the experience of being loved and supported, gaining self-esteem by one's high morale or one's achievements in rehabilitation), the search for a positive meaning (e.g., by reorganizing one's priorities in life): all these strategies may help to reduce feelings of injustice. Examples of such strategies are reported in the studies done by Frankl (1963), Schulz and Decker (1985), Taylor (e.g., Taylor, Wood, & Lichtman, 1983), and others.

Another strategy that can help to avoid the experience of injustice will be discussed in some detail, namely self-blame.[1] One would expect that victims of stressful life events would not burden themselves even more by objectively questionable or even unreasonable self-blame. However, evidence is reported in several studies suggesting that some victims who blamed themselves seemed to cope more successfully with their losses than others (an early discussion was provided by Wortman, 1976).

Self-Blame: Various Emotional Consequences

Bulman and Wortman (1977) are often cited for having evidenced that spinal-cord injured victims of accidents were better adjusted when they considered themselves in some way responsible for the accident. Schulz and Decker (1985) reported similar findings. Comparable results were reported for parents whose children had died of leukemia (Chodoff, Friedman, & Hamburg, 1964), people who had lost their relatives in concentration camps (Rappaport, 1971), rape victims (Burgess & Holmstrom, 1979; Janoff-Bulman, 1979; Medea & Thompson, 1974), and battered women who frequently expressed self-blame rather than outrage about their husbands' brutality (Frieze, 1979; Martin, 1978).

However, there are also contradictory findings. Rogner et al. (1987), for instance, found a poorer course of recovery in accident victims who felt their accident had been avoidable. In a study of rape victims, Meyer and Taylor (1986) found self-blame negatively related to adjustment. Studies of unemployment showed self-blame to have rather dysfunctional effects compared to explaining

---

[1]*The meaning of self-blame:* What is really meant by self-blame that is usually assessed by one item asking for a rating of one's own responsibility? Is it the attribution of a causal contribution to oneself, is it the assumption of foreseeability, avoidability, intentionality, or blameworthiness? Imagine a mountaineer who falls and becomes paralyzed. Whether or not he perceives himself responsible depends on the circumstances of the accident and its foreseeability: Could he have foreseen the actual danger? Did he make an avoidable mistake? If the answer is yes, he is responsible. But even if he feels responsible, he does not have to blame himself as long as he justifies the risks with the challenges and the satisfaction this sport gave him.

What sounds like self-blame may, in fact, often be nothing but the statement: "If I had or had not done this or that, it would not have happened." Is this self-blame? Possibly not in the sense of reproaches or feelings of guilt. After every traffic accident it is easy for the victim to imagine that it would not have happened if he/she had chosen another route, or if he/she had started earlier or later, and so forth. Miller (this volume) and Mark and Folger (1984) argue that the degree of dissatisfaction or anger is higher the easier it is to imagine a better outcome. Thus, it should be less problematic to suffer an accident on one's usual way to work ("I always take this route.") or while fulfilling a duty ("I had to go there.") than during a drive to a soccer game in spite of one's wife's reproaches or inspite of a bad conscience because there was work to be done at home. Why? Carrying out routines or duties either (a) reduces one's perceived freedom of choice, or (b) offers justifications for one's decision. The first reduces one's own responsibility (carrying out routines is an excuse), the latter reduces blameworthiness (the decision made is a justified one). We have to differentiate between the concepts of causation, responsibility, and blameworthiness (cf. Montada, in press; Semin & Manstead, 1983; Shaver, 1985, and in this volume). These concepts are frequently used interchangeably when we talk about blaming oneself or blaming the victim.

one's unemployment by referring to "external" social and economical factors (Jaspars et al., 1983), at least as far as the psychological well-being was concerned (getting a job could be less likely if external factors are objectively given). Yet, evidence of different and even contradictory effects of self-blame is not surprising either. Self-blame may be associated with several different emotional responses having a different impact on adjustment. Some of the possible emotional responses are presented in Figure 8.1.

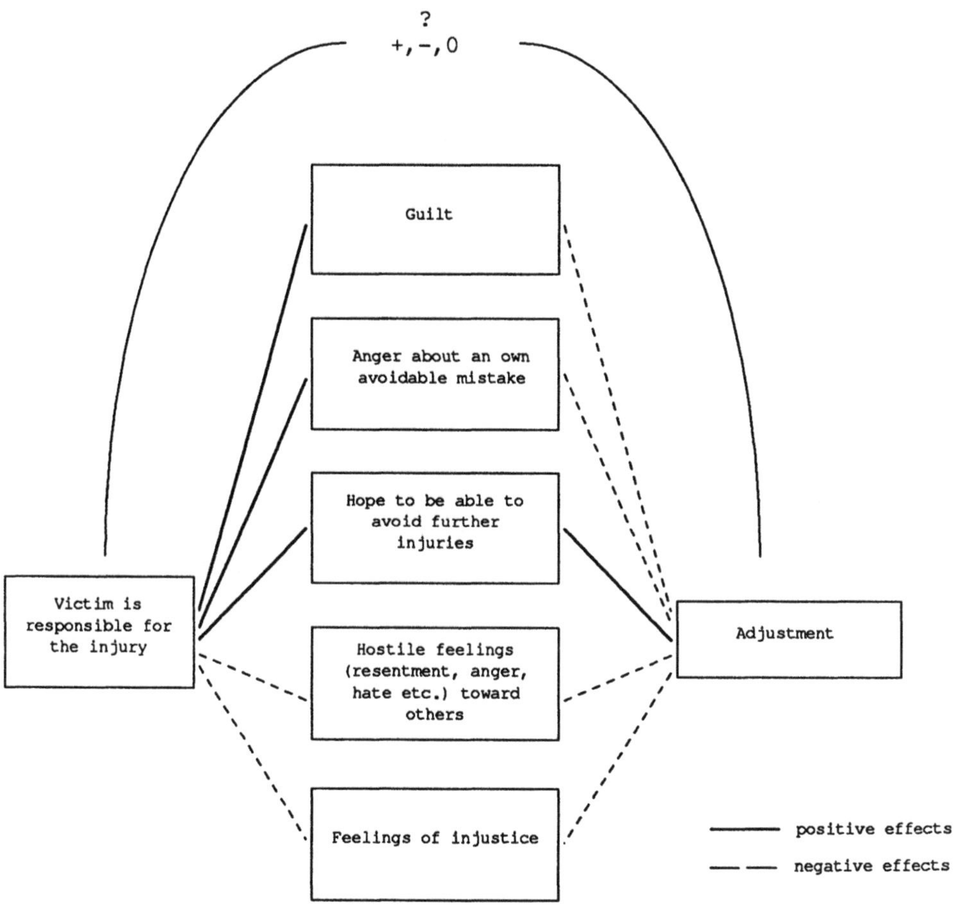

FIG. 8.1. Emotional consequences of attribution of responsibility to oneself and their impact on successful coping.

Confidence in Avoidability and Controllability

The core argument of why self-blame may have a favorable effect on coping with losses is that people who blame themselves for being victimized reinforce at the same time their belief in their ability to avoid incidents of that kind in the future. A woman who considers her carelessness a reason for having been raped may feel safer when she intends to avoid similar careless behavior in the future. Of course, in order to be functional in this sense, self-blame must be related to controllable and changeable performances or characteristics (Janoff-Bulman, 1979).

Moreover, self-blame should be expected to be functional only in cases of recurring or recurrable events. In cases like failures in examinations or victimization by crimes which may occur again, self-blame because of avoidable false behavior may be functional in the sense of mediating a feeling of safety in the future. Other events, like spinal-cord injuries caused by an accident in sports, are not likely to happen to the victim a second time. Why should self-blame be helpful or adaptive in these cases?

Self-blame may help some people to avoid viewing their own lives as being "controlled" by blind fate, a notion that is likely to undermine feelings of security and invulnerability. Chodoff et al. (1964) and Wortman (1983) suggested that some people prefer to blame themselves rather than accept being at the mercy of chance or blind fate.[2]

Avoiding Feelings of Injustice

As pointed out above, self-blame may prevent blaming others, and, consequently, the additional burden of outrage because of suffered injustice, which would constitute a secondary loss. To our knowledge, there are no studies explicitly exploring this function of self-blame. There are, however, several studies—some of them are cited above—that demonstrate negative effects on adjustment when events or losses are attributed to external agents or causes.

Guilt, Shame, and Self-Directed Anger

While self-blame may prevent feelings of helplessness, uncontrollability, and vulnerability as well as outrage against others who are held responsible, it might

[2] *Self-blame and vulnerability*: Victims of bad fate might ask how this could happen, and why it happened to them. Their belief in living safely in a just world is shattered. To become the victim of a critical life event will intensify the perceived vulnerability. People who have never suffered a heavy blow will, on the average, consider themselves rather invulnerable and safe. They underestimate the objective possibility of becoming the victim of a crime, falling dangerously ill, or suffering an accident (for an overview, see Perloff, 1987). This belief is often lost after having been victimized (e.g., Tyler, 1980). Those who previously felt particularly invulnerable to undesirable life events (Wortman, 1976) or who believed that they were able to control the dangerous situation (Scheppele & Bart, 1983) were the ones who seemed to have been especially affected. Losing the belief in invulnerability and losing controllability beliefs are possible secondary losses caused by critical life events. They may be avoided by attributing responsibility for their occurrence to oneself.

also instigate "negative" feelings such as anger about an avoidable own mistake, feelings of shame because of avoidable failure, guilt because of risky or irresponsible own behavior, or fear of being criticized by others. To "choose" self-blame "as a strategy of coping with losses" could, therefore, have unwanted side-effects. Whereas it is reasonable to assume that nonvictimized observers of critical events might regularly gain feelings of security and safety by attributing responsibility to victims, this cannot be expected to be the general effect for victims. Nonvictims want to believe "that such bad things would not happen to them," and "that everybody gets what he or she deserves" and blaming the victim may enable them to preserve these beliefs. For victims, self-blame may have the side-effects of feeling guilty, ashamed, or angry about one's avoidable mistake.

Various Effects of Self-Blame on Adjustment

What conclusions are to be drawn? As can be seen in Figure 8.1, we neither expect a direct nor unidirectional effects of self-blame (attribution of responsibility for an injury to oneself) on successful adjustment. Several emotional reactions may result from attributing responsibility to one's self, such as guilt, self-directed anger, or confidence in being able to avoid future injuries. Other emotions are more or less incompatible with self-blame, such as feelings of injustice and resentment, hate, or anger about others. We hypothesize that self-blame may protect victims from these latter feelings. Therefore, we expect negative correlations between self-blame and these emotions. On the other hand, self-blame may lead to confidence and the hope of being able to avoid a recurrence of the bad event suffered, but it may also lead to guilt or self-directed anger: We expect positive correlations between self-blame and these emotions.

The different emotional responses that may result from self-blame are expected to have different effects on adjustment. Just like self-directed anger, guilt, resentment or anger about others, and feelings of injustice are expected to interfere, the hope to be able to avoid further injury should facilitate good adjustment. Consequently, contradictory effects of self-blame will be expected depending on the resulting emotions that function as mediators between the attribution of responsibility and the success in coping (see Figure 8.1).

A Study on the Effects of Perceived Injustice and Responsibility Attributions

In a pilot study[3] with spinal-cord-injured accident victims we were able to test some of the above hypotheses. This questionnaire study included the assessment of cognitions of losses and gains through the injury in several areas of life, cognitions

[3] The data collection was done by Birgit Albs.

TABLE 8.1

Selected Correlations of Perceived Injustice of Own Fate (Spinal-Cord Injured Victims of Accidents; 34 < N < 47)

Variables	*r with Perceived Injustice*	*Variables*	*r with Perceived Injustice*
Assumed antecedents		*Assumed consequences*	
Activity leading to accident was freely chosen	-.20*	Hostile emotions toward others when thinking about the accident	.44**
Subject's causal contribution to the accident	-.16	Intrusive "hot thoughts" about others when thinking about the accident	.39**
Subject's behavior was risky and unresponsible	-.30	Guilt	.08
Subject's responsibility for the injury	-.30**	Mastering of losses (compared with others)	-.50***
Others' causal contribution to the accident	.11	Contentment with own accomplishments in various areas of life after the accident	-.49***
Others' responsibility for the injury	.21	Emotional balance in various areas of life after the injury (mean scores)	-.28**
Others' behavior was risky and unresponsible	.15	Envy of healthy others with respect to various areas of life (mean scores)	.46***
		Sadness when thinking about various areas of life (mean scores)	.62**

* $p < .10$; ** $p < .05$; *** $p < .01$

of the causation of the accident, appraisals of the responsibility (foreseeability, avoidability) for the accident (the victim him- or herself, other people, technical defects, society, fate, or bad luck), for the spinal-cord injury (again the victim him- or herself, the person causing the accident, helpers, medical staff), appraisals of one's own behavior and the behavior of others while the accident happened (e.g., risky, irresponsible, careless vs. cautious, thoughtful), appraisals of the initiation of the activity that led to the accident (Did it happen while performing a duty, a routine, or on the occasion of a freely chosen activity?), and appraisals of the injustice concerning one's fate.

Furthermore, we assessed the frequency of emotional reactions when thinking about one's own behavior during the accident (e.g., anxiety, anger, guilt, contentment) or when thinking about the behavior of others (e.g., anxiety, resentment, hate, helplessness). Another measure was the frequency of uncontrollable intrusive "hot" thoughts (a) about one's own behavior during the accident and (b) about the behavior of others who were held responsible for the injury.

Finally, we assessed several indicators of adjustment. A first measure was the mean self-rated mastering of the losses experienced in several areas of life (close relationships, sexuality, job, hobbies, social status, financial situation, and so forth). Other measures were the mean self-rated intensity of several emotions when thinking about the actual life situation as a handicapped person with respect to the mentioned areas of life: sadness, anxiety, contentment with one's own achievements, pride in these achievements, resentment of others, envy of nonhandicapped persons, shame, and mental balance. Some emotions were considered to indicate good adjustment (contentment, pride, mental balance), others to indicate poor adjustment (sadness, anxiety, envy, resentment, and shame). In this chapter, mastering losses, contentment, and mental balance were selected as indicators of good adjustment, envy and sadness as indicators of poor adjustment.

The sample: The study was conducted with 48 subjects, 34 were male and 14 were female. Their age ranged from 19 to 66, with a mean of 39.8 years. Seventeen subjects lived together with a partner, 8 were divorced, and 2 were widowed. Seventeen had children, 11 had a job, 12 were on retirement pensions, and 4 were students; 35 had a job before the accident happened, 25 of them were no longer able to work in their former job. Twenty-eight subjects suffered traffic accidents, 8 had work accidents, and 4 were injured in sports. All accidents happened at least two years before the assessment, the mean interval since the accident was 15.4 years.

Perceived Injustice and Successful Coping

The first question concerned antecedents of the perceived injustice of one's fate and the impact of this appraisal on adjustment (Table 8.1). Correlations with the adjustment criteria were as expected: negative to all three selected criteria of successful adjustment (mastering of losses, contentment, and mental balance), positive to the criteria of poor adjustment (sadness and envy of nonhandicapped people). Perceived injustice has a negative impact on adjustment, indicating that it might possibly mean an additional stress to cope with.

The relations of perceived injustice to attributions of responsibility were as expected, too: negative to variables representing own responsibility of the subjects, and positive (not significant) to variables indicating responsibility of others for the accident or the injury (Table 8.1, first part). This is corroborated by the fact that perceived injustice was positively related to hostile emotions toward others – implying attributions of responsibility to them – and to intrusive "hot" thoughts about them (Table 8.1, second part).

Self-Blame and Successful Adjustment

The second question concerned the impact of self-blame on successful adjustment. We assessed several variables belonging to the broad semantic category of "self-blame"[4] (subject's causal contributions to the accident, subject's responsibility for the injury, riskiness, and irresponsibility of subject's behavior): None of these appraisals was correlated positively to any criterion of good adjustment (see Table 8.2, first part). This was expected considering the hypothesis that attribution of responsibility to oneself may have divergent effects on coping depending on the emotions aroused. Consequently, emotional responses should be the better predictors of adjustment.

Emotional Reactions to the Accident and Successful Adjustment

Table 8.2 (second part) shows the correlations of two emotions (guilt and hostile feelings toward others) with five criteria of adjustment: Both are negatively correlated with indicators of successful adjustment, and they are positively correlated with sadness and envy indicating poor adjustment. In a multiple regression analysis, both guilt and hostile feelings toward others contribute significantly to the prediction of good (negative effects) respectively poor adjustment (positive effects). The proportion of the explained variance of the criteria accounted for the emotions is substantial (Table 8.3). The data are compatible with the view that these negative emotions interfere with successful coping. This is further corroborated by the fact that emotionally loaded "hot" intrusive (assumedly negative) thoughts about

[4]*Problematic assessment of self-blame*: However, it is not easy to assess the concepts of causality, responsibility, and blameworthiness differentially. In two of our studies (Albs, 1989; Maes & Montada, in press), it became obvious that the majority of subjects was not able to exactly comprehend the conceptual differences between the terms causality, responsibility, and blameworthiness in a juridical sense, and, therefore, they were not able to make consistent distinctions between these concepts. They seem to use them interchangeably, which can be seen in scaleability analyses and the patterns of interrelationships. Until now, we have not yet solved the problem of adequate assessment (or induction) of these concepts. There are, however, good reasons to assume that in social interactions and communications, most subjects make these distinctions: When they are blamed they use excuses and justifications, while they are not able to distinguish and use correctly the abstract terms causality, responsibility, or blameworthiness.

TABLE 8.2

Prediction of Coping With Losses: Zero-Order Correlations Between Five Criteria of Adjustment and Twelve Predictors (34 < N < 47)

Predictors	*Criteria of adjustment*				
	Mastering of losses	*Contentment with own accomplish-ments*	*Emo-tional balance*	*Envy of healthy others*	*Sadness*
Attribution of causation and responsibility					
Subject´s causal contributions to the accident	-.33**	-.28**	-.27**	.09	.17
Subject´s behavior was risky and irresponsible	-.11	.01	-.08	-.09	.01
Subject´s responsibility for the injury	-.10	-.04	-.17	.10	.09
Others´ causal contributions to the accident	.23*	.15	.03	-.10	-.28
Others´ responsibility for the injury	.13	-.00	-.07	.09	-.09
Others´ behavior was risky and irresponsible	.04	-.18	-.19	.16	.04
Emotions					
Guilt feelings	-.36**	-.30**	-.40***	.49***	.42***
Hostile emotions toward others (hate, anger, ...; mean scores)	-.38**	-.36**	-.20	.27*	.26*

(continued)

TABLE 8.2

(continued)

Predictors	*Criteria of adjustment*				
	Mastering of losses	*Contentment with own accomplish-ments*	*Emo-tional balance*	*Envy of healthy others*	*Sadness*
Emotionally loaded intrusive thoughts					
Intrusive "hot" thoughts about oneself when thinking about the accident	-.32**	-.34***	-.35***	.33**	.33**
Intrusive "hot" thoughts about others when thinking about the accident	-.42***	-.41***	-.16	.23*	.32**

* $p < .10$; ** $p < .05$; *** $p < .01$

oneself and about others are both negatively correlated with criteria of successful adjustment (Table 8.2, third part). Overall, in addition to perceived injustice (Table 8.1), it is the lack of negative emotions and intrusive emotional thoughts that predicts successful adjustment; it is not (directly) the attribution of responsibility.

Attribution of Responsibility, Emotions, and Adjustment

Emotions with similar effects on adjustment may imply different attributions of responsibility: Both guilt and hostile feelings toward others have negative effects on adjustment but guilt, conceptually, implies self-blame (and is expected to have negative correlations to blaming others), while the reverse pattern is expected for hostile feelings. Table 8.4 shows the empirical results: Guilt is positively correlated with indicators of subject's own responsibility ("self-blame"), and negatively with responsibility to others. The opposite pattern was found for hostile feelings toward others.

Thus, guilt and hostility have similar (negative) effects on adjustment but dissimilar (opposite) relations to responsibility attributions. Consequently, contra-

TABLE 8.3

Multiple Regressions From Five Criteria of Adjustment on the Emotions Guilt and Hostile Feelings Toward Others (36 < N < 48)

Predictors	*Criteria of adjustment*				
	Mastering of losses	*Contentment with own accomplish-ments*	*Emo-tional balance*	*Envy of healthy others*	*Sadness*
Guilt					
r	-.36	-.30	-.40	.48	.42
beta	-.44	-.37	-.40	.55	.47
b	-.29	-.25	-.29	.49	.41
F_b	7.67**	4.99*	5.54*	12.95**	8.46**
R^2_{change}	.18	.13	.16	.24	.17
Hostile Feelings toward others					
r	-.38	-.36		.27	.28
beta	-.45	-.43		.36	.34
b	-.43	-.39		.46	.41
F_b	8.26**	6.67*	n.s.[a]	5.72*	4.30*
R^2_{change}	.14	.13		.13	.11
R^2	.33	.26	.16	.37	.28
F_{total}	6.82**	5.00*	5.54*	8.11**	5.52**

[a]beta = .27; p >.10

TABLE 8.4

Selected Correlates of Selected Emotions of Spinal-Cord Injured Victims When Thinking About Their Accident (34 < N < 47)

Assumed antecedents	*Emotions*
Guilt feelings when thinking about the accident	
Subject's causal contributions to the accident	.54***
Subject's behavior was risky and irresponsible	.23*
Subject's responsibility for the injury	.55***
Others' causal contributions to the accident	-.53***
Others' responsibility for the injury	-.38**
Others' behavior was risky and irresponsible	-.05
Hostile emotions (hate, anger, resentment, rage) toward others when thinking about the accident (mean scores)	
Subject's causal contributions to the accident	.02
Subject's behavior was risky and irresponsible	.13
Subject's responsibility for the injury	-.34**
Others' causal contributions to the accident	.32**
Others' responsibility for the injury	.41**
Others' behavior was risky and irresponsible	.40***

* $p < .10$; ** $p < .05$; *** $p < .01$

dictory effects of the same responsibility attributions on adjustment are to be expected depending on the emotion aroused (see Figure 8.1). The overall bivariate correlations between responsibility attributions (including self-blame) and adjustment should, consequently, be low. This expectation is empirically supported (see Table 8.2, first part). Thus, there are conceptual and empirical arguments for basing predictions of adjustment preferentially on the emotional responses and not directly on self-blame or other appraisals of responsibility.

THE OBSERVER PERSPECTIVE

While "self-blame" does not reliably help the victims to cope more successfully with their problems and losses, there is evidence that it does reliably help bystanders to cope with observed victimization. The possible reasons for this were briefly outlined above. Attributing responsibility to the victim helps to avoid cognitions and feelings of injustice, it helps to preserve the belief in a just world (Lerner, 1977), and it helps to preserve the notion of invulnerability as long as the victimization of others is perceived as self-inflicted and avoidable. In this sense, blaming the victim may have defensive functions (Shaver, 1970). What is defended? It appears to be the belief in justice, the belief in one's own invulnerability, and perhaps the belief in the ability to control one's own fate. Data from several of our studies fit well into this conceptual scheme. Data from two of these will be reported here.

Blaming the Victim and Belief in a Just and Controllable World

In the *first study*, subjects rated the responsibilities of various agents or agencies for five categories of events: loss of job, lung cancer, colonic cancer, leukemia, and traffic accidents. They were asked to what percentages of all cases of each category they thought the main responsibility was to be attributed (a) to the victims themselves, (b) to other persons, (c) to the society, (d) to the victims' fates, or (e) to bad luck. Thus, each of the five "agents" could be rated for each event category from 0% to 100%. The interindividual differences in these ratings were included in a broad set of cognitive, emotional, and motivational variables, a few of which will be mentioned here (Maes & Montada, in press).

The sample: The study was conducted with 126 subjects (48% male, 52% female). Age ranged from 17 to 81, with a mean of 34 years. Higher educational and professional levels were somewhat overrepresented.

The results demonstrated that the attribution of responsibility varied with the particular event category (corresponding roughly to the actual common sense views of its controllability), but they also suggested to assume interindividually varying "dispositions" to attribute responsibilities to one of the "agents" across various event categories. Some subjects had a higher tendency to attribute responsibility consistently across event categories while others tended to attribute less responsibility to the victim than the average.

Of particular interest here is the question whether attributions of responsibility to the victims serve as "defensive" functions. For each of the event categories, the subjects had to rate preformulated thoughts and emotional responses when thinking about them. Ratings were made on 6-point scales with the end points of 1 = *that is exactly what I am feeling or thinking* to 6 = *that is not at all what I am feeling or thinking*. The mean ratings of several thoughts and emotions may be used as indicators regarding the effect of responsibility attributions; low successful blaming the victims, for instance, is a "defensive" coping strategy.

As can be seen from Table 8.5, the tendency to blame the victim is positively correlated with optimism, perceived invulnerability, and confidence in being able to master such an event; it is negatively correlated with helplessness and—yet not significantly—with resentment.

These correlations fit well to the defensive attribution hypothesis: Subjects who blame the victim feel more invulnerable, more optimistic, more confident, and less helpless. Furthermore, they tend to experience less resentment toward others (representing feelings of injustice and implying the tendency to blame others who are responsible for the events). For the sake of comparison, the correlations between attributions of responsibility to society, bad luck, and these thoughts and emotions are listed in Table 8.5. Both of these attributions have different patterns of correlations that are mostly insignificant.

Blaming the victim was positively correlated with the belief in a just world (measured with a newly developed scale). The result supports the hypothesis that

TABLE 8.5

Selected Correlates of Attribution of Responsibility for Bad Events to the Victim as Compared to Society or Bad Luck: Scores Aggregated Over Five Kinds of Bad Events (Job Loss, Three Categories of Cancer, Traffic Accident); from Maes, J. and Montada, L. (1989); 31 < N < 124.

Variable	*Responsibility Attributed to*		
	Victim	*Society*	*Bad Luck*
- Helplessness	-.34*	.01	.02
- Optimism	.35*	-.29*	-.02
- Invulnerability	.22*	-.14	.08
- Confidence in the ability to cope with	.43**	-.16	.13
- Perceived ability to avoid the bad event	.30**	-.19	-.23**
- Resentment	-.18	.18	-.01
- Belief in just world	.30*	-.08	.36*

* = p < .05

** = p < .01

the attribution of responsibility to the victim is motivated by the tendency to preserve one's belief in justice. Blaming the victim is also positively correlated with the conviction that one is able to avoid the bad event. To maintain a firm belief in the controllability of one's fate might be another motive which disposes one to blame the victims. Though the data are compatible with the casual hypothesis that justice and controllability beliefs motivate responsibility attributions they are not adequate enough to test.

Blaming the Victim, Perceived Injustice, and Prosocial Engagements

The *second study* focused on the prediction of existential guilt and further emotional reactions (sympathy, moral outrage, anger about the disadvantaged, fear of losing one's own advantages, and others) when confronted with the problems and needs of three groups of socially disadvantaged people: the unemployed, foreign (Turkish) guest workers, and poor people in the developing countries (see also Montada & Schneider, 1989). As potential predictors of emotional reactions we assessed (a) cognitions of injustice, (b) cognitions of responsibility for the existence (e.g., self-infliction by the disadvantaged) and (c) for the reduction of disadvantages (e.g., the subject, the state, the economy), (d) views on principles of distributive justice (e.g., the equity principle and the need principle), (e) the belief in a just world (assessed with both a general scale and a problem-specific scale, the items of which were concerned with the problems of the three groups of disadvantaged persons), and (f) social attitudes toward the disadvantaged. Moreover, several categories of readiness for prosocial commitments to aid the disadvantaged were assessed as potential consequences of emotional reactions.

The sample: The study was done with a sample of 865 subjects all of whom had a relatively privileged status with respect to education, wealth, or social security; 59% were male, 41% female. The age of the subjects ranged from 18 to 86, with a mean of 36 years.

Table 8.6 shows zero-order correlations of perceived injustice relating to the problems and needs of the disadvantaged. It proved to be substantially correlated with three prosocial emotions (existential guilt, moral outrage, sympathy with the disadvantaged), with self-felt responsibility to help the disadvantaged, and with readiness to engage in prosocial acts (ranging from caritative support to political activities). Thus, the perception of injustice seems to instigate altruistic motivations. Who are they, the people who perceive the disadvantages of others as unjust and undeserved? As can be seen from Table 8.6 they are those who prefer the need principle of allocation, reject the equity principle, and do not believe that the world is just (see Table 8.6).

In addition to the zero-order correlations multiple regression analyses were computed which support the theoretical path model shown in Figure 8.2. According to this model, the prosocial emotions moral outrage and existential guilt both show positive paths to prosocial commitments. Empirically, two of the more distal predictors (view of the need principle and positive social attitudes) have not only indirect but also direct effects on prosocial commitments.

Another line of analyses focused on the concept of blaming the victims for having self-inflicted their problems and needs (Montada, Schneider, & Meissner, 1988). The zero-order correlations represented in Table 8.6. evidence that blaming the disadvantaged covaries negatively with perceived injustice and that these two variables have just opposite relations to the other variables: Blaming the disadvantaged covaries with anger about them, with the belief in a just world, with the acceptance of the equity principle of allocation, and with negative social attitudes toward them. It is negatively related to the acceptance of the need principle of allocation, to the three prosocial emotions under study (existential guilt, sympathy, and moral outrage on unjust disadvantages), and it is negatively correlated with self-felt responsibility for the disadvantaged and with readiness to help them improve their situation.

TABLE 8.6

Selected Correlates of Perceived Self-Infliction of Misery and Perceived Injustice of Disadvantages for Several Categories of Needy People (Unemployed People, Turkish Guest Workers, Poor People in the Developing Countries; Bivariate Zero Order Correlations; 862 < N < 797; p < .01).

Correlates	*Perceived Injustice*	*Perceived Self-Infliction*
	*r**	*r**
Social emotions		
Existential guilt	.50	-.20
Moral outrage	.63	-.31
Sympathy	.57	-.20
Anger about the disadvantaged	-.37	.81
Fear of losing one´s advantages	.13	.08*

(continued)

TABLE 8.6
(continued)

Correlates	*Perceived Injustice* r^*	*Perceived Self-Infliction* r^*
Prosocial behavior		
Felt own responsibility to help reduce the disadvantages	.61	-.33
Readiness for prosocial commitments	.45	-.20
Justice-related background variables		
Belief in just world		
- general scale	-.19	.39
- specific scale	-.45	.67
View of the equity principle	-.42	.74
View of the need principle	.63	-.38
Social attitudes toward disadvantaged persons		
Positive attitudes	.44	-.33
Negative attitudes	-.38	.48
Perceived self-infliction	-.42	1.00
Perceived injustice	1.00	-.42

* $p > .01$

These findings are consistent with the following hypotheses: Blaming the less fortunate for having self-inflicted their existing problems and needs is functional for preserving belief in a just world because in cases of self-infliction the issue of justice will not be raised at all. Of course, the best arguments for blaming the

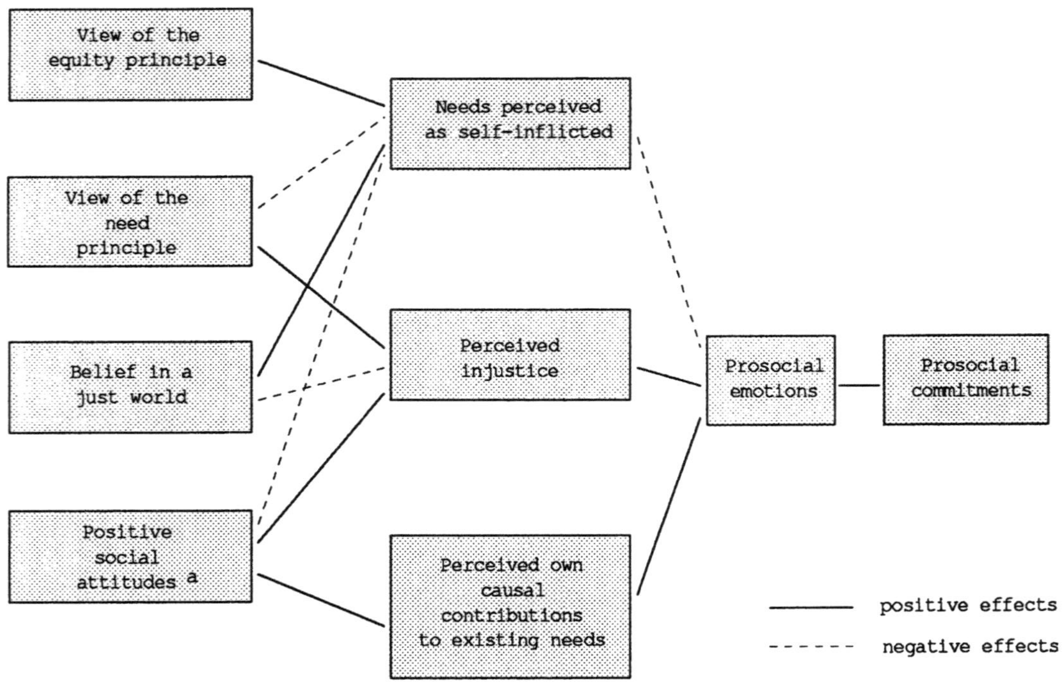

[a] Paths of negative social attitudes have exactly opposite signs. They are omitted to avoid confusion through an overload of paths.

FIG. 8.2. Theoretical path model of variables related to perceived injustice.

disadvantaged are provided by the equity principle, e.g., "The disadvantaged have not worked hard enough." Blaming for self-infliction frequently takes the form of angry reproaches addressed to the victims and interferes with prosocial emotions and accepting responsibility for helping them.

The data fit the interpretation based upon the justice motive theory closely. They offer less support for the hypothesis that blaming the victims is functional for preserving or gaining belief in control over one's own fate. Our assumption was that belief in control over one's fate would lead to optimism and feelings of security and, consequently, would be represented by a lack of fear to lose one's actual advantageous situation. Therefore, we interpreted existing fears of that kind as indicators that belief in control could not be strong. If blaming the victims would have the function to gain or maintain belief in control it should be negatively correlated with fears of that kind. The data reveal, however, that fear of losing one's advantageous situation is positively—yet weakly ($p > .05$, Table 8.6)—correlated with blaming victims for self-infliction.

At first glance, this result seems to be inconsistent with the result of the Maes and Montada study described above. A closer look, however, reveals that the differences do make sense. In the present study, the needs of large (sub-)populations are addressed which may be perceived as objectively threatening those who are actually better off: The misery of the developing countries might indeed have negative consequences for the industrial nations as a whole regardless of the question who may have caused it. There are objective interconnections on a collective societal level which may nourish doubts as to whether or not individuals have control over their individual fates. Blaming the disadvantaged should prevent fear more frequently when an objective interrelatedness of the fates of victims and subjects is lacking or less obvious.

The data reported were aggregated over several categories of events, or groups of disadvantaged respectively. Yet, the category unemployment was included in both studies. With respect to this category, the results were consistent: Blaming the victim was significantly related to a lack of fear. In the line of the proposed interpretation, unemployment seems to be conceived of as individually avoidable by the majority of subjects.

In general, we have to admit that the hypothesis of fear-defensive attribution is theoretically not unequivocally related to fears and to felt security: Fear is expected to motivate "defensive" attributions of responsibility to the victims but the hypothesis does not specify at which point in time these attributions will be effective in reducing fear, or whether they will be effective at all. Therefore, a positive correlation between attributions and fears is not incompatible with the hypothesis because it is not very precise in these respects.

CONCLUSIONS

The main thesis of this chapter was that experiencing loss (as well as observing others who experience loss) often raises issues of justice that are extremely important for coping and adjustment, but that are rarely addressed explicitly in research and theory. I have attempted to bridge this gap in the literature by reinterpreting dimensions that are frequently used to explain the varying riskiness of critical life events: foreseeability, normativeness, and controllability. I have tried to argue that these three dimensions are of particular relevance for appraising a critical event as either just or unjust—the latter case being the more risky one. Furthermore, some coping strategies, such as downward comparisons and seeking a positive meaning in bad events, were interpreted as attempts to avoid feelings of injustice.

Special attention was given to the phenomenon of self-blame to clarify its impact (a) on perceived injustice, (b) on recovery and adjustment. It was argued that self-blame may be related to various emotions, and that it may have divergent effects on adjustment depending on which emotions had been evoked. Some emotions are related positively to self-blame, such as guilt, anger about an avoidable own mistake, and confidence concerning avoidability of such events in the future. Some are related negatively to self-blame, such as feelings of injustice, resentment, or other kinds of hostility toward others. Self-blame may contribute to successful adjustment whenever it is associated with confidence in the future, or when it helps to avoid feelings of injustice or hostile emotions toward others. On the other hand, self-blame will be rather dysfunctional when it is associated with guilt or anger about an avoidable own mistake. Therefore, the effects of self-blame on the experience of stress and loss and on adjustment my vary across incidents. We do not know which the conditions are that moderate the effects, but we would suggest to look at emotional responses to stress and losses. Several emotions imply attributions of responsibility, but they are more reliably related to adjustment than these.

The effects of blaming the victim are less ambiguous *from the perspective of observers*: It may help observers to avoid feelings of injustice, hostility toward others, and guilt, and it may help observers to maintain or gain the belief that they themselves will be able to avoid victimization or to master stressful events. Moreover, blaming the victim may help to deny prosocial responsibility for the victims: Whereas observers who perceive victims as suffering an undeserved fate or harm tend to help and support them, observers who judge the victims' needs to be self-inflicted will not be disposed to engage in altruistic activities.

Empirical evidence from three studies was reported that corroborates these arguments. In the first of the studies the *perspective of the victims* was explored. The results show that accident victims with spinal-cord injuries who perceive their lot as unjust do not cope so well with their fate. Furthermore, "self-blame" (measured by various variables, e.g., perceiving own causal contributions to the accident, perceiving the event as foreseeable and avoidable, appraising one's own behavior during the accident as risky and irresponsible) proved not to be correlated with good or poor adjustment. However, self-blame was correlated with emotional responses of patients when thinking about the accident: positively to guilt and negatively to hostile emotions toward others. Both guilt and hostile emotions toward others have negative effects on adjustment (e.g., mastering of losses, contentment with own accomplishments, emotional balance). This is also true for self-directed anger, which is not so much predicted by indicators of self-blame as by the fact of whether or not the activity having led to the accident was freely chosen.

Taken together, the main hypotheses prove to be corroborated with regard to the role of attributions of responsibility from the perspective of the victim. Taken into account that self-blame does yield divergent effects on adjustment depending on the emotions aroused it can be better understood why the empirical evidence on the effects of self-blame as reported in the literature is so contradictory.

Two studies on the observers' perspectives were reported. Both were concerned with effects of the attribution of responsibility to the victims; the second one also considered the perceived injustice suffered by the victims. Results of the first study supported the view that in general the attribution of responsibility to the victims has positive consequences for observers in terms of feelings of invulnerability, confidence in one's own ability to master stressful events, optimism, lack of helplessness, and lack of feelings of injustice.

The results of the second study are in line with the view that attributing responsibility to the victim interferes with recognizing their fate as an unjust one, with the arousal of prosocial emotions (existential guilt, outrage, and sympathy), with taking responsibility for supporting them and with prosocial commitments. Thus, blaming the victim seems to help observers to maintain their view of a just world, to avoid being affected by the fate of victims or less fortunate people. Moreover, blaming victims can be an adequate means of gaining confidence in one's own abilities to master life's difficulties.

If critical life events (and the consequent stress and losses) are perceived as undeserved and unjust, opposite reactions can be observed: Prosocial emotions arise, and the willingness to engage in prosocial activities to support the victims or the less fortunate is enhanced.

One final remark concerns the focus on emotions in the analysis of critical life events and coping with them: The basic assumption is that focusing on emotions like self-directed anger, resentment about others, guilt, envy, and so forth is more informative than focusing on stress. While it is true that intense emotions are frequently associated with stress, their assessment informs about the type of problem subjects encounter which is not the case when we merely assess stress. Cognitive models of emotions explicate the types of problems that evoke a specific emotion. Components of such models may be, for instance, the goals of subjects, their expectations, aspirations, entitlements, attributions of causality and responsibility, normative beliefs, and so forth (cf. Epstein, 1984; Frijda, 1987; Montada, in press; Scherer 1984; Smith & Ellsworth, 1985; Solomon, 1976). Resentment, for instance, implies or presupposes at least the following appraisals:

(1) Another person or institution has hurt or is hurting a legal or moral norm, a role-bound obligation, or an entitlement of the subject (or of a third person who the subject sympathizes with).

(2) The actual or potential consequences for the victim are not deserved.

(3) The subject attributes responsibility (agency) to the perpetrator, meaning the perpetrator is assumed to have (had) decisional control over his or her actions or omissions.

(4) The subject does not perceive or accept any reasons that justify the deviant act.

Starting from these appraisals that constitute resentment further hypotheses concerning the conditions for their occurrence may be generated concerning, for instance, (a) the development and legitimation of violated norms and entitlements, (b) beliefs about excuses from responsibility such as mental illnesses, youth, inherited traits, extreme affective states, drugs, authority of a commanding third person, and so forth, (c) biases in attributing responsibility like prejudices against the perpetrator or existing identity relationships with the victim (if the subject him- or herself is not the victim). Such hypotheses may be tested empirically.

Cognitive models of emotions not only offer structural schemes for grasping the problems a subject encounters, they also offer ideas and goals for intervention or coping, such as (a) changing normative beliefs, (b) putting entitlements into perspective, (c) changing attitudes toward the resented person or the victim, (d) seriously testing possible excuses the perpetrator might have or justifications for the deviant act, (e) differentiating levels of responsibility, for instance, by distinguishing between intended, not intended, foreseen, or merely foreseeable outcomes, and so forth. All these and more could be used within a blame reduction program supplementing Shaver's self-blame inoculation program (Shaver, this volume).

Emotions might turn into stress when subjects do not have sufficient resources and competences to cope with them successfully. I think we waste information if the kind of problem represented in emotions (more precisely: in the cognitive models of emotions) is not identified. Stress is conceptualized as a nonspecific reaction to dangers or losses. A more precise specification of the problem offers information relevant to explanation, prediction, and intervention. Stress may result from fears, rage, hate, guilt, jealousy, envy, shame, bitterness, and so forth. The quantitative amount of stress may be similar for different stressful problems generating different emotions. The problems themselves are certainly not similar with respect to their structure and with respect to adequate strategies of coping or intervention. Therefore, I call for a focus on emotions whenever we are dealing with critical life events and their associated losses (cf. Thoits, 1984).

The empirical studies reported in this chapter demonstrate that it is useful to specify the "quality" of stress. Specific emotional responses are reliably related to subjects' views and appraisals and they are meaningfully related to success or failure in coping with losses. Thus, focusing emotions seems to be not only of theoretical but also of practical significance. What is usually called "emotion oriented coping" does, of course, not cover the whole scope of possibilities in dealing with the problems that cause an emotional response.

REFERENCES

Affleck, G., Tennen, H., Croog, S., & Levine, S. (1987). Causal attribution, perceived benefits, and morbidity after a heart attack: An 8-year study. *Journal of Consulting and Clinical Psychology, 55*, 29-35.

Albs, B. (1989). *Emotionale Auseinandersetzung mit unfallbedingter Querschnittslähmung.* Unveröffentlichte Diplomarbeit, Universität Trier.

Bulman, R. J., & Wortman, C. B. (1977). Attributions of blame and coping in the "real world": Severe accident victims react to their lot. *Journal of Personality and Social Psychology, 35*, 351-363.

Burgess, A. W., & Holmstrom, L. L. (1979). Adaptive strategies and recovery from rape. *American Journal of Psychiatry, 136*, 1278-1282.

Chodoff, P., Friedman, S. B., & Hamburg, D. A. (1964). Stress, defense, and coping behavior: Observations in parents of children with malignant diseases. *American Journal of Psychiatry, 120*, 743-749.

Epstein, S. (1984). Controversial issues in emotion theory. In P. Shaver (Ed.), *Review of personality and social psychology* (pp. 64-88). Beverly Hills, CA: Sage.

Filipp, S.-H., & Gräser, H. (1982). Psychologische Prävention im Umfeld kritischer Lebensereignisse. In J. Brandtstädter & A. von Eye (Eds.), *Psychologische Prävention* (pp. 155-195). Bern: Huber.

Frankl, U. E. (1963). *Man's search for meaning*. New York: Washington Square Press.

Frieze, I. H. (1979). Perceptions of battered wives. In I. H. Frieze, D. Bar-Tal, & J. S. Carroll (Eds.), *New approaches to social problems: Applications of attribution theory* (pp. 79-108). San Francisco, CA: Jossey-Bass.

Frijda, N. (1987). Emotion, cognitive structure, and action tendency. *Cognition and Emotion, 1*, 115-143.

Goffman, E. (1971). *Relations in public.* Harmondsworth: Penguin.

Janoff-Bulman, R. (1979). Characterological vs. behavioral self-blame: Inquiries into depression and rape. *Journal of Personality and Social Psychology, 37*, 1798-1809.

Jaspars, J., Fincham, F., & Hewstone, M. (1983). *Attribution theory and research: Conceptual, developmental, and social dimensions.* London: Academic Press.

Kelley, H. H. (1973). The process of causal attribution. *American Psychologist, 28*, 107-128.

Lerner, M. J. (1977). The justice motive: Some hypotheses as to its origins and forms. *Journal of Personality, 40*, 1-32.

Lerner, M. J. (1980). *The belief in a just world: A fundamental delusion.* New York: Plenum.

Lerner, M. J., & Simmons, C. H. (1966). The observer's reaction to the "innocent victim": Compassion or rejection? *Journal of Personality and Social Psychology, 4*, 203-210.

Maes, J., & Montada, L. (in press). Verantwortlichkeit für "Schicksalsschläge": Eine Pilotstudie. *Psychologische Beiträge.*

Mark, M. M., & Folger, R. (1984). Responses to relative deprivation: A conceptual framework. In P. Shaver (Ed.), *Review of personality and social psychology* (Vol. 5, pp. 192-218). Beverly Hills, CA: Sage.

Martin, D. (1978). Battered women: Society's problem. In J. R. Chapman & M. Gates (Eds.), *The victimization of women.* Beverly Hills, CA: Sage.

Medea, A., & Thompson, K. (1974). *Against rape*. New York: Farrar, Straus, Girous.

Meyer, C. B., & Taylor, S. E. (1986). Adjustment to rape. *Journal of Personality and Social Psychology, 50*, 1226-1234.

Meyer, J. P., & Mulherin, A. (1980). From attribution to helping: An analysis of the mediating effects of affect and expectancy. *Journal of Personality and Social Psychology, 39*, 201-210.

Montada, L. (1988). Die Bewältigung von "Schicksalsschlägen"—erlebte Ungerechtigkeit und wahrgenommene Verantwortlichkeit. *Schweizerische Zeitschrift für Psychologie, 47*, 203-216.

Montada, L. (in press). Life stress, injustice, and the question "Who is responsible?". In H. Steensma & R. Vermunt (Eds.), *Social justice in human relations. II. Psychological and societal consequences of justice and injustice*. New York: Plenum.

Montada, L., & Schneider, A. (1989). Justice beliefs and emotional reactions toward disadvantaged and victimized people. *Social Justice Research, 3*, 313-344.

Montada, L., Schneider, A., & Meissner, A. (1988). *Blaming the victim: Schuldvorwürfe und Abwertung*. Trier: E.S.- Bericht Nr. 8 (= Berichte aus der Arbeitsgruppe "Verantwortung, Gerechtigkeit, Moral" Nr. 49). Trier: Universität Trier, Fb I - Psychologie.

Moore, B. (1984). *Ungerechtigkeit: Die sozialen Ursachen von Unterordnung und Widerstand*. Frankfurt: Suhrkamp.

Perloff, L. (1987). Social comparison and illusions of invulnerability to negative life events. In C. R. Snyder & C. E. Ford (Eds.), *Coping with negative life events* (pp. 217 - 242). New York: Plenum.

Rappaport, E. A. (1971). "Survivor guilt." Midstream, August/September 1971, pp. 41-47. Cited after Coates, D., Wortman, C. B., & Abbey, A. (1979). Reactions to victims. In I. H. Frieze, D. Bar-Tal, & J. S. Carroll (Eds.), *New approaches to social problems* (pp. 21-52). San Francisco, CA: Jossey-Bass.

Rogner, O., Frey, D., & Havemann, D. (1987). Der Genesungsverlauf von Unfallpatienten aus kognitionspsychologischer Sicht. *Zeitschrift für Klinische Psychologie, 16*, 11-28.

Ross, M., & DiTecco, D. (1975). An attributional analysis of moral judgments. *Journal of Social Issues, 31*(3), 91-109.

Ryan, W. (1971). *Blaming the victim*. New York: Pantheon.

Scheppele, K. L., & Bart, P. B. (1983). Through women's eyes: Defining danger in the wake of sexual assault. *Journal of Social Issues, 39*(2), 63-81.

Scherer, K. R. (1984). Emotion as a multicomponent process: A model and some cross-cultural data. In P. Shaver & L. Wheeler (Eds.), *Review of personality and social psychology* (pp. 37-63). Beverly Hills, CA: Sage.

Schulz, R., & Decker, S. (1985). Long-term adjustment to physical disability: The role of social support, perceived control, and self-blame. *Journal of Personality and Social Psychology, 48*, 1162-1172.

Semin, G. R., & Manstead, A. S. R. (1983). *The accountability of conduct. A social psychological analysis*. New York: Academic Press.

Shaver, K. G. (1970). Defensive attribution: Effects of severity and relevance on the responsibility assigned for an accident. *Journal of Personality and Social Psychology, 14*, 101-113.

Shaver, K. G. (1985). *The attribution of blame: Causality, responsibility, and blameworthiness*. New York: Springer.

Shaver, K. G. (1970). Defensive attribution: Effects of severity and relevance on the responsibility assigned for an accident. *Journal of Personality and Social Psychology, 14*, 101-113.

Smith, C. A., & Ellsworth, P. C. (1985). Patterns of cognitive appraisal in emotion. *Journal of Personality and Social Psychology, 48*, 813-838.

Solomon, R. C. (1976). *The passions*. New York: Anchor Press.

Steil, J. M., & Slochover, J. (1985). The experience of injustice: Social psychological and clinical perspectives. In G. Stricker & R. H. Keisner (Eds.), *From research to clinical practice* (pp. 217-242). New York: Plenum.

Stroebe, W., & Stroebe, M. (1987). *Bereavement and health*. New York: Cambridge University Press.

Taylor, S. E. (1983). Adjustment to threatening events: A theory of cognitive adaptation. *American Psychologist, 38*, 1161-1173.

Taylor, S. E., Wood, J. V., & Lichtman, R. R. (1983). It could be worse: Selective evaluation as a

response to victimization. *Journal of Social Issues, 39*(2), 19-40.
Thoits, P. (1984). Coping, social support, and psychological outcomes. The central role of emotion. In P. Shaver (Ed.), *Review of personality and social psychology* (pp. 219-238). Beverly Hills: Sage.
Tyler, T. R. (1980). Impact of directly and indirectly experienced events: The origin of crime-related judgments and behaviors. *Journal of Personality and Social Psychology, 39*, 13-28.
Walster, E. (1966). Assignment of responsibility for an accident. *Journal of Personality and Social Psychology, 3*, 73-79.
Wortman, C. B. (1976). Causal attributions and personal control. In J. H. Harvey, W. J. Ickes, & R. F. Kidd (Eds.), *New directions in attribution research* (pp. 21-52). Hillsdale, NJ: Erlbaum.
Wortman, C. B. (1983). Coping with victimization: Conclusions and implications for future research. *Journal of Social Issues, 39*(2), 195-221.

9 Blame Avoidance: Toward an Attributional Intervention Program[1]

Kelly G. Shaver
College of William and Mary, Williamsburg

In the half-century since the pioneering work of Cannon (1935) and Selye (1936) the scientific study of stress and coping has grown exponentially. Moreover, it has thoroughly captured the public's imagination. Stress-management seminars are offered by private sector businesses and public agencies alike, controversies regarding the measurement of critical life events receive air time even on rock music stations, and vitamins are advertised as perfect dietary supplements for people who "burn the candle at both ends." When the public embraces the results of research, investigators have a duty to ensure that the findings will replicate; when the tabloids consider a problem solved, theoreticians have a duty to regard the question as open. This chapter is offered in that spirit. Stress has arrived. Our job is to make certain that coping will not be too far behind.

COGNITIVE INFLUENCES ON THE STRESS RESPONSE

Because there are two referents for the term "stress" in the literature, one originating from engineering and one originating from biobehavioral research, it is necessary to say at the outset that by "stress" I will mean the bodily *response* to demands placed on the individual (following Selye, 1976). Such demands, typically external to the

[1]Research reported in this paper was conducted by Nicolette Borek, Debra Drown, with the assistance of Sherry Hamby; their contributions are gratefully acknowledged. The proposal for a blame-inoculation technique is based on ideas developed in collaboration with Debra Drown, and a paper by Shaver and Drown (1985) describing that work in detail was presented at the Fourth International Conference on Justice and Law, Kill Devil Hills, NC, USA.

person, are then called *stressors* (Selye, 1976). It is important to note that a constant intensity stressor stimulus does not produce identical responses either in one person over time, or across people. Rather, the stress response is product of the joint influences of the stressor, the situational context in which that stressor occurs, and a number of individual difference variables (for a more detailed discussion of this position, see Cottington & House, 1987).

Several examples make this point quite clearly. People who believe an intense noise is controllable, whether or not that belief is factually correct, suffer less from continued exposure than do people who think the noise cannot be controlled (Glass & Singer, 1972). Providing thorough descriptions of physiological symptoms to be suffered lessens the discomfort associated with giving blood (Mills & Krantz, 1979). People who are given a nonthreatening attributional locus for their arousal can tolerate higher levels of pain than can people without such an alternative attribution (Nisbett & Schachter, 1966; Ross, Rodin, & Zimbardo, 1969). Although very little of this work involves "hard" physiological outcome measures, such as secretions of epinephrine, norepinephrine, or cortisol, that, too, is changing with the development of new technologies for measurement of plasma catecholamines in field settings (Dimsdale, 1987, reviews the potential, and the limitations, of such measurement procedures). For example, Dimsdale and Moss (1980) found epinephrine levels elevated over baseline among individuals who had just begun giving a public speech, but those elevations returned almost to their original level midway through the speech. This representative sample of research makes it clear that the effective stressor is heavily influenced by cognitive processes (e.g., see Baum, O'Keefe, & Davidson, 1990; Green, 1990; Norris, 1990).

COGNITIVE FACTORS IN COPING

Three Cognitive Theories

Occasionally there is advance warning that a demand is about to be placed on the person, so preparation can be part of adaptation. With or without foreknowledge, the stressor must be dealt with when it occurs. And especially in cases of adult life crises and loss experiences, the chronic psychological pain may linger long after the precipitating event. Consequently, a person's attempts to deal with stressors will encompass preparation, immediate response, and long-term adaptation. The imprint of cognitive processes is apparent in each of these areas.

The conflict-theory model of emergency decision making outlines four key issues that have implications for the effectiveness of response, should the anticipated threat materialize (Janis, 1986; Janis & Mann, 1977). First, if risks of potential danger are not seen as serious enough to warrant any protective action, complacency will leave the person unprepared. Second, if some defensive action is needed, but the most readily available choice is considered acceptable, the undiscovered weaknesses of that choice will remain unknown until too late. Third, if no acceptable plans can be hoped for, the person will defensively avoid considering the potential threat, and will, again, be unprepared. Fourth, if there is hope for a solution, but no time to deliberate among the possibilities, the resulting near panic will lead the person to take hasty action likely to be regretted later. Only if (a) risks are regarded as serious, (b) readily available but unexamined solutions are rejected, (c) there is hope for better alternatives, and (d) time to weigh these options carefully, will the person display the vigilance essential for an effective response if the danger materializes. This is a fundamentally cognitive theory, and its success in guiding interventions with surgical patients indicates the value of cognitive processes in preparing to deal with impending stressors (see a review by Janis, 1986).

No matter how carefully people plan, they will confront stressors that occur without warning. Here, too, cognition plays a role in the emotional upheaval that accompanies the stress response. Specifically, any emotional experience includes *cognitive appraisal* and *reappraisal* of one's "adaptive transactions with the environment" (Lazarus, 1986, p. 400). This theory places the individual in the role of evaluator of his or her dealings with the world, and especially with anticipated or actual threat. Appraisal involves judgments about whether a particular transaction (a) is relevant to well-being, (b) has already produced harm that requires amelioration, (c) may produce such harm in the future, (d) presents a challenge to be overcome, or on a more hopeful note (e) forecasts a positive outcome (Lazarus, 1986; Lazarus & Folkman, 1984). Reappraisal is included in this model to indicate that the person/environment transaction is dynamic, or in the present context, subject to re-evaluation after the stressor has had its initial impact. Again, this highly cognitive theory boasts a research record sufficient to indicate the value of cognition in dealing with ongoing stressors.

Finally, cognitive processes are part of dealing with the aftereffects of an acute stressor now gone, or with the ongoing effects of a chronic stressor still present. A theory of cognitive adaptation to stressors with lingering effects, such as cancer, has been proposed that "rests fundamentally upon the ability to form and maintain a set of illusions" (Taylor, 1983, p. 1161). Such illusions are not deemed to be in opposition to facts, but rather are interpretations that concentrate on three general themes. The first theme is a search for meaning in the experience that involves attributional judgments of causality. The second theme is the attempt to regain a sense of mastery over the stressor in particular and one's life in general. Especially noteworthy in this regard is the high proportion of patients who believe that they can keep the cancer from recurring. The third theme in adjustment is the effort to restore self-worth through a process of self-enhancement, that often involves social comparison.

Control and Responsibility

Whether the person's objective is to prepare for an impending threat, to deal with an ongoing stressor, or to contend with the lasting consequences of a crisis or loss, the cognitive processes are directed at regaining control over the events that affect one's well-being. The psychological state of vigilance is of no use unless actions can take advantage of revealed solutions. Appraisal of an ongoing stressor serves a purpose only if there is some opportunity to ameliorate the harm. An illusion of mastery can be preserved, and can be helpful, only if in some measure it is justified by the facts.

One review of 14 diverse descriptions of ways to deal with trauma argues that all of these formulations can productively be characterized as involving approach and avoidance (Roth & Cohen, 1986). Among those included in the analysis were the conflict-theory model and cognitive appraisal model as discussed above, and several more personological variables such as repression-sensitization (Byrne, 1964), blunting-monitoring (Miller, 1980, 1987), and reducers-augmenters (Petrie, 1978). Roth and Cohen (1986) argue that each of these notions embodies factors that predispose the person either to avoid thinking about, and dealing with, the stressor, or to engage in it actively.

The approach-avoidance categorization serves the valuable heuristic purpose of illustrating similarities among formulations that previously have been known principally for their differences. The analysis can be pushed one step further, to suggest that control is the motivation that drives many approaches. For example, "alertness," "careful planning," "attending to warning signals," "vigilance," "taking self-responsibility," and "integration of threat into the self-system" involve or imply direct action to deal with the stressor.

What has not yet been widely acknowledged is that along with control which most writers endow with therapeutic benefits comes *responsibility* for the outcome. A person who, by whatever description, avoids acknowledging the possibility of stressor amelioration can only be accused of ignorance. But a person who approaches the stressor in an attempt to control its effects can, if the effort is unsuccessful, bear the added liability for failure. The deleterious effects of the original stressor would then be augmented by the burden of culpability. Those of us who believe in the restorative powers of regaining control need to take this risk into account. Before suggesting how this might be done, there are two more matters of definition that need attention.

Stress Management

The reader will have noticed that the section on the stress response began with the customary definition of stress, but that this section has as yet not confronted the thorny problem of defining "coping." There are two problems with almost any definition. First, by whose standards should a person be judged to be coping? An analogy to practicing psychotherapy in a prison is illuminating: Should prisoners be taught to adjust to the abnormal if not inhuman conditions within the penitentiary, or should they be taught to hate the institution, the better to survive in the outside world upon release? In the present context, should a person with terminal cancer be preparing for a lengthy, painful, and institutionalized deterioration, or planning for a quick suicide? Mental health professionals certainly have an aversion to the latter, but who can say which is the better coping strategy *from the victim's perspective*?

The second problem with any definition of coping is suggested by the several cognitive theories reviewed in this section. Should preparation that permits one to avoid a stressor entirely, psychological combat that keeps the person capable despite an ongoing stressor, and social comparison that helps a victim achieve a level of self-esteem higher than the previctimization level all be described by the same term? Probably not. Even the typical dictionary definition of coping as maintaining a contest "usually on even terms *or* with success" (emphasis added) obscures a distinction most psychologists would consider important.

Perhaps a better descriptive term is *stress management*. Compared to "coping," "stress management" more plausibly incorporates preparation, contemporary response, and dealing with the chronic residue from acute episodes. Not only does this term individualize the response more closely to the stressor, it also narrows the range for the criterion. For one thing, "management" is arguably more consistent with the active quality of vigilance, attention, and mastery than is coping. For another, stressors have predictable physiological effects, effects that should be mitigated by effective stress management. Prevailing mental health doctrine then becomes secondary to "hard" physiological data; both "success" and "staying even" can be operationalized in neurochemical terms. Consequently, in the remainder of this chapter I shall speak of stress management, rather than of coping.

ELEMENTS OF CAUSALITY, RESPONSIBILITY, AND BLAMEWORTHINESS

The literature on stress and its aftermath is careful in its definitions of stress and recognizes the complexities inherent in defining coping. Unfortunately, as Shaver and Drown (1986) have noted, similar care has not generally been evident in the usage of "causality," "responsibility," and "blame." Psychology is enamored of the nonobvious, and research on stress has not been immune to this affliction. So the observation by Bulman and Wortman (1977) that "self-blame" was associated with more effective coping was too much for the field to resist. Studies with "self-blame" in the title continue to proliferate, almost without regard for the actual wording of their dependent variables. Careful examination of these dependent variables, however, reveals that the operative word may be "cause," "responsibility," or, much less frequently, "blame." It is no surprise that these diverse operational definitions have produced a literature in which the putative effects of self-blame are sometimes positive, sometimes negative, and sometimes null.

Quite apart from asking that the conceptual content of article titles, introductions, and discussion sections correspond to the operationalization of the dependent variables, one can wonder whether there is any psychologically important difference among these three terms. If the three cannot be distinguished conceptually or empirically, then their interchangeable usage presents no problem. Without repeating the argument I have made elsewhere in detail (Shaver, 1985), let me assure you that the three are conceptually distinct. After examining the notion of causality as used in the philosophy of science, and the idea of personal responsibility as used in moral philosophy, and after reviewing research and theory on the attribution of causality and responsibility, I concluded, as have others (e.g., Fincham & Jaspars, 1980), that an attribution of responsibility presupposes a prior attribution of causality. Furthermore, an attribution of blame presupposes not only a prior attribution of responsibility, but also a failure by the perceiver to accept the actor's excuse or justification for the potentially blameworthy behavior.

In this prescriptive model of the assignment of blame, causality involves the only the production of effects, through forces of nature or the actions of people. Effects of further interest to psychologists involve human agency in some form. By contrast to "the cause," which is an entity possessing an independent existence, "responsibility" is a label applied to the outcome of a process. Where causality is dichotomous, responsibility is variable and multidimensional. More responsibility will be attributed as there are increases in the actor's (a) causal contribution to production of the effect, (b) awareness of the potential consequences of the action being taken, (c) intent to bring about the occurrence (as opposed to the involuntary production of an unintended effect), (d) degree of volition (typically as indicated by lack of external coercion), and (e) appreciation of the moral wrongfulness of the action. Finally, "blame" is the attribution made after the perceiver assesses and refuses to accept the validity of the actor's justification or excuse for an action the perceiver believes was intended. Thus, blame assignment is a *disputed social judgment*.

This theory was developed to serve as a rational and prescriptive model of how blame ought to be assigned to an actor by a perceiver. It is not a description of how blame is assigned in all cases, for two reasons. First, the perceiver may not always be as attentive to the conceptual distinctions involved as is the theory. Perceivers may "blame" others for causing injury through wanton recklessness, rather than intentional action. In a legal metaphor, such perceivers would be convicting for first-degree murder a perpetrator who is technically guilty only of manslaughter. Second, perceivers may attend to the conceptual distinctions, but assign "blame" even where they know it is unwarranted, because to do so serves other psychological purposes. What the model describes is a set of conceptual terms that can provide a common language for the study of blame attribution. Without agreement on terms involved in judgments of culpability whether or not it is my terms that are adopted it will be impossible for researchers to (a) make meaningful comparisons across studies, or (b) discover the "other psychological purposes" hidden among the failures of construct validity.

What is critical, is the requirement that blame, as opposed to responsibility, be reserved for those who have acted intentionally to bring about harm. Thus what has been called "behavioral self-blame" (Janoff-Bulman, 1979) is really a combination of self-causality ("I was, after all, driving the car when the accident happened") and self-responsibility ("I should have foreseen that it was dangerous to be out alone in that place at night"). Similarly, what has been called "characterological self-blame" (Janoff- Bulman, 1979) is also not really blame, because it lacks the critical element of intentionality. In the literature on coping with crisis and loss, only the notion of "anger-in," an element of the current scoring system for the Type A Structured Interview protocol used by Dembroski and his associates, comes close to my view of behavior for which true blame might be appropriate (Dembroski & MacDougall, 1985). Some coronary heart disease patients high on *anger-in* may well engage in intentional actions that at the very least have a high probability of producing damaging side effects, if not damaging direct effects. Most victims of life crises, however, range from being unwitting to being negligent, but not intentional, participants in their victimization. I readily admit that "self-causality" does not have the attention-grabbing power of "self-blame," but the loss of seductive titles is a small price to pay for increased conceptual rigor in a cumulative science.

BLAME INOCULATION

From a social policy perspective, the crucial task is to get people who suffer stress from life crises or loss to seek assistance. There may be, as Kobasa's work suggests, individuals who are sufficiently "hardy" that they are better off managing their stress alone (e.g., Kobasa & Puccetti, 1983). But whether the particular stress-management technique chosen is physical exercise (Blumenthal & McCubbin, 1987), participation in a stress-management program at work, reliance on an informal self-help network, or the seeking of professional advice, most people would do better with some form of social support. In addition to the methodological and conceptual difficulties inherent in studying the effects of social support (see Wortman & Dunkel-Schetter, 1987), a problem insufficiently addressed concerns the stress sufferer's reluctance to seek assistance.

Blame Avoidance

The purpose of this chapter is to identify one factor that might militate against the seeking of assistance in stress management and suggest a kind of intervention that could reduce this reluctance. The argument begins with another legal analogy. Crime victims, especially rape victims, frequently suffer what is known as "secondary victimization" at the hands of the criminal justice system. Victims are forced to (a) recount their stories to police who may be unsympathetic, and to prosecutors who try to be as tough on them as defense attorneys are expected to be, (b) have control over their fate slip out of their hands as the state becomes the aggrieved party, (c) spend considerable time assisting in the investigation and prosecution, and if "fortunate," (d) confront their attackers in court, watching helplessly as the defendant is acquitted, or convicted but given a minimal sentence. No wonder that on the average in the United States some 50% of crimes go unreported.

Now, to the extent that blame assignment is the moral equivalent of a court proceeding (and the description of blame assignment as a "disputed social judgment" certainly makes that point), then people might choose to avoid settings in which responsibility and blameworthiness will be discussed. A sufferer from stress who believes that he or she might have contributed to the occurrence, even in a small way, may avoid the expected accusatory glances of others by "toughing it out alone." In part, the problem arises from a confusion of causality with responsibility with blameworthiness. What a rational theory of blame assignment can do is provide a model for teaching the distinctions to sufferers from stress. Specifically, victims can be taught that causality is the route to regaining control, but that self-*blame* is neither appropriate nor desirable. If the stress-inoculation technique employed by Meichenbaum and Novaco (1986) is any indication of likely success, giving people these cognitive tools early in their experience with the stressor could remove one of the obstacles to seeking the necessary assistance.

But special blame-attribution education is no more likely to be sought than is any other form of social support. For this reason, it must be built into the response system normally encountered by individuals who suffer stress from victimization or major life crises. Rescue squads and hospital emergency rooms, business outplacement services, rape crisis centers, and prosecuting attorneys' offices are just a few of the places that typically serve as the first point of contact for people who have experienced serious life crises. Professionals in these service agencies should be prepared so that blame-inoculation can be a routine part of their interaction with victims. This is an admittedly immodest proposal. But, to borrow a term from business, the "diffusion of innovation" is extremely rapid in the area of stress reduction. The health segments of major syndicated television programs, the health sections in most big-city newspapers, and yes, even the tabloids, can be the researcher's ally. After all, if the Hassles scale (DeLongis, Coyne, Dakof, Folkman, & Lazarus, 1982; Kanner, Coyne, Schaefer, & Lazarus, 1982) can make it to the disk jockey's patter on a rock music station, can other developments in stress reduction be far behind?

Evidence That Differentiation Can Be Taught

Before proceeding with an ambitious program of blame-inoculation research, theory, and practice, there is one fundamental question that must be answered. Can people understand the differences among causality, responsibility, and blameworthiness without a thorough grounding in philosophy or attribution research? Although past research provides mixed results on this issue,[2] I believe that with only minimal instruction people can comprehend the differences, and use them to describe stressful life events.

Let me report two studies that help make this point. The first was an investigation of the long-term effects of parental conflict and divorce (Borek & Shaver, 1988). The general question was whether problems in the parents' intimate relationship might adversely affect the child's close relationship with a dating partner or friend. The specific attributional question was whether the young adult's attribution of blame to either that person's mother or father for the occurrence of parental conflict or divorce reduces the level of intimacy attained in that young adult's own dating relationships. College students who had previously reported either substantial parental conflict or parental divorce were asked to attribute causality, responsibility, and blameworthiness to father, mother, self, and aspects of the family structure as a whole. Half of the subjects were asked to perform this attribution task with no instructions regarding causality, responsibility, and blameworthiness, whereas half of the subjects were given *one*-sentence definitions of each term.

Results overall showed that mother-blame for conflict was associated with lesser intimacy in one's own dating relationships, suggesting that both females and males still learn how to deal with others by watching their mothers, not their fathers. Additionally, we found that self-blame for conflict *increased* intimacy, as if our subjects were determined to overcome what they considered earlier relationship mistakes.[3] What is critical for our present purposes, however, are the effects of simple conceptual definitions on subjects' usage of causality, responsibility, and blameworthiness. If people are not distinguishing among these terms, then all three kinds of ratings should be highly intercorrelated. On the other hand, if people are making the distinctions, the correlations should be reduced. Data on this prediction are presented in Table 9.1. Subjects provided no definitions showed uniformly high intercorrelations among the terms, in judgments of both the father and the mother.

In contrast, when there were one-sentence definitions, the correlations involving blame were significantly reduced from their prior level, regardless of whether the judgment had been made about the father or the mother. As Table 9.1 shows, the

---

[2]For example, Critchlow (1985) found clear empirical distinctions made among the terms when all three were used as dependent variables in a single study, whereas Wortman (1983) reports that accident victims became upset when asked to answer both causality and blameworthiness questions.

[3]In a second study, not yet completed, the attributions and intimacy measures were collected across an academic year, to permit us to assess whether the attributions were predictors of, or were predicted by, current relationship variables.

TABLE 9.1

Judgments of Fault for Parental Conflict: Effects of Providing Definitions

	Intercorrelation		
	Cause Responsibility	*Cause Blame*	*Responsibility Blame*
No definitions (n = 51)			
Father	.81	.88	.88
Mother	.85	.79	.81
With definitions (n = 52)			
Father	.82	.46	.46
Mother	.76	.60	.54

causality-responsibility correlations remained high, and indistinguishable from those obtained without definitions. With definitions, the correlations involving blame remained significantly different from zero, indicating that blameworthiness is based in part on perceived causality and responsibility. Yet these blameworthiness judgments were also significantly different from the blame judgments made in the absence of definitions.

These findings show that people's judgments about others are influenced by simple definitions of the three key terms. But what about judgments concerning the self? After all, the proposed blame-inoculation program is directed toward the alleviation of the perceiver's own stress, not toward changing the perceiver's evaluations of others. The issue of self-attributions was addressed in an important study done by Drown (1985).[4] Her major research question was whether victims of spouse abuse "blame themselves," either for the onset of their victimization, or for its continuation.

Abused women were recruited from an area shelter within a month of their admission (the average was roughly eight days of residence). In addition, a group of women was recruited through laundromat bulletin boards and newspaper advertisements for participation in a study of relationships, and all of them were screened with the Conflict Tactics Scale (Straus, 1979). Those reporting more than two or more instances of partner-inflicted abuse within the preceding year were

[4]This research was supported by a doctoral dissertation grant from the Society for the Psychological Study of Social Issues.

considered abused (while still living with their partners). Those who had never experienced partner-inflicted physical abuse in their adult relationships were considered nonabused.[5]

All women were asked to read, and rate, incidents of spouse abuse developed on the basis of prior interviews with a different set of abuse victims. Women in the study were first asked to give an account of the incidents, using the open-ended technique originated by Harvey, Yarkin, Lightner, and Town (1980). These accounts were coded by two clinical psychologists blind to the hypotheses of the study and the subject's group of origin. Results of the coding showed that overall some 45% of the comments were attributional in nature, with no differences across subject groups in the proportions of attributions. Not surprisingly, the proportion of attributions was higher in accounts of the male's behavior (76%) than in accounts of the female's behavior (18%), $t(53) = 9.18, p < .001$.

Next, all women were given brief definitions of causality ("*produced* the harm, brought it about, made it happen"), responsibility ("*could have done otherwise*, should have known better, should have had better control, should have seen what would happen"), and blame ("*intended*, meant at the outset for the outcome to happen"). Then they were asked to assign causality, responsibility, and blameworthiness to both the male partner and the female partner in the vignettes. Finally, women in the two abused groups were asked to recount an incident of their own victimization and to assign causality, responsibility, and blameworthiness to themselves and their male partners.

Two specific findings from Drown's research are of principal interest here, and both involve only the two abused groups. Because shelters actively attempt to counter the view that women are culpable for their own abuse, these two groups provide a rough test of the potential effectiveness of a blame-inoculation procedure. Ratings of blame to the female partner for the violence in the vignettes, and for its continuation; ratings of blame to the male partner for the violence in the vignettes, and its continuation; and ratings of self-blame for the violence in one's own relationship were subjected to a multiple analysis of variance, with subject group as the independent variable. There was a significant group effect, but univariate analyses showed a difference only on ratings of self-blame: Women in the shelter engaged in significantly less self-blame ($M = 1.60$, on a 7-point scale) than did women remaining in their abusive environments ($M = 3.00, F(1,34) = 8.87, p < .01$). This difference disappeared, however, when an important covariate, violence of the abuse, was taken into account. Abuse severe enough to overcome the many

[5]A total of 77 women responded to the public advertisements. Of these, 16 had been physically abused twice or more during the preceding year; an additional 41 had been abused at least once in an adult relationship, but not twice in the preceding year; the remaining 20 women had not ever experienced abuse. It is worth noting that in our sample overall, 74% of the respondents had suffered some physical abuse. Women who respond to an advertisement about "relationships" may be those who are having relationship problems, but it is still shocking to find three-quarters of such a sample having suffered physical abuse.

impediments to going into hiding, is obviously also severe enough to remove any questions about who should be culpable.

The second finding of interest to a blame-inoculation procedure requires a bit more explanation. Recall that abused women were asked to rate not only the experiences of women in the standard vignettes, but also their own abuse. The specific question is, did abused women use the same principles to evaluate themselves as they use to evaluate other abused victims? The answer, shown in Table 9.2, is that it depends on whether or not they were in the shelter. For those women remaining in their abusive relationships, self-rated causality correlated significantly with rating of causality for the hypothetical female victims; for these women the self-other ratings of responsibility and blameworthiness were also significantly correlated. In short, the women remaining in their abusive relationships appeared to be using the same standards to evaluate their own behavior that they used to rate the behavior of another victim. What about the women housed in the shelter? For these women, the self-other ratings were significantly correlated only for the relatively nonemotional judgment of causality. For ratings of responsibility and blameworthiness, judgments of the other victim were essentially *independent* of judgments of the self. Numerous interpretations could be offered for these differences, but one obvious explanation is that the shelter has engaged in an effective intervention, teaching its new arrivals that regardless of how responsibility and blameworthiness may apply to others, *they* must not hold themselves either responsible or blameworthy for their own victimization. In short, the shelter may have performed a successful blame-reduction therapy.

Outline of a Blame-Inoculation Program

If the conceptual distinctions among causality, responsibility, and blameworthiness can be taught, and if they can be used to mitigate judgments of one's own culpability, then the next task would be to demonstrate that blame-inoculation has

TABLE 9.2

Correlations of Self-Attributions for Abuse with Attributions to Other Female for Her Abuse

	Attributional Judgment		
Subject Group	*Causality*	*Responsibility*	*Blame*
Remaining at Home (n = 16)	.48	.46	.76
Sheltered (n = 20)	.48	.01	.13

positive consequences for stress reduction. This will need to be done to the complete satisfaction of the scientific community, if only to avoid further embarrassment of the sort now produced by the "global" Type A behavior pattern. At the risk of casting aspersions on some of our own data, correlational studies are insufficient for this job. What is required is prospective experimental research, with random assignment of participants to treatment conditions, and dependent variables that include hard physiological measures as well as self-reports.

Several years ago, Shaver and Drown (1985) described how such a study might be conducted with victims of crime.[6] Despite the many differences between criminal victimization and other forms of stressors, the proposal serves as an informative model for what a blame-inoculation program might look like. As noted earlier, victims of crimes, especially victims of violent crimes, often suffer secondary victimization from the criminal justice system. The objective of a blame-inoculation program in this arena would be to reduce secondary victimization by teaching people the differences among causality, responsibility, and blameworthiness, and by making certain that victims understood that *perpetrators* were the only people for whom true blame was justified.

With the full support of the local police, prosecutors, and judges, the inoculation program would have contacted victims of violent crimes such as robbery, rape, and assault within 48 hours of their coming to the attention of the police. Victims who agreed to participate would have been randomly assigned to one of three experimental conditions. In the *basic assistance* condition participants were to receive (a) screening for possible referral to medical or psychiatric services, (b) periodic notification of the progress of their case, (c) volunteer escort and transportation services for court visits, (d) help in arranging day care for children on days of court appointments, (e) an orientation to the courthouse and criminal justice system conducted by volunteer law students, (f) a letter from the prosecuting attorney to their employer requesting release time with no financial penalty for court appointments, and (g) a payment of $20 per day from the project for days of court appointments.

Two experimental conditions would have built upon this basic assistance by adding semistructured, problem-focused group meetings. These six 1 1/2 hour meetings would have taken place over a 3-week period, with no more than three meetings per week, and a maximum of 12 people per group. In the *discussion* condition one of the six meetings would have been devoted to the prevention of future victimization, one would have expanded the orientation to the criminal justice system, and the remaining four would have focused on members' ideas for recovering from their victimization, giving people the opportunity to vent their feelings (in social psychological terms, of course, these are opportunities for social comparison). In the *attribution* condition, one (or perhaps two) of the four unfocused

---

[6]The study was a proposal made to the United States Public Health Service National Institute of Mental Health. The research was not supported, so what follows is the study outline, with no results.

meetings would have been replaced by a session specifically designed to teach the conceptual distinctions among causality, responsibility, and blameworthiness. In the attributional education session(s) the rational theory of blame assignment would have been applied to each victim's case, in turn, and each person would have been encouraged to use the model in his or her future discussions of the response to victimization.

Dependent variables in any blame-inoculation program should include cognitive, affective, and behavioral measures. When the objective is stress reduction, rather than the avoidance of secondary victimization, the dependent variables should be expanded to incorporate physiological measures as well. Examples of possible cognitive measures are locus of control (Paulhus, 1983) and the Impact of Event Scale used clinically with posttraumatic stress disorder (Zilberg, Weiss, & Horowitz, 1982). Examples of the affective measures are the SCL-90-R (Derogatis, 1977), a general measure of psychiatric distress previously used successfully to assess emotional consequences of rape (Kilpatrick, Resick, & Veronen, 1981), and the Profile of Mood States, a measure of transitory negative affective experiences (McNair, Lorr, & Droppelman, 1971). Finally, victims and significant others in their lives could be asked about specific instances of behavioral avoidance, medical or psychiatric hospitalization, time away from work, change in residence, or utilization of long-term psychotherapy. To this set could be added a selected sample of physiological indices of the stress response. Cognitive, affective, and physiological measures should be assessed at least three times: once at the beginning of the project, once immediately following the conclusion of the intervention, and again at a 3- to 6-month follow-up. Behavioral measures of success in stress management could be obtained at the time of the final follow-up. Whether the target is stress or secondary victimization, the attribution condition should produce a significant reduction in stress as compared to either of the other conditions. Such a design would represent a balance between attending to the legitimate needs of the victims and producing data with sufficient rigor to soothe scientific critics.

Could a blame-inoculation program actually work for stress reduction? The answer depends on a number of assumptions. People must be able to distinguish among causality, responsibility, and blameworthiness. Making (or being taught) those distinctions must be shown to have positive psychological benefits for sufferers from stress. And the ability to bring about such benefits from education must be transferable to helping professionals who are the first to encounter the victims of crises. As of this writing, evidence is accumulating that people do respond to differences among the terms. Although the data are by no means univocal, there are hints that knowing the distinctions may assist in the adjustment to loss. Turning these promising leads into an effective blame-inoculation program remains an important challenge for the future.

REFERENCES

Baum, A., O'Keefe, M. K., & Davidson, L. M. (1990). Acute stressors and chronic response: The case of traumatic stress. *Journal of Applied Social Psychology, 20*, 1643-1654.

Blumenthal, J. A., & McCubbin, J. A. (1987). Physical exercise as stress management. In A. Baum & J. E. Singer (Eds.), *Handbook of psychology and health. Vol. V: Stress* (pp. 303-331). Hillsdale, NJ: Erlbaum.

Borek, N., & Shaver, K. G. (1988, April). *Effects of attributions for parental conflict on intimacy*. Paper presented at the meeting of the Eastern Psychological Association, Buffalo, NY.

Bulman, R. J., & Wortman, C. B. (1977). Attributions of blame and coping in the "real world": Severe accident victims react to their lot. *Journal of Personality and Social Psychology, 35*, 351-363.

Byrne, D. (1964). Repression-sensitization as a dimension of personality. In B. A. Maher (Ed.), *Progress in experimental personality research* (Vol. 1, pp. 169-220). New York: Academic Press.

Cannon, W. B. (1935). Stress and strains of homeostasis. *American Journal of Medical Science, 189*, 1.

Cottington, E. M., & House, J. S. (1987). Occupational stress and health: A multivariate relationship. In A. Baum & J. E. Singer (Eds.), *Handbook of psychology and health. Vol. V: Stress* (pp. 41-62). Hillsdale, NJ: Erlbaum.

Critchlow, D.E. (1985). *Metric methods for analyzing partially ranked data*. Berlin: Springer.

DeLongis, A., Coyne, J. C., Dakof, G., Folkman, S., & Lazarus, R. S. (1982). Relationship of daily hassles, uplifts, and major life events to health status. *Health Psychology, 1*, 119-136.

Dembroski, T. M., & MacDougall, J. M. (1985). Beyond global Type A: Relationships of paralinguistic attributes, hostility, and anger-in to coronary heart disease. In T. M. Field, P. M. McCabe, & N. Schneiderman (Eds.), *Stress and coping* (pp. 223- 242). Hillsdale, NJ: Erlbaum.

Derogatis, L. R. (1977). *SCL-90-R manual*. Baltimore, MD: Clinical Psychometric Research.

Dimsdale, J. E. (1987). Measuring human sympathoadrenomedullary responses to stressors. In A. Baum & J. E. Singer (Eds.), *Handbook of psychology and health. Vol. V: Stress* (pp. 25-40). Hillsdale, NJ: Erlbaum.

Dimsdale, J., & Moss, J. (1980). Short-term catecholamine response to psychological stress. *Psychosomatic Medicine, 42*, 493-497.

Drown, D. (1985). *Attributions for violence in relationships: Do battered women blame themselves?* Unpublished doctoral dissertation, Virginia Consortium for Professional Psychology.

Fincham, F. D., & Jaspars, J. M. (1980). Attribution of responsibility: From man the scientist to man as lawyer. In L. Berkowitz (Ed.), *Advances in experimental social psychology* (Vol. 13, pp. 81-138). New York: Academic Press.

Glass, D. C., & Singer, J. E. (1972). *Urban stress: Experiments on noise and social stressors*. New York: Academic Press.

Green, B. L. (1990). Defining trauma: Terminology and generic stressor dimensions. *Journal of Applied Social Psychology, 20*, 1632-1642.

Harvey, J. H., Yarkin, K. L., Lightner, J. M., & Town, J. P. (1980). Unsolicited interpretation and recall of interpersonal events. *Journal of Personality and Social Psychology, 38*, 551-568.

Janis, I. L. (1986). Coping patterns among patients with life-threatening diseases. In C. D. Spielberger & I. G. Sarason (Eds.), *Stress and anxiety. Vol. 10: A sourcebook of theory and research* (pp. 461-476). Washington, DC: Hemisphere.

Janis, I. L., & Mann, L. (1977). *Decision-making: A psychological analysis of conflict, choice, and commitment*. New York: Free Press.

Janoff-Bulman, R. (1979). Characterological versus behavioral self-blame: Inquiries into depression and rape. *Journal of Personality and Social Psychology, 37*, 1798-1809.

Kanner, A. D., Coyne, J. C., Schaefer, C., & Lazarus, R. S. (1982). Comparisons of two modes of stress measurement: Daily hassles and uplifts versus major life events. *Journal of Behavioral Medicine, 4*, 1-39.

Kilpatrick, D. G., Resick, P. A., & Veronen, L. J. (1981). Effects of a rape experience: A longitudinal study. *Journal of Social Issues, 37*(4), 105-122.

Kobasa, S. C. O., & Puccetti, M. C. (1983). Personality and social resources in stress-resistance. *Journal of Personality and Social Psychology, 45*, 839-855.

Lazarus, R. S. (1986). The psychology of stress and coping. In C. D. Spielberger & I. G. Sarason (Eds.), *Stress and anxiety. Vol. 10: A sourcebook of theory and research* (pp. 399-418). Washington, DC: Hemisphere.

Lazarus, R. S., & Folkman, S. (1984). *Stress, appraisal, and coping*. New York: Springer.

McNair, D., Lorr, M., & Droppelman, L. (1971). *Manual. Profile of Mood States*. San Diego, CA: Educational and Industrial Testing Service.

Meichenbaum, D., & Novaco, R. (1986). Stress inoculation: A preventative approach. In C. D. Spielberger & I. G. Sarason (Eds.), *Stress and anxiety. Vol. 10: A sourcebook of theory and research* (pp. 419-435). Washington, DC: Hemisphere.

Miller, S. (1980). When is a little information a dangerous thing? Coping with stressful events by monitoring vs. blunting. In S. Levine & H. Ursin (Eds.), *Coping and health* (pp. 145-169). New York: Plenum.

Miller, S. (1987). Monitoring and blunting: Validation of a questionnaire to assess styles of information seeking under threat. *Journal of Personality and Social Psychology, 52*, 345-353.

Mills, R. T., & Krantz, D. S. (1979). Information, choice, and reactions to stress: A field experiment in a blood bank with laboratory analogues. *Journal of Personality and Social Psychology, 37*, 608-620.

Nisbett, R. E., & Schachter, S. (1966). Cognitive manipulation of pain. *Journal of Experimental Social Psychology, 2*, 227-236.

Norris, F. H. (1990). Screening for traumatic stress: A scale for use in the general population. *Journal of Applied Social Psychology, 20*, 1704-1718.

Paulhus, D. (1983). Sphere-specific measures of perceived control. *Journal of Personality and Social Psychology, 44*, 1253-1265.

Petrie, A. (1978). *Individuality in pain and suffering*. Chicago: University of Chicago Press.

Ross, L., Rodin, J., & Zimbardo, P. G. (1969). Toward an attribution therapy: The reduction of fear through induced cognitive-emotional misattribution. *Journal of Personality and Social Psychology, 12*, 279-288.

Roth, S., & Cohen, L. J. (1986). Approach, avoidance, and coping with stress. *American Psychologist, 41*, 813-819.

Selye, H. (1936). A syndrome produced by diverse nocuous agents. *Nature, 138*, 32.

Selye, H. (1976). *The stress of life* (rev. ed.). New York: McGraw-Hill.

Shaver, K. G. (1985). *The attribution of blame: Causality, responsibility, and blameworthiness*. New York: Springer.

Shaver, K. G., & Drown, D. (1985, June). *Attributions of blame and coping with criminal victimization*. Paper presented at the Fourth International Conference on Justice and Law, Kill Devil Hills, NC.

Shaver, K. G., & Drown, D. (1986). On causality, responsibility, and blameworthiness: A theoretical note. *Journal of Personality and Social Psychology, 50*, 697-702.

Straus, M. A. (1979). Measuring intrafamily conflict and violence: The Conflict Tactics (CT) Scales. *Journal of Marriage and the Family, 41*, 75-88.

Taylor, S. E. (1983). Adjustment to threatening events: A theory of cognitive adaptation. *American Psychologist, 38*, 1161-1173.

Wortman, C. B. (1983). Coping with victimization: Conclusions and implications for future research. *Journal of Social Issues, 39*(2), 195-221.

Wortman, C. B., & Dunkel-Schetter, C. (1987). Conceptual and methodological issues in the study of social support. In A. Baum & J. E. Singer (Eds.), *Handbook of psychology and health. Vol. V: Stress* (pp. 63-108). Hillsdale, NJ: Erlbaum.

Zilberg, N. J., Weiss, D. S., & Horowitz, M. J. (1982). Impact of Event Scale: A cross-validation study and some empirical evidence supporting a conceptual model of stress response syndromes. *Journal of Consulting and Clinical Psychology, 50*, 407-414.

10 The Counterfactual Fallacy: Confusing What Might Have Been With What Ought to Have Been[1]

Dale T. Miller
Princeton University

William Turnbull
Simon Fraser University

Reactions to negative life events—whether they be crimes, accidents, or illnesses—depend on more than the events themselves. Knowing that someone was raped, was severely injured in an accident, or has AIDS is not sufficient to anticipate how either these victims or observers will react to the event. If we are to predict victims' reactions, we must know their perceptions of the event, of themselves, as well as of the broader social world (Janoff-Bulman & Frieze, 1983; Janoff-Bulman & Lang, 1988; Janoff-Bulman & Timko, 1987; Tait & Silver, 1989; Taylor, 1983; Wortman & Silver, 1987). Similarly, predicting observers' reactions to misfortunes requires knowing how they perceive various characteristics of the victim, including the victim's attractiveness, his or her personal responsibility for the event, and so on (Coates, Wortman, & Abbey, 1979; Lerner, 1980; Weiner, Perry, & Magnusson, 1988).

This chapter continues the construal tradition of victimization research by considering another important perceptual determinant of reactions to negative life events: the perceived mutability of a victim's misfortune. By the term mutability, we refer to the extent to which a victim's experience can be imagined otherwise—that is, the extent to which it evokes counterfactual images or scenarios of more positive experiences. Actions and outcomes that strongly evoke counterfactual images in the perceiver are termed mutable, those that do so only weakly as

[1] This chapter is a slightly modified and abbreviated version of a paper that appeared in Social Justice Research, 1990, 4, 1-16. Copyright by Plenum Press. Reprinted by permission. The authors wish to thank Michelle Buck and Darrin Lehman for their comments on an earlier version of this article. The preparation of this article was supported by NIMH grant MH44069 to Dale T. Miller. Correspondence should be addressed to Dale T. Miller, Department of Psychology, Green Hall, Princeton University, Princeton, New Jersey, 08544-1010.

immutable (Kahneman & Miller, 1986). Our thesis is that victims' and observers' reactions to negative life events often are based on the tendency to construe mutable events as events that they can easily imagine otherwise as events that ought not to have happened. Whereas the naturalistic fallacy, as Moore termed it, refers to the confusion of what is the case and what ought to be the case, what we shall term the counterfactual fallacy refers to the confusion of what might have been the case and what ought to have been the case.

We organize the evidence for our thesis into four sections. The first examines the proposition that negative life events preceded by mutable or mentally undoable actions evoke stronger reactions than ones preceded by immutable actions. The second section considers the proposition that negative life events that are presupposed or taken for granted generate weaker reactions than more mutable fates. The third section considers the proposition that when two or more people are involved in a negative life event the person whose actions are perceived to be the most mutable will tend to be assigned most blame for the event. In the final section, we consider the claim that mutable outcomes have a different psychological meaning than unexpected but immutable outcomes. In particular, we argue that mutable outcomes are more difficult to cope with and have greater emotional impact.

ACTIONS THAT NEED NOT HAVE BEEN

Upon hearing of another's misfortune, people often find themselves unable to suppress counterfactual thoughts about how the negative outcome could have been avoided. Indeed, the recurrence or salience of these "if only" thoughts can serve as an index of the poignancy of the misfortune. Frequently such thoughts focus on those actions not taken by the victim that could be viewed as being more rational, responsible, or moral than the one actually taken. For example, an accident caused by an impaired driver might generate the thoughts "if only she had not drunk so much" or "if only he had allowed someone else to drive." The strength with which "if only" thoughts are evoked tends to increase with the assumed strength of the relation between the victim's actions or inactions and his or her resulting misfortune (Miller, Turnbull, & McFarland, 1990). Foreseeability, however, is not a sufficient condition for "if only" thinking. To become included in counterfactual musings, a foreseeably dangerous, reckless, or immoral action must also be mutable; it must be an action that can be imagined otherwise. If it is difficult to imagine the person acting differently, even if the action could have been expected to lead to misfortune, then it is unlikely that the victim or observers would engage in "if only" thinking. One would only say "if only he had allowed someone else to drive" if there were someone else present who could drive and perhaps had offered to drive.

Having argued that actions that are foreseeably related to negative outcomes will evoke counterfactual thoughts only if they are also mutable (i.e., if they are readily construed otherwise), we now wish to make a bolder claim. We propose that the perception of mutability may be sufficient to evoke counterfactual thought. That is, any precipitating action that is mutable, even one that is not foreseeably-linked to the victim's circumstance, will provoke "if only" thinking as well as stronger reactions to the victim. Consider the case of a man who is killed in the crash of a commercial airliner that he had switched to from another flight only minutes before take-off. Most of us will find it difficult to resist the thought that this passenger would not have been killed "if only" he had not switched flights. We may also feel that the death of this person is more poignant or tragic than the death of a passenger who had been booked on the fatal flight for some weeks. These difficult reactions are puzzling. After all, the outcomes are identical in the two cases. Moreover, neither outcome is more or less foreseeable than the other: Switching flights is perceived neither to increase nor decrease one's probability of crashing. Nor do moral prescriptions concerning what one ought to do account for the different affective reactions in the two cases. What then is the difference?

We propose that the differential reactions arise because of the differential availability of a more positive alternative in the two cases (Kahneman & Miller, 1986; Kahneman & Tversky, 1982). The counterfactual world in which the victim escaped his fate is imaginatively closer or more available in the changed flight version of the scenario because the availability of thoughts about how the misfortune could have been avoided (e.g., "If only he had not switched flights") is greater. It is true that the victim in the unchanged flight version of the scenario would have avoided death if he had switched flights but there is little tendency in this case to say "if only he had switched flights." That counterfactual alternative simply does not come to mind readily (Hofstadter, 1979, 1985; Kahneman & Tversky, 1982; Wells, Taylor, & Turtle, 1987). In summary, the fate of a person who was killed in the crash of an airliner that he switched to at the last minute seems especially unfortunate because it is so easy to imagine him not being on that flight; and the perception that he need not have been on the flight fosters the belief that he "ought" not to be dead. More generally, the differential reactions to the two crash victims illustrate the central thesis of this chapter: *The stronger the perception that an event need not have been, the stronger will be the sense that it ought not to have been.*

Miller and McFarland (1986, Study 1) provided evidence that negative outcomes produced by mutable actions (ones easily imagined otherwise) evoke greater sympathy than those produced by immutable actions (ones not easily imagined otherwise). These researchers asked college student subjects to assist them in providing information to a victim compensation board on the public's reaction to various types of victims. The description of the victim and the circumstances of his victimization were identical across two versions of a scenario, with the only difference being the mutability of the victim's misfortune. Mutability was manipulated by describing the action leading to the victimization as being either an exception to, or in accordance with, the victim's routine actions. The victim was a man who had been severely injured during a robbery. In one condition, the robbery took place in the store he most commonly frequented. In a second condition, the robbery took place in a store the victim did not commonly frequent but had decided to go to "for a change of pace." Miller and McFarland (1986) predicted that subjects would experience the misfortune that befell the victim in the unusual store condition as more mutable, and hence more deserving of sympathy, than the misfortune that befell the victim in the usual store condition. Consistent with this hypothesis, subjects recommended significantly more compensation (over $100,000) for the victim's injury when it occurred in the exceptional context than they did when it occurred in the routine context. The greater sympathy for the "exceptional" victim appears to be due to the sense that this victim's misfortune was less inevitable—more mutable. In line with the counterfactual fallacy, his misfortune—because it need not have been—seemed as though it ought not to have been.[2]

Near Misses

We now extend our analysis of fate mutability to include those cases in which there is no particular action of the victim that is linked to his or her fate but the misfortune nevertheless seems highly mutable. We argue, once again, that people tend to assume that mutable negative life events—ones for which counterfactual alternatives are highly available—*ought* not to have been. Consider the deaths of two soldiers: one who is killed on the last day of his tour of duty, and another who is killed on the first day of his tour of duty. If your reactions are similar to ours, the death of the first soldier seems more poignant or tragic than the death of the second. The circumstances of the first soldier's death make scenarios in which he would still be alive much more available (Kahneman & Varey, 1990). One can imagine saying, for example, "he almost made it" or that "he would have been safe if only he could have survived one more day."

A study by Miller and McFarland (1986, Study 2) indicates that observers do respond differently to victims who vary in their perceived closeness to being nonvictims. As with Miller and McFarland's previously described study, the cover story here described subjects' task as that of helping provide information to a victim compensation board on the public's reactions to various types of victims. The description of the victim and the circumstances of his victimization were identical across two versions of a scenario, the only difference being the closeness of a more positive fate. The victim in this study had died from exposure after surviving a plane crash in a remote area. He had made it to within 75 miles of safety in one condition and to within 1/4 mile of safety in a second condition. Based on the assumption that it is easier to imagine an individual continuing another 1/4 mile than another 75 miles, Miller and McFarland predicted that the fate of the "close" victim would be

---

[2] This study also demonstrates the distinction between perceptions of mutability and subjective probability. The different reactions to the two victims in this study are not due to differences in the perceived probabilities of their outcomes. Subjects' judgments of the probabilities of being shot in the two stores were low and indistinguishable from one another.

perceived as more mutable, and hence more deserving of sympathy, than the fate of the "distant" victim. The results confirmed the predictions and, once again, reveal the counterfactual fallacy: Subjects recommended significantly more compensation for the family of the victim whose fate seemed closer to having been avoided.[3]

TAKEN-FOR-GRANTED VERSUS MUTABLE MISFORTUNES

The unusualness of a victim's actions and the psychological closeness of an outcome is only one of the determinants of the perceived mutability of a victim's misfortune. As we shall demonstrate in this section, there are many other factors that dispose individuals to take certain misfortunes for granted and to perceive others as highly mutable. Once again, we argue that the less taken for granted a misfortune is perceived to be, the stronger will be people's reaction to it.

Observer Reactions

A controversial incident that occurred some years ago in France illustrates how social knowledge structures can influence the perceived mutability of an event and, in turn, reactions to the event. The incident was a bomb attack on a synagogue in France that left a number of people injured. France's Prime Minister then publicly denounced the attack and expressed his sympathy for both the Jews who were inside the synagogue and the "innocent passersby." The Prime Minister's differentiation of the victims into Jews and innocent passersby provoked considerable outrage because many interpreted it as implying that he did not consider the Jews to be as innocent as the passersby.

Certainly the term innocent has a strong moral connotation, but should we assume that the Prime Minister's remarks reflect anti-Semitism? Not necessarily. His failure to apply the term innocent to the Jews inside the synagogue may reflect the fact that his mental representation of a synagogue enabled him to mentally remove passersby from the vicinity more easily than the attending Jews. That the passersby were not the intended victims of the attack also makes their injuries less taken for granted and thus easier to undo mentally (although no more or less deserved) than those of the Jews. Once again, the principle of psychologic operating here appears to be: What need not have been, ought not to have been.

[3] Before leaving this section, we should note that it is not only victims who were almost nonvictims who engage in counterfactual thinking; nonvictims who were almost victims also engage in this process. Consider someone who changed flights at the last moment only to learn that their original flight crashed. A variant of this happened in 1989 when a door on a New Zealand 747 blew off in midflight. Only minutes before one of the survivors had switched his original seats with another passenger who was sucked out of the plane when the door flew off. Such an experience can be expected to haunt a person for some time—possibly for life.

Producers of television dramatic shows seem to possess an exquisite sense of the relation between mutability and emotional reaction as is attested to by their fascination with plots of the following type. Attractive young women—models, prostitutes, dancers—are being murdered by a psychopathic serial killer. The hero of the show, generally a male detective, tries to discover the identity of the murderer. The killing of the women, including ones for whom the audience has some sympathy, continues up to the point that the hero discovers the identity of the killer. The main tension of the show centers around the question of whether the hero will catch the now-identified killer before he kills his next victim. For this woman to be killed would be tragic. It is too bad that the others were killed, but because the killer's identity was not known at that time, there is a sense in which nothing could have been done about their deaths. Their deaths are taken for granted. But once the killer's identity is known, the fates of his future victims suddenly become highly mutable. Those targeted as future victims may be no more innocent than the previous victims but their deaths, because they can be avoided, would assume more tragic proportions. For this reason only rarely do the producers allow another victim to be killed after the killer's identity has been discovered—this would be too "heavy" for a weekly dramatic series.[4]

The factors that lead observers to take one negative life events more for granted than another ca be subtle as a study by Miller (1989) demonstrates. Miller found that victims of crimes evoked less sympathy when the harm inflicted on them or their property was necessitated by the goals of their victimizer (even when these goals were reprehensible) than when it was not. When the victim's suffering was produced by actions that were necessitated by the perpetrator's goals the victim's suffering—like the perpetrator's actions—appeared to be taken more for granted by observers. Thus observers were less sympathetic toward, and recommended less compensation for, a victim whose dog had been killed by a burglar when the dog's barking threatened the burglar's mission than when it did not (i.e., the house vacant and isolated). Put differently, when the successful completion of the burglar-script necessitated a particular action, observers reacted to the negative consequences that followed from that action as though they too were neccessary, and thus not unfair.

Victim Reactions

For most misfortunes it is possible to imagine worse alternatives as well as better ones. Whether victims think of others whose lots are better or others whose lots are

---

[4] Interestingly, successful tragedy often exploits for dramatic effect just this type of "unneccessary" death. Much of *King Lear's* dramatic impact, for example, derives from the tension between the audience's awareness that the time between Lear's regaining of his senses and Cordelia's execution is long enough for her to be saved and its realization that a dramatic momentum makes her death immutable. She could be saved in another world, but not in Lear's world. One difference between melodrama and tragedy, then is that the latter extends our sense of what needs to have been. Fates can be seen as immutable not only because of physical and temporal constraints such as whether or not the killer's identity is known, but also because of characterological and dramatic constraints.

worse than their own affects victims' ability to cope with their misfortunes (Gibbons & Gerrard, 1990; Wood, Taylor, & Lichtman, 1985). Indeed, considerable recent attention has been given to the possibility that victims willfully direct their attention to worse-off others (real or imagined) as a means of minimizing the distress they experience (Taylor & Lobel, 1989; Wills, 1981, 1987; Wood, 1989). Our analysis is agnostic on the question of whether victims do or do not strategically downwardly compare but it does suggest that the ease with which they can do so (whether voluntarily or not) will depend on how mutable they perceive their victim status to be.

There are two classes of interpersonal comparisons that a victim can make. One class presupposes the occurrence of the event (e.g., the stroke, the cancer, the paraplegia) and one does not. Thus a breast cancer victim can compare herself either to other women with breast cancer or to other women (or men for that matter) without breast cancer. If she compares herself to other women with breast cancer, she can think of those whose circumstances are either better or worse than her own. The same is true if she thinks of other women who do not have breast cancer. We hypothesize that an important determinant of whether a victim considers alternatives that primarily share his or her victimizing status or ones that do not will be the perceived mutability of the status. Further, we hypothesize that the more immutable a victim perceives his or her victim's status to be, the greater the victim's ability to focus on "worse world" comparisons.

Consider first the circumstance of a breast cancer victim. A victim of breast cancer will be inclined to presuppose her condition because her causal understanding of breast cancer will not permit her to readily imagine how she might have avoided it. The relative difficulty of generating counterfactual thoughts of the type "I would not have breast cancer if only..." means that images of herself (or others) without breast cancer should not be highly available and hence not highly troubling. On the other hand, while having breast cancer may be perceived by the woman to be an immutable aspect of her identity, the conditions under which she has breast cancer will not be. She should be able to readily imagine having breast cancer under many alternative conditions, including many that evoke comforting "it could be worse" thoughts.

Now consider the circumstances of an accident victim. Compared to the occurrence of breast cancer, the occurrence of an accident will frequently be perceived as more mutable: It will be difficult for him or her to avoid intrusive thoughts of how the accident might have been avoided and, as a consequence, thoughts of him or her as a nonvictim (Bulman & Wortman, 1977; Davis, Lehman, Thompson, Silver, & Wortman, 1991). These nonvictim images and comparisons, in turn, can be expected to interfere with accident victims' ability to generate thoughts of how their lot as an accident victim could be worse. In essence, the perceived mutability of the negative life event will constrain whether the event evokes thoughts of an alternative world in which the event did not happen or one in which it happened with even more serious consequences.

Interestingly, victims may see their fate as more mutable than do observers. Consider the experience of a woman who was mugged late one night at a McDonald's restaurant in California (Miller, 1989). This woman reported that one of the most difficult aspects of coping with this experience was the fact that people kept telling her that she was lucky that it was not worse—she was lucky she was not also raped, for example. This type of reaction from others, far from consoling her, enraged her for she did not feel the least bit lucky and resented their telling her that she was.

Let us consider this experience from the perspective of the analysis we have been developing. For this event there are two broad categories of counterfactual alternatives that can be generated. The first category involves her not being mugged; the second involves her being both mugged and worse: for example, raped. Which of these two alternatives will be more easily imagined? To use Markus' terminology (Markus & Kunda, 1986; Markus & Nurius, 1986), which *possible self* will be more available—the nonmugged counterfactual self or the mugged and raped counterfactual self? It appears from the woman's response that the availability of these two alternatives differed markedly for herself and her friends. The alternative constructions of the woman's friends apparently presupposed her mugging and, compared to these scenarios, she did indeed seem lucky. Her own counterfactual constructions, on the other hand, apparently did not presuppose her mugging, and compared to these scenarios she seemed very unlucky. We thus suggest that there may be a general tendency for victims, in contrast to observers, to react more strongly to the probability of the first events happening (e.g., getting mugged when you go to a McDonald's), and less to the probability of the second event happening given the first (e.g., not getting raped given you are mugged). However, even if there is such a general tendency, we suspect that its strength will depend, at least to some extent, on the situation. Clearly victims often do say they were lucky and that it could have been worse. It remains for future research to determine more precisely what type of victimizations lead them to mentally undo their victimization and consider more positive outcomes.

BLAME AND MUTABILITY

Our focus to this point has been the mutability of negative life events and we have argued that both victims and observers react to highly mutable outcomes as they would to those that ought not to have happened. We now consider action sequences involving more than one person that lead to negative outcomes. Our interest here lies not in the mutability of the resulting misfortune, but in the mutability of the actions of the different parties involved in the misfortune. The counterfactual fallacy, we claim, operates in this case as well. Specifically, we propose that the party whose action is most readily imagined otherwise will tend to be blamed the most for the misfortune. Thus we propose a link between the mental modifiability of a person's action and the assignment of blame to that person (Kahneman & Miller, 1986; Miller, Turnbull, & McFarland, 1990).

To illustrate this link consider the following scenario employed by Miller and Gunasegaram (1990).

> Two individuals (Jones and Cooper) are offered the following very attractive proposition. Each individual is asked to toss a coin. If the two coins come up the same (both heads or both tails), each individual wins $1000. However, if the two coins do not come up the same, neither individual wins anything. Jones goes first and tosses a head; Cooper goes next and tosses a tail. Thus the outcome is that neither individual wins anything.

Who would you predict will experience more guilt: Jones or Cooper? And will Jones blame Cooper more or will Cooper blame Jones more for their failure to win $1000? Of course, in a logical sense there should be no difference between Jones and Cooper in either the guilt they experienced or in the desire of observers to blame them since the tossing of a coin constitutes a chance event. Nevertheless, the vast majority of the subjects to whom Miller and Gunasegaram presented this scenario predicted that Cooper would experience more guilt and be blamed more by Jones than *vice versa*. But why? In what sense is Cooper more responsible for their mutual loss than Jones? It is true that if Cooper had tossed a head they would have won the $1000, but it is equally true that they would have won the $1000 if Jones had tossed a tail.

To help us understand this asymmetry, let us return to the concept of mutability. To begin, note that there are two alternative scenarios in which the two individuals could be imagined to be $1000 richer; one would have Jones tossing a tail to match the toss of Cooper and the other would have Cooper tossing a head to match the toss of Jones. However, if the second event is more mutable than the first, these two alternatives should not be equally salient either to the participants or to observers. The scenario in which the second toss matched the first should more readily come to mind than the equally positive and equally probable scenario in which the first toss matched the second. To test this hypothesis subjects were also asked to respond to the following probe: "There are two ways that Jones and Cooper could have won $1000. Which of these alternatives comes more readily to mind: (a) Jones tossing a tail; (b) Cooper tossing a head." The overwhelming majority of the subjects chose the option that modified the second rather than the first toss, supporting the hypothesis that the second event was perceived as more mutable than the first. Given this finding, and the proposed link between mutability and responsibility, we now have an account for why Cooper might feel more guilt and be blamed more than Jones. Cooper is seen to be more responsible for the loss because his behavior is perceived to be more mutable.

Miller and Gunasegaram's (1990) results suggest the following general proposition concerning mutability and blame: As the mutability of a person's actions increases, so does the likelihood that he or she will be blamed for any resulting negative outcome. Consider the well-documented tendency for victims of violence to be assigned an unreasonable degree of blame for their fate (Lerner, 1980; Lerner & Miller, 1978). One explanation for this phenomenon may be that descriptions of a harmful act often present the actions of the perpetrator in a way that makes him or her part of the presupposed background of the story and, as such, relatively immutable. With the victim's actions being perceived as more mutable than those of the perpetrator, counterfactual scenarios in which harm is avoided will tend to be ones that change the victim's past actions but keep the aggressor's behavior essentially constant. The higher availability of counterfactual scenarios that modify the victim's actions, in turn, may induce an impression that the victim is responsible for his or her fate (Kahneman & Miller, 1986). Additional support for this hypothesis comes from the observation that people who live under historically corrupt political rule tend to characterize the abuse and torture of fellow citizens as the result of agitation on the part of the victims rather than as the product of a corrupt political system (Conroy, 1988, cited in McGill, 1989).

The link between mutability and blame will not always be a simple one. Often the implications of events' mutability for blame assignment will conflict with the implications suggested by more formal or legalistic conceptions of responsibility (Hart & Honoré, 1959; Heider, 1958). Under most circumstances it is hard to justify the view that victims of crimes are more responsible for their fates than are the perpetrators of crimes. Thus when observers are asked to apportion responsibility they are unlikely to assign more to victims than to perpetrators. For example, rapists will almost certainly be assigned more responsibility than their victims in any formal request for responsibility attribution. Nevertheless, the greater the perceived mutability of the rape victim's behavior, the more attention her actions will receive. People may say of a rape "Of course, he is to blame." but go on to say "But why didn't she do X?" or "If only she had done X or had not done Y." Thus the fact that the mental undoing of a rape is more likely to focus on the victim than the perpetrator can be expected to affect people's reactions to the victim and their analysis of the victimization; and this will be true even if requests for responsibility attributions elicit more conventional, socially acceptable accounts.

MUTABLE VERSUS UNEXPECTED OUTCOMES

The research we have described demonstrates that an event's impact does not derive solely from its relation to the subjective probabilities and prescriptive standards that the perceiver brings to the event. It depends also on the perceiver's counterfactual constructions that are evoked by the event itself. Furthermore, we demonstrated that the contrasts that arise between an experience and the perceiver's thoughts about what might have been can have effects similar to those produced by contrasts between an experience and a perceiver's expectancies or thoughts about what ought to have been. But precisely how similar are the two types of reactions? Are the counterfactual versions of emotional states such as guilt, regret, and sympathy the same as the noncounterfactual versions? For example, does a person who expresses regret over an out-of-character action actually feel the same type of regret as the person whose regret derives from the perception of having engaged in an irrational or unethical action?

Sanitioso and Miller (unpublished) conducted a study that began to address this question. Employing an extensive list of bipolar trait adjectives, these researchers elicited subjects' emotional reactions to negative life events that were (a) mutable and foreseeable, (b) mutable but unforeseeable, and (c) immutable and unforeseeable. The following vignettes are illustrative of their cases:

Mutable but unforeseeable. John and Eric lived next door to each other and worked in the same downtown area in the city. They had been taking turns driving to the city to save gas and parking expenses. This Monday was John's turn to drive. On the spur of the moment, John decided to take the country road rather than the interstate highway they usually took. They were driving along this country road when a car whose driver seemed to have lost control ran broadside into their car from one of the smaller streets intersecting the road. John suffered only minor injuries, but Eric suffered severe head injuries.

Mutable and foreseeable. John and Eric lived next door to each other and worked in the same downtown area in the city. They had been taking turns driving to the city to save gas and parking expenses. This Monday was John's turn to drive. They were driving along this country road when it began to rain lightly and the road became slippery. John knew that he should slow down but he did not since he was in a hurry to get to work. As they approached a curve, John's car went out of control and skidded into the opposite lane. An approaching car hit his car broadside on the passenger's side. John suffered only minor injuries, but Eric suffered severe head injuries.

Immutable and unforeseeable. John and Eric lived next door to each other and worked in the same downtown area in the city. They had been taking turns driving to the city to save gas and parking expenses. This Monday was John's turn to drive. They were driving along the interstate highway that they take to work everyday when a car whose driver seemed to have lost control ran broadside into their car from one of the on-ramps. John suffered only minor injuries, but Eric suffered severe head injuries.

After reading one of these versions of the scenario, subjects were asked to respond to the bipolar scales as they thought John would respond. The analyses revealed no difference in the *pattern* of subjects' responses to the first two versions of the scenario; that is, there was no difference in the structure of the emotional reactions that the two experiences were expected to elicit. There was, however, a difference in the expected *intensity* of the responses. Subjects who read the mutable-foreseeable version predicted that John would be more miserable, more self-critical, more ashamed, more self-blaming, more angry at himself, and guiltier than did subjects who read the mutable-unforeseeable version. These differences suggest that foreseeability does indeed increase the negative affect generated by a negative life event. On the other hand, the comparison between the first and third version of the scenario provides clear evidence of the existence of the counterfactual fallacy. Subjects in the mutable-unforeseeable condition expected John to be more self-critical, more ashamed, more regretful, more self-blaming, and more angry at himself than did subjects in the immutable-unforeseeable condition.

In summary, it appears that the emotions evoked by fates that are undoable by virtue of their mutability rather than their foreseeableness are similar in kind, if not in intensity, to those evoked by outcomes that are undoable by virtue of their foreseeableness. It is as though people, because they find themselves saying "if only" when they experience unintended negative consequences that were foreseeable, are also disposed to feel responsible in other circumstances in which they find themselves saying "if only." Most importantly, this relation may obtain even when the conventional prerequisites for responsibility assignment (i.e., foreseeability) do not exist. An important task for future research is to explore the ways in which people resolve or cope with the cognitive and affective incoherence that an event's mutability can produce. For example, how do people cope with feeling guilty over a mutable action that they know was neither foolish nor immoral? Does feeling guilty when one knows ones should not feel guilty intensify one's dysphoria? And how does one reconcile feelings of differential sympathy for different victims whose fates one knows cannot be discriminated on moral or rational grounds? These are just some of the intriguing questions that we hope future research will address.

Imposing Meaning on Mutable Versus Unexpected Outcomes

Many authorities have noted the need of both victims and observers to impose meaning on misfortunes (Frankl, 1963; Lerner, 1980; Lifton, 1967; Marris, 1986; Silver, Boon, & Stones, 1983; Silver & Wortman, 1980; Taylor, 1983). How, if at all, does the mutability of the misfortune affect the quest to impose meaning on it? Contrast a person who is the victim of a highly improbable misfortune and one who is a victim of a misfortune that is not only highly improbable but highly mutable as well. Let us say the first victim was the only member of a platoon to be seriously wounded in battle and the second victim was a member of a casualty-ridden platoon who was seriously wounded only minutes before a cease-fire went into effect. In the first case both the victim and observers can be expected to dwell on the contrast between the victim's fate and the more fortunate fates of others. Victims of such misfortunes are inclined to ask "Why me?" (Silver & Wortman, 1980). Without a satisfactory account of how the victim differs from the nonvictims, the victim's fate will seem devoid of meaning to both observers and to the victim him or herself. The reaction to the second, highly mutable fate seems somewhat different. The question for individuals who come close to being nonvictims, such as a soldier wounded minutes before a cease-fire went to effect, would not seem to be why their misfortune happened to them, as opposed to someone else, but why it happened at all. Why were they wounded when they had come so close to being safe? Pondering the role of fate and destiny would seem especially likely in the case of a misfortune that need not to have been.

SUMMARY

This chapter has reviewed evidence for the counterfactual fallacy; the tendency to confuse beliefs about what might have been with beliefs about what ought to have been. Across a wide variety of contexts we demonstrated that the impact of negative life event has on victims and observers depends on the extent to which the event prompts them to think of less negative alternatives. Negative life events vary greatly in the extent to which they prompt thoughts of what might have been and our analysis pointed to a variety of factors that determine how mutable a negative life event will seem. The routineness or necessity of the action preceding the misfortune are two examples of relevant factors. A misfortune preceded by an action that was unusual or unnecessary (even if not foreseeably linked to the misfortune) is especially likely to generate a strong reaction—either of sympathy or blame depending on the particular features of the situation. Both victims and observers of highly mutable misfortunes find it extremely difficult to avoid thoughts about a more positive outcome. Mutable misfortunes evoke intrusive thought—obsessive thoughts of "if only" and "almost" that are not easily ignored or modified. Attempts to comfort victims by telling them it is not their fault, or that there was no way they could have known, do not diminish the belief that what happened to them need not have happened.

Finally, our analysis may also shed light on justice-based reactions more generally. The mutability of a negative life event appears to affect justice-based reactions and coping responses through a form of heuristic processing. People's feelings here, as in other judgment domains, provide them with evaluative information (Schwarz, 1990; Schwarz & Clore, 1988). When people decide how much blame or compensation to assign a victim it appears that they are guided by the strength of their reaction to the outcome. The stronger the feelings evoked by a victim's experience, the more intense are the blame and sympathy reactions. As with other forms of heuristic processing, this process will generally serve people well (Kahneman & Tversky, 1973). Because people's perceptions of a victim's deservingness generally will guide their emotional reaction to the victim—the less deserving, the stronger the reaction—their emotional reaction generally will serve as a reliable index of how deserved they perceive the victim's misfortune to be, and hence how much blame or compensation they should assign. Emotional reactions, however, are not solely determined by the fit between the victim's outcome and beliefs about what is just. The perceived mutability of his or her fate is also important.

REFERENCES

Bulman, R. J., & Wortman, C. (1977). Attributions of blame and coping in the "real world": Severe accident victims react to their lot. *Journal of Personality and Social Psychology, 35*, 351-363.

Coates, D., Wortman, C., & Abbey, A. (1979). Reactions to victims. In I. H. Frieze, D. Bar-Tal, & J. S. Carroll (Eds.), *New approaches to social problems* (pp. 21-52). San Francisco: Jossey-Bass.

Davis, C. G., Lehman, D. R., Thompson, S. C., Silver, R. C., & Wortman, C. B. (1991). *The undoing of traumatic life events.* Unpublished manuscript.

Frankl, V. E. (1963). *Man's search for meaning: An introduction to logotherapy.* New York: Washington Square Press.

Gibbons, F. X., & Gerrard, M. (1990). Downward comparison and coping. In J. Suls & T. Wills (Eds.), *Social comparison: Contemporary theory and research* (pp. 317-346). Hillsdale, NJ: Erlbaum.

Hart, H. L. A., & Honoré, A. M. (1959). *Causation in the law.* London: Oxford University Press.

Heider, F. (1958). *The psychology of interpersonal relations.* New York: Wiley.

Hofstadter, D. R. (1979). *Godel, Escher, Bach: An eternal goldenbraid.* New York: Basic Books.

Hofstadter, D. R. (1985). *Metamagical themas: Questing for the essence of mind and pattern.* New York: Basic Books.

Janoff-Bulman, R., & Frieze, I. H. (1983). A theoretical perspective for understanding responses to victimization. *Journal of Social Issues, 39*(2), 1-17.

Janoff-Bulman, R., & Lang, L. (1988). Coping with disease and accidents: The role of self-blame attributions. In L. Y. Abramson (Ed.), *Social-personal inference in clinical psychology* (pp. 116-147). New York: Guilford.

Janoff-Bulman, R., & Timko, C. (1987). Coping with traumatic life events: The role of denial in light of people's assumptive worlds. In C. R. Snyder & C. E. Ford (Eds.), *Coping with negative life events: Clinical and social psychological perspectives* (pp. 135-159). New York: Plenum.

Kahneman, D., & Miller, D. T. (1986). Norm theory: Comparing reality to its alternatives. *Psychological Review, 93*, 136-153.

Kahneman, D., & Tversky, A. (1973). On the psychology of prediction. *Psychological Review, 80*, 237-251.

Kahneman, D., & Tversky, A. (1982). The simulation heuristic. In D. Kahneman, P. Slovic, & A. Tversky (Eds.), *Judgment under uncertainty: Heuristics and biases* (pp. 201-208). New York: Cambridge University Press.

Kahneman, D., & Varey, C. (1990). Propensities and counterfactuals: The loser that almost won. *Journal of Personality and Social Psychology, 59*, 1101-1110.

Lerner, M. J. (1980). *The belief in a just world: A fundamental delusion.* New York: Plenum.

Lerner, M. J., & Miller, D. T. (1978). Just world research and the attribution process: Looking back and ahead. *Psychological Bulletin, 85*, 1030-1051.

Lifton, R. J. (1967) *Death in life. Survivors of Hiroshima.* New York: Simon and Schuster.

Markus, H., & Kunda, Z. (1986). Stability and malleability of the self-concept. *Journal of Personality and Social Psychology, 51*, 858-866.

Markus, H., & Nurius, P. (1986). Possible selves. *American Psychologist, 41*, 954-969.

Marris, P. (1986). *Loss and change* (rev. ed.). London: Routledge & Kegan Paul.

McGill, A. L. (1989). Context effects in judgments of causation. *Journal of Personality and Social Psychology, 57*, 189-200.
Miller, D. T. (1989). *Counterfactual thinking and reactions to negative life events*. Paper presented at the First International Conference on "Crises and loss experiences in the adult years." Trier, Federal Republic of Germany, July, 1989.
Miller, D. T., & Gunasegaram, S. (1990). Temporal order and the perceived mutability of events: Implications for blame assignment. *Journal of Personality and Social Psychology, 59*, 1111-1118.
Miller, D. T., & McFarland, C. (1986). Counterfactual thinking and victim compensation: A test of norm theory. *Personality and Social Psychology Bulletin, 12*, 513-519.
Miller, D. T., Turnbull, W., & McFarland, C. (1990). Counterfactual thinking and social perception: Thinking about what might have been. In M. P. Zanna (Ed.), *Advances in experimental social psychology* (Vol. 23, pp. 305-331). Orlando, FL: Academic Press.
Schwarz, N. (1990). Feelings as information: Informational and motivational functions of affective states. In E. T. Higgins & R. M. Sorrentino (Eds.), *Handbook of motivation and cognition* (Vol. 2, pp. 527-561). New York: Guilford Press.
Schwarz, N., & Clore, G. L. (1988). How do I feel about it? Informative functions of affective states. In K. Fiedler & J. Forgas (Eds.), *Affect, cognition, and social behavior* (pp. 44-62). Toronto: Hogrefe.
Silver, R. L., Boon, C., & Stones, M. H. (1983). Searching for meaning in misfortune: Making sense of incest. *Journal of Social Issues, 39*(2), 81-101.
Silver, R. L., & Wortman, C. B. (1980). Coping with undesirable life events. In J. Garber & M. E. P. Seligman (Eds.), *Human helplessness* (pp. 279-340). New York: Academic Press.
Tait, R., & Silver, R. S. (1989). Coming to terms with major negative life events. In J. S. Uleman & J. A. Bargh (Eds.), *Unintended thought* (pp. 351-381). New York: Guilford.
Taylor, S. E. (1983). Adjustment to threatening events: A theory of cognitive adaptation. *American Psychologist, 38*, 1161-1173.
Taylor, S. E., & Lobel, M. (1989). Social comparison activity under threat: Downward evaluation and upward contacts. *Psychological Review, 96*, 569-575.
Weiner, B., Perry, R. P., & Magnusson, J. (1988). An attributional analysis of reactions to stigmas. *Journal of Personality and Social Psychology, 55*, 738-748.
Wells, G. L., Taylor, B. R., & Turtle, J. W. (1987). The undoing of scenarios. *Journal of Personality and Social Psychology, 53*, 421-430.
Wills, T. A. (1981). Downward comparison principles in social psychology. *Psychological Bulletin, 90*, 245-271.
Wills, T. A. (1987). Downward comparison as a coping mechanism. In C. R. Snyder & C. Ford (Eds.), *Coping with negative life events: Clinical and social psychological perspectives* (pp. 243-267). New York: Plenum.
Wood, J. V. (1989). Theory and research concerning social comparisons of personal attributes. *Psychological Bulletin, 106*, 231-248.
Wood, J. V., Taylor, S. E., & Lichtman, R. R. (1985). Social comparison in adjustment to breast cancer. *Journal of Personality and Social Psychology, 49*, 1169-1183.
Wortman, C. B., & Silver, R. C. (1987). Coping with irrevocable loss. In G. R. VandenBos & B. K. Bryant (Eds.), *Cataclysms, crises, and catastrophes: Psychology in action* (Master Lecture Series, Vol. 6, pp. 189-235). Washington, DC: American Psychological Association.

III Ways of Dealing With Crises and Losses

11 The Role of Similarity in Coping Through Downward Comparison[1]

Thomas Ashby Wills
Ferkauf Graduate School of Psychology and
Albert Einstein College of Medicine, Bronx

My purpose here is to discuss the role of similarity in how persons cope with life stressors through downward comparison. I begin with a brief exposition of social comparison theory, including the constructs of upward comparison and downward comparison. I suggest how social comparison is involved in coping with crisis and loss experiences and summarize evidence from field and laboratory studies showing how downward comparison is employed as a coping mechanism. Then I consider how similarity between self and other is involved in the comparison process, and suggest some hypotheses about how similarity will operate in downward comparison. The chapter concludes with suggestions for further development of social comparison theory and coping theory.

THEORY OF SOCIAL COMPARISON

Social comparison theory as originated by Leon Festinger (1954a, 1954b) focused on how persons compare with others in order to increase confidence in the accuracy of their self-evaluations and the correctness of their opinions. In this sense, social comparison is a rational process that aims to achieve better self-knowledge through

[1] Preparation of this paper was partly supported by Grant R01-DA-05950-01 from the National Institute on Drug Abuse. Versions of this paper were presented at the Conference on Coping with Crises and Loss Experiences, University of Trier, and the meeting of the American Psychological Association, New Orleans. Thanks to Hans Werner Bierhoff, Frederick X. Gibbons, Jerry Suls, Ladd Wheeler, and Bernard Weiner for their comments on a draft of this paper.

comparison with other persons. One of Festinger's basic postulates was that when persons pursue social comparison, they compare with others who are similar to the self on the attribute in question. For example, a person who wishes to evaluate his/her ability at golf would tend to obtain information about the golf scores of persons who are at the same general level. A golfer of moderate accomplishment would not tend to pursue comparison with either professional golfers or rank beginners, because such comparisons do not provide useful information for assessing where the comparer stands on the dimension of golf ability. Festinger's basic theory has received extensive support (see, e.g., Latane, 1966; Suls & Miller, 1977), and the similarity postulate has been specifically confirmed in several studies (e.g., Gruder, 1971; Wheeler, 1966; Wheeler et al., 1969). Extensions of the original theory have shown that persons use comparison information not only on the focal dimension of comparison (e.g., golf score) but also on attributes related to the performance dimension, such as age, amount of practice, and gender (Feldman & Ruble, 1981; Gastorf & Suls, 1978; Goethals & Darley, 1977; Wheeler, Koestner, & Driver, 1982).

Festinger's model of social comparison was intended to delineate how persons use social information in the service of accurate self-evaluation. Experimental tests of this model did show that people choose information about others who are similar to and slightly better off than the self, a process termed upward comparison. However, the empirical support for the theory derived from situations where subjects were in affectively neutral conditions. An alternative model of social comparison inquires how social comparison is pursued when persons are distressed. This model proposes that when negative affect is aroused the focus of comparison shifts from self-evaluation to self-enhancement, because the dominant psychological need is for reduction of distress and maintenance of self-esteem (Wills, 1981). It is proposed that under such conditions a person will compare with others who are worse-off than the self because the relatively favorable comparison between the self and the (worse-off) other will enable the comparer to feel better about his/her own situation. This process is termed downward comparison because it involves comparing with others who are below, rather than above, the self on the continuum of subjective well-being.

The model of downward comparison delineates how persons can use social information to cope with distressing situations that are not readily controllable.[2] The basic postulate is that in such situations (which would be represented by severe crisis or loss experiences), the motive for accurate evaluation is supplanted by the motive for feeling better about the self. Accurate evaluation would be aversive because the situation is already acknowledged to be bad, and reminding oneself of

[2] The assumption of the theory was that when the situation is controllable or remediable through problem-focused coping, then persons will use these coping mechanisms rather than a cognitive type of coping (cf. Lazarus & Folkman, 1984). For further discussion of how downward comparison is influenced by skill level and situational control see Ruble and Frey (1990) and Major, Testa, and Bylsma (1990).

this assessment presumably is not helpful to the coping process. Rather, a person would pursue comparison information that suggests something relatively positive about the self. This would not only help the person feel better about his/her own situation, but also could help to motivate further coping efforts.

The original version of downward comparison theory proposed that self-enhancing comparison could be pursued in several ways. One is strict downward comparison, that is, finding a comparison target who is considerably worse off than the self. Another is comparing with a person who is not well off but whose misfortune is essentially at the same level as the self, a process that is termed *lateral comparison*. In either case, the obtaining of social information shows that there are other persons who have problems (or worse problems). While this information may not have a long-term impact on a person's self-concept, it could enable the person to feel better about his/her situation, at least for a short time.

The theory of downward comparison does not deny the existence of upward comparison. Rather it was recognized that both upward comparison (for purposes of self-evaluation) and downward comparison (for purposes of self-enhancement) occur, but they occur under different conditions (Wills, 1983, 1987). Upward comparison is predominant when affective conditions are neutral or positive and when comparing with better-off others promises to provide a conclusion that is favorable to the self, i.e., either the self is relatively well off compared to the rest of the population, or will become like the better-off others (Goethals, 1986). However, when a person's life situation is difficult because of negative life events or perceived inadequacies, then self-evaluative comparisons may be avoided because it is clear they will provide a relatively unfavorable conclusion about the self (Wills, in press; Wood & Taylor, 1990). In these conditions, there should be a shift from upward to downward comparison.

SUPPORT FOR DOWNWARD COMPARISON

Before proceeding to discussion of similarity processes, I shall discuss evidence on how downward comparison can be employed as a coping mechanism. This area has been developed through contributions from both laboratory research and field studies.

Studies of Threat and Affiliation

The first experimental demonstration of downward comparison was provided in a study by Hakmiller (1966). College student subjects were given feedback indicating they had either a positive or a negative personality trait ("hostility toward one's parents"), and then were given the opportunity to obtain information about personality attributes of five other persons, who they were told ranged from very maladjusted to very adjusted. Choices of comparison others indicated that subjects who believed they had a negative personality showed a shift toward comparison with a worse-off other, and for subjects who believed their personality to be very negative, the majority of comparison choices (54%) were with the worst-off comparison target. Similar shifts in comparison behavior as a function of ego-threat have been observed in studies by Friend and Gilbert (1973) and Wilson and Benner (1971).

Another line of evidence occurred in studies of fear and affiliation. It was originally demonstrated that when subjects are fearful (e.g., because of anticipated electric shock) they show an increased preference for affiliating with other persons (Schachter, 1959). This was originally interpreted as a process of clarifying one's own emotional reactions through social comparison, but evidence on fear and affiliation was somewhat mixed. My previous discussion (Wills, 1981) suggested that the operative process is one of downward comparison, in which fearful subjects gain enhancement of subjective well-being through comparison with other persons who are exposed to the same threat as the self. This suggestion was sustained by the finding that subjects in fear-affiliation experiments show a preference for affiliation with persons who are actually worse off than the self (Bell, 1978; Darley & Aronson, 1966; Zimbardo & Formica, 1963). It was also noted that subjects show evidence of tension reduction only when the comparison target is exposed to the same fate as the self (Amoroso & Walters, 1969; Kiesler, 1966). When the affiliation person is not expected to experience the same negative fate, different and sometimes opposite effects are observed (e.g., Buck & Parke, 1972; cf. Kenrick & Johnson, 1979; Rotton, Barry, Frey, & Soler, 1978). So in this case, similarity of fate was a crucial determinant of outcomes.

Current interest in laboratory research has focused on the role of threat in evoking downward comparison processes. For example, Levine and Green (1984) tested social comparison choices among a sample of young children. Subjects worked alone at a computer terminal that presented a series of visual tasks. After each trial, the subject could elect to receive either intrapersonal feedback (their own score), interpersonal feedback (the typical score of other children), or both. Through experimental manipulations, subjects experienced either improving vs. declining performance over trials and feedback indicated either superior vs. inferior performance relative to other children. Results showed that in the improving condition, subjects looked equally often at scores of superior and inferior others, whereas in the declining performance condition, subjects looked more frequently at the scores of inferior others, that is, a downward comparison effect. This study showed that downward comparison could be observed in a sample of relatively young children (cf. Ruble, Boggiano, Feldman, & Loebl, 1980).

Pyszczynski, Greenberg, and LaPrelle (1985) examined how subjects' comparison choices were influenced by perceived personal inadequacy. College student subjects were given a test purportedly measuring social competence, were given manipulated feedback about their performance, and then had an opportunity to examine information about the performance of other subjects. Results indicated a general tendency for subjects to avoid information about others who had done better than themselves and to prefer information about others who had done less well than themselves, i.e., downward comparison; choices of worse-performing others were particularly marked among subjects who were told their performance was poor. Similarly, Sherman, Presson, and Chassin (1984) gave subjects manipulated information indicating success vs. failure on a task and then provided an opportunity to make ratings of the performance of other persons. Two studies showed that failure produced a downward shift in subjects' ratings of the performance of other persons, with subjects who failed overestimating the percentage of the population who would fail. Such shifts in consensus perceptions are not found when subjects believe they have desirable behaviors (Sherman, Presson, Chassin, & Agostinelli, 1984); so the implication is the effect is attributable to a self-enhancement mechanism evoked by a threat to personal competence.

The role of depression in social comparison was tested in several laboratory studies (Gibbons, 1986; Gibbons & Gerrard, 1989). Subjects were preselected through screening of a college population using measures of depression and self-esteem. In the experimental procedure, subjects were first induced to experience positive or negative affect and then had an opportunity to read a statement by another person that reflected positive or negative affect. Results indicated that depressed subjects preferred to read negative statements, particularly when negative mood was induced (this preference was reversed among nondepressed subjects). Also, depressed subjects showed an improvement in mood after the downward comparison experience, whereas this effect was not found among nondepressed subjects. These data are consistent with the proposition that downward comparison enhances subjective well-being, and that downward comparison effects occur primarily when subjective distress is present.

Studies of Physical Illness and Stigmatization

In recent years, attention has shifted to investigating comparison processes among persons who are stressed by stigmatizing conditions or physical illness. A field study by Wood, Taylor, and Lichtman (1985) is notable for studying social comparison in a sample of 78 cancer patients, all in active treatment for their illness. Through direct interviews with respondents, Wood et al. obtained comparison measures that included structured ratings of how the respondent rated her own adjustment to illness relative to other patients, and codings of spontaneous statements from the interview protocol. The researchers found that the majority of patients perceived their own coping to compare favorably with that of other patients, consistent with a downward comparison process. The interviews also suggested that respondents tended to compare with another person who was worse off on a related dimension, which the authors termed *dimensional comparison.*

Related findings have been obtained in studies of patients with rheumatoid arthritis, a nonfatal but painful and disabling condition (Affleck & Tennen, 1990; Affleck, Tennen, Pfeiffer, & Fifield, 1988; Affleck, Tennen, Pfeiffer, Fifield, & Rowe, 1987; DeVellis et al., 1990). Interview data indicate that patients tend to perceive their own coping and adjustment in relatively favorable terms, with a focus on perceptions that they are able to remain physically active, to control negative emotions and attitudes, and to maintain an attitude of optimism about the future. In these studies standardized measures of psychological outcomes were obtained and it was found that measures of downward comparison were positively related to adjustment. Covariance analyses indicated that this effect remained significant when the effects of actual disease activity and illness duration were controlled statistically.

At the same time, studies conducted with mentally retarded populations suggested that social comparison theory might clarify some puzzling observations about the self-perceptions of retarded individuals. The initial observation was that retarded individuals in classrooms with nonhandicapped children often had perceptions of their intellectual ability as being comparable to that of nonretarded students, while learning-disabled (but not retarded) students rated themselves lower than nonretarded students (Gibbons, 1985; Harter, 1985; Silon & Harter, 1985). The researchers used direct questions to determine whom the children compared themselves with. They found that mentally retarded students were comparing themselves to retarded peers, thus arriving at a relatively favorable comparison, while learning-disabled students compared with normal students, thus arriving at a relatively unfavorable perception. The inference was that retarded children were arriving at a relatively favorable self-perception through comparison with retarded targets who were perceived to be worse off.

It should be noted that individuals may employ comparison-oriented coping to deal with events that occur to others. Tennen and colleagues studied parents of children in neonatal units (Affleck & Tennen, 1990; Affleck et al., 1987; cf. Tennen, Affleck, & Gershman, 1986). Mothers were interviewed shortly after the birth of a child with perinatal complications, which may produce developmental handicaps. The mother's perception of the condition of her own infant, relative to other infants in the unit, was recorded in addition to her perception of her own coping ability. Spontaneous statements and comparative ratings indicated that mothers perceived the severity of the child's medical condition as less than average and their own coping as better than average. Follow-up data obtained 6 months after the original interview indicated that comparison ratings were related to better adjustment among mothers, findings that remained significant with statistical control for baseline measures.

In summary, recent research has demonstrated downward comparison processes in several contexts. Laboratory research has shown that downward comparison is evoked by threat and results in improvement of subjective well-being. Field studies have shown evidence of downward comparison among persons with physical illness or stigmatizing conditions and have suggested that social comparison is part of the process of coping. Comparison processes that involve direct target choice, comparison on particular dimensions, or cognitive alterations of social information have all been demonstrated. Thus the existence of downward comparison as a process is established, and its role in the coping process seems consistent with theory. There has been less attention to variables that influence the downward comparison process and determine the outcome of the comparison. This issue is addressed in the following section.

SIMILARITY AND DOWNWARD COMPARISON

In Festinger's theory the role of similarity as a variable was strictly specified. The purpose of social comparison was to gain accurate self-evaluation, hence comparison with similar better-off others was posited. The purpose of downward comparison, however, is to increase subjective well-being, so the role of similarity may be different. At present there has been little theoretical development of how similarity would operate in this type of social comparison. When persons are distressed by a life crisis or loss event, will similarity be a factor in determining the types of downward comparisons they make and will it affect the outcome of the comparison process? Here I consider some of the theoretical issues for this question and suggest some hypotheses about the role of similarity in downward comparison.

Lateral Comparison and Downward Comparison

One theoretical question is whether there is a preference for downward comparison (comparison with a person who is worse off than the self) or lateral comparison (comparing with another who is experiencing distress but is at essentially the same level as the self). For example, if a person has been unemployed for three months and is engaging in downward comparison, would he/she have a preference for a comparison target who had been unemployed for three months (lateral) or a target who had been unemployed for a year (downward)? Though this is a basic issue for downward comparison theory, there is little empirical evidence on this issue from either laboratory or field research.

Two issues are relevant for considering the theoretical question. The first concerns the goal of downward comparison. One possibility is that the goal is to maximize the gain in subjective well-being. If this were true, then there would always be a preference for a strict downward comparison. Moreover, it would be expected that the change in subjective well-being after the comparison would be linearly related to the comparison differential, that is, the larger the difference in well-being between the self and the comparison other the greater the increase in subjective well-being for the comparer. I expect there would be boundary conditions for this process, because observing a person who was much worse off than the self would evoke empathic tendencies, which at some point would increase subjective distress.[3] However, the general prediction would be that the larger the comparison differential, the larger the gain in subjective well-being. Were this prediction confirmed, it would suggest a basic aspect of the nature of downward comparison.

The alternative view is that the goal of downward comparison is to decrease feelings of perceived deviance. One of the stressful aspects of crisis events is the perception that one's difficulties are unique, or there are few others who have the same problem (cf. Snyder & Ingram, 1983; Suls & Wan, 1987). For example, a loss event such as widowhood may cause distress because the affected person believes there are few people with a similar problem. In this case, the goal of utilizing social comparison information would be to reduce perceived deviance by finding examples of other persons who have the same problem (but not a worse problem). This model of the comparison process implies a preference for lateral comparison, i.e., obtaining information about other persons with a similar difficulty. This suggests a rather different view of the downward comparison process. It is less a matter of enhancing one's own life satisfaction by finding examples of others who are worse off; rather, it would be a process of enhancing one's own self-esteem through identification with others who have similar difficulties.

Research on coping with crisis experiences thus may help to clarify an important theoretical issue about downward comparison. The empirical approach would be to offer subjects several comparison choices (including lateral and downward comparisons) and to obtain multiple measures of subjective well-being, including life satisfaction, perceived deviance, and self-concept. The contrasting predictions are that social comparison will enhance life satisfaction through observing a large comparison differential (strict downward comparison model) or that comparison will decrease perceived deviance though observing a similar comparison other (lateral comparison model). It is of course possible that both processes occur, which also would be informative since it would suggest that people cope with crisis experiences through multiple comparison mechanisms.

General Similarity and Downward Comparison

Assume the first model of downward comparison, in which a strict downward comparison is the preference. Within this model of the comparison process a second issue occurs: Does the magnitude of the comparison differential show a linear

[3] The question of how the boundary conditions change is itself of interest. When people are very distressed, will they tolerate a larger comparison differential between the self and the worse-off other before they begin to experience empathic concern? Will people tolerate a smaller comparison differential when the target person has the same problem as themselves than when the target person has a different problem?

relationship to change in subjective well-being? An experimental paradigm is generated in which subjects are presented with a number of different comparison targets that vary in comparison differential relative to the subject, i.e., some are slightly worse off, some are moderately worse off, and some are extremely bad off. The question, then, is whether the relationship between comparison differential and change in subjective well-being will be linear.

My argument here is that the effect is not linear. Rather, the prediction is that the greatest net gain in subjective well-being will occur at a moderate comparison differential. The argument is as follows. At a small comparison differential (i.e., the other's fate is quite similar to the subject's) the comparison differential is minimal and hence the change in subjective well-being is minimal.[4] At a moderate comparison differential, there should be substantial change in well-being because the comparison other is still somewhat similar and the comparison differential is considerable. At a large comparison differential (i.e., the other is much worse off than the self) the change in subjective well-being is predicted to be reduced because of several factors. One is that empathic concern with the other's fate may be evoked (cf. Batson, 1987; Berkowitz, 1972). Another is that as the other's fate becomes very different from the subject's, the impact of the comparison may be reduced because there is no longer a sense of identification with the target person's fate. For example, if a person who has been unemployed 6 months observes a person who has been unemployed for 6 years, it may be difficult to engage in a meaningful comparison because the other person's life situation is so different from that of the self. Note that in this prediction two different factors, empathic concern and identification with the other, are posited. For a precise test of the impact of comparison differential, these two factors should be measured separately to determine whether each contributes to the outcome of the comparison process.

The overall hypothesis, then, posits an inverse-U effect, with greatest change in subjective well-being at a moderate comparison differential, less change at either small or large differentials. It is possible that some part of this model is wrong, in which event the graph describing the relation between comparison differential and well-being change would be more rectangular at certain points. For example, it is conceivable that any amount of downward comparison produces a significant impact on well-being, in which case the curve would be equally high at low and moderate comparison differentials but would decline at a large differential. Alternatively, it is conceivable that for distressed persons, large comparison differentials do not evoke empathic concern because the person's attention is focused on his or her own problem (not the other's). In this case the curve might rise to a peak at a moderate comparison differential but would not decline significantly thereafter.

[4] Further, people are ambivalent about engaging in downward comparison at all (see Brickman, 1975; Wills, 1981), which may cause a certain reluctance to initiate downward comparison under ordinary circumstances. Again, this may change with level of distress, so that a person who is very distressed will show little ambivalence about engaging in downward comparison.

Either of these alternative outcomes, however, would say something meaningful about the nature of the comparison process.

There are two possible qualifications to this hypothesis. One is that the comparison process depends on the type of problem. For example, problems that derive from normative life transitions (e.g., bereavement) may be coped with primarily through lateral comparison, whereas for problems that are nonnormative (e.g., unemployment, poverty), strict downward comparison may be the primary coping process. This distinction could be empirically tested. A second is that the shape of the curve may depend on the distress level of the comparer. For example, at a relatively low level of distress the curve may be sharply peaked, at a moderate level of distress it may be linear, and at a high level of distress it may be rectangular. Statistical tests are available to discriminate these alternative processes.

Principle of Mixed Elements

A more articulated question about the role of similarity in downward comparison can be raised by distinguishing theoretically different types of similarity information (Wills, 1990). In principle one can distinguish three types of similarity information: (a) *fate similarity* concerns whether the target person's status is similar to versus worse off than the self at the present time; (b) *future similarity* concerns an assessment of the probability that the comparer would become like the target person in the future; and (c) *personality similarity* is the overall similarity of personality/attitudinal attributes between the comparer and the target person. I believe that these types of similarity have quite different effects on the outcome of the comparison process. I believe that a typical comparison situation provides some mixture of these types of information, so this is termed the *principle of mixed elements* in comparison.

Consider first the interaction of fate similarity and future similarity. By crossing two levels of fate similarity (same status vs. worse status) with three levels of future similarity (better status in the future vs. same status vs. worse status), a 2×3 table is generated which represents possible outcomes of downward comparison as a function of the two types of similarity. The presumption is that for a representative sample of comparison situations, fate similarity and future similarity will be relatively independent, i.e., statistically uncorrelated. The hypothesis is that the outcome of the comparison will be largely determined by the future-similarity factor. To the extent that one's future status is perceived to be worse than present status, negative effects of comparison will occur, that is, people will become more depressed/anxious if they observe a person who is currently worse off than the self but believe they *may become like that person* in the future. To the extent that future status is believed to be dissimilar to the target (i.e., improving), then positive outcomes will derive from comparison and people will be less anxious or depressed. Thus, there should be a significant Fate Similarity × Future Similarity interaction effect. In the six cells of the design, I predict that highly positive outcomes will be observed in some cells whereas highly negative outcomes will be observed in other cells. Downward comparison, then, may not always produce enhancement of subjective well-being. Whether it will do so, theoretically is based on the similarity information presented by a particular comparison situation.

A somewhat different derivation obtains for the interaction of fate similarity and personality similarity. This generates a 2 × 2 table with two levels of fate similarity (same status vs. worse status) and two levels of personality similarity (similar vs. dissimilar). Here I assume there is an implicit linkage between personality similarity and future similarity, that is, people tend to believe that if they are similar to another person in general personality attributes they are more likely to experience the same fate as the other in the future. This perceived linkage of course could be empirically tested. There are some situations where the linkage is not logically necessary; for example the occurrence of cancer to a similar other would not carry strong logical implication that the self is likely to get cancer (though this is psychologically possible).[5]

The basic prediction is that when personality similarity is low, outcomes of downward comparison will be generally positive, with somewhat increased subjective well-being for equal fate similarity and strongly increased well-being when the other's current status is worse off. When personality similarity is high, there may be a mild positive outcome when fate similarity is equal, but when the other is worse off than the self and similar in personality, the prediction is that a negative outcome will occur because the comparison information suggests that one's present status will become worse. This prediction is based on several assumptions, for example that fate and personality similarity are correlated. Also, it is possible that personality similarity operates differently for normative life events than for nonnormative events. It would be necessary to obtain data to check the assumptions in order to obtain a strong test of the prediction.

A further elaboration of this thinking would consider the interaction of fate similarity, future similarity, and personality similarity. The complexity of such predictions is beyond the scope of the present paper, and may be premature. Tests of the two-way interactions seem a necessary preliminary step for building the theory of similarity and comparison.

I should note that the observed outcomes of downward comparison in field studies seem to be uniformly positive, whereas the predicted effects of comparison include some negative outcomes. This raises a question as to why negative outcomes have not been observed in naturalistic settings. There are several possible answers to this, one of which is that the hypothesis presented here is incorrect. However, there are other possibilities. In naturalistic settings, it is possible that

---

[5] At the psychological level, the occurence of a disease to a similar person may evoke a belief that the disease is due to some shared personality or behavioral element (e.g. diet, anxiety). This is also a testable question.

people specifically select comparison targets that will yield positive outcomes. It is also conceivable that some cognitive alteration of key parameters occurs; for example, information about personality similarity and future similarity may be processed in a way that provides a favorable (for the comparison process) combination of these variables. It has also been suggested that instead of selecting actual comparison targets, persons create hypothetical targets who present a combination of attributes that is favorable from the comparison standpoint (cf. Goethals, Messick, & Allison, 1990; Taylor, Wood, & Lichtman, 1983; Wood, 1989). All these alternative explanations are conceivable and deserve detailed investigation in field research.

LOCUS OF PROBLEM

Another type of similarity in downward comparison concerns the locus of the problem. Given that a person is experiencing a particular type of problem and compares with a person having a similar type of problem, several different attributions about the respective loci of the problems (of self and other) are theoretically possible. Following from the theory of attribution and emotion (Kelley, 1973; Weiner, 1985), a given crisis or loss experience could be attributed to causes that are internal (e.g., low competence) versus external (e.g., bad luck). Following this line of thinking, one could predict that the perceived locus of the problem (internal vs. external) will influence the outcome of the comparison process. Other dimensions of attributions concerning problems, for example stable vs. unstable or changeable vs. unchangeable, may also have an impact on the comparison process.

Consider, for example, a case in which a person perceives the cause of his or her own problem to be internal/changeable, and the locus of the other's problem to be internal/unchangeable. The outcome of this comparison theoretically would be quite favorable for the self because it implies that one's own situation is remediable—following from the principle of mixed elements. In contrast, if the locus of one's own problem is perceived as internal/stable whereas the other's problem is perceived as internal/unstable, the outcome of the comparison might not be so positive for the self.

Predictions about external attributions are more complicated to derive. Assume that in a given situation the locus of one's own problem is perceived to be external whereas the locus of the other's problem is perceived to be internal. Other things equal, will this produce a positive comparison outcome? My view is that it might not. Perceiving one's own problem as being attributable to external factors may have some effect for maintaining self-esteem (because the self is not personally responsible for the problem) but believing that the problem locus is external may suggest the problem could occur again, unpredictably; so on the balance the comparison outcome might not be favorable. Perceiving the other's problem as internally caused could tend to produce a favorable comparison outcome because there is a favorable comparison differential between one's own problem (external locus) and the other's problem (internal locus). However, there may be an implicit linkage for perceiving internal-locus problems as also being changeable problems; so here the comparison might favor the other. This argument is somewhat tentative because there is a general self-enhancing tendency in attributions (see Burger, 1981; Snyder & Higgins, 1988; Taylor & Brown, 1988; Zuckerman, 1979), and for the kinds of problems studied in typical coping research there may be a tendency to perceive others' problems (e.g., unemployment) as being due to personality factors that are stable and unchangeable (e.g., incompetence, hostility). Thus because of attributional issues there may be a general tendency in naturalistic settings for downward comparisons to produce positive outcomes. These attributional issues, however, have not been studied in detail.

With several theoretical dimensions of attribution applied to problems of self and other, there are many possible combinations of self- and other-attributions that could theoretically be examined.[6] One simple approach to the problem is to define the attributions for problems as being internal versus external, or controllable versus uncontrollable, and go from there. I think it sufficient to note that this is an interesting question and little is known about how persons tend to perceive the locus of crisis or loss experiences occurring to themselves and to others (cf. Perloff & Fetzer, 1986; Weinstein, 1984). The suggestion, again, is that there is a great deal of perceptual flexibility in the downward comparison process, and much could be learned through studying how attributional variables relate to the outcome of the comparison.

GENERAL DISCUSSION

In this chapter I have summarized current research on social comparison as a coping mechanism. I think the body of evidence from laboratory and field studies shows that downward comparison is a prevalent coping mechanism for persons facing crisis or loss experiences. This is a new development in social comparison theory and seems likely to add to understanding of coping processes (Wills, in press; Wood & Taylor, 1990). At the same time I have suggested that little is understood about how downward comparison works. I think it is not clear what types of comparison are preferred, what outcome dimensions are most affected by the comparison process, or how the outcome of the comparison is determined. Further research is necessary to develop both social comparison theory and coping theory.

---

[6] Also, it is possible that different comparison processes are involved for normative stressors (e.g. widowhood) than for nonnormative life stressors (e.g. unemployment). There are further distinctions between onset and continuation and irrevocable versus reversible losses.

Here I have focused on the role of similarity in the comparison process because I think it raises a number of intriguing questions about downward comparison. One basic issue, whether persons have a preference for lateral or downward comparison, has not really been examined in either laboratory or field research and seems a worthy topic for investigation. The suggestion is that lateral and downward comparison may have quite different effects, possibly on different dimensions, and that each may be most appropriate for a particular type of crisis or loss experience. Further, given that a downward comparison is pursued it is not clear how the self-other comparison differential will affect the net gain in subjective well-being. At present there is little empirical evidence relevant to either issue, so further research would be informative.

Another issue raised in this paper is whether there exist different types of similarity in the downward comparison process. It is proposed that one can distinguish between fate similarity, future similarity, and personality similarity, and that these factors have different effects on the outcome of the comparison process. In theory, a downward comparison could have negative effects such as increased anxiety or depression if certain parameters of similarity are present in the comparison, so research examining for negative outcomes would be interesting. Another intriguing question follows from the observation that in current laboratory and field studies the outcomes of downward comparison seem predominantly positive, that is, increased subjective well-being. One can then ask whether negative comparison outcomes are prevalent in naturalistic settings, and if not, why not. At several points in the present paper I have suggested decisional and cognitive processes that may tend to produce favorable comparison outcomes. However, the role of these processes in naturalistic settings has not been demonstrated, and this also would seem an interesting avenue for research on coping.

Finally, I have suggested that from the standpoint of social psychological theory, similarity also involves consideration of attributional variables. The perceived locus of problems of self and other may have a considerable impact on the outcome of the comparison process. At present, however, few data are available that would shed light on this question. Accordingly, research on the kinds of attributions made for typical crisis or loss experiences would seem informative, and specific tests of how self- and other-attributions influence the comparison process would be useful for comparison theory.

CONCLUSION

The theory of social comparison has developed steadily since its inception, and continues to provide a theoretical base for understanding the processes of self-evaluation and self-enhancement (Suls & Wills, 1990). Currently, social comparison theory is helping to elucidate the process of coping for persons with distress, illness, or stigmatization. Further work on social comparison as a coping mechanism seems promising as an approach to understanding the resources that persons use to cope with adversity and the ways in which suffering can be alleviated.

REFERENCES

Affleck, G., & Tennen, H. (1990). Social comparison and coping with major medical problems. In J. Suls & T. A. Wills (Eds.), *Social comparison: Contemporary theory and research* (pp. 369-393). Hillsdale, NJ: Lawrence Erlbaum Associates.

Affleck, G., Tennen, H., Pfeiffer, C., & Fifield, J. (1988). Social comparisons in rheumatoid arthritis: Accuracy and adaptational significance. *Journal of Social and Clinical Psychology, 6*, 219-234.

Affleck, G., Tennen, H., Pfeiffer, C., Fifield, J., & Rowe, J. (1987). Downward comparison and coping with serious medical problems. *American Journal of Orthopsychiatry, 57*, 570-578.

Amoroso, D. M., & Walters, R. H. (1969). Effects of anxiety and socially mediated anxiety reduction on paired-associate learning. *Journal of Personality and Social Psychology, 11*, 388-396.

Batson, C. D. (1987). Prosocial motivation: Is it ever truly altruistic? In L. Berkowitz (Ed.), *Advances in experimental social psychology* (Vol. 20, pp. 65-122). San Diego: Academic Press.

Bell, P. A. (1978). Affective state, attraction, and affiliation. *Personality and Social Psychology Bulletin, 4*, 616-619.

Berkowitz, L. (1972). Social norms, feelings, and other factors affecting helping and altruism. In L. Berkowitz (Ed.), *Advances in experimental social psychology* (Vol. 6, pp. 63-108). New York: Academic Press.

Brickman, P. (1975). Adaptation level determinants of satisfaction with equal and unequal outcome distributions in skill and chance situations. *Journal of Personality and Social Psychology, 32*, 191-198.

Buck, R. W., & Parke, R. D. (1972). Behavioral and physiological response to the presence of a friendly or neutral person in two types of stressful situations *Journal of Personality and Social Psychology, 24*, 143-153.

Burger, J. M. (1981). Motivational biases in the attribution of responsibility for an accident: A meta-analysis of the defensive-attribution hypothesis. *Psychological Bulletin, 90*, 496-512.

Darley, J. M., & Aronson, E. (1966). Self-evaluation vs. direct anxiety reduction as determinants of the fear-affiliation relationship. *Journal of Experimental Social Psychology, 2*(Suppl. 1), 66-79.

DeVellis, R., Holt, K., Renner, B., Blalock, S., Blanchard, L., Cook, H., Klotz, M., Mikow, V., & Harring, K. (1990). The relationship of social comparison to rheumatoid arthritis symptoms and affect. *Basic and Applied Social Psychology, 11*, 1-18.

Feldman, N. S., & Ruble, D. N. (1981). Social comparison strategies: Dimensions offered and options taken. *Personality and Social Psychology Bulletin, 7*, 11-16.

Festinger, L. (1954a). A theory of social comparison processes. *Human Relations, 7*, 117-140.

Festinger, L. (1954b). Motivation leading to social behavior. In M. R. Jones (Ed.), *Nebraska symposium on motivation, 1954* (pp. 191-219). Lincoln: University of Nebraska Press.

Friend, R. M., & Gilbert, J. (1973). Threat and fear of negative evaluation as determinants of locus of social comparison. *Journal of Personality, 41*, 328-340.

Gastorf, J. W., & Suls, J. (1978). Performance evaluation via social comparison: Performance similarity vs. related-attributes similarity. *Social Psychology, 41*, 297-305.

Gibbons, F. X. (1985). A social-psychological perspective on developmental disabilities. *Journal of Social and Clinical Psychology, 3*, 391-404.

Gibbons, F. X. (1986). Social comparison and depression: Company's effect on misery. *Journal of Personality and Social Psychology, 51*, 140-148.

Gibbons, F. X., & Gerrard, M. (1989). Effects of upward and downward social comparison on mood states. *Journal of Social and Clinical Psychology, 8*, 14-31.

Goethals, G. R. (1986). Social comparison theory: Lost and found. *Personality and Social Psychology Bulletin, 12*, 261-278.

Goethals, G. R., & Darley, J. (1977). Social comparison theory: An attributional approach. In J. M. Suls & R. M. Miller (Eds.), *Social comparison processes: Theoretical and empirical perspectives* (pp. 259-278). Washington, DC: Hemisphere.

Goethals, G. R, Messick, D. M., & Allison, S. T. (1990). The uniqueness bias: Studies of constructive social comparison. In J. Suls & T. A. Wills (Eds.), *Social comparison: Contemporary theory and research* (pp. 149-176). Hillsdale, NJ: Lawrence Erlbaum Associates.

Gruder, C. L. (1971). Determinants of social comparison choices. *Journal of Experimental Social Psychology, 7*, 473-489.

Hakmiller, K. L. (1966). Threat as a determinant of downward comparison. *Journal of Experimental Social Psychology, 2*(Suppl. 1), 32-39.

Harter, S. (1985). The need for a developmental perspective in understanding child and adolescent disorders. *Journal of Social and Clinical Psychology, 3*, 484-499.

Kelley, H. H. (1983). The processes of causal attribution. *American Psychologist, 28*, 107-128.

Kenrick, D. T., & Johnson, G. A. (1979). Interpersonal attraction in aversive environments. *Journal of Personality and Social Psychology, 37*, 572-579.

Kiesler, S. B. (1966). Stress, affiliation, and performance. *Journal of Experimental Research in Personality, 1*, 227-235.

Latane, B. (1966). Studies in social comparison: Introduction and overview. *Journal of Experimental Social Psychology, 2*(Suppl. 1), 1-5.

Lazarus, R. S., & Folkman, S. (1984). *Stress, appraisal, and coping*. New York: Springer.

Levine, J. M., & Green, S. M. (1984). Acquisition of relative performance information: The roles of intrapersonal and interpersonal comparison. *Personality and Social Psychology Bulletin, 10*, 385-393.

Major, B., Testa, M., & Bylsma, W. H. (1990). Responses to upward and downward social comparisons: The impact of esteem-relevance and perceived control. In J. Suls & T. A. Wills (Eds.), *Social comparison: Contemporary theory and research* (pp. 237-260). Hillsdale, NJ: Lawrence Erlbaum Associates.

Perloff, L. S., & Fetzer, B. K. (1986). Self-other judgments and perceived vulnerability to victimization. *Journal of Personality and Social Psychology, 50*, 502-510.

Pyszczynski, T., Greenberg, J., & LaPrelle, J. (1985). Social comparison after success and failure: Biased search for information consistent with a self-serving conclusion. *Journal of Experimental Social Psychology, 21*, 195-211.

Rotton, J., Barry, T., Frey, J., & Soler, E. (1978). Air pollution and interpersonal attraction. *Journal of Applied Social Psychology, 8*, 57-71.

Ruble, D. N., Boggiano, A. K., Feldman, N. S., & Loebl, J. H. (1980). Developmental analysis of the role of social comparison in self-evaluation. *Developmental Psychology, 16*, 105-115.

Ruble, D. N., & Frey, K. S. (1990). Changing patterns of comparative behavior as skills are acquired: A functional model of self-evaluation. In J. Suls & T. A. Wills (Eds.), *Social comparison: Contemporary theory and research* (pp. 79-113). Hillsdale, NJ: Lawrence Erlbaum Associates.

Schachter, S. (1959). *The psychology of affiliation*. Stanford, CA: Stanford University Press.

Sherman, S. J., Presson, C. C., & Chassin, L. (1984). Mechanisms underlying the false consensus effect: The special role of threats to the self. *Personality and Social Psychology Bulletin, 10*, 127-138.

Sherman, S. J., Presson, C. C., Chassin, L., & Agostinelli, G. (1984). The role of evaluation and similarity principles in the false consensus effect. *Journal of Personality and Social Psychology, 47*, 1244-1262.

Silon, E. L., & Harter, S. (1985). Assessment of perceived competence and motivational orientation in segregated and mainstreamed mentally retarded children. *Journal of Educational Psychology, 77*, 217-230.

Snyder, C. R., & Higgins, R. L. (1988). Excuses: Their effective role in the negotiation of reality. *Psychological Bulletin, 104*, 23-35.

Snyder, C. R., & Ingram, R. E. (1983). "Company motivates the miserable": The impact of consensus information on help-seeking for psychological problems. *Journal of Personality and Social Psy-*

chology, 45, 1118-1126.
Suls, J. M., & Miller, R. L. (1977). *Social comparison processes: Theoretical and empirical perspectives.* Washington, DC: Hemisphere.
Suls, J., & Wan, C. K. (1987). In search of the false-uniqueness phenomenon: Fear and estimates of social consensus. *Journal of Personality and Social Psychology, 52,* 211-217.
Suls, J., & Wills, T. A. (Eds.). (1990). *Social comparison: Contemporary theory and research.* Hillsdale, NJ: Lawrence Erlbaum Associates.
Taylor, S. E., & Brown, J. D. (1988). Illusion and well-being: A social psychological perspective on mental health. *Psychological Bulletin, 103,* 193-210.
Taylor, S. E., Wood, J. V., & Lichtman, R. R. (1983). It could be worse: Selective evaluation as a response to victimization. *Journal of Social Issues, 39*(2), 19-40.
Tennen, H., Affleck, G., & Gershman, K. (1986). Self-blame among parents of infants with perinatal complications: The role of self-protective motives. *Journal of Personality and Social Psychology, 50,* 690-696.
Weiner, B. (1985). An attributional theory of achievement motivation and emotion. *Psychological Review, 92,* 548-573.
Weinstein, N. D. (1984). Why it won't happen to me: Perceptions of risk factors and susceptibility. *Health Psychology, 3,* 431-457.
Wheeler, L. (1966). Motivation as a determinant of upward comparison. *Journal of Experimental Social Psychology, 2*(Suppl. 1), 27-31.
Wheeler, L., Koestner, R., & Driver, R. E. (1982). Related attributes in the choice of comparison others: It may be there, but it isn't all there is. *Journal of Experimental Social Psychology, 18,* 489-500.
Wheeler, L., Shaver, K. G., Jones, R. A., Goethals, G. R., Cooper, J., Robinson, J. E., Gruder, C. L., & Butzine, K. W. (1969). Factors determining the choice of comparison others. *Journal of Experimental Social Psychology, 5,* 219-232.
Wills, T. A. (1981). Downward comparison principles in social psychology. *Psychological Bulletin, 90,* 245-271.
Wills, T. A. (1983). Social comparison in coping and help-seeking. In B. M. DePaulo, A. Nadler, & J. D. Fisher (Eds.), *New directions in helping. Vol. 2: Help-seeking* (pp. 109-141). New York: Academic Press.
Wills, T. A. (1987). Downward comparison as a coping mechanism. In C. R. Snyder & C. Ford (Eds.), *Coping with negative life events: Clinical and social-psychological perspectives* (pp. 243-268). New York: Plenum.
Wills, T. A. (1990). Similarity and self-esteem in downward comparison. In J. Suls & T. A. Wills (Eds.), *Social comparison: Contemporary theory and research* (pp. 51-78). Hillsdale, NJ: Lawrence Erlbaum Associates.
Wills, T. A. (in press). Social comparison processes in coping and health. In C. R. Snyder & D. R. Forsyth (Eds.), *Handbook of social and clinical psychology.* New York: Pergamon.
Wilson, S. R., & Benner, L. A. (1971). The effects of self-esteem and situation on comparison choices during ability evaluation. *Sociometry, 34,* 381-397.
Wood, J. V. (1989). Theory and research concerning social comparison of personal attributes. *Psychological Bulletin, 106,* 231-248.
Wood, J. V., & Taylor, K. L. (1990). Serving self-relevant goals through social comparison. In J. Suls & T. A. Wills (Eds.), *Social comparison: Contemporary theory and research* (pp. 23-50). Hillsdale, NJ: Lawrence Erlbaum Associates.
Wood, J. V., Taylor, S. E., & Lichtman, R. R. (1985). Social comparison in adjustment to breast cancer. *Journal of Personality and Social Psychology, 49,* 1169-1183.
Zimbardo, P. G., & Formica, R. (1963). Emotional comparison and self-esteem as determinants of affiliation. *Journal of Personality, 31,* 141-162.
Zuckerman, M. (1979). Attribution of success and failure revisited, or The motivational bias is alive and well in attribution theory. *Journal of Personality, 47,* 245-287.

12 Social Comparison and Affiliation Under Threat[1]

Shelley E. Taylor
University of California, Los Angeles
Bram P. Buunk
University of Nijmegen, The Netherlands
Rebecca L. Collins
University of British Columbia, Vancouver
Geoffrey M. Reed
University of Washington, Seattle

Crises events elicit many forms of coping activity, directed toward such goals as emotion management and problem solving (e.g., Lazarus & Folkman, 1984). Increasingly, social comparison activity has been recognized as an important aspect of such coping efforts. Downward comparisons have been regarded as particularly crucial in dealing with life stress. In an influential paper, Wills (1981) suggested that when individuals are confronted with a threat to self-esteem, they may engage in downward comparisons with less advantaged others in an attempt to improve the way they feel about themselves. In a similar vein, Taylor and her colleagues (Taylor, 1983; Taylor, Wood, & Lichtman, 1983) have emphasized that social comparisons to less fortunate others may constitute a method of restoring self-esteem when facing a life-threatening disease. An expanding literature drawing on these ideas is exploring social comparison activity among individuals experiencing a variety of stressful circumstances. However, considerable theoretical confusion remains regarding how comparisons are used in response to stressful events.

The present paper presents a general model of social comparison activity under threat based upon classic theory and research examining social comparison processes, as well as upon recent studies suggesting that comparison and affiliative activities diverge under conditions of threat. It is argued that social comparisons are indeed prevalent among those confronted with a life crisis, due to the ambiguity,

[1] The research reported in this chapter was supported by three grants from the National Institute of Mental Health to the first author (MH 42258, MH 42918, and MH 42152), and by a grant from The Netherlands Organization for Scientific Research (NWO) to the second author. The fourth author was supported by a National Institute of Mental Health training grant (MH 15750).

uncertainty, and negative emotions caused by such crises. These experiences lead to a search for information as well as a need for self-enhancement, resulting in a general preference for upward contacts and downward comparisons. To substantiate these theoretical ideas, recent evidence from our laboratories, testing these ideas in the areas of cancer, AIDS, and marital stress is reviewed.

CLASSIC CONTRIBUTIONS

The importance of social comparisons for validating and assessing one's standing on a given dimension has long been recognized in social psychology. However, it was not until Festinger's (1954) social comparison theory that a well-developed conceptual framework outlining the nature of social comparison processes was established. This theory maintains that people have a need to evaluate their abilities and beliefs. Festinger argued that individuals prefer to evaluate themselves employing objective and nonsocial standards. However, if such objective information is unavailable, then they will compare themselves to others as a way of establishing a social reality. Originally, the theory maintained that the preferred source of social comparison is a person who is similar to the self-evaluator on the ability or opinion in question. The rationale for this prediction is that comparison with a similar other is maximally informative because it provides a person with a more precise and stable evaluation than would a comparison with someone who is very different. Subsequent additions to and modifications of the theory (Goethals & Darley, 1977) have suggested that under some circumstances, people prefer comparison others who are not similar on the evaluative dimension itself, but on attributes related to that dimension. Thus, in evaluating how one is coping with a marital crisis, one might select a person similar in age, years married, and employment, rather than someone very different on these dimensions.

Early social comparison theory and research did not explicitly address the role of social comparisons under conditions of threat or in the dynamics of coping. However, this extension would seem implicitly to be logical. Festinger (1954) emphasized that informational ambiguity and uncertainty enhance the desire for social comparison, and research on stressful events has found that a central dimension of events that makes them inherently stressful is their ambiguity and uncertainty (e.g., Billings & Moos, 1984; Gal & Lazarus, 1975). Viewed from this standpoint, social comparison processes can be seen as coping efforts initiated when objective information about a situation is lacking. The relation of social comparison processes to stress and coping is explicitly apparent in Stanley Schachter's (1959) book, *The Psychology of Affiliation*. Schachter presented the results of studies demonstrating that fear due to the prospect of having to undergo a stressful event, in this case electric shock, evoked in most subjects the desire to wait with someone else, preferably an individual in the same situation reacting with a similar degree of emotional intensity. After considering a variety of explanations for his findings, Schachter concluded that they were best explained by social comparison, the need to socially compare one's emotional state in order to determine its appropriateness. In subsequent studies adopting the fear-affiliation paradigm, it was shown that, as predicted by Festinger's (1954) theory, the desire for affiliation is particularly fostered by uncertainty about one's own emotional reactions (Gerard, 1963).

DOWNWARD COMPARISON THEORY

Originally, social comparison theory focused on the need for *self-evaluation*. Research and theory assumed that the social comparison process was primarily geared toward obtaining relatively accurate information about one's abilities, opinions, and emotions. Subsequently, researchers (e.g., Hakmiller, 1966; Thornton & Arrowood, 1966) suggested that social comparisons can be made for the purpose of *self-enhancement* (cf. Hakmiller, 1966). That is, social comparison processes cannot only provide people with accurate information about themselves, it can also provide them with information that leads them to feel better about themselves. The need for such information was expected to be especially prominent when self-esteem is threatened. Hakmiller (1966), for example, provided subjects who had taken a personality test with threatening feedback suggesting that they harbored a high level of hostility toward their parents. Other subjects received nonthreatening feedback. Subjects who were threatened responded by comparing themselves with others who had received feedback that they were even more hostile, whereas subjects exposed to less threat compared themselves with others receiving feedback that they were less hostile. These findings were interpreted to mean that, under conditions of threat, self-enhancement may lead people to make downward comparisons with someone worse off than themselves.

Since that hypothesis was initially ventured, a large amount of literature has confirmed the finding that, under conditions of threat, individuals typically make downward social comparisons, i.e., by derogating others, by realizing that others are worse off, or by actually affiliating with less fortunate others (Wills, 1981). For instance, in a laboratory experiment, Crocker, Thompson, McGraw, and Ingerman (1987) found that individuals high in self-esteem (but not those low in self-esteem), reacted to threats to the self-concept by derogating outgroups relative to the ingroup when the group boundaries had implications for self-evaluation (i.e., scoring high versus low on an intelligence test). In a different paradigm, Gibbons and Gerrard (1989) found that learning another was coping poorly or was having severe personal problems improved the mood of low self-esteem subjects. In addition, studies of serious diseases such as spinal cord injuries (Schulz & Decker, 1985), arthritis (Affleck, Tennen, Pfeiffer, Fifield, & Rowe, 1987), and cancer (Wood, Taylor, & Lichtman, 1985) have found that individuals tend to compare themselves with others worse off. Indeed, most individuals confronted with such naturally occurring stressors perceive themselves as relatively better off than most others facing the same or a similar stressor. For instance, in their study of patients with rheumatoid arthritis, Affleck et al. (1987) found that most patients felt they were doing better than the typical patient in terms of the severity of their illness, their degree of disability, and their ability to cope with the illness.

THE DIVERGENCE OF COMPARATIVE AND AFFILIATIVE ACTIVITY UNDER THREAT

The theoretical and empirical work of Schachter (1959) not only made explicit the relation of social comparison processes to stress, but also highlighted the importance of social interaction in social comparison processes. Although Festinger had originally developed the theory as a social one, suggesting that the need for self-evaluation leads people to affiliate with others, the emphasis of both his theorizing and subsequent research was on the *evaluations* of opinions and abilities. Schachter's work, in contrast, gave prominence to the affiliative activity that occurred in response to threat, rather than to the outcomes of social comparison processes, such as the conclusions one draws following comparison with a similar other.

As a result of these joint origins in cognitive and social processes, several different paradigms examining social comparison theory were adopted in the literature. Some studies operationalized social comparison activity as the desire to affiliate with others (see Cottrell & Epley, 1977; Rofe, 1984; and Suls, 1977, for reviews). The need for social comparison has also been operationally defined as the desire for information about selected others and about relevant individual differences (e.g., Rofe, 1984; Suls, 1977; Wheeler & Koestner, 1984; Wheeler, Koestner, & Driver, 1982). In addition, in a number of recent studies, subjects have been asked explicitly to compare their own abilities and outcomes with those of others (e.g., Campbell, 1986; Crocker et al., 1987; Marks, 1984; Tabachnik, Crocker, & Alloy, 1983). These distinctions among different measures of social comparison activity become important in the context of examining social comparison processes as a method of coping with stress.

Despite the support that various studies seem to offer for downward comparison theory, there is increasing evidence that social comparison activity under stress is more complex that this theory assumes. Recently, Taylor and Lobel (1989) analyzed the literature on social comparisons in stressful circumstances, and concluded that in certain groups under threat, comparison activities diverge: Explicit self-evaluation is made against a less fortunate target (downward evaluation), but information and affiliation are sought from more fortunate others (upward contacts). Their review, covering primarily the literature on social comparisons among cancer patients, indicated that, although patients typically made downward comparisons when explicitly evaluating their physical condition or coping (Wood et al., 1985), they did not seek contact with or information about less fortunate others. Rather, emerging evidence suggests that cancer patients seek exposure to other patients who have either overcome their threatening circumstances or have adjusted well to them, and that they avoid exposing themselves to those who are doing poorly (Molleman, Pruyn, & van Knippenberg, 1986; Taylor, Aspinwall, Dakof, & Reardon, 1988; Taylor & Dakof, 1988; see Taylor & Lobel, 1989, for a review).

For example, in a questionnaire study of 506 cancer patients, Molleman et al. (1986) asked respondents if they would like to interact with fellow patients who were much less, slightly less, similarly, slightly more, or much better off physically. Subjects strongly preferred to interact with a fellow patient who was similarly or slightly better off. Patients were also asked how they experienced their interactions with fellow patients. Interactions with fellow patients who were much worse off were experienced most negatively, followed by interactions with patients who were slightly worse off. Interaction with fellow patients who were much better off was experienced the most positively. In fact, these findings are quite compatible with early results based on Schachter's (1959) fear and affiliation studies. For instance, Rabbie (1963) showed that a high fear person was avoided in all conditions of his experiment. Low fear subjects preferred a low fear companion, moderate fear subjects a moderate fear companion, but the high fear subjects also preferred a moderate fear companion (cf. Gerard, 1963). Interestingly, it seems that upward affiliation is particularly characteristic of individuals high in self-esteem (Wilson & Benner, 1971), a finding largely in line with downward comparison theory.

As the foregoing makes clear, under conditions of threat, social comparison activities consist of explicit downward self-evaluation, that is against less fortunate others, and upward affiliative tendencies: Individuals prefer to interact with individuals who are doing better. In their review paper, Taylor and Lobel (1989) suggested that downward evaluations and upward contacts meet different needs. If one assumes that a crises or loss event produces both emotional needs (e.g., fear and anxiety) and problem-solving needs (e.g., efforts to eliminate the problem), then one would expect coping to revolve around these two basic sets of tasks: the regulation of emotional states and problem-solving efforts (Lazarus & Folkman, 1984). Downward evaluations seem to be clear efforts to regulate emotions by making the person feel better in comparison to worse-off others. Upward contacts, however, may be viewed simultaneously as problem-solving efforts, by providing a person with information valuable for potential survival and coping, and as a method for meeting emotional needs, by providing hope, motivation, and inspiration.

Together, these lines of research and theorizing suggest a model of comparison activity under threat. Individuals confronted with a crisis or loss are likely to experience a high degree of uncertainty, a condition likely to elicit social comparisons. In addition, they are faced with two major coping tasks: regulating their emotions and obtaining relevant problem-solving information. The first of these tasks is best addressed through the use of downward, self-enhancing comparisons, while the latter requires affiliation with or information on better-off others.

Several aspects of this model, however, remain untested. First, it has yet to be demonstrated that individuals facing major stressors experience a high degree of uncertainty and a concomitant rise in comparison activity, as compared with individuals in normal circumstances. Second, although there is considerable evidence to document the tendency to self-evaluate in a downward direction, there is less evidence that individuals affiliate upwardly when they are under stress. Third, it is unclear whether downward comparisons and upward affiliations are specific to threatened individuals or are common to all individuals. Various lines of research suggest that most individuals typically engage in downward comparisons by feeling that they are "better" than most others. For instance, most individuals feel they are more capable drivers than most others (Svenson, 1981), run fewer risks on coming down with various diseases (Perloff & Fetzer, 1986), and have a higher chance of being confronted with positive life events (Weinstein, 1980). It may be the case that all people have a need to feel good about themselves, which can be satisfied by downward comparisons. In a similar vein, it is quite possible that most individuals try to get better on dimensions under evaluation by obtaining information about others who are better off. A last point is that there is not yet evidence for the processes motivating downward comparisons and upward contacts: that upward comparisons serve both problem-solving and emotional needs, and downward comparisons primarily emotional needs. Below, we review emerging evidence from our research addressing these questions.

AFFILIATION UNDER THREAT

To assess whether people have a stronger tendency to affiliate upwardly when facing stress and uncertainty, we conducted a study of marital satisfaction and its determinants in a sample of 634 married individuals. These respondents were recruited using announcements placed in local newspapers, and by contacting a random sample of a middle-sized Dutch town (Buunk, VanYperen, Taylor, & Collins, in press). Subjects received a mailed questionnaire which they completed anonymously. To measure marital satisfaction, we employed an eight-item scale developed by Buunk (1990), that has been shown to have high reliability and validity. To assess uncertainty, the respondents were asked to indicate on a five-point scale to what extent they felt uncertain about how things were going in their marriage. To assess the desire for affiliation, subjects indicated on a five-point scale to what extent they felt a desire to talk with others about their marriage. These data were then analyzed as a function of marital satisfaction and uncertainty. The results indicated a significant linear trend, such that people with high levels of marital dissatisfaction and uncertainty were more interested in talking with others about their marriage than those low in dissatisfation and uncertainty. This finding is consistent with Schachter's (1959) point that affiliative preferences increase under threat and uncertainty (cf. Gerard, 1963).

To assess whether upward or downward affiliation was preferred, subjects were asked if they would want to talk with someone with a much worse marriage, a somewhat worse marriage, an equally good marriage, a somewhat better marriage, or a much better marriage than their own. Both men and women showed a linear preference for upward affiliation, as marital dissatisfaction or uncertainty increased. Indeed, only those individuals experiencing strain in their marriage were interested in talking with other who had better marriages, whereas those expressing low levels of dissatisfaction and uncertainty were more interested in talking with people whose marriages were about the same as theirs in satisfaction level. One can, of course, argue that there are simply more marriages available for people with stressful marriages to compare with, and that the upward affiliation pattern is simply a function of the availability pool of good marriages for these people. However, the question was phrased comparatively, so that as long as there are at least some marriages that are better or somewhat better than one's own, upward comparison is a possibility for those without or with marital stress.

This study makes several important points. It is the first study to provide clear evidence of upward affiliation preferences in the face of threat. Perhaps more important, by providing an opportunity to compare those experiencing more versus less threat, the study indicates that the upward affiliation pattern is largely confined to those experiencing high threat. These points provide evidence for the argument that threat is the condition producing the need to affiliate in an upward direction (Taylor & Lobel, 1989). Greater affiliation was desired among the threatened individuals, and it was clearly in the upward direction. Those experiencing less threat had less desire to affiliate overall and preferred those with similar marriages over those with better marriages as affiliative objects.

DIVERGENCE OF EVALUATIVE AND AFFILIATIVE ACTIVITIES

Full support for the model developed in this paper, however, would be provided by evidence showing downward evaluation and upward comparison processes occur simultaneously in the same sample. Such evidence is provided by a study of gay men with AIDS conducted by Reed (1989). These data are based on a study of 24 men with AIDS identified through a larger study on the natural history of AIDS. The mean age of the interview subjects was 38, and all were Caucasian. The mean educational level was some college, and most had been white-collar workers, although some were no longer working at the time of the interview. Three-quarters of the subjects had been initially identified with either Kaposi's sarcoma or pneumocystis carinii pneumonia as the primary AIDS-related condition; the remainder had other AIDS-related diagnoses. At the time the study was conducted, the mean time since diagnosis with AIDS was approximately 19.2 months, making the sample a relatively long-term group. Hereafter, these subjects will be referred to as Persons-Living-With-AIDS (PLAs), the term of choice in the gay community.

To examine the divergence of evaluative and affiliative comparison activities, we constructed a series of questions administered to the PLAs to assess evaluative and affiliative activities. We asked them first about the AIDS patients they preferred to spend time with: "In terms of medical condition, how would you rate the people with AIDS that you would prefer to be around?" They were given a five-point scale ranging from "much worse off than I am" to "much better off than I am." They were then asked the same question in terms of physical appearance and in terms of coping.

Next, questions were asked to assess self-evaluations, namely how they thought they were doing in comparison to other men with AIDS. They were asked about their medical condition, their physical appearance, and their coping with the illness. They rated their responses on a five-point scale, with one indicating "much worse off than others" and five indicating "much better off than others." The results indicated that PLAs preferred to affiliate with other AIDS patients who were about the same of slightly better off than they were in terms of their medical condition ($M = 3.13$), their physical appearance ($M = 3.29$), and their coping ability ($M = 3.29$). In contrast, on the evaluative questions, these men viewed themselves as between somewhat and much better off than other AIDS patients in terms of all three dimensions: their medical condition ($M = 4.35$), their physical appearance ($M = 4.26$), and their coping ability ($M = 4.10$). Thus, the data confirm the hypothesis that, under conditions of stress, people downwardly compare but upwardly affiliate.

It should be noted, however, that the upward affiliation data in this study are quite weak. That is, for the most part, the AIDS patients preferred to be with someone like themselves. This is in contrast to research on cancer patients, who more strongly prefer to be with people who are somewhat or much better off than themselves on the dimensions of physical illness and coping (see Taylor & Lobel, 1989). A possible explanation for this is that AIDS is generally considered to be terminal, while cancer generally offers the hope of successful treatment. Thus, upward affiliation may not have the same meaning for PLAs as for cancer patients. If one has no prospects for getting better, the value of comparisons with people who are doing better may be somewhat muted. Indeed, one of the reasons that PLAs gave in the interviews for not wanting to interact with others who were doing better was not wanting to be "preached to." These men often seemed to perceive AIDS as quite individual and quite veritable, even random, and to see successful others as not necessarily having much informational value. It is easier to identify with persons more similar to oneself, and similar others may be more relevant informationally.

Note that this interpretation is consistent with Taylor and Lobel's argument concerning why self-evaluations and affiliative preferences diverge under threat. If upward contacts are methods for meeting emotional needs and engaging in problem-solving activities, they can do so primarily to the extent that there is a possibility for improving on the dimension under evaluation. In the case of a good prognosis, upward affiliations would clearly be useful. In the case of a terminal illness, the role that upward affiliations can serve in terms of helping people to improve their medical condition, their physical appearance, or their coping, may be considerably more limited. Such comparisons may also make individuals more painfully aware of the tragedy of their own condition.

EFFECTS OF COMPARISONS AND AFFILIATION UNDER THREAT

Our model maintains that evaluative and affiliative preferences diverge under conditions of threat, because the two types of comparison processes serve different needs. Downward comparisons are assumed to make people feel better, whereas upward contacts are assumed to serve problem-solving needs, as well as emotional needs for hope, motivation, and inspiration. There are some inferential data to support this interpretation. Consistent with the idea that upward affiliations are a source of motivation, inspiration, and hope, a study of 663 lymphoma and breast cancer patients (van den Borne, Pruyn, & van den Heuvel, 1987) found improved mood among cancer patients following contacts with fellow patients. Significantly, increased self-esteem was found only among patients who were the worst off (i.e., who were undergoing a second set of treatments). Those who were better off did not show increased self-esteem as a result of contact with fellow patients. This finding tentatively suggests that upward contacts can be esteem-building, particularly for individuals who are facing a significant threat.

Consistent with the idea that upward contacts satisfy informational needs and emotional needs simultaneously, a review of 18 articles by van den Borne, Pruyn, and van Dam-de Mey (1986) found that cancer patients' contacts with fellow cancer patients consistently led to a higher level of information, as well as to a reduction in negative feelings (anxiety, fatigue, tension, and confusion; see also Kulik & Mahler, 1987). However, none of the studies reviewed assessed whether these affiliations were with better-off or worse-off others.

A study conducted by Buunk, Collins, Taylor, vanYperen, and Dakof (in press) addressed the affective consequences of upward and downward social comparisons. The study involved interviews with 55 cancer patients, who were recruited from a pool of 668 cancer patients who had previously participated in a survey of social support needs. The response rate was 93%. Patients were within five years of diagnosis or recurrence and between 30 and 70 years of age. The sample included 30 men and 25 women with a median age of 54. Eighty-three percent were married and 84% had children. Fifty-six percent were employed, and the median family income was between $40,000 and $49,000. Participants had been diagnosed or had sustained a recurrence an average of 3.2 years prior to the interview. Respondents were telephoned and an interview time was arranged, usually at home. The interview covered basic demographic data, the respondent's past and current health status, social support experiences following the cancer diagnosis, perceptions of how life had changed since the cancer diagnosis, and items relevant to social comparison processes and the affective outcomes of those comparisons. Specifically, affective consequences of downward comparisons were assessed as follows. Subjects were told, "Some people have told us when they see cancer patients who are not doing as well as they are, it makes them feel lucky and grateful that they are not in worse shape themselves. Other people have told us, when they see cancer patients who are not as well off as they are, it makes them feel worse. For these people, seeing cancer patients who are worse off only increases their fears and anxieties." Subjects were then asked to rate the frequency with which they had felt lucky or grateful when exposed to worse-off others, on a four-point scale, from one, "never," to four, "often." Subjects were also asked how often they felt fearful or anxious in response to such people, on the same four-point scale. The affective consequences of upward comparisons were assessed next. Subjects were told, "Some people have told us that when they see cancer patients who are doing better than they are, it makes them feel frustrated or depressed. Other people have told us that they feel inspired or comforted when they see other cancer patients who seem to be doing better then they are." Again, subjects rated the frequency of each of these reactions on a four-point scale and provided an example of each.

If, as assumed in our model, social comparison activities are initiated as coping efforts in response of stress, one should find that the preponderance of comparisons made would be positive affect comparisons, both upward and downward. As predicted, eighty-two percent of the respondents made positive affect downward comparisons, and 78% made positive affect upward comparisons. This is in comparison to 59% who made downward comparisons and felt bad as a result and 40% who made upward comparisons and felt bad as a result. Thus, although negative comparisons were altogether lacking and indeed were quite prevalent for some subjects, the preponderance of comparisons in both directions made the respondents feel good, providing some evidence that these social comparison activities are successful coping efforts.

Interestingly, however, these effects were moderated by the perceived control that people felt they had over their cancer. Subjects had been asked to indicate the extent to which they had control over their daily symptoms and the extent to which they felt they could keep the cancer from spreading or coming back. Subjects indicated their answers on five-point scales, ranging from "not at all" to "completely." The model developed in this paper would predict that those who believed they had high control over their illness would be more likely to report feeling good in response to upward comparisons, and less likely to report feeling bad in response to downward comparisons. The rationale for these predictions is that if one believes one has the capacity to maintain or improve one's condition, then upward comparisons should provide one with information relevant to this process and with positive role models. Similarly, contact with those who are deteriorating should be less threatening, given that one assumes one will not have the same fate. No prediction can be made concerning positive affect downward comparisons as a function of control, inasmuch as those both high and low in control could profit affectively from downward comparisons. The predictions were only partially supported. The belief that one has personal control over the course of one's illness or over one's symptoms predicted fewer numbers of negative affect downward comparisons. That is, patients with high feelings of control were less likely to experience negative affect downward comparisons[2]. However, unexpectedly, they were no more likely than those with low feelings of control to make positive affect upward comparisons. As expected, belief that one could control one's illness was unrelated to the frequency of positive affect downward comparisons, which was high for all subjects.

The affective outcomes of social comparisons were also moderated by self-esteem. Self-esteem did not alter the frequency with which positive affect comparisons were made, both upward and downward. However, low self-esteem persons were significantly more likely to experience negative outcome comparisons than were persons of high self-esteem (cf. Crocker et al., 1987).

The study described earlier that involved 634 married individuals from The Netherlands also assessed the affective consequences of social comparisons. Subjects responded to questions similar to those in the cancer study concerning the affect involved in socially comparing their marriages. They were asked how often they felt happy and pleased when they compared their marital relationship with others who had a relationship that was worse. A five-point scale was employed, ranging from "never" to "very often." To assess the frequency of negative affect evoked by downward comparisons, subjects were asked, "How often do you feel unhappy and displeased when you compare your own marital relationship with that of others who have a relationship that is worse than yours?" Similar questions were asked for the negative and positive affect evoked by marriages that were better than one's own. As was the case with the cancer patients, the most common comparisons reported were positive affect downward comparisons, with 95% of subjects reporting such comparisons. Positive affect upward comparisons were also commonly reported (78%). Thus, nearly all individuals had experienced positive feelings when seeing other marriages that were worse than their own, and a large majority had derived satisfaction from observing that other marriages were better. As with the cancer patients, negative affect upward (59%) and negative affect downward comparisons (48%) were less frequent.

On the basis of their scores on the marital satisfaction scale, the subjects were divided into three groups, those with high, medium, and low marital dissatisfaction. Contrary to our predictions, the frequency of both downward negative affect

---

[2] It is not clear whether these patients physically avoided patients who were worse off or whether they were simply more able to avoid the negative implications of such contacts. Further research is needed to differentiate these two possibilities.

comparisons was greater for those in dissatisfying marital relationships than in more satisfying ones. Among women and marginally among men, there was an effect of marital dissatisfaction on the frequency of positive affect downward comparisons. People in less happy marriages felt less positively in response to downward comparisons than those whose marriages were more satisfying. It would appear, then, that the desire or ability to make positive affect social comparisons under conditions of threat may be compromised by threat itself.

SOCIAL COMPARISON PROCESSES UNDER STRESS: DISCUSSION AND CONCLUSIONS

The present paper presents a general model of social comparison activity under threat, based upon classic social comparison theory, as well as upon recent studies on naturally occurring stressors (Taylor & Lobel, 1989). This model suggests that stress generates social comparison activities, due to the ambiguity, uncertainty, and negative emotions that are associated with stress and threat. These social comparison activities are assumed to be guided by both emotional concerns and problem-solving needs. Emotional needs are assumed to be met both by downward comparisons, namely the evaluation of one's situation in comparison to worse-off others, and by upward contacts, which provide inspiration and motivation. In addition, upward affiliation is expected to provide useful information and role models for coping and adjustment. Thus, the model predicts that under conditions of threat, there will be a preference for upward contacts and downward comparisons.

In the face of the data presented in this paper, how well does the model fare? First, as predicted, the study on the married couples showed that individuals experiencing a relatively high degree of uncertainty show a stronger desire for affiliation and heightened comparison activity, as compared with individuals in normal circumstances. The same was true for individuals who were relatively dissatisfied in their marriages, as compared to happily married individuals. Second, the same study showed that individuals with high levels of uncertainty and marital dissatisfaction, clearly preferred upward affiliation more than individuals with low levels of dissatisfaction and uncertainty. Thus, a preference for upward affiliation is, as predicted by our model, specific to threatened individuals, and not common to all individuals. The model also predicts that upward affiliations are in part for the purpose of gaining information relevant to improving one's situation. The muted tendency of AIDS patients to engage in upward comparisons, relative to the other threatened groups we studied, is implicitly consistent with this point. Because AIDS is a terminal illness and creates lesser potential for improvement, upward comparisons may be less able to provide useful information and therefore may not be made as often.

Our data provide only limited support for the assumption that making downward comparisons is an important and effective way of coping with stress. Persons living with AIDS and cancer patients clearly do feel that they are better off than others in the same circumstances. However, a number of findings from our research contradict assumptions derived from Wills' (1981) downward comparison theory. First, our results suggest that individuals facing stress may not make downward comparisons more than individuals in normal circumstances. In our study of married individuals, those in more dissatisfying or uncertain marriages were not more likely to make downward comparisons. Second, Wills' theory predicts that low self-esteem individuals and individuals under threat will derive satisfaction from making downward comparisons. However, our data revealed that individuals who evaluate their own situation negatively (e.g., low self-esteem individuals or those experiencing a high degree of marital dissatisfaction), derive fewer positive and more negative feelings from downward comparisons than individuals in more happy circumstances. As in the study of Crocker et al. (1987), our findings suggest that individuals high in self-esteem and marital satisfaction are better able to use either upward or downward comparisons for the purpose of self-enhancement, as compared to individuals low in self-esteem or marital satisfaction.

Earlier, Taylor and Lobel (1989) had argued that these downward comparisons and upward affiliations help people cope with stressful events. In particular, it has been argued that upward comparisons provide hope and inspiration as well as exposure to information useful for improving on the dimension in question. Downward comparisons improve emotional functioning by enabling people to feel better about themselves. To a degree, this explanation of social comparison patterns under threat has received support. However, both upward and downward social comparisons contain both positive and negative information. An upward comparison may contain information about how circumstances can be improved, but it simultaneously reminds a person that others are better off. Similarly, a downward comparison may allow a person to feel good that he or she is not as badly off as others, but contains the information that it is possible to get worse. Thus, while upward and downward comparisons may provide victims with the positive outcomes predicted by the model, namely the satisfaction of needs for problem-solving and emotional regulation, conditions of threat may also intrude so as to make the negative spectre of both downward comparisons and upward comparisons more salient. In using others to feel better and/or acquire useful information, one may be reminded that one's situation is not as positive as it could be and that it could worsen. Thus, the use of social comparison strategies to bolster self-esteem, restore positive affect, and to develop coping strategies may have both positive and negative effects. Though clearly beneficial in enabling people to derive some benefit from stressful experiences, social comparisons under threat can be a double-edged sword.

REFERENCES

Affleck, G., Tennen, H., Pfeiffer, C., Fifield, J., & Rowe, J. (1987). Downward comparison and coping with serious medical problems. *American Journal of Orthopsychiatry, 57*, 570-578.

Billings, A. C., & Moos, R. H. (1984). Coping, stress, and social resources among adults with unipolar depression. *Journal of Personality and Social Psychology, 46*, 877-891.

Buunk, B. P. (1990). Relationship interaction satisfaction scale. In J. Touliatos, B. F. Perlmutter, & M. A. Straus (Eds.), *Handbook of family measurement techniques* (pp. 106-107). Newbury Park, CA: Sage.

Buunk, B. P., Collins, R. L., Taylor, S. E., VanYperen, N., & Dakof, G. A. (in press). The affective consequences of social comparison: Either direction has its ups and downs. *Journal of Personality and Social Psychology*.

Buunk, B. P., VanYperen, N., Taylor, S. E., & Collins, R. L. (in press). *Social affiliation under threat*. Manuscript submitted for publication.

Campbell, J. D. (1986). Similarity and uniqueness: The effects of attribute type, relevance, and individual differences in self-esteem and depression. *Journal of Personality and Social Psychology, 50*, 281-294.

Cottrell, N. B., & Epley, S. W. (1977). Affiliation, social comparison, and social mediated stress reduction. In J. M. Suls & R. L. Miller (Eds.), *Social comparison processes: Theoretical and empirical perspectives* (pp. 43-68). Washington, DC: Hemisphere.

Crocker, J., Thompson, L. L., McGraw, K. M., & Ingerman, C. (1987). Downward comparison, prejudice, and evaluations of others: Effects of self-esteem and threat. *Journal of Personality and Social Psychology, 52*, 907-916.

Festinger, L. (1954). A theory of social comparison processes. *Human Relations, 7*, 117-140.

Gal, R., & Lazarus, R. S. (1975). The role of activity in anticipating and confronting stressful situations. *Journal of Human Stress, 1*(4), 4-20.

Gerard, H. B. (1963). Emotional uncertainty and social comparison. *Journal of Abnormal and Social Psychology, 66*, 568-573.

Gibbons, F. X., & Gerrard, M. (1989). Effects of upward and downward social comparison on mood states. *Journal of Social and Clinical Psychology, 8*, 14-31.

Goethals, G. R., & Darley, J. M. (1977). Social comparison theory: An attributional approach. In J. M. Suls & R. L. Miller (Eds.), *Social comparison processes: Theoretical and empirical perspectives* (pp. 259-278). Washington, DC: Hemisphere.

Hakmiller, K. L. (1966). Threat as a determinant of downward comparison. *Journal of Experimental Social Psychology*, (Suppl. 1), 32-39.

Kulik, J. A., & Mahler, H. I. M. (1987). Effects of preoperative roommate assignment on preoperative anxiety and recovery from coronary-bypass surgery. *Health Psychology, 6*, 525-543.

Lazarus, R. S., & Folkman, S. (1984). *Stress, appraisal, and coping*. New York: Springer.

Marks, G. (1984). Thinking one's abilities are unique and one's opinions are common. *Personality and Social Psychology Bulletin, 10*, 203-208.

Molleman, E., Pruyn, J., & van Knippenberg, A. (1986). Social comparison processes among cancer patients. *British Journal of Social Psychology, 25*, 1-13.

Perloff, L. S., & Fetzer, B. K. (1986). Self-other judgments and perceived invulnerability to victimization. *Journal of Personality and Social Psychology, 50*, 502-510.

Rabbie, J. M. (1963). Differential preference for companionship under threat. *Journal of Abnormal and Social Psychology, 67*, 643-648.

Reed, G. M. (1989). *Stress, coping, and psychological adaptation in a sample of gay and bisexual men with AIDS*. Unpublished doctoral dissertation, University of California, Los Angeles.

Rofe, Y. (1984). Stress affiliation: A utility theory. *Psychological Review, 91*, 235-250.

Schachter, S. (1959). *The psychology of affiliation*. Stanford, CA: Stanford University Press.

Schulz, R., & Decker, S. (1985). Long-term adjustment to physical disability: The role of social support, perceived control, and self-blame. *Journal of Personality and Social Psychology, 48*, 1162-1172.

Suls, J. M. (1977). Social comparison theory and research: An overview from 1954. In J. M. Suls & R. L. Miller (Eds.), *Social comparison processes: Theoretical and empirical perspectives* (pp. 1-20). Washington, DC: Hemisphere.

Svenson, O. (1981). Are we all less risky and more skillful than our fellow drivers? *Acta Psychologica, 47,* 143-148.

Tabachnik, N., Crocker, J., & Alloy, L. B. (1983). Depression, social comparison, and the false-consensus effect. *Journal of Personality and Social Psychology, 45,* 688-699.

Taylor, S. E. (1983). Adjustment to threatening events: A theory of cognitive adaptation. *American Psychologist, 38,* 1161-1173.

Taylor, S. E., Aspinwall, L. G., Dakof, G. A., & Reardon, K. (1988). *Stress, storytelling, social comparison, and social support: Victims' reactions to stories of similar victims.* Manuscript submitted for publication.

Taylor, S. E., & Dakof, G.A. (1988). Social support and the cancer patient. In S. Spacapan & S. Oskamp (Eds.), *The social psychology of health: The Claremont symposium on applied social psychology* (pp. 95-116). Newbury Park, CA: Sage.

Taylor, S. E., & Lobel, M. (1989). Social comparison activity under threat: Downward evaluation and upward contacts. *Psychological Review, 96,* 569-575.

Taylor, S. E., Wood, J. V., & Lichtman, R. R. (1983). It could be worse: Selective evaluation as a response to victimization. *Journal of Social Issues, 39*(2), 19-40.

Thornton, D. A., & Arrowood, A. J. (1966). Self-evaluation, self-enhancement, and the locus of social comparison. *Journal of Experimental Social Psychology,* (Suppl. 1), 40-48.

van den Borne, H. W., Pruyn, J. F. A., & van Dam-de Mey, K. (1986). Self-help in cancer patients: A review of studies on the effects of contacts between fellow-patients. *Patient Education and Counseling, 8,* 367-385.

van den Borne, H. W., Pruyn, J. F. A., & van den Heuvel, W. J. A. (1987). Effects of contacts between cancer patients on their psychosocial problems. *Patient Education and Counseling, 9,* 33-51.

Weinstein, N. D. (1980). Unrealistic optimism about future life events. *Journal of Personality and Social Psychology, 39,* 806-820.

Wheeler, L., & Koestner, R. (1984). Performance evaluation: On choosing to know the related attributes of others when we know their performance. *Journal of Experimental Social Psychology, 20,* 263-271.

Wheeler, L., Koestner, R., & Driver, R. E. (1982). Related attributes in the choice of comparison others: It's there, but it isn't all there is. *Journal of Experimental Social Psychology, 18,* 489-500.

Wills, T. A. (1981). Downward comparison principles in social psychology. *Psychological Bulletin, 90,* 245-271.

Wilson, S. R., & Benner, L. A. (1971). The effects of self-esteem and situation upon comparison choices during ability evaluation. *Sociometry, 34,* 381-397.

Wood, J. V., Taylor, S. E., & Lichtman, R. R. (1985). Social comparison in adjustment to breast cancer. *Journal of Personality and Social Psychology, 49,* 1169-1183.

13 Employees' Reactions to an Anticipated Plant Closure: The Influence of Positive Illusions[1]

Melvin J. Lerner
University of Waterloo

Darryl G. Somers
Government of Canada

Contemporary trends in the economy force increasing numbers of people to deal with the crisis of job loss. Unemployment created by plant closures and downsizing produces multiple threats to workers' economic and psychological well-being. The displaced workers can anticipate a loss in seniority, reduced pay, and consequently, a lowering standard of living for themselves and their dependents. Typically, the impact of job loss goes beyond direct economic costs. Along with being separated from a familiar daily routine and supportive social contacts, displaced workers must deal with the implicit threats to their sense of self-worth and confidence in an orderly and manageable world (Borgen & Amundson, 1987; Brenner & Bartelli, 1983; Janoff-Bulman & Frieze, 1983; Kaufman, 1982; Kelvin, 1980; Lerner, 1980; Vinokur, Caplan, & Williams, 1988; see Kelvin & Jarrett, 1985, and Warr, 1987, for reviews). These threats create a powerful incentive for the displaced worker to find the best possible re-employment. However, they may also lead to a crippling demoralization and avoidant defenses. The possibility for destructive rather than effective coping responses poses a serious problem for society as well as the victimized worker.

To understand what factors would enable displaced workers to manage the psychological impact of their job loss and find employment, we turned to the recent work of Taylor and her colleagues (Taylor, 1983; Taylor & Brown, 1988; Taylor,

[1]This research was supported by a contract awarded by the Employment Adjustment Branch, Ontario Ministry of Labour to M. J. Lerner. The authors would like to thank the staff of the Employment Adjustment Branch, and especially Lisa Avedon for initially suggesting the need for this research and then providing support during the critical period of data collection. Some of the analyses in this chapter have been reported in Lerner and Somers (1990) and in the unpublished Ph.D. dissertation of Somers (1989).

Wood, & Lichtman, 1983). Contrary to the common view that effective coping must be based upon a realistic appraisal of the situation (e.g., Haan, 1977; Jahoda, 1958; Vaillant, 1977), Taylor and Brown (1988) concluded from a review of recent evidence that certain positive illusions can play a critical role in enabling people to cope with threats posed by serious crises. They argue that to cope effectively people need to maintain a requisite level of self-esteem, personal control, and optimism about the future, even if unsupported by more objective assessments. Presumably, these illusory beliefs would enable displaced workers to avoid immobilizing feelings of despair, and provide the encouragement and incentive necessary to sustain an effective search for employment.

The research reported here examines the role of positive illusions in the coping efforts of workers who had been given six months notice that their plant would be closing. One aspect of this relationship is their influence on the workers' sense of well-being. Do "positive illusions" contribute to maintaining the employees' morale? Most importantly, however, do they promote the incentive and confidence required for the workers to engage in efforts to find re-employment, as Taylor and Brown (1988) suggest?

The strategy employed in answering these and other related questions is based on a two-stage panel design. We administered questionnaires containing measures of optimism, self-esteem, and control to the employees of a plant shortly after they were informed that it would be closing and once again just two weeks prior to the closure. The workers' beliefs were measured both in a general form that is found in the literature and also in a form specific to the crisis facing these employees. The specific form assessed how positively the workers viewed themselves in comparison to their fellow workers, how optimistic they were about finding a job, and how closely their personal credentials matched those needed to find another job. In order to examine the impact of these beliefs on coping, the workers' intentions to find work and their job-seeking efforts were measured at both time periods.

The studies reported here follow preliminary analyses (Somers & Lerner, 1990) that confirmed the expected presence of positive illusions in this sample of workers. Consistent with Taylor and Brown's (1988) analysis of prior evidence the workers, in aggregate, manifested unrealistically high self-esteem (Brown, 1986), optimism about their future (Weinstein, 1980), and confidence that their attributes were those required to obtain re-employment (Kunda, 1987).

Having established the presence of the "positive illusions" in this sample of threatened employees, the first study examines Taylor and Brown's (1988) predictions concerning the relationships among the illusions, the sense of well-being, and the workers' coping responses. The second study will explore some of the issues Taylor and Brown (1988) left unresolved. In particular, the workers' reactions will be examined for suggestions concerning how to integrate the available evidence supporting the potential functional roles of both reality testing and positive illusions: When are people best served by relying on positive illusions and when they are better served by facing the crisis as realistically as possible, however painful the reality might be?

ASSESSING THE FUNCTIONAL CONSEQUENCES OF POSITIVE ILLUSIONS

To test Taylor and Brown's (1988) assertions about the functional role of positive illusions, the "illusions" were treated as sets of beliefs or personal constructs about themselves and their environment which ranged from positive to negative, more to less. A model based upon the following hypotheses was constructed and subjected to a path analysis: The more positive the workers' beliefs about themselves and their environment, including self-esteem, sense of control, and optimism (i.e., termed here, personal constructs), the less the workers will view the plant closure as threatening to their security, and the more they will feel confident in their finding re-employment, thus creating a higher level of general morale. A greater sense of well-being combined with confidence in their ability to find re-employment will in turn provide the incentive and encouragement required to seek employment. Looking for work in this context is a form of active coping.

Method

Subjects

This study involved foundry workers anticipating the closure of their plant. Of the 327 workers at the foundry, 220 were eligible for the study. Temporary workers and permanent workers who were retiring or being transferred within the company were excluded from the sample. One-hundred and fifty-six (70.90%) workers answered the first initial questionnaire two months prior to the closing. This sample was composed of 148 male and eight female workers who had a mean age of 32.83, ranging from 19 to 63. Their mean education level was grade 12. They had worked at the foundry between 1 and 38 years, for a mean of 6.78 years. Their mean total income level was $30,000 to $40,000 a year. Two thirds of the sample were married. At the reassessment 6 weeks later (2 weeks before the scheduled closing) 116 workers from the initial sample (74.36%) completed the second questionnaire. Six workers were absent due to illness or injury, and 11 had quit their jobs, leaving only 22 workers (14.10% of the original sample) who declined to participate.

Procedure

Two months prior to the plant closing date (Time 1) respondents completed questionnaires during 60-minute testing sessions scheduled directly preceding or following their regular work shift. The schedule was arranged so that no more than 12 respondents would be present at a testing session. The second assessment session, two weeks before the plant closing (Time 2), took place during workers regular shifts, and a maximum of eight workers attended each session. Respondents were told that the study was intended to assess workers' thoughts and feelings about the plant closure and their resultant job loss and were assured that the information they provided would be kept completely confidential.

Measures

Three measures were created specifically for this study to assess the workers' beliefs about themselves and the job loss. Measures were also included to assess the respondents' more global sense of self-esteem and locus-of-control, as well as their belief in a just world. Also assessed were the employees' expectations of finding re-employment, perceived severity of the crisis, sense of well-being, plans to find work, and reports of job-search activities. The means, standard deviations, and reliability coefficients, and test-retest correlations for these measures are presented in Table 13.1.[2]

Comparative Self-Evaluations. Based on Brown's (1986) method, subjects rated the extent that three positive adjectives (responsible, bright, and dependable) and three negative adjectives (phoney, cruel, rude) applied to themselves and to other workers at the plant, using 5-point scales ranging from "Not at all true of me/others" to "Very true of me/others." An overall scale was created by summing the differences between the two ratings (self, other), reversing the sign of the values for the negative items so that a higher score indicates more positive comparative self-evaluations.

Comparative Optimism. The workers rated the relative probability that each of four positive events (e.g., enjoy good health) and four negative events (e.g., have a drinking problem) would occur to them in the next 5 years (see Weinstein, 1980). The ratings were done on 5-point scales with endpoints labeled as "Below average" and "Above average." The signs for the negative items were reversed and added to the positive items to form a general scale, with higher scores indicating more comparative optimism.

Functional Attributes. Based on Kunda's (1987) research, subjects first rated how important each of seven attributes was for gaining employment and then, later in the questionnaire, rated how self-descriptive each attribute was (5-point scales with responses from "Not at all" to "A great deal"). A scale measuring subjects' estimation of the self-descriptiveness of an attribute relative to its importance was created by subtracting the importance rating of each attribute from the self-

---

[2]Many subjects did not complete all of the items in the questionnaire, either by choice or accident. For this reason *n*'s in the analyses will vary depending upon the number of respondents who completed the particular items under consideration.

TABLE 13.1

Reliabilities, means, and standard deviations at Time 1 and Time 2.

Measure	*Time 1* *Alpha*	*Time 1* *Mean*	*Time 1* *S.D.*	*Time 2* *Alpha*	*Time 2* *Mean*	*Time 2* *S.D.*	*Test-Retest*
Comparative Optimism	.68	41.10	5.52	.81	39.74	6.40	.46
Functional Characteristics	.74	-1.97	3.51	.57	-2.38	3.24	.57
Comparative Self-evaluations	.56	4.60	4.21	.47	4.42	4.26	.73
Control	.47	20.81	3.49	.65	20.53	3.60	.65
Self-esteem	.80	28.19	3.53	.78	27.93	3.14	.46
Belief in Justice	...	3.06	1.19	...	3.09	1.23	.39
Personal Constructs	...	5.65	2.58	...	5.57	2.31	.53
Positive Affect	.94	35.11	7.20	.95	34.24	6.80	.59
Distress	.94	35.35	12.98	.95	34.67	11.76	.68
Well-being	...	2.14	1.03	...	1.99	1.04	.73
Problem-focused	.73	5.85	2.91	.79	5.99	2.61	.52
Emotion-focused Coping	.72	3.10	2.84	.67	2.76	2.65	.67
Perceived Severity	.36	-10.52	3.85	.34	-7.41	2.77	.52
Subjective Employability	.79	13.05	3.68	.78	13.91	3.20	.65
Expert-rated Employability	.94	30.16	4.35	...	...	...	...
Job-search Intentions	.50	26.71	6.63	.40	27.12	5.83	.63
Job-search Behavior	.29	5.45	2.42	.56	13.36	5.45	.62

descriptiveness rating. Lower scores indicate that important job-relevant attributes were not descriptive of them.

Self-Esteem. Rosenberg's (1965) 10-item scale was included as a general measure of self-esteem; responses varied on a 4-point scale from "Strongly agree" to "Strongly disagree."

Control. A locus-of-control scale, created by Lumpkin (1985) based on the original Rotter (1966) scale for use in questionnaire research, was administered; respondents indicated degree of (dis)agreement on a 5-point scale; a higher score indicates internality of locus of control.

Belief in a Just World. Respondents were asked the extent that they agreed or disagreed with a single item from the Rubin and Peplau (1973) Belief-in-a-Just-World Scale: "Basically, the world is a just place." Higher score indicates more agreement.

Subjective Employability. Respondents' appraisals of their difficulty finding employment was assessed through several questions. Respondents were asked "Compared to most people you work with, how difficult do you think it will be to find a job equal to or better than your present job?" and "How do you think things will go for you in the next few months compared to other workers in this plant?" (1 = Much worse to 6 = Much better). An additional open-ended question asked respondents, "At the present time, what is your best guess about the maximum amount of time it will take you to find a job?". These items were summed to a single index, with a higher score indicating positive perceptions about their employability.

Perceived Severity. Respondents' perceptions of the severity of the situation were assessed by asking them "Considering all of the things that could happen in a person's life, how would you rate being laid-off at this time..." (1 = Among the best, 10 = Among the worst). They were also asked "Compared to workers at other plants with the same skills as you, everything considered, how well off are you at this time?" and "Looking ahead to 5 years from now, compared to other workers in this plant, how will this layoff have affected you?", using 5-point scales ranging from "Much better off" to "Much worse off." These items were summed to form a single index with higher values indicating greater perceived severity.

Well-Being. Respondents' well-being was assessed by combining measures of acute distress and positive affect. Distress was measured using selected subscales from the Brief Symptom Inventory (BSI; Derogatis & Melisaratos, 1983). The subscales used measure somatization, depression, hostility, and anxiety. The respondents rated items using 5-point scales that assessed the extent to which each symptom had caused discomfort in the past week (Not at all to Extremely). The Joy and Contentment subscales of the Affect Balance Scale (ABS; Derogatis, 1975) assessed the respondents' positive affect. Each subscale had five mood adjectives rated on a 5-point scale from "Never" to "Always." Well-being scores were created by subtracting respondent's BSI score from their ABS score. A higher score refers to greater subjective well-being in the sense that respondents experience more positive affect and less distress.

Job-Search Intentions. Measures assessing respondents' intentions to perform problem-solving behavior asked respondents whether they intended to seek retraining (4-point bipolar scale), and whether they intended to speak to other workers, friends, supervisors, union representatives, family, government agencies, nongovernment employment agencies, retraining/counseling centers, or any other source to get information on job opportunities (Not at all, Maybe, Definitely). They were also asked about the extent to which they had made plans to seek employment, and how much they thought about the plant closure situation. These four items were summed into a single index to assess respondents' job-search intentions, with greater scores referring to more intention to engage in job-search behavior.

Job-Search Behavior. Several items were included in the questionnaire to assess problem-solving, job-search behavior: e.g., "How many jobs have you applied for since finding out about the layoff?" (None, 1 or 2, 3 to 5, 6 to 10, More than 10), "Which of the following people have you talked to about your job in the last couple of days?" (e.g., fellow workers, friends outside of work, supervisors, union representatives, family, government representatives, employment agencies, retraining/counseling centers, or any other source). "How useful has each of the following [items on a list of job-search strategies] been to your efforts to find a new job?". This item was scored as a dichotomous variable based on whether or not respondents used the strategy. Respondents were also asked how many job prospects or leads they had managed to find at that time. A higher score on this measure indicates more job-search activity.

Results

The Functional Illusion Model

The functional illusion model based upon Taylor and Brown (1988) predicts that positive paths will lead from the Personal Constructs to Perceived Severity, Well-being, and Subjective Employability. These, in turn, are expected to have positive paths to Behavioral Intentions and Job-search Behavior. Well-being and Subjective Employability are also anticipated to have positive paths to Job-search Behavior through Behavioral Intentions.

Path analyses indicate that the specified paths in this model do provide an adequate account of the relations among the variables, explaining approximately

45% of the variance in Job-search Behavior at both time intervals (Time 1, estimated $\chi^2(10) = 4.71$, n.s., Goodness of Fit = .95; Time 2, estimated $\chi^2(10) = 3.43$, n.s., Goodness of Fit = .80). The standardized path coefficients for Times 1 and 2 are presented in Figures 13.1 and 13.2, respectively.

Within this model, as predicted, there are significant paths between the Personal Constructs and the workers' Perceived Severity (Time 1), their Well-being, and Subjective Employability. Also, consistent with the functional illusion model, there are significant paths between the workers' Well-being and their Subjective Employability. The significant path at Time 1 between the workers' Subjective Employability and their Job-search Behavior provides additional confirmation for this model, although the path does not achieve an acceptable level of significance at the second testing session.

There are further difficulties for the functional illusion model, however. The theoretically important paths between Well-being and Job-search Behavior, though significant, indicate negative relationships rather than the expected positive relationship between these two variables. Apparently, both earlier and later in the crisis, the greater the workers' sense of well-being the less actively they searched for re-employment. Consistent with this unexpected inverse relationship, there is also a negative path between Subjective Employability and Behavioral Intentions early on (Time 1), indicating that the more employable the workers thought they were, the less they intended to actively seek work.

Discussion

The respondents in this study were workers who had been given six months notice that their jobs would no longer be there. For the vast majority of them, the promised financial and technical assistance would not eliminate the economic and psychological threats created by the job loss, nor the demand to find re-employment. Nevertheless, at eight and two weeks before they lost their jobs the workers, in aggregate, believed they had more positive and less negative attributes than others, had a greater control over their environment, and that their future held more promises and less threats than could possibly have been warranted by the facts (Somers & Lerner, 1990).

These optimistic biases, first identified in university undergraduate samples, constitute the positive illusions that Taylor and Brown (1988) propose have a functional relationship to coping with a crisis. In this case, the effective coping response was looking for another job. The workers' responses confirmed the role that these illusions were expected to play in maintaining their morale and expectation of being able to find work. Those with more positive self-regard, a more optimistic view of their future, and greater sense of control reported having fewer worries and less personal distress. They also thought they were more likely than the other workers to find work in the near future. However, this functional aspect of the illusions did not extend beyond the workers' morale and

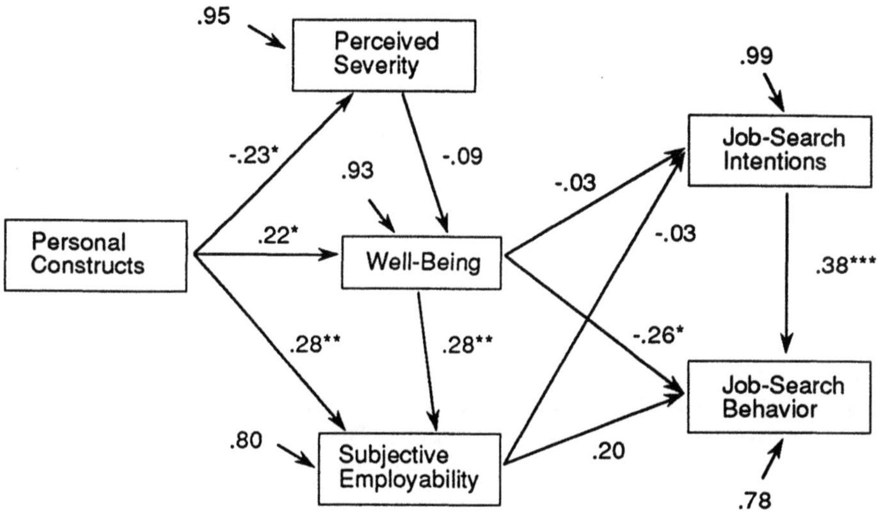

FIG. 13.1. Functional illusion path model (*p <.05; **p <.01; ***p<.001).

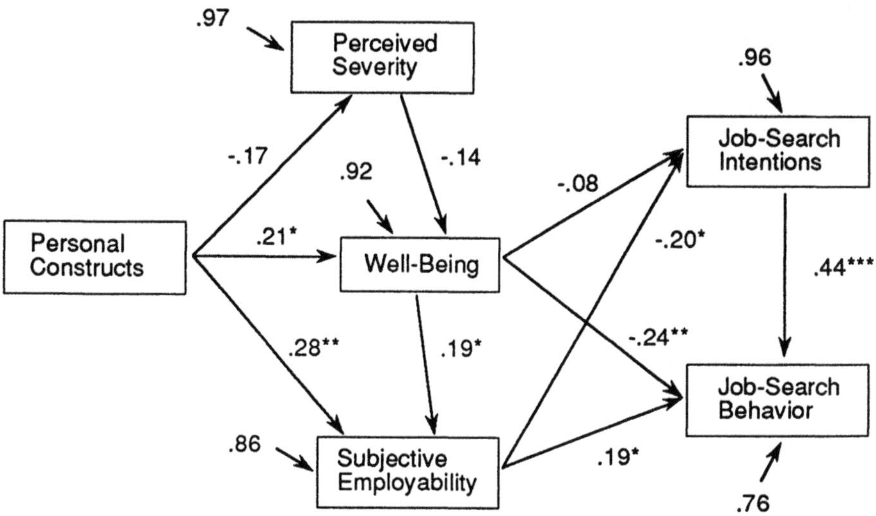

FIG. 13.2. Functional illusion path model for Time 2 (*p <.05; **p <.01; ***p<.001).

optimistic expectations. Both earlier and later in the crisis the workers who experienced the least distress were less, not more, likely to be looking for work.

These findings suggest that contrary to expectations, the positive illusions may have been dysfunctional for these workers, facing this crisis, at this time in their lives. If we accept the implicit causal model, rather than providing the motivational base required to cope with the threat of job loss, the comforting illusions appear to have significantly reduced the workers' incentive to engage in an active job search. Without additional information, however, it is not possible to determine whether this lessened effort to find work is a result of dysfunctional illusions or realistic perceptions. Conceivably, the workers with higher self-esteem and greater feelings of control and optimism were in fact those with better personal and professional qualifications. In that case, their relative contentment and lack of coping efforts in the face of the crisis may have been based upon realistic rather than illusory views of their ability to ultimately find work. On the other side of the same coin, the impending job loss may have constituted a much greater threat to those workers with relatively poor personal qualifications. These workers would have good reason to be upset by the impending job loss and the obstacles they would encounter in finding re-employment. Understandably, they would begin their job seeking in earnest during this pre-closure period.

A dysfunctional illusion explanation recalls earlier distinctions in the stress and coping literature. When faced with a crisis, a person can cope either by reinterpreting and denying the threat, or engaging in efforts to remove or overcome the threatening events. Although Lazarus and his associates (Folkman, Lazarus, Dunkel-Schetter, DeLongis, & Gruen, 1986; Lazarus & Folkman, 1984) have reported the co-occurrence of both emotion-focused and problem-solving coping responses, the more common view (e.g., Goldstein, 1973; Miller, 1981, 1987) holds these as separate alternatives. For example, to the extent that stress reduction is successful it will remove the need for any further coping efforts. In this case, it appears that those workers who were able to persuade themselves that they were better people, with more control and a better future than the other workers, not only became more sanguine about the crisis, they were more certain a job would be on the horizon for them. The positive illusions were functional, then, in reducing experienced stress, but as an unfortunate consequence, they appear to have also dysfunctionally reduced the incentive to find work. Without additional information, it is not possible to decide to what extent the negative paths from well-being to job seeking reflect realistic confidence or a false sense of security created by the positive illusions.

AN EXPLORATORY PATH MODEL OF COPING WITH JOB LOSS

Method

These alternative explanations led to the inclusion of two relevant additional sets of data and the construction of an exploratory model of the workers' reactions to the threat of job loss.

In addition to those used in the test of the functional illusion model, the research questionnaires contained measures assessing the employees' use of emotion-focused and problem-focused coping (Lazarus & Folkman, 1984), with their job-seeking behavior to be examined. Including these two measures would enable us to consider how the employees' coping style was related to their job. A reasonable prediction would be that emotion-focused coping will be inversely related to job-seeking behavior, while problem-focused coping will be positively related. Conceivably, positive illusions are simply another form of what Lazarus and Folkman (1984) consider emotion-focused coping. However, since Taylor and Brown (1988) do not explicitly discuss the relation between positive illusions and the earlier work on emotion-focused coping, it is not possible to determine if they view the positive illusions as independent of emotion-focused responses to stress, or an alternative to them.

Coping Styles—Emotion-Focused and Problem-Focused. To measure these coping styles, four items with the highest item-total correlations for each coping style were selected from the Lazarus and Folkman (1984) Revised Ways of Coping Scale. The resulting scales were relatively independent in this sample, correlating $r = .11$, n.s., at Time 1, and $r = .12$, n.s., at Time 2. Importantly, subjects in this study were asked to indicate the coping strategies they used in the context of the plant closure, rather than being asked to indicate their coping strategies for a past event, as normally done with this scale. Higher scores on these scales imply more use of the particular coping style.

Expert-Rated Employability. Employment counselors were provided with the information they considered necessary to arrive at an informed judgment concerning the employment potential for each worker. This information, as identified in prior research, included: age, income, length of employment, job skills, education level, and availability of appropriate jobs in the community (Hepworth, 1980; Kelvin & Jarrett, 1985). The counselors rated the employee's probability of finding employment, the time it would take, and the level of probable income. The ratings were obtained from six experienced employment counselors. Interclass correlations, the conceptual equivalent of calculating the average correlation between all possible pairs of raters, indicated good reliability among raters, ranging from .77 to .82. A single score was created, with higher values indicating greater realistic prospects for being re-employed as rated by experts. Since these counselors were functionally gate-keepers, as well as employment experts, an index based upon their judgments is a reasonable approximation of the reality facing each worker.

Constructing the Model

The construction of any path model involves assumptions of causal relations. In the initial analysis we articulated a functional model of positive illusions based on Taylor and Brown (1988) which placed the illusions (personal constructs) antecedent to and causing subjective well-being, and both of those influencing the motivation to overcome the threat by finding work. But the inclusion of the two coping styles re-opened the question of all causal links. It seemed most reasonable to place the "expert-rated employability index," as an estimate of the reality they faced, at the beginning of the causal chain. Beyond that there were no strong theoretical bases for any particular model. For example, one could make a case for placing the coping strategies virtually anywhere in the process. Similarly, although Taylor and Brown (1988) explicitly portray the positive illusions as contributing to people's sense of well-being, they also recognize that moods often affect how confidently and optimistically people approach the problems they face (Brown, 1986; Brown & Taylor, 1986).

The availability of plausible alternative causal paths suggested the use of an empirical procedure for establishing the model. To decide the ordering of variables we first performed cross-lagged regression analyses with each possible pair of variables between Time 1 and Time 2 (Kessler & Greenberg, 1981; Markus, 1979) and supported by LISREL analyses where possible (Jøreskog & Sørbom, 1984). The important test was the relative significance of the cross-lag weights. If, for example, as was in fact the case, the cross-lag analysis yielded a significant path from Well-being at Time 1 to the Personal Constructs (illusions) at Time 2, but no significant path occurred between the Personal Constructs at Time 1 and Well-being at Time 2, then we placed Well-being before the Personal Constructs in the path analyses. Since Well-being at an earlier time predicted extent of the Personal Constructs later in the process, in the absence of any other information it seemed most plausible to assume that the workers' level of morale influenced how positively were their "illusions" about themselves and their environment were rather than the opposite, or even reciprocal, relationship.[3]

[3]Although cross-lagged analyses using zero-order and partial correlations to assess the causal order of two variables have been strongly criticized (see Rogosa, 1980), many of the problems can be avoided by using regression analyses. Regression allows comparison of the association of two variables over time, while partialling out the correlations that the variables have with themselves. Although superior to correlation methods, regression analyses are still subject to confounding influence of correlations between error terms for the variables over time, known as autocorrelation. Using LISREL allows this autocorrelation to be estimated, eliminating its confounding effects, but is limited to cases where there are large sample sizes and the constructs are represented by multiple indicators. For these reasons, regression analyses were used to estimate cross-lags for the majority of cases, supplemented by LISREL analyses where possible.

Although not all the cross-lags produced significant results we found no contradictory or conflicting paths, and there were enough meaningful significant results from the cross-lag analyses to provide a reasonable empirical basis for the final ordering. Having established the order of the variables, they were then entered into the exploratory regression path analyses, with the data from Time 1 and Time 2 analyzed separately. Each variable was regressed on all those preceding it in the causal sequence. As well, all variables following the Generalized Beliefs in the model were tested for interactions with Coping Style and Expert-rated Employability.

Results

Based on the sequence of causal effects suggested by the significant cross-lag analyses (presented in Table 13.2), empirically based path models were created separately for Time 1 and Time 2. In order, the variables included in the models were the Expert-rated Employability, Perceived Severity, Well-being, Generalized Belief, Subjective Employability, Emotion-focused and Problem-focused Coping, Job-search Intentions, and finally, Job-search Behavior.[4]

Significant Paths at Time 1: Meaningful Patterns

The Functional Illusion Model. Looking at the path model in Figure 13.3, one configuration of significant paths leads from Well-being to the Personal Constructs, then to Subjective Employability, Problem-focused Coping, Behavioral Intentions, and eventually to Job-search Behavior. This causal chain provides support for a functional interpretation of the role of positive illusions. As Taylor and Brown (1988) might have predicted, the more positive the workers' beliefs about themselves and their environment, the more certain they were of finding employment, and thus the more likely they were to actively cope with the crisis by engaging in planful efforts to find work.

The Central Role of Subjective Employability. Three other sets of significant paths at the initial testing merit noting. One set reveals the central role played by Subjective Employability. The workers' subjective estimates of the likelihood of their finding employment mediates the influence of their Personal Constructs

[4]The negative autocorrelation of Personal Constructs may be attributed to the differential weightings from Time 1 to Time 2 of each of the illusions on the Personal Construct factors at those two time periods. Apparently the relative weights of the illusions became reversed over time. That unanticipated finding is consistent with other results that will be discussed in the final section of the chapter. The placement of Well-being after Personal Constructs in the exploratory path model is supported not only by the significant cross-lag between Personal Constructs at Time 1 and Well-being at Time 2, it is also consistent with the significant cross-lags between components of the Personal Construct variable (Self-esteem and Control) at Time 1 and Well-being at Time 2.

TABLE 13.2.

Significant Regression Cross-lag Analyses.

Time 2 Variable	*Time 1 Variable*	*b*	*Beta*	*F*⁺	*R*
Personal Constructs	Personal Constructs	-.22	-.29		
	Well-being	.48	.39***	37.87***	.50
Well-being	Personal Constructs	.05	.07		
	Well-being	.75	.69***	8.29***	.18
Personal Constructs	Personal Constructs	-.15	-.19		
	Problem-focused Coping	.26	.17	2.59	.06
Problem-focused Coping	Personal Constructs	.09	.19*		
	Problem-focused Coping	.54	.54***	19.48***	.34
Control	Control	.55	.60***		
	Well-being	.15	.24**	41.25***	.52
Well-being	Control	-.07	-.11		
	Well-being	.80	.73***	37.85***	.50
Self-esteem	Self-esteem	.51	.54***		
	Well-being	.08	.20*	25.92***	.41
Well-being	Self-esteem	-.28	-.11		
	Well-being	.80	.74***	38.79***	.51
Functional Characteristics	Functional Characteristics	.62	.63***		
	Job-search Intentions	-.01	-.09	25.27***	.40
Job-search Intentions	Functional Characteristics	1.97	.23**		
	Job-search Intentions	.56	.65***	37.28***	.50
Comparative Optimism	Comparative Optimism	.80	.67*		
	Subjective Employability	-.01	-.08	25.81***	.41
Subjective Employability	Comparative Optimism	1.49	.23*		
	Subjective Employability	.45	.51*	26.62***	.41

(continued)

TABLE 13.2
(continued)

Time 2 Variable	*Time 1 Variable*	*b*	*Beta*	F^{+}	*R*
Job-search Intentions	Job-search Intentions	.53	.62***		
	Job-search Behavior	.19	.08	30.98***	.45
Job-search Behavior	Job-search Intentions	.22	.27*		
	Job-search Behavior	1.02	.45***	28.80***	.43
Well-being	Well-being	.37	.48***		
	Perceived Severity	-.60	-.19a	37.56***	.50
Perceived Severity	Well-being	.01	.05		
	Perceived Severity	.77	.71***	14.60***	.28
Problem-focused Coping	Problem-focused Coping	.53	.53***		
	Job-search Intentions	.01	.08	16.94***	.31
Job-search Intentions	Problem-focused Coping	1.95	.23**		
	Job-search Intentions	.53	.62***	37.35***	.50

Note. Significance levels for b and Beta weights are identical.
[a]p <.06; *p <.05; **p <.01; ***p <.001
+The degrees of freedom for all F tests were all 2 and 77.

(illusions) and Perceived Severity of the crisis, as well as the reality component reflected in the Expert-rated Employability, on Job-search Behavior.

Emotion-Focused and Problem-Focused Coping. A second set of paths show that the workers' use of emotion-focused and problem-focused coping reflect understandable processes. The lower the workers' morale and the more severe they perceived the crisis, the more likely they were to engage in denying and avoidant coping strategies (see Figure 13.3). Alternatively, the greater the workers' estimates of finding employment, the more likely they were to engage in problem-focused coping, leading to a greater intention to find work. The interaction of Problem-focused Coping with Expert-rated Employability to determine Job-search Behavior was particularly revealing. The form of the interaction suggests that Problem-focused Coping has the greatest effect on the Job-search Behavior of

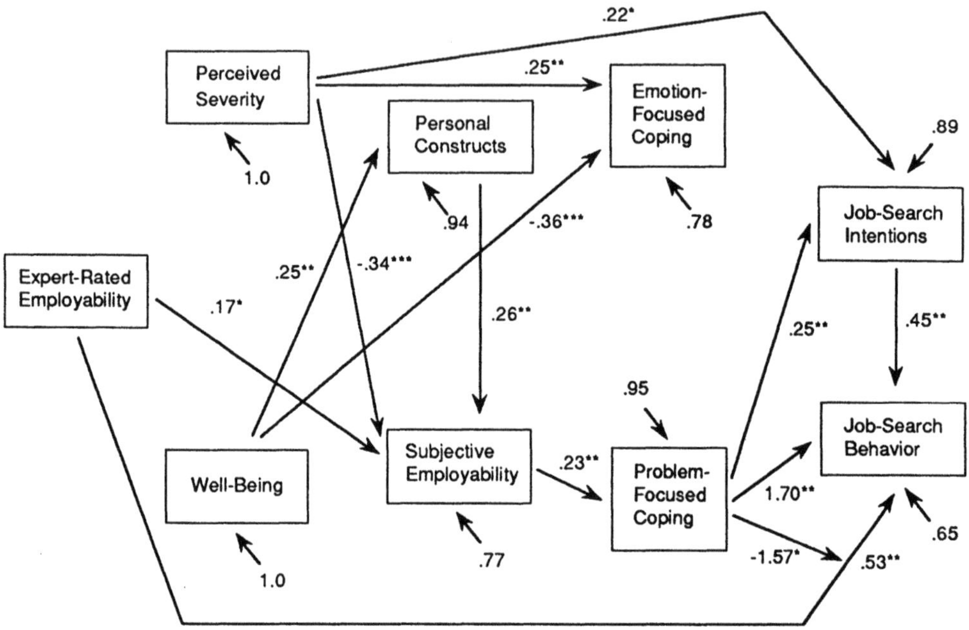

FIG. 13.1. Exploratory path model for Time 1 (*p <.05; **p <.01; ***p <.001).

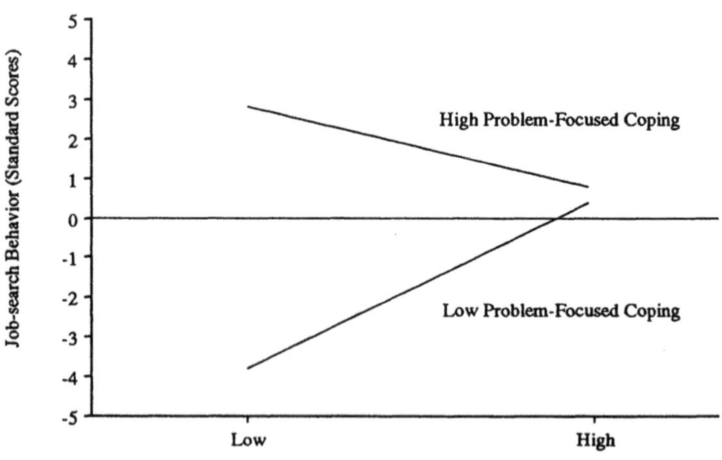

FIG. 13.4. Interaction effect of Problem-focused coping and Expert-rated Employability on Job-search Behavior at Time 1 (scales represent standardized scores).

workers with weaker qualifications, leading them to use greater efforts to find work. That is less true for the more qualified workers (see Figure 13.4).

The Source and Consequences of Workers' Morale. The third set of paths suggests that while the workers' well-being influenced their confidence, and subsequently their coping responses (see Figure 13.3), there were no significant paths linking Well-being to Expert-rated Employability or Perceived Severity. Apparently, at this early stage in the crisis, the workers' morale did not reflect either the genuine or perceived threats they faced from the impending job loss. Conceivably, they were exhibiting their ambient or relatively chronic state of self-esteem, control, and optimism.

Significant Paths at Time 2: Meaningful Patterns

The Alternatives: Reality-Testing vs. Dysfunctional Illusions. One set of significant paths at Time 2, shown in Figure 13.5, directly addresses the alternative interpretations offered for the negative relation between Well-being and Job-search Behavior that was uncovered in the theoretically derived model tested in the first study. At this later time in the crisis, a significant path leads from Expert-rated Employability to Perceived Severity of the crisis, which in turn has negative path

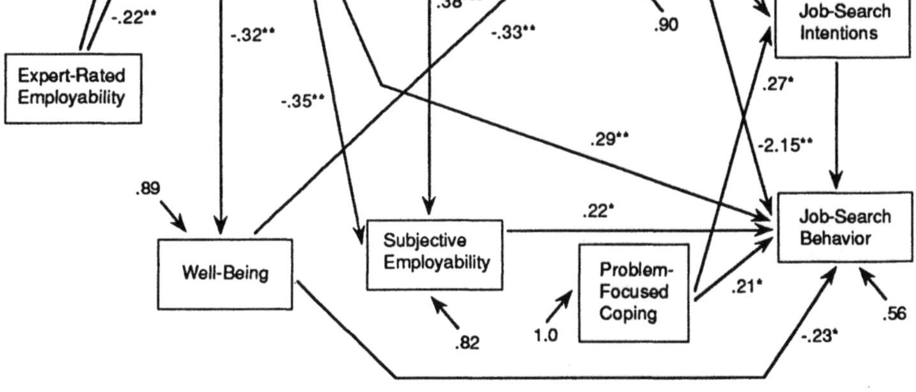

FIG. 13.5. Exploratory path model for Time 2 (*p <.05; **p <.01; ***p <.001).

to Well-being, and both of these have significant paths to Job-search Behavior. Apparently, those workers with better qualifications saw their job loss as less severe, resulting in higher morale, greater optimism about being able to find work, and consequently, less active efforts as the plant closure neared.

The Role of Positive Illusions. At this later period in the crisis, the Personal Constructs (illusions) appear to act in concert with the workers' reality-based estimate of the severity of the crisis to influence their subjective estimates of finding work, eventuating in Job-search Behavior. The more positive and optimistic the workers' outlook, and the better their actual qualifications, the more optimistic they were about finding work and thus more likely to look for a job.

Well-Being and Coping Responses. The workers' sense of well-being, at least partly influenced by the realistic appraisal of the severity of the threat, had no direct path to their Personal Constructs, as had been the case at Time 1. Instead we find a negative path from Well-being to Emotion-focused Coping which in turn has two indirect paths to job seeking. One of those was a positive path through Behavioral Intentions and the second involved an interaction with Expert-rated Employability. Together these paths indicate that to the extent workers' morale was lowered by their recognition of the severity of the crisis they faced, they were more likely to try to deny the crisis and distance themselves from it, which allowed them to feel the security they needed to try to find work. The significant interaction between Emotion-focused Coping and Expert-rated Employability reveals, however, that the denial and withdrawal associated with this type of coping also served as an alternative to adaptive employment seeking for workers with poorer realistic job prospects (see Figure 13.6).

Separate Analyses with each Personal Construct (Illusion). When the individual measures that made up the Personal Constructs measure were placed in the path model, interesting differences appeared. Neither the workers' Comparative Self-evaluations (see Brown, 1986) nor their Functional Characteristics (see Kunda, 1987) revealed significant paths to any of the other variables. Apparently at this later stage in the crisis they played an inconsequential role in the workers' sense of well-being and coping efforts. However, the workers' general Optimism (see Weinstein, 1980), feelings of control (see Lumpkin, 1985; Rotter, 1966), and Self-esteem (Rosenberg, 1965) were all influenced by their level of Well-being (the paths were respectively, .34, .34, and .30). These, in turn, all had positive paths, directly or indirectly, to Job-search Behavior. Self-esteem, in particular, revealed a complex relation with job seeking. It had a direct negative path to Job-search Behavior (path = -.25) but an indirect positive path through Problem-focused Coping (Self-esteem—Problem-focused Coping, path = .23; Problem-focused Coping—Job-search Behavior, path = .23).

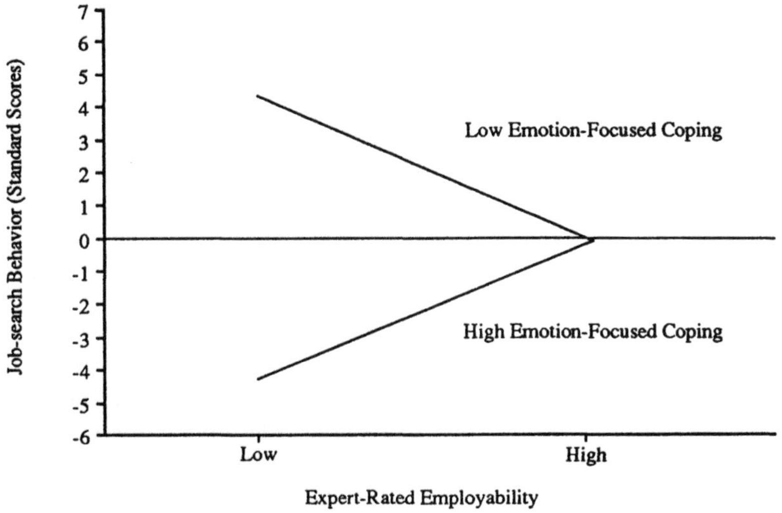

FIG. 13.6. Interaction effect of Emotion-focused coping and Expert-rated Employability on Job-search Behavior at Time 2 (scales represent standardized scores).

FIG. 13.7. Interaction effect of Expert-rated Employability and Belief in a Just World on Job-search Behavior at Time 2 (scales represent standardized scores).

The Belief-in-a-Just-World measure (see Rubin & Peplau, 1973) also presented a complex relationship with Job-search Behavior. The first testing revealed a significant positive path between the workers' Belief in a Just World and their job seeking (path = .15). Six weeks later, in the second testing, that path disappeared and an interaction with the workers' qualifications (Expert-rated Employability) took its place. The interaction revealed that the Belief in a Just World had little influence on the Job-search Behavior of the more qualified workers. However, to the extent that the less qualified workers gave up their Belief in a Just World, they were more likely to engage in active efforts to find work (see Figure 13.7).

Comparing Workers' Reactions to the Crisis at Time 1 and Time 2

The differences in the Time 1 and Time 2 path models suggested the possibility of major changes in the workers' reactions to the crisis during that time period.[5] In fact, we found relatively few significant differences in their reactions (see Table 13.3).

The comparisons revealed no differences in their positive illusions (Personal Constructs), with the exception of Comparative Optimism (see Weinstein, 1980). Although the workers still believed their future lives would be better than that of the average worker, that margin of difference was significantly lessened. This lessened optimism did not appear in changes to their other illusions (i.e., Functional Characteristics, Comparative Self-evaluations, Control, Self-esteem, Belief in a Just World) nor their general sense of well-being. In fact, there are indications that after six weeks the workers saw the crisis as less severe, and although they were less inclined to seek retraining, they applied for more jobs, and thought it would be less difficult to find a job now and within the next few months.

GENERAL DISCUSSION AND SUMMARY

The questions driving this research centered on how functional positive illusions are to the coping process. Initially, we wanted to know whether the illusions of control, self-esteem, and optimism would facilitate the workers' adapting to the crisis, as suggested by Taylor and Brown (1988). In order to answer that question we translated the illusions into dimensions that varied from negative to positive,

---

[5]Analyses were performed to examine whether the sample attrition between Time 1 and Time 2 was related to any of the relevant variables in this study. The analyses indicated no reliable differences in the Time 1 responses between workers who did and did not participate in the second assessment. A multivariate analysis of variance indicated no overall differences between participants and nonparticipants on any of the relevant variables, including age, sex, income, education, job type, Expert-rated Employability, Personal Constructs, and coping styles, $F(29,83) = 0.96$, n.s. Individual t-tests for each major variable indicate, though, that the later nonparticipants had less Comparative Optimism than participants, $t = 2.43$, $p < .02$.

TABLE 13.2

Mean differences across measurement items

	Time 1 Mean	*Time 2 Mean*	*t*	*df*
Personal Constructs				
Comparative Optimism	41.96	39.85	3.48***	113
Functional Characteristics	-2.15	-2.40	.86	110
Comparative Self-evaluations	4.79	4.55	.81	107
Control	20.82	20.63	.67	111
Self-esteem	4.79	4.55	.81	111
Belief in Justice	3.05	3.11	.49	108
Coping Styles				
Problem-focused Coping	5.57	5.96	1.50	110
Emotion-focused Coping	3.08	2.66	1.93	109
Job Search Behavior				
Jobs applied for	2.55	2.77	3.32*	113
People talked to	2.90	3.01	.86	113
Well-being				
Positive affect	35.32	34.64	1.19	109
Distress	34.66	34.66	.00	112
Perceived Severity				
How bad overall	4.12	4.60	2.41**	111
Comparatively how bad	2.71	2.86	1.26	111
Job Search Intentions				
How much think about	3.52	3.61	.87	113
Seeking retraining	2.89	2.73	2.01*	111
Planned job search	2.98	3.05	.63	111
Subjective Employability				
Chance of finding job	4.06	4.12	.44	108
Effects in a few months	2.88	3.31	3.88***	111
Effects in a few years	3.28	3.46	1.76	110
How difficult to find job	2.50	2.76	2.18*	112

* $p<.05$; ** $p<.01$; *** $p<.001$

assessing low to high self-esteem, less to more control, and a pessimistic to optimistic view of the future. Although that procedure does not allow an assessment of the extent to which an employee's beliefs were illusory, it provides the information necessary to test Taylor and Brown's hypotheses. They proposed that positive illusions are adaptive because they maintain the person's optimistic constructions of their ability to confront the threat. They would not insist that the confident optimism must be illusory, but rather that the reality bases of those beliefs are irrelevant to their adaptive consequences. The measures employed in this research, which were based upon studies cited by Taylor and Brown (1988), appear to be reasonable representations of their positive illusions.

Measuring adaptive coping, which is the principal focus of this research, raises other conceptual and methodological issues. We began with the assumption that going through the steps of gaining information and applying for jobs provided the best and clearest evidence of adaptive behavior. Simply put, more adaptive behavior meant more applying for jobs. However, even within the normative demands to find re-employment, making plans for how to go about finding work and intending to implement those plans could also be viewed as quite adaptive, especially during this period prior to the actual closure. A similar case might be made for attending retraining and job-counseling sessions. A factor analysis of these various measures, however, suggested two orthogonal variables: Job-search intentions including such measures as engaging in retraining, while Job-search Behavior included the extent of seeking information and number of job applications.

The LISREL analysis of the cross-lags between the measure of intentions and the measure of Job-search Behavior confirmed the conceptual independence of these two variables. Consistent with common understanding, intentions at Time 1 were highly predictive of behavior at Time 2, while behavior at Time 1 did not predict intentions at Time 2. Additional data collected by representatives of the plant closure committee, supported the construct and external validity of these measures. Among the 45 employees they were able to reach 6 months after the closure, the employees' intentions to find work, as reported 2 weeks prior the plant closure (Time 2) predicted their reported success at finding work within 6 months of the plant closure ($r = .35, p < .02$).

The first phase of this study examined the functional relation between the workers' positive illusions, morale, and adaptive behavior. This approach confirmed part of the Taylor and Brown (1988) model. The more positive their illusions of self-worth, control, and optimism, the less threatened they felt by the closure and the more certain they were of finding re-employment. As a result they maintained relatively high levels of morale, as measured by their overall sense of well-being. However, the workers' responses revealed a more complex than expected relation between these cognitive and affective reactions to the crisis and their job-seeking. The expected positive relationship between their expectations of finding employment and their job-seeking efforts, were both confirmed and contradicted. The findings indicated that the higher their morale, the less they looked for work, while the more certain they were of finding employment, the less they intended to seek re-employment. Obviously more data and theoretical work are needed to integrate these findings and their implications into a more adequate representation of coping behavior.

The subsequent analyses generated a complicated, yet quite meaningful, set of answers to the initial questions, as well as the beginning of an outline for a more comprehensive theory of coping behavior. The seemingly simple question of whether or not the positive illusions facilitated adaptive coping has to be answered differently depending upon which illusions, which people, and the stage in the crisis. The last factor, how long the people have been trying to cope, appears to reveal how the illusions develop and function in the crisis. Earlier in the crisis, a number of factors, including their ambient sense of well-being, perceived severity of the threat, and an awareness of their abilities, converged on the workers' confidence in finding re-employment. That confidence then played a key role in their job-seeking efforts by activating their use of problem-focused coping, which in turn led to more efforts to prepare themselves and actively seek employment. The factor of who the person is, in this case their level of job qualifications, appears at this early stage in the form of problem-focused coping being most functional for those with the poorer qualifications.

Later in the crisis, these qualifying factors take a different form. Although the workers' confidence in their ability to find re-employment and their use of problem-focusing coping continue to support their job-seeking, many other changes have taken place. Focusing first on the positive illusions, we find two major differences from earlier in the crisis. One is that they show signs of functioning differently, both from earlier in the crisis and from each other. Whereas earlier in the crisis the illusions of self-esteem, optimism, and control were sufficiently similar to be considered a single construct, at the later stage important differences appeared. Questions of what illusions have what effects now become important. Apparently, the general illusions of control and optimism continue to promote adaptive behavior, while the more situationally relevant illusions, such as comparative personal qualities and qualifications for re-employment, become irrelevant over time. To complicate and enrich the picture, we found that the workers' level of self-esteem developed a strong negative influence on job seeking, and their belief in a just world became especially dysfunctional for less qualified workers engaging in active coping.

More generally, after six weeks of living with the crisis, the workers revealed a rather different set of coping processes from what emerged initially. At the later time a realistic assessment of their qualifications, and thus the seriousness of the threats associated with the job loss influenced their sense of well-being. In effect, the more poorly qualified the workers were, the lower their morale and the more effort they put in to finding work, as well as trying to reduce their stress through emotion-focused coping. This understandable pattern clearly contradicts the initial theoretical prediction of a positive sense of well-being as necessary to provide the motivation and incentive to find work. In this case, the realistic threats of job loss provided greater incentive to workers with poor prospects for re-employment than did the well-being experienced by the better qualified employees. In retrospect, it is not surprising to find that as people continue to cope with a major crisis, involving serious threats to their security and well-being, they become more realistic about the nature of the threats and what they must do to cope with them. Among these workers whose jobs would be terminated in two weeks that recognition led to greater, not lesser efforts to cope, both by adaptive and stress-reducing responses.

Conceivably, had the dimensions of the crisis been more potentially demoralizing either immediately or over time, then the positive illusions would have played a more functional role in enabling the the victims to muster the energy to engage in coping efforts. Or, if the normative demands were less explicit concerning the appropriate way for these employees to deal with their victimization, then we might have found the demoralized more poorly qualified employees accepting their fate and using more passive means of coping. However, it seems clear from the results of this field study, that the important empirical issues are not whether positive illusions are more or less adaptive than a reality-based coping response. Rather, the next generation of research and theory will need to specify more precisely how particular illusions influence the coping responses of people with a particular set of resources at any stage in a particular crisis.

REFERENCES

Borgen, W. A., & Amundson, N. E. (1987). The dynamics of unemployment. *Journal of Counseling and Development, 66*, 180-184.

Brenner, S. O., & Bartelli, R. (1983). The psychological impact of unemployment: A structural analysis of cross-sectional data. *Journal of Occupational Psychology, 56*, 129-136.

Brown, J. D. (1986). Evaluations of self and others: Self-enhancement biases in social judgements. *Social Cognition, 4*, 353-376.

Brown, J. D., & Taylor, S. E. (1986). Affect and the processing of personal information: Evidence for mood-activated self-schemata. *Journal of Experimental Social Psychology, 22*, 436-452.

Derogatis, L. R. (1975). *The Affect Balance Scale*. Baltimore: Clinical Psychometric Research.

Derogatis, L. R., & Melisaratos, N. (1983). The Brief Symptom Inventory: An introductory report. *Psychological Medicine, 13*, 595-605.

Folkman, S., Lazarus, R. S., Dunkel-Schetter, C., DeLongis, A., & Gruen, R. J. (1986). Dynamics of a stressful encounter: Cognitive appraisal, coping, and encounter outcomes. *Journal of Personality and Social Psychology, 50*, 992-1003.

Goldstein, M. J. (1973). Individual differences in response to stress. *American Journal of Community Psychology, 1*, 113-137.

Haan, N. (1977). *Coping and defending*. New York: Academic Press.

Hepworth, S. J. (1980). Moderating factors of the psychological impact of unemployment. *Journal of Occupational Psychology, 53*, 139-145.

Jahoda, M. (1958). *Current concepts of positive mental health*. New York: Basic Books.

Janoff-Bulman, R., & Frieze, I. H. (1983). A theoretical perspective for understanding reactions to victimization. *Journal of Social Issues, 39*(2), 1-18.

Jøreskog, K., & Sørbom, D. (1984). *LISREL VI: Analysis of linear structural relationships by maximum likelihood, instrumental variables, and least squares methods*. Mooresville, IN: Scientific Software.

Kaufman, H. G. (1982). *Professionals in search of work: Coping with the stress of job loss and underemployment*. New York: Wiley.

Kelvin, P. (1980). Social psychology 2001: The social psychological bases and implications of structural unemployment. In R. Gilmour & S. Duck (Eds.), *The development of social psychology* (pp. 293-316). London: Academic Press.

Kelvin, P., & Jarrett, J. E. (1985). *Unemployment: Its social psychological effects*. Cambridge: Cambridge University Press.

Kessler, R. C., & Greenberg, D. F. (1981). *Linear panel analysis: Models of quantitative change*. New York: Academic Press.

Kunda, Z. (1987). Motivated inference: Self-serving generation and evaluation of causal theories. *Journal of Personality and Social Psychology, 53*, 636-647.

Lazarus, R. S., & Folkman, S. (1984). *Stress, appraisal, and coping*. New York: Springer.

Lerner, M. J. (1980). *The belief in a just world: A fundamental delusion*. New York: Plenum.

Lerner, M. J., & Somers, D. G. (1990). *Positive illusions and coping: Workers' reactions to an anticipated plant closure*. Unpublished manuscript, University of Waterloo.

Lumpkin, J. R. (1985). Validity of a brief locus-of-control scale for survey research. *Psychological Reports, 57*, 655-659.

Markus, G. B. (1979). *Analyzing panel data*. Beverly Hills, CA: Sage.

Miller, S. M. (1981). Predictability and human stress: Toward a clarification of evidence and theory. In L. Berkowitz (Ed.), *Advances in experimental social psychology* (Vol. 12, pp. 203-256). New York: Academic Press.

Miller, S. M. (1987). Monitoring and blunting: Validation of a questionnaire to assess styles of information seeking under stress. *Journal of Personality and Social Psychology, 52*, 345-353.

Rogosa, D. (1980). A critique of cross-lagged correlation. *Psychological Bulletin, 88*, 245-258.

Rosenberg, M. (1965). *Society and the adolescent self-image*. Princeton, NJ: Princeton University Press.

Rotter, J. B. (1966). Generalized expectancies for internal versus external control of reinforcement. *Psychological Monographs, 80*, (1, Whole No. 609).

Rubin, Z., & Peplau, A. (1973). Belief in a just world on reactions to another's lot: A study of participants in the national draft lottery. *Journal of Social Issues, 29*(4), 73-93.

Somers, D. G. (1989). *Employee's reactions to plant closure: Illusions, coping, and job-seeking behavior*. Unpublished doctoral dissertation, University of Waterloo.

Somers, D. G., & Lerner, M. J. (1990). *Illusion and well-being in a field setting*. Manuscript submitted for publication.

Taylor, S. E. (1983). Adjustment to threatening events: A theory of cognitive adaptation. *American Psychologist, 38*, 1161-1173.

Taylor, S. E., & Brown, J. D. (1988). Illusion and well-being: A social psychological perspective on mental health. *Psychological Bulletin, 103*, 193-210.

Taylor, S. E., Wood, J. V., & Lichtman, R. L. (1983). It could be worse: Selective evaluation as a response to victimization. *Journal of Social Issues, 39*(2), 19-40.

Vaillant, G. (1977). *Adaptation to life*. Boston: Little, Brown.

Vinokur, A., Caplan, R. D., & Williams, C. C. (1988). Effects of recent and past stress on mental health: Coping with unemployment among Vietnam veterans. *Journal of Applied Social Psychology, 17*, 710-730.

Warr, P. (1987). *Work, unemployment, and mental health*. Oxford: Oxford University Press.

Weinstein, N. D. (1980). Unrealistic optimism about future life events. *Journal of Personality and Social Psychology, 39*, 806-820.

14 Monitoring and Blunting in the Face of Threat: Implications for Adaptation and Health[1]

Suzanne M. Miller
Temple University

The prospect of loss—as in learning that one is at risk for a serious disease such as cancer or AIDS—can be an agonizingly stressful and threatening crisis. Who fares best in the face of such threats and how can individuals be helped to manage their reactions to terrifying prospects? Recent evidence suggests that the process of adapting to threatening events can be dissected along a number of different dimensions, such as problem- versus emotion-focused coping and active vs. passive coping. Another fundamental approach has to do with the extent to which the individual monitors and confronts the threat or, alternatively, psychologically blunts and avoids the threat.

Beginning with Freud, personality and clinical psychologists have been concerned with the way in which individuals selectively attend to or avoid particular kinds of information in the process of coping with aversive events, as well as how they perceive and express negative affective states. Much in psychoanalytic theory and practice is predicated on the view that a healthy psyche is one in which "repressions" are removed. Consistent with this, a good deal of evidence shows that the use of avoidant coping can be counterproductive, particularly in the long run (Suls & Fletcher, 1985). However, much in contemporary research also points to the adaptive value of selective inattention (Auerbach, 1989).

Recently, several theorists have emphasized the importance of flexibility in coping as the hallmark of adaptive responding (Taylor & Brown, 1988). Indeed, a rigid approach to resolving the problems of everyday living has often been thought to characterize individuals whose levels of stress are chronically elevated—as in

[1] I am indebted to Anand Athavale, Gregg Hurst, Linda Kruus, Rosemary Murphy, Kim Sproat, and Richard Sommers for their assistance. This research was supported in part by NIH grant CA46591.

patients suffering from a variety of anxiety disorders. It is therefore especially challenging to sift out when and for whom avoidance may produce healthy outcomes, as well as to specify when and for whom the opposite might be true. It is also important to identify which outcomes are affected and how they are affected. The present chapter explores the implications of avoidant and confrontive coping modes, beginning with patients' emotional responses to health threats. The adaptive consequences of these attentional modes appear to be complex and to depend on a variety of factors that are not all well-articulated. However, there is some indication that those who typically scan for threat-relevant information ("monitors") may be more at risk for heightened distress in this context than those who typically avoid threat-relevant information ("blunters"), particularly when the stressor is less severe or more transient.

I then go on to explore the applicability of these constructs to the clinical domain, focusing on the anxiety disorders. Recent cognitive formulations of these syndromes emphasize the role played by hypervigilance (monitoring) of external and internal cues about threat in sustaining prolonged and disabling levels of anxiety, especially in response to minor or short-term everyday stressors. However, there also appear to be conditions in which hyperavoidance (blunting) of threatening cues is disadvantageous, as when the individual attempts to adjust to highly traumatic life events. Finally, I explore the consequences of the two attentional modes for the initiation and maintenance of preventive self-regulatory behaviors. Evidence is highlighted which suggests that blunting may be a less efficacious strategy than monitoring for promoting health-related self-protective behaviors. I conclude by attempting to integrate what is known about the personal and situational factors that moderate adaptive coping under conditions of perceived and actual crisis and loss.

IMPLICATIONS OF MONITORING AND BLUNTING FOR ADJUSTMENT TO HEALTH THREATS

Studies of coping in the health-care setting have tended to focus on two main types of populations: patients undergoing more short-term aversive diagnostic and surgical procedures and patients suffering from more long-term chronic diseases. With respect to the first, the type of information provided to subjects is typically varied, and its impact on patients with differing coping styles is sometimes explored. In contrast, studies focusing on chronic disease rarely manipulate situational variables, such as the amount or type of information made available to patients. Instead, the focus tends to be on the differential impact of alternative dispositional styles or, less commonly, on the actual strategies used by patients to negotiate the stressor.

Diagnostic and Surgical Procedures

The results in this area have traditionally been confusing and difficult to interpret within a unified conceptual framework. However, the exact nature of information conveyed to patients—orienting them toward or away from threatening cues—appears to be a critical determinant of patient response. Three main types of information have been explored: general information (which describes the disease, the medical staff, and the hospital), sensory information (which describes the sensations to be experienced), and procedural information (which describes the specific medical procedures to be followed).

Overall, general information does not appear to improve patient outcomes. However, sensory information—both on its own and in combination with procedural information—is superior to procedural information alone and to minimal information (Miller, Combs, & Stoddard, 1989; Suls & Wan, 1989). On the other hand, information (even when it contains strongly reassuring elements) often fares less well in comparison with interventions that more actively induce patients to modulate attention away from the situation at hand (Miller, Combs, & Stoddard, 1989). These latter strategies—which enable patients to selectively avoid cues about threat—include a variety of manipulations, such as teaching patients relaxation techniques, providing them with distractors, and encouraging them to reinterpret the situation by focusing them on its more positive aspects (Langer, Janis, & Wolfer, 1975; Ridgeway & Mathews, 1982; Scott & Clum, 1984).

An important, but often overlooked factor is the interaction of these various attentional and avoidant interventions with dispositional differences in coping style. One variable that has proven to have some utility in this context is the extent to which individuals typically prefer to scan for and "monitor" threat-relevant cues and the extent to which they typically prefer to cognitively distract from and to "blunt" threat-relevant cues. Those who monitor for information, either in health-related contexts specifically or in response to threat more generally, show better adjustment when they receive voluminous sensory and procedural information than when they receive minimal information or circumscribed procedural information. Those who adopt a more blunting style generally show the opposite effects (Auerbach, Martelli, & Mercuri, 1983; Miller & Mangan, 1983; Watkins, Weaver, & Odegaard, 1986). There is also some indication that this latter group may fare best with interventions that facilitate avoidant processes, such as relaxation, distraction, and reinterpretation (Efran, Chorney, Ascher, & Lukens, 1989; Martelli, Auerbach, Alexander, & Mercuri, 1987; Miller & Mangan, 1983).

Attentional dispositions also appear to exert an effect on adaptation to short-term medical stressors, independent of their interaction with situational variables. Research with the monitor-blunter dimension has shown that monitors are generally more distressed in response to health threats, physically and psychologically, than blunters. They also appear to exaggerate the significance of their somatic symptoms and generally represent a more demanding population, desiring greater attention to their stress-related problems as well as more information, support, and advice from their physicians than blunters do. On the other hand, they are typically better informed about their medical problems and adhere more faithfully to medical screening regimens. Data from nonmedical stressors are consistent with these findings. Further, monitors appear to fare better in the face of inevitable, intrusive stressors—such as the pain of childbirth—where preparatory information is more routine (e.g., Weisenberg & Caspi, 1989). Interestingly, during baseline or nonthreat conditions, monitors and blunters do not tend to differ. This suggests that these attentional processes may be activated by specific types of environmental challenges. For reviews of this literature the reader is referred to Miller (1989, 1990, in press).

Chronic Disease

Much of the research on chronic disease focuses on potentially related—but conceptually separable—aspects of coping, such as the use of problem- vs. emotion-focused coping, perceptions of social support, causal attributions, and social comparison processes. One area where attention-avoidance strategies and styles have been researched in some detail is in assessing adjustment to cancer.

A subset of studies on attentional processes in cancer patients have explicitly explored the response to various aversive treatment procedures, such as chemotherapy. One study found that a significantly higher percentage of monitors undergoing chemotherapy experienced nausea than blunters and their episodes of nausea lasted over three times as long (Gard, Edwards, Harris, & McCormack, 1988). These effects are particularly striking, since significantly more monitors than blunters received antiemetic medication designed to reduce the severity of these effects (see also Lerman et al., 1990; Ward, Leventhal, & Love, 1988). Further, among patients about to undergo chemotherapy, teaching patients relaxation techniques proved to be more effective in reducing anticipatory anxiety for blunters than for monitors (Lerman et al., 1990). This suggests that monitors may require more targeted—or more prolonged—stress management interventions in the face of health-related and other stressors (Miller, 1989). Monitors with metastatic cancer have also been found to be more dissatisfied with information provided about their tests, symptoms, and conditions (Steptoe, Sutcliffe, Allen, & Coombes, 1991). Hence, they may also benefit from more intensive information protocols.

Findings obtained on global measures of general adaptation and health have been more conflicting. Several studies have shown that denial tends to facilitate psychological well-being (Meyerowitz, Heinrich, & Schag, 1983). Unfortunately, the instruments used to assess this construct are generally not well-validated. Further, it is unclear how constructs such as denial relate to the monitoring-blunting dimension. With regard to actual health status, there is evidence to suggest that avoidant-like strategies may not be beneficial to health. Some studies have shown that individuals who have trouble experiencing and/or expressing negative feelings (especially anger and hostility) and who, instead, appear more repressed and better adjusted to their disease are more likely to develop cancer in the first place and to die of it at a faster rate (e.g., Derogatis, Abeloff, & Melisaratos, 1979; Greer, Morris, & Pettingale, 1979; Jensen, 1987). However, this effect is not always obtained (e.g., Cassileth, Lusk, Miller, Brown, & Miller, 1985; Levy, Lee, Bagley, & Lippman, 1988). One difficulty in reconciling these findings is that it is not clear exactly which aspects of negative emotion may be toxic: its unconscious repression, its conscious suppression, its strategic nonexpression, or its passive nonexpression. To resolve these inconsistencies, studies are needed that explore—in a more fine-grained manner—exactly what is being attended to or avoided, as well as the mechanisms used to accomplish this.

Discussion

Overall, the results to date are complex and appear to depend on a number of factors. Among the variables that may moderate the effects of attentional processes are: (a) the nature and type of stressful event, such as its duration (short-term or long-term), controllability, and severity; (b) the nature and type of information made available to individuals, such as sensory vs. procedural information, as well as when in the stress cycle the information is made available; (c) the nature and type of alternative strategies available, such as the availability of external distractors or the training of relaxation and reinterpretation approaches; (d) personal factors, such as the individual's dispositional tendency to monitor or to blunt threat-relevant cues; and (e) the nature and type of outcome under consideration, such as psychological distress, medical status, knowledge, and adherence.

In general, the benefits of confrontational approaches appear to be most pronounced when individuals are provided with sensory and procedural information about long-term medical stressors, particularly for those who are characteristically disposed to attend to threatening cues. Such preparation appears to enable individuals to clarify the meaning of situational cues, to exclude threatening interpretations, to actively process incoming events, and to compare them with expected occurrences (Leventhal, 1989). However, information is not always readily available, realistic, or presented in a form that matches—on an ongoing basis—the individuals' informational needs. Indeed, avoidant approaches—which the individual can execute at will—can be useful, especially when dealing with short-term stressors and for individuals who are characteristically disposed to psychologically blunt and attenuate objectives sources of danger.

A virtually unexplored issue in this context is whether there are individuals who are best able to flexibly apply avoidant and confrontational strategies as conditions warrant or specific situational configurations that maximize the use of flexible self-regulatory skills (Auerbach, 1989; Horowitz, 1986). It may well be the case that a dynamic interplay between attentional and avoidant modes is optimal, enabling individuals: (a) to ensure that they are aware of their options and of the extent of their personal control, when initially confronted by the stressor; (b) to activate arousal-reducing strategies when facing short-term or overwhelming events; and (c) to re-evaluate their status and options as the threat persists, remits, increases or diminishes in severity.

The danger for some individuals may be that they become locked into a rigid mode of processing the event, which they cannot modulate effectively. Some evidence from research on the monitoring-blunting dimension suggests that monitors may sometimes be more vulnerable in this context than blunters. For example, among women at risk for cervical cancer, preliminary results show that monitors were more likely to use strategies of an information-oriented nature when dealing with an aversive diagnostic procedure, such as focusing on bodily sensations, talking with the staff about their physical feelings, thinking about what the doctor was doing, and thinking how necessary the procedure was. They were less likely to engage in avoidant-type strategies, such as relaxing or thinking about things other than the procedure or their gynecologic condition. These differences were confirmed by observer ratings of patients' coping strategy during the procedure. However, compared with blunters, they indicated that their coping strategies were less helpful to them (i.e., they did not necessarily make them feel less anxious) but they nonetheless felt compelled to enact them (Miller, Rodoletz, & Stoddard, 1990).

Further, in the days preceding their medical visit, monitors reported that they were more disturbed by intrusive thoughts about their gynecologic situation than blunters were (even though they actually experienced equivalent amounts of intrusive ideation), and engaged in more avoidant strategies as a means of curbing their thoughts. That is, they were more likely to avoid thinking or talking about it, to push thoughts of it out of their minds, and to avoid reminders of it. Among individuals facing more lethal health threats, such as patients who are HIV-positive, monitors report both greater intrusive and avoidant ideation than blunters do (Miller, Robinson, & Combs, 1991).

However, attempts to actively suppress disturbing thoughts may sometimes have the paradoxical effect of increasing intrusive ideation. For example, Wegner, Schneider, Carter, and White (1987) instructed normal subjects to avoid thinking about a white bear and to ring a bell every time they did think about it. The results showed that subjects had difficulty suppressing the thought. Moreover, during a subsequent task in which they were explicitly instructed to think about a white bear, they experienced more thoughts about it than a group who had been asked to think the thought from the outset. Monitors may well be more vulnerable to these effects than blunters are. They may have more difficulty spontaneously suppressing unpleasant cognitions and attempts to do so may be counterproductive for them. Interventions that provide them with a structure or strategy for tuning out disturbing thoughts may be helpful. For example, in the Wegner et al. (1987) study, providing subjects with a specific thought to use as a distractor (the image of a red Volkswagen) during the initial suppression period eliminated later preoccupation with the thought.

These findings suggest that blunters sometimes feel more satisfied with their coping efficacy, less anxious in the face of intrusive ideation, and—perhaps most interestingly—less inclined to initiate attempts to suppress or contain these thoughts. Monitors, on the other hand, appear to be more sensitive to their own ruminative ideation, perhaps because they fear that their inability to modulate this thinking will enmesh them in an ever-increasing monitoring spiral, which they are unable to switch off. This may lead them to overly attend to even minor consequences of the situation or to exaggerate the probability and severity of more major consequences. Consistent with this, recent findings show that monitors are more likely to engage in worrying than blunters are (Davey, 1990). While the construct of worry is complex, it can be described as the persistent awareness of and attention to possible future danger. The relationship between monitoring and worry was found to hold, independent of levels of trait anxiety. This suggests that the adaptiveness of attentionally oriented processes may depend on different aspects of the threat situation. In conditions where information-seeking becomes maladaptive, monitors may benefit from intervention techniques that teach them blunting strategies for tuning out threat. They may also benefit from learning how to monitor in a way that decreases the salience of threat and instead focuses them on the positive and reassuring aspects of the situation.

An important agenda for future research, in both medical and clinical settings, will be to further explore monitors' and blunters' metacognitions and construals not only of the events that befall them but of the meaning and efficacy of their own coping efforts. It will be particularly important to determine the underlying nature of observed self-regulatory differences between monitors and blunters. One possibility is that blunters simply have fewer intrusive thoughts than monitors do. Another is that they are not as disturbed by or as focused on such thoughts when they do have them. In either case, the coping process (involving attempts to somehow avoid such thoughts) may be short-circuited. Alternatively, in the face of intrusive ideation, blunters may be more successful in suppressing disturbing thoughts because they have (or believe they have) a more varied or effective distraction repertoire. These possibilities are now being explored, looking at a range of threatening situations and conditions.

Not only are the differences in attentional styles reviewed here relevant to a broad range of medical outcomes, but they also appear to be relevant to psychological adaptation more generally, even in the absence of exposure to major health or other threats. Indeed, an important component of so-called "failures in coping" may reside in the inappropriate or ineffective use of monitoring and blunting mechanisms. The anxiety disorders represent a major area of psychopathology in which the maladaptive modulation of these modes may be paramount. This issue is discussed in the next section of the paper.

IMPLICATIONS OF MONITORING AND BLUNTING FOR ANXIETY DISORDERS

Originally, mainstream psychological contributions to the understanding of anxiety states centered primarily around behavioral formulations. These models emphasize the importance of faulty learning experiences for the acquisition and maintenance of disorders of anxiety, particularly with respect to phobias and obsessive-compulsive disorders. More recently, cognitive perspectives have emerged, which can account for the etiology and persistence of generalized anxiety disorder and panic disorder, as well as the more traditionally studied forms of anxiety, such as phobias and obsessive-compulsive disorder.

Essentially, cognitive models highlight the ways in which individuals scan for and process cues about perceived or potential threats. Exposure to adverse life events is not a necessary component of the anxiety disorders—with the exception of post-traumatic stress disorder. Nevertheless, stress does appear to play a role in triggering these conditions. Further, anxiety disorders generally arise during early to middle adulthood, a time when the demands for successful accommodation to—and achievement in—life's tasks are high. This section enumerates the different anxiety disorders and the ways in which various informational tendencies have been found to play a role. Almost no evidence currently bears on the role of monitoring-blunting styles for the origins of the anxiety disorders. However, attentional processes appear to have somewhat parallel effects in both nonclinical and clinical contexts. As in the medical setting, findings with anxiety disorders generally implicate the maladaptiveness of monitoring modes of self-regulation, when coping with more minor or perhaps more short-term stressors. In addition, excessive amounts of both monitoring and/or blunting may increase vulnerability to the prolonged effects of highly traumatic or persistent stressors.

Generalized Anxiety Disorder

Generalized anxiety disorder, while still fairly rare in clinical practice, is highly prevalent in the general population. Indeed, of all the anxiety states, it appears to share the closest linkages with everyday ups and downs in anxious mood. The essential feature of generalized anxiety is unrealistic worry or apprehension about two or more areas of one's life. While patients with generalized anxiety disorder tend to worry about aspects of life that are often legitimately troublesome (e.g., money, family, and work), they exaggerate their problems and are rarely free of thoughts about them. They are also far more likely to worry endlessly about fairly trivial or minor aspects of their lives, compared with normal individuals and individuals suffering from other types of anxiety disorders (Sanderson & Barlow, 1986).

Exposure to stressful life events appears to play a role in triggering the disorder. Individuals who report having experienced one or more unexpected, negative, very important life event(s) have a threefold risk of developing the disorder (Blazer, Hughes, & George, 1987). Patients who ultimately develop generalized anxiety disorder appear to be characterized by a style which entails a selective focus on cues about danger, in which they attend intently to cues about threat. This bias has been demonstrated in a series of elegant studies by Mathews and his colleagues, which borrow on sophisticated techniques developed by cognitive psychologists for assessing information-processing (e.g., MacLeod, Mathews, & Tata, 1986; Mathews & MacLeod, 1985). Individuals characterized by such a bias may come to experience their everyday world as being highly personally dangerous (Mathews, Richards, & Eysenck, 1989).

As discussed above, monitors are more likely than blunters to worry about aspects of everyday living (Davey, 1990). Hence, it is possible that generalized anxiety disorder may be more easily triggered for them, especially in the face of threatening or disruptive circumstances. Further, monitors appear to remain more behaviorally engaged in the face of threat. That is, they are more likely to focus on the situation and to keep trying to find a solution to it. However, they do not actually engage in more active coping or planning attempts (e.g., Carver, Scheier, & Weintraub 1989). This is consistent with research showing that when worrying becomes chronic, it actually appears to interfere with effective decision-making and problem-solving (Borkovec, 1985).

Generalized anxiety disorder has proven to be among the most difficult of the anxiety conditions to treat effectively. Neither biological nor behavioral approaches have been especially successful. Relaxation techniques, which attempt to reduce the arousal component of sustained high levels of anxiety, have proven to be of some use. However, a subset of individuals (between 30% and 50%) actually become profoundly anxious when they attempt to relax as instructed (Borkovec, 1985). Recently, more cognitive approaches to the management of generalized anxiety have been attempted and have been found to be effective. Techniques that construe worry as an uncontrolled habit that must be moderated may be especially beneficial for monitors.

Panic Disorder and Agoraphobia

Panic disorder is characterized by the occurrence of panic attacks, which are discrete periods of intense fear or discomfort, that arise unexpectedly. Symptoms of panic include physical components, such as palpitations, dizziness, and trembling; as well as cognitive components, such as fears of dying, going crazy, or losing control. Earlier formulations proposed that panic disorder was secondary to agoraphobia. That is, individuals who had an intense fear of places or situations in which escape might be difficult ultimately panicked when they found themselves trapped in those situations. However, more recent research suggests that the reverse is true: Individuals who are prone to panic ultimately come to avoid situations from which escape might be difficult, should they experience a panic attack (Barlow, 1988).

As with generalized anxiety disorder, panic disorder is often triggered by exposure to stressful life circumstances (Barlow & Craske, 1988). With respect to panic, the cognitive model focuses more on the way in which individuals process information about their own internal bodily sensations and less on the way in which individuals process information about external threats. According to this view, individuals who are prone to panic misinterpret their somatic sensations in a catastrophic way. More specifically, panic-prone individuals are considered to be over-sensitive to certain stimuli, such as bodily sensations. They respond by becoming apprehensive about and hypervigilant to these cues, particularly if no obvious nonthreatening interpretation of their state is available. This makes them anxious, which further heightens bodily symptoms of arousal. As anxiety spirals, a full-blown panic attack can be precipitated (Clark, 1988).

The cognitive perspective thus appears to implicate a negative focus on somatic cues as central to panic. A number of lines of evidence are consistent with this approach (Beck, 1988; Clark, 1988; Teasdale, 1988). It is possible that monitors may be at risk for this disorder, since they appear to attend more intently to their physical symptoms and are more inclined to exaggerate their significance (Miller, Brody, & Summerton, 1988). Whether and under what conditions such a monitoring style (which entails a preoccupation with bodily symptoms) may, or may not, progress to the disabling symptoms of panic remains an issue for future research.

Exposure to feared situations has proven to be an effective treatment strategy for agoraphobia, as well as for other phobias. The effects of exposure appear to be dependent upon the individuals' ability to attend to and access fear-relevant information, thereby enabling them to fully process the event or object. Since monitors are generally more prone to scan for threat than blunters, they may be optimal candidates for this type of therapy (Foa & Kozak, 1986). One study found that monitors appear to respond better to exposure treatment than blunters. Specifically, they showed greater initial arousal to the phobic stimulus, presumably reflecting greater attention to threat. In addition, monitors showed greater habituation of physiological and subjective indices of arousal, both within and across sessions, presumably reflecting increased emotional processing of threat over time (Steketee, Bransfield, Miller, & Foa, 1989).

Exposure to external cues has not fared as well with symptoms of panic. More recent cognitive-behavioral therapies entail exposure to the actual symptoms of panic —by deliberately inducing a state of panic—along with techniques that teach patients to decatastrophize the meaning of these bodily symptoms. Patients are also taught a variety of relaxation, breathing control, and distraction technique (Beck, 1988).

Obsessive-Compulsive Disorder

Obsessive-compulsive disorder is among the most debilitating of the anxiety disorders. Obsessions are persistent ideas, thoughts, images, or impulses that intrude unbidden into the individual's consciousness. Concerns about dirt and contamination are among the most common obsessive thoughts, followed by thoughts of violence and aggression. Compulsions are repetitive, purposeful, and intentional behaviors that are performed according to certain rules or in a stereotypic fashion. They are generally performed in response to obsessive thoughts and are intended to neutralize or prevent the discomfort caused by such thoughts (Marks, 1987). Obsessive-compulsives are often under stress when their symptoms first emerge.

According to current thinking, obsessive-compulsive disorder is the result of faulty information-processing of external cues (Kozak, Foa, & McCarthy, 1988). In most instances, individuals assume that various environmental situations are safe, unless there is firm evidence to the contrary, such as the presence of explicit cues for danger. Obsessive-compulsives operate under the reverse assumption: They assume that a variety of environmental situations is dangerous, unless there are explicit safety signals available. Since such evidence is typically difficult to obtain, obsessive-compulsives associate a wide variety of unrelated stimuli with ideas of threat or danger, hold erroneously high estimates of their probability of occurrence, and exaggerate the aversiveness of the situation, should it befall them. Compulsive behaviors—designed to ward off these presumed threats—help individuals to restore their sense of safety and thereby to increase their feelings of vulnerability and uncertainty. Recent evidence suggests that individuals with a monitoring style are inclined to evaluate potential stressors as more threatening and more unpredictable. They also tend to view them as more uncontrollable and easier to imagine (van Zuuren & Wolfs, 1991). Hence, it is possible that — under certain conditions — they may be more at risk for the development of obsessive symptomatology. This possibility is currently being explored.

Exposure to the relevant anxiety-inducing situations and prevention of accompanying compulsive rituals are the treatments of choice for obsessive-compulsive disorder. Only 10% of patients fail to show any improvement with this regimen (Foa, Steketee, & Ozarow, 1985). This combination of techniques appears to enable patients to habituate to the source of their fear and to reevaluate the unpleasantness and probability of harm in the situation. However, it may leave cognitive style unchanged, such that individuals continue to experience difficulties in making decisions about danger and safety (Kozak et al., 1988). As with phobias, monitoring patients may fare better with exposure treatments. On the other hand, it may be more difficult to change underlying aspects of their cognitive style that have to do with perceptions of predictability and controllability.

Posttraumatic Stress Disorder

Posttraumatic stress disorder represents a maladaptive response to a traumatic event that is outside the range of usual human experience, such as war, rape, floods, fires, and car accidents. There are three main symptoms of this disorder:

1. Persistent reexperiencing of the trauma, as demonstrated by intrusive recollections, distressing dreams or nightmares of the event, feeling like the event is happening all over again, or distress when exposed to reminders of the event.
2. Persistent avoidance of thoughts and feelings that are associated with the trauma, or feelings of numbness, detachment, and loss of interest in important aspects of life.
3. Persistent symptoms of hyperarousal, such as startle responses, hypervigilance, sleep problems, and physiological arousal.

Posttraumatic stress disorder is thus characterized by symptoms reflecting attentional fixation on threat, as well as by symptoms reflecting extreme avoidance of threat (Horowitz, 1986; Keane, Fairbank, Caddell, Zimering, & Bender, 1985). Attentional and avoidance mechanisms may even alternate in a phasic pattern, as the individual struggles (unsuccessfully) to come to terms with the event (Horowitz, 1986).

Recent evidence suggests that whether monitors or blunters are more at risk for symptoms of posttraumatic stress disorder may depend upon the severity and/or timing of the aversive experience. As discussed above, among individuals facing health threats, monitors appear to be at greater risk for both intrusion and avoidance symptoms than blunters are. On the other hand, blunters appear to be more at risk for the perpetuation of such symptoms, especially in the face of highly traumatic conditions (Solomon, Mikulincer, & Arad, in press). When individuals are exposed to an event beyond the realm of normal human experience, they may need to process that event in order to resign themselves to it. Blunters may fail to allow such processing to occur, thereby setting the stage for both the overwhelming intrusion and avoidance of traumatic imagery (Foa, Steketee, & Rothbaum, 1989). Hence, a primarily avoidant approach may sometimes facilitate, and sometimes impede, adaptation to threat. Future research should help to untangle the conditions that determine the impact of attentional versus avoidant processes under stress.

There are two main types of treatment that have been found to be of use in the management of posttraumatic stress disorder. The first involves exposure, usually in imagination, to disturbing thoughts, images, and memories (Foa, Rothbaum, & Steketee, in press; Keane et al., 1985). The second, stress inoculation training, is designed to teach a variety of techniques for directing attention away from the source of threat or increasing emotional self-regulation. These include thought stopping, relaxation and breathing exercises, role playing, and guided self-dialogue (Veronen & Kilpatrick, 1983). Exposure and stress inoculation may be complementary techniques, which target different aspects of the disorder. Exposure may undermine re-experiencing and avoidance symptoms whereas stress inoculation training may undermine chronic hyperarousal (Foa et al., 1989). While monitors may respond more favorably to exposure techniques, and less favorably to stress inoculation training, both may be important to overcome posttraumatic symptomatology.

Discussion

Overall, the cognitive perspectives on anxiety disorders emphasize monitoring processes gone awry, as the process of everyday living unfolds. This formulation implicates the role of hypervigilance to threatening environmental cues (generalized anxiety disorder), catastrophic misinterpretation of bodily cues (panic disorder), and an inability to perceive safety (obsessive-compulsive disorder). It is tempting to speculate that individuals who are disposed to monitor for cues of danger when they are under threat may be more vulnerable to the development of these disorders. At the very least, research into monitoring and blunting processes should help to illuminate certain key aspects of the nature and function of the anxiety disorders. In addition, in response to highly traumatic conditions, either hypervigilance or hyperblunting may interfere with emotional processing and thereby impede adaptation. Future research should explore when a given anxiety disorder is precipitated and whether there are person-by-situation interactions that render individuals more vulnerable to the development or persistence of these disorders.

While treatment approaches include a variety of strategies, they predominantly fall into two main categories. The first set of techniques serves to focus the individual more intently on precipitating internal or external threatening cues. This approach may proceed most smoothly with individuals who are characteristically disposed to monitor for threat. Among the strategies used are exposure to somatic symptoms (panic disorder), exposure to obsessional material (obsessive-compulsive disorder), and exposure to cues and reminders of trauma (posttraumatic stress disorder). These techniques appear to enable the individual to more fully process the event, which ultimately lowers patients' intrusive ideation centering on harm, its probability of occurrence, and its perceived aversiveness.

The second set of techniques serves to focus the individual away from precipitating internal or external threatening cues. This approach may be most beneficial for individuals who are characteristically disposed to psychologically attenuate threat-relevant cues. Cognitive-behavioral strategies, such as relaxation and distraction, direct attention onto neutral or positive stimuli. This enables the individual to restrict worrying (generalized anxiety disorder), reduce a focus on internal anxiety cues (panic disorder), and decrease the hyperarousal associated with trauma (posttraumatic stress disorder). These techniques appear to foster the use and efficacy of emotion-focused strategies, which allow the individual to manage their own anxiety and remain calm in the face of threat, thereby reducing disabling levels of arousal.

IMPLICATIONS OF MONITORING AND BLUNTING FOR SELF-PROTECTIVE BEHAVIORS

With the exception of individuals' responses to highly traumatic stressors, I have concentrated on conditions in which monitoring may generally prove to be a less adaptive, as well as a less flexible, mode of coping than blunting. However, there may also be nontraumatic conditions under which an avoidant approach to threat may become inappropriately inflexible and detrimental. For example, having initially appraised a particular threat as uncontrollable, blunters may subsequently exclude any further incoming information that may bear on it. If aspects of the threat itself become subject to change, blunters will not be in a position to reevaluate the potential controllability or consequences of the situation and so may be at a disadvantage.

In a laboratory study of subjects facing unpleasant but uncontrollable auditory stimulation, blunters were more likely to rigidly avoid information about the stressor than monitors were. Further, blunters who did attend to threat-relevant information showed the highest physiological and subjective arousal, particularly during the early phases of the anticipatory interval (Kohlmann, 1989). Other research has also shown that blunters suffer adverse effects when unwanted information is imposed upon them in apparently uncontrollable circumstances (Miller & Mangan, 1983; Watkins et al., 1986).

In situations where prolonged attention to threat may be important, blunters may be less inclined than monitors to remain vigilant over time and to suffer arousal consequences when they do. Individuals who are at risk for a variety of medical problems (such as cervical cancer or AIDS) typically must adhere to screening regimens. This entails a recurrent focus on threatening cues, as the individual must schedule, attend, and submit to sometimes aversive medical regimens, as well as await the results of these procedures. It has been difficult to find useful individual or situational predictors of health-care negligence (Baumeister & Scher, 1988). One important determinant appears to be the extent to which the individual is attentive to, or concerned about, the relief of painful or annoying symptoms (Haynes, 1976).

Blunters may represent a more vulnerable population in these situations. These individuals tend to downplay the significance of internal and external cues about threat (Miller et al., 1988; Miller, Leinbach, & Brody, 1989). This strategy may thus interfere with adherence to self-protective diagnostic and preventive behaviors. Indeed, among women, blunters have been found to be less likely to perform breast self-examinations or to undergo regular gynecologic screenings (Miller et al., 1990; Steptoe & O'Sullivan, 1986). Recent research suggests that this may bear negatively on the state of their gynecologic health (Miller et al., 1990). Blunters may thus benefit from interventions designed to increase the salience of somatic and other symptoms of threat, perhaps by focusing them on the negative aspects of noncompliance (Meyerowitz & Chaiken, 1987).

CONCLUSIONS

It is true that much has still to be learned about the nature and development of avoidant and attentional informational styles and their implications for the anxiety disorders. Continuing questions remain about their relations to ongoing coping efforts, their sensitivity to variations in situational demands, and their impact on a broad range of adaptational outcomes. Nevertheless, some tentative conclusions do appear to be emerging. This chapter has attempted to provide a clearer delineation of when and under what circumstances avoidant and attentional self-regulatory processes are associated with lower arousal and distress and improved health outcomes and when they are more harmful to health, physically and psychologically.

Overall, monitoring in the face of health and other everyday threats seems to increase distress, because of an overattention to the potential severity, probability, and consequences of one's situation. Indeed, a style which entails heightened sensitivity to—and over-interpretation of—ongoing experience (especially when dealing with more minor stressors) appears to be implicated in the maintenance, and possibly the origins, of the anxiety disorders. Conversely, blunting appears to exacerbate maladjustment in the face of highly traumatic stressors and to undermine the individual's commitment to undertake appropriate self-protective behaviors in response to health threats. It is possible that monitoring-blunting styles increase the risk for the development and/or the persistence of clinical anxiety, in the wake of exposure to certain stimulus conditions and experiences. Alternatively, various minor and major life events may trigger monitoring- and blunting-type processes, independent of individual dispositions. In either case, research on information-seeking and avoidance in nonclinical situations may help to shed some light on the role of attentional processes in patient populations.

Perhaps it is not simply the particular strategy that is engaged that is critical, but how well—or selectively—it is engaged. With respect to monitoring, adverse effects seem to result when the attention to threat merely serves to repeatedly re-expose the individual to threatening cues and hence stokes the fires of fear. Beneficial effects result when the event is confronted in a manner that enables individuals to thoroughly process and assimilate it, thereby simultaneously resigning themselves to its occurrence and more realistically reevaluating its nature and consequences (Foa & Kozak, 1986). Similarly, blunting may be maladaptive when it merely pushes thoughts of threat out of immediate experience, which can also seriously hinder attempts to effectively process threat. It is more advantageous when it entails strategies to reduce arousal, so that the processing of threat can proceed in a less overwhelming fashion.

There is probably no royal road to the management of emotional and instrumental responses in the face of a variety of perceived or actual life crises and losses (Wortman & Silver, 1989). Individuals who are most flexible may well be those whose primary strategy—attentional or avoidance—is efficiently enacted, freeing them of the need to rigidly adhere to their particularly preferred mode. Further, situational factors may determine which primary strategy is most efficacious. In conditions where the threat is more minor or short-term, blunting may be the most adaptive mode, interspersed with attentional phases that enable the individual to scan for any alterations in the nature or controllability of the stressor. In situations where the threat is more major or long-term, monitoring may be the most adaptive mode, interspersed with avoidant phases that enable the individual to reduce arousal and thereby maintain distress within tolerable limits. In future research, it will be important not only to identify—but also to try to predict—these kinds of fine-grained interactions and to explore their potential health and clinical applications.

REFERENCES

Auerbach, S. M. (1989). Stress management and coping research in the health care setting: An overview and methodological commentary. *Journal of Consulting and Clinical Psychology, 57*, 388-395.

Auerbach, S. M., Martelli, M. F., & Mercuri, L. G. (1983). Anxiety, information, interpersonal impacts, and adjustment to a stressful health care situation. *Journal of Personality and Social Psychology, 44*, 1284-1296.

Barlow, D. H. (1988). *Anxiety and its disorders: The nature and treatment of anxiety and panic*. New York: Guilford Press.

Barlow, D. H., & Craske, M. (1988). The phenomenology of panic. In S. Rachman & J. D. Maser (Eds.), *Panic: Psychological perspectives* (pp. 11-35). Hillsdale, NJ: Lawrence Erlbaum Associates.

Baumeister, R. F., & Scher, S. J. (1988). Self-defeating behavior patterns among normal individuals: Review and analysis of common self-destructive tendencies. *Psychological Bulletin, 104*, 3-22.

Beck, A. T. (1988). Cognitive approaches to panic disorder: Theory and therapy. In S. Rachman & J. D. Maser (Eds.), *Panic: Psychological perspectives* (pp. 91-111). Hillsdale, NJ: Lawrence Erlbaum Associates.

Blazer, D., Hughes, D., & George, L. D. (1987). Stressful life events and the onset of a generalized anxiety syndrome. *American Journal of Psychiatry, 144*(1), 178-1183.

Borkovec, T. D. (1985). The role of cognitive and somatic cues in anxiety and anxiety disorders: Worry and relaxation-induced anxiety. In A. H. Tuma & J. Maser (Eds.), *Anxiety and the anxiety disorders* (pp. 463-478). Hillsdale, NJ: Lawrence Erlbaum Associates.

Carver, C. S., Scheier, M. F., & Weintraub, J. K. (1989). Assessing coping strategies: A theoretically based approach. *Journal of Personality and Social Psychology, 56*, 267-283.

Cassileth, B. R., Lusk, E. J., Miller, D. S., Brown, L. L., & Miller, C. (1985). Psychosocial correlates of survival in malignant disease. *New England Journal of Medicine, 312*, 1551-1555.

Clark, D. M. (1988). A cognitive model of panic attacks. In S. Rachman & J. D. Maser (Eds.), *Panic:*

Psychological perspectives (pp. 71-90). Hillsdale, NJ: Lawrence Erlbaum Associates.

Davey, G. (1990). *The characteristics of worrying*. Unpublished manuscript, City University, London, England.

Derogatis, L. R., Abeloff, M. D., & Melisaratos, N. (1979). Psychological coping mechanisms and survival time in metastatic breast cancer. *Journal of the American Medical Association, 242*, 1504-1508.

Efran, J. S., Chorney, R. L., Ascher, L. M., & Lukens, M. D. (1989). Coping styles, paradox, and the cold pressor task. *Journal of Behavioral Medicine, 12*, 91-103.

Foa, E. B., & Kozak, M. (1986). Emotional processing of fear: Exposure to corrective information. *Psychological Bulletin, 99*, 20-35.

Foa, E. B., Rothbaum, B. O., & Steketee, C. S. (in press). Treatment of rape victims. *Journal of Interpersonal Violence*.

Foa, E. B., Steketee, G. S., & Ozarow, B. J. (1985). Behavior therapy with obsessive-compulsives: From theory to treatment. In M. Mavissakalian (Ed.), *Obsessive-compulsive disorder: Psychological and pharmacological treatments* (pp. 49-129). New York: Plenum.

Foa, E. B., Steketee, G., & Rothbaum, B. O. (1989). Behavioral/cognitive conceptualizations of post-traumatic stress disorder. *Behavior Therapy, 20*, 155-176.

Gard, D., Edwards, P. W., Harris, J., & McCormack, G. (1988). Sensitizing effects of pretreatment measures on cancer chemotherapy nausea and vomiting. *Journal of Consulting and Clinical Psychology, 56*, 80-84.

Greer, S., Morris, T., & Pettingale, K. W. (1979). Psychological response to breast cancer: Effect and outcome. *Lancet, 2*, 785-787.

Haynes, R. B. (1976). A critical review of the 'determinants' of patient compliance with therapeutic regimens. In D. L. Sackett & R. B. Haynes (Eds.), *Compliance with therapeutic regimens* (pp. 26-39). Baltimore: Johns Hopkins University Press.

Horowitz, M. J. (1986). Stress response syndromes: A review of post-traumatic and adjustment disorders. *Hospital and Community Psychiatry, 37*, 241-249.

Jensen, M. J. (1987). Psychobiological factors predicting the course of breast cancer. *Journal of Personality, 55*, 317-342.

Keane, T. M., Fairbank, J. A., Caddell, J. M., Zimering, R. T., & Bender, M. E. (1985). A behavioral approach to assessing and treating post-traumatic stress disorder in Vietnam veterans. In C. R. Figley (Ed.), *Trauma and its wake* (pp. 257-294). New York: Brunner/Mazel.

Kohlmann, C. W. (1989, July). *Rigid and flexible modes of coping and the goodness-of-fit hypothesis: The role of coping preferences*. Paper presented at First European Congress of Psychology, Amsterdam, Netherlands.

Kozak, M. J., Foa, E. B., & McCarthy, P. R. (1988). Obsessive-compulsive disorder. In C. G. Last & M. Hersen (Eds.), *Handbook of anxiety disorders* (pp. 87-108). New York: Pergamon.

Langer, E. J., Janis, I., & Wolfer, J. (1975). Reduction of psychological stress in surgical patients. *Journal of Experimental Social Psychology, 11*, 155-165.

Lerman, C., Rimer, R., Blumberg, B., & Cristinzio, M. S., Engstrom, P.F., McElwee, N. O'Connor, K., & Seay, J. (1990). Effects of coping style and relaxation on cancer chemotherapy side effects and emotional responses. *Cancer Nursing, 13*, 308-315.

Leventhal, H. (1989). Emotional and behavioral processes in the study of stress during medical procedures. In M. Johnston & L. Wallace (Eds.), *Stress and medical procedures* (pp. 3-35). Oxford: Oxford Science and Medical Publications.

Levy, S. M., Lee, J., Bagley, C., & Lippman, M. (1988). Survival hazards analysis in first recurrent breast cancer patients: Seven-year follow-up. *Psychosomatic Medicine, 50*, 520-528.

MacLeod, C., Mathews, A., & Tata, P. (1986). Attentional bias in emotional disorders. *Journal of Abnormal Psychology, 95*, 15-20.

Marks, I. M. (1987). *Fears, phobias, and rituals: Panic, anxiety, and their disorders*. Oxford: Oxford University Press.

Martelli, M. F., Auerbach, S. M., Alexander, J., & Mercuri, L. G. (1987). Stress management in the health care setting: Matching interventions with patient coping styles. *Journal of Consulting and*

Clinical Psychology, 55, 201-207.
Mathews, A., & MacLeod, C. (1985). Selective processing of threat cues in anxiety states. *Behavior Research and Therapy, 23,* 563-569.
Mathews, A., Richards, A., & Eysenck, M. (1989). Interpretation of homophones related to threat in anxiety states. *Journal of Abnormal Psychology, 98,* 31-34.
Meyerowitz, B. E., & Chaiken, S. (1987). The effect of message framing on breast self-examination attitudes, intentions, and behavior. *Journal of Personality and Social Psychology, 52,* 500-510.
Meyerowitz, B. E., Heinrich, R. L., & Schag, C. C. (1983). A competency-based approach to coping with cancer. In T. G. Burish & L. A. Bradley (Eds.), *Coping with chronic disease* (pp. 137-158). New York: Academic Press.
Miller, S. M. (1989). Cognitive informational styles in the process of coping with threat and frustration. *Advances in Behavioral Research and Therapy, 11,* 223-234.
Miller, S. M. (1990). To see or not to see: Cognitive informational styles in the coping process. In M. Rosenbaum (Ed.), *Learned resourcefulness: On coping skills, self-regulation, and adaptive behavior* (pp. 96-126). New York: Springer.
Miller, S. M. (in press). Individual differences in the coping process: What to know and when to know it. In B. Carpenter (Ed.), *Personal coping: Theory, research, and application.* New York: Praeger.
Miller, S. M., Brody, D. S., & Summerton, J. (1988). Styles of coping with threat: Implications for health. *Journal of Personality and Social Psychology, 54,* 345-353.
Miller, S. M., Combs, C., & Stoddard, E. (1989). Information, coping, and control in patients undergoing surgery and stressful medical procedures. In A. Steptoe & A. Appels (Eds.), *Stress, personal control, and health* (pp. 107-204). Chichester: Wiley.
Miller, S. M., Leinbach, A., & Brody, D. S. (1989). Coping style in hypertensive patients: Nature and consequences. *Journal of Consulting and Clinical Psychology, 57,* 333-337.
Miller, S. M., & Mangan, C. E. (1983). The interacting effects of information and coping style in adapting to gynecologic stress: Should the doctor tell all? *Journal of Personality and Social Psychology, 45,* 223-236.
Miller, S. M., Robinson, R., & Combs, C. (1991). *Styles of coping with HIV-positive status.* Unpublished manuscript, Temple University, Philadelphia, PA.
Miller, S. M., Rodoletz, M., & Stoddard, E. (1990). *Adjustment, coping, and compliance in women at risk for cervical cancer.* Unpublished manuscript, Temple University, Philadelphia, PA.
Ridgeway, V., & Mathews, A. (1982). Psychological preparation for surgery: A comparison of methods. *British Journal of Clinical Psychology, 21,* 271-280.
Sanderson, W. C., & Barlow, D. H. (1986, November). *Domains of worry within the DSM-III-R generalized anxiety disorder category: Reliability and description.* Paper presented at the annual meeting of the Association for the Advancement of Behavior Therapy, Chicago.
Scott, L. E., & Clum, G. A. (1984). Examining the interaction effects of coping style and brief interventions in the treatment of postsurgical pain. *Pain, 20,* 279-291.
Solomon, Z., Mikulincer, M., & Arad, R. (in press). Styles of information-seeking under threat: Implications for combat-related post-traumatic stress disorder. *Journal of Traumatic Stress.*
Steketee, G., Bransfield, S., Miller, S. M., & Foa, E. B. (1989). The effect of information and coping style on the reduction of phobic anxiety during exposure. *Journal of Anxiety Disorders, 3,* 69-85.
Steptoe, A., & O'Sullivan, J. (1986). Monitoring and blunting coping styles in women prior to surgery. *British Journal of Clinical Psychology, 25,* 143-144.
Steptoe, A., Sutcliffe, I., Allen, B., & Coombes, C. (1991). Satisfaction with communication, medical knowledge, and coping style in patients with metastatic cancer. *Social Science Medicine, 32,* 627-632.
Suls, J., & Fletcher, B. (1985). The relative efficacy of avoidant and non-avoidant coping strategies: A meta-analysis. *Health Psychology, 4,* 249-288.
Suls, J., & Wan, C. K. (1989). The effects of sensory and procedural information on adaptation to stressful medical procedures and pain: A meta-analysis. *Journal of Consulting and Clinical Psychology, 57,* 372-379.
Taylor, S. E., & Brown, J. D. (1988). Illusion and well-being: A social psychological perspective on

mental health. *Psychological Bulletin, 103*, 193-210.

Teasdale, J. (1988). Cognitive models and treatments for panic: A critical evaluation. In S. Rachman & J. D. Maser (Eds.), *Panic: Psychological perspectives* (pp. 189-203). Hillsdale, NJ: Lawrence Erlbaum Associates.

van Zuuren, F. J., & Wolfs, H. M. (1991). Styles of information seeking under threat: Personal and situational aspects of monitoring and blunting. *Personality and Individual Differences, 12*, 141-149.

Veronen, J. L., & Kilpatrick, D. G. (1983). Stress management for rape victims. In D. Meichenbaum & M. E. Jaremko (Eds.), *Stress reduction and prevention* (pp. 361-374). New York: Plenum.

Ward, S. E., Leventhal, H., & Love, R. (1988). Repression revisited: Tactics used in coping with a severe health threat. *Personality and Social Psychology Bulletin, 14*, 735-746.

Watkins, L. O., Weaver, L., & Odegaard, V. (1986). Preparation for cardiac catheterization: Tailoring the content of instruction to coping style. *Heart and Lung, 15*, 382-389.

Wegner, D. M., Schneider, D. J., Carter, III, S. R., & White, T. L. (1987). Paradoxical effects of thought suppression. *Journal of Personality and Social Psychology, 53*, 5-13.

Weisenberg, M., & Caspi, Z. (1989). Cultural and educational influences on pain of childbirth. *Journal of Pain and Symptom Management, 4*, 13-19.

Wortman, C. B., & Silver, R. C. (1989). The myths of coping with loss. *Journal of Consulting and Clinical Psychology, 57*, 349-357.

15 Reality Negotiation and Valence/Linkage Self-Theories: Psychic Showdown at the "I'm OK" Corral and Beyond

Charles R. Snyder
Lori M. Irving
Sandra T. Sigmon
Sharon Holleran
The University of Kansas, Lawrence

On October 26, 1881, in the frontier town of Tombstone, Arizona, there was the most famous gunfight in the history of the American "wild west" (Trachtman, 1974). The "good guys," as the story goes, were the Earp brothers (City Marshal Virgil, Assistant City Marshal Wyatt, and Morgan) and Doc Holiday. The "bad guys" were the Clanton (Ike and Billy) and McLaury (Tom and Frank) brothers. After the Clantons and McLaurys had repeatedly disparaged the positive image of the Earp brothers, the tensions had reached a peak on this late October day. Clearly, something needed to happen in order to stop this afront to the Earps' reputations. Sensing a showdown, the townspeople cleared the streets as the Earps and Holiday set off to find the Clantons and McLaurys. The confrontation occurred near the stalls of the OK Corral on Fremont Street. The results were heralded in the headline of the newpaper, the Tombstone Daily Epitaph, the next day: "Three Men Hurled Into Eternity in the Duration of a Moment." Frank and Tom McLaury, along with Billy Clanton, were killed, and Ike Clanton was last seen running away through the OK Corral. The Earp brothers and Doc Holiday had defended the threat to their reputations in a blaze of gunfire.

This sort of physical showdown, when viewed a century later, may seem very violent and dramatic, but it parallels more subtle psychological showdown processes that modern people face throughout their lives as they react to information that threatens their personal sense of self. In the present chapter, we will elaborate a model of how people engage in psychological reality negotiations in order to preserve and sometimes enhance their personal theories of who and what they are in the face of threatening input.

POSITIVE VALENCE/LINKAGE SELF-THEORIES: THE "I'M OK" CORRAL

The idea that people have theories about their "selves" has a long and distinguished heritage, including such noted thinkers as Freud (1894/1953), James (1910), Adler (1931), Cooley (1902), Mead (1934), Lecky (1945), Snygg and Combs (1949), Hilgard (1949), Rogers (1951), Sarbin (1952), Sullivan (1953), Allport (1955), Kelly (1955), Gergen (1968), Epstein (1973/1980), Rosenberg (1979), Stryker (1980), Greenwald (1980), Schlenker (1980), and Markus and Nurius (1986), to name but a few. These writers have implicitly or explicitly tackled the following three questions:

1. On what dimensions is the self charted?
2. Where do people appraise themselves on those dimensions?
3. What motive or motives underlie the person's self-theory?

In the present section, we will present our views about each of these questions in the exposition of our model. Because of space limitations, we will not describe the similarities of our model to all of the previous writers, but we will highlight the closest ideas from previous work.

On What Dimensions is the Self Defined?

We assume that the individual's theory of self is built upon two fundamental dimensions: linkage-to-act and valence-of-act (see Snyder, 1989). These dimensions reflect a schema against which the person evaluates himself or herself. For our present purposes, a schema is "a cognitive structure that represents organized knowledge about a concept or type of stimulus" (Fiske & Taylor, 1984, p. 140). The stimulus in this particular instance is the person's self. Definitionally, the linkage-to-act dimension "reflects the degree to which the person believes that he or she is yoked to a particular act or outcome" (Snyder, 1989, p. 134). As shown on the abscissa of Figures 15.1a and 15.1b, the perceived linkage to any given act may vary from the extremes of none to total.

A very young child must increasingly learn causal reality relative to the external world. To obtain a sense of competence (see White, 1959), the developing child must achieve an understanding of what events are causally or associatively linked with each other. To the newborn, the sense of contingency between antecedent and consequent events is largely unknown. Over time, however, these fundamental lessons are learned and the maturing child understands the surrounding environment and the causal role that he or she plays in it. In this latter vein, the person's perceived linkage to events forms one of the building blocks upon which the sense of self is erected.

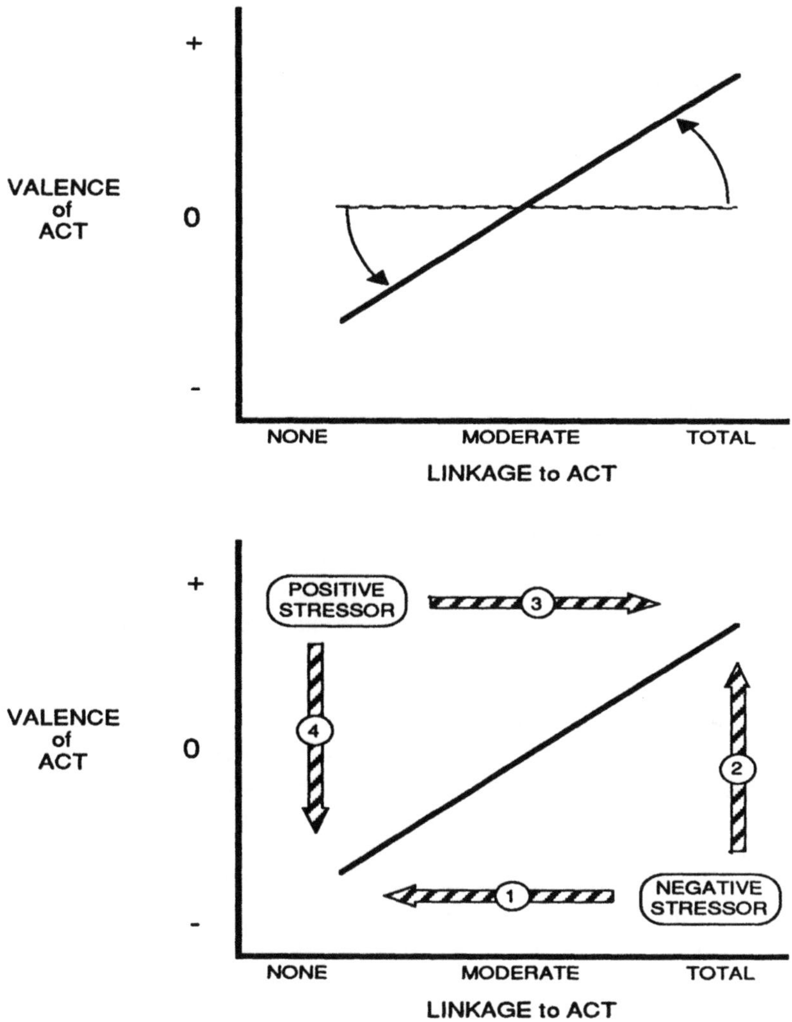

FIG.15.1a. The positive valence/linkage self-theory rotation
FIG. 15.1b. Reality negotiation dynamics of the positive valence/linkage self-theory rotation

The second basic dimension of appraisal is valence-of-act. As shown on the ordinate of Figure 15.1, the valence-of-act dimension reflects the degree to which any given outcome is considered to be negative to positive. Given the fashion in which the linkage and valence dimensions are arrayed in Figure 15.1, it can be seen that these two sources of appraisal are intertwined when the self is the target. Indeed, it is our premise that this matrix provides the essential coordinates by which people plot themselves from the earliest years. For example, something very favorable may have happened, and we perceive ourselves as being strongly linked to it, or we may perceive no linkage; moreover, for some very negative outcome, we may or may not see any linkage. Indeed, it is difficult to imagine the linkage evaluation *not* being accompanied by the valence appraisal. In this vein, Rogers (1951) defined the self as a "consistent pattern of perceptions of characteristics and relationships of the 'I' or the 'me', *together with the values attached to these concepts*" (p. 498, emphasis added). If one were to plot a person's perceived linkage to a series of outcomes that vary in valence from positive to negative, this matrix would provide a phenomenological representation of that person's self. Such an exercise can be undertaken with children and adults, and the scatterplot gives a visual portrayal of the particular self. We expand this point in the next section.

Where Do People Appraise Themselves on These Dimensions?

Consider, for a moment, the recurring lessons of childhood in which parents teach the difference between good and bad acts. Such valence-of-act instruction does not occur in a vacuum, however, in the sense that the child typically is reinforced for increased linkage to positive outcomes and decreased linkage to negative outcomes. Thus, as shown in Figure 15.1a, the wavy line showing no greater linkage to acts of varying valence reflects the tabula rasa of the newborn before the linkage/valence lessons have been learned.[1] When it comes to the self, therefore, the usual developmental result is the positive valence-linkage rotation that we have pictured in Figure 15.1a. Here, it can be seen that the normal development of the self-theory increasingly involves the perception that one is associated with positive outcomes and is not associated with negative outcomes. If we are good boys and girls, we live our lives in ways so that we actually are associated more with positive than negative outcomes. The psychological and physical reinforcements both contribute to such positive self-theories. In the words of Epstein (1980, p. 86), "The self-system develops out of the desire of the child to gain approval and avoid disapproval." To return to our original tale of the wild west, this sense of self appears to be the "I'm OK" corral in that it encapsulates the fact that most people see themselves as "good and in control."

The linkage and valence dimensions reflect two human motives—control and esteem, respectively—that have been chronicled throughout the history of psychology (for reviews of the control and esteem motives, see Arkin & Baumgardner, 1986; Epstein, 1973, 1980; Greenberg, Pyszczynski, & Solomon, 1986; Greenwald, 1980; Langer, 1983; Snyder, Higgins, & Stucky, 1983; Taylor & Brown, 1988). We would argue that this parallel is not by accident. Rather, the linkage and valence

---

[1] As we will note later, the wavy line also may reflect an adult selftheory in which there is equal perceived linkage to outcomes of varying valence.

dimensions provide the instruments for mapping the self, and the control and esteem motives provide the impetus for one's placement on these dimensions. That is, the very dimensions on which the self is encoded are also the ones whereby normal people are motivated to achieve a sense of linkage to positively valenced outcomes. A recent review of a multitude of studies involving nonpsychiatric samples by Taylor and Brown (1988) suggests that people use two dimensions, control and esteem, as they form appraisals of themselves.[2] Additionally, Taylor and Brown provide compelling evidence that normal people are biased in their appraisals in that they assign an exaggerated sense of control and esteem to themselves. This latter exaggeration process further contributes to the positive valence-linkage rotation that we have depicted in Figure 15.1a.

As should be obvious from the above discussion, we are suggesting that the linkage and valence dimensions operate together to determine the sense of self. Greenwald (1980) has argued for a similar underlying motive, which he calls beneffectance, for the formation of the self. Beneffectance is defined as "the tendency to take credit for success while denying responsibility for failure" (Greenwald, 1980, p. 605). The inherent interactive properties of the control and esteem motives, and the propensity to increasingly attribute linkage to outcomes of more positive valence, have been described by other writers as the "self-serving attributional bias" (Weary, 1979), "egocentric attributions" (Schlenker & Miller, 1977), "ego-defensive attributions" (Miller, 1976), "attributional egotism" (Snyder, Stephan, & Rosenfield, 1978), and "subjective competence" (Bowerman, 1978).

What Motives Underlie the Self-Theory?

The answer to the question posed as the lead to this section is inherent in the discussion of the control and esteem motives in the previous section. That is to say, the interactive esteem-driven valence appraisals and the control-driven linkage appraisals provide the underlying motivational source for the presently-hypothesized self-theories. Some further elaboration of these ideas is warranted, however, in order to place this motive question in the context of two related debates that have appeared in the study of the self.

A first debate involves the question of whether the self is a structure, a process, or both. Our view is that the linkage/valence dimensions provide a structure for charting the self, *and* they are accompanied by motivational processes that operate on these dimensions. This latter view about the dual nature of the self-schemata as a structure *and* a process is increasingly being advocated by self-theorists and researchers (e.g., Epstein, 1973, 1980; Markus & Sentis, 1982; Markus & Wurf, 1987; Neisser, 1976). In terms of our metaphor, the "I'm OK" corral is both a structure and a working arena.

---

[2] The authors also note a third biasing motive that they call unrealistic optimism, but it is our view that this reflects a combination of the control and esteem motives.

A second debate begins with the assumption that the self is both a structure and a process, but thereafter focuses on the issue of whether self-consistency or self-enhancement provides the better explanation for the operation of the self-theory (for rcviews, see Jones, 1973; Moreland & Sweeney, 1984; Shrauger, 1975). Once people have a theory of self, according to the self-consistency explanation, the primary motivation is to preserve that theory; according to the self-enhancement explanation, the primary motive is to increase the overall positiveness of the self-theory. The emerging resolution to this latter debate, and one that we also advocate, it that the consistency and enhancement motives are not independent, nor are they necessarily antithetical (see Epstein, 1973; Greenwald, 1980; Trope, 1986). Because the typical person maintains a positive valence/linkage rotation, for example, the consistency motive would suggest that the person would try to *maintain* this positive self-theory in the face of disconfirming input (i.e., at least preserve the positive valence/linkage slope as shown in Figure 15.1a); moreover, in the absence of such disconfirming input, the person may actually attempt to *enhance* the perceived linkage to positive outcomes (i.e., increase the positive valence/linkage slope as shown in Figure 15.1a). The operations of these consistency and enhancement motives in conjunction with a positive self-theory will be detailed in the next section. Returning to our analogy one more time, the "I'm OK" corral is an arena that is protective and potentially expansive.

The Positive Valence/Linkage Rotation in Context

As may be obvious, the hypothesized positive valence/linkage rotation is the prototypical self-theory for a normal person who is coping with the stressors of life. Thus, it is our contention, and one that is borne out by related research (see reviews by Snyder, 1989; Taylor & Brown, 1988), that this positive self-model is adaptive. As such, the present positive valence/linkage model probably taps those persons who are at the adaptive end of many of the present individual differences measures. Included here would be persons scoring higher in optimism (Scheier & Carver, 1985, 1987), hope (Snyder et al., in press), resourcefulness (Rosenbaum, 1980; Rosenbaum & Jaffe, 1983), and hardiness (Kobasa, 1979; Kobasa, Maddi, & Kahn, 1982), as well as those with an internal locus of control (Lefcourt & Davidson-Katz, in press), positive affectivity (Watson & Clark, in press), and an external/variable/specific attributional style for negative events (Abramson, Seligman, & Teasdale, 1978; Burns & Seligman, in press). Stated another way, in statistical terms, the slope of the valence/linkage regression line should be positively correlated with more adaptive or healthy scores on these various indices. As such, there may be many ways to measure the "I'm OK" corral.

REALITY NEGOTIATION AND THE POSITIVE VALENCE/ LINKAGE ROTATION SELF-THEORY

Having described the basic premises of the positive valence/linkage rotation self-theory, in the present section we will turn to a discussion of how such self-theories operate when people must deal with feedback that is relevant to the self. First, we will define the overarching reality negotiation mechanism, as well as specific processes that operate in conjunction with the positive valence/linkage rotation self-theory.

Definition of Reality Negotiation

Reality negotiation is any psychological process whereby the person preserves or amplifies the personal theory of self. In the instance of the normal person with a positive valence/linkage rotation, the psychological reality negotiation dynamics serve to maintain the positive slope in reaction to discrepant negative self-relevant information, and to increase the slope if possible. Reality negotiation may take one or two general forms, which may be used sequentially or perhaps even simultaneously. First, the person may decrease the perceived linkage to a negative outcome, or increase the linkage to a positive outcome; such reality negotiation maneuvers occur on the linkage-to-act dimension. Second, the person may increase the positiveness of a negative outcome to which he or she is linked, or decrease the positiveness of a positive outcome to which he or she is not linked; these latter reality negotiation processes operate on the valence-of-act dimension. Examples of each of these types of reality negotiation, which provide the dynamics for the "psychic showdown," will be presented subsequently.

Before detailing the actual reality negotiation processes, we would like to review the role of various audiences on such processes. Reality negotiation may proceed in an automatic fashion that is generally not within awareness when the person is operating in settings without an external audience. This assertion must be tempered, however, by the fact that the normal developmental maturation process of the self probably involves the inculcation of important external audiences (e.g., parents, authorities, etc.) into a "looking glass self" (see Cooley, 1902; Mead, 1934) that provides an imagined external audience even when one is not physically present. The operation of reality negotiation processes on the valence/linkage dimensions will be biased in the sense that the normal person will be motivated to preserve and even enhance the positive slope, but it should be recognized that this must be done in a fashion so as to attend to the constraints of any imagined or real audiences. Especially in this latter vein, when an actual external audience is involved, we need to "achieve a biased compromise between what we want to perceive about ourselves and what outside persons will not question seriously" (Snyder & Higgins, 1990, pp. 212-213). In the degree to which there is an obvious and potentially powerful external audience, the individual's reality negotiation processes should move from a low to high level of awareness.

Reality Negotiation With Nondiscrepant Feedback

Looking at the slope shown in Figure 15.1, nondiscrepant information would reflect strong linkage to a positive outcome, or no linkage to a negative outcome. In other words, the input is plotted directly on the slope. In such instances where the person receives feedback that is consistent with the positive valence-linkage rotation, there is no stressor placed on the self-theory, and there is no strong need for the maintenance type reality negotiation processes. In terms of information processing, our prediction is that persons should process nondiscrepant self-related feedback more quickly and certainly than discrepant feedback; similarly, persons should exhibit better recognition and recall of nondiscrepant as compared to discrepant feedback.[3]

Although the nondiscrepant feedback does not produce any need for the *maintenance* type of reality negotiation, it is possible in such circumstances that the person may attempt to *enhance* the slope even more. This may be accomplished by increasing the already strong linkage to the positive outcome, and/or increasing the already acknowledged positiveness of the outcome to which one is linked. In the theater of one's own mind, such strategies may be useful, but public displays of such tactics may yield the counterproductive feedback that the person is too boastful.

Reality Negotiation With Discrepant Negative Feedback

Discrepant feedback can either be positive or negative. In the latter scenario, a negative stressor would reflect information that strongly links the person to a negatively valenced outcome. As shown in the lower right portion of Figure 15.1b, the negative stressor clearly is off the positive valence/linkage slope, and as such it tends to produce reality negotiation processes that involve the lessening of the linkage, and/or the increasing of the positiveness of the outcome. We will describe each of these self-maintenance processes next.

Lessening Linkage to Negative Outcome

Perhaps the first and most rudimentary reality negotiation tactics involve attempts to diminish the perceived linkage to the negative outcome. This lessening of linkage is shown in the # 1 arrow of Figure 15.1b. It is our belief that this is one of the first defensive strategies employed (e.g., the classic "I didn't do it" of the child

---

[3] This prediction is consistent with the finding that events that are incongruous with well-developed self-schemata are likely to be forgotten or ignored (Hastie, 1981; Markus, 1980).

caught with the hand in the cookie jar). Further, even with adults who naturally tend to use more sophisticated tactics, the most prevalent tactic may be to decrease the linkage to a negative outcome.

The archetypical reality negotiation process for lessening the linkage to a negative outcome is excuse-making. Tracing the linguistic roots of this term, "ex" means "out of," and "causa" signifies "causality." In other words, excuses seek to shift the causal linkage away from the person who is yoked to a negative outcome. Because we have described the robustness and diversity of such excuse-making strategies elsewhere (e.g., Snyder et al., 1983), in the present context we will first synopsize two general types of excuses, and thereafter will discuss their effectiveness.

The first type of excuses is aimed at lessening the apparent linkage. This is a rudimentary approach, and it attempts to totally sever the linkage between the person and the bad act (the prototypical phrase is "I didn't do it"). Pleas of innocence or denial fit this category, and it should be noted that these strategies have parallels in the legal system (e.g., Hart, 1968). The person may augment the innocence plea by blaming some other person (e.g., Schlenker & Miller, 1977) or object (Bowerman, 1978), or by not wearing any identifying apparel that labels the person as being part of a group that has performed poorly (e.g., "cutting off reflected failure," Snyder, Lassegard, & Ford, 1986). If one can truly convince oneself and the external audience that there is no apparent linkage, then the predicted salutory effects on the positive self-theory should be realized. It should be noted, however, that the blaming of others, especially if one must continue to interact with those others, actually has a backfiring effect in that it makes one appear in a even more negative light (Higgins & Snyder, 1989).

The second type of excuse is aimed at lessening the transformed linkage. In those instances in which it is clear that the person is linked to the negative act (i.e., the apparent linkage is irrefutable), the person may attempt to lessen the perceived psychological linkage (the prototypical beginning is "Yes, but...," in which the "but" is followed by the operative phrase). This may be accomplished by raising the consensus regarding the degree to which most people in the same situation also would have been linked to the negative outcome ("Yes, but everyone was doing it"), thereby shifting some of the causal linkage from the particular person to the situation. Or, the person may lower the perceived consistency of being linked to the bad outcome ("Yes, but I only did it once"), thereby again implicitly suggesting that there was something in the particular situation that accounted for the poor performance rather than something that is characteristic of that person. Interestingly, these transformed linkage excuses, with their psychologically sophisticated logic, appear to preserve the positive self-theory, both in the eyes of the individual (Mehlman & Snyder, 1985) and the observing audience (Weiner, Amirkhan, Folkes, & Verette, 1987). Additionally, in a recent review of the effectiveness of excuses, we have concluded that the evidence generally supports the contention that they do have beneficial effects for persons' self-theories (Snyder & Higgins, 1988). Thus, excuses appear to play the hypothesized protective role.

Decreasing Unfavorable Valence of Negative Outcome

If one cannot lessen the linkage to the negative outcome, a second set of reality negotiation strategies may be invoked to lessen the negative valence of the outcome. This type of lessening of negative valence is shown in the # 2 arrow of Figure 15.1b. The inherent logic in these strategies is that the person is arguing to the self and external audiences that "It wasn't so bad."

The first subtype within this category of reality negotiation involves memory-based distortions whereby that the protagonist recalls a negative event in a more benign light (see Greenwald, 1980; Ross & Conway, 1986). In the theater of the mind, the person with a positive valence/linkage self-theory will misremember events so as to lessen their negativeness. The second subtype involves direct minimizations, wherein the person connected to a negative outcome voices arguments as to why it is not as bad as it seems. These strategies are simplistic, and are probably evidenced early by children. Included here would be such examples as, "Oh, come on, it didn't hurt that much," and "It's not as bad as it looks." As a third subtype, language serves as a powerful vehicle for customizing the negative outcome. Two examples are: "She is a tramp, you are a flirt, I have a warm affectionate personality," or "He is sneaky, you are crafty, I am subtle" (Hammond, 1972, p. 89). A somewhat more sophisticated fourth subtype involves a contextualizing process in which the person places the seemingly bad outcome in a context that makes it appear more positive. This contextualizing is similar to what others have labelled as "embedding" (Jellison, 1977) or "exonerative moral reasoning" (Wrightsman & Deaux, 1981, p. 220). In this latter vein, consider the following words of the bombardier of the airplane that dropped the atomic bomb that is believed to have killed 100,000 Hiroshima residents toward the end of World War II: "I'm not proud of killing all those people, but I'm proud of saving all the lives that we did" (*Kansas City Star*, 1975, p. 4B). A fifth subtype for undermining the negativeness of an outcome relates to derogation of the sources of feedback for the negative outcome. Research consistently shows that the receipt of negative feedback results in derogations of the source of evaluative feedback when the source is an instrument such as a classroom test (Snyder & Clair, 1976), a personality test (Snyder & Shenkel, 1976), or a person (Snyder & Clair, 1976).

Although there is considerable research demonstrating that people are motivated to lessen the negativeness of the poor outcome with which they are associated, the question regarding the effectiveness of these "It wasn't so bad" strategies is largely unexplored. The one exception is a study by Burish and Houston (1979), where derogation of an examiner, relative to no such derogation, appeared to diminish the sense of anxiety and depression associated with a poor performance on an achievement test. This area obviously is ripe for a pre-post self-esteem measurement in order to verify the theorized protective effects of such reality negotiation strategies. Such studies would clarify whether these strategies do result in the self-maintenance that we have posited.

Reality Negotiation With Discrepant Positive Feedback

A discrepant, positive stressor would reflect information that shows little or no linkage between the person and a positively valenced outcome. As shown in the upper left portion of Figure 15.1b, the positive stressor clearly is off the positive valence/linkage slope, and as such it tends to produce reality negotiation processes that involve the increasing of the linkage (a self-enhancement process), and/or the decreasing of the positiveness of the outcome (a self-maintenance process). We turn to a discussion of these processes next.

Increasing Linkage to Positive Outcome

The objective response to positive information that has no obvious linkage to the person would be to merely acknowledge the excellent outcome, and do nothing to increase the linkage to that outcome. Of course, this latter response may not be the preferred one. Rather, there is a variety of reality negotiation maneuvers whereby the person increases the linkage to the positive outcome. These dynamics aimed at increasing the linkage to positive acts are shown in arrow # 3 in Figure 15.1b. As one example of these processes, consider the group setting where people are working together toward an outcome. In the instance in which the final group outcome is very successful, each individual participant strongly tends to overestimate his or her contribution to this winning effort. The person may accomplish this by ascribing more responsibility to himself or herself than to a partner (e.g., Johnston, 1967), or to an average other group member (Schlenker, 1975; Wolosin, Sherman, & Till, 1973). Interestingly, even when the individual group is given sufficient information so as to infer a more equitable sharing of the credit for a group success, that individual nevertheless tends to overaccentuate his or her contribution (Schlenker & Miller, 1977).

In the aforementioned examples the person does have some, albeit slight, linkage to the positive outcome in that she or he was a part of the group that attained the success. It may be the case, however, that the linkage of the person is even less obvious to the positive outcome (or person). For example, people appear to expend some efforts in describing how they grew up in the same town as a famous person, or were on an airplane with a superstar athlete. In other words, people attempt to increase their linkage to successful others by accentuating physical, ethnic, or religious similarities (Cialdini et al., 1976; Cialdini, Finch, & DeNicholas, 1990; Richardson & Cialdini, 1981), even when the linkage to such persons is seemingly meaningless or incidental. This "basking in reflected glory" phenomenon is defined as the "tendency for people to publicize a connection with another person who has been successful" (Cialdini et al., 1976, p. 366).

Cialdini et al. (1976) have found support for this phenomenon in three studies. In a first, a higher percentage of college students were found to wear school-identifying apparel on days after their university football team had won as compared to days after losses. In a second study, students described victorious games in terms of "we won," while they tended to describe losing games with the phrase "they lost," and this effect was amplified when the students were given failure feedback on cognitive intellectual task (thereby threatening their positive self-theories). This latter finding was replicated in a third study. Perhaps, the reader can remember a recent athletic event in which the everpresent television camera scanned the spectators of the championship team. These fans can be seen pointing their index fingers skyward, shouting "We're # 1." One almost gets the impression that the fans were down on the playing field scoring the critical touchdowns or goals. Although studies have not taken the next step of ascertaining whether such basking persons truly enhance their positive self-theories, their smiles and jubilation suggest that they do.

A phenomenon that bears some similarity to basking involves a bandwagon effect, wherein the protagonist increasingly becomes linked to a point of view or a behavior that appears to be successful or popular. This type of reality negotiation may involve mere verbal statements aligning the protagonist with the successful outcome; moreover, beyond the verbalizations, the protagonist may actually begin to display other behavioral manifestations so as to join the bandwagon. In this sense, the adage "Victory has a hundred fathers" may apply both to basking and to bandwagoning.

Decreasing Positiveness of Outcome to Which One is Not Linked

If one cannot increase the linkage to a positive act, then the positive discrepant outcome may be denigrated in order to bring it more into line with the positive valence/linkage self-theory rotation (see dynamic depicted in arrow # 4 of Figure 15.1b). That is, because the positive self-theory posits that negative events are not linked to the person, and the particular outcome is not linked to the person, therefore that outcome must be rather negative. This logic is essentially that "It can't be much good if I wasn't associated with it." While this may strike the reader as being an extremely narcissistic and childlike reality negotiation process, it is sufficiently understood among laypeople that it has been given a name. In this vein, we all know what "sour grapes" means.

Because the "sour grapes" term conjures images of petty gossiping, it may well be the case that this is the last reality negotiation tactic resorted to by persons with positive valence/linkage self-theories. Although there is a literature involving the derogation-related processes that accompany the negative outcomes to which people are linked, we could not find any literature on the mirror-like process of denigrating the positive outcome to which another person is linked. Given the rather ungracious nature of "sour grapes," this topic may have been somewhat taboo as a serious focus for psychological inquiry. Obviously, our hypothesis is that "sour grapes" does occur in normal, healthy people, and although it may be difficult to get people to verbalize this reality negotiation process in experimental settings, this remains a worthy topic for future research.

Psychic Showdown at the "I'm OK" Corral in Perspective

The four dynamics depicted in arrows # 1 through # 4 in Figure 15.1b reflect the reality negotation processes used by normal people as they deal with the multitude of life stressors. The processes shown in arrows # 1, # 2, and # 4 all reflect protective reality negotiations, while the process shown in arrow # 3 is an enhancing one. This illustrates our contention that reality negotiation can at times be related to the maintenance of the positive self-theory, and at other times it can be related to enhancement. It should also be noted that some persons may be more prone to employ one of these four reality negotiation processes more frequently. Additionally, in many instances there may be double plays in which at least two of the processes are employed simultaneously. For example, the consensus-raising excuse (e.g., "Everyone in that same situation would do as badly") not only lessens the linkage by shifting the attributional cause to the situation, but it also decreases the negativeness of the outcome by implicitly raising the base-rate for the behavior. Finally, it should be noted that the sophisticated person may vary the reality negotiation processes to match the situation. When it comes to the psychic showdown, therefore, the normal person has a varied and powerful armamentarium.

NEGATIVE VALENCE/LINKAGE SELF-THEORIES: THE "I'M NOT OK" CORRAL

To this point, we have described the valence/linkage rotation that typifies normal people as they develop and sustain their positive self-theories across their lives. There is a different valence/linkage rotation, however, that is possible because of genetic, developmental, or environmental factors. Instead of the positive valence/linkage rotation shown in Figure 15.1b, the child may perceive that he or she is not anymore strongly linked to positive negative outcomes. This neutral self-theory would be represented by the horizontal wavy line displayed in Figure 15.2a. In yet another developmental scenario, the child may progressively learn that he or she is associated with negative outcomes and tends *not* to be linked to positive outcomes. This hypothetical negative valence/linkage rotation can be seen in Figure 15.2a. Despite the usual genetic and environmental dynamics, as well as perceptual biases,

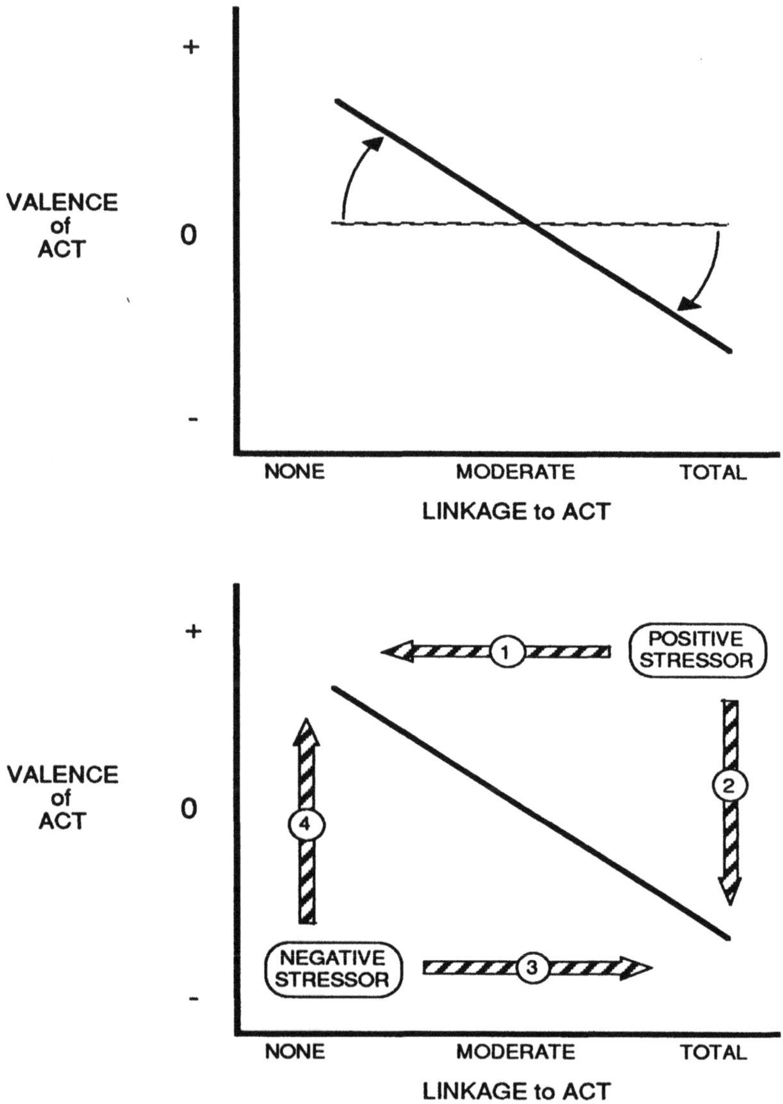

FIG. 15.2a. The negative valence/linkage self-theory rotation.
FIG. 15.2b. Reality negotiation dynamics of the negative valence/linkage self-theory rotation.

that tend to produce a majority of citizens with a positive valence/linkage rotation, some small percentage of children may not realize this positive self-theory. For such persons, the early environmental factors both within the immediate home and surrounding neighborhood may contribute to a sense of being linked more to negative than to positive outcomes. Indeed, for some, the self-theory that evolves is most accurately described as the "I'm *not* OK" corral.

The discussion as to why a small minority of people in general may develop a negative valence/linkage self-theory rotation is beyond the focus of the present chapter, but it should be noted that most theories about the etiology of "abnormal" or "dysfunctional" behavior, although not using this valence/linkage matrix, are essentially addressing this issue. Likewise, persons who are at the very extreme *maladaptive* end of the previously mentioned individual differences measures (e.g., optimism, hope, hardiness, resourcefulness, locus of control, and attributional style) should manifest this negative valence/linkage self-theory rotation.[4]

One example of negative valence/linkage self-theory rotations may be revealed by depressed persons. Depressed as compared to nondepressed persons do not appear to show the typical positive biases of an exaggerated sense of control (Abramson & Alloy, 1981) and self-esteem (Coyne & Gotlib, 1983; Ruehlman, West, & Pasahow, 1985; Watson & Clark, 1984). Beck (1967) argues that depressed persons have self-schemata that place a negative bias on self-related information. This latter view raises the issue of whether the negative valence/linkage self-theory rotation is driven by consistency, enhancement, or both. Although researchers presently do not agree over the underlying motive of depressed persons' self-schemata, it is our view that both motives are operative. That is, at times the person with a negative valence/linkage self-theory may merely attempt to maintain this theory, while at other times the person may actually enhance the theory (i.e., make it even more negative).

REALITY NEGOTIATION AND THE NEGATIVE VALENCE/LINKAGE ROTATION SELF-THEORY

Before exploring the hypothetical reality negotiation processes whereby the "I'm not OK" self-theories are sustained in this section, we would like to address one question that may be on the reader's mind at this point. It may seem questionable, especially given the fact that most readers will have a positive self-theory about themselves, that we are asserting that a person actually may be motivated to maintain a negative self-theory. The answer to this seeming inconsistency lies in understanding that the self-theory, even a negative one, is a source of stability that enables one to make sense of oneself in one's world. Thus, "basic beliefs in a theory of reality become self-fulfilling prophesies, and ... even an unpleasant, but predictable, world is preferable to a chaotic one. It follows that there are some people who

[4] Given the generally adaptive and successful histories of college students, it may not be possible to obtain persons with truly negative valence/linkage self-theory rotations, even if one were to sample students at the very negative end of these individual differences dimensions. It may be necessary to sample actual clinical populations in order to obtain persons with the negative valence/linkage self-theory rotations.

can only feel secure when they are miserable" (Epstein, 1987, p. 48).

Reality Negotiation With Nondiscrepant Feedback

As shown in the slope of Figure 15.2a, nondiscrepant information reflects strong linkage to a negative outcome, or no linkage to a positive outcome. In such instances, the input matches the slope. When the person receives feedback that is consistent with the negative valence-linkage rotation, there is no stressor placed on the self-theory, and similarly there is no apparent need for reality negotiation processes. Schema nondiscrepant feedback should be processed more quickly and certainly than discrepant self-related feedback; likewise, the recognition and recall of nondiscrepant as compared to discrepant feedback should be superior. These are the same predictions as those generated for the positive self-theory, but in this case they apply to the negative self-theory.

Reality Negotiation With Discrepant Positive Feedback

As shown in the upper right portion of Figure 15.2b, a positive stressor is located away from the negative valence/linkage slope, and it therefore should produce reality negotiation processes that involve the lessening of the linkage, and/or the decreasing of the positiveness of the outcome. We describe each of these self-maintenance processes next.

Decreasing Linkage to Positive Outcome

For the individual with a negative self-theory, perhaps the first reality negotiation process that is invoked when the person is strongly linked to a positive outcome involves attempts to diminish the linkage. This dynamic is depicted in arrow # 1 in Figure 15.2b. Although there is no literature to corroborate our speculations at this point, we would predict that the person would engage in excuse-like reality negotiation processes similar to those that we described earlier in this chapter. (Realize, however, that the previous literature involved persons with positive self-theories who were lessening their linkage to negative outcomes, while in the present case the persons with a negative self-theory are lessening their linkage to positive outcomes.)

The apparent responsibility excuses are aimed at breaking any obvious linkage between the person and the outcome, and as such one might hear simple denials for the positive outcome (e.g., "It couldn't have been me!"), or the giving of credit to another (e.g., "Zach really did it. I didn't have anything to do with it."). The more sophisticated transformed responsibility excuse acknowledges some linkage to the act, but attempts to transfer the linkage to something in the situation. In this latter vein, consider the consensus-raising excuse "Yes, but anyone in that situation would have done well." These and other excuses are legendary in clinical work, where the client seems to do everything possible to *not* accept any linkage to some positive event in his or her life.

Decreasing Positiveness of Outcome to Which One is Linked

Another reality negotiation process whereby the person with the negative self-theory deals with a positive stressor is to lessen the favorability of the positive outcome to which the person is linked. This dynamic is depicted in arrow # 2 of Figure 15.2b. The logic inherent in this type of reality negotiation process is captured in the phrase "It's not as good as it looks."

The forms of these reality negotiation processes should be similar to those exhibited for decreasing the negativeness of outcomes exhibited by the positive self-theory persons, but in this case the negative self-theory people are decreasing the positiveness of the outcomes. Included in such processes would be (a) memory-based distortions whereby the positive outcome is recalled in a more negative light, (b) direct minimizations (e.g., "It's not really very good"), (c) derogation of the sources of feedback (e.g., "Everyone gets glowing reviews from her"), etc.

Reality Negotiation With Discrepant Negative Feedback

A discrepant, negative stressor would reflect information that shows little or no linkage between the person and a negatively valenced outcome. As shown in the lower left portion of Figure 15.2b, the negative stressor is situated away from the negative valence/linkage slope, and accordingly it should elicit reality negotiation processes that involve the increasing of the linkage to the negative outcome (a self-enhancement process), and/or the decreasing of the negativeness of the negative outcome to which one is not linked (a self-maintenance process). These processes are examined next.

Increasing Linkage to Negative Outcome

In this scenario, the negative self-theory person is confronted with feedback that he or she is not linked to some negative outcome. This is an unusual state of affairs because the negative self-theory person is accustomed to viewing herself or himself as being linked to bad outcomes. The response, in this case shown in the dynamic of arrow # 3 of Figure 15.2b, is to increase the linkage to the bad outcome. To the outside observer, and to the clinician who may be working with such a person, the tendency to link oneself to bad outcomes may seem nonsensical, if not psychotic in its implications. For example, a person may blame himself for some natural or person-made disaster in which there is absolutely no rationale basis to make any link to the accident. Even if the person cannot ascribe linkage for the causation of the event, that person may nevertheless be racked with guilt-based accountability for some other aspect of the bad outcome (e.g., "I should have warned the people that the skywalk was going to collapse"). For those clinicians working with families, it is common to find that the children of divorcing couples take unreasonable responsibility for the breakup. The basic logic in this type of reality negotiation, therefore, is "If it is bad, I must have had something to do with it." This tactic is an enhancement one in that it actually may pull down the negative self-theory slope further.

Increasing Favorable Valence of Negative Outcome to Which One is Not Linked

If the person cannot increase the linkage to the bad outcome, the next reality negotiation tactic of the negative self-theory person may be to decrease the perceived negativeness of bad outcome (i.e., make it more positive). This dynamic is shown in arrow # 4 of Figure 15.2b. The underlying logic here is "If I didn't have anything to do with it, it can't be so bad." In other words, if someone else did it, the negative self-theory person will cast the event in a much more benign light because it surely cannot be as bad as the outcomes associated with the protagonist. Thus, other people may be given the benefit of the doubt. The essence of this dynamic demands a new term, which we will call "sweet lemons." In a mirror image to the previously described dynamic of sour grapes, sweet lemons inherently suggests that the person sees something more positive in an outcome associated with another person than is the prevalent view of that outcome.

Psychic Showdown at the "I'm Not OK" Corral in Perspective

The four dynamics depicted in arrows # 1 through # 4 in Figure 15.2b reflect the reality negotiation processes used by a small minority of people as they attempt to cope with stressors across their entire lives, or at some point in their lives. These processes are predicated on a negative valence/linkage selftheory. For some people, this negative self-theory is one that is operative for their entire lives, and as such they may occupy what professionals call the chronic, abnormal end of the mental health spectrum. Or, it may be that a profound life stressor has plunged the person with a normally positive self-theory into a temporary negative self-theory that may or may not endure over the subsequent course of that person's life. From a clinical perspective, it is important to understand whether the negative self-theory is long-term or short-term. As may be obvious in our presentation of the dynamics that govern the maintenance of the negative self-theory, it is our belief that a variety of somewhat counterintuitive behaviors begin to make sense in the context of the present model. Indeed, it should be remembered that the "I'm not OK" corral was constructed for understandable reasons; furthermore, the reality negotiation dynamics continue because they allow the person to face the psychic showdowns of contemporary life.

CAVEATS, CORRALS, AND REALITY NEGOTIATIONS

Having described our theory of self and the processes that accompany it, we would close by acknowledging what we do not know. Although the literature certainly makes a case for the existence and operation of the valence-of-act and linkage-to-act dimensions of appraisal, we have only begun to measure these in our laboratory. We have begun by developing a methodology for plotting the extent to which people perceive that they are linked (the linkage dimension) to outcomes of varying favorability (the valence dimension). Preliminary work with college students (Snyder, Irving, Holleran, & Sigmon, 1990) supports our contention that, in general, individuals exhibit a positive valence/linkage self-theory rotation across a number of life domains (i.e., problem solving, academics, health, personality, physical appearance, relationships, work, leisure, and political/social events). This promising result must be followed by studies of samples wherein greater variation in valence/linkage rotation is likely to be found. For example, the measurement of self-theories of persons with varying degrees of psychological problems should provide us with further insight regarding the utility of the valence/linkage plot, particularly among depressed individuals whom we propose may link themselves to negative events and divorce themselves from positive outcomes. To understand whether the individual's self-theory is of the "I'm OK" or the "I'm not OK" type is the critical first step in unravelling the kinds of reality negotiation strategies that should be expected. To date, there is little experimental research on the operation, and even less on the sequelae of the various reality negotiation processes that are posited to accompany the "I'm OK" and the "I'm not OK" types. These issues will form the agenda for our subsequent research program. Although our view is that the present model allows one to understand complex human coping responses to the inevitable stressors of life, at this point this perspective may reflect only our own reality negotiation attempts. We will be armed with data for future showdowns. Look for us at high noon near the "I'm OK" corral.

REFERENCES

Abramson, L. Y., & Alloy, L. B. (1981). Depression, non-depression, and cognitive illusions: A reply to Schwartz. *Journal of Experimental Psychology, 110*, 436-447.

Abramson, L. Y., Seligman, M. E. P., & Teasdale, J. (1978). Learned helplessness in humans: Critique and reformulation. *Journal of Abnormal Psychology, 87*, 32-48.

Adler, A. (1931). *What life should mean to you.* Boston: Little, Brown.

Allport, G. (1955). *Becoming: Basic considerations for a psychology of personality.* New Haven: Yale University Press.

Arkin, R. M., & Baumgardner, A. H. (1986). Self-presentations and self-evaluations: Processes of self-control and social control. In R. F. Baumeister (Ed.), *Public self and private self* (pp. 75-97). New York: Springer.

Beck, A. T. (1967). *Depression: Clinical, experimental, and theoretical aspects.* New York: Hoebner.

Bowerman, W. R. (1978). Subjective competence: The structure, process, and function of self-referent causal attributions. *Journal for the Theory of Social Behaviour, 8*, 45-75.

Burish, T. G., & Houston, B. K. (1979). Causal projection, similarity projection, and coping with threat to self-esteem. *Journal of Personality, 47*, 57-70.

Burns, M. O., & Seligman, M. E. P. (in press). Explanatory style, helplessness, and depression. In C. R. Snyder & D. R. Forsyth (Eds.), *Handbook of social and clinical psychology: The health perspective.* Elmsford, NY: Pergamon.

Cialdini, R. B., Borden, R. J., Thorne, A., Walker, M. R., Freeman, S., & Sloan, L. R. (1976). Basking in reflected glory: Three (football) field studies. *Journal of Personality and Social Psychology, 39*, 406-415.

Cialdini, R. B., Finch, J. F., & DeNicholas, M. E. (1990). Strategic self-presentation: The indirect route. In M. J. Cody & M. L. McLaughlin (Eds.), *The psychology of tactical communication* (pp. 194-206). Clevedon, England: Multilingual Matters.

Cooley, C. H. (1902). *Human nature and the social order.* New York: Scribner.

Coyne, J. C., & Gotlib, I. H. (1983). The role of cognition in depression: A critical appraisal. *Psychological Bulletin, 94*, 472-505.

Epstein, S. (1973). The self-concept: Or, a theory of a theory. *American Psychologist, 28*, 404-416.

Epstein, S. (1980). The self-concept: A review and the proposal of an integrated theory of personality. In E. Staub (Ed.), *Personality: Basic issues and current research* (pp. 82-132). Englewood Cliffs, NJ: Prentice-Hall.

Epstein, S. (1987). Implications of cognitive self-theory for psychopathology and psychotherapy. In N. Cheshire & H. Thomae (Eds.), *Self, symptoms, and psychotherapy* (pp. 43-58). New York: Wiley.

Fiske, S. T., & Taylor, S. E. (1984). *Social cognition.* Reading, MA: Addison-Wesley.

Freud, S. (1894/1953). *Sigmund Freud: Collected papers* (Vol. 1). London: Hogarth Press.

Gergen, K. J. (1968). Personal consistency and the presentation of the self. In C. Gordon & K. J. Gergen (Eds.), *The self in social interaction* (Vol. 1, pp. 299-308). New York: Wiley.

Greenberg, J., Pyszczynski, T., & Solomon, S. (1986). The causes and consequences of a need for self-esteem: A terror management theory. In R. F. Baumeister (Ed.), *Public self and private self* (pp. 189-212). New York: Springer.

Greenwald, A. G. (1980). The totalitarian ego: Fabrication and revision of personal history. *American Psychologist, 35*, 603-618.

Hammond, V. C. (1972). *The Saturday Evening Post, 244*, 89.

Hart, H. L. A. (1968). *Punishment and responsibility: Essays on the philosophy of law.* New York: Oxford University Press.

Hastie, R. (1981). Schematic principles on human memory. In E. T. Higgins, C. P. Herman, & M. P. Zanna (Eds.), *Social cognition: The Ontario Symposium on personality and social psychology* (Vol. 1, pp. 39-88). Hillsdale, NJ: Erlbaum.

Higgins, R. L., & Snyder, C. R. (1989). Excuse gone awry: An analysis of self-defeating excuses. In R. C. Curtis (Ed.), *Self-defeating behaviors: Experimental research, clinical impressions, and practical implications* (pp. 99-130). New York: Plenum.

Hilgard, E. R. (1949). Human motives and the concept of the self. *American Psychologist, 4*, 374-382.

James, W. (1910) *Psychology: The briefer course*. New York: Holt.

Jellison, J. M. (1977). *I'm sorry I didn't mean to, and other lies we love to tell*. New York: Chatham Square Press.

Johnston, W. A. (1967). Individual performance and self-evaluation in a simulated team. *Organizational Behavior and Human Performance, 2*, 309-328.

Jones, S. (1973). Self and interpersonal evaluations: Esteem theories versus consistency theories. *Psychological Bulletin, 79*, 185-199.

Kansas City Star. (1975). August 3, 4B.

Kelly, G. A. (1955). *The psychology of personal constructs*. New York: Norton.

Kobasa, S. C. (1979). Stressful life events, personality, and health: An inquiry into hardiness. *Journal of Personality and Social Psychology, 37*, 1-11.

Kobasa, S. C., Maddi, S. R., & Kahn, S. (1982). Hardiness and health: A prospective study. *Journal of Personality and Social Psychology, 42*, 168-177.

Langer, E. J. (1983). *The psychology of control*. Beverly Hills, CA: Sage.

Lecky, P. (1945). *Self-consistency: A theory of personality*. Long Island, NY: Island Press.

Lefcourt, H. M., & Davidson-Katz, K. (in press). Locus of control and health. In C. R. Snyder & D. R. Forsyth (Eds.), *Handbook of social and clinical psychology: The health perspective*. Elmsford, NY: Pergamon.

Markus, H. (1980). The self in thought and memory. In D. M. Wegner & R. R. Vallacher (Eds.), *The self in social psychology* (pp. 102-130). London: Oxford University Press.

Markus, H., & Nurius, P. (1986). Possible selves. *American Psychologist, 41*, 954-969.

Markus, H., & Sentis, K. (1982). The self in social information processing. In J. Suls (Ed.), *Psychological perspectives on the self* (Vol. 1, pp. 41-70). Hillsdale, NJ: Lawrence Erlbaum Associates.

Markus, H., & Wurf, E. (1987). The dynamic self-concept: A social psychological perspective. *Annual Review of Psychology, 38*, 299-337.

Mead, G. H. (1934). *Mind, self, and society*. Chicago: University of Chicago Press.

Mehlman, R. C., & Snyder, C. R. (1985). Excuse theory: A test of the self-protective role of attributions. *Journal of Personality and Social Psychology, 49*, 994-1001.

Miller, D. T. (1976). Ego involvement and attribution for success and failure. *Journal of Personality and Social Psychology, 34*, 901-906.

Moreland, R. L., & Sweeney, P. D. (1984). Self-expectations and reactions to evaluations of personal performance. *Journal of Personality, 52*, 156-176.

Neisser, U. (1976). *Cognition and reality*. San Francisco: Freeman.

Richardson, K. D., & Cialdini, R. B. (1981). Basking and blasting: Tactics of self-presentation. In J. T. Tedeschi (Ed.), *Impression management theory and social psychological research* (pp. 41-53). New York: Academic Press.

Rogers, C. R. (1951). *Client-centered therapy*. New York: Houghton-Mifflin.

Rosenbaum, M. (1980). A schedule for assessing self-control behaviors: Preliminary findings. *Behavior Therapy, 11*, 109-121.

Rosenbaum, M., & Jaffe, Y. (1983). Learned helplessness: The role of individual differences in learned resourcefulness. *British Journal of Social Psychology, 22*, 215-225.

Rosenberg, M. (1979). *Conceiving the self*. New York: Basic Books.

Ross, M., & Conway, M. (1986). Remembering one's own past: The construction of personal histories. In R. M. Sorrentino & E. T. Higgins (Eds.), *Handbook of motivation and social cognition: Foundations of social behavior* (pp. 122-144). New York: Guilford.

Ruehlman, L. S., West, S. G., & Pasahow, R. J. (1985). Depression and evaluative schema. *Journal of Personality, 53*, 46-92.

Sarbin, T. R. (1952). A preface to a psychological analysis of the self. *Psychological Review, 59*, 11-22.
Scheier, M. F., & Carver, C. S. (1985). Optimism, coping, and health: Assessment and implications of generalized outcome expectancies. *Health Psychology, 4*, 219-247.
Scheier, M. F., & Carver, C. S. (1987). Dispositional optimism and physical well-being: The influence of generalized outcome expectancies on health. *Journal of Personality, 55*, 169-210.
Schlenker, B. R. (1975). Group members' attributions of responsibility for prior group performance. *Representative Research in Social Psychology, 6*, 96-108.
Schlenker, B. R. (1980). *Impression management: The self-concept, social identity, and interpersonal relations*. Monterey, CA: Brooks/Cole.
Schlenker, B. R., & Miller, R. S. (1977). Egocentrism in groups: Self-serving biases or logical information processing? *Journal of Personality and Social Psychology, 35*, 755-764.
Shrauger, J. S. (1975). Responses to evaluation as a function of initial self-perceptions. *Psychological Bulletin, 82*, 581-596.
Snyder, C. R. (1989). Reality negotiation: From excuses to hope and beyond. *Journal of Social and Clinical Psychology, 8*, 130-157.
Snyder, C. R., & Clair, M. S. (1976). Effects of expected and obtained grades on teacher evaluations and attribution of performance. *Journal of Educational Psychology, 18*, 62-67.
Snyder, C. R., Harris, C., Anderson, J. R., Holleran, S., Irving, L. M., Gibb, J., Yoshinobu, L., Langelle, C., & Harney, P. (in press). The development and validation of an individual differences measure of hope. *Journal of Personality and Social Psychology.*
Snyder, C. R., & Higgins, R. L. (1988). Excuses: Their effective role in the negotiation of reality. *Psychological Bulletin, 104*, 23-35.
Snyder, C. R., & Higgins, R. L. (1990). Reality negotiation and excuse-making: President Reagan's March 4, 1987 Iran arms scandal speech and other literature. In M. J. Cody & M. L. McLaughlin (Eds.), *The psychology of tactical communication* (pp. 207-228). Clevedon, England: Multilingual Matters.
Snyder, C. R., Higgins, R. L., & Stucky, R. J. (1983). *Excuses: Masquerades in search of grace*. New York: Wiley-Interscience.
Snyder, C. R., Irving, L. M., Holleran, S., & Sigmon, S. T. (1990). *Self-theories of college students: A methodology for measuring valence/linkage rotations*. Unpublished manuscript, University of Kansas, Lawrence, KS, 66045.
Snyder, C. R., Lassegard, M., & Ford, C. E. (1986). Distancing after group success and failure: Basking in reflected glory and cutting off reflected failure. *Journal of Personality and Social Psychology, 51*, 382-388.
Snyder, C. R., & Shenkel, R. J. (1976). Effects of "favorability," modality, and relevance on acceptance of general personality interpretations prior to and after receiving diagnostic feedback. *Journal of Consulting and Clinical Psychology, 44*, 34-41.
Snyder, M. L., Stephan, W. G., & Rosenfield, D. (1978). Attributional egotism. In J. H. Harvey, W. J. Ickes, & R. F. Kidd (Eds.), *New directions in attribution research* (vol. 2, pp. 91-117). Hillsdale, NJ: Lawrence Erlbaum Associates.
Snygg, D., & Combs, A. W. (1949). *Individual behavior*. New York: Harper & Row.
Stryker, S. (1980). *Symbolic interactionism*. Menlo Park, CA: Benjamin Cummings.
Sullivan, H. S. (1953). *The interpersonal theory of psychiatry*. New York: Norton.
Taylor, S. E., & Brown, J. D. (1988). Illusion and well-being: A social psychological perspective on mental health. *Psychological Bulletin, 103*, 193-210.
Trachtman, P. (1974). An epic showdown at the O.K. Corral. In G. Constable (Ed.), *The gunfighters* (pp. 15-51). Alexandra, VA: Time-Life.
Trope, Y. (1986). Self-enhancement and self-assessment in achievement behavior. In R. M. Sorrentino & E. T. Higgins (Eds.), *Handbook of motivation and social cognition: Foundations of social behavior* (pp. 350-378). New York: Guilford.
Watson, D., & Clark, L. A. (1984). Negative affectivity: The disposition to experience aversive emotional states. *Psychological Bulletin, 96*, 465-490.

Watson, D., & Clark, L. A. (in press). Extraversion and its positive emotional core. In S. Briggs, W. Jones, & R. Hogan (Eds.), *Handbook of personality psychology*. New York: Academic Press.
Weary, G. (1979). Self-serving attributional biases: Perceptual or response distortions? *Journal of Personality and Social Psychology, 37*, 1418-1420.
Weiner, B., Amirkhan, J., Folkes, V. S., & Verette, J. A. (1987). An attributional analysis of excuse giving: Studies of a naive theory of emotion. *Journal of Personality and Social Psychology, 31*, 415-421.
White, R. W. (1959). Motivation reconsidered: The concept of competence. *Psychological Review, 66*, 296-335.
Wolosin, R. J., Sherman, S. J., & Till, A. (1973). Effects of cooperation and competition on responsibility attribution after success and failure. *Journal of Experimental Social Psychology, 9*, 220-235.
Wrightsman, L. S., & Deaux, K. (1981). *Social psychology in the 80s* (3rd ed.). Monterey, CA: Brooks/Cole.

IV Developmental Perspectives on Coping With Loss

16 Coping With Discrepancies Between Aspirations and Achievements in Adult Development: A Dual-Process Model

Jochen Brandtstädter
Gerolf Renner
University of Trier

Life histories are a mixture of changes and events that are partly intended and expected, partly unintended and surprising, and that—in terms of the individual's developmental aspirations and life themes—involve gains as well as losses. What are the basic strategies and processes that individuals apply in order to keep this balance favorable over the life span? Our theoretical approach to this question is based on the assumption that the cognitions, evaluations, and actions involved in a person's construction of developmental gains and losses are dynamically interrelated. For example, the emotional valences of perceived developmental outcomes critically depend on whether we assume personal responsibility for them or consider them as unrelated to our actions and intentions; these appraisals may be influenced by our desire to maintain a favorable view of ourselves. Furthermore, we do not only attune our actions to developmental goals but also, in turn, adjust our system of goals to perceived developmental potentials and capacities; and we tend to give up developmental options that appear unattainable or definitively blocked and to replace them with new ones. By such strategies and processes, which may partly involve automatic and subpersonal levels of functioning, we protect ourselves more or less successfully against permanent dissatisfaction, depression, and grief. As Brim (1988) has pointed out: "That process of arranging and managing our lives to keep the right balance between achievement and capacity is ... one of the most important, fascinating, and overlooked aspects of adult development" (p. 50).

The perceived relationship between aspirations and achievements, as well as the perceived scope for improving this balance, deeply influences a person's subjective quality of life (e.g., Brandtstädter, 1989). When we look at development in middle and later adulthood, however, we come upon some apparent inconsistencies. The subjective ratio of developmental gains and losses seems to worsen progressively (cf. Heckhausen, Dixon, & Baltes, 1989), and the perceived impact of uncontrollable influences upon personal development tends to increase (cf. Brandtstädter & Baltes-Götz, 1991). Irreversible losses, uncontrollable events, and chronic strains cumulate in later life (Seligman & Elder, 1986). Given this rather bleak scenario, it seems surprising that longitudinal and cross-sectional research has largely failed to establish a general or pervasive decline in subjective quality of life; meta-analyses of pertinent findings even indicate a moderate increase in life satisfaction (cf. Mayring, 1987; Stock, Okun, Haring, & Wilter, 1983). Contrary to what might be theoretically expected, for example, on the grounds of learned helplessness and self-efficacy formulations (cf. Bandura, 1989; Peterson & Seligman, 1984), there is also no consistent evidence for a growing prevalence of depression in later life; Lewinsohn, Hoberman, Teri, and Hautzinger (1985, p. 338) even claim a "counterintuitive decrease of depression" beyond the age of 50.

In our view, these seeming paradoxes may be resolved by differentiating two basically different modes of coping with frustrating discrepancies between aspirations and factual outcomes in personal development. On the one hand, such discrepancies may induce active attempts to change one's developmental circumstances and prospects in order to bring them into a closer correspondence with personal goals and aspirations. On the other hand, the individual's system of preferences and aspirations may be adjusted to situational constraints so that initially aversive situations lose their negative valence. Whereas developmental problems are *solved* in the former case, they are, as it were, neutralized or *dissolved* in the latter.[1]

We have designated these complementary forms of optimizing one's developmental prospects as "assimilative" and "accommodative" respectively (cf. Brandtstädter, 1989; Brandtstädter & Renner, 1990). In the following, we will elaborate this distinction theoretically and compare it with related constructs. Then we will outline some implications for theories of depression. Finally, we will discuss the relevance of assimilative and accommodative processes for maintaining and regaining a satisfying life perspective in adulthood and old age.

---

[1] We do not claim priority for this basic assumption; as a matter of fact, the notion of "neutralizing" problems by a readjustment of preferences can be traced back to ancient stoic philosophy. Already Seneca stated that "Quicquid vult habere nemo potest, illud potest nolle quod non habet" ("No man can have what he will, he may choose whether he will desire what he has not;" quoted from Burton's "Anatomy of Melancholy," 1621, p. 131).

ASSIMILATIVE AND ACCOMMODATIVE PROCESSES IN THE CONTEXT OF DEVELOPMENT-RELATED CONTROL ACTIVITIES

Assimilative and accommodative processes are not mutually exclusive, but may operate simultaneously in concrete coping episodes. We do assume, however, that they correspond to different stages of the coping process. Accommodative tendencies should become predominant to the degree that active-assimilative attempts to alter the situation turn out to be futile or to involve intolerable costs (in a broad sense). Feelings of hopelessness or helplessness that result from repeated unsuccessful problem-solving attempts thus appear as important parameters in the shift from assimilative to accommodative processes. We further assume that the temporal dynamics of these processes depend on the interaction of dispositional factors (e.g., self-efficacy cognitions, generalized outcome expectancies) and situational characteristics.

Assimilative Processes of Coping

Figure 16.1 shows the postulated interrelationships between cognitive and affective appraisals of personal developmental prospects, subjective control potentials, and assimilative action tendencies, and delineates the conditions that induce a shift from the assimilative to the accommodative phase. In its structural features, the model can be compared to a complex Test-Operate-Test-Exit sequence (in the sense given by Miller, Galanter, & Pribram, 1960).

It is assumed that assimilative activities presuppose a self-monitoring process: Personal developmental prospects are assessed and evaluated with reference to developmental goals and life designs (see model components 1, 2). Here, defensive or counterdefensive distortions may intrude that may strengthen or diminish assimilative or self-corrective tendencies (cf. Bandura, 1982; Taylor & Brown, 1988). A high degree of contentment or satisfaction with one's developmental situation will generally lower the tendency to alter established patterns of action (2,+; 3; to simplify matters, we assume alternative outcomes at the different branching points of the model).

Assimilative efforts are initially motivated by a discrepancy between aspirations and actual achievements or life circumstances (2,-), which is typically accompanied by negative emotions such as disappointment or anger. The ensuing process largely depends on the perceived scope for altering the situation and on subjective potentials of control (4; 5). If these are considered sufficient (5,+), corrective actions are prepared and executed (6). This phase may involve intermediary explorative and heuristic processes; here, our model gives only a simplified picture (see also Carver & Scheier, 1981).

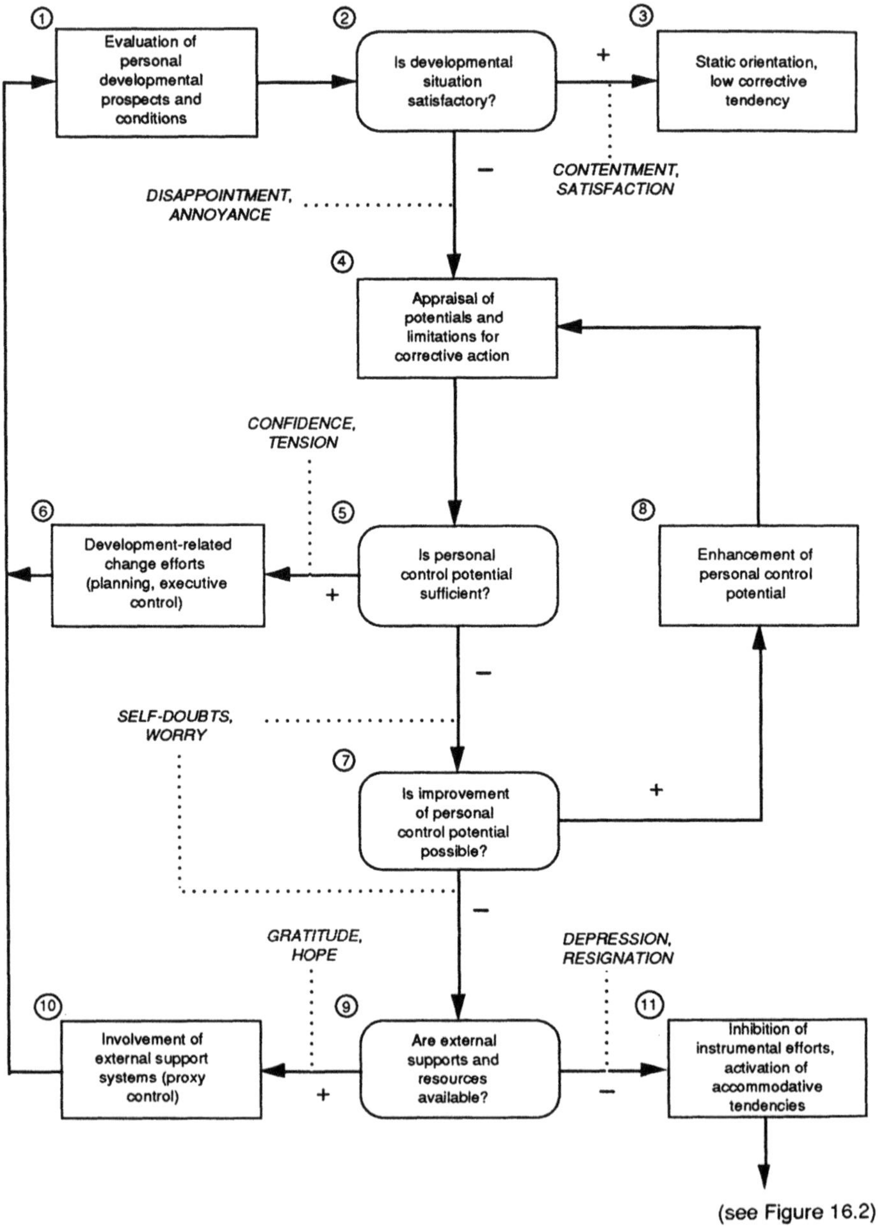

FIG. 16.1. The assimilative phase of coping with developmental losses and deficits: Cognitive, affective, and behavioral implications.

If personal potentials of control are seen as deficient (5,-), this may not necessarily inhibit further assimilative efforts. Rather, our model assumes that, in this case, individuals will first try to enhance their capacities for efficient action and control by searching for relevant information, acquiring new skills, and so forth, provided that such options are available (5,-; 6,+). Activation of such competence-building tendencies is a well-known phenomenon in critical life situations. If such efforts turn out to be unavailing (7,-; 9), the individual may eventually look for external help to manage the difficulty (proxy control; cf. Bandura, 1982).

The different phases of assimilative action are linked to distinctive emotional states; such links are already suggested by the conceptual structure of emotion terms (cf. Brandtstädter, 1985). Negative emotions like anger, worry, or disappointment are related to a limitation or worsening of personal developmental perspectives and of personal potentials for action (2,-; 5,-). Feelings of helplessness and hopelessness arise when opportunities for meliorative intervention seem exhausted (2,-; 5,-; 7,-; 9,-). This critical stage may be characterized by an intense inner preoccupation with unattainable goals and by growing disorientation and depression (cf. Horowitz, 1979; Klinger, 1975). We assume that under these conditions accommodative tendencies gain dominance, which enhance the disengagement from barren options and a readjustment of developmental goals and life themes.

Accommodative Processes of Coping

Figure 16.2 ties in with Figure 16.1 at the point at which repeated and unsuccessful attempts at problem-oriented intervention have led to an inhibition of further assimilative efforts.

The diagram in Figure 16.2 first focuses on processes that aim at a devaluation of blocked developmental options and a positive reappraisal of initially aversive circumstances. These accommodative processes basically involve a reorganization of belief structures and goal systems; cognitions and valuations that contribute to a palliative reappraisal of the situation have to be strengthened; those that generated (or have been generated by) distress and depression have to be weakened accordingly (cf. model elements 2; 3,+; 4). A critical factor is the availability of such palliative reinterpretations, which may differ interindividually and between situations; when palliative interpretations are not initially available, they may eventually be generated through further exploratory processes (2; 3,-; 5,+; 6; 3,+; 4). Let's have a closer look at these processes.

Palliative reappraisals involve a shift in the meanings that are ascribed to a given situation. We can differentiate between instrumental and semantic aspects of meaning. The former refer to the representation of personally relevant consequences and side-effects of a given event or situation, the latter to its semantic encoding or placement into a conceptual structure (these interpretative processes may be functionally interdependent). For example, older persons may partly revise

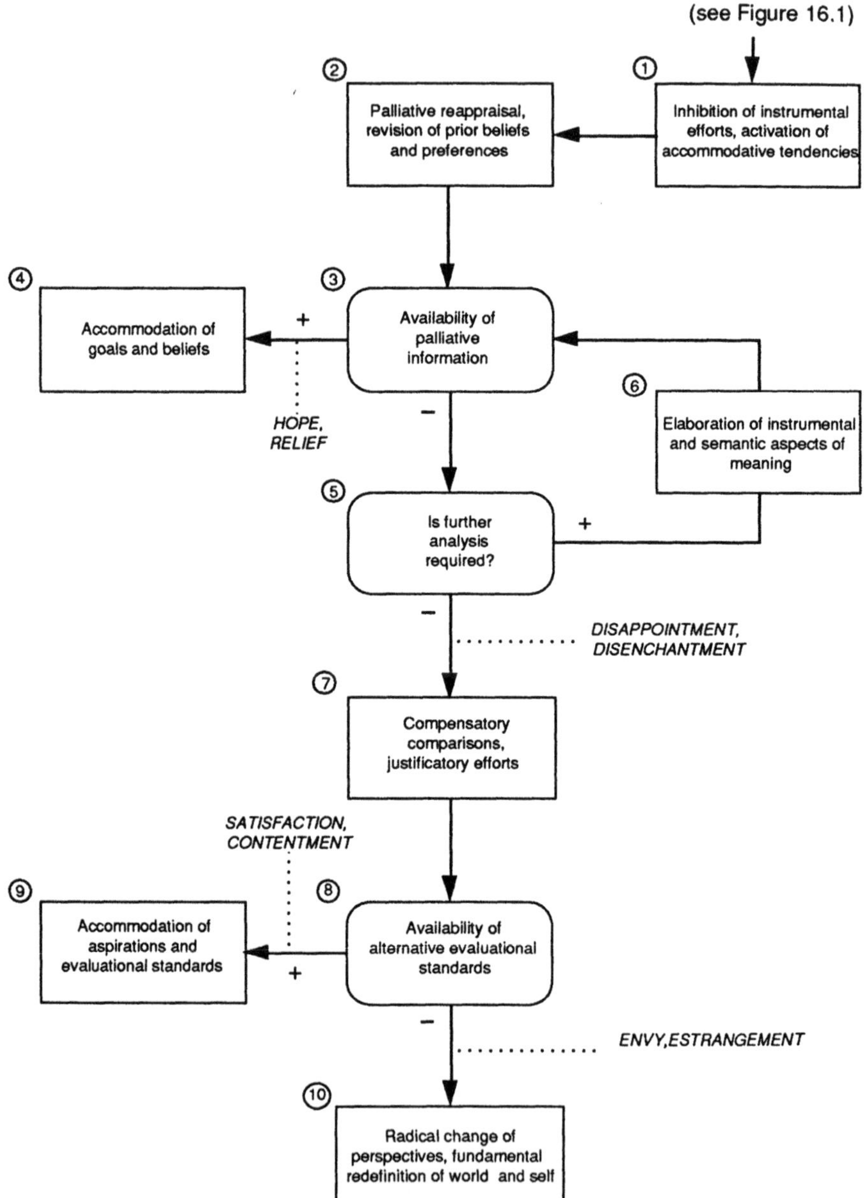

FIG. 16.2. The accommodative phase of coping with developmental losses and deficits: Cognitive, affective, and behavioral implications.

their concept of intelligence so that positively age-related competences (life experience, expertise) are more heavily weighted than competences that tend to deteriorate with age (e.g., mnemonic skills, spatial abilities, etc.); this shows how the experience of a loss and corresponding threats to the person's self-concept may be neutralized, or even positively reinterpreted, by a reorganization of semantic structures (cf. Greve, 1989). Instrumental meanings of a situation, on the other hand, may be changed by focusing selectively on specific consequences, rejecting specific evidences as irrelevant, doubting the credibility or validity of information, or by adopting alternative causal or theoretical beliefs with new predictive implications (cf. Bandura, 1982). These processes may, but do not necessarily, lead to a biased perception of oneself and the world; they may also bring to attention new and hitherto neglected aspects of the situation. In any case, concepts and evidences are often fuzzy enough to leave scope for revisions and plausible alternative interpretations.

If palliative interpretations are not available, individuals may eventually rescale or critically revise their evaluative standards (7; 8). Losses in a certain personally important domain may be balanced against gains in other domains. In comparative evaluations, the choice of a reference point is crucial; our situation may appear more acceptable when we compare it against a hypothetical worse world (Taylor, Wood, & Lichtman, 1983). In particular, we may compare ourselves with persons in a similar or worse position ("downward comparison"; Wills, 1987). For example, debilitating developmental changes in old age may appear more tolerable when we focus on same-aged persons rather than comparing ourselves with younger people (or with ourselves at an earlier age). Personal and social conceptions of fairness and justice may make some comparisons more available than others. Generally, the availability of palliative comparisons is enhanced by the diversity of potential dimensions for comparison; "everyone is better off than someone else as long as one picks the right dimension" (Taylor, 1983, p. 1166). In our view, however, it would be mistaken to conceive of such comparison processes as deliberately applied strategies. As Kahneman and Miller (1986) have shown, normative comparisons involve the recall of episodes, scenarios, or counterfactual alternatives that are most closely associated with a particular type of event or situation; these retrieval processes are fast, automatic, and do not involve any reflective decisions.

With regard to the dynamics of accommodative reappraisals, it seems plausible to expect that they involve those parts of the individual's system of beliefs and preferences that are most amenable, or least resistant, to change. Firmly entrenched convictions are, by definition, more resistant to change than uncertain hypotheses, and valuations that are central or fundamental to the individual's self-conception and life design will be defended more forcefully than peripheral or derived preferences. When palliative reappraisals that are compatible with fundamental conceptions of self and the world are not available, only radical shifts in identity, life design, and world view can establish new and satisfying developmental prospects (see Figure 16.2: 3,-; 5,-; 7; 8,-; 10).

We should note that during the phase of depression and disorientation, which in our model sets the stage for accommodative processes, the availability of palliative interpretations is reduced by a tendency to generate mood-congruent cognitions (e.g., Blaney, 1986). Depressed individuals may be willing to consider positive aspects of their situation, but they are typically unable to successfully adopt this perspective. How can this tendency be overcome or counteracted? We assume that such accommodative tendencies have to be related to certain dynamic constraints in cognition and information processing.

First, a mechanism of attention regulation seems important. We may call this the *relevance principle*: Attention is directed to those aspects of a situation that are relevant to current action plans and to their successful execution (cf. Cranach von, 1982). According to this principle, aversive aspects of a situation will tend to demand attention as long as the individual sees some chance of managing the problem. Already from an evolutionary point of view, a permanent blocking of working memory with action-irrelevant contents would seem dysfunctional. This suggests that attention tends to withdraw from negative situational aspects as soon as they appear definitely irreversible, that is, as soon as active-assimilative tendencies are sufficiently eroded. This process may be self-reinforcing by its palliative effect. Conversely, if problem-focused ruminations persist although there is little hope to alter the situation, we may infer that the problem is of high personal or existential importance.

Changes in belief systems are further subject to an epistemic *consistency principle*. As has been amply documented in social psychological and cognitive research, empirical evidence is more easily accepted or held true when it conforms to the system of prior beliefs; revisions of prior beliefs are induced by epistemic conflicts and aim at resolving such conflicts (cf. Taylor & Crocker, 1981). The integration of evidence into a cognitive structure seems subject to constraints analogous to those Quine (1951) has postulated for the dynamics of scientific theories: "...our natural tendency [is] to disturb the system as little as possible" (p. 41). According to the consistency principle, certain fundamental beliefs and attitudes (e.g., the belief in a just or benevolently organized world) should facilitate the availability of palliative cognitions.

The willingness to accept or to reject certain interpretations and aspects of meaning, however, depends not only on their coherence with established beliefs but also on their personal valence. Here, a further dynamic constraint—call it the *optimism principle*—comes into play. Situational interpretations that have positive implications for our self-conception and personal view of the world are, *ceteris paribus*, accepted more easily and abandoned more reluctantly (cf. Greenwald, 1980; Janoff-Bulman & Timko, 1987). Thus, when individuals explore the implications and consequences or gather new information about a given situation or event, self-enhancing scenarios should be more readily adopted. Within the boundaries of rationality, there is usually scope for a trade-off between the consistency and the optimism principle. Our perceptual and cognitive system, however, is realistic enough to accept information that is incompatible with prior opinions and preferences, provided the evidence is sufficiently strong and unambiguous (so that its rejection would violate other strong epistemic beliefs). It follows that cognitive and affective acceptance of information may diverge (cf. Swann, Griffin, Predmore, & Gaines, 1987). In certain cases, evidence may be too strong to reject and too aversive or threatening to accept. Such cases may considerably strain belief systems and preference structures and thus invoke a radical redefinition of world and self—akin to a paradigm shift in science.

RELATED THEORETICAL NOTIONS

The basic arguments presented so far are, in essence, not novel. The antagonism between active-offensive and complacent-accepting modes of coping with life problems is a traditional topic in philosophical anthropology (cf. the distinction between "offensive" and "defensive" conceptions of happiness; Tatarkiewicz, 1976). There are, of course, also points of convergence with more recent psychological conceptions of coping and control. More specifically, we should mention here: (a) the theory of primary and secondary control (Rothbaum, Weisz, & Snyder, 1982); (b) the distinction beween problem-focused and emotion-focused coping (Lazarus, 1977; Lazarus & Launier, 1978; cf. Moos & Billings, 1982); and (c) the theory of the incentive-disengagement cycle (Klinger, 1975, 1977).

Primary and secondary control: This distinction has been proposed by Rothbaum et al. (1982; cf. also Weisz, Rothbaum, & Blackburn, 1984). The authors argue that typical inward behaviors such as passivity, submissiveness, or withdrawal should not simply be taken as signs of relinquished control. Rather, when efforts to bring the environment into line with personal wishes (primary control, "changing the world") have proven futile, people may attempt to gain or maintain control by adjusting to situational forces or constraints (secondary control, "changing the self"). Without going into details of this conception, similarities to our theoretical approach should be obvious. There are, however, some points of divergence, too. We accord with the basic assumption that when possibilities of active or instrumental control are limited, individuals may maintain a sense of control or personal power by adjusting personal preferences to the range of feasible options. Since getting what one wants is central to the concept of power (cf. Elster, 1983), this claim can already be defended on purely conceptual grounds. However, categorizing both "primary" and "secondary" modes of coping under a sweeping notion of control seems to overstretch the concept. This use of terms blurs the fundamental difference beween deliberate efforts at control and reactive or nonintentional processes that may enhance self-percepts of efficacy and control but are not themselves subject to personal control. We are not generally able to modify our personal beliefs and preferences merely because it seems advantageous to do so. Rather, such changes happen to us under certain circumstances and, thus, are counterexamples of personally controlled action. The equivocal use of the control concept leads to ambiguities in distinguishing between cases of primary and secondary control. Given the explications provided by Rothbaum et al. (1982), it is difficult to decide, for example, whether intentional strategies of self-management, which may aim at a more efficient realization of personal goals, should be considered as examples of primary or secondary control (cf. also Flammer, Züblin, & Grob, 1988).

Problem-focused versus emotion-focused coping: In his "transactional" paradigm of stress and coping, Lazarus (1977; cf. also Lazarus & Launier, 1978; Folkman, 1984; Moos & Billings, 1982) has proposed a distinction between coping strategies that involve active transformation of the threatening situation ("problem-focused coping"), and activities that aim at alleviating the negative emotions induced by stressful situations ("emotion-focused coping"). It is argued that "situations in which the person thinks something constructive can be done . . . favor problem-focused coping, whereas those having to be accepted favor emotion-focused coping" (Folkman & Lazarus, 1980, p. 219). The problem-focused mode of coping encompasses concrete problem-solving efforts, exploratory activities, and so forth, and may be compared to our "assimilative" mode of coping as defined above. In contrast, the category of "emotion-focused coping" comprises deliberately chosen instrumental actions as well as reactions beyond personal control; in this respect, it seems wider or more heterogeneous than our notion of accommodative coping. As operationalized by the "Ways of Coping Checklist" (Folkman & Lazarus, 1980), the concept of emotion-focused coping comprises such diverse behaviors as palliative reappraisals of the situation through defensive processes (denial, suppression), as well as self-therapeutical strategies to alleviate emotional strain (e.g., using sedatives, relaxation techniques)—which may even impede accommodative reorientations in the sense given above.

Incentive-disengagement cycle: According to Klinger (1975, 1977) any action is directed toward "incentives," that is, toward states or objects with attractive valence. At the onset of an instrumental action sequence, specific "commitments" or goal orientations centering on incentives are established. The action sequence is terminated by attainment of incentives and disengagement from previous commitments. Such disengagement, however, may also result from frustration, e.g., when difficulties in pursuing an incentive appear, or when the intended course of action is definitively blocked. Klinger (1975) assumes that the ensuing cognitive, motivational, and behavioral reactions are organized in a regular, cyclic pattern. The initial phase of the postulated "incentive-disengagement cycle" is characterized by intensified efforts to overcome the obstacle (increased concentration, exploratory activity, heightened attractiveness of the blocked incentive). If these efforts are fruitless, the pattern of reactions is likely to become more primitive and turn into destructive aggression. Under prolonged and unrelieved frustration, reactions of invigoration and aggression eventually merge into a phase of depression that involves feelings of resignation and helplessness as well as a gradual devaluation of the barren incentives, and, finally, disengagement from blocked goals. In contrast to helplessness formulations, the incentive-disengagement model conceives of depression and disengagement not as the terminal outcome of perceived loss of control, but rather as a functional phenomenon that enhances recovery and the buildup of new and meaningful perspectives for action and personal development. As detailed below, this partly converges with our dual-process conception.

IMPLICATIONS FOR A THEORY OF DEPRESSION

Cognitive theories of depression such as the model of Beck (1976) or the theory of learned helplessness (Abramson, Seligman, & Teasdale, 1978; Peterson & Seligman, 1984) have significantly contributed to our understanding of the etiology of depressive disorders and of dispositional factors that increase the vulnerability for depression. These models are, however, less informative when it comes to explaining the processes and conditions that lead to the termination of a depressive episode. Considering the high rate of spontaneous recovery from depression—Stern and Mendels (1980) estimate that the majority of cases recovers within six months without therapeutic aid—this seems a serious theoretical deficit (cf. also Coyne & Gotlib, 1980). From a learned helplessness perspective, it seems particularly difficult to understand how individuals recover from depression in cases in which they are confronted with permanent and definitely irreversible loss.

The theoretical distinction of assimilative and accommodative processes may provide an answer to this puzzling question. It suggests that severity and duration of depressive reactions depends not only on specific attributional styles and control beliefs—as explicated in helplessness theory—but also on the capability or readiness to revise and readjust personal life perspectives and developmental options. Such accommodative readjustments may depend on trait-like dispositional factors as well as on situational aspects such as personal importance, centrality, or substitutability of blocked developmental options. From this theoretical point of view, disengagement from blocked goal perspectives does not mark a pathological end state, but rather paves the way for the construction of new and satisfying life perspectives (cf. Janoff-Bulman & Brickman, 1982; Wrubel, Benner, & Lazarus, 1981; Klinger, 1975).

In support of this argument, several findings may be cited that, however, partly deviated from the investigators' expectations. In a study on coping in stressful episodes, Coyne, Aldwin, and Lazarus (1981, p. 439) found—to their own surprise—that depressed persons were less prone "to appraise situations as requiring their acceptance." Findings by Becker (1985) and Pyszczynski and Greenberg (1987) hint in a similar direction. Collins, Baum, and Singer (1983) investigated psychological reactions to the reactor calamity at Three Mile Island. They found that persons favoring a problem-focused style of coping reported higher depression. Such evidence does not easily fit into the framework of learned helplessness theory or related control-theoretical notions but converges with our dual-process conception of coping. In line with these results, observations from our own research indicate that nondepressed individuals tend to downgrade the importance of developmental goals with increasing goal distances, whereas depressed persons are less prone to do so (cf. Brandtstädter, 1989; Brandtstädter & Baltes-Götz, 1991). Of special interest in this context are results by Miskimins and Simmons (1966) indicating that older persons with depressive disorders tend to cling to developmental goals that generally are more characteristic for younger age groups. "I can no longer do what I want to do, and yet I still want to do those things"—this statement of a depressed patient (quoted from Melges & Bowlby, 1969, p. 694) epitomizes the potentially adverse effects of rigidly adhering to barren developmental options and life designs. When confronted with factually uncontrollable events or irreversible losses, persons having a strong sense of personal efficacy may experience particular difficulties in adjusting their goals and life plans to the new circumstances. Thus, we may contrast a pathogenic, premature resignation with a "pathology of high expectations" (Janoff-Bulman & Brickman, 1982) that impedes flexible accommodations of the personal goal system.

AGE-RELATED CHANGES IN PREFERRED COPING STYLES

Up to now, research on changes in coping strategies across the life span has failed to reveal clear developmental trends (cf. Folkman, Lazarus, Pimley, & Novacek, 1987; Lazarus & DeLongis, 1983; McCrae, 1982; Saup, 1987). Summarizing his findings, McCrae (1982, p. 459) concludes that "... older people ...cope in much the same way as younger people, and where they employ different mechanisms, it appears largely to be a function of different types of stress they face." It seems problematic, however, to take the lack of evidence for age-related changes as evidence for the lack of such changes. Before jumping to such conclusions, one should consider the possibility of theoretical deficiencies.

Surprisingly, the theoretical discussion of age-related changes in coping patterns has largely neglected the "paradoxes" mentioned earlier. How can we explain that older people do not report a general or dramatic loss in life quality and satisfaction, even though they face severely restricted developmental prospects and an increasingly unfavorable balance of developmental gains and losses? We assume that this phenomenon might be due to a gradual age-related shift from active-offensive to accommodative strategies of coping that involve flexible reorganization of developmental goals and readjustments in aspiration levels.

We have investigated this assumption by means of a questionnaire designed to assess preferences for assimilative and accommodative modes of coping on a dispositional level (for psychometric features and details of the construction procedure, see Brandtstädter & Renner, 1990). This instrument comprises two statistically independent scales: Tenacious Goal Pursuit (TGP) and Flexible Goal Adjustment (FGA). The TGP scale assesses a tendency to pursue goals tenaciously even in the face of obstacles and under high risk of failure (or, at the opposite pole, the tendency to give up readily); according to our conception, this reflects an assimilative mode of coping as defined above. The FGA scale comprises items indicating a tendency to reinterpret initially aversive situations positively and to disengage easily from barren commitments; this corresponds to an accommodative mode of coping as defined above.[2] In spite of their statistical independence, both scales correlate positively with various indicators of subjective quality of life such as optimism, lack of depression, and life satisfaction (interestingly, these relations are more pronounced for FGA; see Brandtstädter & Renner, 1990). Results from an independent study with coronary disease patients indicate that persons with high FGA values show less difficulties in changing their life-style (Scherler, 1989).

Figures 16.3 and 16.4 show cross-sectional age gradients for Flexibility and Tenacity. The data were obtained in the third wave of a larger cross-sequential research project focusing on changes in subjective developmental perspectives and control orientations in adulthood (see Brandtstädter, 1989; Brandtstädter, Krampen, & Heil, 1986).[3] For cross-sectional comparisons, subjects were grouped into five age cohorts (34 to 39 years, $N = 165$; 40 to 45 years, $N = 158$; 46 to 51 years, $N = 189$; 52 to 57 years, $N = 177$; 58 to 63 years, $N = 177$). A three-factor ANOVA with the factors cohort, gender, and coping style (TGP vs. FGA) yielded significant interactions of coping style with cohort, $F(4,856) = 8.14$, $p < .001$, and gender, $F(1,856) = 12.49$, $p < .001$. The structure of the Coping × Cohort interaction confirms our theoretical expectations: FGA shows an age-related increment, while TGP decreases over the age range studied. The opposite developmental gradients for FGA and TGP are particularly remarkable considering the low variance overlap of these variables and their convergent relationship with indicators of a high subjective quality of life.

From a methodological point of view, cross-sectional differences may confound cohort effects with genuine age-related change. We have, however, offered

---

[2] Sample items from TGP scale: The harder a goal is to achieve, the more desirable it often appears to me; I can be very persistent in pursuing my goals; Even if everything seems hopeless, I still look for a way to master the situation; If I run into problems, I usually double my efforts. Sample items from the FGA scale: Even if everything goes wrong, I still can find something positive about the situation; I can adapt quite easily to changes in a situation; After a serious disappointment, I soon turn to new tasks; I usually recognize quite easily my own limitations.

[3] This research was supported by a grant from the German Research Foundation.

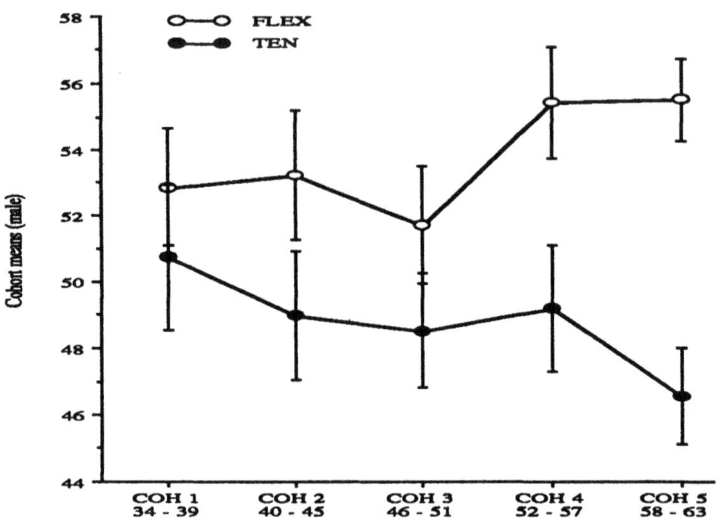

FIG. 16.3. Age gradients for Tenacious Goal Pursuit and Flexible Goal Adjustment (male sample, $N = 444$; cohort means are given with .95 confidence intervals).

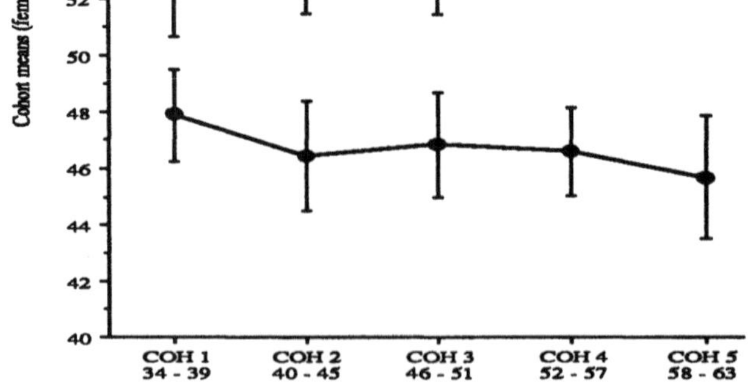

FIG. 16.4. Age gradients for Tenacious Goal Pursuit and Flexible Goal Adjustment (female sample, $N = 422$; cohort means are given with .95 confidence intervals).

theoretical reasons that, for the present case, strongly favor an interpretation in terms of ontogenetic or age-graded change. We should note that there are some scattered findings in the literature that point in a similar direction (cf. Fleishman, 1984; Folkman et al., 1987; Gutmann, 1964). These earlier findings were, however, partly interpreted as evidence for an insidious trend toward resignation and regression in old age. We consider that view—which, however, is suggested by a popular stereotype of successful development centering on notions of competitive achievement and assertiveness—as misleading. The ability to flexibly adjust preferences to life circumstances, to replace blocked developmental goals, and to positively reinterpret aversive situations rather seems to facilitate coping with developmental losses and to promote maintenance of a meaningful life perspective in old age (cf. Brim, 1988; Clark & Anderson, 1967; Taylor, 1983).

We can substantiate this assumption by some further observations. Considering the presumed palliative implications of accommodative processes, we should expect that the effect of perceived developmental deficits on life satisfaction is less detrimental for high levels of flexibility (FGA). Data obtained from the panel described above allow a test of this postulated moderator effect. Figure 16.5 shows the conditional regressions of life satisfaction (measured by selected items from scales by Neugarten, Havighurst, & Tobin, 1961) on the sum of perceived goal distances with respect to 17 developmental goals for five levels of FGA (for the selection of goals and details of the rating procedure, see Brandtstädter, 1989). For the whole sample, the correlation between the sum of perceived distances from developmental goals—which is taken here as an indicator of subjective developmental deficits—and life satisfaction is clearly negative (-.43, $p < .001$). This negative correlation, however, is less pronounced for higher levels of flexibility (FGA), which indicates that persons scoring high on FGA obviously are less negatively affected by developmental deficits and losses.

The conditional regressions shown in Figure 16.5 were obtained by means of hierarchical regression analysis (cf. Cohen & Cohen, 1983); the interaction term is significant ($t = 3.67, p < .001$). An analogous effect is obtained with measures of depression as a target variable. These results lend further support to the assumption that accommodative tendencies, as measured by the FGA scale, contribute to the maintenance of a positive life perspective in the face of irreversible developmental losses that are typical for the later phases of life.

SUMMARY

Perceived discrepancies between desired and factual courses of personal development may activate two distinct but interrelated modes of coping: A first mode involving the active adaptation of developmental circumstances to personal goals and preferences (assimilative tendency), and a second mode involving an adjust-

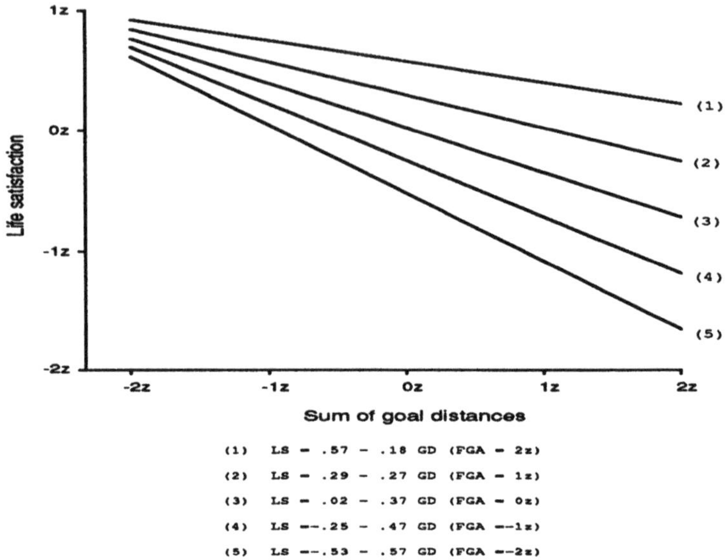

FIG. 16.5. Conditional regressions of Life Satisfaction (LS) on subjective developmental deficits (sum index of perceived distances from 17 developmental goals, GD) for different levels of Flexible Goal Adjustment (FGA).

ment of goal systems and belief structures to situational constraints (accommodative tendency). Assimilative and accommodative processes are integrated into a model of personal self-regulation of development and related to control- and coping-theoretical formulations. The model suggests that severity and duration of depressive reactions to developmental deficits or losses depends not only on perceived deficits in control over subjectively relevant areas of life but also on the adaptive flexibility of personal aspirations and goal systems. Age comparisons indicate a gradual shift from assimilative to accommodative modes of coping in middle and later adulthood. It is argued that this shift contributes to maintaining a positive outlook on personal development even in the face of an increasingly unfavorable balance of developmental gains and losses.

REFERENCES

Abramson, L. J., Seligman, M. E. P., & Teasdale, J. (1978). Learned helplessness in humans: Critique and reformulation. *Journal of Abnormal Psychology, 87*, 49-74.

Bandura, A. (1982). Self-efficacy in human agency. *American Psychologist, 37*, 122-147.

Bandura, A. (1989). Perceived self-efficacy in the exercise of personal agency. *The Psychologist: Bulletin of the British Psychological Society, 10*, 411-424.

Beck, A. T. (1976). *Cognitive therapy and the emotional disorders.* New York: International Universities Press.

Becker, P. (1985). Bewältigungsverhalten und seelische Gesundheit. *Zeitschrift für Klinische Psychologie, 14,* 169-184.

Blaney, P. H. (1986). Affect and memory: A review. *Psychological Bulletin, 99,* 229-246.

Brandtstädter, J. (1985). Emotion, Kognition, Handlung: Konzeptuelle Beziehungen. In L. H. Eckensberger & E.-D. Lantermann (Eds.), *Emotion und Reflexivität* (pp. 252-261). München: Urban & Schwarzenberg.

Brandtstädter, J. (1989). Personal self-regulation of development: Cross-sequential analyses of development-related control beliefs and emotions. *Developmental Psychology, 25,* 96-108.

Brandtstädter, J., & Baltes-Götz, B. (1991). Personal control over development and quality of life perspectives in adulthood. In P. B. Baltes & M. M. Baltes (Eds.), *Successful aging. Perspectives from the behavioral sciences* (pp. 197-224). New York: Cambridge University Press.

Brandtstädter, J., Krampen, G., & Heil, F. E. (1986). Personal control and emotional evaluation of development in partnership relations during adulthood. In M. M. Baltes & P. B. Baltes (Eds.), *The psychology of aging and control* (pp. 265-296). Hillsdale, NJ: Lawrence Erlbaum Associates.

Brandtstädter, J., & Renner, G. (1990). Tenacious Goal Pursuit and Flexible Goal Adjustment: Explication and age-related analysis of assimilative and accommodative strategies of coping. *Psychology and Aging, 5,* 58-67.

Brim, O. G. (1988, September). Losing and winning. *Psychology Today, 22,* 48-52.

Burton, R. (1621). *The anatomy of melancholy.* Oxford: Cripps (reprinted: 1977. New York: Vintage Books).

Carver, C. S., & Scheier, M. F. (1981). *Attention and self-regulation: A control-theory approach to human behavior.* New York: Springer.

Clark, M., & Anderson, B. G. (1967). *Culture and aging: An anthropological study of older Americans.* Springfield, IL: C.C. Thomas.

Cohen, J., & Cohen, P. (1983). *Applied multiple regression/correlational analysis for the behavioral sciences* (2nd ed.). Hillsdale, NJ: Lawrence Erlbaum Associates.

Collins, D. L., Baum, A., & Singer, J. E. (1983). Coping with chronic stress at Three Mile Island: Psychological and biochemical evidence. *Health Psychology, 2,* 149-166.

Coyne, J. C., Aldwin, C., & Lazarus, R. S. (1981). Depression and coping in stressful episodes. *Journal of Abnormal Psychology, 90,* 439-447.

Coyne, J. C., & Gotlib, I. H. (1980). The role of cognition in depression: A critical appraisal. *Psychological Bulletin, 94,* 472-505.

Cranach, M. von (1982). The psychological study of goal-directed action: Basic issues. In M. von Cranach & R. Harré (Eds.), *The analysis of action. Recent theoretical and empirical advances* (pp. 35-74). Cambridge: Cambridge University Press.

Elster, J. (1983). *Sour grapes. Studies in the subversion of rationality.* London: Cambridge University Press.

Flammer, A., Züblin, C., & Grob, A. (1988). Sekundäre Kontrolle bei Jugendlichen. *Zeitschrift für Entwicklungspsychologie und Pädagogische Psychologie, 20,* 239-262.

Fleishman, J. A. (1984). Personality characteristics and coping patterns. *Journal of Health and Social Behavior, 25,* 229-244.

Folkman, S. (1984). Personal control and stress and coping processes: A theoretical analysis. *Journal of Personality and Social Psychology, 46,* 839-852.

Folkman, S., & Lazarus, R. S. (1980). An analysis of coping in a middle-aged community sample. *Journal of Health and Social Behavior, 21,* 219-239.

Folkman, S., Lazarus, R. S., Pimley, S., & Novacek, J. (1987). Age differences in stress and coping processes. *Psychology and Aging, 2,* 171-184.

Greenwald, A. G. (1980). The totalitarian ego. *American Psychologist, 35,* 603-618.

Greve, W. (1989). *Selbstkonzeptimmunisierung. Verteidigung und Entwicklung zentraler Selbstkonzeptbereiche im Erwachsenenalter.* Unpublished doctoral dissertation, Universität Trier.

Gutmann, D. L. (1964). An exploration of ego configurations in middle and late life. In B. Neugarten (Ed.), *Personality in middle and late life* (pp. 114-148). New York: Atherton.

Heckhausen, J., Dixon, R. A., & Baltes, P. B. (1989). Gains and losses in development throughout adulthood as perceived by different adult age groups. *Developmental Psychology, 25*, 109-121.

Horowitz, M. J. (1979). Psychological responses to serious life events. In V. Hamilton & D. M. Warburton (Eds.), *Human stress and cognition* (pp. 235-264). Chichester: Wiley.

Janoff-Bulman, R., & Brickman, P. (1982). Expectations and what people learn from failure. In N. T. Feather (Ed.), *Expectations and actions* (pp. 207-237). Hillsdale, NJ: Lawrence Erlbaum Associates.

Janoff-Bulman, R., & Timko, C. (1987). Coping with traumatic life events. In C. R. Snyder & C. E. Ford (Eds.), *Coping with negative life events* (pp. 135-159). New York: Plenum.

Kahneman, D., & Miller, D. T. (1986). Norm theory: Comparing reality to its alternatives. *Psychological Review, 93*, 136-153.

Klinger, E. (1975). Consequences of commitment to and disengagement from incentives. *Psychological Review, 82*, 1-25.

Klinger, E. (1977). *Meaning and void. Inner experiences and the incentives in people's lives.* Minneapolis, MN: University of Minnesota Press.

Lazarus, R. S. (1977). Cognitive and coping processes in emotion. In A. Monat & R. S. Lazarus (Eds.), *Stress and coping* (pp. 145-158). New York: Columbia University Press.

Lazarus, R. S., & DeLongis, A. (1983). Psychological stress and coping in aging. *American Psychologist, 38*, 245-254.

Lazarus, R. S., & Launier, R. (1978). Stress-related transactions between person and environment. In L. A. Pervin & M. Lewis (Eds.), *Perspectives in interactional psychology* (pp. 287-327). New York: Plenum.

Lewinsohn, P. M., Hoberman, H. M., Teri, L., & Hautzinger, M. (1985). An integrative theory of depression. In S. Reiss & R. R. Bootzin (Eds.), *Theoretical issues in behavior therapy* (pp. 331-362). New York: Academic Press.

Mayring, F. (1987). Subjektives Wohlbefinden im Alter. Stand der Forschung und theoretische Weiterentwicklung. *Zeitschrift für Gerontologie, 20*, 367-376.

McCrae, R. R. (1982). Age differences in the use of coping mechanisms. *Journal of Gerontology, 37*, 454-460.

Melges, F. T., & Bowlby, J. (1969). Types of hopelessness in psychopathological processes. *Archives of General Psychiatry, 20*, 690-699.

Miller, G. A., Galanter, E., & Pribram, K. H. (1960). *Plans and the structure of behavior*. New York: Holt, Rinehart & Winston.

Miskimins, R. W., & Simmons, W. L. (1966). Goal preference as a variable in involutional psychosis. *Journal of Consulting and Clinical Psychology, 30*, 73-77.

Moos, R. H., & Billings, A. G. (1982). Conceptualizing and measuring coping resources and processes. In L. Goldberger & S. Breznitz (Eds.), *Handbook of stress: Theoretical and clinical aspects* (pp. 212-230). New York: Free Press.

Neugarten, B. L., Havighurst, R. J., & Tobin, S. S. (1961). The measurement of life satisfaction. *Journal of Gerontology, 16*, 134-143.

Peterson, C., & Seligman, M. E. P. (1984). Causal explanations as a risk factor for depression: Theory and evidence. *Psychological Review, 91*, 347-374.

Pyszczynski, T., & Greenberg, J. (1987). Depression, self-focused attention, and self-regulatory perseveration. In C. R. Snyder & C. E. Ford (Eds.), *Coping with negative life events* (pp. 105-129). New York: Plenum Press.

Quine, W. V. O. (1951). Two dogmas of empiricism. *The Philosophical Review, 60*, 20-43.

Rothbaum, F., Weisz, J. R., & Snyder, S. S. (1982). Changing the world and changing the self. A two-process model of perceived control. *Journal of Personality and Social Psychology, 42*, 5-37.

Saup, W. (1987). Coping im Alter. Ergebnisse und Probleme psychologischer Studien zum Bewältigungsverhalten älterer Menschen. *Zeitschrift für Gerontologie, 20*, 345-354.

Scherler, J. (1989). *Entwicklungserleben bei Patienten mit koronaren Herzkrankheiten.* Unpublished master's thesis, Universität Trier.

Seligman, M. E. P., & Elder, G. (1986). Learned helplessness and life-span development. In A. B. Sfrensen, F. W. Weinert, & L. Sherrod (Eds.), *Human development and the life course: Multidisciplinary perspectives* (pp. 377-428). Hillsdale, NJ: Lawrence Erlbaum Associates.

Stern, S. L., & Mendels, J. (1980). Affective disorders. In A. E. Kazdin, A. S. Bellack, & M. Hersen (Eds.), *New perspectives in abnormal psychology* (pp. 204-226). New York: Oxford University Press.

Stock, W. A., Okun, M. A., Haring, M. J., & Wilter, R. A. (1983). Age and subjective well-being: A meta-analysis. In R. J. Light (Ed.), *Evaluation studies: Review annual* (Vol. 8, pp. 279-302). Beverly Hills, CA: Sage.

Swann, W. B., Griffin, J. J., Predmore, S. C., & Gaines, B. (1987). The cognitive-affective crossfire: When self-consistency confronts self-enhancement. *Journal of Personality and Social Psychology, 52,* 881-889.

Tatarkiewicz, W. (1976). *Analysis of happiness.* The Hague, Netherlands: Martinus Nijhoff.

Taylor, S. E. (1983). Adjustment to threatening events. *American Psychologist, 38,* 1161-1173.

Taylor, S. E., & Brown, J. D. (1988). Illusion and well-being: A social psychological perspective on mental health. *Psychological Bulletin, 103,* 193-210.

Taylor, S. E., & Crocker, J. (1981). Schematic bases of social information processing. In E. T. Higgins, C. P. Herman, & M. P. Zanna (Eds.), *Social cognition* (pp. 89-134). Hillsdale, NJ: Lawrence Erlbaum Associates.

Taylor, S. E., Wood, J. W., & Lichtman, R. R. (1983). It could be worse: Selective evaluation as a response to victimization. *Journal of Social Issues, 39*(2), 19-40.

Weisz, J. R., Rothbaum, F. M., & Blackburn, T. C. (1984). Standing out and standing in: The psychology of control in America and Japan. *American Psychologist, 39,* 955-969.

Wills, T. A. (1987). Downward comparison as a coping mechanism. In C. R. Snyder & C. E. Ford (Eds.), *Coping with negative life events* (pp. 243-268). New York: Plenum.

Wrubel, J., Benner, P., & Lazarus, R. S. (1981). Social competence from the perspective of stress and coping. In J. Wine & M. Singer (Eds.), *Social competence* (pp. 61-99). New York: Guilford.

17 Is it Coping or is it Growth? A Cognitive-Affective Model of Contentment in the Elderly[1]

Melvin J. Lerner
Monique A. M. Gignac
University of Waterloo

If we try to imagine what could be learned from studying the elderly, two characteristics might come readily to mind. The first is that the elderly possess more "wisdom" than younger members of our society. Having recently recognized the intriguing psychological aspects of this problem, a few investigators have engaged in creative preliminary efforts to define and understand what forms such wisdom might take (Baltes, Smith, Staudinger, & Sowarka, in press; Clayton & Birren, 1980; Dittmann-Kohli & Baltes, in press; Holliday & Chandler, 1986; Meacham, 1982). Other developmental theorists have avoided the difficult definitional problems posed by the concept of wisdom, by translating the elderly's potentially unique ways of viewing the world into theories of "postformal operational" thought processes (Arlin, 1975; Basseches, 1980; Commons, Richards, & Armon, 1984; Commons, Richards, & Kuhn, 1982; Labouvie-Vief, 1982; Riegel, 1973). Eventually, we will return to this special quality of the elderly and how we, somewhat indirectly, came upon our own theory of the wise elderly. But first, we will consider the second distinguishing characteristic, the elderly as society's quintessential victims, and their intriguing reactions to this victimization.

Aging in our society often implies a tragic scenario in which the elderly are increasingly victimized by social and biological processes until their progressive

[1]The development of this theory and the preparation of this chapter were supported in part by a "Population Aging" grant from the Social Sciences and Humanities Research Council of Canada (SSHRC) to Melvin J. Lerner (1982-1983), and a University of Waterloo administered SSHRC grant to M. J. Lerner and Monique Gignac (1988-1989). Michael Ross, Kenn Rubin, Nancy Adler, and many graduate students at the University of Waterloo, responded to an earlier version (Lerner, 1983) and thus helped to shape the ideas presented here.

deterioration is interrupted by death. Butler and Lewis (1977) portray this normal component of aging as one where:

> The elderly are confronted by [with] multiple losses, which may occur simultaneously; death of a partner, older friends, colleagues, relatives; decline of physical health and coming to terms with personal death; loss of status, prestige and participation in society; and for large numbers of the older population, additional burdens of marginal living standards. (p. 34)

Considering these deprived and deteriorating circumstances, we might expect to find the majority of elderly living out their remaining years as increasingly demoralized victims. However, although the evidence does indicate a slightly greater risk of becoming clinically depressed (Butler & Lewis, 1982; Kay & Bergmann, 1980), most elderly describe themselves as leading useful lives with surprisingly little anxiety and depression (Birren & Renner, 1980; Rosow, 1974; Tobin & Lieberman, 1976). Psychologists typically attribute this remarkable state of relative equanimity to the elderly's use of "functional illusions" (Tobin & Lieberman, 1976) or "working fictions" (Lazarus & Golden, 1981). In other words, the elderly achieve contentment, or at least avoid demoralization, by employing familiar defense mechanisms to deny their victimization. They find illusory reason to hope in spite of their inexorably deteriorating conditions (Pfeiffer, 1977; Rosow, 1974).

The observations of gerontologists, however, suggest an alternative image of at least some elderly who avoid depression and achieve a degree of contentment. Birren and Renner (1980) describe elderly who, rather than distorting or denying the painful realities of their lives, have an "inner structure that enables them to be strong yet flexible, feeling yet controlled, living in the present yet planning for tomorrow, and less needing to justify their past views and behavior" (p. 27). Kaufman (1986), in the course of her research, found elderly who integrate a wide range of experiences, unique situations, structural forces, values, cultural pathways, and knowledge of an entire life span to construct a current and viable identity.

Although these descriptions suggest the availability of an enriched, more completely integrated life as an alternative to avoidance and illusions, they leave unexplained the processes enabling the increasingly victimized elderly to arrive at this seemingly undefended peaceful state. Such an achievement would require a qualitative change in responding to the unalterable deterioration in virtually all aspects of their lives. Instead of avoiding demoralization through distortion or denial, the elderly would need to accept and frame those painful realities in a context which neutralizes the threat. But how is that possible? What psychological processes might account for this rather remarkable way of dealing with unalterable threats and losses?

PAIN, SUFFERING, AND EVALUATING PERSPECTIVES

The answer offered here begins with the recognition of a crucial difference between pain and suffering. Pain, a relatively simple and direct sensory experience, can become suffering or, alternatively, part of excitement or ecstasy, depending upon how the person views and interprets the pain and the meaning he or she gives it (Lazarus, 1982). For example, pains in child-birth or competitive sports can be an intrinsic, and even enhancing, aspect of the excitement experienced by a mother or competitor (Zillman, Katcher, & Milavsky, 1972). Similarly, people living under the most minimal and meager conditions, as assessed by objective criteria, will not feel deprived if they believe they are entitled to no more than what they presently have (Crosby, 1976; Gurr, 1968; Stouffer, Suchman, DeVinney, Star, & Williams, 1949). In effect, whether people's pains and losses lead to their experiencing suffering rather than a neutral or even positive reaction appears to depend upon their tacit judgment of what should be happening to them and of what is an appropriate, if not intrinsically desirable, fate for them.

The next question, then, is how do people decide whether a particular pain or loss is an appropriate fate for them? The answer, in general terms, is that people understand and evaluate their fates from a particular perspective or referent point (Folger, 1986; Suls & Miller, 1977). By adulthood, most people have a vast repertoire of perspectives available, derived from their culture, personal experiences, and comparison with particular others (Olson, Herman, & Zanna, 1986). In the course of their daily lives, people will typically adopt perspectives in response to the salient cues in each situation. However, they may also change perspectives, or referents, to facilitate important goals. Common examples of goals where a change in perspective might occur include maintaining self-esteem, being effective in the situation, and, of course, reducing stress and suffering (Suls & Miller, 1977; Taylor & Brown, 1988).

The research of Taylor and her colleagues (Taylor, 1983; Taylor, Wood, & Lichtman, 1983; Wood, Taylor, & Lichtman, 1985), conducted with women who were coming to terms with breast cancer, compellingly illustrates this process. Faced with the threat of disfigurement and possibly death, many of the patients eased their distress by comparing themselves with women who were worse off than they, a "downward comparison." Taylor et al. (1983) conclude:

> Under conditions of threat, the goal of the comparison process, namely to make one's self look good can be achieved by juggling ... either the comparison target or the comparison attribute. The point of course is that everyone is better off than someone as long as one picks the right dimension. (pp. 29-30)

This research (Taylor, 1983; Taylor et al., 1983) documented an important psychological effect: Realizing that one is better off than others reduces the suffering associated with having been unfairly victimized. Even more importantly, the findings describe a basic process linking emotions to cognitions. Any one individual can experience a range of emotional reactions to a terrible event, such as having cancer. A person's emotional reactions to the threat at any given time will depend upon the perspective he or she adopts. Furthermore, in response to an unalterable life crisis, people can and do alter their emotional reactions by changing their perspective in ways that make them feel better. This process of altering perspectives to find a relatively comforting view of one's fate provides a useful description of the dynamics underlying the effective use of "working fictions" or "functional illusions." However, a more careful consideration of how perspectives develop and appear in people's lives will provide a theoretical framework for understanding the achievement of contentment without distorting or denying the objectively deteriorating circumstances. In the next section, we will begin to develop this theoretical framework by considering the development of differing levels of knowing one's world as provided by social role taking and a psychological alternative to simply changing one's perspective.

COGNITIVE BASES OF EMOTIONAL REACTIONS: FROM PREOPERATIONAL TO SOCIAL ROLE TAKING

A considerable amount of research and theory in the area of cognitive development provides information concerning the origin and types of perspectives people adopt toward their world. Structural theorists, in particular, (Chandler & Boyes, 1982; Flavell, 1985; Flavell, Botkin, Fry, Wright, & Jarvis, 1968; Piaget & Inhelder, 1956, 1968) have described an orderly and cumulative development of levels of knowing. These include: (a) the direct experiencing and reacting to events in our world known as presymbolic, or sensorimotor reactions; (b) a symbolic level involving concrete operations where events and objects in one's world are categorized and classified, and (c) an ordered mental manipulation of the symbolic representations of events and objects. Here, a person engages in planful and reflective thought at the metarepresentational level of formal operations.

In the normal course of development, adults acquire the ability to employ formal operational thought processes in their planning and decision making. However, their reactions to many events continue to be influenced by sensorimotor cognitions such as direct and immediate response to smells, tastes, and the ugly or beautiful appearance of others (Dion, Berscheid, & Walster, 1972; Dion & Dion, 1987). In addition, routine interactions comprising most socially organized behavior often occur as virtually "mindless" acting out of scripted reactions to socially defined cues with some, but relatively little, involvement of formal operational thought. Getting dressed in the morning, driving to work, and having lunch in a restaurant provide just a few examples of this well scripted, "mindless" behavior (Langer, 1978; Langer, Blank, & Chanowitz, 1978; Rozin, Millman, & Nemeroff, 1986).

Apparently, though developed in an ordered cumulative process, earlier levels of knowing continue to appear in adults' reactions to typical everyday encounters (Bibace & Walsh, 1979; Riegel, 1973; Sinnott, 1984; Werner, 1948). This observation helps to explain the relation between people's rather automatic emotional reactions to critical events and their more dispassionate reasoned responses. Research, too, suggests that our emotional reactions are influenced in predictable ways not only by the content of the cognitive representation of an event, but also by the form or level of the construction. For example, when responding at the metarepresentational level the person can engage in a form of social role taking with the potential for radically different emotional consequences (Damon, 1977; Hoffman, 1983; Schachter & Singer, 1962).

As an illustration of the influence of levels of cognition, consider the following hypothetical example: An adult comes upon two children having a fight. One of them looks menacing and the other is crying, sobbing bitterly. At the preoperational level, the child's crying elicits a virtually automatic empathic reaction and an impulse to comfort the crying child (Hoffman, 1983). At the same time, the cues in the situation (menacing boy, crying girl) evoke prototypes of the aggressive boy persecuting the innocent little girl (concrete operations-symbolic level). As a consequence, the adult becomes angry and intends to punish the nasty harm-doer, the boy. However, most adults, instead of acting on these feelings, have the ability to decenter and view the situation from differing perspectives. Through role taking the boy's as well as the girl's perspectives, the adult might then discover the boy's intentions were to protect himself or retaliate for the girl's unprovoked prior assault. As a result of this formal operational analysis of the causal sequence, the adult's emotional reaction would almost certainly be different from one elicited solely by the cues of the girl's weeping or the boy's menacing stance.

All three reactions, empathic comforting of the girl, desire to punish the aggressive boy, and the more dispassionate understanding of the bases of the conflict, represent alternatives available to the adult emanating from levels of their cognitive construction of the event. However, the cognitive act of decentering and taking the perspectives of the various participants enables the adult to transcend the emotional reaction elicited by the girl's tears and the symbolic meaning associated with the menacing posture of the boy. The adult, without denying or distorting the validity of each perspective, and through role taking and then cognitively representing the various perspectives, can then integrate them to achieve a more complete picture of what had transpired.

This hypothetical example highlights a number of relevant points. Most adults, when in a critical, emotionally charged situation, have the ability to imaginally represent alternative perspectives, accept them as valid, but limited representations, and then achieve a systematically organized construction of the event. Secondly, adults' subsequent reactions, including their emotional responses, can differ appreciably from the responses emanating from any one of the perspectives involved in creating the composite image. Finally, adults can, and often do, alter their reactions to emotionally charged events by performing formal operations on a multiply represented array of relevant perspectives. In short-hand terms, this can be referred to as social role taking.

SOCIAL ROLE TAKING

To fully appreciate the psychological implications of this process, we have to consider again what occurs when people engage in social role taking. Through decentering and imaginally representing another perspective, people are able to recreate to some extent the experiential consequences emanating from that perspective. Decentering further places those experiences in systematic relation to other relevant ways of viewing and reacting to the same event. As a consequence, people generate a more encompassing cognitive representation of the event. How they subsequently think and feel about what has transpired and the participants involved, will evolve from their systematic integration of the composite perspectives. Most importantly, for our purposes, they recognize at some level of awareness, the possibility of multiple perspectives of the same event, and thus alternative ways of feeling, each of which can be a valid, but of necessity, only a limited part of reality. In this manner, adults are able to transcend stimulus-bound, egocentric, or social category-based reactions and achieve a fuller appreciation of the origins and meaning of other people's acts. The answer to the initial question of how people, especially those elderly undergoing inalterably deteriorating circumstances, can find contentment may be simply the extension of this same decentering, role taking process brought to bear on themselves and their own reactions.

Levels of Cognitive Construction and Emotional Reactions to Cancer

To describe this process of self-role taking and its relation to the more familiar defensive changes in perspectives, we will employ another hypothetical example, this time, an increasingly familiar crisis in our lives—the invasion of the body by a cancerous tumor. On the basis of what has been described thus far, we can assume that for most victims, all three levels of cognitive construction will appear sooner or later in the recognition and systematic appraisal of what it means to have a tumor (see Figure 17.1).

To begin, the level of direct sensorimotor experience may be triggered by cues emanating from direct palpation of an alien or deforming bulge in some part of the body. The sensation of a strange and recurring pain may have prompted that discovery. Although some decoding of sensory cues has taken place even by this point, the next level of abstraction (symbolic, concrete operations) appears in the integrating organization of those direct experiences in order to find an appropriately

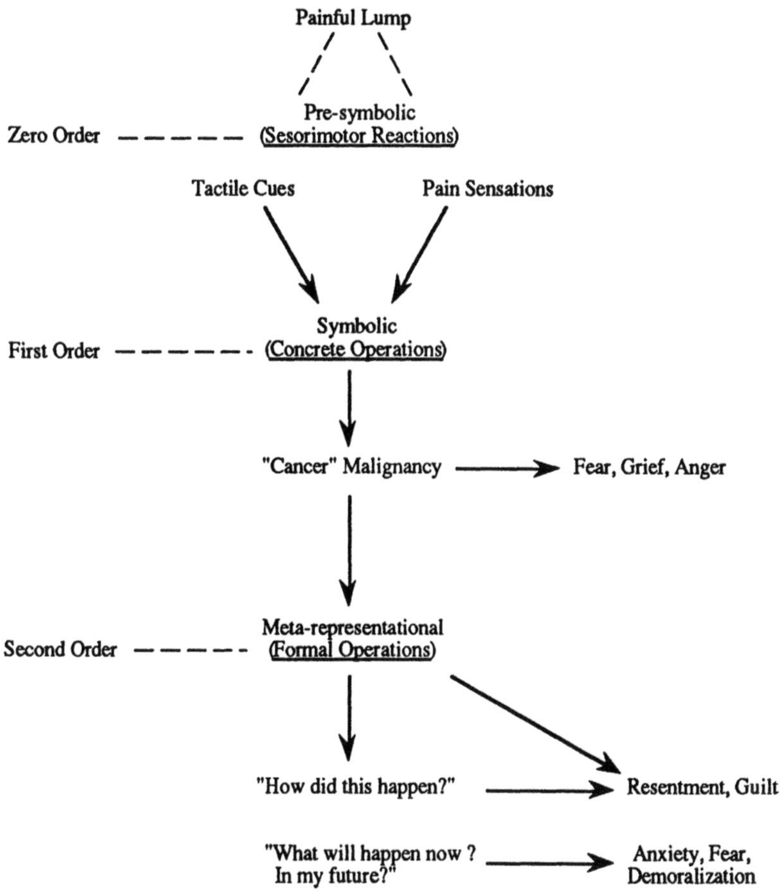

FIG. 17.1. Initial constructions of cancer: Levels of cognition and associated affect.

matching category or familiar descriptive label for what up to this point has been an aggregate of tactile and affective sensations. Once receiving the diagnosis or seriously entertaining the possibility of malignant cancer, the sufferer experiences a flood of associated emotions, characterized often by a combination of fear, anxiety, anger, and resentment.

These emotions elicited by the symbolic cue, the label of cancer, will eventually blend with others as victims undertake the metarepresentational analysis of what the cancerous growth means in their lives. Often this subsequent use of formal operations focuses on the attempt to generate a causal explanation (why me?) and to anticipate what the future holds (Bibace & Walsh, 1979). Negative emotions associated with this process may include guilt, grief, dread, and demoralization.

In brief, then, the initial reactions to the critical event probably include three levels of "knowing" the cancer and three associated sets of aversive emotional reactions, from the simplest rather direct experience of pain to the more complex anguished and grieving reactions that appear as the meaning of the event unfolds following the diagnostic labeling and thoughtful examination of what the label of cancer implies.

Thus far, the victim in this example has focused on the "event," reacting to the painful lump. His or her emotional reactions have emanated rather directly from their construction and understanding of the "cancer." But now the victim must deal with both the critical event, the cancer, and his or her powerfully aversive reactions to the cancer. Naturally, most people will attempt to remove the stressor and alleviate their painful emotional reactions by employing what Lazarus (Lazarus & Folkman, 1984) would term a "problem-focused" coping response. However, failing to eliminate the threat completely, as is the case with many of the inalterable losses facing the elderly, victims will turn to "emotion-focused" coping responses. As the stressor cannot be removed, victims have no alternative but to put their major efforts into reducing or eliminating the emotional trauma created by the inalterable crisis.

The most commonly employed emotion-focused coping responses are understandable manifestations of the perspectives victims take with respect to their emotional reactions to the painful lump, cancer, and threat to their future. For example, at the simplest cognitive level, victims can find relief from all of the aversive states—pain, suffering, and anxiety—by simply not acknowledging the presence of the cancer; by blotting it out of their consciousness (see Column 1, Figure 17.2). Personality theorists would refer to these *sensorimotor, presymbolic* coping responses as denial, repression, suppression, or simply avoiding thinking about the cancer by finding compelling distractions. Considerable evidence confirms the ability of these presymbolic coping responses to relieve some degree of the pain, threat, and dread, at least in the short term (Lazarus & Folkman, 1984).

The stress and coping literature also contains many examples of victims who find relief from their suffering by changing the meaning or the label of the crisis. These represent responses at the *symbolic* level of *concrete operations* (Bulman & Wortman, 1977; Glick, Weiss, & Parkes, 1974; Lazarus & Folkman, 1984; Taylor, 1983; Taylor et al., 1983; see Column 2, Figure 17.2). Relabeling their fate now allows people to either minimize their suffering or find compensating benefits. The paraplegic accident victims in Bulman and Wortman's research (1977) may have used this coping mechanism when they relabeled their their paralysis as a transforming benefit in their lives. Despite the severity of their disability, many of these people commented that this was "the best thing that could have happened," it "brought me closer to God," and it "taught me the error of my ways" (Bulman & Wortman, 1977).

Initial Constructions of the Crisis: Levels of Cognition and Affect	Self-Reflexive Cognitive Reactions: Pre-Symbolic Sensori-Motor (Denials)[a]	Symbolic Concrete Operations (Defensive-Alter Perspectives)[b]	Metarepresentation Formal Operations ("Bracket and Comment Upon")
Pre-Symbolic Direct Experience Pain	Avoid direct Experience	"Minimize" by Comparative Redefinig: Pain and Loss	Detach - Separate "Self" from "Pain"
Symbolic Label-Categorize Grief - Suffering	Denial of "Event"	"Minimize" Suffering; Find Compensating Benefits	Recognize and be Released from Perspective-Affect Association
Metarepresentation Cause and Implications Fear - Demoralization	Deny - Avoid "Implications"	Discover Future Compensations and Relief	Reintegration of Past: Control over Future Affect

a See Lazarus and Golden (1982) for more complete description.
b See Taylor (1983) and Silver and Wortman (1981) for more complete description.

FIG. 17.2. Summary table of emotion-focused reactions to life crises: Levels of cognitive construction.

The coping literature also includes reports of many victims who coped with an inalterable crisis by reinterpreting its meaning and future implications. Their responses are best described as being at the *metarepresentational level of formal operations* (see Column 3, Figure 17.2). Many people afflicted with cancer, permanently disabling accidents, or the sudden death of their child generated more comfortable causal explanations for their suffering, while others found compensating benefits by redefining what the future held for them, including for some, the after-life (Bulman & Wortman, 1977; Glick et al., 1974; Lazarus & Folkman, 1984; Taylor, 1983; Taylor et al., 1983).

As Taylor (1983) and others (Lazarus & Folkman, 1984) have described, when faced with an inalterable crisis, people selectively adapt their coping responses like avoidance, denial, redefining, downward comparison, generating faith in the future, etc., to whichever response or combination of responses is most available and effective in reducing their stress. Quite understandably then, other things being equal, the next crisis, illness, or loss will elicit a similar set of coping responses. Victims will avoid, and/or redefine the crisis until the pain, anguish, and suffering are rendered tolerable, if not completely eliminated. Not surprisingly, this habitual and continually reinforced reliance on familiar defenses prevents the appearance of other ways of dealing with crises.

SELF-ROLE TAKING AND THE GROWTH PROCESS. APPRECIATING THE INFLUENCE OF PERSPECTIVES ON ONE'S EMOTIONAL REACTIONS

But what about the process whereby people, especially the elderly, achieve contentment without distorting the reality of their circumstances by relabeling or denying them? How might that occur? The key cognitive act involved in this developmental process is the ability to decenter as in social role taking. The person sequentially adopts various perspectives with respect to the same phenomenon, imaginally represents these alternatives, cognitively brackets and comments upon them, recognizing that each produces a valid but limited view of the event, and finally, generates a systematic ordering and integrating of these various perspectives (Chandler & Boyes, 1982; Flavell, 1985; Piaget & Inhelder, 1956, 1968).

Adults, of course, are capable of this level of metarepresentational appreciation of others' behavior, just as they are capable of social role taking. However, because of the influence of social custom, personal habit, and possibly need, they rarely focus upon their own reactions long enough to engage in the sequential decentering needed to appreciate the influences that determined their cognitive-affective reactions to an inalterable crisis. Although victims of tragic events will often ask themselves "How did this happen and what does this mean in my life?", they seldom experience the transforming consequences that follow from self-reflectively examining how their own answer determines their emotional state. Psychologically, this requires stepping back and appreciating how their emotional responses to a tragic event—their grief, suffering, fears, or even sense of well-being—are generated by a particular perspective or way of viewing and evaluating their fate. Such recognition may require the relatively contiguous altering of perspectives with their attendant changes in emotional response to the same event.

Let us return to our example to illustrate this process. What if the cancer victim, Mrs. V., realizes that given the comparatively terrible fate of the woman down the hall, Mrs. D., her own suffering could have been much worse. Viewing her own fate from this "downward comparison" provides some genuine, welcome relief for Mrs. V. Then, while Mrs. V. is feeling somewhat better, Mrs. U. enters the room announcing she has had a close scare but the doctors have found no cancer at all. As a result, she is now happily off to celebrate with friends. Quite likely, the news of Mrs. U.'s good fortune jolts Mrs. V. into viewing herself and her fate from the perspective of someone who is much better off. She is automatically reminded of how unjust and terrible it all is. Mrs V. now feels much worse. Taking our example to the extreme, let's assume Mrs. V. is then visited by Mrs. M., whom she has admired for years, in part because she seems to radiate an inner strength and a sense of peace and contentment. Mrs. M. informs her that she, too, had been diagnosed as having a similar cancer, and that it has transformed her, enabling her to experience the beauty of her life as never before. Her coming to terms with death freed her to enjoy her remaining life. Now, Mrs. V., vicariously caught up in this more optimistic, almost euphoric, way of viewing her fate, feels much better again.

Conceivably, the contiguous juxtaposition of these three events with their vividly differing emotional experiences could provide the occasion for Mrs. V. to decenter and imaginally represent all three perspectives. This self-role taking would allow her to recognize what they all have in common, in other words, to cognitively bracket these three experiences. They all provided a different perspective and way of viewing the same event. Each perspective, the downward comparison, then the upward comparison, then the optimistic model resulted in different evaluation and emotional reaction to having cancer. The bracketing, or recognizing the common element, created the conditions for Mrs. V. to appreciate how the perspective she adopted, not the cancer, determined her degree of distress or contentment. The full appreciation of this recognition provided the opportunity and, in fact, the first step toward contentment. It would then be possible for Mrs. V. to generalize this recognition to other sources of worry, grief, regrets, and anxieties. They, no less than her reactions to the cancer, were generated by the perspectives she adopted toward a particular crisis or failure.

In summary, until they recognize the connection between the perspective taken and their emotional reactions, people automatically take on and alter perspectives, defining and then redefining the meaning of events in ways that are most familiar and comfortable. However, having engaged in self-role taking people should be able to find relief from the most frightening perspectives by stepping back and appreciating several different perspectives and their emotional concomitants. They can then have more control over their experiences and freedom from the dictates of any one way of viewing present or past "realities" in their lives. Armed with this control and sense of freedom, people should be able to react more directly and openly to the events happening around them without unconsciously imposing evaluative standards.

Finally, having realized and appreciated the availability of various ways of viewing what has happened or may happen and how these perspectives have predictably different emotional consequences, the person will eventually decide that not all perspectives are "equal" or "valid" for him or her. Some will appear foolish, bizarre, immoral, strange, or uncomfortable because they violate the person's values or are alien to his or her self-concept. For the same reasons, other perspectives will appear right, comfortable, and obviously true and good. The ability to discover which perspectives are "best" for them will enable people to more explicitly articulate who they are in terms of what values, goals, and ways of viewing themselves and the world they wish to maintain, or wish to change. This psychological process of self-discovery and affirmation has been termed "recentering" in contrast to the relativism acquired through the earlier decentering and self-role taking (Chandler, 1975; Turner, 1973).

At this point in the developmental process, people have reexamined, evaluated, modified, and reaffirmed who they are, what they believe is true and good, and thus what perspectives they will and will not adopt. No longer dictated to by imposed perspectives, they now are able to recognize the choices available to them and to affirm their own identity when they choose how to view what is happening to them and around them. As well, they can now accept the personal validity of others' perspectives and choices. This process may not always eventuate in less grief, suffering, and anxiety in response to any new crisis, but people will know their chosen experiences, the painful even more than the pleasurable, are an act of affirmation or reaffirmation of their selves. They are no longer helpless victims, but are active respondents to the events confronting them.

Why Is Self-Role Taking Less Likely to Develop at Younger Ages?

Given the common development of social role taking and formal operational thought usually by adolescence or early adulthood, it is reasonable to wonder why this form of self-role taking seems to occur so rarely and has been principally identified among the elderly. A plausible answer to this question may be found in the social milieu in which this development occurs. Social institutions in contemporary society—family, occupation, citizen, community member, and so on—provide each member with consensually supported, well elaborated perspectives. As described earlier, for the most part, people automatically adopt these perspectives and act out the behaviors appropriate to functioning in their routine activities. How we behave at breakfast, how we get to the office or school, what we wear, and how we behave toward others are all, for the most part, automatic, "mindless" reactions to a series of cues and symbols.

In effect, most of the time, people function at the presymbolic level or symbolic level of concrete operations (Dion & Dion, 1987; Langer, 1978). Those periods during which they engage in formal operations are limited in time and scope. When forced by circumstances, surprises, disappointments, or opportunities to consider alternative perspectives or to arrive at decisions, people typically adopt a perspective they believe will enable them to perform more effectively or maintain their self-esteem. They may even simply adopt the most situationally salient perspective. All of these, except for the attempt to maintain one's self-esteem, are directed toward dealing with the world out there (Olson et al., 1986; Suls & Miller, 1977). The need to operate effectively on the environment becomes the predominant expectation and the overriding demand that impinges on adolescents and adults in our society (Lefcourt, 1982; White, 1974).

Adopting perspectives to meet the demands for effective performance and to maintain one's self-esteem are an appropriate, if not inevitable, means of adapting to the social environment with which people are confronted. However, although these perspectives were functional for building a career and being a responsible parent, they may have inhibited the development of the form of self-role taking necessary for producing the next possible stage of development.

The elderly, with more time and reason to reflect upon the crises in their lives, are in a better position to arrive at effective self-role taking. Our social system requires the elderly, in increasingly compelling terms, to relinquish attempts to accomplish and be effective actors in their world. These factors, together with the inalterable nature of their physical crises and personal losses, may lead the elderly to seek alternatives to the most familiar means of denying or distorting the nature of their crises. Unfortunately, however, given the strength of habit, even under these propitious circumstances, we cannot expect to find a great number of elderly who have fully developed the processes of self-role taking and subsequent self-affirmation. And yet, however rare, their presence provides a valuable opportunity to study developmental processes potentially available to people at all ages.

SUMMARY

The developmental process presented here differs somewhat from prior models of adult development (Baltes et al., in press; Dittmann-Kohli & Baltes, in press; Labouvie-Vief, 1982; Riegel, 1973; Ryff, 1982) in that we took a specific intriguing problem as the focus of our theoretical efforts: how to explain the psychological processes enabling some elderly to find contentment without distorting or denying the increasing pains and losses in their lives. The search for that process led, initially, to the psychology of perspectives and levels of cognitive constructions with their associated affective consequences as exhibited in social role taking. A decentering and social role taking explanation of how people evaluate and react emotionally to the behavior of others was extended to provide a theoretical description of self-role taking in response to the crises and losses endemic to the lives of the elderly. By identifying the cognitive underpinnings of the familiar emotion-focused coping strategies we demonstrated their relation to the appearance *self-role taking*. An elaboration of the psychological consequences of self-role taking provided the explanatory solution to the riddle of the contented but undefended elderly victims. Through self-role taking, victims recognize and understand how their own perspectives determine their emotions, that is, whether they suffer, are indifferent, or are pleased. This recognition enables them to oversee their ways of viewing what has transpired and thus gain control over their emotional lives. Ultimately, they are able to reassess and choose those perspectives which express their identity. At this point in the developmental process, they are able to accept pains and losses as nothing more than direct experiences, unless and until they choose to react with suffering or grief as an expression of their personal identity. As Neugarten (1977) describes so compellingly:

> In old age there are also the triumphs of survivorship; the recognition that one has savored a wide range of experiences and therefore knows about life in ways no younger person can know: The knowledge that in having lived through physical and psychological pain, one recovers and can deal also with the contingencies that lie ahead: and a sense that one is now the possessor and conservator of the eternal truths ... With the passage of time, life becomes more, not less complex: it becomes enriched, not impoverished. (Neugarten, 1977, pp. 890-891)

Hopefully, this theoretical model, intended to explain how such enrichment may occur, will promote future research into these processes both in the laboratory and the field. One such study, being undertaken by the present authors, would undertake a careful analysis of the cognitive styles of the contented elderly, with a particular focus on discovering whether those who achieve contentment through the elaborate use of defenses can be reliably distinguished from those who have "grown" through self-role taking to a state of contentment. The latter should be considerably more spontaneous, open, and accepting of others. Similarly, it should be possible to examine, even experimentally to create, the decentering process that is at the core of the self-role taking described in this theory.

REFERENCES

Arlin, P. K. (1975). Cognitive development in adulthood: A fifth stage? *Developmental Psychology, 11,* 602-606.

Baltes, P. B., Smith, J., Staudinger, U. M., & Sowarka, D. (in press). Wisdom: One facet of successful aging? In M. Perlmutter (Ed.), *Late-life potential.* Washington, DC: Gerontological Society of America.

Basseches, M. (1980). Dialectical schemata: A framework for the empirical study of the development of dialectical thinking. *Human Development, 23,* 400-421.

Bibace, R., & Walsh, M. B. (1979). Developmental stages in children's conceptions of illness. In G. C. Stone, F. Cohen, & N. E. Adler (Eds.), *Health psychology* (pp. 285-302). San Francisco, CA: Jossey-Bass.

Birren, J. E., & Renner, V. J. (1980). Concepts and issues of mental health and aging. In J. E. Birren & R. B. Sloane (Eds.), *Handbook of mental health and aging* (pp. 3-33). Englewood Cliffs, NJ: Prentice-Hall.

Bulman, R. J., & Wortman, C. B. (1977). Attributions of blame and coping in the "real world": Severe accident victims react to their own lot. *Journal of Personality and Social Psychology, 35,* 351-363

Butler, R. N., & Lewis, M. I. (1977). *Aging and mental health: Positive psychosocial approaches.* Saint Louis: Mosby.

Butler, R. N., & Lewis, M. I. (1982). *Aging and mental health: Positive psychosocial and biomedical approaches.* Saint Louis: Mosby.

Chandler, M. J. (1975). Relativism and the problem of epistemological loneliness. *Human Development, 18,* 171-180.

Chandler, M. J., & Boyes, M. (1982). Social-cognitive development. In B. B. Wolman (Ed.), *Handbook of developmental psychology* (pp. 387-402). Englewood Cliffs, NJ: Prentice-Hall.

Clayton, V. P., & Birren, J. E. (1980). The development of wisdom across the life span: A re-examination of an ancient topic. In P. B. Baltes & O. G. Brim (Eds.), *Life-span development and behavior* (Vol. 3, pp. 103-135). New York: Academic Press.

Commons, M. L., Richards, F. A., & Armon, C. (Eds.). (1984). *Beyond formal operations.* New York: Praeger.

Commons, M. L., Richards, F. A., & Kuhn, D. (1982). Meta-systematic reasoning: A case for a level of systematic reasoning beyond Piaget's stage of formal operations. *Child Development, 53,* 1058-1069.

Crosby, F. A. (1976). A model of egoistical relative deprivation. *Psychological Review, 83,* 85-113.

Damon, W. (1977). *The social world of the child.* San Francisco: Jossey-Bass.

Dion, K. K., Berscheid, E., & Walster, E. (1972). What is beautiful is good. *Journal of Personality and Social Psychology, 24,* 285-290.

Dion, K. L., & Dion, K. K. (1987). Belief in a just world and physical attractiveness stereotyping. *Journal of Personality and Social Psychology, 52,* 775-780.

Dittmann-Kohli, F., & Baltes, P. B. (in press). Toward a neo-functionalist conception of adult development: Wisdom as a prototypical case of intellectual growth. In C. Alexander & E. Langer (Eds.), *Beyond formal operations: Alternative endpoints of human development.* New York: Oxford University Press.

Flavell, J. H. (1985). *Cognitive development.* Englewood Cliffs, NJ: Prentice-Hall.

Flavell, J. H., Botkin, P. I., Fry, C. C., Wright, J. W., & Jarvis, P. G. (1968). *The development of role-taking and communication skills in children.* New York: Wiley.

Folger, R. (1986). A referent cognitions theory of relative deprivation. In J. M. Olson, C. P. Herman, & M. Zanna (Eds.), *Relative deprivation and social comparison: The Ontario Symposium* (Vol. 4, pp. 35-36). Hillsdale, NJ: Erlbaum.

Glick, I. O., Weiss, R. S., & Parkes, C. M. (1974). *The first year of bereavement.* New York: Wiley.

Gurr, T. R. (1968). A causal model of civil strife: A comparative analysis using new indices. *American Political Science Review, 62,* 1104-1124.

Hoffman, M. L. (1983). Developmental synthesis of affect and cognition and its implications for altruistic motivation. In W. Damon (Ed.), *Social and personality development: Essays on the growth of the child* (pp. 258-277). New York: Norton.

Holliday, S. G., & Chandler, M. J. (1986). *Wisdom: Explorations in adult competence*. Basel: Karger.

Kaufman, S. R. (1986). *The ageless self*. Madison, Wisconsin: University of Wisconsin Press.

Kay, D. W. K., & Bergmann, K. (1980). Epidemiology of mental disorders among the aged in the community. In J. E. Birren & R. B. Sloane (Eds.), *Handbook of aging and mental health* (pp. 34-56). Englewood Cliffs, NJ: Prentice-Hall.

Labouvie-Vief, G. (1982). Dynamic development and mature autonomy. *Human Development, 25*, 161-191.

Langer, E. J. (1978). Rethinking the role of thought in social interaction. In J. Harvey, W. Ickes, & R. Kidd (Eds.), *New directions in attribution research* (Vol. 2, pp. 36-58). Hillsdale, NJ: Lawrence Erlbaum Associates.

Langer, E. J., Blank, A., & Chanowitz, B. (1978). The mindlessness of ostensibly thoughtful action: The role of "placebic" information in interpersonal interaction. *Journal of Personality and Social Psychology, 36*, 635-642.

Lazarus, R. S. (1982). Thoughts on the relations between emotion and cognition. *American Psychologist, 9*, 1019-1024.

Lazarus, R. S., & Folkman, S. (1984). *Stress, appraisal, and coping*. New York: Springer.

Lazarus, R. S., & Golden, G. Y. (1981). The function of denial in stress, coping, and aging. In J. L. McGaugh & S. K. Kiesler (Eds.), *Aging: Biology and behavior* (pp. 283-307). New York: Academic Press.

Lefcourt, H. (1982). *Locus of control: Current trends in theory and research*. Hillsdale, NJ: Erlbaum.

Lerner, M. J. (1983). *Coping and growth in old age: Social cognitive approach to life-span development*. Report to Social Sciences and Humanities Research Council of Canada.

Meacham, J. A. (1982). Wisdom and the context of knowledge: Knowing that one doesn't know. In D. Kuhn & J. A. Meacham (Eds.), *On the development of developmental psychology* (pp. 111-134). Basel: Karger.

Neugarten, B. L. (1977). Personality and aging. In J. E. Birren & K. W. Schaie (Eds.), *Handbook of the psychology of aging* (pp. 626-649). New York: Van Nostrand Reinhold.

Olson, J. M., Herman, C. P., & Zanna, M. P. (Eds.). (1986). *Relative deprivation and social comparison: The Ontario Symposium* (Vol. 4). Hillsdale, NJ: Erlbaum.

Pfeiffer, E. (1977). Psychopathology and social pathology. In J. E. Birren & K. W. Schaie (Eds.), *Handbook of the psychology of aging* (pp. 650-671). New York: Van Nostrand Reinhold.

Piaget, J., & Inhelder, B. (1956). *The child's conception of space*. London: Routledge and Keagan Paul.

Piaget, J., & Inhelder, B. (1968). *The psychology of the child*. New York: Basic Books.

Riegel, K. F. (1973). Dialectic operations: The final period of cognitive development. *Human Development, 16*, 346-370.

Rosow, I. (1974). Socialization structures in old age. In I. Rosow (Ed.), *Socialization to old age* (pp. 120-148). Berkeley: University of California Press.

Rozin, P., Millman, L., & Nemeroff, C. (1986). Operation of the laws of sympathetic magic in disgust and other domains. *Journal of Personality and Social Psychology, 50*, 703-712.

Ryff, C. D. (1982). Successful aging: A developmental approach. *The Gerontologist, 22*, 209-214.

Schachter, S., & Singer, J. E. (1962). Cognitive, social, and physiological determinants of emotional state. *Psychological Review, 69*, 379-399.

Sinnott, J. D. (1984). Postformal reasoning: The relativistic stage. In M. L. Commons, F. A. Richards, & C. Armon (Eds.), *Beyond formal operations: Late adolescent and adult cognitive development* (pp. 298-325). New York: Praeger.

Stouffer, S. A., Suchman, E. A., DeVinney, L. C., Star, S. A., & Williams, R. M. (1949). *The American soldier: Adjustment during army life* (Vol. 1). Princeton, NJ: Princeton University Press.

Suls, J. M., & Miller, R. L. (Eds.). (1977). *Social comparison processes: Theoretical and empirical perspectives*. Washington, DC : Hemisphere.

Taylor, S. E. (1983). Adjustment to threatening events: A theory of cognitive adaptation. *American Psychologist, 11,* 1161-1173.
Taylor, S. E., & Brown, J. D. (1988). Illusion and well-being: A social psychological perspective on mental health. *Psychological Bulletin, 103,* 193-210.
Taylor, S. E., Wood, J. V., & Lichtman, R. R. (1983). It could be worse: Selective evaluation as a response to victimization. *Journal of Social Issues, 39*(2), 19-40.
Tobin, S., & Lieberman, M. (1976). *Last home for the aged.* San Francisco: Jossey-Bass.
Turner, T. (1973). Piaget's structuralism. *American Anthropologist, 75,* 351-373.
Werner, H. (1948). *Comparative psychology of mental development.* New York: International Universities Press.
White, R. W. (1974). Strategies of adaptation: An attempt at systematic description. In G. V. Coelho, D. A. Hamburg, & J. E. Adams (Eds.), *Coping and adaptation* (pp. 47-68). New York: Basic Books.
Wood, J. V., Taylor, S. E., & Lichtman, R. R. (1985). Social comparison in adjustment to breast cancer. *Journal of Personality and Social Psychology, 49,* 1169-1183.
Zillman, D., Katcher, A. H., & Milavsky, B. (1972). Excitation transfer from physical excitation to subsequent aggressive behavior. *Journal of Experimental Social Psychology, 8,* 247-259.

V Searching for Protective Factors

18 Reconsidering Assumptions About Coping With Loss: An Overview of Current Research

Camille B. Wortman
State University of New York

Roxane Cohen Silver
University of California

In this chapter, we provide an overview of our research program on how people cope with sudden, irrevocable losses. Irrevocable losses are those life events involving permanent change, and over which we have little, if any, control. In particular, our research has focused on how people come to terms with serious physical disability (see, e.g., Bulman & Wortman, 1977; Silver, 1982), and the death of a spouse or child (Downey, Silver, Wortman, & Hermann, 1990; Lehman, Wortman, & Williams, 1987). We believe that such events share a number of characteristics that make their study particularly interesting. Permanent losses often disrupt a person's hopes and plans for the future (cf. Silver & Wortman, 1980). Such losses also challenge people's beliefs and assumptions about themselves and their world (Janoff-Bulman & Frieze, 1983; Wortman, 1983). In our judgment, such losses provide an excellent arena in which to study basic processes of stress and adaptation to change, in order to enrich theoretical development in this rich and complex area.

We begin this chapter by tracing the development of theoretical ideas that we have used in studying loss events. We will describe three very different theoretical approaches to the study of loss: the learned helplessness model, stage models of grief and loss, and the stress and coping model, and we will consider the advantages and disadvantages of each. In so doing, we will illustrate how our own theoretical perspective on loss events has changed over the past decade.

Of course, the test of a good theory is whether it can account for data concerning how people respond to major losses in their lives. We next summarize two longitudinal studies that were conducted to test our theoretical ideas: a study on coping with physical disability as a result of a serious spinal cord injury, and a study on coping with the sudden, unexpected loss of an infant as a result of Sudden Infant Death Syndrome.

In each of these studies, we focused on respondents' early emotional reactions to the loss, and how these reactions changed over time. To our surprise, the findings we obtained did not fit neatly into any of the theoretical models that have been advanced to date. One such finding was the prevalence of positive emotions, such as happiness, following a major loss. A second, parallel finding was that many of the respondents we interviewed did not seem to be as devastated by the loss, initially, as we might have expected. Since obtaining these findings, we have carefully examined our own, as well as others', data in an effort to understand their theoretical significance.

Taken together, these data suggest the need for a careful re-examination of current theoretical perspectives on reactions to irrevocable outcomes. In the concluding section of the paper, we highlight the theoretical questions raised by the findings. We then briefly describe two prospective studies of reactions to loss that have been designed to clarify the theoretical questions raised by our earlier work. Finally, we spell out the implications of our analysis for treatment and interventions for those who have endured losses.

DEVELOPMENT OF OUR THEORETICAL PERSPECTIVE

Initial Theoretical Orientation: The Learned Helplessness Model

As social psychologists, we have been interested in reactions to uncontrollable outcomes, including irrevocable losses, since our graduate school days. The discipline of social psychology has devoted considerable attention to understanding reactions to outcomes that are stressful or unpleasant. At that time, the majority of those studies were conducted in laboratory settings, and focused on reactions to such stressors as noise bursts, electric shocks, and failure on problem-solving tasks (see, e.g., Glass & Singer, 1972). Most of these studies have been conducted to test predictions from the learned helplessness model developed by Seligman and his associates (see, e.g., Abramson, Seligman, & Teasdale, 1978). This model had its origins in Seligman's work on Pavlovian fear conditioning with infrahuman species, where it was found that exposure to uncontrollable aversive stimulation subsequently interferes with the acquisition of escape-avoidance learning. If naive dogs are placed in a two-compartment shuttle box, they quickly learn to jump from one compartment to the other and thus avoid electric shocks. However, this is not the case for dogs who have previously received uncontrollable electric shocks. These dogs are very slow to learn to avoid or escape the shocks. They seem to give up and passively accept as much shock as the experimenter chooses to give. On the basis of these studies, Seligman and his associates proposed that exposure to uncontrollable outcome results in learned helplessness. The organism is said to have learned that its outcomes are not contingent on its responses. According to Seligman, this state is characterized by a motivational deficit and passivity, thereby interfering with subsequent learning that one's behavior can influence one's outcomes (Seligman, Maier, & Soloman, 1971).

When investigators began testing the model on human subjects, the results were inconsistent. Exposure to insoluble problems or uncontrollable noise bursts or shocks did not always result in passivity, performance decrements, or depressed mood, as the model would predict (see Miller & Norman, 1979, for a review). Over the years, there have been many reformulations of the original model, the most important of which was proposed by Abramson et al. (1978). These investigators argued that the nature of the helplessness effects depends on the attributions of causality that a person makes when confronted with an uncontrollable outcome. They maintained that attributions can be categorized according to three orthogonal dimensions: internality, stability, and globality. They predicted that attributions to internal factors (e.g., "I'm stupid") are characterized by loss of self-esteem, while attributions to external factors (e.g., "These problems are impossible") are not. Attributions to stable factors (e.g., "I was mugged because the streets of New York are never safe") are hypothesized to produce greater subsequent performance deficits than attributions to unstable factors (e.g., "I was mugged because I was unlucky"). Attributions to global factors, or those which occur across many situations (e.g., "My business failed because I am completely incompetent") should lead to deficits which generalize further than attributions to more specific factors (e.g., "My business failed because it was in the wrong location").

What are the implications of this theoretical approach for the study of reactions to irrevocable losses? In our view, the most significant feature of this model is that it suggests a theoretical mechanism through which exposure to a loss event could result in subsequent difficulties. The basic underlying idea is that exposure to uncontrollable outcomes alters people's beliefs about themselves and their ability to influence their environment. Of course, in the original laboratory research on which the model is based, subjects were exposed to several trials of uncontrollable stimulation. Is this theory applicable to loss events that are experienced outside the laboratory, like disability and death? In such cases, people encounter a single, irrevocable event that is monumental in its implications. To what extent does losing a spouse alter a person's beliefs about his or her ability to influence future outcomes, and thus result in decreased persistence or passivity in the face of later goals? We have always felt that this was an intriguing possibility—one deserving of serious research attention (see Silver, Wortman, & Klos, 1982).

As we continued our work within this theoretical tradition, however, we became aware of a number of limitations. First, the model focuses exclusively on the conditions under which exposure to uncontrollable outcomes leads to depression. In 1980, we completed a systematic review of studies examining emotional reactions to stressful life events (Silver & Wortman, 1980). This review provided clear evidence that among those who encounter a major loss, such as the death of their spouse, anxiety is also a common reaction. Moreover, anger is also experienced following many major life events. We felt that ideally, a theoretical model should incorporate a broad spectrum of emotional reactions. Second, those working within the learned helplessness paradigm have focused their attention on determining when individuals continue their efforts to solve a particular problem, and when they give up. Intrapsychic coping mechanisms, such as denying the problem, or interpreting it in a more positive light, have received limited attention (see Wortman & Dintzer, 1978). Finally, the model has attempted to identify the conditions under which exposure to uncontrollable outcomes results in depression. In understanding reactions to irrevocable loss, we have come to feel that this may be the wrong question. In our judgment, a much more important issue concerns the process of adaptation or recovery. How do individuals move from a state of helplessness or depression toward recovery and resolution of the loss?

Theories of Grief and Loss: Stage Models of Adaptation

Because of these limitations in the learned helplessness model, we began to search for a theoretical framework that would be more appropriate for understanding reactions to major, irrevocable losses. Through a careful and systematic review of available work, we learned that most investigators who had focused on such losses had adopted a theoretical framework involving stages of emotional response (Silver & Wortman, 1980). One theoretical model that has been extremely influential is the attachment model of grief originally developed by Bowlby (1961, 1973, 1980). In this formulation, Bowlby drew heavily from psychodynamic thought, from the developmental literature on young children's reactions to separation, and from work on the mourning behavior of animals. Bowlby maintained that when close affectional bonds are threatened, powerful attachment behaviors are activated, such as clinging, crying, and angry protest. He argued that bereavement can be conceptualized as an unwilling separation that gives rise to many forms of attachment behavior.

Drawing in part from these theoretical notions and in part from available research, Bowlby (1980) maintained that effective mastery of bereavement involves passing through four stages, or phases, of mourning. Initially, individuals are expected to go through a phase of numbness or feeling stunned. This is followed by a phase of yearning or searching, where the bereaved may show manifestations of a strong urge to find, recover, and reunite with the lost person. During this period, the individual may experience anger as a result of the loss, as well as general restlessness and irritability. Bowlby argued that, over time, those behaviors aimed at re-establishing the attachment bond usually cease, and individuals enter the third phase of the mourning process. According to Bowlby, this phase is characterized by giving up the attempts to recover the deceased. The bereaved person typically experiences depression, and feels a disinclination to look to the future. Eventually, individuals enter the final phase, in which they are able to break down their attachment to the lost loved one and start to establish new ties to others. In this phase of reorganization or recovery, there is a gradual return of former interests.

In the literature, a number of other theorists also have proposed models which, like Bowlby's, involve phases or stages of reactions to loss (see, e.g., Horowitz, 1976, 1985). Among health care providers and lay persons, perhaps the most well-known model is the one proposed by Kubler-Ross (1969) in her highly influential book, *On Death and Dying*. Although offered to explain dying patients' reactions to their own impending death, Kubler-Ross identified five stages of emotional response to anticipated loss: denial, anger, bargaining, depression, and ultimately, acceptance. Each year, Kubler-Ross's stage models have been taught, in her estimation, in 125,000 courses in colleges, seminaries, medical schools, hospitals, and social work institutions (Rosenbaum, 1982).

Over the past two decades, descriptions of stage models of reactions to loss have also appeared in numerous textbooks and articles written by and for physicians, nurses, therapists, social workers, clergymen, and patients and their families (see Silver & Wortman, 1980). As a result, these models have become firmly entrenched among health care professionals. There is evidence that professionals sometimes use the stages as a kind of yardstick to assess progress and evaluate how a given individual is doing. In our view, the consequences of applying the stage models in this manner are not always positive. As Pattison (1977) has written concerning the care of the dying: "... dying persons who did not follow these stages were labeled 'deviant,' 'neurotic,' or 'pathological dyers.' Clinical personnel became angry at patients who did not move from one stage to the next ... I began to observe professional personnel demand that the dying person 'die in the right way.'" (p. 304).

Given the strong beliefs in such models by health care providers, we were interested in whether there was any empirical evidence to support the view that people go through stages. Over the years, we have systematically reviewed dozens of studies on coping with stressful life events (Silver & Wortman, 1980; Wortman & Silver, 1989). While there have been few studies that have systematically assessed several affective reactions following a major loss, the available data do not support, and sometimes contradict, the stage approach. A close examination of these studies suggests that there is considerable variability in the intensity of the emotional response, in the kinds of specific emotions that are experienced, and in their sequence (see Wortman & Silver, 1987, for a more detailed discussion).

It should be noted that stage models of emotional response are difficult to test empirically. Unless individuals are monitored quite frequently, it is impossible to determine whether they are not showing a particular emotional reaction because they have already "passed through" this stage, or whether they have not yet arrived at it. Moreover, many of the stage models are presented in such a way that they are difficult to disconfirm. Some theorists have maintained, for example, that people may experience more than one stage simultaneously, may move back and forth among the stages, and may skip certain stages completely (e.g., Klinger, 1975, 1977; Kubler-Ross, 1969).

Because of the problems in subjecting such models to a rigorous empirical test, and because of the lack of evidence in support of such models, there is growing speculation that such models are not as useful as was previously believed. In fact, an authoritative review of bereavement research recently issued by the Institute of Medicine cautioned against the use of the word "stages" of response. It noted that this term "might lead people to expect the bereaved to proceed from one clearly identifiable reaction to another in a more orderly fashion than usually occurs. It might also result in . . . hasty assessments of where individuals are or ought to be in the grieving process" (Osterweis, Solomon, & Green, 1984, p. 48).

Despite these shortcomings, we have found the work of the major stage theorists—particularly Bowlby (1980) and Horowitz (1976, 1985), to be extremely useful in a descriptive sense. Unlike the helplessness model, stage models focus on the full range of negative emotions likely to be experienced following a loss. The stage models also focus considerable attention on the processes through which individuals move from emotional distress to adaptation or recovery. In our view, the major weakness of this theoretical approach is that it proposes no mechanisms through which loss may exert an influence on subsequent mental or physical health. For this reason, the stage models have no way of accounting for the diversity of outcomes that occur in response to loss events—no way of explaining, for example, why one person is devastated by a given loss event, while another person emerges relatively unscathed.

The Stress and Coping Model

The stress and coping approach had its origins in the work of Cannon (1939) and Selye (1956). According to these theorists, life change creates a disequilibrium which imposes a period of readjustment. They maintained that the readjustment period can leave the person more vulnerable to stress and its consequences. They also held that this was true of both positive and negative events. As Selye (1956) put it, even a kiss can be stressful.

In order to assess the relation between exposure to stress and subsequent mental or physical health problems, it was necessary to have a measure of how much stress a particular individual had encountered. In the late 1960s, such a scale was developed by Holmes and Rahe (1967). This scale listed 43 different life events, ranging in seriousness from the death of a spouse to minor violations of the law, and included positive (e.g., marriage) as well as negative events. The Holmes and Rahe scale, and several other life events scales that were developed by other researchers (e.g., Brown & Harris, 1978; Coddington, 1972; Dohrenwend, Krasnoff, Askenasy, & Dohrenwend, 1978; Paykel, Prusoff, & Uhlenhuth, 1971) were very effective in spurring research on the impact of stress exposure, because they could easily be incorporated into large-scale surveys of community residents. Indeed, in the first year of its existence, the Holmes and Rahe scale alone was used in over 1,000 publications, many of them concerned with the cumulative impact of various types of events.

Respondents in such surveys are typically asked to indicate which events on the list they have experienced over a particular time period, such as the past year. They are also asked to complete validated inventories of psychological distress and/or physical symptoms. From the life events scale, it is possible to derive a score assessing the individual's cumulative exposure to stress. In arriving at a score, some individuals (including Holmes and Rahe) have emphasized the importance of weighting the events so that individuals who experience more serious events (e.g., bereavement) receive a higher score than individuals who experience more minor events (see Thoits, 1983, for a more detailed discussion of the weighting issue). In many early studies, significant associations were found between the amount of life stress experienced and mental and/or physical health (see Rabkin & Struening, 1976; and Thoits, 1983, for representative reviews).

However, the relations that have been documented are extremely small. Rabkin and Struening (1976) estimated that no more than 9% of the variance in health outcomes is explained by life events. Early attempts to account for the disappointingly weak relation between life events and disturbance focused on methodological shortcomings of the research (see Dohrenwend & Dohrenwend, 1981). For example, one problem in interpreting an association between life stress and functioning is that prior emotional difficulties can bring about some events, such as divorce or job loss, thus leading to ambiguity in the causal meaning of associations between events and disorder. Indeed, a substantial percentage of the events in standard life event inventories have been judged by a sample of clinicians to be symptoms of emotional disorder (Dohrenwend, Dohrenwend, Dodson, & Shrout, 1984). Moreover, respondents who are distressed may recall more events than nondistressed individuals in order to explain their current distress (Brown, 1974). In order to avoid these problems, investigators have recognized the importance of collecting data on life events and functioning at two separate points in time (e.g., Turner & Noh, 1982), and of limiting their analysis to events judged unlikely to have resulted from prior psychopathology (e.g., Brown & Harris, 1978). Several other methodological improvements also have been introduced in the measurement of life events, such as specifying ambiguously worded items with respect to their desirability, and independently verifying events by a second party in order to insure accuracy of recall. However, these and other refinements have not substantially increased predictive power.

Consequently, researchers have attempted to conduct a more systematic analysis of the features of events that are most likely to result in particular types of disorder. This approach has proved to be somewhat fruitful. It has been found, for example, that positive or desirable events are unlikely to have an impact on subsequent mental health (see Thoits, 1983, for a more detailed discussion), and that uncontrollable events increase vulnerability to depression. Nonetheless, the relation between life change and subsequent disorder remains a very modest one. The vast majority of people who experience life events do not become mentally or physically ill. In fact, there is emerging evidence that stressful encounters can sometimes promote coping capacity (see Haan, 1982, for a review).

For these reasons, the major thrust of current research in the stress and coping area involves the identification of variables—so-called vulnerability or resistance factors—that can account for the variability that exists in response to stress. Several different types of factors have been examined in the literature, including various personality predispositions such as neuroticism (e.g., Depue & Monroe, 1986), and dispositional optimism (e.g., Scheier & Carver, 1985); resources, such as intellectual capacity, cognitive flexibility, and financial assets (Menaghan, 1983); coping strategies, such as reinterpretation of the situation as positive, or denial that a problem exists (e.g., Lazarus & Folkman, 1985), and social support (see Kessler, Price, & Wortman, 1985, for a review).

Much of the research on the impact of life events was guided by a general model of the life stress process originally developed by Barbara Dohrenwend and her colleagues (see, e.g., Dohrenwend, 1978; Dohrenwend & Dohrenwend, 1981). This model, which is depicted in Figure 18.1 in a slightly modified version, focuses attention on the precise theoretical mechanisms through which exposure to stress leads to subjective perceptions of distress, to short-term psychological and physiological responses to these perceptions, and to changes in mental or physical health (see Kessler et al., 1985, or Martin, Dean, Garcia, & Hall, 1989, for a more detailed discussion of the model). This general model has been enormously influential during the past decade. As Martin et al. (1989) have noted, it was adopted as a heuristic guide by the Institute of Medicine panel on Stress and Life Events in 1981 (Elliot & Eisdorfer, 1982).

In this model, it is generally assumed that once a stressful life event is encountered, the appraisal of that stressor, as well as mental and physical health consequences, will depend on the individual's vulnerability or resistance factors. Thus, unlike the stage models discussed earlier, a major advantage of the stress and coping approach is that it can account for variability in response. An implicit assumption underlying the stage models is that everyone will recover from a stressful life experience. However, according to the stress and coping model, those with more coping resources, such as social support, are likely to recover more quickly and completely than those with fewer resources.

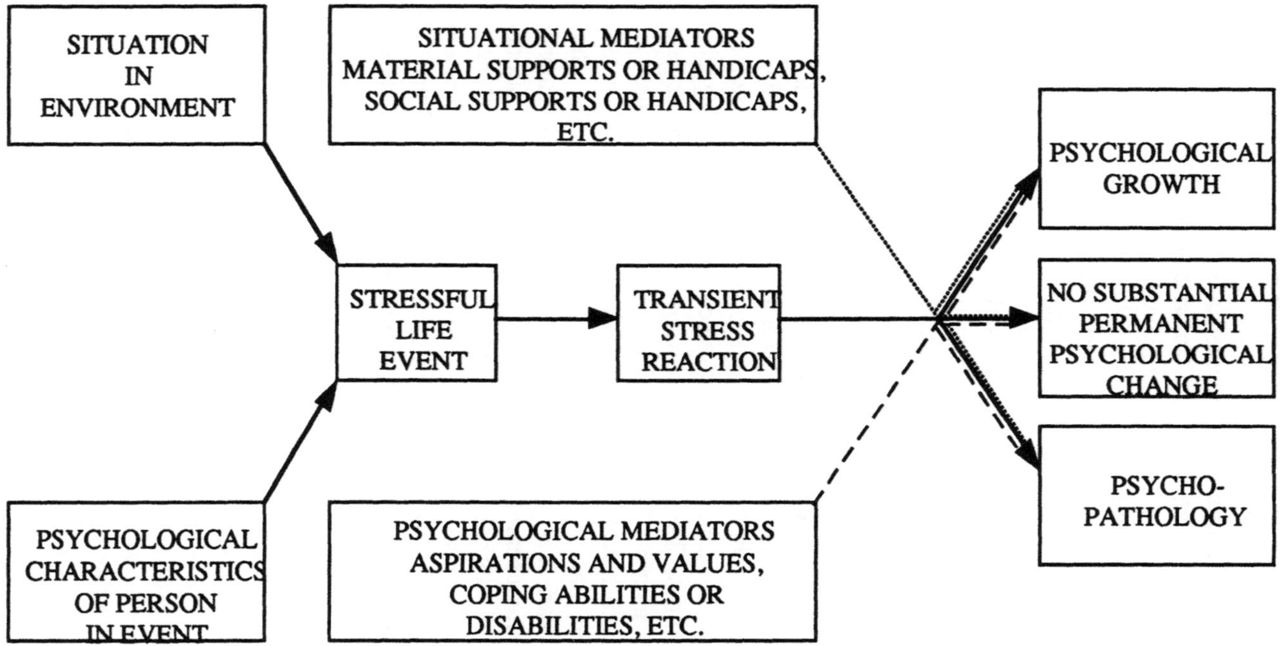

FIG. 18.1 A model of the relationship between life stress and psychopathology. Adapted from B.S. Dohrenwend (1978).

INITIAL EMPIRICAL WORK

We were strongly influenced by the above theoretical models, particularly the stress and coping model, in planning our initial empirical work. We designed two longitudinal studies in order to assess how people cope with irrevocable losses: one on individuals who became physically disabled following an accident; and one on parents who have suddenly and unexpectedly lost a child. On the basis of our earlier review (Silver & Wortman, 1980), it was clear that our research should focus on mediating variables which might account for the variability in reactions to a major loss. In addition, drawing from the stage models of grief and loss, we felt it important to include an assessment of a full array of different emotions at specific points in time following the loss. Finally, on the basis of the learned helplessness model, we were curious about whether irrevocable losses might lead individuals to change their view of themselves or their world, and hence become passive in the face of later goals.

In the first study, we conducted interviews with approximately 125 individuals from Northwestern Memorial Hospital who became physically disabled following a sudden, traumatic accident (Silver, 1982). Respondents were injured in many different kinds of accidents, including motor vehicle accidents, sporting accidents, falls, and violent crimes. The subjects also varied in terms of the severity and permanence of their injuries. Two-thirds of the respondents experienced injuries to the spinal cord, with approximately one-half of those suffering permanent loss of sensation and function and the other half sustaining injuries for which the prognosis was unclear. The spinal cord injured group was also comprised of approximately equal numbers of paraplegics and quadriplegics. The final one-third of the sample suffered neck or back injuries but no damage to their spinal cords. The majority of the respondents were between the ages of 21 and 25, approximately 80% were male, and about 80% were white. Subjects were interviewed 1, 3, and 8 weeks following their accidents. To measure emotional response to the injury, respondents were asked to report how often in the previous week they had experienced four different affective states: anxiety, depression, anger, and happiness.

In the second study, we focused on parents who had lost an infant to Sudden Infant Death Syndrome (SIDS; see Wortman & Silver, 1987). SIDS is the most common cause of death among infants under the age of 1 (Beckwith, 1977), and is diagnosed in those cases where the death is unexpected and where a postmortem examination fails to reveal any pathology. In most cases, the parents find the baby dead in his or her crib and have had no prior warning that the death might occur (Beckwith, 1970). In this study, approximately 125 parents in Wayne County, Michigan, and Cook County, Illinois, who had lost an infant to SIDS were interviewed at 3 weeks, 3 months, and 18 months after the death had occurred. The parents in the sample were relatively young (the average age was 25), about 70% were women, and about 60% were black. In this study, we included a more extensive measure of how frequently respondents experienced positive and negative emotions. All respondents were asked to complete the Affects Balance Scale (Derogatis, 1975), which includes 40 adjectives designed to measure each of four positive and four negative affective states. We also included a more extensive battery of outcome measures than was possible in the spinal cord injury study, where our time with respondents was quite limited due to the gravity of their injuries.

Emotional Reactions to the Loss

Much of our initial analyses focused on identifying the emotional reactions that were most predominant at various points in time following the event. As noted above, there have been few systematic studies in the literature that have followed individuals at various points in time after a major loss, and assessed a wide range of emotions. In our assessment, we not only included a variety of different negative emotions, but assessed positive emotions as well. While at Northwestern University in the 1970s, we had the opportunity to discuss the possible role that positive emotions might play in the coping process with Brickman, who had written several papers on happiness (see, e.g., Brickman, Coates, & Janoff-Bulman, 1978). As a result of these conversations, we began to wonder whether individuals might experience moments of happiness or joy relatively soon after experiencing a significant loss. If such positive emotions were experienced, we became curious about whether they could sustain hope, and perhaps facilitate adjustment, among individuals who had encountered loss. With notable exceptions (Brickman et al., 1978; Lazarus, Kanner, & Folkman, 1980) few researchers had considered these issues, and we were not able to locate a single study on reactions to a major loss in which positive emotions were assessed. Interestingly, when we shared our assessment battery with staff from Northwestern Memorial Hospital, we encountered extreme resistance to the idea of including measures of happiness. Many staff members felt it was "ridiculous" to ask respondents about happiness within a few days of a major traumatic injury. In addition, our own interviewers were quite reluctant to question respondents about positive feelings. As one of our interviewers expressed it, "If you think I'm going to go in there and ask that quadriplegic how many times he's felt happy in the past week, you're crazy." It took considerable effort and some careful pilot work to convince the staff and our own interviewers that such assessment was feasible, ethical, and worthwhile.

The data illustrating the frequency with which anxiety, depression, anger, and happiness was reported among respondents in the physically disabled study sample are portrayed in Figure 18.2. At Time 1, which was just 1 week after the accident, anxiety was the most frequently reported emotion. However, we were struck by the prevalence of positive emotions at all three time points. By the Time 2 assessment, at 3 weeks after the accident, subjects reported happiness more frequently than

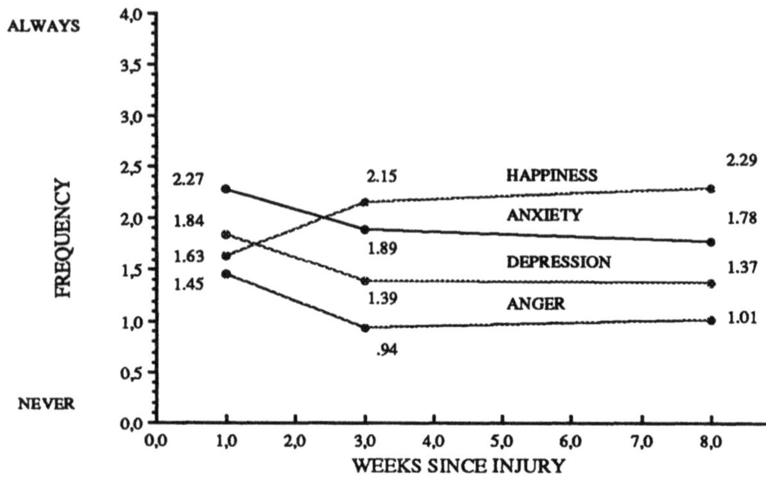

FIG. 18.2. Spinal cord injury study. Frequency of positive and negative affect (from Silver & Wortman, 1990a).

anxiety, depression, or anger, and it continued to be the most frequently reported emotion at the 8-week interview. When asked what had triggered their feelings of happiness, subjects reported that the most common source of positive emotion was social contacts (see Silver & Wortman, 1990b, for a more detailed discussion). For example, one respondent said, "I was surprised by some letters and calls I got from people who I thought wouldn't care."

An obvious way to account for these data is to attribute them to denial. In order to shed some light on this issue, respondents were asked a number of questions about their future expectations concerning their physical limitations. Patients' expectations did become more realistic, that is, more in line with their actual prognosis, over the course of the study (Silver, 1982). Nonetheless, negative affect was highest at the first interview and decreased significantly over time. Because feelings of happiness did not coexist with unrealistic expectations, the happiness data do not appear to be merely a function of denial.

Although our respondents reported more happiness than we or others might have expected (Silver & Wortman, 1990b), it is important to note that patients were not always cheerful following the accidents that left many permanently paralyzed. In fact, a few patients were quite distraught and mentioned thoughts of suicide in the interview. As shown in the frequency data in Figure 18.2, at 3 and 8 weeks after their accident, most respondents reported feeling happy "sometimes" during the previous week. In addition, compared to a normative sample of nondisabled individuals who were approximately the same age as the disabled group, patients reported significantly less happiness than the norms at 1 and 3 weeks postinjury. However,

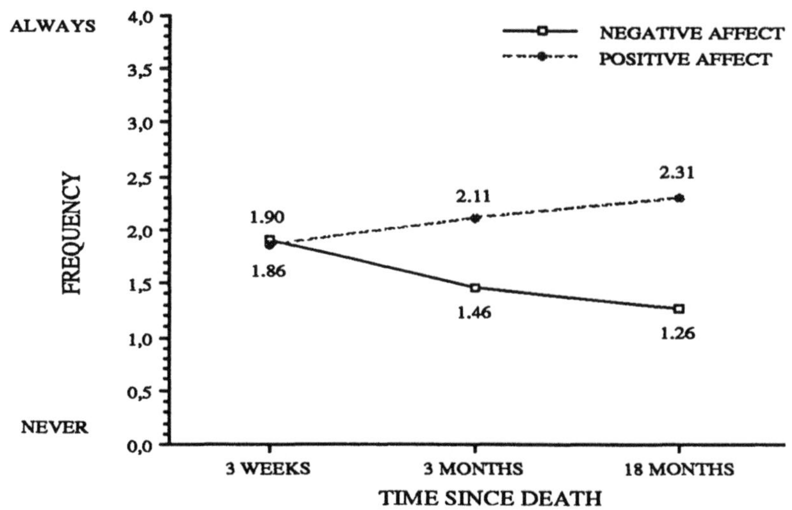

FIG. 18.3. SIDS study: Frequency of positive and negative affect (from Silver & Wortman, 1990a).

while the disabled sample reported less happiness than the normative sample at the interview conducted at 8 weeks postinjury, the difference was not statistically significant. Nonetheless, subjects appeared to experience happiness either as frequently, or more frequently, than feelings such as anxiety, depression, and anger, which are expected to be more common during the early weeks postinjury.

Because these results were unexpected, a replication was attempted in our research on how parents cope with the loss of an infant to SIDS. The results of this study are portrayed in Figures 18.3 and 18.4. As shown in Figure 18.3, the data on frequency of emotion are highly similar to the findings from our study of patients with physical disabilities. By the second interview, conducted 3 months after the infant's death, positive affect was more prevalent than negative affect, and this continued to be the case at the third interview, 18 months after the loss.

One question that might be raised concerning these results is whether negative affect, although less frequent than positive affect, may simply be more intense. In order to determine whether this was the case, SIDS parents were asked questions designed to probe the intensity of their feelings (see Silver & Wortman, 1990b). If respondents said that they had felt happy or sad during the previous week, they were asked to indicate how intense these feelings were. In Figure 18.4, the same pattern of results is shown for the intensity measure as for the frequency measure. At all three interviews, feelings of happiness were at least as intense as feelings of sadness for all respondents. Moreover, at the second and third interviews, respondents reported that their feelings of happiness were significantly more intense than their

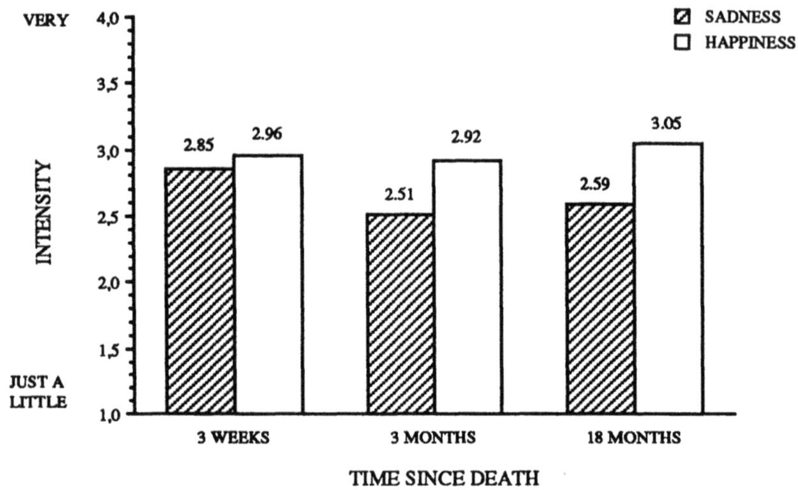

FIG. 18.4. SIDS study. Intensity of positive and negative affect (from Silver & Wortman, 1990a)

feelings of sadness. Taken together, these studies provide converging evidence that although people do experience distress following a loss, they experience positive emotions as well.

The Inevitability of Depression or Emotional Distress

In addition to investigating the prevalence of positive emotions, a second major goal in conducting these longitudinal investigations was to gain a clearer understanding of the prevalence of intense distress, or depression, following a major loss. As noted above, many health care professionals currently recognize that relying on the stages concept alone is too simplistic. Nonetheless, it is generally assumed that virtually all individuals who experience an important loss will go through a grieving process, beginning with a phase of intense distress and ultimately followed by recovery as the person comes to terms with the loss. In fact, there is believed to be a "near-universal occurrence of intense emotional distress following bereavement, with features similar in nature and intensity to those of clinical depression" (Osterweis et al., 1984, p. 18).

As noted above, our study on coping with SIDS loss had included a more complete assessment of key outcome variables, including depression, than was possible in our work with physically disabled patients. In order to examine the prevalence of depression, parents were classified as exhibiting high or low depression at the initial interview 3 weeks after their baby died, and again at approximately 18 months after the loss. This classification was made on the basis of respondents' scores on the depression subscale of the Symptom Check List-90 (SCL-90; Derogatis, 1977).

On the basis of this initial classification, we were surprised to find that a significant minority of our respondents (26.2%) did not evidence intense depression at either of these two assessment periods. To determine the generality of these findings, we also have made an effort to identify other methodologically sound data sets that include a rigorous assessment of depression, and that follow respondents longitudinally over time. To date, we have examined four such data sets in addition to our own (see Wortman & Silver, in press, for a more detailed discussion). Each of these data sets focuses on the loss of a spouse. Without exception, these data sets provide clear evidence that an initial period of depression following loss is by no means universal. In one study, Clayton, Halikas, and Maurice (1972) interviewed 109 widows and widowers anywhere from 1-5 weeks after losing their spouse. Using strict diagnostic criteria to assess depression, Clayton et al. (1972) found that only a minority of respondents (35%) could be classified as definitely or probably depressed. Similarly, Vachon et al. (1982a) interviewed 162 widows and found that 1 month after the loss, 30% of the widows they studied scored below 5 on the General Health Questionnaire (GHQ)—a score considered insufficient to warrant further psychiatric assessment. In their sample of primarily Mormon elderly bereaved individuals, Lund, Caserta, and Dimond (1986) reported that only 14.6% of the men and 19.2% of the women they studied at 3-4 weeks post-loss evidenced "at least mild" depression on the Zung Depression Scale (Zung, 1965).

Available evidence also provides little support for the assumption that those who fail to experience distress shortly after the loss will have difficulties later. In our study of SIDS parents, there were almost no respondents (only 2.5%) who showed delayed grief—that is, low distress at 3 weeks, but high distress at the 18-month assessment period. In addition, those who evidenced low distress at 3 weeks post-loss were extremely likely to be doing well 18 months later. In the previously mentioned study of bereavement by Clayton et al. (1972; see Bornstein, Clayton, Halikas, Maurice, & Robins, 1973), widows and widowers were followed longitudinally, and interviewed at 1 month, 4 months, and 13 months post-loss. As noted above, the majority of respondents (65%) emerged in the first month of bereavement with minimal depressive symptoms. Moreover, only 3 of the 71 respondents interviewed at 4 months had become depressed by that time, and only 1 subject evidenced depression for the first time at 13 months post-loss. These results lead the investigators to conclude that "delayed" grief is relatively rare. Similar findings were obtained in the longitudinal study of 99 widows conducted by Vachon et al. (1982b). Over 30% of these women were classified as "low distress" by virtue of their scores on the GHQ 1 month post-loss, and 94% of that group continued to evidence "low distress" when interviewed 2 years later. In fact, only 2 women in the study who had low distress scores at 1 month had high distress scores at the 2-year interview. Moreover, each of these women had experienced a new life event, such as the development of a major health problem or the loss of a job, in the interval

(Vachon, personal communication, 1989). In the previously mentioned study of elderly bereaved conducted by Lund et al. (1986), only 12.5% to 20% of the sample reported scores exceeding the cutoff score delineated as indicating depression at any of six different assessment points from 3-4 weeks to 2 years post-loss (see also Zisook & Shuchter, 1986).

At present, we are continuing our analyses of data from these data sets in order to enhance our understanding of those respondents who fail to show a typical grief reaction to the loss of their loved one. For example, we are attempting to determine whether those who failed to show the normal pattern of grieving were faced with situations involving an extended illness and/or caretaking responsibilities for their spouse. If so, such individuals may have grieved for their spouse prior to the death. Another possibility is that as individuals become older, they are more likely to anticipate the loss of their spouse, and may not show grief because they have already "worked through" the implications of the loss. In fact, those studies with the largest concentration of older respondents were the ones where absence of intense distress was the most predominant reaction (Wortman & Silver, in press).

In clinical lore, the assumption that distress should occur following loss is so powerful that a variety of negative attributions may be made toward those who fail to become significantly depressed (Wortman & Silver, 1989). One such attribution is lack of attachment. A person who fails to grieve following the loss of a spouse or child may be labeled as a shallow, superficial individual who is incapable of deep attachments. Alternatively, the absence of distress may be dismissed as indicative of denial of the reality of the loss. Across these various data sets, we have carefully examined the hypothesis that those who showed low distress at Time 1 were not really attached to their loved ones. The data provide no support for this view. For example, in our study of coping with loss of an infant to SIDS, parents who initially showed low distress did not differ from those who initially evidenced high distress on such indicators as whether they reported it to have been a good time to be pregnant or whether the pregnancy had been unplanned or difficult to accept. Furthermore, these groups did not differ in their positive evaluations of their babies while alive. Although a detailed discussion of these findings is beyond the scope of this chapter, our analyses have also failed to support the notion that low initial distress can be dismissed as simply denial. Finally, there is little evidence in these data to support the widely held assumption that those who do not exhibit distress initially will show subsequent health difficulties or symptoms.

Implications of our Findings for Research and Intervention

The data reviewed above suggest that, across several studies, a substantial proportion of respondents do not experience intense distress following the loss of a loved one. In addition, positive emotions were found to be more predominant than might have been expected. However, these studies were not designed to explore the process of coping with loss as a function of respondents' early emotional reactions. Thus, they leave many questions unanswered about individuals who appear to be well-adjusted following a loss. For example, do such individuals experience classic signs of grief and mourning despite their lack of distress? Are they preoccupied with thoughts about the loss? Do such individuals devote significant energy to avoiding reminders of the loss, or are they able to encounter reminders with equanimity? What is the relation between failure to experience intense distress, and the ability to experience positive emotions following a major loss? Are those individuals who experience little distress likely to report feeling "numb" or "empty," and hence experience little positive emotion, as some investigators have suggested (cf. Deutsch, 1937). At present, we are examining these and other questions among respondents in our study of coping with SIDS loss. To date, our analyses suggest that individuals who fail to experience distress following the loss are not preoccupied with thoughts about it, nor do they avoid reminders of the baby (see Silver & Wortman, 1990a).

It has traditionally been assumed by clinicians that "the absence of grieving phenomena following bereavement represents some form of personality pathology" (Osterweis et al., 1984, p. 18). Those who do not show intense distress are expected to show subsequent physical or mental health problems. For example, Marris (1958) has argued that "grieving is a process which 'must work itself out'...if the process is aborted from too hasty a readjustment ...the bereaved may never recover" (p. 33). To date, the results of our analyses have not supported this grim view. Nonetheless, more careful and systematic work is necessary before we can abandon these firmly entrenched notions. Are people who fail to show intense distress more vulnerable to subsequent minor losses, as some theorists have suggested? Are they more likely to develop somatic symptoms or physical health problems, or problems in other areas of their lives, such as at work or in their interpersonal relationships? Conversely, does the ability to experience positive emotions in the face of a major loss serve a protective function? In collecting such data, it will be important to go beyond the self-report methodology that is used almost exclusively in current research on reactions to loss. Individuals who indicate that they are not distressed immediately after a loss, and report predominantly positive affect, may also be unwilling to admit experiencing subsequent problems in other areas of their lives. In subsequent research, it will be important to supplement self-reports of symptomatology with more objective indicators of behavioral and physiological functioning—for example, from physical health records or from observational ratings made by family members or supervisors at work.

Taken together, these findings have important implications for treatment and intervention among those who have endured loss. Among laypersons, the expectation that those who have experienced a loss must be distressed may lead to judgmental behavior toward them if they evidence positive emotions, or if they fail to display appropriate grief. During the initial months following a loss, expressions of happiness or enjoyment are not well tolerated. Members of peer support groups for the recently bereaved have told us that only within the confines of the support group walls were they free to laugh without risking censure from members of their social environment. Friedman, Chodoff, Mason, and Hamburg (1963) reported that parents of a dying child reported to have been expected to appear grief stricken all the time. According to these investigators, "parents were not expected to take part in normal social activities or be interested in any form of entertainment" (p. 619). A mother who planned a birthday party for another one of her children was challenged by relatives who "could not understand how my family could have a party at a time like this" (p. 619).

Among health providers, the expectation that individuals must go through a period of distress may lead them to push those who have encountered loss into such a reaction. For example, regarding spinal cord injury, Nemiah (1957) recommended that "it is often necessary to confront the patient gently but firmly with the reality of his situation, and force him into a period of depression while he works out his acceptance of his loss" (p. 146). Similarly, the belief that distress is necessary may lead health care providers to withhold treatment that may bring relief from the raw distress that may accompany a major loss. In a manual for grief counselors, for example, Doyle (1980) has discouraged the use of tranquilizers or antidepressants by the bereaved during the early stages of grief, since grief "needs to be felt in all its ramifications" (p. 15). At this time, it is unknown whether such recommendations are likely to be beneficial or counterproductive.

ONGOING THEORETICAL AND EMPIRICAL WORK

If results obtained from further studies are consistent with the findings reviewed herein, we must acknowledge the possibility that a sizable minority of people may come through a major loss relatively unscathed. What are the theoretical implications of this conclusion? Such results are incompatible with current theories of grief and loss, which assume latent pathology among those who fail to show intense distress following irrevocable losses. However, by dismissing such a reaction as indicative of pathology, attention appears to have been deflected away from identifying strengths or coping resources that may protect people from distress.

As we detailed earlier, a strength of the stress and coping model is that it emphasizes the importance of coping resources in explaining why some people may take longer than others to recover from the effects of a major loss. However, the stress and coping model is based on the assumption that a major loss or change *will* cause a state of disequilibrium. Hence, this model has no way of accounting for the fact that for a substantial minority of individuals, major loss events do not seem to bring about such a period of disequilibrium. Taken together, the findings suggest that some people may have something in place beforehand—perhaps a religious or philosophical orientation, or a certain view of the world—that enables them to be less vulnerable to the effects of loss.

At present, our theoretical work is focused on the role that might be played by philosophical perspectives, or assumptions about the world, in coping with a major loss (Janoff-Bulman & Frieze, 1983; Wortman, 1983). We believe that such events may be particularly likely to result in intense distress, and subsequent problems in mental and physical health, when they shatter a person's assumptions about the world. As Lilliston (1985) has indicated, this can happen when a person experiences a sudden, traumatic injury: "A suddenly disabled person who was the victim of accident or disease is given a horrifying and permanent reminder of the world's injustice. If the person formerly believed in a just world, he [or she] must somehow harmonize the dissonance between what he [or she] expected life to be, and what it now has revealed itself to be" (p. 8). We would predict that sudden and unexpected losses are more likely to shatter such assumptions than losses that occur at an expected time in the life span, or losses for which there is time for psychological preparation (see Wortman & Silver, in press). With respect to bereavement, Parkes and Weiss (1983) have written that sudden, unexpected losses are particularly debilitating, largely through their "transformation of the world into a frightening place, a place in which disaster cannot be predicted and accustomed ways of thinking and behaving have proven unreliable and out of keeping with the actual world" (p. 245).

To date, researchers in the stress and coping tradition are focusing much of their attention on such variables as personality and social support. In our view, such variables are unlikely to account for the finding that a substantial minority of individuals fail to become significantly distressed following a major loss. We suspect that certain views of the world may serve a protective function in allowing individuals to incorporate a major tragedy. If so, an analysis of life events in terms of their impact on previously held world views could account for the failure to experience initial depression. For example, a person who holds a firm belief that all things are part of God's larger plan may show less distress following the loss of a spouse than a person who does not hold this view. The belief that one will be reunited with the loved one for all of eternity may also serve a protective function. Similarly, individuals who have the perspective that bad things can happen at any time, and that suffering is part of life, may find it easier to cope with loss than those individuals who believe that if they work hard and are good people, they will be protected from misfortune (cf. Janoff-Bulman & Frieze, 1983). In our judgment, religious or philosophical orientations that might lead individuals to incorporate loss events into their view of the world, and hence be protected from distress, are in need of considerably more research.

Our earlier review showed that by one month following the loss, there is already marked variability in response to the loss of a loved one, with some individuals reacting with intense distress, and others showing more strength and confidence in their ability to deal with the loss. As noted above, these early reactions appear to be highly predictive of long-term adjustment. Clearly, in studies beginning after the loss event, it is impossible to determine the antecedents of initial adjustment. Moreover, it is difficult to determine whether variables assessed after the event, such as respondents' mental health or social networks, have been altered by the loss. Because of such interpretive difficulties, it has been suggested that the logical next step in advancing our understanding of the relation between stressful life events and health outcomes is a prospective study, which would assess relevant risk factors and potential confounding variables (e.g., initial health status) prior to the stressor. In fact, a major conclusion drawn in the recent report on bereavement completed by the Institute of Medicine is that "prospective longitudinal studies that begin before and run for several years after bereavement are needed" (Osterweis et al., 1984, p. 11)!

Over the past few years, we have had the opportunity to become involved in two prospective studies of reactions to loss that provide a unique opportunity to clarify the issues raised above. The first study is being conducted in conjunction with a large-scale investigation of stress and coping across the life span called the Americans' Changing Lives study.[1] In 1986, personal interviews were conducted with a representative sample of 3,617 U.S. adults from age 25 to 92 in 70 different areas around the United States. The interviews focused on respondents' stressful life experiences, and information about various coping resources such as personality, self-esteem, and social support. Information about physical and mental health and functioning was also obtained from all respondents. An attempt was made to reinterview all respondents in 1989.

Between the first and second interviews, approximately 75 of the respondents became widowed. Preloss information concerning risk factors and moderating variables is available from the Wave I interview. At the Wave II interview, those respondents who lost a spouse were questioned about their reactions to the loss. They also provided information about their current health and functioning.

The second prospective study is being conducted in the Detroit, Michigan area. In 1987, baseline information was collected on approximately 1,530 respondents who were at risk for bereavement (couples where the spouse is 65 years or older). The baseline interview provides a careful assessment, prior to the loss, of potential risk factors, confounding variables, and coping resources such as social support. Michigan death records are being monitored to determine when deaths occur among this sample. It is projected that approximately 200 respondents will become bereaved by 1992. These respondents will be contacted and invited to participate in a study of conjugal bereavement. If they agree, they will be interviewed at 6 to 8 months, 18 months, and 30 months after the loss. A control group of married respondents matched on age, sex, race, age of (deceased) spouse, and spouse's prior

[1] This project is being conducted in collaboration with an interdisciplinary team of researchers including James House and Ronald Kessler, sociologists; James Morgan, an economist; and Robert Kahn and Toni Antonucci, psychologists, among others.

physical health will be selected from those who participated in the baseline interview, and they will be interviewed at parallel time points to provide comparison data concerning functioning. In addition, a separate interview is being conducted with a subset of our respondents to collect biomedical, physical, and cognitive functioning data. Such information, including blood and urine samples, will be obtained from all of the baseline respondents who are age 70 or older, and all respondents who become bereaved, as well as on matched controls.

CONCLUSIONS

In this chapter, we have provided an overview of our research program on how people cope with irrevocable losses, and have traced the development of the theoretical ideas we have considered while studying loss. Each of the theoretical models we have employed—the learned helplessness model, stage models of emotional reaction to loss, and the stress and coping model—have important strengths. Nonetheless, none of these models can account for an intriguing phenomenon that we have detected in studies of reactions to loss conducted by ourselves and others. Taken together, past studies suggest that a minority of individuals, ranging from around 25% of respondents to over 75% of respondents (see Wortman & Silver, in press) do not appear to experience intense distress following a loss. In fact, these individuals may possess coping resources that allow them to incorporate the loss of a loved one almost immediately following the loss.

At present, we are attempting to develop a theoretical model that can account for this unexpected finding, and that can also account for the striking variability in reaction to loss that we and others have observed. This model is based on the assumption that when a major loss is experienced, its impact on subsequent health and functioning will depend largely on whether it can be incorporated into the respondent's view of the world. Respondents who can incorporate events within their world view are expected to experience far less distress than individuals whose world views are shattered by the event. We would predict that such factors as the suddenness of the loss, its untimeliness, and the conditions under which the loss is perpetrated, can contribute to the shattering of world views. Losses that are perpetrated by others who intend to do harm, or who are grossly negligent, may be particularly likely to violate assumptions about the world.

We would expect the shattering of world views to have profound consequences for mental and physical health, and for the initiation of subsequent coping efforts. Those individuals who believe that good behavior and hard work are rewarded may be particularly vulnerable to events in which the fruits of their efforts are unexpectedly destroyed. Such a reaction may be experienced by, for example, a person who loses a spouse or child to a drunk driver who receives no punishment or censure for his or her crime (Lehman et al., 1987). Following such a loss, individuals may be deeply distressed by their recognition that they cannot control the important things in their lives. They may be reluctant to engage in subsequent coping efforts, since the event has shown them that all of their efforts can be taken away in a matter of seconds.

Once an individual has experienced a loss that shatters the assumptions on which his or her world is based, we are interested in the mechanisms through which some individuals are able to develop a new world view that eventually allows them to continue a meaningful and rewarding life. In contrast, others may come to see the world as generally uncontrollable, may feel vulnerable to subsequent tragedy, and may view most people as generally untrustworthy. We are also interested in the conditions under which the world views developed in response to major losses are adaptive in the face of subsequent losses, and the conditions under which they are maladaptive.

We believe that a theoretical account of the process of coping with loss that considers the impact of such losses on one's world view has a number of advantages over previous formulations. First, as noted above, such a model can account for the paradoxical finding that a substantial minority of respondents do not appear to become intensely distressed following a major loss. Second, such a model can account for the striking variability in response that is often seen in response to a single life crisis, such as cancer (see Silver & Wortman, 1980, for a more detailed discussion). A person who viewed illness as preventable through diet and exercise, and who went to considerable lengths to eat the right foods and get regular exercise, may be far more likely to experience a challenge to his or her world view than a person who sees the development of disease as a more random and multidetermined process. Third, the model can help to account for the paradoxical finding that sometimes relatively trivial events seem to perpetuate major distress. For example, Brown and Harris (1978) report that depressive episodes are frequently brought about by relatively small events that challenge one's view of reality, such as learning that a close friend cannot be trusted. Fourth, our analysis suggests a new way of thinking about vulnerability to major losses. In the past, vulnerability has been assumed to be a function of the coping resources that one possesses—for example, one's self-esteem, socioeconomic status, beliefs in the ability to control one's environment, social support, etc. Our analysis suggests that people who appear to have considerable coping resources—successful, control-oriented people who have a history of accomplishment, and who have generally been rewarded for their efforts—may be particularly vulnerable to certain kinds of sudden, undesirable life events. Such people may be more devastated by a loss that challenges the view that efforts are generally rewarded than those who possess considerably less coping resources.

At present, we are engaged in research designed to test the theoretical ideas delineated here. In the prospective studies described above, we are attempting to measure people's views of the world prior to experiencing a major loss. We expect that these designs will help us to clarify the conditions under which particular world views are protective in the face of loss. Ultimately, we hope to present a model of world views that delineates how they are initially formulated, as well as how they are affected by the experience of a major loss.

REFERENCES

Abramson, L. Y., Seligman, M. E. P., & Teasdale, J. D. (1978). Learned helplessness in humans: Critique and reformulation. *Journal of Abnormal Psychology, 87,* 49-74.

Beckwith, J. B. (1970). Observations on the pathological anatomy of Sudden Infant Death Syndrome. In A. Bergman, J. Beckwith, & C. Ray (Eds.), *Sudden Infant Death Syndrome: Proceedings of the second international conference on causes of Sudden Infant Death in infants* (pp. 83-101). Seattle, WA: University of Washington Press.

Beckwith, J. B. (1977). *The Sudden Infant Death Syndrome.* Washington, DC: U.S. Department of Health, Education and Welfare.

Bornstein, P. E., Clayton, P. J., Halikas, J. A., Maurice, W. L., & Robins, E. (1973). The depression of widowhood after thirteen months. *British Journal of Psychiatry, 122,* 561-566.

Bowlby, J. (1961). Processes of mourning. *International Journal of Psychoanalysis, 42,* 317-340.

Bowlby, J. (1973). *Attachment and loss: Vol. 2. Separation: Anxiety and anger.* New York: Basic Books.

Bowlby, J. (1980). *Attachment and loss: Vol. 3. Loss: Sadness and depression.* New York: Basic Books.

Brickman, P., Coates, D., & Janoff-Bulman, R. (1978). Lottery winners and accident victims: Is happiness relative? *Journal of Personality and Social Psychology, 36,* 917-927.

Brown, G. W. (1974). Meaning, measurement, and stress of life events. In B. S. Dohrenwend & B. P. Dohrenwend (Eds.), *Stressful life events: Their nature and effects* (pp. 217-243). New York: Wiley.

Brown, G. W., & Harris, T. (1978). *Social origins of depression: A study of psychiatric disorder in women.* New York: Free Press.

Bulman, R. J., & Wortman, C. B. (1977). Attributions of blame and coping in the "real world": Severe accident victims react to their lot. *Journal of Personality and Social Psychology, 35,* 351-363.

Cannon, W. B. (1939). *The wisdom of the body.* New York: Norton.

Clayton, P. J., Halikas, J. A., & Maurice, W. L. (1972). The depression of widowhood. *British Journal of Psychiatry, 120,* 71-78.

Coddington, R. D. (1972). The significance of life events as etiologic factors in the diseases of children — II. A study of a normal population. *Journal of Psychosomatic Research, 16,* 205-213.

Depue, R. A., & Monroe, S. M. (1986). Conceptualization and measurement of human disorder in life stress research: The problem of chronic disturbance. *Psychological Bulletin, 94,* 36-51.

Derogatis, L. R. (1975). *The Affects Balance Scale.* Baltimore: Clinical Psychometric Research.

Derogatis, L. R. (1977). *SCL-90: Administration, scoring and procedures manual.* Baltimore: Clinical Psychometric Research.

Deutsch, H. (1937). Absence of grief. *Psychoanalytic Quarterly, 6,* 12-22.

Dohrenwend, B. S. (1978). Social stress and community psychology. *American Journal of Community Psychology, 6,* 1-14.

Dohrenwend, B. S., & Dohrenwend, B. P. (1981). Life stress and illness: Formulation of the issues. In B. S. Dohrenwend & B. P. Dohrenwend (Eds.), *Stressful life events and their contexts* (pp. 1-27). New York: Neale Watson Academic Publications.

Dohrenwend, B. S., Dohrenwend, B. P., Dodson, M., & Shrout, P. E. (1984). Symptoms, hassles, social supports and life events: The problem of confounded measures. *Journal of Abnormal Psychology, 93,* 222-230.

Dohrenwend, B. S., Krasnoff, L., Askenasy, A. R., & Dohrenwend, B. P. (1978). Exemplification of a method for scaling life events: The PERI life events scale. *Journal of Health and Social Behavior, 19,* 205-229.

Downey, G., Silver, R. C., Wortman, C. B., & Hermann, C. (1990). *Reconsidering the attribution-adjustment relation following a major negative event: Coping with the loss of a child.* Manuscript submitted for publication.

Doyle, P. (1980). *Grief counseling and sudden death: A manual and guide.* Springfield, IL: Charles C. Thomas.

Elliot, G. R., & Eisdorfer, C. (Eds.). (1982). *Stress and human health: Analysis and implications of research.* New York: Springer.

Friedman, S. B., Chodoff, P., Mason, J. W., & Hamburg, D. A. (1963). Behavioral observations on parents anticipating the death of a child. *Pediatrics, 32,* 610-625.

Glass, D. C., & Singer, J. E. (1972). *Urban stress.* New York: Academic Press.

Haan, N. (1982). The assessment of coping, defense, and stress. In L. Goldberger & S. Breznitz (Eds.), *Handbook of stress: Theoretical and clinical aspects* (pp. 254-269). New York: The Free Press.

Holmes, T. H., & Rahe, R. H. (1967). The Social Readjustment Rating Scale. *Journal of Psychosomatic Medicine, 11,* 213-218.

Horowitz, M. J. (1976). *Stress response syndromes.* New York: Aronson.

Horowitz, M. J. (1985). Disasters and psychological responses to stress. *Psychiatric Annals, 15,* 161-167.

Janoff-Bulman, R., & Frieze, I. H. (1983). A theoretical perspective for understanding reactions to victimization. *Journal of Social Issues, 39*(2), 1-17.

Kessler, R. C., Price, R. H., & Wortman, C. B. (1985). Social factors in psychopathology: Stress, social support, and coping processes. *Annual Review of Psychology, 36,* 531-572.

Klinger, E. (1975). Consequences of commitment to and disengagement from incentives. *Psychological Review, 82,* 1-25.

Klinger, E. (1977). *Meaning and void: Inner experience and the incentives in people's lives.* Minneapolis, MN: University of Minnesota Press.

Kubler-Ross, E. (1969). *On death and dying.* New York: Macmillan.

Lazarus, R. S., & Folkman, S. (1985). *Stress, appraisal, and coping.* New York: Springer.

Lazarus, R. S., Kanner, A. D., & Folkman, S. (1980). Emotions: A cognitive-phenomenological analysis. In R. Plutchik & H. Kellerman (Eds.), *Theories of emotion* (pp. 189-218). New York: Academic Press.

Lehman, D. R., Wortman, C. B., & Williams, A. F. (1987). Long-term effects of losing a spouse or child in a motor vehicle crash. *Journal of Personality and Social Psychology, 52,* 218-231.

Lilliston, B. A. (1985). Psychosocial responses to traumatic physical disability. *Social Work in Health Care, 10,* 1-13.

Lund, D. A., Caserta, M. S., & Dimond, M. F. (1986). Gender differences through two years of bereavement among the elderly. *The Gerontologist, 26,* 314-319.

Marris, P. (1958). *Widows and their families.* London: Routledge and Kegan Paul.

Martin, J. L., Dean, L., Garcia, M., & Hall, W. (1989). The impact of AIDS on a gay community: Changes in sexual behavior, substance abuse, and mental health. *American Journal of Community Psychology, 17,* 269-293.

Menaghan, E. (1983). Marital stress and family transitions: A panel analysis. *Journal of Marriage and the Family, 45,* 371-386.

Miller, I. W., & Norman, W. H. (1979). Learned helplessness in humans: A review and attribution theory model. *Psychological Bulletin, 86,* 93-118.

Nemiah, J. C. (1957). The psychiatrist and rehabilitation. *Archives of Physical Medicine and Rehabilitation, 38,* 143-147.

Osterweis, M., Solomon, F., & Green, M. (Eds.). (1984). *Bereavement: Reactions, consequences, and care.* Washington, DC: National Academy Press.

Parkes, C. M., & Weiss, R. S. (1983). *Recovery from bereavement.* New York: Basic Books.

Pattison, E. M. (1977). *The experience of dying.* Englewood Cliffs, NJ: Prentice-Hall.

Paykel, E. S., Prusoff, B. A., & Uhlenhuth, E. H. (1971). Scaling of life events. *Archives of General Psychiatry, 25,* 340-347.

Rabkin, J. G., & Struening, E. L. (1976). Life events, stress and illness. *Science, 194,* 1013-1020.

Rosenbaum, R. (1982, July). Turn on, tune in, drop dead. *Harpers,* pp. 32-42.

Scheier, M. F., & Carver, C. S. (1985). Optimism, coping, and health: Assessment and implications of generalized outcome expectancies. *Health Psychology, 4,* 219-247.

Seligman, M. E. P., Maier, S. F., & Soloman, R. L. (1971). Unpredictable and uncontrollable aversive events. In F. R. Brush (Ed.), *Aversive conditioning and learning* (pp. 347-400). New York: Academic Press.

Selye, H. (1956). *Stress of life.* New York: McGraw-Hill.

Silver, R. C. (1982). *Coping with an undesirable life event: A study of early reactions to physical disability.* Unpublished doctoral dissertation, Northwestern University, Evanston, IL.

Silver, R. C., & Wortman, C. B. (1980). Coping with undesirable life events. In J. Garber & M. E. P. Seligman (Eds.), *Human helplessness: Theory and applications* (pp. 279-340). New York: Academic Press.

Silver, R. C., & Wortman, C. B. (1990a). *Is "processing" a loss necessary for adjustment? A study of parental reactions to the death of an infant.* Unpublished manuscript, University of California, Irvine.

Silver, R. C., & Wortman, C. B. (1990b). *The role of positive emotions in the coping process.* Manuscript submitted for publication.

Silver, R. C., Wortman, C. B., & Klos, D. S. (1982). Cognitions, affect, and behavior following uncontrollable outcomes: A response to current human helplessness research. *Journal of Personality, 50,* 480-514.

Thoits, P. A. (1983). Multiple identities and psychological well-being: A reformulation and test of the social isolation hypothesis. *American Sociological Review, 48,* 147-187.

Turner, R. J., & Noh, S. (1982, August). *Social support, life events, and psychological distress: A three-wave panel analysis.* Paper presented at the American Sociological Association, San Francisco, CA.

Vachon, M. L. S., Rogers, J., Lyall, W. A. L., Lancee, W. J., Sheldon, A. R., & Freeman, S. J. J. (1982a). Predictors and correlates of adaptation to conjugal bereavement. *American Journal of Psychiatry, 139,* 998-1002.

Vachon, M. L. S., Sheldon, A. R., Lancee, W. J., Lyall, W. A. L., Rogers, J., & Freeman, S. J. J. (1982b). Correlates of enduring stress patterns following bereavement: Social network, life situation, and personality. *Psychological Medicine, 12,* 783-788.

Wortman, C. B. (1983). Coping with victimization: Conclusions and implications for future research. *Journal of Social Issues, 39*(2), 195-221.

Wortman, C. B., & Dintzer, L. (1978). Is an attributional analysis of the learned helplessness phenomenon viable? A critique of the Abramson-Seligman-Teasdale reformulation. *Journal of Abnormal Psychology, 87,* 75-90.

Wortman, C. B., & Silver, R. C. (1987). Coping with irrevocable loss. In G. R. VandenBos & B. K. Bryant (Eds.), *Cataclysms, crises, and catastrophes: Psychology in action.* (Master Lecture Series, Vol. 6; pp. 189-235). Washington, DC: American Psychological Association.

Wortman, C. B., & Silver, R. C. (1989). The myths of coping with loss. *Journal of Clinical and Consulting Psychology, 57,* 349-357.

Wortman, C. B., & Silver, R. C. (in press). Successful mastery of bereavement and widowhood: A life course perspective. In P. B. Baltes & M. M. Baltes (Eds.), *Successful aging: Perspectives from the behavioral sciences.* New York: Cambridge University Press.

Zisook, S., & Shuchter, S. R. (1986). The first four years of widowhood. *Psychiatric Annals, 15,* 288-294.

Zung, W. W. K. (1965). A self-rating depression scale. *Archives of General Psychology, 13,* 508-516.

19 Mutual Impacts of Toughening on Crises and Losses

Richard A. Dienstbier
University of Nebraska

It is usually expected that if we are overwhelmed by an episode of crisis or loss that we may temporarily cope ineffectively, whereas when we are exposed to a sequence of challenges and stressors that are managable, we learn gradually to become better able to cope with such events. The "toughness" concept relates to analogous processes at the physiological level. The concept is based upon a wide variety of research with both animals and humans that is reviewed in detail elsewhere (Dienstbier, 1989). The focus of this chapter will instead be upon how toughness influences both physiological and psychological responses to life's crises and losses, and upon how those crises and losses in turn influence toughness.

The premise underlying toughness, is that while experience with overwhelming stressors will temporarily disrupt ideal physiological balances in the short term, regular exposure to challenges and stressors followed by adequate recovery periods can cause peripheral and central physiological changes that will increase one's future capacity for more positive forms of arousal and the suppression of more costly forms of arousal; resistance to depletion of some neuroendocrines will be enhanced. These relationships will be explicated more fully after a brief section on definitions and an introduction to the elementary physiological concepts at issue.

My definitions of terms relevant to stress follow largely those of R.S. Lazarus. Following Lazarus and colleagues, both "challenge" and "stress" imply "a relationship between the person and the environment that is appraised by the person as relevant to his or her well-being and in which the person's resources are taxed or exceeded" (Folkman & Lazarus, 1985, p. 152). "Challenge" is experienced when one anticipates success and the likelihood of the associated positive emotions; challenge holds the eventual potential for growth. "Stress" is divided into "loss," or injury already done, and "threat," understood as the potential for harm or loss.

(Unlike Lazarus, I define "challenge" separately from "stress," including within my use of "stress" only the negative components of threat and harm/loss.) Finally, it is assumed that life crises may hold the potential for challenge as well as for stress.

Since modern research has shown most of the neural transmitters of interest here to have hormonal qualities, and the hormones to be used by some neurons as transmitters, the term "neuroendocrine" is used here to include both functions. Two neuroendocrine systems are central to this discussion:

The first peripheral arousal system, associated with the catecholamines (adrenaline, noradrenaline, and dopamine), emphasizes hypothalamic stimulation of the sympathetic nervous system (SNS) with associated release of noradrenaline, the transmitter of the SNS with hormonal action on nonneural tissue; SNS stimulation of the adrenal medulla causes the release of the neuroendocrine adrenaline. When the peripheral arousal function of this system is emphasized, it will be referred to as the "SNS-adrenal-medullary system." This peripheral arousal system is closely associated with the catecholamines of the central nervous system (CNS), of which noradrenaline and dopamine are of primary importance. Levels of central catecholamines often parallel peripheral catecholamine levels, though the mechanism for this correlation is not certain (Anisman & LaPierre, 1982; Potter, Ross, & Zavadil, 1985). For a number of reasons in this chapter I emphasize the positive adaptive character of episodic SNS-adrenal-medullary arousal in contexts of challenge/stress situations. As indicated below, such arousal stimulates desirable forms of energy at minimal physical and psychological cost, and it is capable of ending quickly when no longer required, as the peripheral catecholamines have a half-life of under 2 minutes in the human body.

The second arousal system depends upon hypothalamic stimulation of the pituitary, which releases adrenocorticotropin (ACTH). Carried by the circulatory system to the adrenal cortex, ACTH stimulates the release of cortisol, the adrenal-cortical steroid of primary importance in humans. This system will be referred to as the "pituitary-adrenal-cortical system." I emphasize here the negative consequences of the pituitary-adrenal-cortical system. High levels of cortisol are associated with feelings of anxiety and depression, and result in suppression of the immune sytem. The half life of cortisol in the human body is around 90 minutes, so that when no longer needed, the quick reduction of pituitary-adrenal-cortical arousal to base-rate levels is not possible.

THE TOUGHNESS PATTERN AND HOW ONE ACHIEVES IT

The following paragraphs sketch only sections of research (reviewed thoroughly in Dienstbier, 1989) showing how toughening occurs, and once toughened, how the individual differs from those who are less fit. In summary, these studies show that in subsequent challenge/stress situations, the toughened individual will have an increased capacity to central catecholamine depletion. (This perspective is opposed to the common assumption that peripheral physiological arousal in all forms is usually harmful.) With increased peripheral and CNS catecholamine capacities, in those future challenge/stress contexts the more physiologically and psychologically costly pituitary-adrenal-cortical arousal is suppressed. Between episodes of challenge/stress, toughness is associated with generally lowered arousal base-rates.

Central Toughness: Animals that have been subjected to manipulations designed to induce behavioral suppression (or "learned helplessness," e.g., Weiss, Glazer, Pohorecky, Brick, & Miller, 1975) and depressed humans (e.g., van Praag, 1986) show evidence of central catecholamine depletion. In the case of the behavioral suppression literature with animals, such depletions follow directly from short-term experience with stressors over which the animal had little or no control. On the other hand, daily handling or shocking throughout the early development of young animals (e.g., Meaney et al., 1987) or subjecting adult animals to a 14-day regime with stressors of the same type that cause short-term depletion of central catecholamines, or even inducing a 14-day central catecholamine depletion sequence with drugs (Glazer, Weiss, Pohorecky, & Miller, 1975) results in long-term resistance to central catecholamine depletion and in resistance to behavioral suppression.

In summary, whether induced behaviorally or chemically, systematically exposing organisms to manipulations that cause central catecholamine depletion results in an increased ability of the organism to generate central catecholamines with resistance to central catecholamine depletion in the context of a future episode of challenge/stress.

Peripheral Toughness: Systematic aerobic training in humans (e.g., Hull, Young, & Ziegler, 1984) and in animals (e.g., Brown & Van Huss, 1973) causes an increase in the capacity of the organism to generate peripheral catecholamines when tested under maximum exercise conditions. That is, although training leads to increased physical efficiency, so that lower neuroendocrine levels are needed in the trained individual to achieve the same amount of work, training increases the capacity for more work and for more SNS-adrenal-medullary arousal. It will be shown later why this increased capacity is similarly important in response to *psychological* challenges and stresses. Fortunately, we have been able to show that following a 3-month period of aerobic training in college students, catecholamines generated in the context of psychological challenge/stress are increased compared to untrained controls and compared to themselves prior to training (Dienstbier, LaGuardia, Barnes, Tharp, & Schmidt, 1987).

As individuals become tougher, with increased central and peripheral catecholamine capacity, they also become more sensitive to peripheral catecholamines; that is, a given amount infused into the body stimulates a greater arousal response; (this response is dependent upon the beta-receptors becoming more responsive to the catecholamines; Harri, 1979; Sklar & Anisman, 1981). This increased sensivity is balanced by lower SNS-adrenal-medullary arousal base-rates during rest in the tough than in the unfit individual.

With increased catecholamine capacity, tough organisms show a reduced pituitary-adrenal-cortisol response in challenge/stress contexts. This reciprocal relationship between increased catecholamine capacity and reduced cortisol probably depends upon the inhibition of central ACTH generation being mediated by noradrenergic neurons in the CNS (Ganong, Kramer, Reid, Boryczka, & Shackelford, 1976).

The various manipulations that have been shown to lead to some of the elements of toughening in adult animals include daily training with swimming in cold water, aerobic exercise, electric shock, and chemical depletion of catecholamines. Manipulations effectively used with young animals include daily handling, shocking, or living with adults of other species. Manipulations shown to be effective with humans include daily aerobic training and seasonal exposure to cold.[1] For both animals (Ritter & Pelzer, 1978) and humans (Faucheau, Bourlière, Baulon, & Dupuis, 1981) aging leads to a physiological pattern that is like that of less fit organisms.

While some of these findings relate to central and some to peripheral catecholamine capacity increases in the tough, the distinction between central and peripheral arousal is blurred, for peripheral catecholamines often correspond with central catecholamine levels, and peripheral catecholamines have been shown to have a profound impact upon central functioning. For example, McGaugh (1983) has shown that in animals that have just completed a learning task, retention is facilitated when peripheral catecholamines are increased, while retention is severely reduced when peripheral catecholamine depletion occurs. A discussion of the means for such peripheral arousal influences on CNS functioning will be given below in the section on toughness and energy.

In summary of more research that has been reviewed here (but for more complete treatment, see Dienstbier, 1989), in contrast to less fit individuals, tough individuals show lower SNS-adrenal-medullary and lower pituitary-adrenal-cortical base-rates of arousal, but in response to an episode of challenge or threat they show a faster and stronger SNS-adrenal-medullary arousal; pituitary-adrenal-cortical arousal is delayed. Following the challenge/stress situation, arousal declines faster in the tough than in the less fit. With loss or continuous threat, sufficient central catecholamine levels are maintained in the tough for longer periods than in the less fit (i.e., depletion is delayed), and again, cortisol arousal is delayed. Aging leads to

[1]The toughness concept is derived from a synthesis of research from many different research traditions with animals and humans. No single research project has attempted to show that any one manipulation leads to all of the physiological elements of toughness discussed here, nor has any single effort attempted to show a relationship between all of the physiological elements of toughness and the several personality, performance, and stress-tolerance dimensions discussed below.

arousal patterns that are like those of the less fit, suggesting that as we age the behaviors that lead to toughening become increasingly important.

IMPLICATIONS OF TOUGHNESS FOR PERSONALITY AND PERFORMANCE

An analysis of the relevant research shows that certain activities or manipulations lead to a physiological syndrome (as described above) that in turn improves performance capabilities, personality (primarily emotional stability), and stress tolerance. (A discussion of how the physiological syndrome also impacts the immune and circulatory systems will be presented later.)

Two kinds of research derived from both animal and human subjects explicate these relationships. The first branch of research ignores the physiological mediators, showing that certain activities or manipulations that lead to toughening cause positive changes in the performance, personality, and stress tolerance variables. The second branch of research demonstrates relationships between elements of the physiological pattern of toughness and variables related to performance, personality, or stress tolerance.

Manipulations Leading to Personality-Performance Changes

In research with animals, the early-experience literature, cited briefly above, showed that even though such manipulations increased adrenal-gland weight (Levine, 1960) and catecholamine capacity (Pfeifer, 1976) those animals exposed to frequent stressors were more emotionally stable than controls. Similarly, the increased central catecholamine capacity shown in response to toughening manipulations in the 14-day programs of the research by Weiss and colleagues led to resistance to behavioral suppression or "helplessness." In research with humans, two decades of relatively weak research with regular aerobic exercise has shown the impact of such programs on increased emotional stability (for a review, see Dienstbier, 1984).

Physiological Toughness Correlates with Personality and Performance

Two research traditions with humans most closely addressed these issues: In the first, Frankenhaeuser and associated Scandinavian researchers have shown positive relationships between increases in catecholamines during mental challenge/stress situations on the one hand and positive emotional adjustment on the other. (These relationships tend to be larger for adrenaline than for noradrenaline and larger for men than for women.) For example, children with higher adrenaline levels during an exam were rated by teachers as better adjusted, were more satisfied with school, and were more emotionally stable (Johansson, Frankenhaeuser, & Magnusson, 1973). Older children with higher metriculation-exam catecholamine levels were similarly found to have lower psychosomatic symptomotology and, for boys, lower anxiety and higher achievement (Rauste-von Wright, von Wright, & Frankenhaeuser, 1981). Catecholamine increases during exams were associated with higher MMPI measured ego strength in American male medical students (Roessler, Burch, & Mefferd, 1967), and larger catecholamine increases during laboratory-induced stress situations were associated with lower neuroticism in Swedish male college students (Forsman, 1981).

Performance benefits are also associated with greater catecholamine (again stronger with adrenaline) increases during challenge/stress tasks. For example, the children in the Johansson et al. (1973) study whose catecholamines increased in the math test had fewer errors, particularly toward the end of that 45-minute test, than did the other children; similar relationships were found by Rauste-von Wright et al. (1981), particularly for boys (for a more extensive review, see Frankenhaeuser, 1979). Research by Ursin, Baade, and Levine (1978) with Norwegian paratrooper trainees measured catecholamine increases from before to after individual jumps from a training tower. Catecholamine increases correspond with higher performance in both written and jump-performance measures across an 11-day training period.

In summary, the research (sketched in the "Toughness Pattern" section, previously) shows that exposure to manipulations or activities consisting of regular sessions of either active (e.g., aerobic exercise programs) or passive (e.g., daily shocking or handling) activities that tax the central catecholamine capacities and/or peripheral SNS-adrenal-medullary systems lead to the "tough" syndrome of physiological responses (detailed earlier). Research sketched in this section has shown first that those same activities are related to emotional stability, positive performance in challenge/stress situations, and resistance to behavioral suppression (and presumably resistance to depression as well) and the research has shown secondly that the mediating physiological syndrome is associated with that same pattern of emotional stability, positive performance, and so forth. The complete nomological net of relationships between these various elements is drawn in Dienstbier (1989).

HOW TOUGHNESS RELATED TO ENERGY, PERFORMANCE, AND PERSONALITY

Contrary to the often repeated speculations about the archaic nature of human emotional responses, high episodic arousal in response to mental challenge/stress situations is potentially beneficial. Although only a few percent of body weight, the brain is a major energy consumer, accounting for approximately 20% of our at-rest metabolism (Smith, 1970), with increases to over 25% when challenging mental activities such as mental math are untertaken (Brod, 1970). Increased energy for mental activities is facilitated by peripheral as well as CNS arousal.

Both adrenaline and noradrenaline play a positive role in energy supply to the brain through circulatory system adjustments and through their role in the release and metabolism of glucose (where a primary role is played by adrenaline; Krotkiewski et al., 1983; Martin, 1985). Since glucose is the fuel of the nervous system and is directly influenced by adrenaline, the association between mental performance and adrenaline increases noted in the (largely) Scandinavian research is apparent.

On the other hand, noradrenaline increases correspond more highly with physical rather than mental activity (Frankenhaeuser, 1979). Noradrenaline is more involved than is adrenaline in the regulation of free fatty acids, and (with thyroxin) in regulating the conversion of fats to energy (Jansky, Mejsnar, & Moravec, 1976). In combination with the SNS- and noradrenaline-mediated blood pressure increases, necessary for major muscle functioning, noradrenaline is ideally suited for increasing energy and efficiency when high levels of physical activity are required.

The relationship of toughness with the personality dimension of emotional stability is also apparent taking the foregoing into account. Consider the association of emotional instability (i.e., chronic anxiety or neuroticism) and depression on the one hand with high arousal base-rates, high cortisol levels (Anisman & LaPierre, 1982; Persky, 1975), and lower SNS-adrenal-medullary response (Lader, 1983) on the other. The low arousal base-rates and delayed pituitary-adrenal-cortical responses and higher SNS-adrenal-medullary arousal (in challenge/stress situations) of the tough individual are physiological conditions associated therefore with emotional stability.

In addition to the impact of physiological toughness on performance and personality through the rather direct relationship of the tough neuroendocrine pattern leading both to mental and physical energy and to hormonal patterns associated with emotional stability, physiological toughness also apparently influences performance through its impact on appraisals or attributional processes. That influence is best understood by first considering the approach of Lazarus (1968) to coping.

IMPLICATIONS FOR COPING WITH LIFE CRISES AND LOSSES

In the Lazarus system, in the context of challenge or threat an individual makes a primary appraisal of the seriousness of the situation and its potential for positive or negative outcomes. That appraisal is followed by secondary appraisals of the skills and resources available for coping. The secondary appraisal in turn influences the primary appraisal, and so forth. My consideration of the importance of physiological toughness leads to a focus on energy levels as a principal resource that is taken into account in making secondary appraisals. That is, when coping will require a significant amount of energy (including situations in which only mental effort ist required), the physiological pattern of toughness will facilitate coping and, in an experienced individual, will be taken into account in making secondary appraisals. It is at this point that one of the fascinating relationships between mind and body becomes salient: When appraisals are made that success is likely (i.e., appraisals that the situation is a challenge more than a threat), the physiological pattern that results resembles, in the short term, the pattern described here as tough. Specifically, in the context of an appraisal of challenge, catecholamine levels increase while cortisol levels are held at base-rate levels or even reduced. Conversely, for an unfit individual with a history of low energy levels in the face of crises, the appraisals that are likely are that threat rather than challenge is imminent. With such an expectation, cortisol levels tend to increase along with catecholamine increases (Frankenhaeuser, Lundberg, & Forsman, 1980).

Thus, appraisals of challenge or threat carry an element of self-fulfillment, not only at the psychological level, where different levels of effort and styles of coping are likely to follow, but more directly at a physiological level, with each inducing a different pattern of phyiological response—responses with challenge that are associated with energy without tension (see Figure 19.1) or with threat that are associated more with tension and anxiety than only energy (see Figure 19.2). For

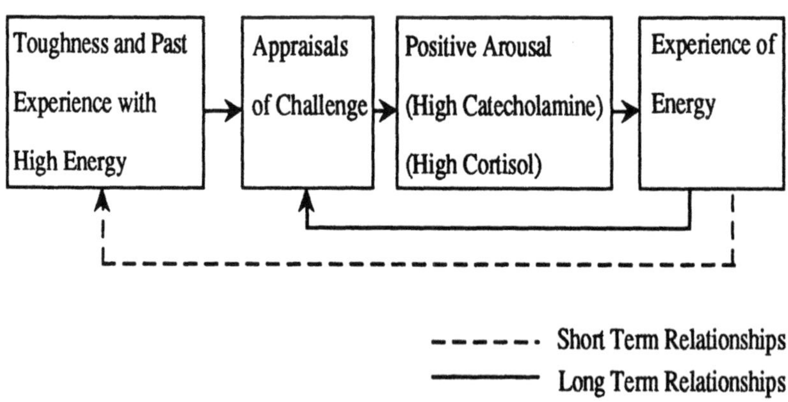

FIG. 19.1. Past experience being tough leads to appraisals of challenge, with a subsequent physiological arousal pattern that leads to energy and reinforcement of the expectation of success.

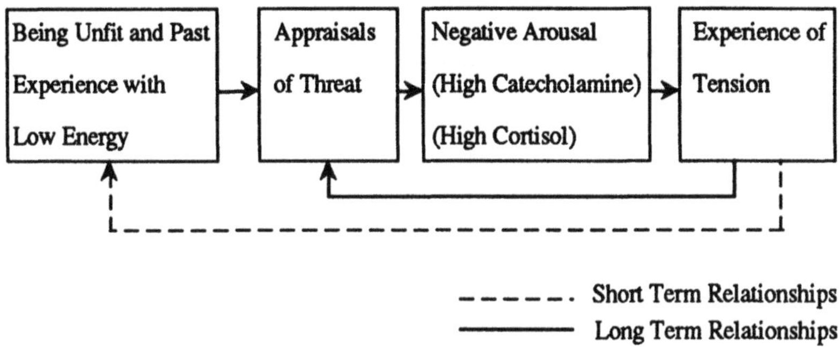

FIG. 19.2. Past experience of low energy in challenge/stress situations leads to appraisals of threat with a subsequent physiological arousal pattern that leads to tension and reinforcement of the expectation of failure.

reviews of the remarkable research underlying these observations, see Frankenhaeuser (1982) and Forsman (1983).

In the long term, expectations of success from challenge/threat situations are likely to lead to one seeking out stimulating situations. Regular experience with such stimulating situations is likely to lead, in turn, to toughening, increasing the potential for success in future situations, and leading to more adventurousness, etc. These relationships between appraisals and physiological responses in the short and long terms are shown in Figure 19.3, as are some relationships between toughness and immune processes to be discussed below.

Situations involving loss are almost by definition situations that are aversive without permitting effective instrumental activities. Such situations tend to lead to brain catecholamine depletion (in animal research such as that of Weiss & Glazer, 1975) and to high cortisol secretion levels (as shown by human research such as that of Rodin, 1980).

The research by Weiss and colleagues on behavioral suppression, reviewed above, clearly shows direct physiological benefits from toughness. In the context of even inescapable stressors, tougher individuals sustain less depletion of central catecholamines (Weiss et al., 1975) and delayed pituitary-adrenal-cortical responses (Starzec, Berger, & Hesse, 1983). Since CNS catecholamine exhaustion and high cortisol levels are both associated with depression and since cortisol levels are associated with suppression of the immune system, toughness is likely to result in delay of onset and perhaps avoidance of the problems of both mental and physical health that are associated with severe loss experiences.

In loss situations as in crises, the tough individual may gain advantages through the modified attributions that are likely to follow from a history of energy in difficult situations and from reduced depression. If a history of success leads to even a mistaken belief that one has control, then the pattern of physiological arousal will tend more to resemble that associated with toughness.

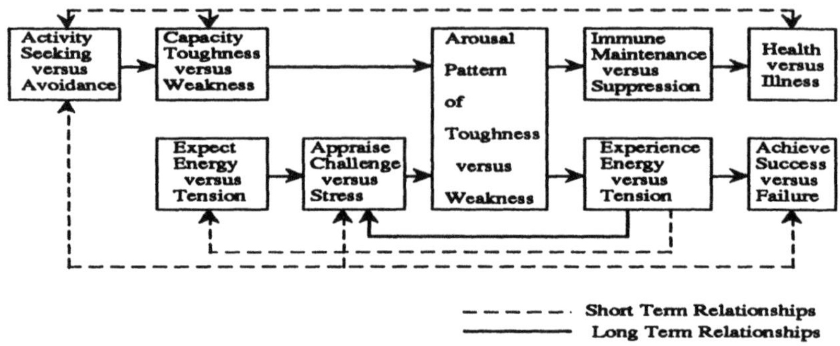

FIG. 19.3. Interrelationships between toughness (versus weakness) and the behavioral, psychological and physiological concomitants.

HOW TOUGHNESS RELATES TO HEALTH

Toughness and the Immune System

Most acute laboratory stressors used with animals, including shock, cold, or social stressors such as crowding, suppress immune functioning and cause susceptibility to all phases of tumor growth (Calabrese, Kling, & Gold, 1987; Sklar & Anisman, 1981). Long-term "crises" for humans such as living near the site of a nuclear power plant accident (Three Mile Island) and losses such as bereavement or being assigned to a nursing home similarly increase morbidity and mortality (Baum, 1986; Rodin, 1980).

Apparently the most damaging aspect to the immune system of the physiological response to stressful situations is the suppression of immune function by cortisol. Since toughness is associated with delayed cortisol responses, toughening should result in less disease when individuals experience crises or loss. Research with animals strongly supports this prediction. Sklar and Anisman (1981) noted that *regular* exposure to most laboratory stressors (from shock to cold, but *not* to social stressors) results in enhanced immune function and resistance to all phases of cancerous growth. Such positive effects from chronic stress are enhanced if the stress occurs before or soon after exposure to experimentally induced pathogens and if the animals have some control (Solomon, Kay, & Morley, 1986) over the stressors.[2]

---

[2]Cortisol suppresses immune system functioning by inhibiting the secretion of lymphokines (including interferons and interlukins) and depressing helper T-cell functioning. However, central and peripheral catecholamine availability enhances natural killer cell activity. Exposure to toughening manipulations leads to inhanced interferon production (Calabrese, Kling, & Gold, 1987; Sklar & Anisman, 1981; Solomon, Kay, & Morley, 1986).

These data support the frequently heard informal observation of individuals enjoying recently acquired exercise habits that their disease resistance is thereby strengthened, and suggest that a history of toughening activities before crises or loss will be prophylactic for both mental and physical health.

Toughness, Crises, and Cardiovascular Health

My analysis of the role played by toughness in the maintenance of cardiovascular health during crises or loss is based largely upon the literature on Type A personality.

Once it was noted that there is a connection between Type A personality disposition (time-concern, competitiveness, and hostility, labelled "Type A") and various cardiovascular diseases (hereafter coronary heart disease or CHD), researchers began to search for the expected mediating physiological variables (Matthews et al., 1986; Williams, 1986). Recent research indicates that higher peripheral physiological arousal or greater cardiovascular and neuroendocrine "responsivity" is often found for Type A's, especially in circumstances of difficult or challenging tasks (Holmes, McGilley, & Houston, 1984), previous "warmups" in other stimulating tasks (Ortega & Pipal, 1984), very competitive situations (Chesney & Rosenman, 1983), or understimulation (Lundberg, 1983).

Since toughness is associated with increased SNS-adrenal-medullary responsivity, toughness and the response characteristics of Type A persons look superficially similar, suggesting enhanced risks from toughness, particularly with frequent experiences of crises or losses. A superficial look at the literature appears to support this bleak conclusion, for there is a large and growing literature on the association of CHD with cardiovascular and autonomic reactivity to stressors (e.g., Matthews et al., 1986). For example, autonomically responsive animals show atherosclerosis of coronary arteries, elevated blood pressure, and similar unhealthy states (e.g., Manuck & Krantz, 1986). However, while most of the studies in this area define cardiovascular responsivity by base-rate to stressor-condition increases, few provide information about catecholamine or cortisol levels, and few provide data on speed of recovery from arousal (Matthews, 1986).

The recovery information is a crucial, since the tough recover quickly from SNS-adrenal-medullary arousal. Fortunately for the tough, reviews of studies of monkeys (e.g., Clarkson, Manuck, & Kaplan, 1986), and humans (e.g., Goldstein & McDonald, 1986; Ursin, 1978) have similarly concluded that it is the total duration of heightened arousal over long time periods (months or years) that leads to CHD. Other research has shown that unlike tough individuals, Type A persons recover more slowly from SNS-adrenal-medullary arousal, as demonstrated by slower T-wave response recovery in Type A's than B's following infusion of noradrenaline (Williams, 1986).

Additional differences between Type A's and the tough relate to arousal base-rates. That is, arousal base-rates on several parameters are higher in Type A's; those same arousal characteristics are associated with neuroticism and hostility—personality characteristics often associated with Type A's. On the other hand those arousal base-rates tend to be lower in the tough, especially as measured by urinary catecholamines (Forsman, 1981). In the context of challenges or crises, cortisol levels are higher for Type A's in contrast to others, while delayed cortisol secretion is a characteristic of toughness. For example, in studies of neuroendocrine responses to mental math, Williams (1986) noted that while Type A's gave higher adrenaline and noradrenaline responses, even greater differences in cortisol levels developed between Types A and B (with A's higher). Williams suggested that testosterone and cortisol hyper-responsivity were probably the major factors in CHD risk. Ursin and Knardahl (1985) reached similar conclusions, noting that Type A's with family histories of CHD had higher cortisol levels than other Type A's. Finally, in a review of neuroendocrine mechanisms in CHD, Herd (1986) cited more experimental evidence for the involvement of cortisol than for the catecholamines in fostering the vascular conditions leading to heart disease.

In conclusion, although "hyperresponsive" Type A's are prone to CHD, and although at first glance the tough seem similar, with their increased SNS-adrenal-medullary responsivity in challenge/stress situations, Type A's and the tough differ on the physiological and personality dimensions that seem crucial. That is, in contrast to Type A's (and to a lesser extent in contrast to the less fit) the tough have lower arousal base-rates and lower cortisol responsivity with quicker recovery from arousal. While Type A is associated with neuroticism, associated with lower rather than higher SNS-adrenal-medullary responses to challenge/stress albeit higher SNS base-rates (Lader, 1983), and with higher cortisol responsivity (Persky, 1975), toughness is associated with emotional stability.

These observations would suggest that in times of crisis and loss, when health risks are potentially increased by high arousal base-rates and by pituitary-adrenal-cortical arousal, that toughness is prophylactic rather than a risk factor in CHD.

RESEARCH ON LIFE EVENTS FROM THE PERSPECTIVE OF TOUGHNESS

The crises and losses that are the topic of this volume are usually major negative life events, and so they will usually be associated with health problems, as suggested by the foregoing section. However, like challenge/threat situations generally, in addition to causing short-term health problems, in the long term some life events may have the potential to toughen.

Researchers in the "life events" area originally endeavored to show that major negative or *positive* changes in life requiring "restructuring" result in increased incidences of illness (Holmes & Rahe, 1967). Indeed, they were initially quite successful as reflected in the association of life changes or "events" with illness being accepted in most introductory psychology texts. But research reviewed above suggests that regular or frequent exposure to positive life events (often experienced as challenges) and even frequent exposure to stressors that evoke SNS-adrenal-medullary arousal should lead to toughness, eventually impacting immunological function positively, and causing no CHD problems (e.g., Sklar & Anisman, 1981). How are these differences to be resolved?

The life-events field has been characterized by an increasing proportion of articles focusing upon methodological problems (Kasl, 1983). Early critiques of retrospective studies emphasized the problems of defining causal direction (e.g., would current illnesses bias recall of life events). Current critiques of the more recent prospective studies and of more objectively anchored retrospective studies still emphasize causal problems. For example, Kasl noted that third factors are frequently ignored (e.g., while certain medical specialities characterized by higher stress also show higher CHD, the physicians in those fields smoke more; young people sustain many more life events and have more illnesses than older individuals, so that the life events to illness correlation may be due to age as a third factor). Finally, many life events (e.g., divorce, job loss) may develop over long time periods and may be influenced by health rather than the reverse.

In Kasl's analysis, to eliminate such problems, one must eliminate from the life-events inventories those events that are possibly influenced by health and those that are under the individual's control (i.e., related to life style). With the 43-item Holmes and Rahe (1967) scale, one is then left with death of spouse, close family member. Schroeder and Costa (1984) argue that when the vague life-events items are eliminated, results do not support a general "life events to illness" hypothesis, and that prospective studies using objective measures of illness fail to show the predicted effects.

By itself, Kasl's (1983) thorough critique is devastating for most life-events research. Other critics have approached the methodological problems from different perspectives, with similar impact. For example, although both positive and negative life events are included in most scales (such as the Holmes and Rahe scale, 1967), those studies that have compared their impacts generally find no correlations between positive events and illness (see the review by Thoits, 1983). For example, in Theorell's (1976) large-scale prospective study of almost 10.000 building construction workers, only life events causing "discord" were found to be related to later illness incidences. In their review of depression, Anisman and LaPierre (1982) noted that only undesirable or unpleasant life events (rather than change per se) are associated with depression. Rabkin and Struening (1976) go further by suggesting that a relationship between life events and illness is evident only when positive life events are *substracted* from negative ones.

In summary, the toughening concept predicts no negative impacts from life events other than those life crises and losses that cause high levels of distress (and that therefore deplete catecholamines and/or increase cortisol). Toughness, whether through genetic predisposition or through experience with regular challenge/stress situations, should attenuate those negative impacts from crises and losses. In fact, this model predicts health benefits from frequent exposure to positive life events, particularly those associated with a feeling of control. In studying job environments, Karasek, Russell, and Theorell (1982) have identified challenging occupations with high control as leading to some of the same physiological changes associated with toughness.

WHAT EXPERIENCES LEAD TO TOUGHENING?

Apparently tough individuals are able to face crises and losses with less negative impact on their mental and physical health than are the less fit. At issue in this section is the question of what kinds of experiences or perceptions of experience may have the most positive impact on the development of physiological toughness.

Research reviewed above has shown that regular stress such as electric shock and regular exercise effectively stimulate the development of toughness in laboratory animals. Exposure to cold and aerobic exercise have been shown to lead to similar results in humans. I have suggested elsewhere that the association of the humor response with catecholamine generation (Fry, 1986) in individuals who are bed-ridden suggests that humor may toughen, and research by Karasek et al. (1982) suggests in a preliminary way that occupational challenge (with control) may lead to toughening. I would speculatively add to this list that positive forms of social interaction that are high in stimulation quality may serve similar functions.

In the abstract, the toughening of any physiological system seems dependent upon a rhythm of regular stimulation followed by an interval during which recovery (eventually beyond initial levels of capability) is possible. I suspect that the reason that social stressors such as crowding are not effective (in laboratory animals; Sklar & Anisman, 1981) is that the necessary recovery intervals are missing.

In human life, if our "crises" are daily events (e.g., demanding deadlines as in editing a newspaper), they should toughen us unless we are unable to stop worrying once each "crisis" has been met. Major losses, on the other hand, are likely to be infrequent and to elicit pituitary-adrenal-cortical responses as much or more than SNS-adrenal-medullary responses. If they preoccupy us for long periods, such as is often the case with deaths, they are likely to provide insufficient recovery periods for toughness to develop and to cause depletion of catecholamines, rather than increased neuroendocrine resources.

In conclusion, it has been popular to say that we need some "stress" in our lives to remain appropriately stimulated and to grow. Terms such as Selye's (1956) "eustress" have been coined to suggest this positive aspect of stress. In my terms, as defined in this chapter, we will certainly benefit by becoming tougher through regular exposure to challenges that are physical, and probably as well through exposure to those that are mental; we will probably benefit through periodic exposure to some milder life crises—situations that may threaten us, provided we have recovery periods, probably at nearly daily intervals (precluding extensive worrying). On the other hand, while we will face any challenge, threat, or harm/loss situation with more energy and with higher neuroendocrine reserves if we are tough, we should not expect to toughen from severe harm/losses.

REFERENCES

Anisman, H., & LaPierre, Y. (1982). Neurochemical aspects of stress and depression: Formulations and caveats. In R. W. Neufeld (Ed.), *Psychological stress and psychopathology* (pp. 179-217). New York: McGraw-Hill.

Baum, A. S. (1986, August). *Chronic and extreme stress: Psychobiological influences on health.* Paper presented at the annual meeting of the American Psychological Association, Washington, DC.

Brod, J. (1970). Haemodynamics of emotional stress. In M. Koster, H. Musaph, & P. Viser (Eds.), *Psychosomatics in essential hypertension* (pp. 13-37). Basel: Karger.

Brown, B. S., & Van Huss, W. (1973). Exercise and rat brain catecholamines. *Journal of Applied Physiology, 34,* 664-669.

Calabrese, J. R., Kling, M. A., & Gold, P. W. (1987). Alterations in immunocompetence during stress, bereavement, and depression: Focus on neuroendocrine regulation. *American Journal of Psychiatry, 144,* 1123-1134.

Chesney, M. A., & Rosenman, R. H. (1983). Specificity in stress models: Examples drawn from Type A behavior. In C. L. Cooper (Ed.), *Stress research: Issues for the eighties* (pp. 21-34). New York: Wiley.

Clarkson, T. B., Manuck, S. B., & Kaplan, J. R. (1986). Potential role of cardiovascular reactivity in atherogenesis. In K. A. Matthews, S. M. Weiss, T. Detre, T. M. Dembroski, B. Falkner, S. B. Manuck, & R. B. Williams, Jr. (Eds.), *Handbook of stress, reactivity, and cardiovascular disease* (pp. 35-48). New York: Wiley.

Dienstbier, R. A. (1984). The effect of exercise on personality. In M. L. Sachs & G. B. Buffone (Eds.), *Running as therapy: An integrated approach* (pp. 253-272). Lincoln: University of Nebraska Press.

Dienstbier, R. A. (1989). Arousal and physiological toughness: Implications for mental and physical health. *Psychological Review, 96,* 84-100.

Dienstbier, R. A., LaGuardia, R. L., Barnes, M., Tharp, G., & Schmidt, R. (1987). Catecholamine training effects from exercise programs: A bridge to exercise-temperament relationships. *Motivation and Emotion, 11,* 297-318.

Faucheau, B. A., Bourlière, F., Baulon, A., & Dupuis, C. (1981). The effects of psychosocial stress on urinary excretion of adrenaline and noradrenaline in 51- to 55- and 71- to 74-year-old men. *Gerontology, 27,* 313-325.

Folkman, S., & Lazarus, R. S. (1985). If it changes it must be a process: Study of emotion and coping during three stages of a college examination. *Journal of Personality and Social Psychology, 48,* 150-170.

Forsman, L. (1981). Habitual catecholamine excretion and its relation to habitual distress. *Biological Psychology, 11,* 83-97.

Forsman, L. (1983). *Individual and group differences in psychophysiological responses to stress—With emphasis on sympathetic-adrenal medullary and pituitary-adrenal corticol responses.* Unpublished doctoral dissertation, University of Stockholm, Sweden.

Frankenhaeuser, M. (1979). Psychoneuroendocrine approaches to the study of emotion as related to stress and coping. In H. E. Howe, Jr., & R. A. Dienstbier (Eds.), *Nebraska Symposium on Motivation, 1978: Human emotion* (Vol. 27, pp. 123-161). Lincoln: University of Nebraska Press.

Frankenhaeuser, M. (1982). Challenge-control interaction as reflected in sympathetic-adrenal and pituitary-adrenal activity: Comparison between the sexes. *Scandinavian Journal of Psychology*, (Suppl. 1), 158-164.

Frankenhaeuser, M., Lundberg, U., & Forsman, L. (1980). Dissociation between sympathetic-adrenal and pituitary-adrenal responses to an achievement situation characterized by high controllability: Comparison between Type A and Type B males and females. *Biological Psychology, 10*, 79-91.

Fry, W. R., Jr. (1986). Humor, physiology, and the aging process. In L. Nahemow, K. A. McCluskey-Fawcett, & P. E. McGhee (Eds.), *Humor and aging* (pp. 91-98). Orlando, FL: Academic Press.

Ganong, W. F., Kramer, N., Reid, I. A., Boryczka, A. T., & Shackelford, R. (1976). Inhibition of stress-induced ACTH secretion by norepinephrine in the dog: Mechanism and site of action. In E. Usdin, R. Kvetnansky, & I. J. Kopin (Eds.), *Catecholamines and stress* (pp. 139-144). Oxford, England: Pergamon.

Glazer, H. I., Weiss, J. M., Pohorecky, L. A., & Miller, N. E. (1975). Monoamines as mediators of avoidance-escape behavior. *Psychosomatic Medicine, 37*, 535-543.

Goldstein, D. S., & McDonald, R. H. (1986). Biochemical indices of cardiovascular reactivity. In K. A. Matthews, S. M. Weiss, T. Detre, T. M. Dembroski, B. Falkner, S. B. Manuck, & R. B. Williams, Jr. (Eds.), *Handbook of stress, reactivity, and cardiovascular disease* (pp. 187-203). New York: Wiley.

Harri, M. N. E. (1979). Physical training under the influence of beta-blockade in rats. II: Effects on vascular reactivity. *European Journal of Applied Physiology, 42*, 151-157.

Herd, J. A. (1986). Neuroendocrine mechanisms in coronary heart disease. In K. A. Matthews, S. M. Weiss, T. Detre, T. M. Dembroski, B. Falkner, S. B. Manuck, & R. B. Williams, Jr. (Eds.), *Handbook of stress, reactivity, and cardiovascular disease* (pp. 49-70). New York: Wiley.

Holmes, D. S., McGilley, B. M., & Houston, B. K. (1984). Task-related arousal of Type A and Type B persons: Level of challenge and response specifity. *Journal of Personality and Social Psychology, 46*, 1322-1327.

Holmes, T. H., & Rahe, R. H. (1967). The Social Readjustment Rating Scale. *Journal of Psychosomatic Research, 11*, 213-218.

Hull, E., Young, S., & Ziegler, M. (1984). Aerobic fitness affects cardiovascular and catecholamine responses to stressors. *Psychophysiology, 21*, 253-260.

Jansky, L., Mejsnar, J., & Moravec, J. (1976). Catecholamines and cold stress. In E. Usdin, R. Kvetnansky, & I. J. Kopin (Eds.), *Catecholamines and stress* (pp. 419-434). Oxford, England: Pergamon.

Johansson, G., Frankenhaeuser, M., & Magnusson, D. (1973). Catecholamine output in school children as related to performance and adjustment. *Scandinavian Journal of Psychology, 14*, 20-28.

Karasek, R. A., Russell, R. S., & Theorell, T. (1982). Physiology of stress and regeneration in job-related cardiovascular illness. *Journal of Human Stress, 8*(1), 29-42.

Kasl, S. V. (1983). Pursuing the link between stressful life experiences and disease: A time for reappraisal. In C. L. Cooper (Ed.), *Stress research: Issues for the eighties* (pp. 79-102). New York: Wiley.

Krotkiewski, M., Mandroukas, K., Morgan, L., William-Olsson, T., Feurle, G. E., von Schenck, H., Bjorntorp, P., Sjostrom, L., & Smith, U. (1983). Effects of physical training on adrenergic sensitivity in obesity. *Journal of Applied Physiology, 55*, 1811-1817.

Lader, M. (1983). Anxiety and depression. In A. Gale & J. A. Edwards (Eds.), *Physiological correlates of human behavior. Vol. III: Individual differences and psychopathology* (pp. 155-167). London: Academic Press.

Lazarus, R. S. (1968). Emotions and adaptation: Conceptual and empirical relations. In W. J. Arnold (Ed.), *Nebraska Symposium on Motivation* (Vol. 16, pp. 175-266). Lincoln: University of Nebraska Press.

Levine, S. (1960). Stimulation in infancy. *Scientific American, 202*, 80-86.

Lundberg, U. (1983). Psychoneuroendocrine aspects of mental work as related to Type A behaviour. In H. Ursin & R. Murison (Eds.), *Biological and psychological basis of psychosomatic disease* (pp. 193-207). Oxford: Pergamon.

Manuck, S. B., & Krantz, D. S. (1986). Psychophysiologic reactivity in coronary heart disease and essential hypertension. In K. A. Matthews, S. M. Weiss, T. Detre, T. M. Dembroski, B. Falkner, S. D. Manuck, & R. B. Williams, Jr. (Eds.), *Handbook of stress, reactivity, and cardiovascular disease* (pp. 11-34). New York: Wiley.

Martin, C. R. (1985). *Endocrine physiology*. New York: Oxford University Press.

Matthews, K. A. (1986). Summary, conclusions, and implications. In K. A. Matthews, S. M. Weiss, T. Detre, T. M. Dembroski, B. Falkner, S. B. Manuck, & R. B. Williams, Jr. (Eds.), *Handbook of stress, reactivity, and cardiovascular disease* (pp. 461-473). New York: Wiley.

Matthews, K. A., Weiss, S. M., Detre, T., Dembroski, T. M., Falkner, B., Manuck, S. B., & Williams, R. B., Jr. (Eds.). (1986). *Handbook of stress, reactivity, and cardiovascular disease*. New York: Wiley.

McGaugh, J. L. (1983). Preserving the presence of the past: Hormonal influences on memory storage. *American Psychologist, 38*, 161-174.

Meaney, M. J., Aitkens, D. H., Berkel, C., Bhatnagar, S., Sarrieau, A., & Sapolsky, R. M. (1987). *Post-natal handling attenuates age-related changes in the adrenocortical stress response and spatial memory deficits in the rat*. Paper presented at the 17th Annual Meeting of the Society of Neuroscience, New Orleans.

Ortega, D. F., & Pipal, J. E. (1984). Challenge seeking and the Type A coronary-prone behavior pattern. *Journal of Personality and Social Psychology, 46*, 1328-1334.

Persky, H. (1975). Adrenocortical function and anxiety. *Psychoneuroendocrinology, 1*, 37-44.

Pfeifer, W. D. (1976). Modification of adrenal tyrosine hydroxylase activity in rats following manipulation in infancy. In E. Usdin, R. Kvetnansky, & I. J. Kopin (Eds.), *Catecholamines and stress* (pp. 265-270). Oxford, England: Pergamon.

Potter, W. Z., Ross, R. J., & Zavadil, A. P., III (1985). Norepinephrine in the affective disorders: Classic biochemical approaches. In C. R. Lake & M. G. Ziegler (Eds.), *The catecholamines in psychiatric and neurologic disorders* (pp. 213-233). Boston: Butterworth.

Rabkin, J. G., & Struening, E.L. (1976). Life events, stress, and illness. *Science, 194*, 1013-1020.

Rauste-von Wright, M., von Wright, J., & Frankenhaeuser, M. (1981). Relationships between sex-related psychological characteristics during adolescence and catecholamine excretion during achievement stress. *Psychophysiology, 18*, 362-370.

Ritter, S., & Pelzer, N. L. (1978). Magnitude of stress-induced brain norepinephrine depletion varies with age. *Brain Research, 152*, 170-175.

Rodin, J. (1980). Managing the stress of aging: The role of control and coping. In S. Levine & H. Ursin (Eds.), *Coping and health* (pp. 171-202). New York: Plenum.

Roessler, R., Burch, N. R., & Mefferd, R. B. (1967). Personality correlates of catecholamine excretion under stress. *Journal of Psychosomatic Research, 11*, 181-185.

Schroeder, D. H., & Costa, P. T., Jr. (1984). Influence of life event stress on physical illness: Substantive effects or methodological flaws? *Journal of Personality and Social Psychology, 46*, 853-863.

Selye, H. (1956). *The stress of life*. New York: McGraw-Hill.

Sklar, L. S., & Anisman, H. (1981). Stress and cancer. *Psychological Bulletin, 89*, 369-406.

Smith, C. U. M. (1970). *The brain*. New York: Putnam.

Solomon, G. S., Kay, N., & Morley, J. E. (1986). Endorphins: A link between personality, stress, emotions, immunity, and disease? In N. P. Plotnikoff, R. E. Faith, A. J. Murgo, & R. A. Good (Eds.), *Enkephalins and endorphins: Stress and the immune system* (pp. 129-144). New York: Plenum.

Starzec, J. J., Berger, D. F., & Hesse, R. (1983). Effects of stress and exercise on plasma corticosterone, plasma cholesterol, and aortic cholesterol levels in rats. *Psychosomatic Medicine, 45*, 219-226.

Theorell, T. (1976). Selected illnesses and somatic factors in relation to two psychosocial stress indices: A prospective study on middle-aged construction building workers. *Journal of Psychosomatic Research, 20*, 7-20.

Thoits, P. A. (1983). Dimensions of life events that influence psychological distress: An evaluation and synthesis of the literature. In H. B. Kaplan (Ed.), *Psychosocial stress: Trends in theory and research* (pp. 33-103). New York: Academic Press.

Ursin, H. (1978). Activation, coping, and psychosomatics. In H. Ursin, E. Baade, & S. Levine (Eds.), *Psychobiology of stress: A study of coping men* (pp. 201-228). New York: Academic Press.

Ursin, H., Baade, E., & Levine, S. (Eds.). (1978). *Psychobiology of stress: A study of coping men*. New York: Academic Press.

Ursin, H., & Knardahl, S. (1985). Personality factors, neuroendocrine response patterns, and cardiovascular pathology. In J. F. Orlebeke, G. Mulder, & L. J. P. van Doornen (Eds.), *The psychophysiology of cardiovascular control* (pp. 715-731). New York: Plenum.

van Praag, H. M. (1986). Monoamines and depression: The present state of the art. In R. Plutchik & H. Kellerman (Eds.), *Emotion: Theory, research, and experience. Vol. 3: Biological foundations of emotion* (pp. 335-361). Orlando, FL: Academic Press.

Weiss, J. M., & Glazer, H. I. (1975). Effects of acute exposure to stressors on subsequent avoidance-escape behavior. *Psychosomatic Medicine, 37*, 499-521.

Weiss, J. M., Glazer, H. I., Pohorecky, L. A., Brick, J., & Miller, N. E. (1975). Effects of chronic exposure to stressors on avoidance-escape behavior and on brain norepinephrine. *Psychosomatic Medicine, 37*, 522-534.

Williams, R. B., Jr. (1986, August). *Beyond Type A: Psychological and physiological refinements*. Paper presented at the meeting of the American Psychological Association, Washington, DC.

20 Constructive Thinking and Mental and Physical Well-Being[1]

Seymour Epstein
University of Massachusetts at Amherst

Constructive thinking is defined as the ability to solve problems in everyday life at a minimal cost in stress. Recently, a promising measure of constructive thinking, the Constructive Thinking Inventory (CTI), was introduced (Epstein & Meier, 1989). The most recent version of the CTI contains a global scale plus the following 6 specific scales: Emotional Coping, Behavioral Coping, Categorical Thinking, Superstitious Thinking, Naive Optimism, and Esoteric Thinking. These scales, although moderately independent, are all, with the exception of Naive Optimism, significantly interrelated. The scales were all derived from the factor analysis of a large sample of items that described everyday adaptive and maladaptive thinking. The finding of a general factor, from which the global scale was derived, is of considerable interest as it indicates that there is a *g* of constructive thinking analogous to the *g* factor in intelligence. People who are good constructive thinkers in one way tend to be good constructive thinkers in other ways. The specific scales indicate, again like intelligence, that constructive thinking is composed of a limited number of separate abilities in addition to a highly general ability.

Emotional Coping and Behavioral Coping were derived from the two largest factors, by far, in the factor analysis. This indicates that the domain of automatic constructive and destructive thinking can largely be divided into coping with the external world of events and the world of inner experience, corresponding to Lazarus and Folkman's (1984) conceptualization of problem-focused and emotion-focused coping. Unlike Emotional and Behavioral Coping, the scales of Categori-

---

[1]Preparation of this manuscript and the research reported in it were supported by NIMH Research Grant MH01293 and NIMH Research Scientist Award K)5 MH00363.

I wish to acknowledge the contribution of Carolyn Holstein, who did the computing on most of the studies that were reported.

cal Thinking and Superstitious Thinking describe processes rather than content. Categorical Thinking refers to all-or-none, or black-and-white thinking. A typical item is, "There are basically two kinds of people in this world, good and bad." The items in the Superstitious Thinking scale refer to private superstitions, such as that if something good happens it will be balanced by something bad, and not to conventional superstitions, such as bad luck being associated with black cats and Friday the 13th. These private superstitions are all negative and suggest a way of thinking that attempts to reduce the sting of adversity by dampening positive expectations and preparing for adversity in advance. It is therefore not surprising that high scores on the scale have been found to be associated with feelings of depression and helplessness. The scale of Naive Optimism includes mainly references to positive overgeneralization. The optimism is therefore highly unrealistic. There is also a pollyannaish quality about several of the items. Naive Optimism has produced nonsignificant correlations with measures of adjustment, probably because the positive thinking aspect is cancelled out by the unrealistic aspect. The Esoteric Thinking scale contains items that refer to belief in the unusual. Included are beliefs in astrology, ghosts, omens, clairvoyance, and thought projection.

Although the CTI is a relatively new test, a considerable amount of research has been done with it (Epstein, 1990; Epstein & Katz, 1990; Epstein, Lipson, Holstein, & Huh, 1990; Epstein & Meier, 1989; Katz & Epstein, 1990). It has been found that the CTI is more highly correlated with a wide variety of criteria of success in living, including success in the work place, success in social and romantic relationships, and mental and physical well-being, than any of the other measures with which it has been compared, including the I-E scale (Rotter, 1966), the Hardiness scales (Kobasa, Maddi, & Courington, 1981), the Attribution Style Questionnaire (ASQ; Peterson et al., 1982), the Social Support Questionnaire (SSQ; Sarason, Levine, Basham, & Sarason, 1983), and measures of neuroticism and intelligence (described in Epstein, 1990, and in Epstein & Meier, 1989).

The present article extracts relevant results from four studies with respect to relations among constructive thinking, stress, and mental and physical well-being. The studies represent a variety of approaches, including retrospective reports, daily observations, and laboratory investigations. Each has its limitations and advantages. Convergences across the different approaches are therefore of particular interest. In addition, the article discusses issues of special interest with respect to conducting research on stress and coping, such as the confounding between measures of everyday life stress, coping, and symptoms.

CONSTRUCTIVE THINKING AND EMOTIONAL AND PHYSICAL WELL-BEING AS DETERMINED BY RETROSPECTIVE RECALL

An advantage to retrospective recall studies of stress, coping, and well-being is that they are easy to conduct. Not surprisingly, these are the most widely reported studies. The findings from such studies have consistently demonstrated significant positive relations between self-reported measures of stress and of symptoms and significant negative relations between self-reported measures of coping ability and of symptoms. The results have been mixed with respect to demonstrating a significant interaction between coping ability and stress on symptoms, which, if found, would support the hypothesis that coping moderates the effect of potential stressors on symptoms. Not only is the issue of whether there is a significant interaction unresolved, but the interpretation of the main effects is also unclear. It has become evident that a serious problem in studies that rely on retrospective self-recall is that a general tendency to report negative affect, or a general neuroticism factor, can account for most of the findings that have been reported (Costa & McCrae, 1987; Watson & Pennebaker, 1989). That is, people who have negative reporting styles can be expected to report that they experience more stress than others, that they are poorer copers, and that they have more symptoms than others regardless of the objective facts. Even the use of what may appear to be more objective criteria, such as number of visits to a medical facility, does not escape this criticism, because the same people who are biased to report negatively are more likely to seek medical help than others because they view the same symptoms as more serious. The best solution to this problem is to obtain objective data, such as medically verified symptoms of disease or direct measures of physiological reactions (Contrada, 1989; Costa & McCrae, 1987). However, the opportunity to obtain such data is not always available, and therefore restricting research by the requirement that only objective data be regarded as valid would seriously limit the research on stress, coping, and symptoms. An alternative approach is to take into account the patterning of symptoms. If it can be demonstrated that people report symptoms in a differentiated, coherent manner, then the results cannot be explained away by a diffuse negative reporting bias. This is the approach that was taken in the first study to be described.

In a study conducted by Epstein and Meier (1989), several measures of coping style (the CTI, the ASQ, and the I-E), a measure of social support (the SSQ), and a measure of intelligence (the Shipley Hartford scales of vocabulary and abstract thinking) were administered to 174 undergraduate college students. The students also responded to questionnaires that elicited information on various criteria of success in living and on the students' physical and mental health. In responding to a medical checklist, the frequency with which a number of symptoms were experienced during the past year was reported. Table 20.1 presents the correlations of the three most important CTI scales (Global Constructive Thinking, Emotional

Coping, and Behavioral Coping), the I-E scale, the three most important ASQ scales, the three SSQ scales, and three measures of intelligence with the sums of four kinds of symptoms: psychological symptoms, physical symptoms, self-discipline problems, and alcohol and drug problems.

It can be seen in Table 20.1 that the CTI scales produce stronger negative correlations with all four kinds of symptoms than any of the other self-report questionnaires or the measures of intelligence. Moreover, there is considerable differentiation within the various scales as to which scales are most strongly associated with which symptoms.

The CTI Emotional Coping Scale produces a substantial correlation ($r = -.46$, $p < .001$) with psychological symptoms, which is considerably higher than the correlations with psychological symptoms produced by the CTI Behavioral Coping

TABLE 20.1

Correlations Between Major Scales and Symptoms

Scale	*Psychological Symptoms*	*Physical Symptoms*	*Self Discipline Problems*	*Alcohol and Drug Problems*
CTI Global Scale	-.39***	-.22**	-.25***	-.22**
CTI Emotional Coping	-.46***	-.28***	-.11	-.23
CTI Behavioral Coping	-.31***	-.18*	-.25***	-.15*
I-E Scale+	.21**	.17*	.15	.09
A S Q Overall Composite	-.05	-.02	-.13	-.06
A S Q Negative Composite	.16*	.13	-.12	.15
A S Q Positive Composite	.07	.09	-.07	.05
S S Q Overall Support	-.09	.01	.00	-.14
S S Q Satisfaction w/Support	.03	.17*	-.04	-.18*
S S Q Quantity of Support	-.04	-.02	-.01	-.15
Total IQ	.17*	-.04	-.14	-.02
Vocabulatory IQ	.14	-.08	-.22**	-.02
Abstract Thinking IQ	.11	-.01	-.02	-.03

+Scored in the direction of externality

*p <.05

**p <.01

***p <.001

Scale and by any of the scales in other inventories. When the best predicting scale from each inventory is entered into a regression equation for predicting psychological symptoms, and the CTI Emotional Coping scale is entered last, it displaces all other scales.

Turning to physical symptoms, which include mainly minor ailments, such as stomach aches, headaches, muscle pains, colds, influenza, etc., the pattern of results is similar, although the correlations are less strong. The highest correlation is produced by the CTI Emotional Coping scale ($r = -.28, p < .001$). The highest correlation produced by a scale from another inventory is .17 ($p < .05$), which is produced by both the I-E and the SSQ. However, it is noteworthy that the positive correlation with the SSQ scale is in the opposite direction of a buffering effect, and indicates that those with the most physical symptoms are most satisfied with the social support they receive, possibly because of their ailments. The correlation with the I-E scale is in the expected direction, with those with an external locus of control reporting the greatest amount of symptoms. When the best predicting scale in the expected direction from each inventory is entered in a regression equation for predicting physical symptoms, as in the case with psychological symptoms, the CTI Emotional Coping scale displaces all other scales.

Self-discipline problems include frequency of overeating to the point of discomfort, undisciplined study habits, discrepancy between actual and ideal body weight, and frequency of overindulging in drugs and alcohol. The CTI Behavioral Coping scale produces the highest correlation among all the scales with self-discipline problems ($r = -.25, p < .001$). None of the scales from the other self-report inventories is even significantly correlated with self-discipline problems. Moreover the correlation of self-discipline problems with the Behavioral Coping scale is considerably higher than its correlation with the CTI Emotional Coping scale ($r = -.11$). For alcohol and drug problems, which is a subset of self-discipline problems, the CTI Emotional Coping scale produces the highest correlation ($r = -.23, p < .01$). The only significant correlation with alcohol and drug problems by a scale from another inventory is a correlation of -.18 ($p < .05$) with the SSQ. People who are more satisfied with their social support report fewer self-discipline problems than people who are less satisfied.

There are four important conclusions from the above findings. The first is that the CTI is much more strongly related to mental and physical well-being than any of the other measures. The second is that the different pattern of correlations established by the CTI Emotional and Behavioral Coping scales attests to the discriminant validity of the CTI scales. Moreover, the findings which are the bases of both of these conclusions cannot be attributed to differences in reliability, because the comparative relations remain unchanged when the measures are adjusted for unreliability. The third conclusion, which follows from the first two, is that the results cannot be accounted for by the existence of a global negativity, or neuroticism, factor. As further support for this conclusion, the correlation of neuroticism and the CTI scales accounts for less than half of their common variance after adjusting for unreliability of measurement, which indicates that constructive thinking and neuroticism are not equivalent concepts. Finally, it can be concluded that the results support a genuine relationship between various kinds of symptoms, mental, physical, and behavioral, and trait measures of coping ability.

CONSTRUCTIVE THINKING, HARDINESS, STRESS, PRODUCTIVE LOAD, AND MENTAL AND PHYSICAL WELL-BEING AS DETERMINED BY RETROSPECTIVE RECALL

A problem with much of the research that has investigated the relations between stress, coping, and symptoms is that the measures of stress have been confounded with maladaptive behavior (Dohrenwend & Dohrenwend, 1978). For example, in the Daily Hassles scale (Kanner, Coyne, Schaefer, & Lazarus, 1981), subjects are asked to indicate whether certain stressors occurred, and, if so, to rate them for how distressing they were experienced to be. Since distress itself is an index of maladjustment, it is no wonder that scores on the Daily Hassles scale are associated with symptoms and coping. Scales such as the Daily Hassles scale are, therefore, as much a trait measure of coping ability as they are of the occurrence of stressors independent of coping ability. Consider, further, the inclusion of items such as "misplacing or losing things," "legal problems," and "problems getting along with fellow workers." All of these can result from an individual's maladaptive behavior and are therefore reflective of a relatively stable trait of poor constructive thinking, or coping ability. It follows that, if one wishes to study stress independent of coping style, it is important to discriminate between stressors that can be instigated in whole or in part by an individual's own behavior and stressors that occur independently from an individual's behavior.

In a recent study, Epstein and Katz (1990) separately examined the correlates of "externally produced stress," defined as stress produced by events unlikely to be influenced by the individual, such as death of a loved one; "self-produced stress," defined as stress that might have been produced by the individual; and "total stress," which was a combination of the two. In addition, the concept of "productive load" was introduced and measured. Productive load was operationally defined as the sum of an individual's socially and personally constructive accomplishments of all kinds. It included items such as total academic credits carried, time devoted to working for pay, time devoted to philanthropic, political, and social organizations, positions of leadership held, such as club treasurer or secretary, social activities engaged in, and time devoted to athletics and exercise. A final purpose of the study was to compare the strengths of the relations produced by the CTI and Hardiness scales with self-produced stress, load, and symptoms. A total of 450 college student volunteers, all of whom took the CTI, participated in the study. Hardiness was

TABLE 20.2

Correlations of Constructive Thinking Inventory & Hardiness Scales with Stress and Load Variables

	Stress and Load Variables			
	Total Stress	*Self-produced Stress*	*Externally produced Stress*	*Productive Load*
CTI Scales				
Global Scale	-.21**	-.23**	-.02	.18**
Emotional Coping	-.20**	-.20**	-.08	.09
Behavioral Coping	-.10	-.12*	.07	.29**
Categorical Thinking	.08	.10	-.04	-.01
Personal Superstitious Thinking	.20**	.21**	.02	-.04
Naive Optimism	-.04	-.01	-.02	-.00
Esoteric Thinking	.19**	.18**	.11	-.10
Hardiness Scales				
Total Hardy	-.21**	-.21**	-.06	.12
Commitment	-.20**	-.21**	-.04	.09
Control	-.15	-.16*	-.02	.13
Challenge	-.14	-.13	-.09	.07

Note. Sex is partialled out of all correlations. The correlations for the CTI are based on the entire sample of subjects who took the CTI (*N*=438), which is considerably greater than those who took the Hardiness Scales (*N*=281). When the sample of subjects for the CTI is restricted to those who also took the Hardiness scales, the correlations for the CTI scales increase. The comparisons in the above table, therefore, are biased in favor of the Hardiness scales.

*$p < .05$
**$p < .01$

measured by the Personal Views Survey (Kobasa et al., 1981), a 50-item self-report inventory. Different subsets of subjects took different batteries of tests.

Table 20.2 presents the correlations of the CTI and Hardiness scales with total stress, self-produced stress, externally produced stress, and productive load. It can be seen that the CTI and Hardiness scales both produce significant correlations with total stress and self-produced stress, and neither produces a significant relation with externally produced stress. These findings support the hypothesis that good constructive thinkers and hardy individuals experience less stress in living than others because they behave in ways that are less stress-producing (e.g., they are less likely to provoke others into hassling them, and they are less likely to lose things and make careless errors).

It can also be seen in Table 20.2 that only the CTI produces significant correlations with productive load. One of the criticisms leveled against the Hardiness scales is that they measure an absence of maladaptive behavior rather than the presence of adaptive behavior (Hull, Van Treuren, & Virnelli, 1987; Rhodewalt & Zone, 1989). The present findings are consistent with this criticism as one would expect hardy individuals to carry heavier productive loads than less hardy individuals.

Evidence of the discriminant validity of the CTI scales is provided by the different pattern of correlations produced by the Emotional Coping and Behavioral Coping scales with the load and stress variables. It can be seen in Table 20.2 that emotional coping is significantly associated with total stress ($r = -.20, p < .001$) and self-produced stress ($r = -.20, p < .001$), but not with productive load ($r = .09$), whereas behavioral coping is significantly associated with productive load ($r = .29, p < .001$), but not with total stress ($r = -.10$), and only weakly ($r = -.12$), although reliably ($p < .001$), with self-produced stress.

Table 20.3 presents the relations of the CTI and Hardiness scales with various kinds of symptoms reported to have been experienced over the past year. It can be seen that the CTI scales produce significant correlations with a variety of symptoms, whereas the Hardiness scales produce significant correlations with only total emotional symptoms and satisfaction with health. Moreover, the CTI scales produce considerably stronger correlations with emotional symptoms than the Hardiness scales. The highest correlation of emotional symptoms with a CTI scale is -.39 in comparison to -.27 for the highest correlation with a Hardiness scale, the former correlation accounting for twice the amount of variance as the latter. Only on the measure of satisfaction with health, the most subjective measure among the symptom variables, do the Hardiness scales produce as strong correlations as the CTI scales. (It should be noted that the correlations in Table 20.3 are for the entire sample of subjects who took the CTI, which is considerably larger than those who took the Hardiness questionnaire. When the sample of subjects for the CTI is restricted to those who also took the Hardiness questionnaire, the correlations for the CTI scales increase. The comparisons in Table 20.3 are therefore biased in favor of the Hardiness scales.) When the best predicting scales from the CTI and

TABLE 20.3

Correlations of Constructive Thinking Inventory and Hardiness Scales with Symptoms

	Symptoms						
	Total Emotional Symptoms	*Total Physical Symptoms*	*Infectious Disease*	*Skin Problems*	*Sleep Problems*	*Accidents*	*Satisfaction with Health*
CTI Coping Scales (N=408)							
Global Scale	-.35***	-.18***	-.17***	-.16**	-.15**	-.17***	.26***
Emotional Coping	-.39***	-.18***	-.12**	-.14**	-.11	-.15**	.24***
Behavioral Coping	-.24***	-.13**	-.11	-.12**	-.10	-.14**	.28***
Categorical Thinking	.01	-.00	-.01	.01	.04	.04	-.02
Superstitious Thinking	.23***	.15**	.12**	.10	.14**	.14**	-.19***
Naive Optimism	-.05	-.04	.01	-.06	-.03	.04	.07
Esoteric Thinking	.07	.15**	.08	.06	.21***	.12**	-.05
Hardiness Scales (N=250)							
Hardy Total	-.22***	-.09	-.05	-.07	-.08	-.04	.26***
Hardy Commitment	-.27***	-.09	-.05	-.08	-.13	-.08	.25***
Hardy Control	-.19**	-.13	-.06	-.11	-.07	-.06	.26***
Hardy Challenge	.07	.01	.00	.02	.00	.05	-.10

Note. Only scales of symptoms for which there is at least one significant correlation are included. Sex is partialled out of all correlations.

*p <.01

**p <.001

Hardiness questionnaires are entered into regression equations in which the predicted variables are emotional and physical symptoms, the Hardiness scales add nothing to the CTI scales. The CTI Emotional Coping scale by itself accounts for 17% of the variance of emotional symptoms, and the Hardiness scale by itself accounts for 4% of the variance. Together they account for 17% of the variance. For physical symptoms, the Emotional Coping scale by itself accounts for 5% of the variance and the Hardy Control scale by itself accounts for 2% of the variance. Together, they account for 5% of the variance.

The above findings indicate that good constructive thinkers have fewer emotional and physical symptoms than poor constructive thinkers. Correlations, of course, reveal nothing about causal relations. First there is the possibility that symptoms influence constructive thinking, rather than the reverse, although this seems highly unlikely. Assuming that constructive thinking influences symptoms, the question still remains as to how. There are several ways in which constructive thinking can affect symptoms. One is that good constructive thinkers may take better care of themselves. They may eat better, exercise more, smoke less, take drugs less, drink alcoholic beverages less, and visit physicians and dentists appropriately. Another is that they may behave in ways that are less stress-inducing. Thus, they may be less likely to provoke others into hassling them, and they may be less likely to frustrate themselves by their own careless and undisciplined behavior. That this is likely the case is supported by the highly significant negative relation between total stressful events experienced and constructive thinking (see Table 20.2). A third possibility is that good constructive thinkers interpret potential stressors when they arise in a less stressful way than poor constructive thinkers. What is a poor constructive thinker's overwhelming threat may be a good constructive thinker's interesting challenge. Finally, having made an interpretation of an event as stressful, good constructive thinkers, because of superior emotional and behavioral coping skills, are likely to cope with it more effectively than poor constructive thinkers, thereby experiencing less stress. The first reason explains why good constructive thinkers should experience fewer symptoms apart from stress. The second reason explains why good constructive thinkers should experience the occurrence of fewer stressors in their lives. The last two reasons explain why good constructive thinkers, even if they interpret certain events as threatening, will experience less total stress following the events than poor constructive thinkers.

To the extent that good constructive thinking is associated with less stress-inducing interpretive and coping reactions than poor constructive thinking, it should have a buffering effect on the influence of potential stressors on mental and physical well-being. Such a buffering effect on symptoms should be exhibited by an interaction between constructive thinking and stressful events. Unfortunately, the experimental design in the present study is a weak one for testing interaction effects because many of the symptoms that were reported could have preceded rather than followed the stressful events that were reported.

For the reasons discussed above, the present design is more suitable for demonstrating main effects of constructive thinking and stressors than interactive effects between them. It is also suitable for testing the hypothesis that there is greater independence between constructive thinking and external stress than between constructive thinking and self-produced, and therefore also total stress, in their contribution to emotional and physical symptoms.

To obtain information on the relative independent contributions of the different main effects and their interactions, hierarchical regression analyses were conducted in which the predictor variables were entered in the order of external stress (or self-produced or total stress), CTI Emotional Coping, and their interaction, and the predicted variable was either total emotional or total physical symptoms. In all cases, the stress and constructive thinking variables made significant independent

TABLE 20.4
Comparison of Stress and CTI Emotional Coping as Predictors of Emotional and Physical Symptoms

Independent Variable	*R-Square*	*df*	*F*
Dependent Variable: Emotional Symptoms			
External Stress Alone	.03	1/429	12.37**
CTI Emotional Coping Alone	.17	1/429	88.54**
External Stress + CTI Emotional Coping	.19	2/428	49.78**
Self-produced Stress Alone	.10	1/418	45.72**
CTI Emotional Coping Alone	.17	1/418	86.27**
Self-produced Stress + CTI Emotional Coping	.23	2/416	62.11**
Dependent Variable: Physical Symptoms			
External Stress Alone	.02	1/424	9.71*
CTI Emotional Coping Alone	.05	1/424	21.21**
External Stress + CTI Emotional Coping	.06	2/423	14.70**
Self-produced Stress Alone	.06	1/418	26.10**
CTI Emotional Coping Alone	.05	1/418	20.91**
Self-produced Stress + CTI Emotional Coping	.09	2/417	20.05**

*p <.01

**p <.001

contributions to the prediction of both kinds of symptoms. In no case was there a significant interaction.

In accounting for total emotional symptoms, CTI Emotional Coping scores made a considerably larger contribution than either external stress or self-produced stress (see Table 20.4). In accounting for total physical symptoms, CTI Emotional Coping made a considerably larger contribution than external stress, but a slightly smaller contribution than self-produced stress. Not surprisingly, in the equations predicting both emotional and physical symptoms, there is considerably greater overlap between Emotional Coping and self-produced stress than between Emotional Coping and externally produced stress. This is indicated by a comparison of the sum of the separate contributions of the CTI scale and the stress measure to their combined contribution in the regression equation. The sum of the separate contributions of the variables (3% + 17% = 20% for emotional symptoms; 2% + 5% = 7% for physical symptoms) and their combined contribution in the regression equation (19% for emotional symptoms; 6% for physical symptoms) are nearly the same when the measure of stress is externally produced stress. When it is self-produced stress, the sum of the separate variables exceeds their combined contribution to a greater extent, indicating that self-produced stress and constructive thinking share considerable overlapping variance. The results for total stress need not be separately discussed as they are highly similar to those for self-produced stress.

It may be concluded, as suggested earlier, that unless special attention is given to selecting items that are not under the control of the individual, daily stress measures can be expected to be highly confounded with a trait of coping ability. An alternative strategy for separately investigating the influence of stress and coping ability is to partial the contribution of each out of the other. It is noteworthy, in this respect, that despite its considerable overlap with constructive thinking, self-produced stress and total stress made strong contributions to symptoms after constructive thinking was partialled out, one that was greater than the contribution of external stress. The reason for this is the much lower incidence of externally than of self-produced stress.

It was hypothesized that a major way in which constructive thinking influences physical health is through its influence on the occurrence and interpretation of stressors, and thereby through the amount of stress experienced. Stress, in turn, is associated with negative emotional states, which have physiological and biochemical consequences, and therefore can produce symptoms, either directly, as in tension headaches and stomach aches, or indirectly through influencing the endocrine and immune systems. Thus, an important path from constructive thinking to symptoms is assumed to be through negative emotions. To test this hypothesis, a hierarchical regression analysis was conducted in which the independent variables were gender, as a control variable, total stress, Global Constructive Thinking, and emotional symptoms, in that order, and the independent variable was total physical symptoms. It was hypothesized that initially significant relations between stress and physical symptoms and between constructive thinking and physical symptoms would be severely reduced or eliminated when emotional symptoms were entered into the equation. This is exactly what happened. Before the sum of emotional symptoms was entered into the equation, gender, total stress, and constructive thinking were all highly significant and together accounted for 10% of the variance. After the sum of emotional symptoms was entered into the equation, it displaced all other variables and, by itself, accounted for 32% of the variance. The results thus indicate that although stress and constructive thinking are themselves associated with symptoms, the association is the result of their relation with negative emotions, thereby supporting the hypothesis that negative emotions are the connecting link through which constructive thinking and stress influence physical symptoms.

It may be concluded from this study that (a) the CTI is more strongly associated with symptoms and productive load than the Hardiness inventory, that (b) the CTI scales have discriminant validity, that (c) the frequency of potential stressors that occur in people's lives is itself largely determined by a trait of coping ability (e.g., constructive thinking, hardiness), so that if one wishes to investigate the influence of stressors unconfounded with a trait of coping ability, it is necessary to either select stressors that are not under the control of the individual or to partial out coping ability, that (d) both stress and coping ability, despite some degree of overlap, also make independent contributions to mental and physical well-being, and that (e) a major path through which poor constructive thinking influences physical symptoms is through negative emotions.

THE RELATION OF CONSTRUCTIVE THINKING TO DAILY RECORDS OF SYMPTOMS

A serious limitation in studies that rely on the retrospective recall of symptoms over a prolonged period is that the reporting, to an unknown degree, is apt to be inaccurate. Ideally, this would only increase the noise of measurement, but there is also the possibility that the results are systematically biased. There is sufficient evidence for the operation of self-serving biases in a wide range of situations to lead one to suspect that they operate in symptom reporting. As noted earlier, this concern is supported by evidence that a broad factor of negative reporting can account for many of the relations that have been reported between stress, coping, and symptoms (Costa & McCrae, 1987; Watson & Pennebaker, 1989). In the two studies reported above, the possibility that a diffuse factor of negative reporting, or neuroticism, could account for the significant relations between stress, coping, and symptoms could be ruled out because of the patterns of relations that were observed. This, of course, does not negate the desirability of increasing the accuracy of reporting, but simply indicates that retrospective recall is not completely without virtue.

It is reasonable to assume that the shorter the memory interval for reporting symptoms, the more accurate should the reporting be, and that a relatively high degree of accuracy can be expected if subjects keep daily records of their symptoms. If someone says she now has, or that earlier in the day she had, a headache, and if there is nothing to be gained by dissimulating, the likelihood that she actually has or had a headache is very high. Such a report certainly is a far cry from an estimate of the average frequency of headaches over the past year. Each procedure has its advantages and disadvantages. Estimates of symptoms over a prolonged period suffer from a reduction in accuracy but have the virtue of covering a long time interval. With daily recording, the advantages and disadvantages are reversed.

In a recently completed study, not yet written up for publication, 40 undergraduates in two successive classes of 20 subjects filled out a battery of self-report tests, including the Constructive Thinking Inventory (CTI), and kept daily records on special forms of their daily moods and of the most stressful event of the day each day for 30 days. It was emphasized in the class, which was on coping with stress, that if the students wished to learn anything of value for improving their coping with stress, it was important that they keep accurate records. This, then, provided a strong incentive for accuracy in reporting. After records were obtained for 30 days, the data were computer-analyzed and the results, in the form of means, standard deviations, and correlations among response categories, were returned to the students, who wrote a report on what they learned. With the aid of the instructor, they then prepared a remedial program for improving their coping with stress.

For each event, subjects rated the amount of stress they experienced, their construal of the event, as indicated by ratings of whether, and to what extent, the event involved any of a number of situational variables that were listed, such as rejection, failure, attack, loss of relationship, etc. They also rated the extent to which they experienced each of the emotions presented in a list and the degree to which they employed any of a number of mental and behavioral coping strategies that were listed. In addition, they reported whether they had experienced any of a number of common symptoms, and, if so, the intensity of the symptoms and whether the symptoms had continued from the day before or had their onset on the day of the event they were reporting. If a symptom occurred on the day of the event, they noted whether its onset preceded or followed the event. Since the average frequency of specific symptoms was very low, the symptoms were combined into broader categories. Results will be reported only for the following major categories: total physical symptoms, psychophysiological symptoms (e.g., back pain, stiff neck, constipation, diarrhea, vomiting, headaches, and stomach aches), sleep disturbance, and female symptoms (e.g., menstrual problems and infections of, or pain associated with, reproductive organs).

In order to obtain measures of mental well-being, a factor analysis was conducted of daily moods. Semi-independent factors of positive and negative mood were found, and these were developed into scales by selecting items with loadings of at least .30 and then retaining only those that enhanced the internal-consistency reliability (coefficient alpha) of a scale.

Table 20.5 presents the correlations of the CTI scales with the symptom variables averaged over 30 days. Sex of subjects was partialled out of all correlations in order to prevent the occurrence of spurious correlations as a result of mean differences between males and females. The correlations of overall physical symptoms and psychophysiological symptoms are presented according to whether the symptoms occurred on the day of a stressful event following the event, preceding the event, or were a continuation of the symptom from a previous day. It would not be reasonable to present correlations with disturbances of sleep, female symptoms, and moods according to these same divisions, so they are presented only for total incidence of occurrence.

It can be seen in Table 20.5 that the categories of physical symptoms and psychophysiological symptoms that occurred on the day of a stressful event after the event were significantly correlated with Global Constructive Thinking, Emotional Coping, Behavioral Coping, and Categorical Thinking. Among these, the strongest correlations were with Emotional Coping (r = -.44). None of these CTI scales is significantly associated with physical or psychophysiological symptoms that occurred before the stressful event or that had continued from the previous day. These findings suggest that the symptoms were produced on the day of the event by the stressful event, which supports the hypothesis that constructive thinking has a buffering effect on the influence of stress on symptoms.

In contrast to the other scales, Superstitious Thinking produced significant correlations with psychophysiological symptoms only for continuing symptoms and for symptoms that occurred before the stressful event. The correlation of .50 for Superstitious Thinking with continuing psychophysiological symptoms is the highest correlation between a CTI scale and psychophysiological symptoms over the three periods. One interpretation of this finding is that the psychophysiological symptoms of those with high scores on Superstitious Thinking are triggered by inner thoughts rather than external events. It is noteworthy, in this respect, that the Superstitious Thinking scale does not include formal superstitions, but rather items that refer to private superstitions, many of which serve the purpose of reducing the sting of disappointment by accepting negative outcomes in advance. It may be that those with high scores on Superstitious Thinking tend to react to their elaborations of events long after they have occurred. Superstitious Thinking is also correlated significantly with sleep disturbance and female symptoms. Since one of the symptoms of depression is sleep disturbance, the finding with sleep disturbance is consistent with the observation that Superstitious Thinking is associated with depression.

For the correlations of the CTI scales with positive and negative mood, total amount of emotional reactivity was partialled out. The reason for doing this was that for several sets of variables, including moods, total magnitude of responses was found to be a complicating variable that resulted in anomalous findings. When totals were partialled out, anomalies vanished, and the coherence of the results improved. Partialling out totals, in effect calibrates each subject for his level of

TABLE 20.5

Correlations of Daily Symptoms and Moods Aggregated Over 30 Days with Constructive Thinking Inventory (N=40)

	PHYSICAL WELL-BEING								EMOTIONAL WELL-BEING	
CTI Scales	*All Physical Symptoms*			*Psychophysiol Symptoms*			*Total Sleep*	*Total Female Symptoms*	*Pos Mood*	*Neg Mood*
	C	*B*	*A*	*C*	*B*	*A*				
Global CT			-.39**			-.39**		-.34*	.38*	-.54***
Emot. Coping			-.44**			-.44**			.35*	-.49**
Beh. Coping			-.32*			-.33				-.36*
Categ. Thkg.			.33*			.32*				.42
Superst. Thkg.				.50**	.37*		.45**	.62**	-.34*	.41**
Naive Optim.										
Esoteric Thkg.								.42**		

Note. Only correlations significant at the .05 level are included. C = Continuing symptom; B = Symptom occured before event; A = Symptom occured after event. Sex is partialled out of all correlations with symptoms. Sex and sum of magnitude of all mood ratings is partialled out of all correlations with moods.

*$p < .05$
**$p < .01$
***$p < .001$

responding, thereby making the data ipsative in the sense that the pattern of responses becomes all that is important.

With respect to mental well-being, not surprisingly, good constructive thinkers report experiencing more positive moods and less negative moods than poor constructive thinkers. In Table 20.5, it can be seen that all CTI scales except Naive Optimism and Esoteric Thinking produce significant correlations with negative mood. The CTI scales most strongly associated with negative mood are Global Constructive Thinking ($r = -.54, p = .001$) and Emotional Coping ($r = -.49, p < .01$). There are three scales significantly associated with positive mood, Global Constructive Thinking ($r = .38, p < .05$), Emotional Coping ($r = .35, p < .05$), and Superstitious Thinking ($r = -.34, p < .05$). To test the hypothesis that poor constructive thinking is associated with exposure to increased stress, correlations were obtained between the aggregated ratings of event-induced stress over the 30 days and the CTI scales. In support of this hypothesis, significant correlations with stress were found for Global Constructive Thinking ($r = -.31, p < .05$) and Emotional Coping ($r = -.35, p < .05$).

Other information relevant to event-produced stress is event-instigated negative emotions. Subjects rated the intensity of the specific emotions they experienced as a result of the stressful events they reported. Their ratings of anger-out, anger-in, sadness, and fear were aggregated over 30 days and correlated with their scores on the CTI scales. Anger-out was not significantly associated with any of the CTI scales. Anger-in was most strongly associated with Superstitious Thinking ($r = .30$). Frightened was most strongly associated with Categorical Thinking ($r = .61$), Emotional Coping ($r = -.49$), Global Constructive Thinking ($r = -.47$), and Behavioral Coping ($r = -.31$).

A caveat is in order about interpreting the relative magnitudes of the specific relations between mood and CTI scales. Namely, it is unknown how specific they are to the particular group investigated. By aggregating over 30 days, very high reliability coefficients are obtained for almost all variables, which makes it possible to obtain highly reliable relations with other variables even in small samples. The limiting factor is in generalizing to other samples of individuals. The present study investigated a sample of students who registered for a course on coping with stress, often for personal reasons. It remains to be seen how general the patterns of relations are for other kinds of groups. In any event, whether or not specific relations are found to be general across different populations, the findings, consistent with those in the previous studies, make a strong case for the association of the CTI with emotional and physical well-being.

In summary, the findings from this study indicate that when self-report data consist of daily records of symptoms, the results are similar to the findings from retrospective self-report studies over a more extended time period. Namely there are highly reliable correlations between the scales of the CTI and measures of emotional and physical well-being. There is also evidence in both kinds of studies for the discriminant validity of the CTI scales, which indicates that the results cannot be attributed to a global factor of neuroticism or negative-reporting bias.

CONSTRUCTIVE THINKING AND COGNITIVE, AFFECTIVE, AND PHYSIOLOGICAL RESPONSES TO STRESS IN THE LABORATORY

The advantage to laboratory studies of stress is that stressors can be introduced independent of the coping skills of the subjects. It is therefore possible in such studies to straightforwardly test the hypothesis that coping ability moderates the influence of stressors on mental and physical well-being without having to rely on statistical controls and inferences from interactions, the demonstrations of which have been inconsistent.

Katz and I conducted a laboratory study for the purpose of elucidating the links between constructive thinking, stress, and mental and physical well-being (Katz & Epstein, 1990). We were particularly interested in examining the thought processes of good and poor constructive thinkers, and in obtaining objective as well as subjective measures of reactions to a known stressor. We were also interested in determining whether there is a relation between cognitive responses to a stressor in the laboratory and symptoms in everyday life.

Out of a pool of 556 undergraduates who completed the CTI, extreme groups of 26 good and 26 poor constructive thinkers who agreed to participate in further research were selected. Subjects were exposed to two laboratory stressors: counting backwards from 400 by 7s out loud as quickly as possible and tracing a maze that could only be seen in a mirror. Whenever a subject made an error in subtraction or in crossing a line in the mirror-tracing task, the error was announced and the subject was required to continue from the last correct response. Performance was measured by number of correct subtractions and length of the path correctly traversed. Physiological responses, ratings of emotions, and ratings of four kinds of thoughts (negative and positive thoughts related and unrelated to the experiment) were obtained for four points in time: a prestress period, a stress period, a first recovery period, and a second recovery period. The reason for the two recovery periods was that it had been reported (Allred & Smith, 1989; Van Treuren & Hull, 1987) that good may exhibit greater physiological reactivity than poor copers during and immediately after a stress test because of their greater involvement with the task. It was decided, therefore, to examine poststress responses over two time periods to allow the effects of engagement with the task to dissipate. At the end of the stress period, subjects rated their reactions to the stressful tasks on several dimensions, including amount of stress experienced and estimated level of performance. They also rated how they believed the examiners regarded them. Systolic and diastolic blood pressure, heart rate, and finger and wrist temperature were monitored at each of the four periods. At the end of the experiment, a structured interview was

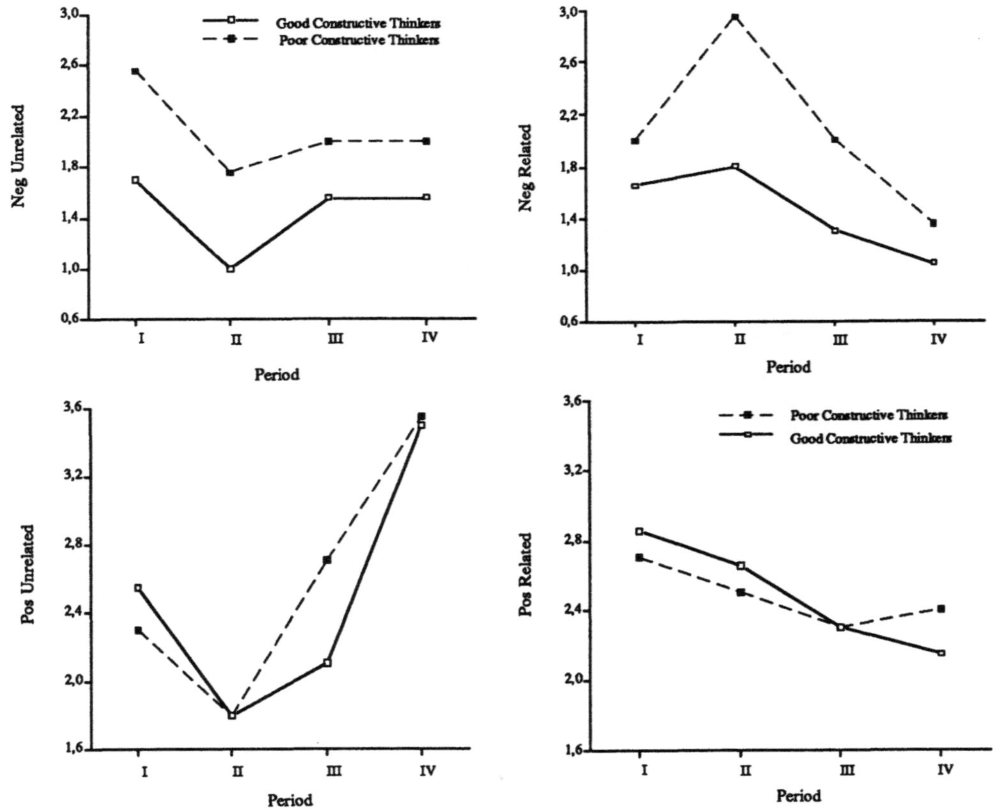

FIG. 20.1. Frequency of positive and negative thoughts related and unrelated to the experiment for good and poor constructive thinkers at four periods: I, prestress; II, stress; III, first recovery period; IV, second recovery period.

conducted, after which subjects indicated the frequency with which they had experienced each of the symptoms listed in a symptom checklist during the past 4 months. The examiners, who were uninformed about group-membership, rated the subjects on how friendly, relaxed, helpful, and self-confident they appeared to be.

Separate analyses of variance were conducted for positive and negative thoughts as a function of groups, periods, and whether the thoughts were related or unrelated to the experiment. The results on positive and negative thoughts related and unrelated to the experiment are presented in Figure 20.1. There were no significant differences between the groups on positive thoughts regardless of whether they were related or unrelated to the experiment. For both groups, positive thoughts related to the experiment decreased throughout the experiment, whereas positive thoughts unrelated to the experiment decreased from the prestress to the stress period, then increased over the remainder of the experiment.

Highly significant group differences were found for negative thoughts of both kinds. Poor constructive thinkers reported a higher incidence of negative thoughts related and unrelated to the experiment in all four periods. There was also a significant interaction between constructive thinking and period on negative thoughts related to the experiment. Poor constructive thinkers exhibited a much sharper increase in negative thoughts related to the experiment from the prestress to the stress period than good constructive thinkers (see Figure 20.1).

Two scales were derived, by factor analysis, from the adjective checklist of emotions: negative affect and engagement. The groups did not differ significantly on engagement, but for negative affect there was a significant group main effect and a significant Group × Period interaction. In Figure 20.3, it can be seen that poor constructive thinkers reported more negative affect than good constructive thinkers at all periods. The interaction was produced by a sharper increase in negative affect from the prestress to the stress period in the poor than in the good constructive thinkers. It is noteworthy that the results for negative affect are highly similar to those for negative thoughts related to the experiment (compare Figures 20.1 and 20.2), which is consistent with the assumption that negative automatic thoughts are a major source of negative affect.

For the measures of physiological reactivity, significant group differences were observed for finger temperature and diastolic blood pressure. In both cases, the greatest group difference occurred in the second recovery period. It can be seen in Figure 20.3 that the poor constructive thinkers had lower finger temperature and higher diastolic blood pressure, both indicative of increased arousal, during this period than during the preceding period. It is noteworthy that the curve of diastolic blood pressure over the four periods for the good constructive thinking group conforms to the self-report data of negative affect and to what was expected: an increase during the stress period and a decrease over the two recovery periods. The curve of diastolic blood pressure for the poor constructive thinking group, on the other hand, is paradoxical in two ways. There is a decrease in blood pressure from the prestress to the stress period and an increase in blood pressure from the first to

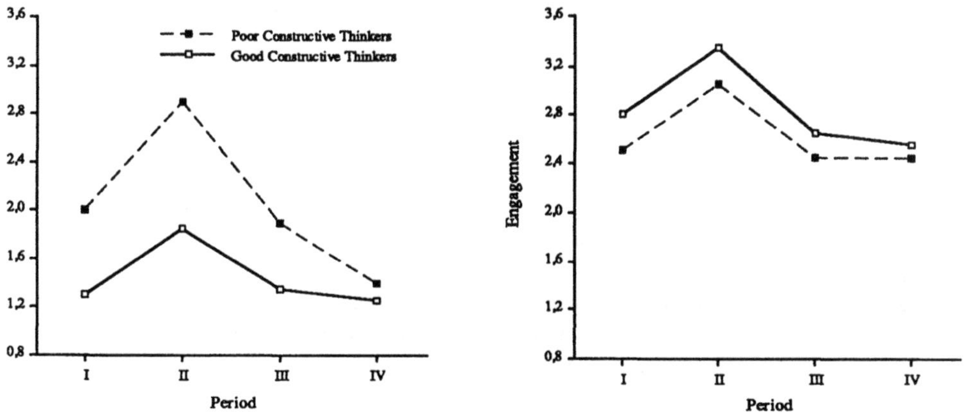

FIG. 20.2. Self-rated negative affect and engagement good and poor constructive thinkers at four periods: I, prestress; II, stress; III, first recovery period; IV, second recovery period.

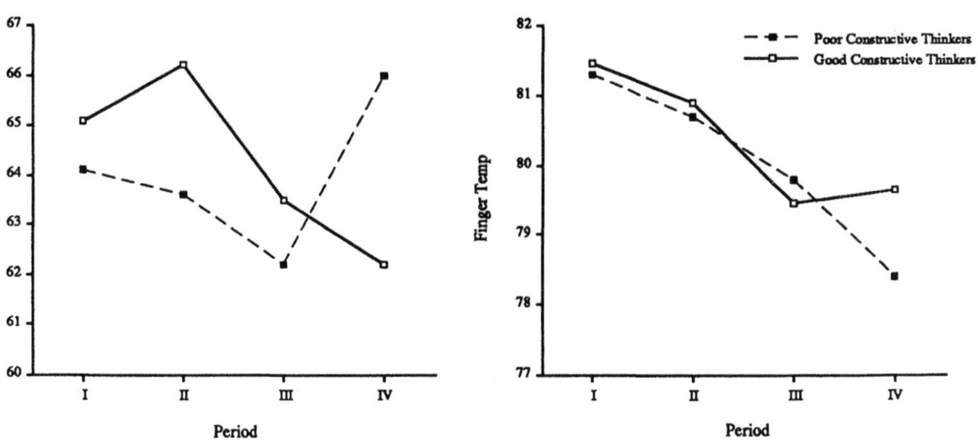

FIG. 20.3. Physiological reactions of good and poor constructive thinkers at four periods: I, prestress; II, stress; III, first recovery period; IV, second recovery period.

the second recovery period. One possible interpretation of these findings is that the decrease in the stress period is due to an inhibitory effect and the increase in the recovery period is due to a disinhibition of the inhibitory effect (Epstein, 1967).

The ratings of various kinds of evaluative reactions during the stress period were of considerable interest. Although poor constructive thinkers performed as well as good constructive thinkers, they judged their performance as poorer, and they were more concerned about having made a poor impression on the examiner than good constructive thinkers. Poor constructive thinkers also judged their performance as particularly poor against their own high standards. Good constructive thinkers judged their performance more favorably, and were less concerned about meeting high personal standards and about the evaluation of the examiner. Not surprisingly, given these differences in self-evaluation and in concern about the views of the examiner, poor constructive thinkers rated the tasks as significantly more stressful than good constructive thinkers.

Ratings of the subjects' behavior and appearance by the examiners significantly discriminated between the groups on one attribute: self-confidence. Poor constructive thinkers appeared to the examiners to be less self-confident than good constructive thinkers.

Turning to the symptoms reported in daily life, poor constructive thinkers reported a significantly higher frequency of both emotional (e.g., depressive episodes, anxiety reactions, and irritability) and physical symptoms over the past four months than good constructive thinkers. In addition to significant differences on these composite variables, there were also significant differences on a number of individual symptoms. Given the large number of comparisons, only differences significant at the .01 level will be reported. The poor constructive thinkers reported significantly more acne, rashes, headaches, dizziness, anxiety, and depression during the past four months than the good constructive thinkers. Were the kinds of thoughts subjects had in the laboratory related to their symptoms in everyday life? To answer this question, positive and negative thoughts related and unrelated to the experiment were correlated with the symptoms reported to have been experienced in the four months preceding the experiment. Negative thoughts that were related to the experiment were highly significantly ($p < .01$) associated with the frequency of reported symptoms over the past 4 months, whereas negative thoughts unrelated to the experiment were not significantly associated with symptoms. Thus, certain kinds of negative thoughts, such as concern about performance and acceptance by others, appear to be more strongly associated with symptoms than other kinds of negative thoughts that are less personal, such as thinking about unpleasant chores that remain to be done.

Perhaps the two most important contributions of this study are that it provides information on the kinds of negative thinking that poor constructive thinkers engage in when confronted with a known stressor, and it provides objective data on the differences between good and poor constructive thinkers that go beyond self-report. The findings from this study support the hypothesis that the relation between constructive thinking and symptoms is mediated by stress. Evidence was presented that poor constructive thinkers think in a manner, when confronted with a known stressor, that leads to an increase in negative emotions and physiological arousal. Their negative thinking in the experiment was also demonstrated to be associated with an increased incidence of common psychosomatic symptoms. Although these results do not unequivocally establish all the hypothesized links between poor constructive thinking as a trait variable, the occurrence of potential stressors, the interpretation of events as stressful, the experience of elevated levels of stress and negative affect, and the final outcome in symptoms, the findings are completely in accord with such an interpretation.

SUMMARY AND CONCLUSIONS

The Constructive Thinking Inventory (CTI) is a measure of coping ability that contains a global scale and six specific scales. The scales have been found to be significantly correlated with a wide variety of criteria of success in living, including work success, social success, love success, and the achievement of mental and physical well-being. The present article focused on the relation of the CTI with mental and physical health. Four studies were reviewed, including studies that examined retrospective recall of symptoms, daily records of symptoms, and physiological, cognitive, and emotional reactions to laboratory-induced stress.

The major findings of the four studies can be summarized as follows:

1. The CTI is more strongly associated with mental and physical well-being than the other measures with which it was compared, including the Attribution Style Questionnaire, the Hardiness scales, the Rotter I-E scale, and the Sarason Social Support Questionnaire.
2. The CTI scales have discriminant validity as indicated by different relations of its scales with different kinds of symptoms, such as physical symptoms, emotional symptoms, and behavioral symptoms. The relations between constructive thinking and symptoms therefore cannot be accounted for by a general factor of negative reporting, or neuroticism.
3. It was demonstrated that unless items are selected over which individuals have no control, measures of stressors, such as the Daily Hassles scale, are apt to be highly confounded with measures of coping ability, such as the CTI. They are thus trait measures as much as measures of external events. Because they apparently are both, even when constructive thinking is partialled out, scores on such measures are still related to mental and physical health, although not nearly as strongly as when constructive thinking is not partialled out.
4. Not only do good constructive thinkers experience fewer stressors in everyday living than others, but they also carry higher productive loads without an increase in symptoms.

5. When confronted with a laboratory stressor, good constructive thinkers have fewer negative thoughts, experience less stress and distressing emotions, and exhibit less physiological arousal than poor constructive thinkers.
6. Negative thoughts that poor constructive thinkers have in response to laboratory stressors are associated with their proneness to have symptoms in everyday life.

The overall findings from the four studies are consistent with the following chain of influence of constructive thinking on physical symptoms: Poor constructive thinking is a trait variable that is associated with stressor-instigating behaviors, stress-enhancing construals, and maladaptive mental and behavioral coping, which, in combination, result in distressing emotions and elevated levels of physiological arousal that are a direct source of everyday minor symptoms, such as headaches, muscle spasms, and stomachaches. The samples of subjects investigated were not appropriate for investigating more serious, chronic illness. It is hypothesized, however, that when negative physiological states resulting from poor constructive thinking are sufficiently prolonged, they can produce enduring maladaptive physiological and biochemical reactions that make the individual increasingly susceptible to serious illness.

REFERENCES

Allred, K. D., & Smith, T. W. (1989). The hardy personality: Cognitive and physiological responses to evaluative threat. *Journal of Personality and Social Psychology, 56,* 257-266.

Contrada, R. J. (1989). Type A behavior, personality hardiness, and cardiovascular responses to stress. *Journal of Personality and Social Psychology, 57,* 895-903.

Costa, P. T. Jr. & McCrae, R. R. (1987). Hypochondriasis, neuroticism, and aging: When are somatic complaints unfounded? *American Psychologist, 40,* 19-28.

Dohrenwend, B. S., & Dohrenwend, B. P. (1978). Some issues in research on stressful life events. *Journal of Nervous and Mental Disease, 166,* 7-15.

Epstein, S. (1967). Toward a unified theory of anxiety. In B. Maher (Ed.), *Progress in experimental personality research* (Vol. 4, pp. 1-89). New York: Academic Press.

Epstein, S. (1990). Cognitive-experiential self-theory. In L. Pervin (Ed.), *Handbook of personality theory and research.* New York: Guilford.

Epstein, S., & Katz, L. (1990). *Constructive thinking, hardiness, stress, productive load, and mental and physical well-being.* Unpublished manuscript.

Epstein, S., Lipson, A., Holstein, C., & Huh, E. (1990). *Irrational reactions to negative outcomes: Evidence for two conceptual systems.* Unpublished manuscript.

Epstein, S., & Meier, P. (1989). Constructive thinking: A broad coping variable with specific components. *Journal of Personality and Social Psychology, 57,* 332-350.

Hull, J. G., Van Treuren, R. R., & Virnelli, S. (1987). Hardiness and health: A critique and alternative approach. *Journal of Personality and Social Psychology, 53,* 518-530.

Kanner, A. D., Coyne, J. C., Schaefer, C., & Lazarus, R. S. (1981). Comparison of two modes of stress measurement: Daily hassles and uplifts versus major life events. *Journal of Behavioral Medicine, 4,* 1-39.

Katz, L., & Epstein, S. (1990). *Constructive thinking and coping with laboratory-induced stress.* Unpublished manuscript.

Kobasa, S. C., Maddi, S. R., & Courington, S. (1981). Personality and constitution as mediators in the stress-illness relationship. *Journal of Health and Social Behavior, 22*, 368-378.

Lazarus, R. S., & Folkman, S. (1984). *Stress, appraisal, and coping*. New York: Springer.

Peterson, C., Semmel, A., von Bayer, C., Abramson, L. Y., Metalsky, G. I., & Seligman, M. E. P. (1982). The Attribution Style Questionnaire. *Cognitive Therapy and Research, 6*, 287-299.

Rhodewalt, F., & Zone, J. B. (1989). Appraisal of life change, depression, and illness in hardy and nonhardy women. *Journal of Personality and Social Psychology, 56*, 81-88.

Rotter, J. B. (1966). Generalized expectancies for internal versus external control of reinforcement. *Psychological Monographs, 8* (1, Whole No. 609).

Sarason, I. G., Levine, H. M., Basham, R. B., & Sarason, B. R. (1983). Assessing social support: The Social Support Questionnaire. *Journal of Personality and Social Psychology, 44*, 127-130.

Van Treuren, R. R., & Hull, J. G. (1987). *Hardiness and the perception of symptoms*. Paper presented at the 95th Annual Convention of the American Psychological Association, New York.

Watson, D., & Pennebaker, J. W. (1989). Health complaints, stress, and distress: Exploring the central role of negative affectivity. *Psychological Review, 96*, 234-254.

21 Trust and Trustworthiness

Hans Werner Bierhoff
University of Marburg

Trust develops when a person must rely on the promises of another person without being able to verify the message. Trust implies uncertainty and, as a consequence, might be the definition of trust proposed by Deutsch (1958).

> An individual may be said to have trust in the occurrence of an event if he expects its occurrence and his expectation leads to behavior which he perceives to have greater negative motivational consequences if the expectation is not confirmed than positive motivational consequences if it is confirmed. (p. 266)

The risk of failure is due to the fact that the positive motivational consequences depend on the benevolence of the other person in the future. The problem of uncertainty in social relationships is a universal issue that pervades social life because certainty is only possible in the present (Luhmann, 1973, pp. 11-12). The multitude of alternatives that lie in the future constitute a threatening complexity. As a result, people try to reduce the complexity by several mechanisms (e.g., stereotypes, schemata). With respect to close personal relationships and social relationships in general, interpersonal trust offers the promise to bring order into a complex social environment (Luhmann, 1973; Petermann, 1985). Therefore, trust can be conceived as a social mechanism which reduces the overwhelming complexity of social reality. As a result, an easily comprehensible schema of the social world is constructed by the trusting individual which offers the opportunity to act with high subjective certainty.

The decision to trust or distrust another person depends in part on situational cues that suggest that the other person is reliable or unreliable. This aspect is included in the definition of trust proposed by Schlenker, Helm, and Tedeschi (1973, p. 419): "Interpersonal trust may be defined as a reliance upon information received from another person about uncertain environmental states and their accompanying outcomes in a risky situation." This definition may serve as a guide for trust research. It emphasizes the informational dependency of the trusting person on the one hand and the uncertainty in a risky situation on the other hand. In addition, the focus is on a specific situation that forces a person to trust another person.

The significance of trust for human development was highlighted by Erikson (1968) who described human development dependent on certain psychosocial crises. The first basic dilemma which the child encounters is—according to Erikson—the issue of trust and distrust toward the parents. Erikson (1968) considers trust to be the basis of personality development, especially with respect to the formation of personal identity. He assumes that personality development is dependent on continuous satisfaction of the child's needs. As a consequence, the perception of the world als a stable and predictable social environment emerges. On the negative side, deficits in the development of trust are related to interpersonal anxieties and inhibitions (Erikson, 1968).

From personality theorists (Rotter, 1967, 1971, 1980) to sociologists (Luhmann, 1973) there is considerable agreement in the assumption that without interpersonal trust an efficient transaction with the social environment is highly unlikely. With respect to coping with life crises and losses the derivation suggests itself that interpersonal trust alleviates some of the subjective feelings of strain by fostering interpersonal openness and frequent communication. Our results which are presented below indicate for example that high trust is associated with a high level of communication in close relationships.

The emphasis on trust as a protective factor in coping with stress should not be interpreted as a plea for gullibility. Empirical studies indicate that trusting people are not necessarily gullible (Rotter, 1980). Trust might be carried to the point where it is more or less pathological. Deutsch (1973, p. 145) refers to the "pathology of trust" as the tendency to be trusting where the social situation does not warrant trust (at least in the eye of neutral observers). Such a pathology of trust is not a valid description of people who are trusting in terms of Rotter's (1967) interpersonal trust scale.

MAJOR THEMES OF TRUST RESEARCH

Conceptual Framework

A conceptual framework for trust was proposed by Kee and Knox (1970). In their model (Figure 21.1), subjective trust is understood as an intervening state depending on the perceptions and attributions of the subject (P) concerning the motives and

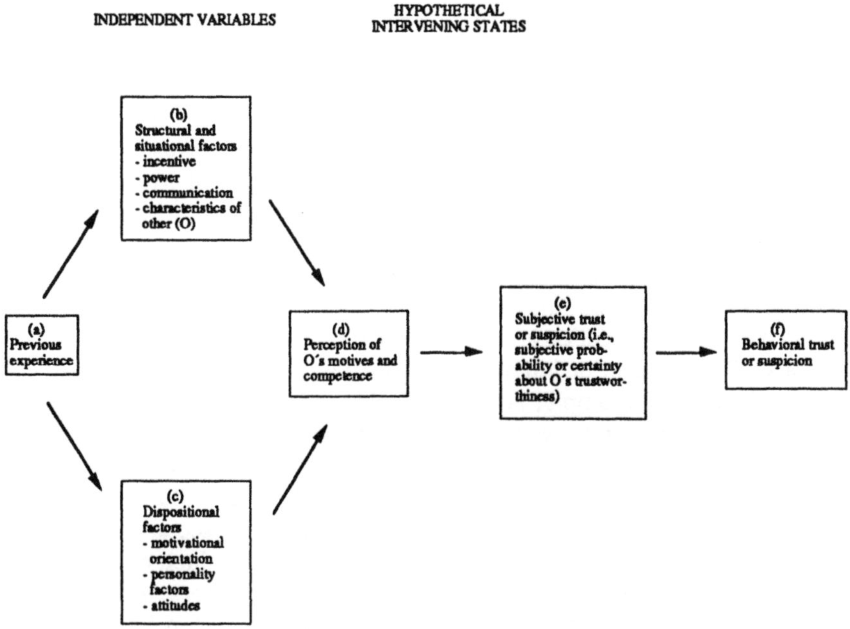

FIG. 21.1. A conceptual model for the study of trust (adapted from Kee & Knox, 1970).

competence of the other person (O), and that precedes the development of subjective trust or suspicion.

The model comprises three classes of independent variables: previous experience, situational determinants, and dispositional determinants. Previous experience refers to positive or negative outcomes that occurred either after trusting or suspicious behavior.

Previous experiences are assumed to influence perceptions and attributions directly and—in addition—indirectly via structural/situational variables and dispositional variables. For example, a person might be inclined to attribute benevolent motives to O because he or she has acquired such a habit in the past. In addition, previous experiences might indicate that trust is most likely to pay when O's cooperative behavior is rewarded (Webb & Worchel, 1986). Finally, previous experience might set in motion processes leading to general expectancies that elicit an inclination to trust or distrust other persons.

Situational determinants refer to the structure of interdependence between parties, available communication channels, and perceived characteristics of the other. For example, simultaneous choice of P and O in a prisoner's dilemma situation elicits, under certain conditions, less trust than alternating choices

(Brickman, Becker, & Castle, 1979). The provision of communication channels facilitates the development of trust (Dawes, 1980). Knowledge that O has cooperated in earlier interactions with other persons or knowledge that O is rewarded for cooperation may increase the expectation that O will cooperate and enhance the trustworthiness of O (Pruitt & Kimmel, 1977).

Relevant dispositional variables include interpersonal trust, perceived locus of control, and competitive or cooperative orientations. While interpersonal orientations might be elicited by instructions (Deutsch, 1949), interpersonal trust and locus of control are understood as generalized expectancies that influence the perception of the motives and performances of O.

For example, a dispositional attribution offers the possibility to infer something about the personality of the other (Jones & Davis, 1965). Lindskold (1978) assumed that a dispositional attribution is a prerequisite for the inference on the trustworthiness of O. The concept of interpersonal trust might be further subdivided into separate facets. For example, Amelang, Gold, and Külbel (1984) differentiate between four factors of interpersonal trust: trust in public institutions, trust in other people, trust in experts, and perception of discrepancies between what people say and what they do. Furthermore, Krampen, Viebig, and Walter (1982) describe three facets of interpersonal trust: perceived reliability of others, social distrust/social anxiety, and distrust with respect to the content which is transmitted by mass media.

Further facets of trust include trust in the fairness of others, trust in others' willingness to reciprocate a favour, and—more general—trust in others' willingness to conform with social norms. These facets of interpersonal trust which comprise partially overlapping clusters should be related to different aspects of coping with stress in major life crises. For example, trust in experts should be a precondition for successful informative support which is based on special competencies of the helpers. The results of an empirical study by Cohen, Sherrod, and Clark (1986) indicate that trust facilitates the obtainment of social support.

The conceptualization of trust and suspicion by Kee and Knox (1970) is the starting point for a more comprehensive model of trust that specifies some of the important consequences of trusting and nontrusting behavior (Figure 21.2). Most empirical evidence is available for the assumption that trust leads to cooperation (Pruitt & Kimmel, 1977; Webb & Worchel, 1986). In addition, social support by O and veridical communication between P and O are among the most important consequences of trusting behavior.

In addition, two parallel hypothetical states are assumed to occur; these are labeled trustworthiness and self-disclosure. Trustworthiness refers to the perceived honesty of O. Perceived trustworthiness of O is the other side of P's trust.

Self-disclosure refers to communications that reveal personal information (Jourard, 1971, p. 2; Spitznagel, 1986). Self-disclosure might be conceptualized as a behavior (Archer, 1987). In addition, self-disclosure refers to a readiness to reveal personal information. In this second sense, self-disclosure is a subjective state.

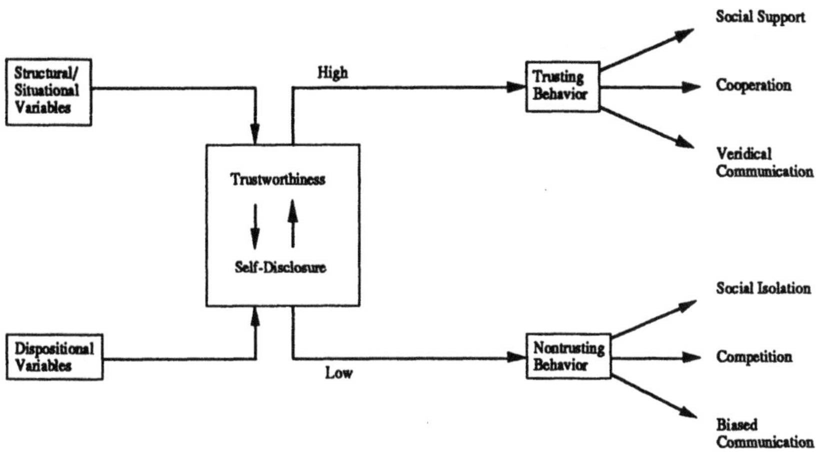

FIG. 21.2. A diagram of the concept of trust.

Self-disclosure serves different functions (Archer, 1987). For example, it expresses self's feelings and opinions, fosters self-clarification, and renders social validation of personal feelings and opinions possible (Archer & Earle, 1983; Derlega & Grzelak, 1979). These are the functions that are most closely related to trustworthiness. (Other functions are related to strategic purposes like self-presentation.) O's trustworthiness and P's self-disclosure (excluding the strategic uses) are so closely intertwined that both states might be conceptualized as parts of the same underlying dimension (see later).

Trust as a Determinant of Coping Processes and Strain

Figure 21.3 highlights the role of trust for coping with stressful life events. The diagram is structured after a model by Kobasa (1982) that describes the role of the personality variable hardiness in coping with stress.

In this model of stress resistance, trust is assumed to affect strain on a direct path and on an indirect path via coping. The model illustrates the possible role of trust for the selection of coping strategies and the experience of strain. At present it is speculative and mainly has a heuristic value. The model implies specific research issues and strategies (see later). In addition, the emphasis on the functions of trust corresponds with the conceptions of self-disclosure proposed by Archer (1987) and by Derlega and Grzelak (1979).

From this perspective, trust can be conceived as a protective factor against the negative effects of life crises and loss experiences. Although the concept of trust has been largely neglected in current theory and research on coping with stress, its potential as a protective factor is obvious. Trust stands for an important facet of the interpersonal dimension which is nearly associated with a high level of self-

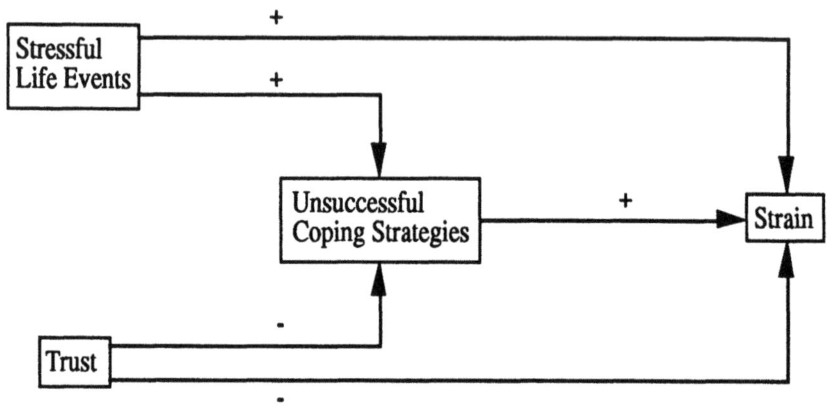

FIG. 21.3. Direct and indirect effects of trust and stressful life events.

disclosure (see following) which is a prerequisite for interpersonal communication which might foster mutual understanding, clarification of needs and expectations, and social support.

With respect to social support, several subtypes were differentiated by Cohen et al. (1986) and Wills (1985):

- *Emotional support* which primarily enhances self-esteem. Emotional support seems to be successful in severe life crises (Wortman & Lehman, 1985). With respect to potential trust correlates it seems likely that self-disclosure is an important factor in eliciting emotional support.
- *Material support* which includes activities like supervising children and material aid. The success of tangible support heavily depends on the willingness of the help-recipient to accept the help offered. In terms of trust, it is more likely that material aid is accepted if the help-recipient infers that the motives of the helper are sincere and altruistic. Therefore, trust in the altruistic motives of the helper is an important determinant of the success of social support. In general, material aid will not be accepted readily if it does not fit the normative expectations of the persons in the existing relationship (Montada & Bierhoff, 1990).
- *Social contact and affiliation.* Positive experiences which derive from social leisure activities and—more general—from the availability of others which whom to do things might reduce negative feelings which stem from major loss experiences (Cohen & Hoberman, 1983). It is likely that the perceived reliableness of the others is a factor which mitigates any tendencies to draw back.
- *Informational support.* There are many problems which can clearly be better solved by experts than lay persons (Bierhoff, 1990). Since informational

support easily is misunderstood as arrogant know-all (Wortman & Lehman, 1985), its successful implementation critically depends on trust in the expertise and competence of the helper. It is likely that perceived trustworthiness of the helper should facilitate informational support.

- *Motivational support* which encourages the help-recipient to hold on. Although the efficiency of this type of support is controversial, it clearly depends on the credibility of the helper. The problems which arise with this kind of support resemble the problems of the moral model of helping which emphasizes that the victim him-/herself is responsible for his/her misfortune and the alleviation of its consequences (cf. Bierhoff, 1990; Brickman et al., 1982). Nevertheless, encouragement for self-help is an important contribution to building up a positive motivation of the help-recipient. This is emphasized in Brickman's compensatory model of helping which stresses the responsibility to take the initiative for one's own welfare while the responsibility for the cause of the problem is attributed to external factors. Therefore, the credibility of motivational support and the availability of persons who make one feel competent and determined contribute to the willingness to hold on with self-help attempts in the face of early failure.

Various Concepts of Trust

In this section, I will discuss the meaning of trust more systematically. First, a distinction must be drawn between generalized trust as a personality variable and trustworthiness of a specific person. Generalized trust was introduced by Rotter (1967, 1971) as a personality variable. Generalized expectancies for interpersonal trust refer to public institutions, political leadership, and experts. The items included in the scale for the measurement of interpersonal trust do not refer to specific persons. Instead, they refer to people in general. Examples are "In dealing with strangers one is better off to be cautious until they have provided evidence that they are trustworthy" and "Most elected public officials are really sincere in their campaign promises."

Interpersonal trust is not equivalent to "foolish trust" or gullibility (Rotter, 1980). High trusters are no more gullible than low trusters when there is a strong reason to distrust another person. The concept of trust as generalized expectancy is related to social learning theory. Rotter (1955) considered the relationship between three variables: behavior potential, expectancy, and reinforcement value. He assumed that the potential for behavior x in a specific situation in relation to reinforcement a is a function of the expectancy of the occurrence of reinforcement a and of the reinforcement value of reinforcement a in the specific situation.

From this perspective, experiences with the confirmation of such expectancies in the past constitute an important class of individual difference variables. The individual's past experience leads to differences in personality. People differ in their expectancies that the promised reinforcements will occur in the future (Rotter, 1967). In this context, Rotter (1967, p. 651) defined interpersonal trust "as an expectancy held by an individual or a group that the word, promise, verbal or written statement of another individual or group can be relied upon."

While this approach focuses on trust as an attitude toward people in general, it does not apply to trust as an attitude toward a specific person that is influenced by specific characteristics of O. While generalized trust is an abstraction derived from past experiences with many people, specific trust is based on the stimulus qualities of one specific target person. These stimulus qualities of the target person include appearance, verbal statements of intention, and past events that have elucidated the willingness of the target person to act in agreement with his or her promises and announcements. O's stimulus qualities constitute the basic ingredients of his or her trustworthiness.

Therefore, the measurement of interpersonal trust as a generalized expectancy must be supplemented by a self-scoring measure of trust toward a specific O. Such scales were developed by Johnson-George and Swap (1982) and Rempel and Holmes (1986). In addition, Buck and Bierhoff (1986) performed extensive psychometric analyses with a German version of Johnson-George and Swap's questionnaire. A principal axis factor analysis on the basis of the data of 235 respondents revealed that the German items yielded two factors. (The results of a maximum likelihood factor analysis were nearly equivalent.) The factor solutions of males and females were very similar.

Factor 1 appeared to focus on reliableness, which refers to keeping promises and commitments. The reliableness scale formed on the basis of the factor analysis has 9 items (item example: "If my alarmclock was broken and I asked N.N. to wake me up at a certain time, I could rely on it.") The internal consistency was high (Cronbach's *alpha* = .90).

Factor 2 was designated trustworthiness. Items that load highly on this factor refer to emotional investments and discretion/secrecy (item example: "I could confide in N.N. with the certainty that he or she will listen to me.") The 10-item scale that is supposed to measure trustworthiness achieved a satisfactory internal consistency (*alpha* = .85).

In an experimental study, it was shown that the manipulation of the reliableness of the target person as high or low affected only the reliableness scale, while the manipulation of the trustworthiness of the target person resulted only in significant effects on the trustworthiness scale (Buck & Bierhoff, 1986). The effects on perceived reliableness were considerably attenuated when trustworthiness of the target person was varied and vice versa (see also Bierhoff & Klein, 1989). These results demonstrate that reliableness and trustworthiness can be differentiated on a conceptual level.

The two factors resemble similar dimensions that were described by Johnson-George and Swap (1982) for males and females. In addition, these authors obtained an additional factor for males that was interpreted as overall trust. Gender differences did not emerge in our studies. Whether or not males respond in a more global manner than females on trust items remains an open question. The issue of gender differences is complex. Situational factors, sex-role attitudes (traditional or liberal), sex-role identity (expressive or instrumental), and sex-role norms must be taken into account (Hill & Stull, 1987).

In some of our studies, which are described later in more detail, we used specific interpersonal trust scales developed by Rempel and Holmes (1986) and Rempel, Holmes, and Zanna (1985). Their questionnaire contains three subscales:

1. Predictability, which relates "to the knowledge that your partner acts in consistently positive ways" (Rempel & Holmes, 1986, p. 28; item example: "I know how my partner is going to act. My partner can always be counted on to act as I expect"),
2. Dependability, which relates to the expectation that the other protects and supports P in dangerous and difficult situations (item example: "I have found my partner is a thoroughly dependable person, especially when it comes to things that are important"), and
3. Faith, which is "a sense of emotional security in the face of an uncertain future" (Rempel & Holmes, 1986, p. 31; item example: "Though times may change and the future is uncertain, I have faith that my partner will always be ready and willing to offer me strength, come what may").

The facets of specific interpersonal trust measured with the specific trust questionnaire correlated positively. The subscales tap interrelated facets of trust. Therefore, global measures of trustworthiness like the Counselor Rating Form (Barak & LaCrosse, 1975) might be employed. The trustworthiness scale of the Counselor Rating Form contains adjective pairs like "honest-dishonest," "reliable-unreliable," and "responsible-irresponsible." In the study by Barak and LaCrosse (1975), twelve traits and their antonyms were attributed to three interviewers who were famous psychotherapists. The internal consistency of the trustworthiness scale was high (Spearman-Brown $r = .91$). Trustworthiness was highly correlated with perceived attractiveness and perceived expertness of the interviewers (LaCrosse & Barak, 1976).

In what areas of research is it useful to apply specific interpersonal trust scales? One area of research that may profit from the use of specific trust scales focuses on close relationships (see Steck, Levitan, McLane, & Kelley, 1982). In empirical studies (Bierhoff, Fink, & Montag, 1988; Rempel et al., 1985), the importance of specific trust for relationship satisfaction was demonstrated. This research will be discussed later in this chapter.

In addition, specific interpersonal trust plays an important role in helping relationships (see also Petermann, 1985). For example, the Counselor Rating Form was developed as a device for measuring client perceptions of counselors (Barak & LaCrosse, 1975). In his book on an eclectic approach to psychotherapy, Garfield (1980) described trustworthiness of the counselor as a prerequisite for clients' self-disclosure. In addition, trustworthiness of the counselor might be related to more favorable expectations of the clients and less client dropout during counseling. Especially when, after a first phase in the course of the client-counselor relationship, ambivalence and contradictory feelings are aroused in the client, trustworthiness of the counselor contributes to a steady commitment of the client during the course of the psychotherapy.

One strategy to induce client trust and self-disclosure is to encourage the counselor/therapist to disclose personal information (e.g., "I remember having to make it on my own and I felt so lonely"; McCarthy, 1982). Another strategy employs self-involving statements that immediately communicate the counselor's feelings and reactions to the client (e.g., "I appreciate the way you are relating to me right now"; McCarthy, 1982).

The research on counseling and self-disclosure is excellently reviewed by Hendrick (1987). We cannot go into detail here. Therefore, we only pursue the question whether self-referent statements of the counselor facilitate the development of client trust.

Empirical evidence indicates that self-involving statements elicited more perceived trustworthiness (measured on the Barak & LaCrosse Scale) than self-disclosing statements (McCarthy, 1979; McCarthy & Betz, 1978). Unfortunately, no control group was included in these studies employing a low-intimacy self-disclosure (McCarthy, 1982).

In a later study (McCarthy, 1982), results indicated that the effects on perceived counselor trustworthiness of high-intimacy self-disclosure and high self-involvement were similar, while a counselor who disclosed personal information at a low-intimacy level was assessed as less trustworthy. Additional data indicated that—although high self-disclosing and high self-involving therapists elicited similar responses on the Counselor Rating Form—the high self-disclosing therapists elicited more affective words in client responses. This might be important when the expression of feelings is considered essential. In summary, self-referent responses of the counselor enhanced client perceptions of trustworthiness.

Wills (1982) discussed the common elements of specific treatment methods in psychotherapy as nonspecific factors in helping relationships. Under the heading self-esteem enhancement, he mentioned helper qualities like warmth, positive regard, and respect that seem to be related to therapy outcome. These variables are related to the self-involving counselor style investigated by McCarthy (1982). Self-involving counselors are quite successful in eliciting the image of a trustworthy interviewer.

According to Wills (1982), trustworthiness of lay helpers might even surpass the rating of professional helpers. In support of this hypothesis, McCarthy (1982) reported that paraprofessional counselors were perceived as more trustworthy than professional counselors.

In the following paragraphs, I shall discuss three issues that are relevant for a fuller understanding of the meaning of interpersonal trust:

First, does trust lead to self-disclosure? I assume that trust and self-disclosure are related concepts. Self-disclosure is the most important consequence of trust and, in addition, enhances the development and maintenance of the trusting relationship.

Second, does trust develop according to the norm of reciprocity? This would imply that pair correlations should be positive. A related issue is self-disclosure reciprocity, which refers to a mutual exchange of information at the same level of intimacy.

Third, what does generalized trust imply for specific interpersonal trust?

Finally, two issues are raised that point to the role of trust in the process of coping with stress (see Figure 21.3). The investigation of the impact of trust in close relationships shows that specific trust of the partners is related to conflict and disagreement. Close relationships are especially well-suited for an analysis of the effects of trust because they introduce a very high level of vulnerability "in the face of an uncertain future." In addition, the relevance of trust in therapeutic settings is considered. The role of trust and client self-disclosure in the treatment of psychological distress illustrates the relevance of trust research for applied settings.

TRUST AS A SOCIAL PSYCHOLOGICAL VARIABLE

Trust and Self-Disclosure

Perceived trustworthiness and willingness to disclose intimate information are interrelated variables. Without high trustworthiness of the listener, high-intimacy self-disclosure would be unlikely. In addition, high-intimacy self-disclosure indicates that the discloser perceives the listener as a trustworthy person.

This theoretical framework was described more fully by Schneider (1976). In his model, self-disclosure encourages the development of trust, while higher trust levels enhance self-disclosure (Figure 21.4).

In an empirical study focusing on the perception of a client-helper relationship, self-disclosure and specific trust were measured as dependent variables (Bierhoff & Kliem, 1986). Trust in the therapist was assessed by the Counselor Rating Form (Barak & LaCrosse, 1975). Self-disclosure was measured by a 21-item questionnaire assessing willingness to self-disclosure at high, medium, and low levels of intimacy (Jourard, 1971).

Results are summarized in Table 21.1. Correlations indicated that trustworthiness and willingness to self-disclosure are highly interrelated.

To facilitate comparison, the intercorrelations of the self-disclosure subscales are also included in Table 21.1. All correlations were substantial. Trust correlated with self-disclosure at the same level of association as self-disclosure subscales correlated with each other. In addition, the internal consistencies (Cronbach's *alpha*) of all scales were satisfactory.

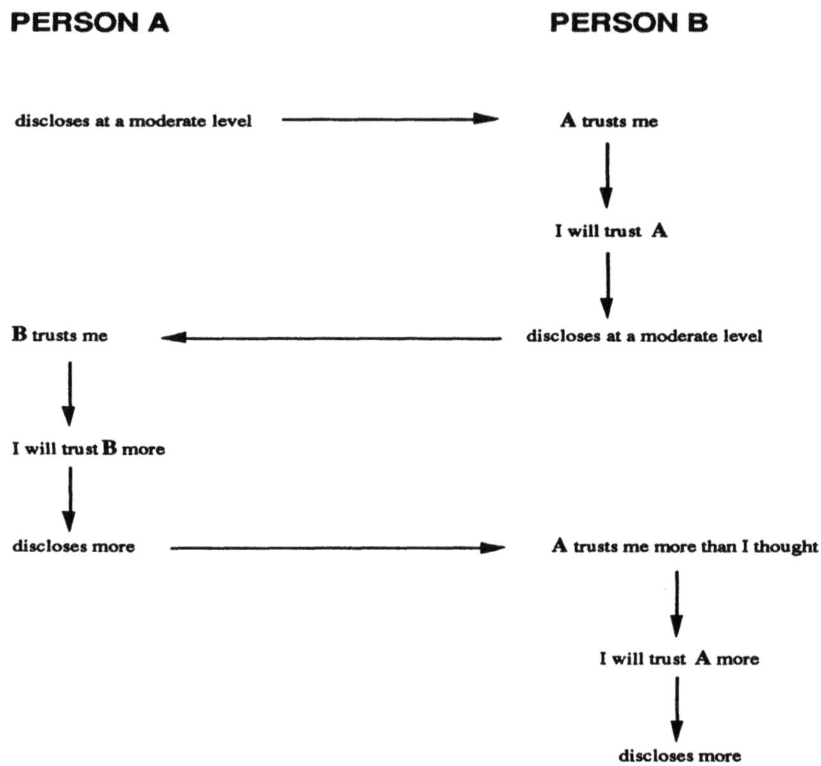

FIG. 21.4. Reciprocity and trust (adapted from Schneider, 1976).

Self-disclosure was conceptualized by Cohen et al. (1986) as a social skill measure. In their study, self-disclosure correlated consistently with social support measured on the Interpersonal Support Evaluation List (ISEL) from Cohen and Hoberman (1983). In addition, self-disclosure predicted change in social support over time. Therefore, self-disclosure—and by implication trust—leads to more social support—at least among college freshmen who were the subjects in the study by Cohen et al. (1986).

Future research might separate samples into groups who are and who are not susceptible to stress symptoms under conditions of stress. One hypothesis states that trusting individuals cope more effectively with stress than nontrusting individuals. This effect might be mediated by different levels of self-disclosure associated with different levels of trust.

The assumption that trust and self-disclosure are variables that refer to the same underlying dimension holds only when self-disclosure is understood as serving a self-expressing, self-clarifying, or self-validating function (Archer, 1987). Self-disclosure that is part of strategic self-presentation is presumably unrelated—or

TABLE 21.1

Correlations of Trustworthiness With Self-Disclosure

	Self-disclosure		
Measures	Low intimacy	Medium intimacy	High intimacy
Trustworthiness	.45 (99)	.76 (99)	.77 (99)
Self-disclosure			
Low intimacy	-	.66 (100)	.62 (100)
Medium intimacy		-	.93 (100)
High intimacy			-

Note. Number of subjects in parentheses. All correlations are signifcant beyond the .001 level.

even negatively related—to trust. It might be useful to use the term impression management for this strategic type of self-disclosure. While impression management is frequently the consequence of ulterior motives (e.g., to gain approval), self-disclosure reflects more genuine motives (e.g., to express one's feelings).

Trust Reciprocity

The study of trust reciprocity depends on the definition of reciprocity (Hill & Stull, 1982). The most narrow meaning of reciprocity is equivalent exchange. In this sense, trust reciprocity depends on the equivalence of the breadth or depth of trust. A less restrictive definition of reciprocity focuses on pair correlations. Hill and Stull (1982) refer to covariant exchange in this context. As the term indicates, changes in the trust of P covary with changes in the trust of O. The broader definition is of special significance for the issue of trust reciprocity because the norm of reciprocity is understood by many researchers as predicting a high covariance of the scores of P and O and not necessarily as implying equivalence of absolute level of behavior. Note that equivalent exchange is a special case of covariant exchange (Hill & Stull, 1982).

The theoretical framework of Schneider (1976) implies positive pair correlations among trust measures. In agreement with this prediction, Butler (1983) reported a high pair correlation for persons who are in a long-term relationship. He investigated the trust scores of professionals (e.g., attorneys, school principals) and their secretaries. The results supported a trust reciprocity hypothesis. In addition, bosses trusted their secretaries more than secretaries trusted their bosses. Therefore, covariant exchange but not equivalent exchange was established.

In a study on close relationships in 76 heterosexual pairs, we found positive correlations of $r = .47^{***}$ for predictability, $r = .21^{*}$ for dependability, and $r = .27^{*}$ for faith (Bierhoff et al., 1988). In a second study with 50 heterosexual pairs, the pair correlations were $r = .46^{***}$, $r = .51^{***}$, and $r = .25^{*}$, respectively ($^{*}p < .05$; $^{***}p < .001$). Therefore, the conclusion is justified that trust follows the principle of covariant exchange.

In addition, the mean trust values of males and females were remarkably similar. For example, the predictability means were $M_{\text{males}} = 4.84$ and $M_{\text{females}} = 5.04$ in the first study. The means for dependability and faith exhibited the same pattern of no significant difference. These results suggest that partners in close relationships follow a norm of reciprocity that is based on equivalence. It makes good sense that boss-secretary pairs who exhibit power inequalities show less indications of equivalent exchange than close relationships among equals (Bierhoff, Schreiber, & Klein, 1989).

Specific Trust and Generalized Trust

In several studies, we investigated whether specific trust is a function of generalized trust. Our hypothesis was that specific trust will correlate positively with generalized trust because generalized trust may be conceived as an abstraction from past experiences (Bierhoff & Buck, 1986). I will only report one study on the perception of counselors in counselor-client relationships. The results were replicated in later studies already mentioned above.

Interpersonal trust was measured with a German version of the Wrightsman scales for the measurement of generalized trust and cynicism (distrust; Stack, 1978). Trustworthiness of the counselor was measured with the Counselor Research Form (Barak & LaCrosse, 1975), and self-disclosure at low, medium, and high levels of intimacy with the Jourard (1971) scale.

The results (Table 21.2) indicated a weak but consistent negative relationship between generalized trust and specific trust/self-disclosure. Cynicism was related neither to specific trust nor to self-disclosure.

In this study, subjects also responded to a German version of the locus-of-control questionnaire that consisted of three subscales: Internal Control, Powerful Others, and Chance. Krampen's (1981) German adaptation of Levenson's (1973) revised scales was used. These permitted a distinction between two types of external orientation (i.e., control by chance and control by powerful others).

The results indicated that the chance scale and the powerful others scale correlated negatively with self-disclosure and with specific trust, respectively (Table 21.2). Therefore, externals were less willing to disclose personal information on all levels of intimacy and attributed less trustworthiness to the counselor. In addition, internals tended to respond more trustingly on the trustworthiness scale (Table 21.2).

These results are surprising. They indicate that generalized trust does not enhance specific trust. Generalized trust might be understood as an ideology that is separated from the perception of interaction partners. In fact, under certain circumstances, those who favor a trust ideology attribute less trustworthiness than those who are more sceptical on an ideological level. Generalized trust might be understood as a belief system that is no longer applied to person perception. Instead, generalized trust serves the function of evaluating social events in general and developing an open or cautious attitude that guides the planning of one's life on a more abstract level.

One implication of these results is that the measurement of specific trust is not redundant with the measurement of generalized trust. Both trust measures apply to different areas of judgment. In the following, two questions are pursued:

TABLE 21.2

Trustworthiness, Self-Disclosure, Generalized Trust and Locus of Control

	Generalized Trust	Cynicism	Locus of Control		
			Internal Control	Powerful Others	Chance
Trustworthiness (Counselor-Rating-Form)	-.23**	.07	.19*	-.32***	-.36**
Self-Disclosure					
Low intimacy	-.11	.08	-.03	-.15	-.11
Medium intimacy	-.27**	.12	.07	-.28**	-.27**
High intimacy	-.27**	.14	.14	-.26**	-.25**

*p<.05 **p<.01 ***p<.001

1. What is the relationship between specific trust and strain in close relationships?
2. Under what conditions does trust develop in a counselor-client relationship?

CONSEQUENCES OF TRUST

Trust and Strain in Close Relationships

Is there a positive correlation between trust and effectiveness of interpersonal coordination in close relationships? For example, is a trusting relationship more harmonious and less distressed by interpersonal conflicts than a relationship that elicits less trust?

We collected data in two studies of opposite-sex friendships that addressed this issue. Men and women assessed their trust in the partner on the Rempel and Holmes scales and the Buck and Bierhoff scales. In addition, they described the course of their relationship in the past using scales that measure the amount of communication, disagreement, and tenderness (Close Relationships Questionnaire; Hahlweg, 1979).

Both studies were mentioned above with respect to pair correlations that tended to be positive. The first study included 76 pairs. The influence of dependability and faith on the relationship variables was especially pronounced. For example, *high dependability* was associated with less disagreements (Figure 21.5). *High predictability* was positively related to common interests (Figure 21.6). In addition, subjects who assumed higher dependability of the partner were more satisfied with their relationship (Figure 21.7).

High faith was associated with less disagreements and better communication (Figure 21.5 and Figure 21.6). In addition, faith was strongly associated with a measurement of relationship satisfaction on a 6-point scale (Figure 21.7).

This pattern of results was replicated in a second study with 50 pairs. In this study, our trust scales (reliableness, trustworthiness) were included. Although both scales were associated with disagreements, the effects were more pronounced and consistent for trustworthiness.

In addition, trustworthiness was significantly related to common interest/communication. Higher trustworthiness led to higher values on this scale. The same pattern of results—although less pronounced—was obtained for reliableness as a predictor of common interest/communication.

Finally, trustworthiness but not reliableness was related to relationship satisfaction. Respondents who scored higher on trustworthiness tended to express more satisfaction. In summary, in distressed couples, individuals expressed less trust in the partner than in nondistressed couples. Therefore, trust is a concomitant and

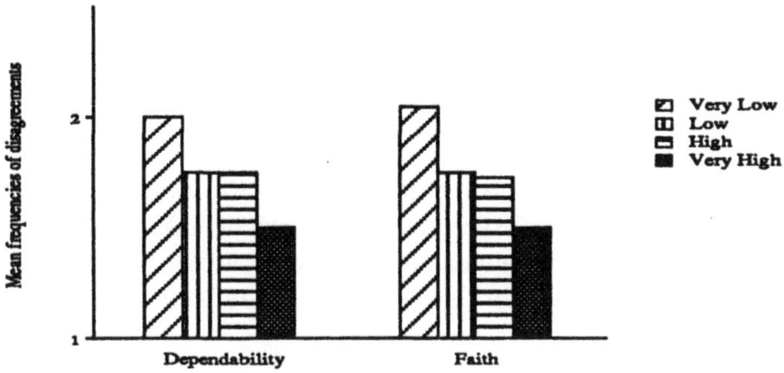

FIG. 21.5. Mean frequencies of disagreements as a function of dependability and faith ($N = 150$).

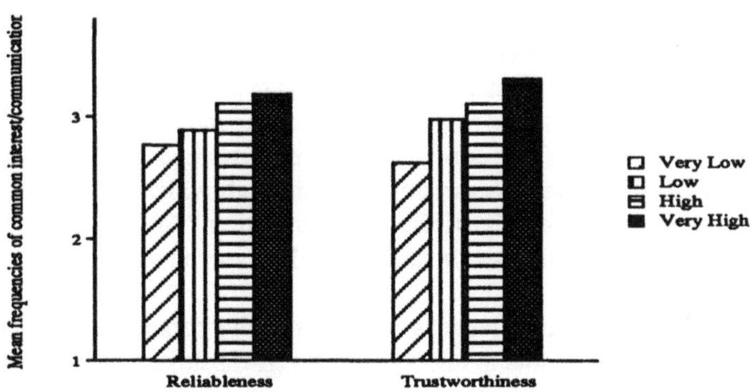

FIG.21.6. Common interest/communication as a function of predictability, dependability, and faith ($N = 150$).

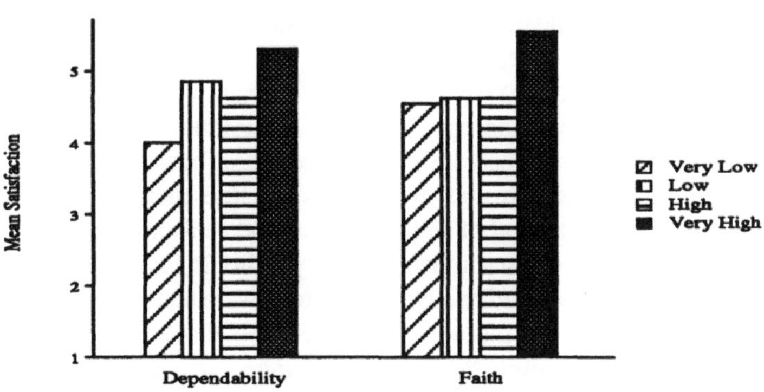

FIG. 21.7. Relationship satisfaction as a function of dependability and faith ($N = 150$).

possibly a determinant of marital problems (see also Bierhoff, in press; Rempel et al., 1985).

Determinants of Trustworthiness

How might a person promote his/her trustworthiness? Ellison and Firestone (1974) varied the interviewer behavior in an interviewer-student dialogue. In the *intrusive*-style condition, the interviewer appeared as active, assertive, and dominant. In the *reflective*-style condition, the interviewer appeared as reflective, quite passive, and indirect.

The intrusive-reflective variation of the interviewer style is related to the nondirective dimension described by Rogers (1959). Ellison and Firestone (1974) measured self-disclosure on a 22-item scale containing 11 high-intimate and 11 low-intimate topics. They reported that interviewer style influenced subjects' willingness to self-disclose on items that were prerated as high on the intimacy dimension. But the difference between the means was fairly small.

Another aspect of the interpersonal exchange process that was emphasized by Berg (1987) is related to the responsiveness of the interacting persons. Miller and Berg (1984, p. 193) defined conversational responsiveness as "behaviors made by the recipient of another's communication through which the recipient indicates interest in an understanding of the communication." Obviously, the concept of conversational responsiveness is similar to self-involvement (McCarthy, 1982) and trust reciprocity.

Conversational responsiveness is related to the personality characteristics of high openers who are able to elicit intimate self-disclosure. They are presumably listeners who are more attentive and more responsive to their partners than low openers. Therefore, high openers are able to encourage their partners to disclose more intimately (Miller, Berg, & Archer, 1983).

A concept that is also closely related to responsiveness is positive regard. Rogers (1959, p. 208) defined positive regard as an interpersonal attitude that includes warmth, sympathy, and acceptance.

A variety of approaches to psychotherapy, for example, psychoanalysis, group therapy, and client-centered therapy, depend on the willingness of the clients to trust other persons and to disclose intimate personal information. Client-centered therapy emphasizes warmth and genuineness of the therapist as a necessary condition for the enhancement of self-disclosure and self-exploration. In addition, the expectation is implied that a nondirective style should facilitate self-disclosure.

In one of our empirical studies, two hypotheses were tested. First, high positive regard elicits more trust and more intimate client self-disclosure than low positive regard. Second, a nondirective therapist elecits more trust and more intimate self-disclosure than an directive therapist. In an experimental study, we employed

TABLE 21.3

Mean Ratings of Self-Disclosure and Trustworthiness by Positive Regard

Dependent Measure	Positive Regard	
	High	Low
Low Self-Disclosure	3.27	2.55
Medium Self-Disclosure	3.01	1.77
High Self-Disclosure	2.44	1.15
Trustworthiness	3.08	4.65

Note. N = 99. Higher values indicate more self-disclosure and less trustworthiness. The self-disclosure measure could vary from 0 to 5, the trustworthiness scale from 1 to 7.

positive regard (high/low) and nondirective style (high/low) as independent factors. Dependent measures tapped trust and willingness to disclose intimately.

Subjects listened to a tape recording of a dialogue between a client and a therapist. In all versions, the client reported that she suffered from depressive symptoms, had problems with her boyfriend, and difficulties with other people in general. A pretest indicated that the two experimental variables were manipulated successfully and independently. Subjects were 100 female college students.

Because the dependent variables were highly correlated, a MANOVA was performed using the trustworthiness scale (derived from Barak & LaCrosse, 1975) and the three self-disclosure scales (Jourard, 1971) as dependent variables. The analysis yielded a highly significant main effect of positive regard. No other main effect or interaction even approached significance. Additional ANOVAs calculated for each dependent variable separately showed that the positive-regard main effect was significant for each of the dependent variables. Subjects in the high positive regard condition indicated more trust and more willingness to disclose intimately (see Table 21.3).

There was only scattered evidence of systematic effects of nondirective style. Although the multivariate *F* was not significant, univariate analyses of variance indicated a significant main effect for self-disclosure at the medium level of intimacy. At this level, self-disclosure tended to be higher in the nondirective style condition. This evidence corroborates the results of Ellison and Firestone (1974).

SUMMARY

Specific interpersonal trust comprises two partially overlapping variables that may be labeled reliableness and trustworthiness. Specific interpersonal trust is determined by dispositional and situational variables. Among the dispositional variables, locus of control must be emphasized because internals tend to score higher on the trustworthiness measure while externals tend to score lower. In addition, high self-monitoring is related to high levels of specific trust (Ludwig, Franco, & Malloy, 1986). Surprisingly, generalized trust seems to be unrelated to specific trust. Therefore, the general beliefs about trust do not determine the willingness to trust a specific target person. In fact, the evidence supports the inference that generalized trust and specific trust are correlated slightly negatively.

Specific trust and self-disclosure are highly related. Self-disclosure—and by implication trust—functions as a social skill that enhances coping with stressful life events. In general, trust leads to self-disclosure, while higher levels of self-disclosure induce more trust. As a consequence, pair correlations of trust in dyads tend to be positive. In close and long-lasting relationships, covariant exchange and—under certain conditions—equivalent exchange of rewards seems to be the rule.

Another determinant of trust is the conversational responsiveness and self-involvement of the target person that resembles positive regard, warmth, and an accepting attitude. A target person (O) who expresses high positive regard enhances P's self-disclosure and O's perceived trustworthiness.

Therefore, positive regard seems to facilitate the development of trust. Although the prerequisites for the development of trust in close relationships are not fully understood, factors like positive regard, predictability of future behavior, and consistency between saying and doing are likely to play a major role in the formation of specific interpersonal trust.

Our theoretical model of trust (Figure 21.2) includes several consequences of trust, for example, social support, cooperation, and veridical communication. Results from close-relationship studies show that trust is systematically associated with the frequency of disagreements and communications. High trust is associated with few disagreements and many communications. In addition, high trust coincides with high levels of satisfaction with the relationship. Other studies indicate that specific trust facilitates the obtainment of social support (Cohen et al., 1986) and the development of cooperative relationships (Pruitt & Kimmel, 1977).

Following Kobasa (1982), we have described the role of specific interpersonal trust in close relationships with regard to crises and loss experiences (Figure 21.3). Trust might influence strain after stressful life events either directly or indirectly via coping strategies. The subtle implications of the model might be tested empirically with sophisticated techniques like path analysis. Stressful life events might be measured with respect to major life events and daily hassles and trust with respect to supporting members of the social network. The coping strategies might include social skills. Strain includes such variables as depression, anxiety, and negative affect. We plan empirical studies in an attempt to use this model as a framework for the understanding of the interplay between stress experiences, trust, and coping.

REFERENCES

Amelang, M., Gold, A., & Külbel, E. (1984). Über einige Erfahrungen mit einer deutschsprachigen Skala zur Erfassung zwischenmenschlichen Vertrauens. *Diagnostica, 30*, 198-215.

Archer, R. L. (1987). Commentary. Self-disclosure, a very useful behavior. In V. J. Derlega & J. H. Berg (Eds.), *Self-disclosure: Theory, research, and therapy* (pp. 329-342). New York: Plenum.

Archer, R. L., & Earle, W. B. (1983). The interpersonal orientations of disclosure. In P. B. Paulus (Ed.), *Basic group processes* (pp. 289-314). New York: Springer.

Barak, A., & LaCrosse, M. B. (1975). Multidimensional perception of counselor behavior. *Journal of Counseling Psychology, 22*, 471-476.

Berg, J. H. (1987). Responsiveness and self-disclosure. In V. J. Derlega & J. H. Berg (Eds.), *Self-disclosure: Theory, research, and therapy* (pp. 101-130). New York: Plenum.

Bierhoff, H. W. (1990). Attribution of responsibility and helpfulness. In L. Montada & H. W. Bierhoff (Eds.), *Altruism in social systems* (pp. 105-129). Toronto: Hogrefe.

Bierhoff, H. W. (in press). Liebe. In M. Amelang, H. J. Ahrens, & H. W. Bierhoff (Eds.), *Brennpunkte der Persönlichkeitsforschung* (Vol. 3). Göttingen: Hogrefe.

Bierhoff, H. W., & Buck, E. (1986). Spezifisches interpersonelles Vertrauen in der Personenwahrnehmung. In M. Amelang (Ed.), *Bericht über den 35. Kongreß der Deutschen Gesellschaft für Psychologie in Heidelberg 1986* (Vol. 1, p. 238). Göttingen: Hogrefe.

Bierhoff, H. W., Fink, A., & Montag, E. (1988). Vertrauen, Liebe und Zufriedenheit in partnerschaftlichen Beziehungen. In W. Schönpflug (Ed.), *Bericht über den 36. Kongreß der Deutschen Gesellschaft für Psychologie in Berlin 1988* (Vol. 1, pp. 409-410). Göttingen: Hogrefe.

Bierhoff, H. W., & Klein, R. (1989). Expectations, confirmation bias, and suggestibility. In V. A. Gheorghiu, P. Netter, H. J. Eysenck, & R. Rosenthal (Eds.), *Suggestion and suggestibility. Theory and research* (pp. 337-346). New York: Springer.

Bierhoff, H. W., & Kliem, B. (1986). *Selbstenthüllung in der Gesprächspsychotherapie*. Unpublished manuscript.

Bierhoff, H. W., Schreiber, C., & Klein, R. (1989). *Trust and social interaction*. Unpublished manuscript.

Brickman, P., Becker, L. J., & Castle, S. (1979). Making trust easier and harder through two forms of sequential interaction. *Journal of Personality and Social Psychology, 37*, 515-521.

Brickman, P., Rabinowitz, V. C., Karuza, J., Coates, D., Cohn, E., & Kidder, L. (1982). Models of helping and coping. *American Psychologist, 37*, 368-384.

Buck, E., & Bierhoff, H. W. (1986). Verläßlichkeit und Vertrauenswürdigkeit: Skalen zur Erfassung des Vertrauens in eine konkrete Person. *Zeitschrift für Differentielle und Diagnostische Psychologie, 7*, 205-223.

Butler, J. K. (1983). Reciprocity of trust between professionals and their secretaries. *Psychological Reports, 53*, 411-416.

Cohen, S., & Hoberman, H. M. (1983). Positive events and social supports as buffers of life change stress. *Journal of Applied Social Psychology, 13*, 99-125.

Cohen, S., Sherrod, D. R., & Clark, M. S. (1986). Social skills and the stress-protective role of social support. *Journal of Personality and Social Psychology, 50*, 963-973.

Dawes, R. M. (1980). Social dilemmas. *Annual Review of Psychology, 31*, 169-193.

Derlega, V. J., & Grzelak, J. (1979). Appropriateness of self-disclosure. In G. J. Chelune (Ed.), *Self-disclosure: Origins, patterns, and implications for openness in interpersonal relations* (pp. 151-176). San Francisco: Jossey-Bass.

Deutsch, M. (1949). A theory of cooperation and competition. *Human Relations, 2,* 129-152.

Deutsch, M. (1958). Trust and suspicion. *Journal of Conflict Resolution, 2,* 265-279.

Deutsch, M. (1973). *The resolution of conflict.* New Haven, CT: Yale University Press.

Ellison, C. W., & Firestone, I. J. (1974). Development of interpersonal trust as a function of self-esteem, target status, and target style. *Journal of Personality and Social Psychology, 29,* 655-663.

Erikson, E. H. (1968). *Identity, youth, and crisis.* New York: Norton.

Garfield, S. L. (1980). *Psychotherapy. An ecclectic approach.* New York: Wiley.

Hahlweg, K. (1979). Konstruktion und Validierung des Partnerschaftsfragebogens PFB. *Zeitschrift für Klinische Psychologie, 8,* 17-40.

Hendrick, S. S. (1987). Counseling and self-disclosure. In V. J. Derlega & J. H. Berg (Eds.), *Self-disclosure: Theory, research, and therapy* (pp. 303-327). New York: Plenum.

Hill, C. T., & Stull, D. E. (1982). Disclosure reciprocity: Conceptual and measurement issues. *Social Psychology Quarterly, 45,* 238-244

Hill, C. T., & Stull, D. E. (1987). Gender and self-disclosure. Strategies for exploring the issues. In V. J. Derlega & J. H. Berg (Eds.), *Self-disclosure: Theory, research, and therapy* (pp. 81-100). New York: Plenum.

Johnson-George, C., & Swap, W. C. (1982). Measurement of specific interpersonal trust: Construction and validation of a scale to assess trust in a specific other. *Journal of Personality and Social Psychology, 43,* 1306-1317.

Jones, E. E., & Davis, K. E. (1965). From acts to dispositions: The attribution process in person perception. In L. Berkowitz (Ed.), *Advances in experimental social psychology* (Vol. 2, pp. 219-266). New York: Academic Press.

Jourard, S. M. (1971). *Self-disclosure. An experimental analysis of the transparent self.* New York: Wiley.

Kee, H. W., & Knox, R. E. (1970). Conceptual and methodological considerations in the study of trust and suspicion. *Journal of Conflict Resolution, 14,* 357-366.

Kobasa, S. C. (1982). Commitment and coping in stress resistance among lawyers. *Journal of Personality and Social Psychology, 42,* 707-717.

Krampen, G. (1981). *IPC-Fragebogen zu Kontrollüberzeugungen.* Göttingen: Hogrefe.

Krampen, G., Viebig, J., & Walter, W. (1982). Entwicklung einer Skala zur Erfassung dreier Aspekte von sozialem Vertrauen. *Diagnostica, 28,* 242-247.

LaCrosse, M. B., & Barak, A. (1976). Differential perception of counselor behavior. *Journal of Counseling Psychology, 23,* 170-172.

Levenson, H. (1973). Multidimensional locus of control in psychiatric patients. *Journal of Consulting and Clinical Psychology, 41,* 397-404.

Lindskold, S. (1978). Trust development, the GRIT proposal, and the effects of conciliatory acts on conflict and cooperation. *Psychological Bulletin, 85,* 772-793.

Ludwig, D., Franco, J. N., & Malloy, T. E. (1986). Effects of reciprocity and self-monitoring on self-disclosure with a new acquaintance. *Journal of Personality and Social Psychology, 50,* 1077-1082.

Luhmann, N. (1973). *Vertrauen.* Stuttgart: Enke.

McCarthy, P. R. (1979). Differential effects of self-disclosing versus self-involving counselor statements across counselor-client gender pairings. *Journal of Counseling Psychology, 26,* 538-541.

McCarthy, P. R. (1982). Differential effects of counselor self-referent responses and counselor status. *Journal of Counseling Psychology, 25,* 251-256.

McCarthy, P. R., & Betz, N. E. (1978). Differential effects of self-disclosing versus self-involving counselor statements. *Journal of Counseling Psychology, 25,* 251-256.

Miller, L. C., & Berg, J. H. (1984). Selectivity and urgency in interpersonal exchange. In V. J. Derlega (Ed.), *Communication, intimacy, and close relationships* (pp. 161-205). Orlando, FL: Academic Press.

Miller, L. C., Berg, J. H., & Archer, R. L. (1983). Openers: Individuals who elicit intimate self-disclosure. *Journal of Personality and Social Psychology, 44,* 1231-1244.

Montada, L., & Bierhoff, H. W. (1990). Studying prosocial behavior in social systems. In L. Montada & H. W. Bierhoff (Eds.), *Altruism in social systems* (pp. 1-26). Toronto: Hogrefe.

Petermann, F. (1985). *Vertrauen*. Salzburg: Müller.

Pruitt, D. G., & Kimmel, M. J. (1977). Twenty years of experimental gaming: Critique, synthesis, and suggestions for the future. *Annual Review of Psychology, 28*, 363-392.

Rempel, J. K., & Holmes, J. G. (1986). How do I trust thee? *Psychology Today, 20*(2), 28-34.

Rempel, J. K., Holmes, J. G., & Zanna, M. P. (1985). Trust in close relationships. *Journal of Personality and Social Psychology, 49*, 95-112.

Rogers, C. R. (1959). A theory of therapy, personality, and interpersonal relationships, as developed in the client-centered framework. In S. Koch (Ed.), *Psychology: A study of a science* (Vol. 1, pp. 184-256). New York: McGraw-Hill.

Rotter, J. B. (1955). The role of the psychological situation in determining the direction of human behavior. In M. R. Jones (Ed.), *Nebraska Symposium on Motivation* (Vol. 3, pp. 245-269). Lincoln, NE: University of Nebraska Press.

Rotter, J. B. (1967). A new scale for the measurement of interpersonal trust. *Journal of Personality, 35*, 651-665.

Rotter, J. B. (1971). Generalized expectancies for interpersonal trust. *American Psychologist, 26*, 443-452.

Rotter, J. B. (1980). Interpersonal trust, trustworthiness, and gullibility. *American Psychologist, 35*, 1-7.

Schlenker, R. B., Helm, B., & Tedeschi, J. T. (1973). The effects of personality and situational variables on behavioral trust. *Journal of Personality and Social Psychology, 25*, 419-427.

Schneider, D. J. (1976). *Social psychology*. Reading, MA: Addison-Wesley.

Spitznagel, A. (1986). Selbstenthüllung: Formen, Bedingungen und Konsequenzen. In A. Spitznagel & L. Schmidt-Atzert (Eds.), *Sprechen und Schweigen. Zur Psychologie der Selbstenthüllung* (pp. 17-46). Bern: Huber.

Stack, L. C. (1978). Trust. In H. London & J. E. Exner (Eds.), *Dimensions of personality* (pp. 561-599). New York: Wiley.

Steck, L., Levitan, D., McLane, D., & Kelley, H. H. (1982). Care, need, and conceptions of love. *Journal of Personality and Social Psychology, 43*, 481-491.

Webb, W. M., & Worchel, P. (1986). Trust and distrust. In S. Worchel & W. G. Austin (Eds.), *Psychology of intergroup relations* (2nd ed., pp. 213-228). Chicago, IL: Nelson-Hall.

Wills, T. A. (1982). Nonspecific factors in helping relationships. In T. A. Wills (Ed.), *Basic processes in helping relationships* (pp. 381-404). New York: Academic Press.

Wills, T. A. (1985). Supportive functions of interpersonal relationships. In S. Cohen & S. L. Syme (Eds.), *Social support and health* (pp. 61-82). Orlando, FL: Academic Press.

Wortman, C. B., & Lehman, D. R. (1985). Reactions to victims of life crises: Support attempts that fail. In I. B. Sarason & B. R. Sarason (Eds.), *Social support: Theory, research, and applications* (pp. 463-489). Dordrecht: Martinus Nijhoff.

22 Social Support and Mental Health: A Conceptual and Empirical Overview[1]

Ralf Schwarzer
Anja Leppin
Freie Universität Berlin

Prior research on the impact of life stress on subjective well-being and health has yielded interesting results, but the amount of explained outcome variance remained limited until attention shifted to resistance and resource factors that either may serve as buffers in the coping process or may directly improve well-being (Cohen & Wills, 1985; Hobfoll, 1988). Among such protective factors, social network variables and social support have received a great deal of attention.

According to recent reviews of empirical evidence which has been compiled within the last two decades, it seems, however, as if social relationships might have rather inconsistent effects on health (Cohen, 1988; Ganster & Victor, 1988; House, Umberson, & Landis, 1988; Israel & Rounds, 1987; Rodin & Salovey, 1989; Röhrle, 1989; Schwarzer & Leppin, 1989a, 1989b). One of the main reasons for such inconsistent findings might be due to the considerable heterogeneity of existing theoretical formulations, including a lack of conceptual clarity as well as deficits in measurement. Instruments which are psychometrically unsound or which have evolved from different concepts of social support produce diverse results.

The present paper proposes a reconceptualization of social support by establishing a causal model which treats the major areas of social relationships in terms of their possible impact on the stress and illness process. This theoretical perspective may help to explain the inconsistency of empirical findings and to overcome shortcomings in future investigations. First, a taxonomy of social relationships is described. Second, the conceptual associations between social relationships and the pathogenic process are explored, taking temporal factors into consideration.

[1]The authors are grateful to Chris Dunkel-Schetter and Richard Lazarus, who have made valuable comments on a previous draft of this chapter.

Finally, empirical findings are reported to give an impression of the strength or weakness of social factors in predicting depression.

A TAXONOMY OF SOCIAL RELATIONSHIPS

Many authors have pointed to the necessity of reconceptualizing the global social support construct (e.g., Cohen & McKay, 1984; Cohen & Syme, 1985; Veiel, 1985, 1987; Wortman & Dunkel-Schetter, 1987). House et al. (1988) argue for a theoretical subdivision of social relationships into social integration, social networks, and relational content. *Social integration* refers to the mere existence or quantity of social relationships and comprises the size of a network and the frequency of contact. The number of active social ties determines one's degree of embeddedness with social isolation being one extreme endpoint. Social integration has also been conceptualized as the number of important roles persons hold, such as being a friend or a boss or being married (Thoits, 1983). Marital status has been used as an indicator in prospective epidemiological studies, such as the Alameda County Study (Berkman & Syme, 1979) or the Tecumseh Community Health Study (House, Robbins, & Metzner, 1982). There is empirical evidence that being married is beneficial to health, and a lower degree of social integration is associated with higher mortality from all causes.

Social network structure has been defined as a set of relational properties such as density, reciprocity, sex composition, durability, or homogeneity of one's network. The presence of women in one's network, for example, might facilitate coping with stress because, on the average, women are regarded as being more supportive than men. According to House et al. (1988, p. 304), networks of small size, strong ties, high density, high homogeneity, and low dispersion are advantageous for maintaining identity and, indirectly, for well-being and health. If a change in identity appears to be necessary, e.g., during or after a divorce, larger networks with weaker ties, low density, and greater social and cultural heterogeneity may be more beneficial.

Relational content comprises social support, social regulation and control, and social demands and conflicts. This refers to the function and nature of social relationships with various sources, such as spouse, boss, friends, or relatives. House et al. (1988, p. 302) reserve the term support for the "positive, potentially health-promoting or stress-buffering, aspects of relationships." Social regulation or control, on the other hand, may either promote or impair health, depending on the circumstances. Relational demands and conflicts represent negative qualities of relationships and may contribute to poor health or lack of well-being. This distinction can be considered as useful for breaking down the many inconsistent results or for counterbalancing positive and negative relational content to determine the net effect of specific aspects of relationships. Attention has to be paid to the processes of support, conflict, and regulation that may take place in response to stressful life events or to daily routines. Deleterious effects due to negative content or lack of support may be greater than beneficial effects caused by helpful actions.

The above distinctions made by House et al. (1988) represent a sociological view, whereas the psychological perspective mainly deals with positive relational content, i.e., the function and quality of beneficial social relationships. One can make a further subdivision of function and quality into categories such as emotional support, instrumental support, informational support, tangible support (aid), esteem support, and appraisal support, among others. Several social support measures illustrate this (for an overview see Heitzmann & Kaplan, 1988; Tardy, 1985; Vaux, 1988).

Not only are the objective interactions important, but also the subjective interpretation of expected or enacted support. Cobb (1976), for example, emphasized the latter aspect by describing support as information that makes the person believe that she is cared for and loved, is esteemed and valued, and belongs to a network of communication and mutual obligation. Health and well-being are dependent on what the person sees and believes, be it accurate or biased.

The perceived availability of support also has to be distinguished from the activation of support when needed. It has been convincingly demonstrated (Dunkel-Schetter, 1984; Dunkel-Schetter & Bennett, 1990; Dunkel-Schetter, Folkman, & Lazarus, 1987; Newcomb, 1990) that both concepts are almost orthogonal in studies where perceived and received support were measured simultaneously. This discriminant validity was very high for tangible and informational support, and less for emotional support. McCormick, Siegert, and Walkey (1987) applied confirmatory factor analysis to two scales, one for received and one for perceived support. Five factors emerged, three of which included only items of received support whereas the remaining two were established by perceived support items exclusively.

Perceived and received support differ in terms of the point in time when they become important. After encountering a stressful event, support may be mobilized, serving as a buffer against deleterious health consequences. At this point support receipt may differ from support expected prior to the event, either because the network does not respond in an appropriate manner, or because the available support has been underestimated. For these reasons it appears to be justified to separate the two domains of social support from the previously discussed social environment variables (Figure 22.1).

The first box in Figure 22.1 displays a hierarchy where relational content is based on social network structure, and the latter, in turn, is based on social integration or network size. A second box is drawn for perceived or *cognitive social support*, which denotes the amount of support that is expected to be available in case of need. A sample item could be: "If I were in a bind, I could rely on my (spouse, friend, etc.)." A subset of this is the evaluative component or satisfaction with anticipated support. A typical item is: "When X helps you to solve the problem Y, how would you feel?" Responses range from "feel worst possible" to "feel best possible."

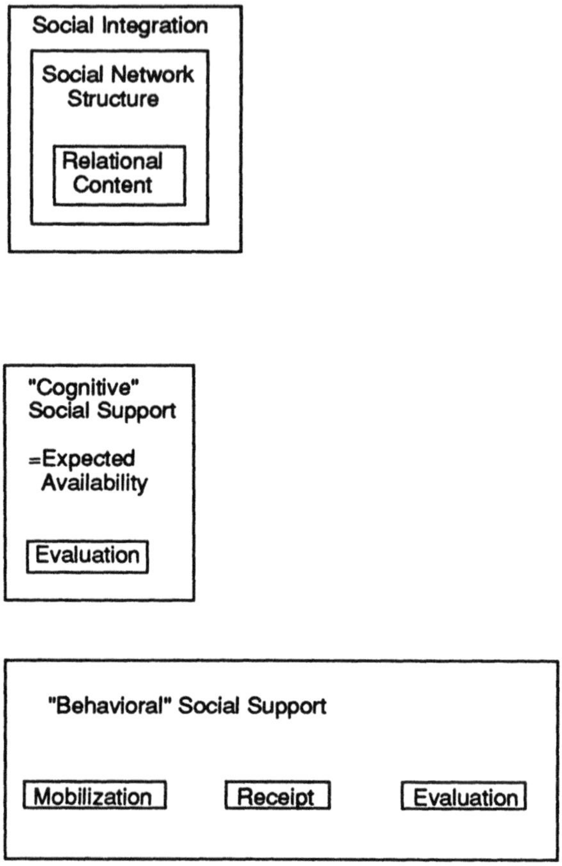

FIG. 22.1. Social interaction and social support: A taxomomy.

It has been questioned whether measures of perceived social support truly reflect the actual availability of support in one's social environment. A cognitive bias might lead to over- or underestimation of one's social resources. Several studies have attempted to determine the validity of the perceived support measures by using indicators of social interaction frequency as a criterion for validity. According to Cohen (1989), Cutrona (1986a, 1986b, 1989), and Vinokur, Schul, and Caplan (1987), there is evidence that verbal reports are rather accurate.

The third box in Figure 22.1 refers to *behavioral social support* and includes the activation of one's network in times of stress, the actual receipt of support—be it emotional, instrumental, or material—and the evaluation of the appropriateness and comfort of the support provided. Mobilizing social support can be considered a coping strategy. The Ways of Coping Questionnaire (Folkman & Lazarus, 1988), for example, contains the subscale "Seek Social Support" with six items, such as "I talked to someone to find out more about the situation."

Received emotional support may be measured in the following way: First, respondents select a stressful episode in the past month. They identify which of several possible persons provided assistance in the situation, and are then asked: "In this situation, how much did each of these persons make you feel he or she cared about you?" (Dunkel-Schetter, Feinstein, & Call, 1987). Although these sample items make clear that it is not the real social behavior that is observed here, but reported behaviors instead, the term "behavioral social support" is preferred to underscore the time perspective: Cognitive support is anticipatory, whereas behavioral support is retrospective after behavior has been initiated. In both cases, however, the subjective view of the recipient is of primary interest.

Although evaluation is considered a subset of cognitive as well as of behavioral support and often is measured as part of its superset, it has to be kept in mind that it refers to a concept of its own. Both sets are empirically only moderately interrelated: Sarason, Pierce, and Sarason (1990), for example, report correlations between .30 and .40.

The three boxes in Figure 22.1 represent groups of variables with very low intercorrelations. For example, marital status, available emotional support, and received aid are almost unconnected with each other. Seeman and Berkman (1988) have shown that measures of network size and measures of available support are only weakly associated, and Dunkel-Schetter and Bennett (1990) as well as McCormick et al. (1987) have pointed to the fact that perceived and received support are empirically almost unrelated. In contrast, measures within the boxes share a considerable amount of variance. Researchers who focus on "cognitive support," for example, have discovered that the corresponding measures are highly intercorrelated and are associated with personality characteristics (Sarason, Shearin, Pierce, & Sarason, 1987). They conclude that perceived social support can be conceived of as a stable individual difference variable which is based on a sense of acceptance. "... perceived social support is a measure of a person's belief that he or she is valued not for superficial characteristics or performance, but as someone independently worthy of this status without contingency. This then is best defined as the sense of acceptance, an inherent, stable personality characteristic that contributes to the perception of social support separately from what the environment actually offers at any particular time" (Sarason, Pierce, & Sarason, 1990, p. 110). Cohen, Lichtenstein, Mermelstein, Baer, and Kamarck (1988, p. 230) state that "at least part of the variance in perceived support measures is probably explained by stable individual differences," but in the same context they also maintain that "support is primarily a reflection of the social environment." This raises a theoretical question: To what degree can social support either be a personality characteristic or an environmental variable ("resources provided by others")? The clue to the answer lies in the above classification: Cognitive social support can be strongly influenced by personality predispositions and, thus, can acquire the status of an individual difference variable, but social integration as well as "behavioral support" would remain either truly social or transactional variables determined by the specific patterns of social exchange.

Dunkel-Schetter and Bennett (1990) have reported the empirical evidence for discriminant validity and have given four alternative theoretical explanations for the discrepancies between cognitive and behavioral support:

1. One obvious reason for discrepancies would be simply the over- or underreporting of help received due to inaccurate perception or memory failure.
2. Expectations that are too high would be derived from conditions that provoke unexpected and undesired provider behavior. In a study by Peters-Golden (1982), for example, enacted support experienced by breast cancer patients was compared to support expected by a group of healthy individuals in case they should be confronted with a cancer diagnosis. The latter reported a great deal of available support, but the actual patients seemed to experience lack of support or inept support attempts. There appears to be an optimistic bias in the normal population, resulting in disappointment when life events strike. In the face of very stressful life events, network members may fail to extend appropriate support because (a) they feel threatened themselves or do not know what kind of help is likely to be effective, (b) they have misconceptions about the coping process, or (c) they blame the victim (Bennett & Dunkel-Schetter, this volume; Silver, Wortman, & Crofton, 1990; Wortman & Dunkel-Schetter, 1987; Wortman & Lehman, 1985).
3. Another reason for the discrepancy between cognitive and behavioral support may lie in too modest expectations. Particularly in the case of positive life changes, such as having a baby, the network may unexpectedly provide an abundant amount of assistance.
4. Finally, initial support may dissipate because network members cannot cope with the burden in the long run: They are frustrated when a chronic illness progresses in spite of skillful support, and feel burned out by lack of reciprocal affection or missing signs of gratitude.

The discrepancy between cognitive and behavioral support could be caused by the social network structure: (a) A large network with low density could be perceived as a potential for available support, but in times of stress each network member might assume that someone else is available and therefore would not feel obliged to deliver services (diffusion of responsibility). (b) The degree of intimacy with one's relationships could be misperceived in that one feels very close to someone who does not reciprocate the feelings, resulting in less support than expected. (c) Partly, the expectation of available support stems from a baseline of prior experience with support, but predictions of future help may fail when the social context has changed (Dunkel-Schetter & Bennett, 1990).

SOCIAL SUPPORT, PERSONALITY, STRESS, AND COPING

A Causal Model

The previous section has dealt with three aspects of social relationships (social integration, cognitive social support, and behavioral social support), which were themselves subdivided into further categories. The following section deals with the possible mechanisms through which social relationships may influence the development of health and health behavior. Prior attempts to deal with the complex causality problem in this field have not been very convincing because of conceptual deficits in the support construct itself: It has been mainly used as a single predictor instead of as a set of rather orthogonal factors (see Barrera, 1986, 1988; Cohen & Wills, 1985).

The present perspective is organized as a composition of hierarchies and pathways (Figure 22.2) with the essential feature of separating three aspects of social relationships and relating them to personality, stress appraisals, and coping.

Individual differences. Individual differences in personality would contribute to the observed discrepancy between cognitive and behavioral support. Persons high in self-esteem might be prone to expect more available support than would actually materialize later in case of stress. Social competence, the propensity to seek help by communicating skillfully with network members, would be a prerequisite for support mobilization. The willingness to accept help without feeling inferior or feeling obliged to retaliate could differ among recipients. Shyness represents a barrier for seeking and accepting help. In Figure 22.2, a personality dimension is postulated which influences both cognitive and behavioral support. Poor social competence, for example, reduces the likelihood of network activation, whereas poor self-esteem would lead to underestimation of available support.

Stress Appraisals. How might social support be related to stress appraisals? Lazarus and Folkman (1984) distinguish between primary and secondary appraisals, which deal with different sources of information and have different functions. During primary appraisal, the person perceives the demand characteristics of a stressful event and decides what and how much is at stake. Primary appraisal can be of four types: harm/loss, threat, challenge, or benefit (Lazarus & Folkman, 1987). Secondary appraisals are evaluative judgments about one's coping options. Both kinds of appraisals are intertwined, occur simultaneously, and influence each other. Stakes and coping options are considered as transactional variables because they depend on the environment and on the personality, as well. Coping options are based on two kinds of antecedent variables, that is, environmental resources and a person's hierarchy of goals, beliefs, and commitments. With respect to appraisal, *personal resources* such as competence, coping styles, hardiness, skills, self-efficacy expectancy, or self-esteem may operate as influential factors on secondary appraisals and on coping (Filipp & Aymanns, 1987). However, Cohen and Edwards

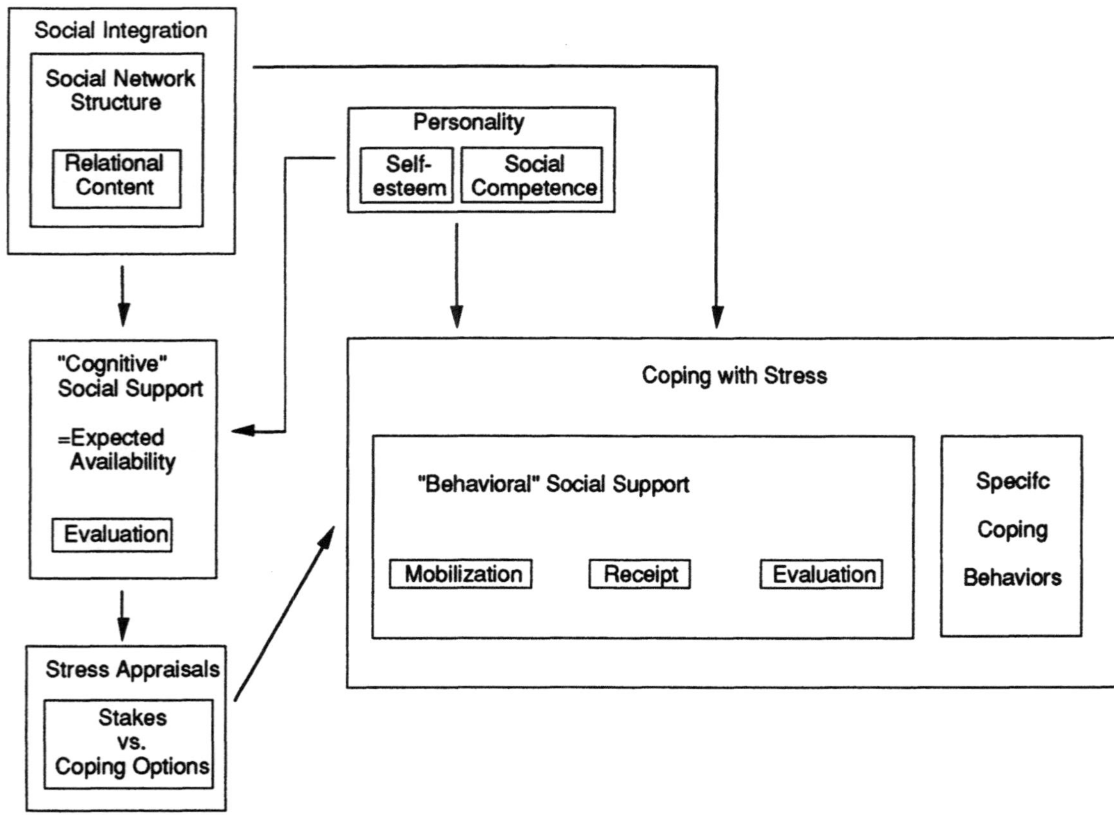

FIG. 22.2. Social relationships, personality, and stress.

(1989) have reviewed the literature and have come to the conclusion that such personal resources do not produce buffer effects on symptomatology. Only generalized expectancies of control could be tentatively assigned a stress-buffering role.

In the present context, *social environment resources* are the critical antecedent variables in coping. If someone feels that he or she can control a difficult situation with the help of close network members, then the appraisal process would result in a lower level of stress intensity. The perceived availability of a social network represents a coping option and therefore would make appraisals of harm/loss, threat, or challenge less severe or even nonexistent. On the other hand, perceived social isolation would imply the lack of one coping option, namely seeking help, with the person having to rely exclusively on other, nonsocial options. Appraisals of loss mean that stress and lack of support coincide which typically results in severe emotional distress. "By losing a loved one we lose the source of our most valued resources and the one provider who can most effectively help us replace the loss and reinstate the sense of fallen self-esteem and self-efficacy that accompanies the loss" (Hobfoll, 1988, p. 157).

The amount of stress which is experienced depends on two kinds of transactional variables, stakes and coping options, and is only indirectly determined by antecedent variables. Objective social integration is an antecedent variable which exerts an indirect influence, but the direct influence stems from "cognitive" social support, i.e., the way a person perceives the availability of a social network, be it in times of stress or in general daily life. The expected availability of social support and its positive evaluation may prevent stress emotions because a well-embedded person would feel less vulnerable.

Thus, social support can be considered a stress-protective factor. In the context of stress appraisal, the person interprets available support along with a number of coping competencies and skills to mobilize support. An example has been given in a study by Pearlin, Menaghan, Lieberman, and Mullan (1981). They have related disruptive job events to subsequent depression and have found by path analyses that more job stress resulted in loss of self-esteem and a reduced sense of mastery, and this in turn was a direct facilitator of depression. Social support produced a stress-buffering effect by operating against the impairment of self-esteem and mastery. The points here are that (a) depression is not an immediate consequence of stress alone, but is dependent on coping deficiencies and appraisals, and (b) social support makes its impact neither on stress nor on depression, but on these mediators. The cognitive appraisal of stressful events considers a number of resources where social support is seen as one resource among others. It represents a resource potential for compensating the loss of other resources. An ecological approach where social resources interact with other resources in buffering stress has been proposed by Hobfoll (1988, 1989).

Coping behaviors. Coping behaviors depend on stress appraisals and, therefore, are indirectly influenced by "cognitive" social support. Problem-focused coping, as compared to emotion-focused coping (Lazarus & Folkman, 1984, 1987), includes

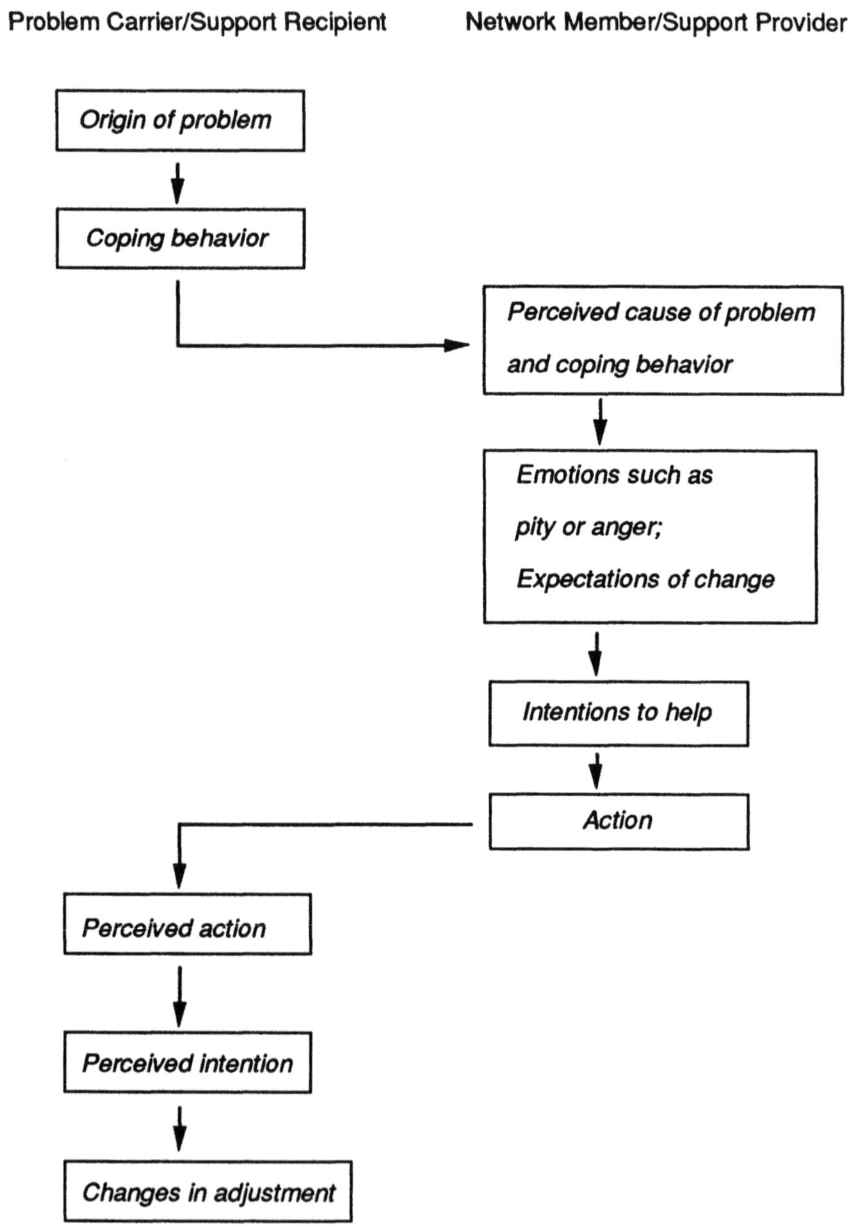

FIG. 22.3. A transactional model of the dyadic support relationship.

instrumental actions that contribute to changing the stressful encounter and to solving the problem at hand. A specific kind of coping behavior is the mobilization of social support and its acceptance when it is provided. One of the eight subscales of the Ways of Coping Questionnaire (Folkman & Lazarus, 1988) is called "Seeking Social Support." Thoits (1985, 1986) has defined social support as "coping assistance." Reaching out to obtain support from one's network, therefore, can be conceived of as one kind of possible coping strategies. Also, in order to benefit from help, persons should be able to accept social support without feeling inferior or being obliged to give the same amount of help in return.

An interesting question in this context is how active coping with stress or illness is related to the *likelihood of receiving support* from onlookers. This changes the perspective from the recipient to the provider. Social support research has dealt mainly with the recipient's perspective, but in order to get the full picture we should consider both. Does it make a difference for the network members' willingness to extend help if the victim of a crisis is actively coping or not? This question leads to a theoretical analysis of the transactional process which involves the support provider and the recipient (Figure 22.3).

In an experimental simulation study (Schwarzer & Weiner, 1990, in press), subjects responded to a number of vignettes in which eight diseases were varied with respect to onset cause and coping behavior of the patient. The "problem carrier" (how the person could be called before he or she becomes a support recipient) may be either responsible for the onset of a problem or a victim of an externally caused misfortune. For example, someone may have developed cancer because he did not comply with wearing regulation-prescribed clothing while working with cancer-producing chemicals. This person would have responsibility for the onset of the disease, but another person who was living unknowingly in an area which was once a toxic waste dump of cancer-producing chemicals would not. Independent of this distinction, the person could either cope with the disease instrumentally, or not. He could undergo chemotherapy and radiotherapy, and take all possible efforts to regain health, including changes in diet and life-style and reading self-help books on coping with cancer. On the other hand, he could deny the severity of the disease, not wanting to learn about it, and not showing up at appointments scheduled for further diagnosis.

The network member who regards the victim as responsible for the disease will develop emotions depending on the attributions made, for example pity or anger, and his expectancies about the stability of the problem. An intention to help also depends on these attributions, and the network member then might become a support provider by taking helpful actions.

The problem carrier, on the other hand, who has now become the support recipient, will probably perceive the supportive action and may correctly understand the underlying intention. If no undesired side-effects of the help emerge, the recipient should experience positive changes in adjustment and improvement of functioning.

One research question of the experiment was which would be a stronger predictor of the support intentions of the network member: perceived onset cause or perceived coping. It turned out that coping made the major impact: Patients who coped well themselves turned out to be more likely to obtain additional help from their social environment (Schwarzer & Weiner, 1990, in press). In a field study, Dunkel-Schetter et al. (1987) found that problem-solving coping in particular was related to the receipt of help, which underscores the notion that instrumental actions may be major determinants of support receipt. On the other hand, well-intended help may make the recipient feel inferior, and misperceptions of intentions may lead to undesired side-effects. The role of the perceived intention of aid still remains to be determined. Shumaker and Brownell (1984), for example, propose that, by definition, the intention should be an essential ingredient of social support.

Recently, the social support research paradigm has been extended to the investigation of reciprocal dyadic processes, helpful encounters, and close relationships more generally (e.g., Clark & Reis, 1988; Dakof & Taylor, 1990; Duck, 1990). According to this line of reasoning, the issue of matching support from an appropriate social source gains particular importance (Cutrona & Russell, 1990; Hobfoll, 1988).

The present transactional model, involving both the support recipient and the support provider has to be extended to a broader time frame. Continued transactions tend to alter subsequent resources and perceptions. Some resources may be depletable, others may grow when called upon, and their appropriateness may change. Provider burnout or loss of control or self-esteem, induced in the recipient by assistance, may diminish the frequency of further interactions. The same result is likely when support is inefficient. It is also possible that different sources of help might compete with each other, either in terms of quantity or specific quality, matching thc actual needs at a certain stage of coping, and the subject may turn to the one who provides the most benefit compared with the costs. The reason for our brief digression into this research perspective was to point to the connections between coping behavior and indirect support mobilization. The bottom line is: A patient or victim is more likely to obtain social support when he presents himself in a way that triggers effort attributions in the potential support provider.

Linking Mental Health to the Causal Model

In this section, the present model is extended by inclusion of an outcome dimension, i.e., psychological adjustment or functioning. Mental health variables found in many studies on social relationships refer to either well-being or to negative affect such as depression, anger, and anxiety. Social integration, cognitive social support, and behavioral social support have been related to both well-being and depression (Aneshensel & Frerichs, 1982; Blöschl, 1984, 1987; Brown & Bifulco, 1985; Dean, Lin, & Ensel, 1981; Goldberg, Natta, & Comstock, 1985; Holahan & Holahan,

1987; Krause, 1986, 1987; Lin, Dean, & Ensel, 1986; Wittchen & Hecht, 1987; for reviews see Röhrle, 1989, and Schwarzer & Leppin, 1989a). LaRocco, House, and French (1980), for example, have found correlations of depression with coworker support of -.38, with boss support of -.29, and with spouse support of -.23, respectively. Cohen, McGowan, Fooskas, and Rose (1984) have found correlations of depression with perceived support of -.51, and with received support of -.14. There are studies, however, that did not find an association between social support variables and indicators of mental health or only a negligible one (Frese, 1989). It is obvious that social relationships imply benefits as well as costs, and that the assumed benign impact of support on well-being depends on the context and on the causal pathways that connect social relationships with the observed outcome variables.

The present model postulates a variety of links among the constructs (Figure 22.4). First, it is assumed that there are direct effects from both cognitive and behavioral social support on mental health. If someone believes in the availability of support, she or he would have good reason to feel good; if someone obtains tangible help or caring attention from a network member, she or he also may have reason to feel good. Reality, however, is not that unambiguous. Satisfaction with support, either expected or received, is a prerequisite for well-being. If, for example, material aid from parents is evaluated as being an attempt to gain control over their child, feelings of dependence may emerge that compensate for the benign effect of the aid.

Second, there are indirect effects to be considered, for example, personality as an antecedent variable of cognitive and behavioral social support. People who are characterized by a trait-like negative affect, including neuroticism, anxiety, and depression, usually do not find anything enjoyable in the world and will hardly be satisfied with expected support or received support. They are preoccupied with evaluating their social relationships in negative terms, which might become a self-fulfilling prophecy because others will avoid neurotic individuals, preferring to direct their attention toward more enjoyable companions.

It is well-known that caregiver burnout is facilitated by negative affect on the part of the patient. Thus, mentally disturbed or socially difficult subjects who need help get less of it because they create an unattractive and stressful situation. Social integration, in this model, is again considered a distal predictor whereas cognitive and behavioral social support are psychologically closer, therefore representing the appropriate proximal predictors of mental health. In times of stress, cognitive appraisal is a mediator, for reasons discussed above.

The problem of confounding social support with trait-like negative affect has been recently addressed by Krause, Liang, and Yatomi (1989), who have studied the relationship between depression and support satisfaction at two points in time. It may be possible that initial depression affects the evaluation of support and thus does not allow to estimate the additional impact of support on later depression. In order to disentangle these influences, the authors have applied a cross-lagged panel

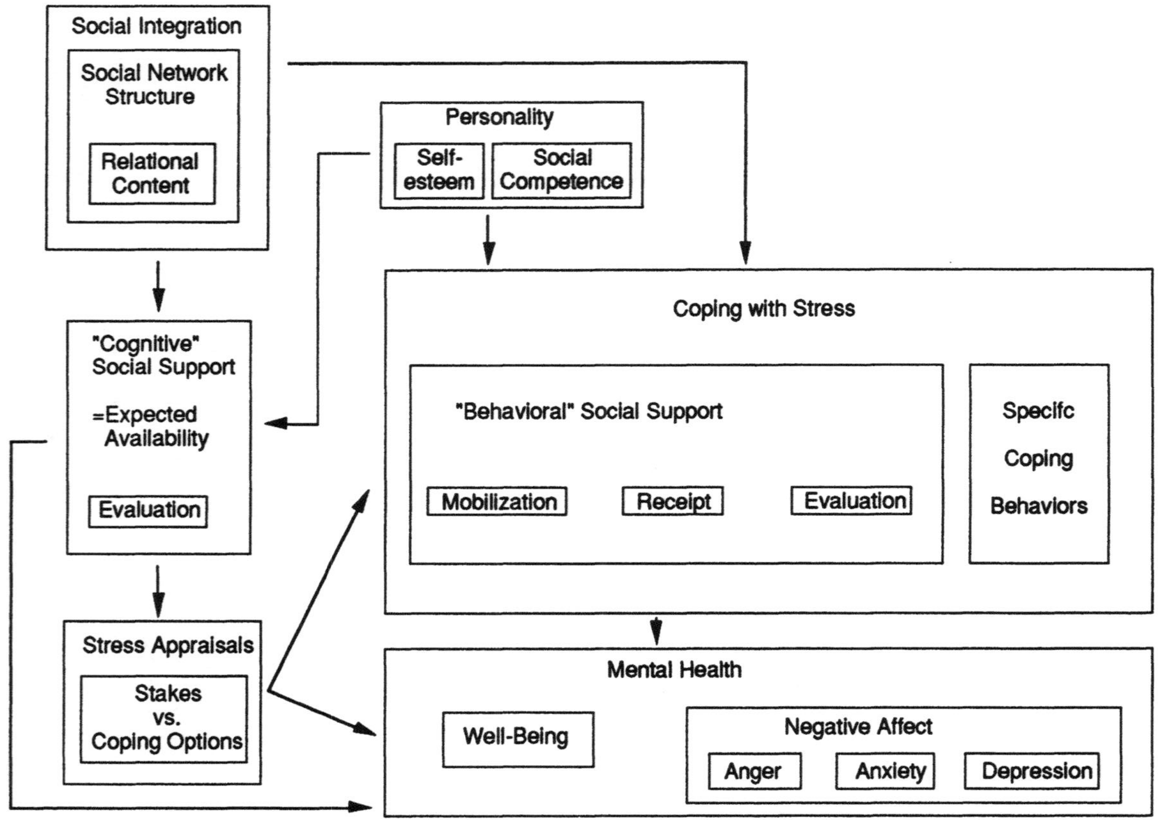

FIG. 22.4. Social support and mental health: A structural model.

design with four latent variables ($N = 252$). In fact, at the first point in time, the unbiased correlation between both constructs was .48, but over time there was a significant causal path from initial support to later depression (.20), whereas there was no relation from initial depression to later support (.013). This finding can be seen as a first step to determine the causal direction among the variables involved.

Research on *widowhood* has demonstrated the devastating effects of personal loss experiences (Stroebe & Stroebe, 1983, 1987). In general, marriage is regarded as being beneficial to human functioning (Depner & Ingersoll-Dayton, 1985), and, therefore, loss of a spouse represents a breakdown of one's social network with serious psychological consequences. There is empirical evidence that bereaved persons experience an immediate health decline after the loss of a spouse (Ferraro, 1985). The mortality risk for widows and widowers is increased compared to married people, being greatest for men during the first six months of bereavement. One reason for this, among others, may be the lack of coping assistance from close network members. When they feel socially isolated during the grieving process men may develop severe loneliness and depression which in turn may lead to further consequences; first, they might be of greater risk for committing suicide and, second, in a more long-term perspective, their immune system or cardiovascular health may be affected resulting in illness and, eventually, in death. Widowed people show impaired psychological and social functioning, including depression. Length of time anticipating the death of a spouse seems to be related in a curvilinear way to perceived health. "Sudden and unexpected loss of a spouse creates special problems, but so may attempting to provide care for a spouse over several years. Death stings in most cases, but the former resembles a sharp pain demanding reorganization while the latter is a dull, chronic pain that delays life reorganization" (Ferraro, 1989, p. 76).

Social Support and Depression: A Meta-Analysis

Most research on social support and mental health indicators does not distinguish accurately between different kinds of social relationships and does not test complex causal models or parts of them. Therefore, it is not astonishing that the empirical evidence is inconsistent. In a series of meta-analyses, one of which investigated the depression-support relationship, we have tried to synthesize what has been found between 1976 and 1987 (see Schwarzer & Leppin, 1989a), compiling 70 studies which include appropriate data on the support-depression relationship, based on 26,619 subjects. There were 89 independent samples allowing to determine 89 effect sizes r (correlations), ranging from -.66 to +.39 (Figure 22.5).

After weighting all effect sizes with their corresponding sample size, a population effect size (or weighted average) of -.22 resulted. This correlation corresponds to almost half a standard deviation ($d = .45$): If those without social support would score at the median of a depression scale, then those with social support would have

−.9	
−.8	
−.7	
−.6	6
−.5	0
−.4	223347
−.3	0012244446677888899
−.2	01122234445667779
−.1	00111224445555566667899
−.0	1456688999
+.0	0245579
+.1	8
+.2	4
+.3	039
+.4	
+.5	
+.6	
+.7	
+.8	
+.9	

FIG. 22.5. Stem-and-leaf display for 89 correlations.

a percentile of 33 only, i.e., they would be considerably less depressed (for the analysis method, see Hunter, Schmidt, & Jackson, 1982, and Schwarzer, 1989). This served as a starting point for subsequent analyses with specific potential moderator variables. One distinction made was between social integration and social support—without distinguishing between cognitive and behavioral support. There were 19 samples with 6,430 subjects for the social integration-depression relationship, resulting in an estimate of -.10, whereas there were 41 samples with 14,675 subjects for the support-depression relationship, resulting in a weighted mean of -.27. As expected, the functional aspect relates more closely to depression than the mere network size or similar indicators of social integration (see Figure 22.6).

As a next step, meta-analysis was applied to the distinction between cognitive and behavioral social support. Cognitive social support is more closely connected with depression (-.30) than behavioral support (-.14). This was valid not only for the entire data base in which 23 samples with received support ($N = 4{,}441$) were contrasted to 51 samples with perceived support ($N = 16{,}207$), but also for all

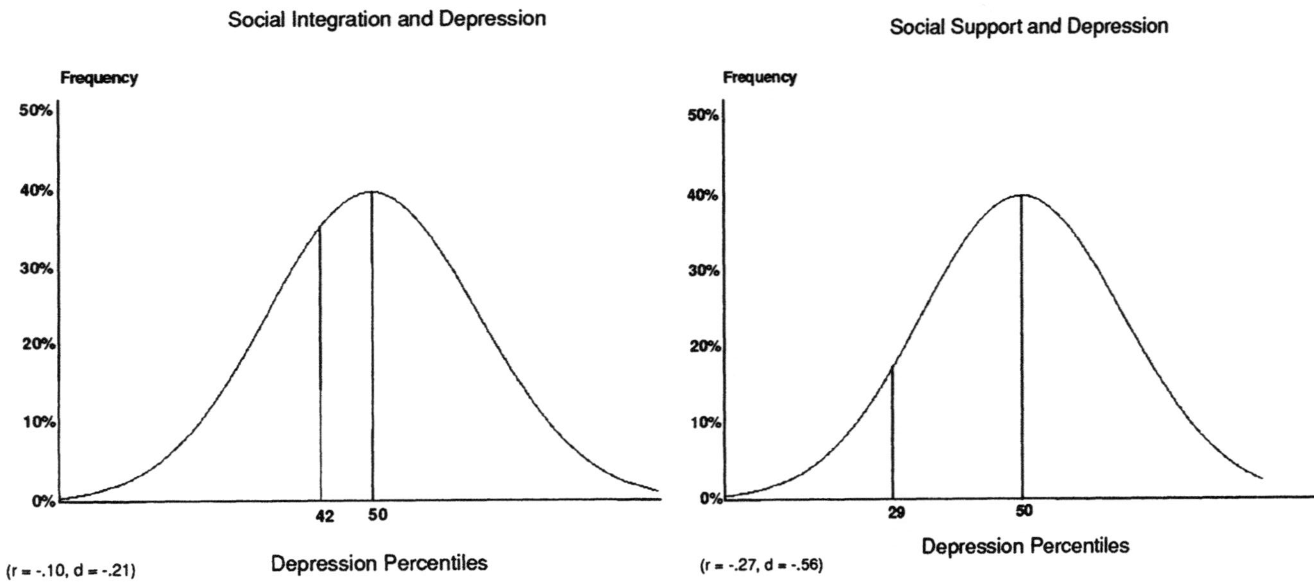

FIG. 22.6. A comparison of social integration and social support as they relate to depression.

subsets which had been separately established in order to obtain more reliable results. Two of these subanalyses are summarized in Table 22.1.

The expected availability of instrumental support correlated -.28 with depression, whereas the enacted instrumental support correlated only -.11. When one specific operationalization of depression was selected, namely Beck's Depression Inventory, then -.30 was contrasted to -.20. Only two of the meta-analytic findings in Table 22.1 are sufficiently homogeneous (82% and 100% variance explained by sampling error). The others are not, indicating that their estimated population effect sizes cannot be considered reliable. There is a great deal of unexplained systematic variance due to unknown moderators. The present theory suggests that there are unique contributions by factors such as support mobilization or support evaluation which have not been explicitly investigated in the original studies.

In sum, there is no doubt that social support is negatively related to depression, and that cognitive social support is more closely related to it than self-reported behavioral support. Also, the data confirm that social integration is a weaker predictor, which may be attributed to its more remote position in the chain of events. The role of personality remains undetermined because most studies did not control for prior depression or for trait-like negative affect. It also has to be established in how far buffer effects can be responsible for the association between support and mental health. Finally, a meta-analysis is not yet available on the support and well-being relationship. The present data are restricted to depression only.

TABLE 22.1

The Relationship Between Depression and Cognitive Behavioral Social Support (SS): Meta-Analytic Findings

Variable	*k*	*N*	*rw*	*% Homogeneity*
Cognitive SS	51	16,207	-.30	9
Behavioral SS	23	4,441	-.14	42
Cognitive SS (instrumental)	5	452	-.28	100
Behavioral SS (instrumental)	7	2,299	-.11	40
Cognitive SS (Beck#s Depression)	7	683	-.30	36
Behavioral SS (Beck#s Depression)	7	862	-.20	82

DISCUSSION

We have established a taxonomy of social relationships which separates *social integration*, with its subcomponents social network structure and relational content, from *cognitive social support*, including its evaluation, and from *behavioral social support*, with subdimensions of mobilization, receipt, and evaluation. These constructs are part of a causal model in which they are related to personality, stress appraisals, coping, and health. We have also presented some findings from a recent series of meta-analyses, but the data of the original studies were far from being sufficient to confirm the entire pattern of associations. There was evidence, however, that social integration is indeed a more remote factor which is mediated by social support to become effective.

Cognitive social support appears to be more closely related to mental health than behavioral social support. The reason for this might lie in the universal importance of perceptions and beliefs for one's well-being and health, but it can also be due to a bias when considering that the outcome measures themselves were subjective reports (Slavin & Compas, 1989). The "illusion of well-being" might correspond to an overestimation of support (Taylor & Brown, 1988). Also, discrepancy in size of both sets of correlations could be partly due to differences in reliability: Traditional measures of support receipt are somewhat less reliable than measures of perceived support. Future meta-analyses with more complete data bases should correct for attenuation in order to control this possible bias.

There are two good reasons to believe that relationships among all kinds of social support and mental health may be empirically underestimated. First, negative and positive correlations cancel each other out when averaged. Although in the majority of cases support is associated with less depression, there may be substantial positive correlations under specific conditions. More negative affect is associated with more support, for example, when life events strike and, as a consequence, one's network is mobilized. At a later point in time this spurious correlation may disappear, but most studies do not control for changes over time. It also may be that a reactive depression initially mobilizes a network until caregiver burnout reduces support again. If all positive correlations would be due to such a "mobilization effect," then they would represent a category of their own and should not be collapsed with negative correlations from studies where different causal mechanisms are at work.

Second, the relationship between support and mental health is underestimated in studies which fail to specify an appropriate causal model or where health behaviors are held constant. Social support operates partly through other variables and exerts indirect effects on health that may exceed the straightforward direct effect. Social support can prompt health behavior such as adherence to medical regimens. The same applies when the effect of social isolation on illness is studied with partialling out all other risk factors such as smoking, lack of exercise, and substance use. The latter could be mediators of social isolation and, therefore, contribute to its total effect on illness. Partialling out risk factors may at least obscure the causal relationship between social resource factors and health outcomes.

One limitation of the present meta-analysis is that buffer effects were not included because the corresponding data base was too small for a quantitative synthesis of exactly the same type of buffer effects. On the other hand, the effect sizes would not be higher with buffer effects combined because the interaction terms in the studies reviewed almost never explained more than one percent of the depression variance.

The prior distinction between main effects and buffer effects may be seen as simplistic and obsolete when compared to more complex causal models which allow the inclusion of more than three variables, specify more accurate directions of influence, and consider several points in time (Barrera, 1986, 1988). Cohen and Wills (1985), for example, have hypothesized that cognitive social support is more likely to exert a main effect while behavioral support would rather produce buffer effects. Wethington and Kessler (1986) have found the opposite pattern in their study. Wills (1985) has proposed that social integration, status support, companionship, and information support would be prone to have main effects, while instrumental and appraisal support would be more appropriate for buffer effects.

Research results will remain inconsistent as long as no complex causal models are applied to longitudinal data. Also, studies have to be more fine-grained with respect to the timing of support and to the appropriateness of aid from different sources. Cohen and McKay (1984) have stated that, in order to prove effective, social support must match the specific needs of the recipient. The needs differ with respect to the kind of stressor and time of exposure. If, for example, someone has lost a spouse, it may be inappropriate to offer money in the early stage of bereavement, but at a later stage such aid may assist in readjustment, especially if the loss implies an economic hardship. Lehmann, Ellard, and Wortman (1986) have demonstrated that provider and recipient differ considerably in their perspective in what is seen as helpful in case of bereavement.

This discussion refers to the concept of multiple supportive actions within a dyadic or network relationship. It would make sense not only to ask retrospectively how much help has been accumulated over a specified period of time, but to obtain a series of data pertaining to different support constructs accompanying the flow of events during a possibly helpful transaction in times of stress. Researchers often state that social support operates in complex ways but, in contrast, they continue to report zero-order correlations among overall variables and, thus, further contribute to obscuring of the causal pathways. We need not compile additional cross-sectional correlation studies on global support - health relationships but should conduct more theory-guided process analyses.

REFERENCES

Aneshensel, C. S., & Frerichs, R. R. (1982). Stress, support, and depression: A longitudinal causal model. *Journal of Community Psychology, 10*, 363-374.

Barrera, M. (1986). Distinctions between social support concepts, measures, and models. *American Journal of Community Psychology, 14*, 413-445.

Barrera, M. (1988). Models of social support and life stress: Beyond the buffering hypothesis. In L. H. Cohen (Ed.), *Life events and psychosocial functioning* (pp. 211-236). London: Sage.

Berkman, L. F., & Syme, S. L. (1979). Social networks, host resistance, and mortality: A nine-year follow-up study of Alameda county residents. *American Journal of Epidemiology, 109*, 186-204.

Blöschl, L. (1984). Research on social contact and social support in depression. *Studia Psychologica, 26*, 299-304.

Blöschl, L. (1987). The present state of research on social contact and social support in depression: A critical analysis. In J. P. Dauwalder, M. Perrez, & V. Hobi (Eds.), *Controversial issues in behavior modification* (pp. 173-178). Amsterdam: Swets & Zeitlinger.

Brown, G. W., & Bifulco, A. (1985). Social support, life events, and depression. In I. G. Sarason & B. R. Sarason (Eds.), *Social support: Theory, research, and applications* (pp. 349-370). Dordrecht: Martinus Nijhoff.

Clark, M. S., & Reis, H. T. (1988). Interpersonal processes in close relationships. *Annual Review of Psychology, 39*, 609-672.

Cobb, S. (1976). Social support as a moderator of life stress. *Psychosomatic Medicine, 38*, 300-314.

Cohen, L. H., McGowan, J., Fooskas, S., & Rose, S. (1984). Positive life events and social support and the relationship between life stress and psychological disorder. *American Journal of Community Psychology, 12*, 567-587.

Cohen, S. (1988). Psychosocial models of the role of social support in the etiology of physical disease. *Health Psychology, 7*, 269-297.

Cohen, S. (1989). Social support and physical health: Symptoms, health behaviors, and infectious disease. In M. Cummings, A. L. Greene, & K. H. Karraker (Eds.), *Life-span developmental psychology: Perspective on stress and coping* (pp. 235-283) Hillsdale, NJ: Erlbaum.

Cohen, S., & Edwards, J. R. (1989). Personality characteristics as moderators of the relationship between stress and disorder. In R. W. J. Neufeld (Ed.), *Advances in the investigation of psychological stress* (pp. 235-283). New York: Wiley.

Cohen, S., Lichtenstein, E., Mermelstein, R., Baer, J. S., & Kamarck, T. W. (1988). Social support interventions for smoking cessation. In B. H. Gottlieb (Ed.), *Marshalling social support. Formats, processes, and effects* (pp. 211-240). Beverly Hills, CA: Sage.

Cohen, S., & McKay, G. (1984). Social support, stress, and the buffering hypothesis: A theoretical analysis. In A. Baum, S. E. Taylor, & J. E. Singer (Eds.), *Handbook of psychology and health* (Vol. 4, pp. 253-267). Hillsdale, NJ: Erlbaum.

Cohen, S., & Syme, S. L. (1985). Issues in the study and application of social support. In S. Cohen & S. L. Syme (Eds.), *Social support and health* (pp. 3-22). New York: Academic Press.

Cohen, S., & Wills, T. A. (1985). Stress, social support, and the buffering hypothesis. *Psychologial Bulletin, 98*, 310-357.

Cutrona, C. E. (1986a). Behavioral manifestations of social support: A microanalytic investigation. *Journal of Personality and Social Psychology, 51*, 201-208.

Cutrona, C. E. (1986b). Objective determinants of perceived social support. *Journal of Personality and Social Psychology, 50*, 349-355.

Cutrona, C. E. (1989). Ratings of social support by adolescents and adult informants: Degree of correspondence and prediction of depressive symptoms. *Journal of Personality and Social Psychology, 57*, 723-730.

Cutrona, C. E., & Russell, D. (1990). Type of social support and specific stress: Toward a theory of optimal matching. In I. G. Sarason, B. R. Sarason, & G. R. Pierce (Eds.), *Social support: An interactional view* (pp. 319-366). New York: Wiley.

Dakof, G. A., & Taylor, S. E. (1990). Victims' perceptions of social support: What is helpful from whom? *Journal of Personality and Social Psychology, 58*, 80-89.

Dean, A., Lin, N., & Ensel, W. M. (1981). The epidemiological significance of social support systems in depression. *Research in Community and Mental Health, 2*, 77-109.

Depner, C. E., & Ingersoll-Dayton, B. (1985). Conjugal social support: Patterns in later life. *Journal of Gerontology, 40*, 761-766.

Duck, S. (Ed.). (1990). *Personal relationships and social support.* London: Sage.

Dunkel-Schetter, C. (1984). Social support and cancer: Findings based on patient interviews and their implications. *Journal of Social Issues, 40*(4), 77-98.

Dunkel-Schetter, C., & Bennett, T. L. (1990). The availability of social support and its activation in times of stress. In I. G. Sarason, B. R. Sarason, & G. R. Pierce (Eds.), *Social support: An interactional view* (pp. 267-296). New York: Wiley.

Dunkel-Schetter, C., Feinstein, L., & Call, J. (1987). *A self-report inventory for the measurement of social support.* Unpublished manuscript, Los Angeles, UCLA, Department of Psychology.

Dunkel-Schetter, C., Folkman, S., & Lazarus, R. S. (1987). Correlates of social support receipt. *Journal of Personality and Social Psychology, 53*, 71-80.

Ferraro, K. F. (1985). The effect of widowhood on the health status of older persons. *International Journal of Aging and Human Development, 21*, 9-25.

Ferraro, K. F. (1989). Widowhood and health. In K. S. Markides & C. L. Cooper (Eds.), *Aging, stress, and health* (pp. 69-90). Chichester, England: Wiley.

Filipp, S.-H., & Aymanns, P. (1987). Die Bedeutung sozialer und personaler Ressourcen in der Auseinandersetzung mit kritischen Lebensereignissen. *Zeitschrift für Klinische Psychologie, 16*, 383-396.

Folkman, S., & Lazarus, R. S. (1988). *Manual for the Ways of Coping Questionnaire.* Palo Alto, CA: Consulting Psychologists Press.

Frese, M. (1989). *The function of social support for the relationship between stress at work and psychological dysfunctioning: Cross-validation and a longitudinal study with objective measures.* Unpublished manuscript, University of Munich.

Ganster, D. C., & Victor, B. (1988). The impact of social support on mental and physical health. *British Journal of Medical Psychology, 61*, 17-36.

Goldberg, E. L., Natta, P. V., & Comstock, G. W. (1985). Depressive symptoms, social networks, and social support of elderly women. *American Journal of Epidemiology, 121*, 448-455.

Heitzmann, C. A., & Kaplan, R. M. (1988). Assessment of methods for measuring social support. *Health Psychology, 7*, 75-109.

Hobfoll, S. E. (1988). *The ecology of stress.* Washington, DC: Hemisphere.

Hobfoll, S. E. (1989). Conservation of resources: A new attempt at conceptualizing stress. *American Psychologist, 44*, 513-524.

Holahan, C. K., & Holahan, C. J. (1987). Self-efficacy, social support, and depression in aging: A longitudinal analysis. *Journal of Gerontology, 42*, 65-68.

House, J. S., Robbins, C., & Metzner, H. L. (1982). The association of social relationships and activities with mortality: Prospective evidence from the Tecumseh Community Health Study. *American Journal of Epidemiology, 116*, 123-140.

House, J. S., Umberson, D., & Landis, K. R. (1988). Structures and processes of social support. In W. R. Scott & J. Blake (Eds.), *Annual review of sociology* (Vol. 14, pp. 293-318). Palo Alto, CA: Annual Reviews.

Hunter, J. E., Schmidt, F.L., & Jackson, G.B. (1982). *Meta-analysis. Cumulating research findings across studies.* Beverly Hills, CA: Sage.

Israel, B. A., & Rounds, K. A. (1987). Social networks and social support: A synthesis for health educators. In W. B. Ward (Ed.), *Advances in health education and promotion* (Vol. 2, pp. 311-351). Greenwich, CT: JAI Press.

Krause, N. (1986). Social support, stress, and well-being among older adults. *Journal of Gerontology, 41*, 512-519.

Krause, N. (1987). Life stress, social support, and self esteem in elderly population. *Psychology and Aging*, *2*, 349-356.

Krause, N., Liang, J., & Yatomi, N. (1989). Satisfaction with social support and depressive symptoms: A panel analysis. *Psychology and Aging*, *4*, 88-97.

LaRocco, J. M., House, J. S., & French, J. R. P. (1980). Social support, occupational stress, and health. *Journal of Health and Social Behavior*, *21*, 202-218.

Lazarus, R. S., & Folkman, S. (1984). *Stress, appraisal, and coping*. New York: Springer.

Lazarus, R. S., & Folkman, S. (1987). Transactional theory and research on emotions and coping. *European Journal of Personality*, *1*, 141-170.

Lehmann, D. R., Ellard, J. H., & Wortman, C. B. (1986). Social support for the bereaved: Recipients' and providers' perspectives on what is helpful. *Journal of Consulting and Clinical Psychology*, *54*, 438-446.

Lin, N., Dean, A., & Ensel, W. (Eds.). (1986). *Social support, life events, and depression*. New York: Academic Press.

McCormick, I. A., Siegert, R. J., & Walkey, F. H. (1987). Dimensions of social support: A factorial confirmation. *American Journal of Community Psychology*, *15*, 73-77.

Newcomb, M. D. (1990). What structural equation modeling can tell us about social support. In B. R. Sarason, I. G. Sarason, & G. R. Pierce (Eds.), *Social support: An interactional view* (pp. 26-63). New York: Wiley.

Pearlin, L. I., Menaghan, E. G., Lieberman, M. A., & Mullan, J. T. (1981). The stress process. *Journal of Health and Social Behavior*, *22*, 337-356.

Peters-Golden, H. (1982). Breast cancer: Varied perceptions of social support in the illness experience. *Social Science and Medicine*, *16*, 483-491.

Rodin, J., & Salovey, P. (1989). Health psychology. *Annual Review of Psychology*, *40*, 533-579.

Röhrle, B. (1989). *The quality of social support and depression: A meta-analysis*. Unpublished paper, University of Marburg.

Sarason, B. R., Pierce, G. R., & Sarason, I. G. (1990). Social support: The sense of acceptance and the role of relationships. In B. R. Sarason, I. G. Sarason, & G. R. Pierce (Eds.), *Social support: An interactional view* (pp. 97-128). New York: Wiley.

Sarason, B. R., Shearin, E. N., Pierce, G. R., & Sarason. I. G. (1987). Interrelations of social support measures: Theoretical and practical implications. *Journal of Personality and Social Psychology*, *52*, 813-832.

Schwarzer, R. (1989). *Meta-analysis programs. Version 4.0*. Raleigh, NC: National Collegiate Software Clearinghouse.

Schwarzer, R., & Leppin, A. (1989a). *Sozialer Rückhalt und Gesundheit: Eine Meta-Analyse*. Göttingen: Hogrefe.

Schwarzer, R., & Leppin, A. (1989b). Social support and health: A meta-analysis. *Psychology and Health: An International Journal*, *3*, 1-15.

Schwarzer, R., & Weiner, B. (1990). Die Wirkung von Kontrollierbarkeit und Bewältigungsverhalten auf Emotionen und soziale Unterstützung. *Zeitschrift für Sozialpsychologie*, *21*, 118-125.

Schwarzer, R., & Weiner, B. (in press). Stigma controllability and coping as predictors of emotions and social support. *Journal of Social and Personal Relationships*.

Seeman, T. E., & Berkman, L. F. (1988). Structural characteristics of social networks and their relationships with social support in the elderly: Who provides support. *Social Science and Medicine*, *26*, 737-749.

Shumaker, S. A., & Brownell, A. (1984). Toward a theory of social support: Closing conceptual gaps. *Journal of Social Issues*, *40*(4), 11-36.

Silver, R. C., Wortman, C. B., & Crofton, C. (1990). The role of coping in support provision: The self-presentational dilemma of victims of life crises. In I. G. Sarason, B. R. Sarason, & G. R. Pierce (Eds.), *Social support: An interactional view* (pp. 397-426). New York: Wiley.

Slavin, L. A., & Compas, B. E. (1989). The problem of confounding social support and depressive symptoms: A brief report on a college sample. *American Journal of Community Psychology*, *17*, 57-66.

Stroebe, M. S., & Stroebe, W. (1983). Who suffers more? Sex differences in health risks of the widowed. *Psychological Bulletin, 93*, 279-301.

Stroebe, W., & Stroebe, M. S. (1987). *Bereavement and health*. New York: Cambridge University Press.

Tardy, C. H. (1985). Social support measurement. *American Journal of Community Psychology, 13*, 187-202.

Taylor, S. E., & Brown, J. D. (1988). Illusion and well-being: A social psychological perspective on mental health. *Psychological Bulletin, 103*, 193-210.

Thoits, P. A. (1983). Dimension of life events as influences upon the genesis of psychological distress and associated conditions: An evaluation and synthesis. In H. B. Kaplan (Ed.), *Psychosocial stress: Trends in theory and research* (pp. 33-103). New York: Academic Press.

Thoits, P. A. (1985). Social support processes and psychological well-being: Theoretical possibilities. In I. G. Sarason & B. R. Sarason (Eds.), *Social support: Theory, research, and applications* (pp. 51-72). Dordrecht: Martinus Nijhoff.

Thoits, P. A. (1986). Social support as coping assistance. *Journal of Consulting and Clinical Psychology, 54*, 416-423.

Vaux, A. (1988). *Social support: Theory, research, and intervention*. New York: Praeger.

Veiel, H. O. F. (1985). Dimensions of social support: A conceptual framework for research. *Social Psychiatry, 20*, 156-162.

Veiel, H. O. F. (1987). Einige kritische Anmerkungen zum Unterstützungskonzept. *Zeitschrift für Klinische Psychologie, 16*, 397-399.

Vinokur, A., Schul, Y., & Caplan, R. D. (1987). Determinants of perceived social support: Interpersonal transactions, personal outlook, and transient affective states. *Journal of Personality and Social Psychology, 53*, 1137-1145.

Wethington, E., & Kessler, R. C. (1986). Perceived support, received support, and adjustment to stressful life events. *Journal of Health and Social Behavior, 27*, 78-89.

Wills, T. A. (1985). Supportive functions of interpersonal relationships. In S. Cohen & S. L. Syme (Eds.), *Social support and health* (pp. 61-82). New York: Academic Press.

Wittchen, H. U., & Hecht, H. (1987). Social support und Depression. Modellvorstellungen in der ätiologisch orientierten Forschung. *Zeitschrift für Klinische Psychologie, 16*, 321-338.

Wortman, C. B., & Dunkel-Schetter, C. (1987). Conceptual and methodological issues in the study of social support. In A. Baum & J. E. Singer (Eds.), *Handbook of psychology and health. Vol. 5: Stress* (pp. 63-108). Hillsdale, NJ: Erlbaum.

Wortman, C. B., & Lehman, D. R. (1985). Reactions to victims of life crises: Support attempts that fail. In I. G. Sarason & B. R. Sarason (Eds.), *Social support: Theory, research, and applications* (pp. 463-489). Dordrecht: Martinus Nijhoff.

VI Understanding Social Responses to Victims

23 The Cost of Social Support Following Negative Life Events: Can Adversity Increase Commitment to Caring in Close Relationships?[1]

John E. Lydon
McGill University, Montreal

Mark P. Zanna
University of Waterloo

Social scientists have given substantial attention to the processes by which victims cope with negative life events. In a review of the literature, Taylor (1986) characterized the coping process in terms of the appraisal process and the internal and external resources and impediments that influence coping. One of the external resources that moderates the stress-coping relation is social support. Taylor concluded: "On balance social support is clearly advantageous. It reduces the experiences of stress, enhances the ability to cope, can reduce the prospect of mental and physical distress or illness, and speeds recovery when illness does occur" (pp. 210-211).

The evolution of empirical questions in the social support literature is reminiscent of the evolution of questions in the attitude-behavior literature. First, researchers wanted to know if social support is positively related to adjustment and coping (Cobb, 1976; House, 1981). Then the question became: "When is social support positively related to adjustment and coping?" (the debate about a main effect versus the buffering hypothesis; Cohen & Wills, 1985; Thoits, 1982). Recently, researchers have begun to ask how social support influences adjustment and coping (Wortman & Dunkel-Schetter, 1987).

Interestingly, the victim or recipient of social support has, for the most part, been the focus of attention in each of these generations of research. However, a reconsideration of traditional, naturalistic sources of social support (i.e., family and friends) raises interesting questions about the psychology of the caregiver and the

[1]We gratefully acknowledge the comments of John G. Holmes on an earlier version of this manuscript. Requests for reprints should be sent to John Lydon, now at the Department of Psychology, McGill University, 1205 Dr. Penfield Avenue, Montreal, Quebec H3A 1B1, Canada.

relationship between the caregiver and victim. For example, researchers have considered the role-related strains of caregivers, expecially women (Kessler, McLeod, & Wethington, 1985; Thoits, 1986). Moreover, Coyne, Wortman, and Lehman (1988) discussed the overinvolvement, and, in turn, ineffectiveness of caregivers when they are providing social support over the long period of time that is often required following negative life events.

Because negative life events often occur in the context of close relationships, it might be useful to begin by asking what property (or properties) of close relationships, expecially marital relationships, might influence the quality and/or the persistence of social support given by the caregiver (cf. Eggert, 1987). Are there aspects of the caregiver's relationship with his or her spouse *prior* to the negative life event that influence the caregiver's response to the negative life event? And in turn, how does the caregiver's response then influence the relationship? Specifically, we can ask how antecedent properties of the relationship influence the caregiver's motivation and/or ability to give social support in response to the negative life event, and, in turn, how the provision of social support may influence the mental health of the victim and the caregiver.

One property of close relationships that might be an important determinant of the quality and/or persistence of social support is the potential caregiver's "commitment to the relationship" both before and, especially, after the negative life event. But what determines the caregiver's commitment to the relationship and, within the relationship, the caregiver's commitment to provide social support?

COMMITMENT IN THE FACE OF ADVERSITY

To answer these questions we turn to social psychological theory and research on the psychology of commitment. Recently, we proposed that when people are faced with adversity, or occur great costs, they will feel especially committed to projects diagnostic of, or central to, their identities—their self-conceptions (Lydon & Zanna, 1990).

The importance that facing adversity, experiencing stress, or incurring costs as for the study of commitment is not new. For example, Staw and his colleagues (Fox & Staw, 1979; Staw, 1976) demonstrated that decision makers are more likely to escalate their commitment to an investment by putting more money into it when the investment is losing money than they are when the investment is making money. More recently, Brickman (1987) proposed a model of commitment in which the salience of negative elements is essential. In fact, Brickman, Dunkel-Schetter, and Abbey (1987) stated: "If no negative elements or contradictions to the decision become salient, we do not think of it as commitment" (p. 175).

We argue: Not only does adversity increase commitment, as Staw and Brickman and others have emphasized, but adversity also *reveals* latent differences in commitment. Adversity allows us to detect qualitative differences in people's expressed commitment that might not be apparent under favorable conditions. In methodological terms stress or adversity serves, what Snyder and Ickes (1985) call, a *precipitating* condition for a test of commitment.

Imagine, for example, that we surveyed 100 newlyweds and asked them to rate, on a 7-point scale, their commitment to their relationships. What do you think the mean response would be, maybe 6.8 with very little variance? Those who have been married a little longer may think: "These newlyweds, let's just wait and see how committed they feel after they have experienced some of the naturally-occurring hassles and stressors that long-term close relationships inevitably present." It would seem that a report of commitment that has been tested by adversity is a report of commitment that we, as observers, may feel is a more reliable indicant of felt commitment. Put simply, we have more confidence in a person's report of commitment when that commitment has been tested.

But, can we identify a variable *present under favorable conditions* that subsequently will predict commitment in the face of adversity? Here we draw on the reformulations of cognitive dissonance theory by Aronson (1969) and, more recently, Steele (1988), which suggest that behavior inconsistent with one's *self-concept* is arousing and even aversive. Interestingly, Steele has demonstrated that giving an individual an opportunity to affirm self-relevant values reduces his or her dissonance, even when the values are unrelated to the dissonant act (e.g., Steele & Liu, 1983). If the powerful effects of dissonance are attributable, at least in part, to concerns about self-conceptions, then (by inverting the logic of self-affirmation) it seems plausible that a person would feel committed to pursuits that affirm or are diagnostic of self-relevant values. The alternative, to renege on a value-laden pursuit, might be too threatening to one's self-conception. Therefore, we reasoned that, in the face of adversity, people will feel more committed to a course of action, but only if it has implications for, or is perceived to be relevant to, one's values.

COMMITMENT TO PERSONAL PROJECTS

To test this hypothesis, we first asked university subjects to indicate eight personal projects (Little, 1983) or courses of action they were currently working on. Some of their personal projects included: "controlling stress," "writing some letters to friends," "improving my relationship with God," "exercising more," "losing ten pounds," "redecorating my room," and "trying to overcome my shyness." Then, in order to assess perceived value relevance and adversity we asked subjects to indicate, for two randomly selected projects, the extent to which the project was consistent with the values that guide their lives and how stressful and how difficult the project was to carry out.

Finally, under the guise of a separate experiment, subjects completed three items designed to measure commitment. Following Brickman (1987), who characterized some commitments as "enthusiastic" and others as "reluctant," we included items which asked subjects how attached they were to their personal projects, how obligated they felt to pursue their projects, and our benchmark item, "To what extent do you feel committed to this project?"

The first step in analyzing the data was to check the indices of adversity and commitment. The stress and difficulty items were correlated, $r = .48$, and consequently were averaged together to form the adversity measure. Although attachment and obligation were both highly correlated with the commitment item (r's of .58 and .61, respectively), interestingly, these items were only moderately correlated with each other, $r = .33$. Thus, it appears that both attachment and obligation were contributing to the measurement of commitment but in somewhat different ways. By averaging subjects' responses to the attachment, obligation and commitment items it was hoped that a broader and more reliable representation of felt commitment would be obtained.

For the main analysis, subjects' responses to their two personal projects were averaged because they were not independent.[2] Value relevance and adversity were entered simultaneously in the first step of a hierarchical regression analysis with the commitment index as the criterion variable. Collectively, the two predictors explained 19.5% of the variance with both variables being positively related to commitment.

However, these main effects subsequently were qualified by the predicted interaction, which explained an additional 9.2% of the variance, $F(1,38) = 4.92, p < .05$.[3] To represent this effect graphically the values one standard deviation above and below the mean were used to represent high and low points on each dimension. These values were entered into the regression equation to predict commitment. As can be seen in Figure 23.1, under low adversity, values made very little difference in predicting expressed commitment. However, as predicted, under high adversity, values made a considerable difference. In the face of adversity, the more subjects believed their projects were relevant to their values, the more committed they felt. This study, then, demonstrated correlationally that value relevance predicts commitment in the face of adversity across a variety of on-going personal projects.

However, the nature of the results raises some questions about the causal direction of the commitment process. For example, it may be that a person first feels committed to a project and then infers value relevance. Relatedly, the results do not reveal whether perceived value relevance prior to the experience of adversity

[2]The data were also analyzed treating subjects' responses to each project as separate cases. The results were consistent with the method of averaging we used. Moreover, a canonical analysis revealed that the relation between the predictors and the criterion was consistent among projects.

[3]All interaction Fs from the regression analyses reported in this chapter are based on the F change, not the cumulative F. Thus, the F represents the unique contribution of the interaction, or product term, independent of main effects for the predictor variables.

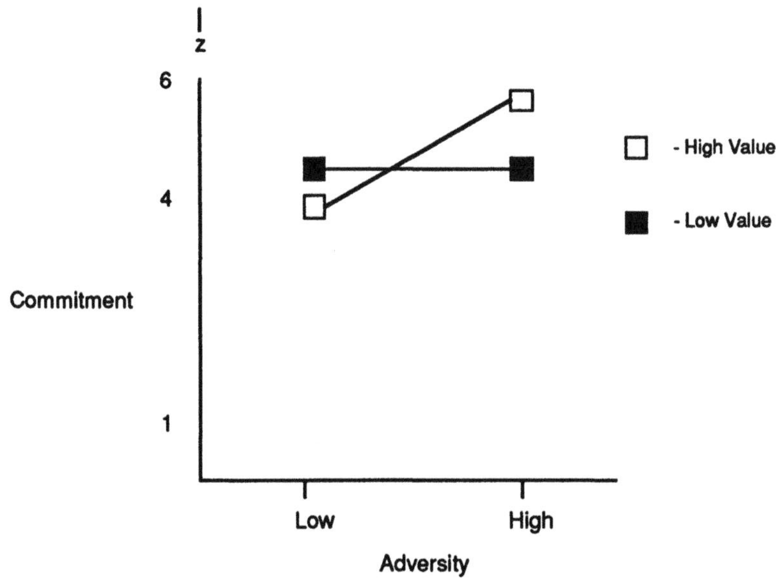

Note. Expected values are based on the equation using the b weights for values, adversity and values by adversity.

FIG. 23.1. Regression lines for commitment in Study 1. Copyright 1990 by the American Psychological Association. Reprinted with permission.

predicts subsequent commitment. An alternative explanation is that adversity influences perceived valued relevance. Indeed, the Brickman model suggests that projects acquire value relevance in the face of adversity. Thus, although offering preliminary evidence supporting the notion that value relevance predicts commitment in the face of adversity, the data also are consistent with alternative explanations of the causal sequence. In a sense, then, these findings cry out for a longitudinal study. Can a measure of value relevance during the initiation of a personal project predict subsequent commitment as one later encounters adversity in the pursuit of the project?

A LONGITUDINAL STUDY OF COMMITMENT

A second study was designed to address this question. The goal was to identify a particular personal project people were initiating, measure the value relevance of the project at the outset, and then measure the adversity subsequently experienced.

The hypothesis was that value relevance at the outset would predict commitment to the project in the face of subsequent adversity. Whereas the first study demonstrated the generality of the relationship, this second study was designed to identify the causal pattern more precisely.

A course in Therapeutic Recreation, in which students were required by their instructor to do eight weeks of volunteer work, provided an ideal context for the longitudinal study. Many of the students were involved in projects with the physically and mentally challenged. Others worked with the elderly, the homeless, or with young offenders. An initial "in-class" testing session was conducted early in the term followed six to eight weeks later by individual lab sessions. The strategy was to measure value relevance during the initial session as students began their volunteer projects, and then, during the lab session, to measure the adversity they subsequently had experienced throughout the term. The hypothesis was that value relevance at the beginning of the term would predict felt commitment at the end of the term for those who experienced stress and difficulty working on their projects.

In order to develop a more reliable measure of value relevance, a set of five items were embedded in the initial questionnaire. The items were based primarily on Steele's conceptualization of self-affirmation. The items were: (a) to what extent is volunteer work a reflection of your value system; (b) to what extent is volunteer work a statement about your view of the world; (c) to what extent is the primary concern of volunteer work something or someone other than yourself; (d) to what extent does volunteer work reveal something about your identity; and (e) to what extent is doing volunteer work important to your self-worth.[4]

Value relevance (measured in the initial session) and adversity (measured in the follow-up session) were entered simultaneously in the first step of a hierarchical regression analysis to predict commitment (also measured in the follow-up session). Collectively, these two variables explained 14.7% of the variance in commitment. However, this effect was qualified, once again, by the predicted interaction of values and adversity which explained an additional 39.5% of the variance. As can be seen in Figure 23.2, those who saw their volunteer work as expressing their values came to feel more committed to it as they faced more adversity. In contrast, those who did not see their projects as value expressive, not surprisingly, felt less committed as they faced more stress and difficulty.

Similar results were found for behavioral intentions. Values and adversity, entered as main effects, predicted intentions to "continue this activity (their volunteer project) beyond the 8-week requirement," explaining 22.5% of the variance. Again, this was qualified by the interaction of values and adversity which added significantly to the regression equation by explaining an additional 14.5% of the variance. As can be seen in Figure 23.3, in the face of adversity, the value relevance expressed six to eight weeks earlier was highly predictive of behavioral intentions.

---

[4] Adversity and commitment were assessed with the same items employed in the first study.

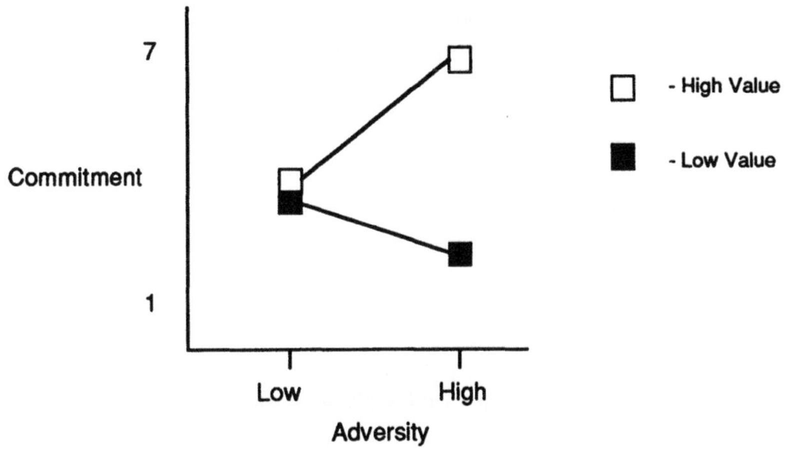

Note. Expected values were generated by the equation using the b weights for values, adversity and the interaction term of values by adversity.

FIG. 23.2. Regression lines for commitment in Study 2. Copyright 1990 by the American Psychological Association. Reprinted with permission.

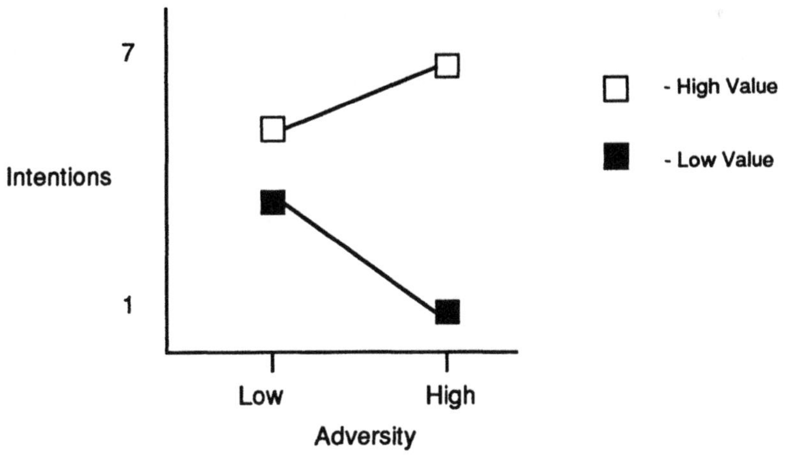

Note. Expected values were generated by the equation using the b weights for values, adversity and the interaction term.

FIG. 23.3. Regression lines for behavioral intentions in Study 2. Copyright 1990 by the American Psychological Association. Reprinted with permission.

The longitudinal analysis in this second study, by uncoupling temporally the measures of value relevance and commitment, offers stronger evidence for the hypothesized direction of the value-commitment relation. However, an alternative explanation might be that commitment was highly stable and the results were due to a high correlation between value relevance and commitment at the outset. Did value relevance predict a change in expressed commitment?

To address this question, initial commitment, which was measured in the initial session, was entered first in a hierarchical regression analysis as a covariate of later commitment. Not surprisingly, initial commitment accounted for 19.9% of the variance in later commitment. The main effects for value relevance and adversity were entered next. Neither of these explained a significant proportion of variance above and beyond the covariate. Finally, the predicted interaction term was entered. The interaction of values and adversity explained an additional 54% of the variance. Thus, value relevance did, indeed, predict, in a positive direction, subsequent perceptions of commitment when faced with adversity, independent of initial commitment.

To summarize, in the first study, the hypothesized relationship between value relevance and commitment in the face of adversity was demonstrated across a wide variety of personal projects. Subsequently, the direction of the relationship was demonstrated more powerfully in the longitudinal study, in which value relevance at the outset of a volunteer project predicted commitment in the face of adversity two months later. Moreover, to the extent that the adversity subjects faced was due to change, one could even conceive of nature, to a degree, randomly assigning subjects to conditions in a way that we would not do ethically. Finally, entering initial perceptions of commitment as a covariate provided a statistical test that advanced the notion that value relevance, in fact, predicts commitment in the face of subsequent adversity.

COMMITMENT TO CAREGIVING

Returning to the issue of social support, this model of commitment suggests that a negative life event experienced by a loved one creates a behavioral forced-choice situation for the caregiver. The negative life event challenges and tests commitment to the relationship and commitment to providing social support by dramatically increasing the costs of maintaining the relationship and providing support.

The model further suggests that there will be a strong positive relation between the caregiver's belief that his or her relationship with the victim is relevant to important values (i.e., diagnostic of self-identity) and the caregiver's commitment to the relationship. This is due in part to the behavioral forced choice created by the negative life event. It is no longer possible to ignore or take for granted one's commitment. According to the model, latent feelings of commitment are likely to be manifest by the precipitating condition that the negative life event creates. Moreover, the veneer of a commitment (not value-laden) when there is no adversity may be stripped away by the negative life event. Thus, the negative life event may reveal the *quality* of the relationship that may have previously been obscured or dormant during the daily routine of an ordinary life. In this sense, the seeds of a value-laden commitment may exist already but then germinate and blossom because of the negative life event.

However, the negative life event may not only reveal latent feelings of commitment previously obscured, but it also may transform and increase those feelings of commitment. In this sense, adversity may challenge caregivers to "rise to the occasion," and "go the extra mile." This may be especially apparent when providing social support inevitably begins to entail high costs.

What then will *sustain* commitment despite continued (and possibly increased) costs? Again, the model suggests that we need to know how the caregiver conceptualizes the relationship to the victim and the social support provided. Previously, we saw in Figure 23.2 that the value-commitment relation increased as adversity increased. Therefore, if the caregiver believes that the relationship and/or support are diagnostic[5] of his or her self-identity then we would expect commitment to increase as the costs increase.

To summarize, then, we are suggesting:

1. A significant other (O) may see the relationship to the person (P) as diagnostic of important values and thus feel committed to the relationship.
2. The significant other (O) may see providing social support as diagnostic and thus feel committed to social support.
3. The person (P) experiences a negative life event.
4. O, the significant other, is especially likely to express his or her commitment to the relationship.
5. That commitment may be expressed by increased social support, especially if O is committed to social support.
6. The inevitable costs of caring arise, we would expect to see.
7. Increases in O's commitment to the relationship and/or support is diagnostic of core identities.
8. Increase P's, the victim's, ability to cope with the negative life event.
9. To the extent that O's motivation to help does not translate into an ability to help, commitment could negatively impact on P's adjustment and, interestingly, O's mental health as well.

---

[5]Diagnostic information includes causal information but it is more broadly based on a simple correlation between two variables (Quattrone & Tversky, 1984). Information diagnostic of the self may create or reveal self-conceptions (causal) or it may confirm self-conceptions (correlational).

Although the present model points to the general conditions under which a caregiver might persist in providing social support for his or her partner in a close relationship, several more specific conditions remain unspecified. For example, it was assumed that increases in commitment to a relationship will automatically lead to increases in motivation to provide social support. But because there are undoubtedly many ways to maintain a sense of commitment to a loved one when the loved one has been victimized besides providing social support, variables which moderate the "commitment to the relationship-social support" relation will need to be determined. Those close to the victim may be trying to affirm their commitment to the victim, while simultaneously responding to other demands within their social network (Kessler & McLeod, 1984; Silverstone, 1979). Thus, we need to consider the various cognitive strategies that those close to the victim may invoke, in lieu of direct, tangible social support, as a means of affirming important values and core identities.

Here, we may find evidence at an interpersonal level for what Taylor describes as functional illusions (Taylor, 1983; Taylor & Brown, 1988). Taylor and Brown characterized these illusions as "a more general, enduring pattern of error, bias, or both that assumes a particular direction or shape" (Taylor & Brown, 1988, p. 194). It would seem that a concept such as social support that professionals struggle to quantify (Dunkel-Schetter & Bennett, 1990) would be especially vulnerable to the biases and errors of caregivers. For example, consider the work of Lerner (Lerner, Somers, Reid, & Tierney, 1989) on the egocentric bias of adult siblings describings their relative contributions of support to a dependent, elderly parent. This bias may protect one's feelings of commitment to the parent and help maintain a self-conception of a caring and loving child (although in the long run, such an illusion may be damaging to the sibling relationship).

Of course, for many, the cognitive strategies will not suffice. Those who see social support as diagnostic of the relationship are likely to be more motivated to provide social support, which then is more likely to lead to persistence of social support. However, to the extent that caregivers are acting on their own personal agenda (because their own identities are at stake), we may find them less responsive to the specific requests of the victim (Batson & Gray, 1981) and their support attempts may be inappropriate and frustrated. Moreover, their commitment to the victims may increase their own anxiety and psychological distress which Lehman, Ellard, and Wortman (1986) speculated was a mediator of unhelpful social support. Thus, high motivation and good intentions of committed caregivers may be positively related to persistence of social support but unrelated (or maybe even negatively related) to the quality of the support over time.

Clearly, we would expect persistent but unhelpful social support to have a negative effect on the health outcomes of the victims. However, our model of commitment suggests an additional prediction about how attempts to provide social support that fail may influence the mental health of the caregivers. We have proposed that those who perceive support for a loved one as particularly diagnostic of core identities will feel especially committed to caregiving. Support attempts that fail, in such cases, may be particularly threatening to the caregiver's sense of self as good and capable, creating feelings of psychological distress (cf. Brockner & Rubin, 1985; Steele, 1988).

The vulnerability of committed caregivers is illustrated by Brown, Bifulco, and Harris (1987). In a prospective study, 303 women were interviewed at length about five areas of their lives (children, marriage, housework, employment, and other activities outside the home), and their commitment to these roles or activities was rated by the interviewer. Those women who experienced a negative life event in a life domain that they characterized a year earlier as a *committed* domain were almost three times more likely to be depressed than those with a negative life event in a relatively less committed life domain. Moreover, Kessler and McLeod (1984) found that women's greater vulnerability to negative life events is due more to life events occurring to loved ones than to the women themselves. To the extent that women see relationships and social support as especially diagnostic of their self-identity, they would be expected to be especially committed caregivers (cf. Thoits, 1987). Thus, women's increased vulnerability to negative life events may reflect an increased vulnerability of committed caregivers.

In sum, commitment may energize caregivers (increasing motivation) and, at the same time, make them vulnerable. We can say then that not only may the incurred costs of the relationship (because of the negative life event) increase commitment, but also that commitment may increase the costs incurred.

LACK OF COMMITMENT

Just as costs may be incurred because of a caregiver's commitment, so too costs may be incurred because of a lack of commitment. The perception that one has not been committed is likely to have a deleterious effect on a person when the commitment (or lack thereof) is diagnostic of fundamental values and core identities. For example, the cultural norm and expectation that the oldest daughter provides for a dependent elderly parent will make the provision of social support more diagnostic for her than younger male siblings. Her identity as a loving daughter may be at stake. Thus living in another part of the country may be especially difficult and distressing for her. However, her younger male siblings may maintain an identity as caring sons (and the values concomitant with that identity) by phoning each weekend and providing financial support.

We can imagine then that in a marital relationship, a caregiver's perception of a lack of commitment may be quite damning, arousing an array of feelings such as anger, guilt, and worthlessness. Even those whose commitment to caregiving may seem high to an observer may feel a personal lack of commitment. Their standards of evaluation are likely to be higher the closer their relationship to the victim. While adversity increases commitment to caregiving, we might expect that it also increases the expectations of the caregiver. When the latter outpaces the former then the caregiver will feel a lack of commitment.

HEALTHY COMMITMENTS: BEYOND CONTROL

When the expectations of the caregiver and/or the victim are too high, a failure experience for the caregiver seems inevitable. Moreover, when the costs incurred are sustained and even increasing over a long period of time (particularly the case with chronic disease), again it seems almost inevitable that the costs will wear down the caregiver and create a failure experience for those who feel especially committed to caregiving. In some instances, the committed caregiver often becomes the bereaved, a victim in his or her own right (cf. Parkes & Weiss, 1983).

In turn, it would seem that commitment makes caregivers vulnerable because "success" is contingent upon the recovery of the victim and factors beyond the caregiver's control. Whereas the victim's illusions of control may serve mastery needs quite well (Taylor, 1983), it is not clear how long and how effectively committed caregivers can evoke and maintain illusions of control. The caregiver may receive comfort and consolation by identifying other life domains that are more controllable. Yet, the *committed* caregiver is still challenged by the relationship to the victim despite a lack of control.

Brickman and Karuza (1987) offer an important insight in distinguishing commitment from control. They note that commitment creates meaning and value, whereas control creates reinforcement. When commitment is at stake it is not necessarily control over behavioral outcomes or predictability that is at stake. People feel committed to those experiences that render meaning to their self-identities (Lydon & Zanna, 1988; Steele, 1988).

Personal control may make one's experiences more understandable, interpretable, meaningful. However, one may derive meaning despite a lack of control. Liu and Steele (1986) offer data suggesting that concerns with uncontrollability and helplessness belie more fundamental and general concerns with self-affirmation. They state, "When a valued self-image had been affirmed, subjects were able to tolerate whatever uncontrollability the helplessness training caused them to expect without mood depression" (p. 539).

Control then may be one way to affirm the self. We have proposed and demonstrated that commitment is another way to affirm the self. Furthermore, we have implied that commitment and control may become braided together, yielding potentially destructive ends. A caregiver who invokes a controlling kind of commitment may be especially vulnerable to failed support attempts. By trying to control the victim, the caregiver may not permit the victim to express feelings (Wortman & Lehman, 1985). The victim's efforts to regain self-respect and feelings of autonomy may be undermined. A controlling kind of commitment may be too focused on the instrumental aspects of social support when the expressive aspects are equally important (Coyne et al., 1988). Thus, attempts by the caregivers to personally control the adjustment of the victim may, in fact, undermine the adjustment of the victim.

Alternatively, commitment to caregiving free from control transforms the caregiving and the caregiver. The caregiver *empowers* the victim and finds meaning in the experience (cf. Brickman et al., 1982). A healthy commitment to caregiving then may entail a relinquishment of control as the standard of evaluation. In fact, by focusing more on empowerment, meaning and the expression of feelings than the controlling of the victim's behavior, it would seem that the caregiver is more fully realizing the essence of commitment to a close relationship.

CONCLUSION

The present paper suggests that researchers who study coping with negative life events do so by taking into account the broader social context, especially the interpersonal relationships, within which the negative life events occurs. In doing so, it is further suggested that the important properties of close relationships, such as commitment, be considered. Hopefully, models, such as the one presented herein, will motivate a greater collaboration between those working in the area of negative life events and those working in the area of close relationships to the mutual benefit of each.

REFERENCES

Aronson, E. (1969). The theory of cognitive dissonance: A current perspective. In L. Berkowitz (Ed.), *Advances in experimental social psychology* (Vol. 4, pp. 1-34). New York: Academic Press.

Batson, C. D., & Gray, R. A. (1981). Religious orientation and helping behavior: Responding to one's own or to the victim's needs? *Journal of Personality and Social Psychology, 40*, 511-520.

Brickman, P. (1987). *Commitment, conflict, and caring*. Englewood Cliffs, NJ: Prentice Hall.

Brickman, P., Dunkel-Schetter, C., & Abbey, A. (1987). The development of commitment. In C. B. Wortman & R. Sorrentino (Eds.), *Commitment, conflict, and caring* (pp. 145-221). Englewood Cliffs, NJ: Prentice Hall.

Brickman, P., & Karuza, J. (1987). Control or commitment? In C. B. Wortman & R. Sorrentino (Ed.), *Commitment, conflict, and caring* (pp. 106-144). Englewood Cliffs, NJ: Prentice Hall.

Brickman, P., Rabinowitz, V. C., Karuza, J., Coates, D., Cohn, E., & Kidder, L. (1982). Models of helping and coping. *American Psychologist, 37*, 368-384.

Brockner, J., & Rubin, J. Z. (1985). *Entrapment in escalating conflicts: A social psychological analysis*. New York: Springer.

Brown, G. W., Bifulco, A., & Harris, T. O. (1987). Life events, vulnerability, and onset of depression: Some refinements. *British Journal of Psychiatry, 150*, 30-42.

Cobb, S. (1976). Social support as a moderator of life stress. *Psychosomatic Medicine, 38*, 300-314.

Cohen, S., & Wills, T. A. (1985). Stress, social support, and the buffering hypothesis. *Psychological Bulletin, 98*, 310-357.

Coyne, J. C., Wortman, C. B., & Lehman, D. R. (1988). The other side of support: Emotional overinvolvement and miscarried helping. In B. H. Gottlieb (Ed.), *Marshalling social support: Formats, processes, and effects* (pp. 305-330). Newbury Park, CA: Sage.

Dunkel-Schetter, C., & Bennett, T. L. (1990). Differentiating the cognitive and behavioral apsects of social support. In I. G. Sarason, B. R. Sarason, & G. R. Pierce (Eds.), *Social support: An interactional view* (pp. 267-296). New York: Wiley.

Eggert, L. L. (1987). Support in family ties: Stress, coping, and adaptation. In T. L. Albrecht & M. B. Adelman (Eds.), *Communicating social support* (pp. 80-104). Newbury Park, CA: Sage.

Fox, F., & Staw, B. (1979). The trapped administrator: The effect of job insecurity and policy resistance upon commitment to a course of action. *Administrative Science Quarterly, 24*, 449-471.

House, J. S. (1981). *Work stress and social support*. Reading, MA: Addison-Wesley.

Kessler, R. C., & McLeod, J. D. (1984). Sex differences in vulnerability to undesirable life events. *American Sociological Review, 49*, 620-631.

Kessler, R. C., McLeod, J. D., & Wethington, E. (1985). The costs of caring: A perspective on the relationship between sex and psychological distress. In I. G. Sarason & B. R. Sarason (Eds.), *Social support: Theory, research, and applications* (pp. 491-506). Dordrecht: Martinus Nijhoff.

Lehman, D. R., Ellard, J. H., & Wortman, C. B. (1986). Social support for the bereaved: Recipients' and providers' perspectives on what is helpful. *Journal of Personality and Social Psychology, 54*, 438-446.

Lerner, M. J., Somers, D. G., Reid, D. W., & Tierney, M. C. (1989). A social dilemma: Egocentrically biased cognitions among filial caregivers. In S. Spacapan & S. Oskamp (Eds.), *The social psychology of aging* (pp. 53-80). Newbury Park: Sage.

Little, B. R. (1983). Personal projects. A rationale and method for investigation. *Environment and Behavior, 15*, 273-309.

Liu, T. J., & Steele, C. M. (1986). Attribution as self-affirmation. *Journal of Personality and Social Psychology, 51*, 531-540.

Lydon, J. E., & Zanna, M. P. (1988). *Commitments and adjustments to experiences diagnostic of values: A self-affirmation approach*. Paper presented at the annual meeting of the Canadian Psychological Association, Montreal, Quebec, Canada.

Lydon, J. E., & Zanna, M. P. (1990). Commitment in the face of adversity: A value-affirmation approach. *Journal of Personality and Social Psychology, 58*, 1040-1047.

Parkes, C. M., & Weiss, R. S. (1983). *Recovery from bereavement*. New York: Basic Books.

Quattrone, G., & Tversky, A. (1984). Causal versus diagnostic contingencies: On self-deception and on the voter's illusion. *Journal of Personality and Social Psychology, 46*, 237-248.

Silverstone, B. (1979). Issues for the middle generation: Responsibility, adjustment, and growth. In P. K. Ragan (Ed.), *Aging parents* (pp. 107-115). Los Angeles: University of Southern California, Ethel Percy Andrus Gerontology Center.

Snyder, M. L. & Ickes, W. (1985). Personality and social behavior. In G. Lindzey & E. Aronson (Eds.), *The handbook of social psychology* (3rd ed., Vol. 2, pp. 883-948). New York: Random House.

Staw, B. (1976). Knee-deep in the big muddy: A study of escalating commitment to a chosen course of action. *Organizational Behavior and Human Performance, 16*, 27-44.

Steele, C. (1988). The psychology of self-affirmation: Sustaining the integrity of the self. In L. Berkowitz (Ed.), *Advances in experimental social psychology* (Vol. 21, pp. 261-302). New York: Academic Press.

Steele, C. M., & Liu, T. J. (1983). Dissonance processes as self-affirmation. *Journal of Personality and Social Psychology, 45*, 5-19.

Taylor, S. E. (1983). Adjustment to threatening life events: A theory of cognitive adaptation. *American Psychologist, 38*, 1161-1173.

Taylor, S. E. (1986). *Health psychology*. New York: Random House.

Taylor, S. E. & Brown, J. (1988). Illusion and well-being: Some social psychological contributions to a theory of mental health. *Psychological Bulletin, 103*, 193-210.

Thoits, P. A. (1982). Conceptual, methodological, and theoretical problems in studying social support as a buffer against life stress. *Journal of Health and Social Behavior, 23*, 145-159.
Thoits, P. A. (1986). Multiple identities: Examining gender and marital status differences in distress. *American Sociological Review, 51*, 259-272.
Thoits, P. A. (1987). *On merging identity theory and stress research.* Paper presented at the annual meeting of the Eastern Sociological Society, Boston, MA.
Wortman, C. B., & Dunkel-Schetter, C. (1987). Conceptual and methodological issues in the study of social support. In A. Baum & J. E. Singer (Eds.), *Handbook of psychology and health* (Vol. 5, pp. 63-108). Hillsdale, NJ: Erlbaum.
Wortman, C. B., & Lehman, D. R. (1985). Reactions to victims of life crises: Support attempts that fail. In I. Sarason & B. Sarason (Eds.), *Social support: Theory, research, and applications* (pp. 463-489). Dordrecht: Martinus Nijhoff.

24 Coping With Rape: A Social Psychological Perspective[1]

Barbara Krahé
Freie Universität Berlin

When an individual experiences a negative life event, such as an accident, illness, or bereavement, others typically respond with compassion and sympathy to his or her plight. For a woman who has been raped, the situation is often dramatically different. Rather than receiving the comfort and support dearly needed after a traumatizing experience such as rape, she may find that many people around her treat her claim with suspicion and challenge her status as victim of a sexual assault. The idea that many, if not most, rape victims precipitate the attack through their behavior or appearance and thus have to accept at least part of the responsibility for what happened is firmly ingrained in the common stereotype about the crime and its victims (Katz & Mazur, 1979). For a raped woman this means that she has to come to terms not only with the psychological aftermath of the attack itself but also with "the reactions of people, especially the negative subjective reactions based on the myth and stereotypes that surround the subject of rape" (Burgess, 1987, p. 3).

Over the last ten years or so, a growing body of evidence has become available demonstrating the long-term psychological consequences of rape and sexual assault. For the most part, this research has been located in the field of clinical psychology, concentrating on the impact of the victimization experience on various aspects of psychological functioning, such as depression, sexual problems, anxiety, and changes in life style subsequent to the assault (e.g., Burgess & Holmstrom, 1985; Cohen & Roth, 1987; Kilpatrick, Veronen, & Best, 1985; Myers, Templer, & Brown, 1984; Whiston, 1981).

[1] The present chapter was prepared when the author was a Visiting Fellow at the University of Sussex, Brighton, UK. This stay was facilitated by a Heisenberg Fellowship awarded by the Deutsche Forschungsgemeinschaft (Kr 972/1-1).

In contrast, the work reported in this chapter is based on a social psychological perspective. This perspective highlights the victim's confrontation with the negative attitudes and stereotypical beliefs about rape held in her social environment as a central factor in the coping process. By investigating the determinants and consequences of what is often described by rape victims as a "second assault" (Williams & Holmes, 1981), the social psychological approach addresses an important aspect of sexual victimization. To illustrate the scope of this approach, let us consider Burt's (1983) outline of a conceptual framework for victimological research in which she distinguishes four stages in the victimization process:

> In Stage 1, the person experiences harm, suffering, or injury caused by another person or institution.
>
> If the person experiences the harm as unjust, then self-labeling as "victim" occurs in Stage 2.
>
> Following the self-labeling, the person will then claim to be acknowledged as victim by others in Stage 3.
>
> Finally, Stage 4 of the victimization process involves the recognition of the victim's role claim and thus the attainment of "real victim status" in the eyes of society.

Applying this framework to sexual victimization, it is clear that social attitudes and stereotypes bear upon each of Stages 2, 3, and 4. Cultural beliefs related to rape, sexuality, and male-female relations in general have a decisive impact on whether or not a raped woman perceives herself as an innocent victim, whether she attempts to claim victim status from significant others and/or members of relevant institutions, and whether those other people are prepared to acknowledge the legitimacy of her claim.

The present chapter examines some of the social psychological variables involved in the perception and evaluation of rape victims. Following a summary of the main findings from previous research, the first part of the chapter will focus on a series of empirical studies examining the factors that influence people's attributions of responsibility to victims of rape. In the second part, evidence will be presented on police officers' subjective definitions of rape that convey their implicit theories about the crime and its victims. Whilst the vast majority of research on these issues has been conducted in the United States, the studies reported in this chapter were carried out in Great Britain and Germany, thus allowing an examination of the cross-national replicability of some of the major findings.

SOCIAL STEREOTYPES AND RESPONSIBILITY ATTRIBUTIONS TO VICTIMS OF RAPE

The much cited study by Jones and Aronson (1973) marks the beginning of a prolific research tradition in social psychology directed at the issue of responsibility attributions to victims of rape. Attributing responsibility is a central aspect of evaluating a rape incident both within and outside the criminal justice system and has been found to be prevalent not just among third persons but also among rape victims themselves (Janoff-Bulman, 1979; Meyer & Taylor, 1986). Holding a raped woman at least partly responsible for the assault is tantamount to questioning her status as victim of a criminal act. Thus, it is essential to identify the variables that affect the attribution of responsibility to victims of rape. Evidence from a diverse range of studies suggests that in forming an impression about a specific rape incident, people typically go beyond the information given and draw upon general social stereotypes to assess the roles of victim and offender. Such stereotypical notions about, e.g., a woman's social respectability or acceptable patterns of female behavior, provide a powerful basis for inferring the credibility of a rape claim and the responsibility of the victim.

The variety of background variables that have been examined in terms of their impact on judgments of responsibility can be classified broadly into three categories: information regarding (a) the victim and (b) the assailant involved in a sexual attack and (c) the personal characteristics and attitudes of the observer/subject judging the event. The following paragraphs illustrate this evidence by discussing one variable from each of the three categories: victim respectability, assailant social status, and sex of observer.

Jones and Aronson (1973) examined the impact of information about the "respectability" of a rape victim on the assessment of victim responsibility. Respectability was defined in terms of the victim's marital status, whereby the respectable victim was described as either a virgin or a married woman whereas the less respectable victim was introduced as a divorcee. Based on Lerner's (1970) concept of "belief in a just world," it was predicted that more responsibility would be attributed to the more respectable victims. According to Lerner, there is a general human desire to believe in the world being a just place. This belief, it is argued, serves a self-protective function by suggesting that negative events happen only to those people who deserve them in one way or another. Learning that a respectable woman has become a victim of rape threatens the validity of the belief in a just world. To restore it, some reason has to be found why she deserved the misfortune after all. Attributing responsibility to a respectable rape victim, i.e. suggesting that she did something to precipitate the attack, is one way of upholding one's belief in a just world. In line with this reasoning, Jones and Aronson showed that the two respectable victims were attributed more responsibility for the attack than the less respectable divorcee.

Subsequent studies, however, have failed to replicate this finding. While some failed to find any influence of victim respectability on attributions of responsibility (e.g., Kahn et al., 1977; Kanekar & Kolsawalla, 1977; Kerr & Kurtz, 1977), others found support for the reverse relationship, with more responsibility being attributed to the less respectable victim (e.g., Alexander, 1980; Feldman-Summers & Lindner, 1976; Luginbuhl & Mullin, 1981; Smith, Keating, Hester, & Mitchell, 1976). A conclusive interpretation of this evidence, however, is hampered by the fact that no consistent operational definition of victim respectability has been used, with examples ranging from marital status over occupation and dress to past sexual history.

Social status has also been found to be a critical variable on the part of the assailant influencing responsibility attributions. Observers were shown to be less certain about the guilt of a high status assailant than of a low status assailant (Deitz & Byrnes, 1981) and to recommend more lenient sentences for high status defendants (Feild & Barnett, 1978). The physical attractiveness of an alleged rapist was shown to exert a parallel influence (Deitz & Byrnes, 1981; Jacobson, 1981). In a study by Yarmey (1985) comparing attributional judgments of older and younger adults, young people were found to attribute greater responsibility for an assault to a woman who resisted a well-dressed attacker than when she resisted a poorly dressed attacker. Altogether, however, the number of studies looking at information about the assailant is small compared to those concerned with either victim or observer variables.

Among the observer variables, the most obvious and most widely explored aspect is that of sex differences. Here, the overall pattern of findings suggests that males attribute more responsibility to rape victims than females (e.g., Calhoun, Selby, Cann, & Keller, 1978; Thornton, Robbins, & Johnson, 1981; Thornton & Ryckman, 1983). However, a number of studies either failed to obtain sex differences (e.g., Acock & Ireland, 1983; L'Armand & Pepitone, 1982) or demonstrated a stronger tendency for females to blame the victim (Howard, 1984) as well as greater leniency by female probation officers in recommending sentences for rapists (Walsh, 1984). Recent studies point to the importance of rape-related attitudes, such as "rape myth acceptance," as facilitating a more fine-grained analysis of the gender-related aspects of responsibility judgments (Bunting & Reeves, 1983; Burt, 1980; Quackenbush, 1989).

As mentioned earlier on, the information currently available on the social judgment of rape victims and assailants has been collected almost exclusively in North America. Thus, very little is known about the cross-national or indeed cross-cultural generality of the findings summarized above. Therefore, the first study to be reported below was conducted with a view to replicating some of the findings obtained in previous research with a West German sample.

Attributing Responsibility to Rape Victims: A German Study

This study (Krahé, 1985) was designed to examine the impact of three variables on ratings of responsibility to the victim and the assailant in a rape case: the victim's social status, the assailant's social status, and the sex of the subject. On the basis of previous evidence, it was predicted that

1. High status victims would be attributed less responsibility than low status victims;
2. High status assailants would also be attributed less responsibility than low status assailants; and finally
3. Male subjects would attribute more responsibility to the victim and less to the assailant than female subjects.

Procedure

A total of 69 undergraduates (42 females and 27 males) from a small West German university participated in the study. They were shown a brief passage from a popular TV program calling upon the support of the audience in investigating crimes. In the videotaped scene, a woman stood with her back to the camera and told the audience how she had picked up a hitch-hiker who had then forced her to drive into an isolated copse where he raped her. Following the videotape, subjects received a booklet with further information about the case which contained the manipulation of victim and assailant social status. The high status victim was introduced as a school teacher, while the low status victim was described as a shop assistant. The assailant was described as a medical student in the high status condition and as an unskilled worker in the low status condition. Two dependent measures were employed. The first, attribution of responsibility to the victim, was obtained in two steps: Subjects were first asked to make a dichotomous "yes/no" judgment of victim responsibility to allow them a forthright rejection of the idea that the woman had done anything to precipitate the attack. Those subjects who thought the victim had some responsibility were then asked to rate that responsibility on a percentage scale ranging from "0%" to "100%" with decimal subdivisions. The remaining subjects were assigned a score of "0" on the percentage scale. Ratings of the second dependent variable, assailant responsibility, were obtained on an independent percentage scale also ranging from "0%" to "100%."

Results and Discussion

Separate 2 × 2 × 2 (Victim Status × Assailant Status × Sex of Subject) analyses of variance were computed for the two dependent variables. For the ratings of victim responsibility, the analysis yielded a marginally significant effect of victim status as predicted in Hypothesis 1 ($F(1,61) = 3.65, p < .07$). The high status victim was attributed less responsibility ($M = 5.2\%$) than the low status victim ($M = 10.2\%$). None of the remaining effects approached statistical significance. For the dependent variable of assailant responsibility, the only significant effect was the main effect for assailant social status ($F(1,61) = 6.02, p < .02$). However, the direction of this effect ran counter to Hypothesis 2, with the high status assailant being attributed greater responsibility ($M = 94.2\%$) than the low status assailant ($M = 87.8\%$).

Thus, it may be concluded that the findings from this study lend only partial support to the hypotheses derived from the body of evidence generated in North America. Neither the sex of the subject nor the social status of the assailant had an influence on the perception of the victim's causal role in the assault. However, information about a rape victim's social status was found to affect observers' perceptions of responsibility in line with the majority of previous findings: Victims of comparatively lower social status are attributed greater responsibility for being raped than victims of higher status. It should be noted that the two occupations selected in the present study (school teacher vs. shop assistant) did not differ dramatically in terms of the social status attached to them compared to some of the earlier studies using more drastic manipulations such as "topless dancer versus nun" (e.g., Smith et al., 1976). The fact that even this relatively weak manipulation of the victim's social status produced an effect on responsibility attributions reveals how firmly the perception of rape is embedded in the social values and stereotypes of society.

This conclusion receives further backing from the findings of the next study to be reported that examined the link between subjects' rape-related attitudes and their processing of information about a rape victim's role-conforming vs. role-discrepant behavior prior to the assault.

Rape Myth Acceptance and Responsibility Judgments: A British Study

As noted above, a number of studies have shown that a person's readiness to endorse stereotypical beliefs about rape, i.e., "rape myths" (Burt, 1980), is a powerful determinant of his or her responsibility attributions. Rape myths are conceptualized in terms of a set of general beliefs about rape for which there is no factual basis and which predispose an individual to adopt a negative, unsympathetic view toward the victims of specific rape incidents. This view is reflected, not least, in the person's appraisal of the victim's responsibility for the attack. The extent to which people accept such rape myths to be true is thought to be directly related to the amount of responsibility they attribute to a victim of rape.

Going beyond this straightforward hypothesis, the study reported in this section explored the proposition that rape myth acceptance not only exerts a direct influence on judgments of responsibility but also affects the way people treat information that is causally irrelevant to the rape incident. The starting point for the study was provided by a previous investigation (Best & Demmin, 1982) showing that victims who engaged in provocative or role-discrepant behavior (i.e., "drinking alone in a bar") prior to the assault were attributed greater responsibility than victims who engaged in role-conforming behavior (i.e., "studying alone in the library"). The rapist, on the other hand, was attributed significantly less responsibility if the victim's prerape behavior had been role-discrepant than when it had been role-conforming.

Apart from attempting to replicate this finding with a British sample, the present study includes the concept of rape myth acceptance to test the idea that persons showing a high acceptance of rape myths should be particularly susceptible to information about a rape victim's role-conforming vs. role-discrepant behavior prior to the attack in their assessments of victim responsibility. Accordingly, two hypotheses were advanced in this study:

1. The victim who is engaged in role-discrepant behavior prior to the rape is attributed greater responsibility than the victim who is engaged in role-conforming behavior.
2. High rape myth acceptance leads to greater responsibility attributed to the victim, especially to the victim engaging in role-discrepant behavior.

The sex of the subject was again included as an independent variable to examine whether the lack of sex effects in Study 1 was replicated with an independent sample in a different country.

Procedure

Thirty-six males and 37 females volunteered to participate in the study. The study was conducted in Brighton, UK. All participants were members of the general public in the age range of 20 to 35 who were approached at various public places. The average age was 26.4 years.

Subjects were presented with a questionnaire containing a brief rape vignette. The vignette described how a women was attacked when she walked across a car park to get to her car. It focused solely on the course of events in the situation and did not contain any background information about the victim and the assailant except for the manipulation of the victim's prerape behavior which was contained in the introductory sentence of the vignette. In the role-conforming condition, this sentence read "After having finished work in her office, the victim was on her way to the car park where her car was parked." In the role-discrepant condition, the first sentence read "After having had a drink on her own in a pub, the victim was on her way to the car park where her car was parked." The text then described the rape incident. Following the rape vignette, subjects were asked to give three responses: (a) to indicate, in a forced choice format, whether or not they thought the victim had any responsibility at all for the attack; (b) those who answered "yes" to the first question were then asked to rate the extent of victim responsibility on a percentage scale ranging from "0%" to "100%." The remaining subjects were assigned a score of "0" on the percentage rating; (c) finally, all subjects rated the assailant's responsibility on another percentage scale.

In the second part of the questionnaire, subjects were asked to complete the "Rape Myth Acceptance Scale" (RMAS) developed by Burt (1980). The RMAS consists of 19 items tapping respondents' agreement with a number of stereotypical beliefs about rape, such as "In the majority of rapes the victim is promiscuous and has a bad reputation." The reliability and validity of the RMAS for use with a British sample had been established in a previous study (Krahé, 1988, Study 1).

Results and Discussion

On the basis of their responses to the RMAS, subjects were classified as either high or low on rape myth acceptance by median split. Separate 2 × 2 × 2 analyses of variance were performed for victim and assailant responsibility with sex of subject, rape myth acceptance, and victim's role conformity as independent variables. The cell means for ratings of victim responsibility are presented in Table 24.1.

The analysis of variance produces a highly significant main effect for rape myth acceptance, ($F(1,65) = 12.32$, $p < .001$), and a significant interaction between victim's role conformity and subjects' rape myth acceptance, ($F(1,65) = 4.26$, $p < .05$), indicating that differential information about victim's prerape behavior only affected the attributions of subjects scoring high on rape myth acceptance. None of the remaining main effects and interactions were significant.

The means for the ratings of assailant responsibility are presented in Table 24.2.

The only significant effect that emerged from this analysis was the interaction between victim's role conformity and subjects' rape myth acceptance, ($F(1,65) =$

TABLE 24.1
Mean Ratings of Victim Responsibility

Subject Gender		*M*		*F*	
Rape Myth Accept.		*High*	*Low*	*High*	*Low*
	Role-Conf.	6.25	0.00	3.75	1.67
Victim's Pre-Rape Behavior					
	Role-Discr.	15.45	0.00	17.00	0.00

Note. The response scales for these ratings ranged from 0% to 100%.

6.31, $p < .02$): Subjects high on rape myth acceptance attributed more responsibility to the assailant than those low on rape myth acceptance when the victim had engaged in role-conforming behavior prior to the rape. The reverse pattern was obtained when the victim had behaved in a role-discrepant fashion prior to the attack.

Thus, no support was obtained for the first hypothesis stating that information about a victim's role-conforming vs. role-discrepant behavior affects the perception of victim responsibility in terms of higher responsibility being attributed to the role-discrepant victim. However, there was support for the second hypothesis postulating an interaction between victim's role conformity and subject's rape myth acceptance: People who accept stereotypic ideas about rape are more ready to take victim's behavior into account as an aggravating or attenuating factor in assessing both victim and assailant responsibility. As in Study 1, the sex of the subject did not have an effect on responsibility attributions.

In conclusion, results from this study confirm earlier evidence in demonstrating that rape myth acceptance is a critical determinant of responsibility attributions to rape victims and assailants. A person's general attitude about what constitutes rape and under what circumstances it can occur at all systematically influences his or her evaluation of a specific rape incident. At the same time, a person who believes in rape myth is also more likely to draw upon general stereotypes of gender-appropriate behavior when asked to evaluate a rape incident. Although the rape vignettes used in this study did not imply in any way that victim prerape behavior was causally related to the subsequent attack, subjects high on rape myth acceptance did utilize this information in their responsibility attributions.

TABLE 24.2

Mean Ratings of Assailant Responsibility

Subject Gender		*M*		*F*	
Rape Myth Accept.		*High*	*Low*	*High*	*Low*
	Role-Conf.	94.38	86.25	96.25	93.33
Victim's Pre-Rape Behavior					
	Role-Discr.	84.55	97.78	73.00	97.86

Note. The response scales for these ratings ranged from 0% to 100%.

Considered in combination, the two studies reported so far provide conclusive evidence that people's perceptions of a victim's causal role in rape are guided by an implicit, socially shared image of the "ideal" victim who is a respectable, that is high status, person and whose behavior is generally in accordance with female role-prescriptions. Whether or not a raped woman is acknowledged as victim rather than precipitator of a sexual attack depends on the extent to which she approximates the image of the ideal victim as well as on the extent to which the context of the attack conforms to the general stereotype of the "classic" rape situation as occurring between strangers, outdoors, and at night (e.g., Burt & Albin, 1981; Gilmartin-Zena, 1983; J. E. Williams, 1984). L. S. Williams (1984) has shown that this stereotype of the classic rape even affects the victims' own perceptions of the assault and their causal role in it, with victims raped under less typical circumstances questioning their role and responsibility in the attack and being less likely to report it to the police.

POLICE OFFICERS' DEFINITIONS OF RAPE

The tendency to be suspicious of rape claims by women whose lifestyle and social background is at odds with societal conceptions of female decency is not limited to those subject populations, i.e., university students, that are most widely represented in the existing body of research. There is evidence that jurors in rape and sexual assault cases are equally affected by such social background information in their perceptions of rape cases (e.g., Feild & Bienen, 1980; LaFree, Reskin, & Visher, 1985). Even before a rape complaint comes to court, the handling of rape cases by members of the criminal justice system, most notably the police, was shown to reflect the impact of social stereotypes and normative beliefs on defining the "real rape" (e.g., Feild, 1978; Feldman-Summers & Palmer, 1980; LaFree, 1980; Rose & Randall, 1982). What these studies suggest is that well-defined legal definitions of rape become blurred by the simultaneous operation of more ambiguous common sense conceptions of the crime and its victims that critically affect the collection, evaluation, and further processing of information concerning a rape complaint. One way of looking at these common sense conceptions is to conceptualize them as cognitive schemata that facilitate a quick and parsimonious assessment of a specific rape incident. In this vein, some authors (e.g., Howard, 1984; Jackson, 1978) suggest that social knowledge about crime is cognitively organized in terms of scripts, specifying the typical features and events that characterize the "normal crime." In this sense, the "normal rape" script can be seen as providing a standard for evaluating a specific case, whereby the more a case deviates from the script the more a woman's claim to the victim role is likely to be rejected.

A Study on Cognitive Prototypes of Rape

The final study to be reported in this chapter also adopts a social cognitive perspective to explore common sense notions about rape. More specifically, it refers to the concept of "cognitive prototypes" to explore the subjective definitions of rape held by police officers. At the core of the prototype concept is the idea that the categories used in natural language to classify objects, persons, and situations have fuzzy boundaries rather than being mutually exclusive (e.g., Cantor & Mischel, 1979). This means that each category contains both highly typical and less typical members, with the less typical members sharing a number of characteristics with those of adjacent categories. The meaning of a category is best captured by its "prototype," defined in terms of those features that are consensually assigned to the category in question.

In the present study, the prototype concept is used as basis for eliciting and comparing the characteristic features of different rape situations as defined by police officers. In line with the proposition that rape has multiple meanings, each associated with a different set of characteristics, a total of six different situations was examined:

1. The typical, i.e. most common rape situation.
2. The credible rape complaint where there is no doubt about the truth of the victims' allegations.
3. The dubious rape complaint where there are serious doubts about the truth of the victims' allegations.
4. The rape experience that is particularly hard for the victim to cope with.
5. The rape experience that is comparatively easy for the victim to cope with.
6. the false rape complaint.

Procedure

One-hundred-and-fifty police officers from the West Berlin police force participated in this study. Questionnaires were distributed to respondents at police stations in different parts of the city to ensure a representative coverage of inner city and suburban areas. One-hundred-and-eight completed questionnaires were returned, leading to a final sample of 85 males and 23 females. Their average age was 35.7 years, while the average number of years in the police was 17.1. Ninety-two (85.2%) of the respondents reported that they had to deal with rape cases as part of their duties, with the average number of cases being estimated at 4.2 per year.

Subjects received a questionnaire containing a random combination of three of the six rape situations listed above. Following each situation, they were presented with a list of 27 characteristics potentially relevant to the description of a rape situation. These characteristics were selected on the basis of a previous study[2] asking an independent sample to generate lists of questions about the victim, the assailant, and the circumstances of a rape incident that they considered to be relevant to the evaluation of a specific case. Subjects were instructed to tick all those features they thought to be characteristic of the situation in question, thus providing a descriptive profile for each situation. For example, they were asked to consider the age of the victim as a potentially relevant feature in each situation. For this feature, four response options, i.e., age ranges, were presented: under 20 years of age, between 20 and 40, between 40 and 60, and over 60. If, for any situation, subjects thought that victim would predominantly belong to one (or more) of the age groups provided, then they would tick the appropriate option(s). If they considered victim age to be irrelevant, none of the options was ticked.

Results and Discussion

To establish the prototypical "profile" of each of the six rape situations, frequencies of the different response options within each feature category were computed. If no response option was ticked by the subject for a particular feature, then the response was coded as "irrelevant". Those options which had been named most frequently were included in the consensual feature list defining the prototype of the respective situation. For example, the distribution of frequencies for the "victim age" feature in the "typical rape" situation was as follows: Of the 51 respondents who looked at this situation, 11 (18.6%) selected the "under 20" age group, 38 (64.4%) regarded the "20-40" age range as typically characterizing this situation, and 2 (3.4%) selected the "40-60" age range. Finally, 8 respondents (13.6%) did not tick any response option, and their responses were coded as reflecting the irrelevance of the feature of "victim age" in describing the typical rape situation. On the basis of these data, the feature of "victim age between 20 and 40" was included into the consensual feature list, i.e. the prototype, for the typical rape situation. In the same way, the characteristic features to be included in the prototype were determined for the remaining categories of victim, assailant, and circumstance characteristics.

The prototypes obtained for each of the six situations are displayed in Table 24.3. Since each respondent received only three situations and not all questionnaires were returned sample sizes differ slightly across the situations.

The characteristics listed in Table 24.3 reflect the police officers' understanding of the features that distinguish a particular kind of rape situation. Blank cells indicate that none of the response options was regarded as distinctive for the situation in question. In terms of the prototype approach, each column of Table 24.3 represents a set of consensual features that define the prototypical example of a

[2]Krahé, B. (1990). *Police officer's definitions of rape: A prototype study*. Manuscript submitted for publication.

TABLE 24.3

Prototypes of the Six Rape Sitiuations

		Typical	*Credible*	*Dubious*	*Hard*	*Easy*	*False*
		S1	*S2*	*S3*	*S4*	*S5*	*S6*
Victim	Age	20-40	20-40	over 40	under 40	20-40	20-40
	Dress		nondist.	nondist.			
	Sexual Exp.	occas.			none	regular	occas.
	Resistance	verbal	physical	none	physical	none	none
	Psych. Conseq.	serious	serious	slight	serious	slight	slight
	Alcohol	slight	none	heavy	none	none	slight
	Injuries	minor	minor	none	serious	none	none
	Escape Attempt		yes	no	yes	no	no
	Communication with A.	yes	yes	yes			yes
Attacker	Age	20-40	20-40	20-40		20-40	20-40
	Sexual Exp.	occas.	occas.			occas.	occas.
	Psych. Dist.	dist.	dist.	not dist.		not dist.	not dist.
	Crim. Record			none		none	
	Alcohol	slight	slight	heavy		slight	slight
	Threat	viol.	viol.	no thr.	death t.	no thr.	viol.
	Use of Weapons	thrat	threat	none	threat	none	none
	Physical Constit.	average	average	weak		average	average
Circumstances	Place	outdoors	outdoors	man´s/ woman´s		man´s/ woman´s	man´s/ woman´s
	Witnesses	none	none	none	none	none	none
	Acquaintance	unknown	unknown	friends	unknown	unknown	met br.
	Time	night	night	night		night	night
	N of Attackers	one	one	one	several	one	one
	Identification	yes	yes	yes	yes	yes	yes
	N	51	50	54	57	54	54

given category. These data lend themselves to both qualitative and quantitative interpretation. The former perspective leads to a comprehensive description of the exact nature of respondents' prototypes of each situation, while the latter provides a numerical index of the similarity between prototypes. The frequency analyses showed that marital status and nationality of both victim and assailant had been regarded as irrelevant with respect to all six situations. Even though this is an interesting finding, these aspects fail to differentiate between the situations and were therefore dropped from any further analysis. In two further categories, namely the presence of witnesses ("none") and the woman's confidence in identifying the attacker ("yes"), the same options were named for all situations and thus also failed to discriminate between them. However, they were retained in the analysis because unlike the irrelevance judgments they contribute positive information to the prototypes.

The findings in Table 24.3 can be interpreted in two complementary ways. Comparing the feature profiles for different situations illustrates how two or more situations differ in terms of the pattern of characteristics that are peculiar to them. At the same time, one can look at each feature individually to determine its significance across the total range of situations.

In characterizing the *typical* rape situation, the police officers in the present sample confirm some of the stereotypical notions about rape as a crime involving an attack, out in the open, after dark, by a stranger, who is psychologically disturbed. At the same time, they perceive the psychological consequences for the victim to be severe, even though they think of the victim in a typical rape situation as being slightly drunk and suffering only minor physical injuries. It is interesting to note that the typical rape situation is described by very much the same features as the *credible* rape situation except that in the latter situation the victim is perceived as having made an attempt to escape and not being intoxicated.

In contrast, the prototype of the *dubious* rape complaint is substantially different from the typical rape. Here, respondents think that the victim is generally older, heavily drunk, and does not show any resistance or attempt to escape. The assailant, at the same time, is also regarded as being heavily drunk, yet not psychologically disturbed. A dubious rape complaint is further characterized by the feature that the man and the woman involved used to be friends and by typically occurring at either the man's or the woman's place.

Compared to the first three situations, the rape that is *particularly hard for the victim to cope with* is characterized by a smaller number of features. Victim age is crucial, with victims under 20 years of age being regarded as most likely to find the rape experience particularly hard to cope with. Other distinctive features in this prototype are the physical resistance shown by the victim, her lack of previous sexual experience, and the suffering of serious injuries, while on the assailant side the severity of threat used in the situation is an outstanding factor. Finally, being raped by several attackers is an essential feature associated with this type of rape experience.

Prototypes of the last two situations, i.e., the *false rape complaint* and the rape experience, that is *comparatively easy for the victim to cope with* show a high degree of feature overlap both amongst each other and with the dubious rape complaint. For the easy to cope with situation, a victim's regular sex life is seen as a critical feature. As expected, psychological consequences for the victim in this type of situation are perceived as being only slightly negative. The false rape complaint differs from the previous situations in that, by definition, it refers to a victim's account of events that did not actually happen. So respondents had to think of characteristics that a woman pretending to have been raped would put forward to tell a convincing story. This may explain, at least in part, why a relatively high degree of overlap was found between the false complaint and the typical rape situation. However, it is interesting to note where the two prototypes differ. In the false rape complaint, the place of the alleged attack is typically seen as being either the man's or the woman's home, with both parties having met briefly in the past. While respondents think it most likely for the woman to report she had been threatened, she is considered unlikely to claim that a weapon was involved.

The findings in Table 24.3 already give some indication of the similarities between the prototypes. To obtain more precise evidence of prototype similarity, a quantitative analysis of feature overlap was conducted[3]. Each pair of situations was compared in terms of their shared and distinctive features, whereby the greater the number of shared features, the greater the overall similarity between two situations. The resulting pattern of similarity between the six rape prototypes is presented in Table 24.4.

The findings show that by far the highest similarity exists between the prototypes of the typical and the credible rape situation. The greatest dissimilarities emerge between the rape situation that is particularly hard to cope with and the dubious and false complaints, respectively. Medium levels of similarity were found between the dubious rape complaint on the one hand and the easy to cope with and false complaint situations on the other. It should be pointed out, however, that the meaning of these quantitative measures of prototype similarity can only be fully understood in conjunction with the qualitative findings reported in Table 24.3. So, for instance, the prototype of the most common rape situation is equally dissimilar from those of the dubious and the hard to cope with situations, yet the nature of the dissimilarities differs greatly with regard to the two situations.

---

[3]In accordance with previous work on cognitive prototypes, the following formula was used to arrive at a quantitative index of similarity between rape situations (cf. Eckes, 1986):

$$S(A,B) = \frac{f(A \cap B)}{f(A \cap B) + f(A-B) + f(B-A)}$$

whereby S(A,B) is the similarity between the prototypes of Situations A and B, f (A Ô B) is the number of shared features in A and B, f (A-B) is the number of features in contained A, but not in B, and f(B-A) is the number of features contained in B, but not in A. S(A,B) can range from 0 to 1, with a score of 0 reflecting complete dissimilarity (i.e., no shared features at all) and a score of 1 reflecting complete similarity (i.e., no distinctive features at all).

TABLE 24.4
Similarity between Situation Prototypes

Situations		*S1*	*S2*	*S3*	*S4*	*S5*
Typical	S1					
Credible	S2	.78				
Dubious	S3	.17	.20			
Hard to cope	S4	.18	.25	.06		
Easy to cope	S5	.32	.35	.50	.14	
False complaint	S6	.46	.35	.45	.06	.62

Altogether, the findings show that the police officers participating in this study perceive rape as a serious criminal offence with lasting consequences for the victim. This is reflected most clearly in the prototype of the typical rape situation that is characterized by the majority of respondents as involving long-term psychological problems for the victim as well as the use of threat by the assailant. The high degree of overlap between the prototypes of the typical and the credible rape situation also fails to support the predominantly negative public image of the police in dealing with rape victims. Thus, the present findings join research by Holmstrom and Burgess (1978) and LeDoux and Hazelwood (1985) in demonstrating that police officers generally adopt a view of rape that acknowledges the severe effects of the assault on the victim. At the same time, however, they also corroborate the tendency found by these authors for police officers to become suspicious if a rape complaint contains certain critical features. As Table 24.3 reveals, previous encounters between the victim and the assailant are perceived as typical features of the dubious and false rape complaints. Similarly, a rape complaint is likely to be treated with suspicion if the alleged assailant does not have a history of psychological disturbance and the attack took place at either the man's or the woman's place. This evidence suggests that the credibility of a rape victim is likely to be called in question whenever her account includes features that are consensually perceived as characterizing the dubious or false rape complaint.

CONCLUSION

The work reported in this chapter originated from a social psychological perspective on the problem of coping with rape. Central to this perspective is the proposition that a victim's confrontation with societal beliefs about rape makes her attempts at overcoming the crisis of sexual victimization even more difficult. Stereotypical conceptions about the "real rape" as well as normative standards of appropriate female behavior affect both the victim's perception of her own role in the attack and the willingness of other people to accept her claim to the victim status.

The three studies presented above addressed different facets of the influence of rape-related stereotypes on the evaluation of rape victims. While the first study demonstrated the impact of information about a victim's social status on observers' perceptions of victim precipitation, the second study illustrated how observers' general attitudes toward rape predispose them to selectively attend to information about a rape victim's conformity or nonconformity to female role prescriptions. Both sets of data reveal that the scope of what is considered to be a "legitimate rape claim" is defined in rather narrow terms, especially by those persons who show a high acceptance of rape myths. The third study further extended this perspective by looking at the subjective definitions of different rape situations held by police officers. While the present findings fail to support the negative image of the police as being generally unsympathetic to victims of rape, it became clear that police officers share a number of the common sense conceptions of rape, and it is reasonable to assume that these conceptions also influence the way they approach specific rape complaints.

In conclusion, the work reported in this chapter joins a large body of evidence in the social psychological literature on rape in showing that sexual victimization is not limited to the rape attack itself. It continues in the form of social processes in the victim's network of interpersonal relationships as well as in the criminal justice system. At the core of these processes is the explicit or implicit negotiation of her role as "victim" which is inextricably linked to the wider framework of normative beliefs and values prevalent in a society. Exploring when and why this negotiation process is likely to preclude a fair and sympathetic treatment of a victim of rape and thus add to her distress is a prime task for a social psychology of sexual violence.

REFERENCES

Acock, A. C., & Ireland, N. K. (1983). Attribution of blame in rape cases: The impact of norm violation, gender, and sex-role attitude. *Sex Roles, 9,* 179-193.

Alexander, C. S. (1980). The responsible victim: Nurses' perceptions of victims of rape. *Journal of Health and Social Behavior, 21,* 22-33.

Best, J. B., & Demmin, H. S. (1982). Victim's provocativeness and victim's attractiveness as determinants of blame in rape. *Psychological Reports, 51,* 255-258.

Bunting, A. B., & Reeves, J. B. (1983). Perceived male sex-role orientation and beliefs about rape. *Deviant Behavior, 4,* 281-295.

Burgess, A. W. (1987). Public beliefs and attitudes concerning rape. In R. R. Hazelwood & A. W. Burgess (Eds.), *Practical aspects of rape investigation. A multidisciplinary approach* (pp. 3-18). New York: Elsevier.

Burgess, A. W., & Holmstrom, L. (1985). Rape trauma syndrome and post-traumatic stress response. In A. W. Burgess (Ed.), *Rape and sexual assault: A research handbook* (pp. 46-60). New York: Garland.

Burt, M. R. (1980). Cultural myths and support for rape. *Journal of Personality and Social Psychology, 38,* 217-230.

Burt, M. R. (1983). A conceptual framework for victimological research. *Victimology, 3,* 261-269.

Burt, M. R., & Albin, R. S. (1981). Rape myths, rape definitions, and probability of conviction. *Journal of Applied Social Psychology, 11,* 212-230.

Calhoun, L. G., Selby, J. W., Cann, A., & Keller, G. T. (1978). The effects of victim physical attractiveness and sex of respondent on social reactions to victims of rape. *British Journal of Social and Clinical Psychology, 17,* 191-192.

Cantor, N., & Mischel, W. (1979). Prototypes in person perception. In L. Berkowitz (Ed.), *Advances in experimental social psychology* (Vol. 12, pp. 4-52). New York: Academic Press.

Cohen, L. J., & Roth, S. (1987). The psychological aftermath of rape: Long-term effects and individual differences in recovery. *Journal of Social and Clinical Psychology, 5,* 525-534.

Deitz, S. R., & Byrnes, L. E. (1981). Attribution of responsibility for sexual assault: The influence of observer empathy and defendant occupation and attractiveness. *The Journal of Psychology, 108,* 17-29.

Eckes, T. (1986). Eine Prototypenstudie zur natürlichen Kategorisierung sozialer Situationen. *Zeitschrift für Differentielle und Diagnostische Psychologie, 7,* 145-161.

Feild, H. S. (1978). Attitudes toward rape: A comparative analysis of police, rapists, crisis counselors, and citizens. *Journal of Personality and Social Psychology, 36,* 156-179.

Feild, H. S., & Barnett, N. J. (1978). Simulated jury trials: Students vs. "real people" as jurors. *Journal of Social Psychology, 104,* 287-293.

Feild, H. S., & Bienen, L. B. (1980). *Jurors and rape.* Lexington, MA: Lexington Books.

Feldman-Summers, S., & Lindner, K. (1976). Perceptions of victims and defendants in criminal assault cases. *Criminal Justice and Behavior, 3,* 135-149.

Feldman-Summers, S., & Palmer, G. E. (1980). Rape as viewed by judges, prosecutors, and police officers. *Criminal Justice and Behavior, 7,* 19-40.

Gilmartin-Zena, P. (1983). Attribution theory and rape victim responsibility. *Deviant Behavior, 4,* 357-374.

Holmstrom, L. L., & Burgess, A. W. (1978). *The victim of rape: Institutional reactions.* New York: Wiley.

Howard, J. A. (1984). The "normal" victim: The effects of gender stereotypes on reactions to victims. *Social Psychology Quarterly, 47,* 270-281.

Jackson, S. (1978). The social context of rape: Sexual scripts and motivation. *Women's Studies International Quarterly, 1,* 27-38.

Jacobson, M. B. (1981). Effects of victim's and defendant's physical attractiveness on subjects' judgments in a rape case. *Sex Roles, 7,* 247-255.

Janoff-Bulman, R. (1979). Characterological versus behavioral blame: Inquiries into depression and rape. *Journal of Personality and Social Psychology, 37,* 1798-1809.

Jones, C., & Aronson, E. (1973). Attribution of fault to a rape victim as a function of respectability of the victim. *Journal of Personality and Social Psychology, 26*, 415-419.

Kahn, A., Gilbert, L. A., Latta, R. M., Deutsch, C., Hagen, R., Hill, M., McGaughey, T., Ryen, A. H., & Wilson, D. W. (1977). Attribution of fault to a rape victim as a function of respectability of the victim: A failure to replicate or extend. *Representative Research in Social Psychology, 8*, 98-197.

Kanekar, S., & Kolsawalla, M. B. (1977). Responsibility in relation to respectability. *Journal of Social Psychology, 102*, 183-188.

Katz, S., & Mazur, M. A. (1979). *Understanding the rape victim*. New York: Wiley.

Kerr, N. L., & Kurtz, S. T. (1977). Effects of a victim's suffering and respectability on mock juror judgments: Further evidence on the just world theory. *Representative Research in Social Psychology, 8*, 42-56.

Kilpatrick, D. G., Veronen, L. J., & Best, C. L. (1985). Factors predicting psychological distress among rape victims. In C. R. Figley (Ed.), *Trauma and its wake: The study and treatment of post-traumatic stress disorder* (pp. 113-141). New York: Brunner & Mazel.

Krahé, B. (1985). Verantwortungszuschreibungen in der sozialen Eindrucksbildung über Vergewaltigungsopfer und -täter. *Gruppendynamik, 16*, 169-178.

Krahé, B. (1988). Victim and observer characteristics as determinants of responsibility attributions to victims of rape. *Journal of Applied Social Psychology, 18*, 50-58.

Krahé, B. (in press). Police officers' definitions of rape: A prototype study. *Journal of Community and Applied Social Psychology, 1*.

LaFree, G. D. (1980). Variables affecting guilty pleas and convictions in rape cases: Toward a social theory of rape processing. *Social Forces, 58*, 833-850.

LaFree, G. D., Reskin, B. F., & Visher, C. A. (1985). Juror's responses to victims' behavior and legal issues in sexual assault trials. *Social Problems, 32*, 389-407.

L'Armand, K., & Pepitone, A. (1982). Judgments of rape: A study of victim-rapist relationship and victim sexual history. *Personality and Social Psychology Bulletin, 8*, 134-139.

LeDoux, J. C., & Hazelwood, R. R. (1985). Police attitudes and beliefs toward rape. *Journal of Police Science and Administration, 13*, 211-220.

Lerner, M. L. (1970). The desire for justice and reactions to victims. In L. Macaulay & L. Berkowitz (Eds.), *Altruism and helping behavior* (pp. 205-229). New York: Academic Press.

Luginbuhl, J., & Mullin, C. (1981). Rape and responsibility: How and how much is the victim blamed? *Sex Roles, 7*, 547-559.

Meyer, C. B., & Taylor, S. E. (1986). Adjustment to rape. *Journal of Personality and Social Psychology, 50*, 1226-1234.

Myers, M. B., Templer, D. I., & Brown, R. (1984). Coping ability of women who become victims of rape. *Journal of Consulting and Clinical Psychology, 52*, 73-78.

Quackenbush, R. L. (1989). A comparison of androgynous, masculine sex-typed, and undifferentiated males on dimensions of attitudes toward rape. *Journal of Research in Personality, 23*, 318-342.

Rose, V., & Randall, S. C. (1982). The impact of investigator perceptions of victim legitimacy on the processing of rape/sexual assault cases. *Symbolic Interaction, 5*, 23-36.

Smith, R. E., Keating, J. P., Hester, R. K., & Mitchell, H. E. (1976). Role and justice considerations in the attribution of responsibility to a rape victim. *Journal of Research in Personality, 10*, 346-357.

Thornton, B., Robbins, A., & Johnson, J. A. (1981). Social perception of the rape victim's culpability: The influence of respondents' personal-environmental causal attribution tendencies. *Human Relations, 35*, 225-237.

Thornton, B., & Ryckman, R. M. (1983). The influence of a rape victim's physical attractiveness on observers' attributions of responsibility. *Human Relations, 36*, 549-562.

Walsh, A. (1984). Gender-based differences: A study of probation officers' attitudes about, and recommendations for, felony sexual assault cases. *Criminology, 22*, 371-387.

Whiston, S. K. (1981). Counseling sexual assault victims: A loss model. *The Personnel and Guidance Journal*, *59*, 363-366.
Williams, J. E. (1984). Secondary victimization: Confronting public attitudes. *Victimology*, *9*, 66-81.
Williams, J. E., & Holmes, K. A. (1981). *The second assault: Rape and public attitudes*. Westport, CT: Greenwood Press.
Williams, L. S. (1984). The classic rape. When do victims report? *Social Problems*, *31*, 459-467.
Yarmey, A. D. (1985). Older and younger adults' attributions of responsibility toward rape victims and rapists. *Canadian Journal of Behavioural Science*, *17*, 327-328.

25 Negative Social Reactions to Victims: An Overview of Responses and Their Determinants

Tracy Bennett Herbert
Christine Dunkel-Schetter
University of California at Los Angeles

> A breast cancer patient finds that her daughter is not as accepting of her as she was prior to her cancer diagnosis. She feels like a stranger around her daughter.
>
> An AIDS patient is told by his sister that he isn't welcome to stay in her house, or even to eat there anymore.
>
> A childless woman dealing with infertility is advised by her husband's relatives that she should divorce him so he can have children with someone else.
>
> Three brothers test positive for HIV. After word spreads of their infection, their barber refuses to cut their hair, and their minister suggests that they stay away from Sunday church services. Eventually, the family's house is burned down.

These quotes do not represent hypothetical examples. They are real instances taken from newspaper articles, and interviews with victims of negative life events. The behavioral and emotional responses these quotes illustrate can be defined as negative social reactions to people who are suffering or distressed. Unfortunately, they are responses that occur reasonably frequently when someone experiences a negative life event. What prompts negative social reactions from network members? This chapter addresses this question.

Although the overriding tendency of people is to try to help or support others who are suffering, responses to victims are often also hurtful. The "victimization perspective" suggests that when negative life events occur, network members may have difficulty providing effective social support, and may therefore react in unhelpful and negative ways (e.g., Coates, Wortman, & Abbey, 1979; Dunkel-Schetter & Bennett, 1990; Dunkel-Schetter & Wortman, 1981, 1982; Silver, Wortman, & Crofton, 1990; Solomon, 1986; Wortman & Dunkel-Schetter, 1979;

Wortman & Lehman, 1985). The victimization perspective was first developed in social psychological research on innocent suffering (Lerner, 1971; Shaver, 1970; Walster, 1966; Wortman, 1976), and in research on cancer patients (Dunkel-Schetter & Wortman, 1982; Wortman & Dunkel-Schetter, 1979). Since then, it has become clear that other victimized populations also experience negative social reactions from network members, mixed together with supportive responses (e.g., Blasband, 1989; Cohen & Lichtenstein, 1990; Lehman, Ellard, & Wortman, 1986; Manne & Zautra, 1989). Wortman and colleagues have offered some reasons why negative or unhelpful responses might occur, including a social network member's feelings of vulnerability (Dunkel-Schetter & Wortman, 1981; Wortman & Dunkel-Schetter, 1979), uncertainty about how best to help (Wortman & Lehman, 1985), and misconceptions about how victims "typically" react to negative life events (Silver & Wortman, 1980). However, a complex set of circumstances operate for victims and their network members in the context of a negative event. In order to more clearly understand the social ramifications of life events, there is a need for greater precision in specifying both the social reactions of network members and the factors that are important determinants of them.

To this end, this chapter details several negative reactions that victims encounter, and describes the way victims also experience inconsistencies in social reactions. Then, based on the available empirical research and theoretical work, the determinants of these negative social reactions to victims are discussed. Literature from several different research traditions has been integrated, including psychological research on "victims" (e.g., rape victims, cancer patients, bereaved persons), the interdisciplinary social support literature, and the social-psychological helping literature. In addition, because victims of negative life events are often distressed or depressed as a result of their victimization, the research on social reactions to depressed people has been included where appropriate.

The use of the term "victim" may seem derogatory but this is not intended. It is used for convenience and for lack of a better term, and is meant to distinguish individuals for whom major negative life events occur from their social network members. Further, the term connotes some element of uncontrollability in the event, and that the event causes suffering or distress for the victim.

A TYPOLOGY OF SOCIAL REACTIONS TO VICTIMS

Many studies find that victims experience both positive and negative social reactions, often from the same network member (e.g., Blasband, 1989; Cohen & Lichtenstein, 1990; Dakof & Taylor, 1990; Dunkel-Schetter, 1984; Lehman et al., 1986; Manne & Zautra, 1989; Meyerowitz, Yarkin-Levin, & Harvey, 1990; Tempelaar et al., in press). In addition, studies find that the negative or stressful social interactions that occur with network members are important predictors of adjustment. For example, Rook (1984) found that in a sample of elderly widows, well-being was more strongly related to these women's perceptions that their privacy was invaded, that they were taken advantage of, that promises of help were broken, and that others consistently provoked conflict or anger, than to the amount of companionship or emotional support they received. Other studies, operationalizing negative social interactions in a variety of ways, have reported similar effects (Abbey, Abramis, & Caplan, 1985; Fiore, Becker, & Coppel, 1983; Pagel, Erdly, & Becker, 1987; Sandler & Barrera, 1984).

It is important then, to elucidate the negative reactions, as well as the positive ones, experienced by victims. Figure 25.1 depicts the categories of social reactions we have identified from the literature. Reactions frequently mentioned in the literature have been included, but the list may not be exhaustive. It should be noted that the likelihood of experiencing each of these reactions will probably vary with a number of factors, including the nature of the relationship between the victim and social network member (Dakof & Taylor, 1990; Dunkel-Schetter & Skokan, 1990).

In Figure 25.1, negative social reactions are distinguished from support attempts. Support attempts can be further distinguished in terms of those that are effective in leading the recipient to feel helped from those that are perceived as ineffective or unhelpful. Most studies investigating the frequency and type of effective support attempts find that victims report an overwhelming amount of helpful social support, with the most helpful kind being emotional support (e.g., Blasband, 1989; Dakof & Taylor, 1990; Dunkel-Schetter, 1984; Dunkel-Schetter, Blasband, Feinstein, & Herbert, in press; Lehman et al., 1986; Lichtman & Taylor, 1986). These studies, however, also find that many victims experience ineffective support attempts, including overprotection, overinvolvement (Coyne, Wortman, & Lehman, 1988), blocking open communication (Silver & Wortman, 1980; Wortman & Silver, 1987), and advice that conveys a negative attribution of the victim, including attributions of incompetence, blame, or failure (Dunkel-Schetter et al., in press). An example of the latter type of ineffective support attempt was provided by an AIDS patient whose friend attempted to cheer him up at a time when he was suicidal, by saying "Well, you just don't have a fighting spirit" (Blasband, 1989; for an in-depth discussion of ineffective support attempts, see Dunkel-Schetter et al., in press).

The distinction between negative reactions to victims and ineffective support attempts is a critical one. Ineffective support attempts might be viewed as behaviors that are altruistically motivated, but are not perceived by the recipient as helpful. Brickman et al. (1982) call this "secondary victimization," in the sense that victims are victimized a second time by awkward or ineffective efforts to help them. In contrast, egoistic (or self-serving) motivations probably underlie most negative reactions (Batson, O'Quin, Fultz, Vanderplas, & Isen, 1983). In the case of many negative responses, however, the underlying intent is not obvious and, therefore, must be imputed by the victim. For example, when network members block communication or the discussion of feelings around the event, it may be because they believe it is in the victim's best interests (i.e., altruistic motivation; Silver & Wortman, 1980; Wortman & Silver, 1987), or because the focus of discussion is too personally distressing (i.e., egoistic motivation; Gottlieb, in press). Social network member behaviors that could be perceived by victims as either negative reactions or ineffective support attempts (depending upon the intent the victim imputes) have been categorized in Figure 25.1 in terms of the way they are most frequently viewed in the literature. For example, blocked communication is usually considered an ineffective support attempt.

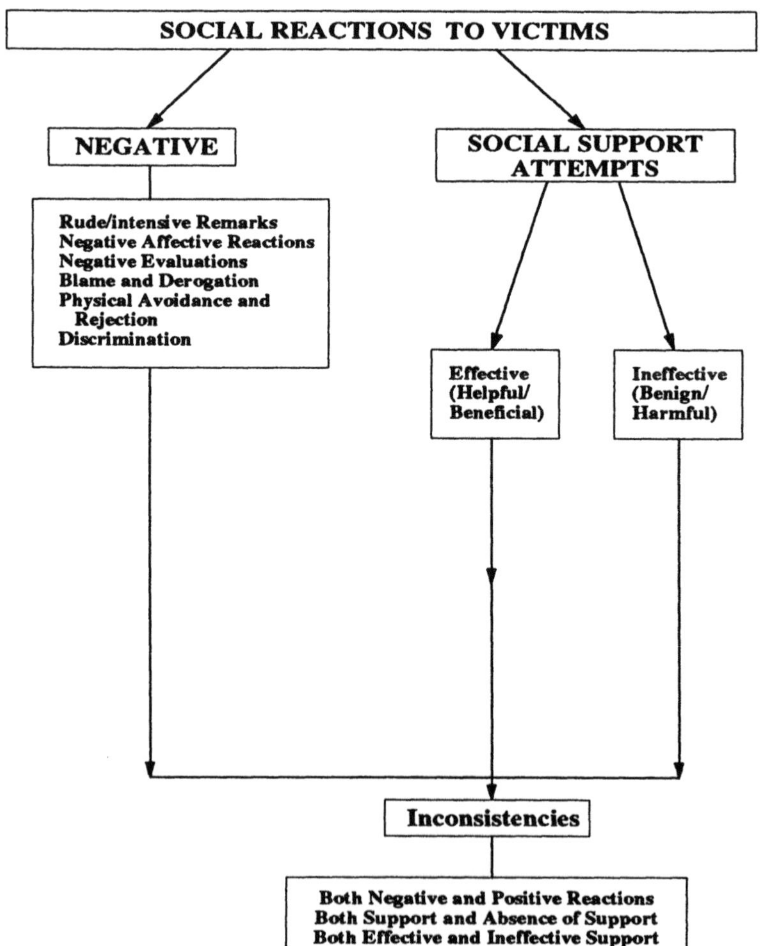

FIG. 25.1. A taxonomy of the possible negative and positive reactions of social network members to victims of negative life events.

Negative Social Reactions

Two types of research have been conducted to investigate negative social reactions to victims: (a) simulation and laboratory studies (e.g., Coates et al., 1979; Coyne, 1976a; Dunkel-Schetter, Silver, & Wortman, 1988; Lerner, 1971; Silver et al., 1990; Weiner, Perry, & Magnusson, 1988), and (b) studies that conduct in-depth interviews to gather information about the negative interactions victims report (e.g., Blasband, 1989; Dakof & Taylor, 1990; Dunkel-Schetter, 1984; Gottlieb, 1978; Lehman et al., 1986; Meyerowitz et al., 1990). Figure 25.1 depicts the six categories of negative social reactions that were extracted from these two paradigms:

1. Rude or insensitive remarks.
2. Negative affective reactions.
3. Negative evaluations.
4. Victim blame and derogation.
5. Physical avoidance and rejection.
6. Discrimination.

Rude, insensitive, and inappropriate remarks of others are one common type of negative social reaction. For example, the cancer patients interviewed by Dunkel-Schetter (1984) reported being upset by being asked about "what their chances were," or whether the cancer was "all out." Rude or insensitive remarks are also common among the bereaved (Lehman et al., 1986) and AIDS patients (Blasband, 1989). For example, one AIDS patient told of a friend asking "What are you going to do when you die? What's gonna happen with your stuff?" Another AIDS patient reported, "One friend said—'What are you doing out? You're tainted'—He was joking but it hurt."

A second common negative social response involves the negative affective reactions of others, which might occur either in response to the victim or in response to the victim's circumstances. For example, an AIDS patient reported that "A friend seemed angry, almost as if I betrayed her" (Blasband, 1989), while a cancer patient interviewed by Dunkel-Schetter (1984) said that "my sister-in-law cried and cried, as if I were dead already." In laboratory studies, negative affective reactions have been operationalized as the mood of subjects following interactions with depressed versus nondepressed partners. Subjects are often found to be significantly more depressed, anxious, and hostile following an interaction with a depressed partner than with a nondepressed partner (Gurtman, 1986).

Third, following interactions with victims, others also often evaluate them negatively. This is illustrated most clearly by laboratory studies where subjects' perceptions of victims are assessed on typical person perception measures following an interaction (e.g., Coates et al., 1979; Coyne, 1976a; Dunkel-Schetter et al., 1988; Silver et al., 1990; Strack & Coyne, 1983). For example, Strack and Coyne (1983) found that following an interaction with depressed persons, subjects rated them more negatively on a variety of dimensions. They were seen as more unpleasant, bad, uncomfortable, weak, cold, unattractive, passive, and unfriendly than nondepressed interaction partners.

Fourth, victims often report blaming or derogating remarks from network members. A typical remark is one that implicitly blames the victim for the occurrence of the event, and is illustrated by a person whose children were tragically killed saying, "[someone called] my wife an unfit mother for letting them [the children] go away with their aunt" (Lehman et al., 1986, p. 446). Two responses from AIDS patients to questions about unhelpful interactions (Blasband, 1989) also illustrate this phenomenon: "Family saying it was my just reward. Mom said it's my behavior that caused it," and "When I told my sister about having AIDS, I got a lecture about drugs, what I'm doing to myself, that I didn't have anyone to blame but myself. On one recent visit, she didn't want to see me."

This last example also illustrates a fifth set of negative behaviors—the physical avoidance and rejection by social network members that victims report experiencing. This type of negative reaction is not uncommon. For example, in the 40 AIDS patients he interviewed, Blasband (1989) found that 25% of the men reported physical avoidance by friends and family. Further, in the sample of cancer patients that Meyerowitz et al. (1990, Study 2) interviewed, 27% reported physical avoidance by family or friends following their diagnosis, while 43% reported that their family or friends withdrew emotionally. In one extreme case, a patient's spouse left him when she learned of the diagnosis. In another sample of female cancer patients, 17% reported that their daughters became emotionally withdrawn, hostile, or rejecting following their diagnosis (Lichtman et al., 1985). In laboratory studies, physical avoidance and rejection of victims has also been found, but has been operationalized in terms of a lack of willingness to interact with the victim in the future (e.g., Coyne, 1976a; Dunkel-Schetter et al., 1988; Sacco & Dunn, 1990; Silver et al., 1990).

Finally, an extreme negative social reaction that victims report is outright discrimination. Two examples from AIDS patients (Blasband, 1989) illustrate this phenomenon: "I lost my job ... He [boss] said, 'I can't have you around here. You'd be a detriment if customers found out you have AIDS,'" and "Our landlord kicked us out. 'You're sick. I want you out of my house.' He gave us an eviction notice and screwed us out of $500."

Inconsistencies in Social Reactions

In addition to negative reactions, three kinds of inconsistencies in network member behaviors have been noted in the past (e.g., Coates & Wortman, 1980; Coyne, 1976b; Dunkel-Schetter & Wortman, 1981, 1982; Heller, 1979; Sacco & Dunn, 1990; Shinn, Lehman, & Wong, 1984; Shumaker & Brownell, 1984; Strack & Coyne, 1983; Suls, 1982). Because victims typically interact with network members on multiple occasions, it provides the opportunity for them to react in a variety of different ways. Over time, as stress persists, the likelihood of network member behavioral and emotional inconsistencies increases (Dunkel-Schetter & Bennett, 1990; Dunkel-Schetter & Wortman, 1982). These inconsistencies in network member reactions may be especially difficult for victims to deal with because they leave them uncertain and confused about what to expect from others, and about how they might best elicit the supportive responses they desire. Inconsistencies might be especially likely to come from family members or intimates, since these are the people who have the most sustained contact with victims.

The three types of inconsistent network member reactions are outlined in Figure 25.1: (a) mixed positive and negative reactions; (b) alternating support and an absence of support; and (c) a combination of effective and ineffective support attempts. For example, a cancer patient whose daughter said "Does your arm hurt, mother? Well, don't tell me if it does" (Dunkel-Schetter & Wortman, 1982) illustrates a person being supportive to a victim one moment and rejecting the next. Discrepancies may also occur between behaviors in different situations and at different times (Dunkel-Schetter & Wortman, 1982), as, for example, a friend who provides a great deal of attention to a victim immediately following an event, but subsequently does not visit or call at all. There may also be discrepancies between a person's expressed intentions and their subsequent behaviors (Dunkel-Schetter & Wortman, 1982). For example, people may promise to call or visit but then fail to fulfill these promises. Finally, an example of the combination of providing emotional support but blocking open communication is provided by the husband of a breast cancer patient who said "I've always kind of played [the cancer] down, rather than to get into any involved conversations over it. I let her know that I consider that it could be serious, but that I'm sure she'll come out of it all right" (Lichtman, 1982).

Summary

The overview of negative social responses presented above is the product of an integration of two relatively extensive and disparate literatures: simulation and laboratory studies, and studies that conduct in-depth interviews to gather information about the negative interactions victims report. Six types of negative social reactions were distinguished and illustrated, including rude or insensitive remarks, negative affective reactions, negative evaluations, victim blame and derogation, physical avoidance and rejection, and discrimination. In the remainder of this chapter, possible determinants of these negative social reactions are discussed.

DETERMINANTS OF NEGATIVE SOCIAL REACTIONS TO VICTIMS

A variety of factors might determine whether social network members respond negatively to victims. The factors investigated thus far include characteristics of the victim, characteristics of the social network member, and the mere presence or occurrence of a victim status.

Victim Factors

Two factors specific to victims have been shown to lead to different sorts of social reactions. Specifically, displays of victim distress and victim coping attempts have been separately related to the occurrence of negative social reactions.

Victim Distress

There is considerable evidence that negative social reactions are elicited by a person displaying depressed affect. This line of research began with Coyne (1976a, 1976b), who randomly assigned students to have a brief telephone conversation with either a depressed or nondepressed partner. In these brief encounters, reactions to clinically depressed persons were more negative in a variety of ways, including derogation, negative evaluations, and affective reactions.

Since this early research, many studies have been conducted which suggest that depressed persons are likely to be rejected by others (e.g., Boswell & Murray, 1981; Hammen & Peters, 1978; Robbins, Strack, & Coyne, 1979; Sacco & Dunn, 1990; Strack & Coyne, 1983; Winer, Bonner, Blaney, & Murray, 1981). Measures of rejection have included unfavorable perceptions, unwillingness to interact in the future, and blame. Gurtman (1986), in a review summarizing the findings of these studies, concluded that the rejection of depressed persons is consistent across the different types of dependent measures (e.g., questionnaire or behavioral), subtle variations in target characteristics (e.g., clinical in- or out-patient, student, confederate, hypothetical), and method of exposure to the depressed person (e.g., taped interview, telephone conversation, face-to-face interaction, transcript or recorded description).

Other studies suggest, however, that negative responses are not only elicited by depression. Simply expressing negative affect as a result of one's life circumstances also elicits negative social reactions. For example, one study (Coates et al., 1979) found that rape victims who expressed negative affect over a rape that had occurred six months previously were rated as significantly less attractive and experienced more derogation and rejection than victims who expressed positive affect. Another study (Winer et al., 1981) also found that individuals expressing negative affect like sad mood, pessimism, and feelings of helplessness following two different negative life events (rejection from law school or a relationship breakup), were rated as less attractive and experienced more rejection than those who did not express these negative feelings.

Dunkel-Schetter et al. (1988) conducted a telephone interaction study modeled closely after Coyne's (1976a) study. In this study, depressed or nondepressed college students spoke with other nondepressed college students over the telephone. The results of the study indicated that perceiving any deviant or depressive behavior in one's interaction partner was associated with consistently more negative reactions. Specifically, perceiving that one's interaction partner was experiencing difficulties, dwelling on the negative aspects of his or her situation, or was exhibiting a high self-focus, led to less willingness to interact in the future, less favorable impressions, more negative feelings during the call, and more anger and depression afterwards. These findings were intriguing in that it was not specifically the "depressed" interaction partners who elicited these negative reactions, but *any* caller who appeared distressed. Thus, nondepressed college students who exhibited any deviant affective behavior experienced negative social reactions as a result.

Finally, a recent study (Silver et al., 1990) manipulated how well actual female cancer patients appeared to have adjusted to their illness and investigated the responses of others interacting with them. The patients either communicated no information about the distress they currently experienced over their cancer, that they experienced little distress, that they experienced a great deal of distress, or that there were times when they felt distressed and other times when they did not. Silver et al. (1990) labeled these conditions "no-information about coping," "good coping," "poor coping," and "balanced coping," respectively. In addition, a healthy comparison condition was included. Responses of the interaction partners were assessed in a variety of ways, including behavioral, nonverbal, and written assessments. Results suggested that relative to the targets who presented themselves as "good" or "balanced copers," subjects reported significantly less attraction toward the "poor coper," sat further away from her during the interaction, reported more distress following the interaction, and expressed less willingness to interact with her in the future. In addition, more nonverbal signs of discomfort were seen in subjects who interacted with cancer patients who communicated a great deal of distress. Thus, the rejection of victims showing difficulty in adjustment was multifaceted and included behavioral avoidance, nonverbal signals of discomfort, and negative evaluations.

A provocative implication of the results of Silver et al. (1990) is that even victims who communicate no distress about their circumstances may be targets of negative social reactions. In particular, cancer patients who communicated little distress elicited more nonverbal signs of discomfort during the interaction than did those who portrayed a more balanced picture, and subjects expressed significantly less interest in future contact with these "good copers." It appears then that victims who display either too little or too much distress as a result of their circumstances are likely to elicit negative reactions from others. Silver et al. (1990) suggest that those who interact with victims displaying too little distress may believe that the victim is simply concealing their distress. Thus, subjects' lack of interest in future contact might be a result of wanting to avoid the distress that they expect would be revealed in future encounters.

Victim Coping Behavior

Evidence has accumulated for the link between the specific coping behaviors of victims and the subsequent negative social responses they experience. Schwarzer and Weiner (in press) recently completed a study that manipulated the apparent coping behavior of victims, and assessed subjects' reactions to them. Specifically, Schwarzer and Weiner used a within-subjects Latin Square design, where each subject received four versions of scenarios depicting an individual who had experienced one of eight stigmatizing events: cancer, AIDS, drug abuse, coronary heart disease, anorexia, depression, obesity, or child abuse. Coping behavior was manipulated by describing the victim as either engaging in situation-specific problem solving behaviors or failing to do so. Responsibility for the onset of the event was also manipulated, by describing the victim as having had control over the cause of the problem, or as having been an innocent victim. Results suggested that both more onset responsibility and less active coping efforts on the part of the victim were related to negative social reactions, but that coping behavior was more strongly related. Specifically, victims portrayed as actively coping with the event were blamed less, were attributed a better chance of improvement, and were less stressful for others socially.

One specific coping behavior that victims might employ to decrease their experience of negative social reactions is to alter their social interactions to avoid the negative reactions. They might do this by withdrawing from social interaction, by not revealing their victim status, or by avoiding mentioning their circumstances around those who are already aware of them. There is some suggestive empirical evidence that supports this, although we could find no direct empirical support. For example, Brewin, MacCarthy, and Furnham (1989) investigated whether victims' perceptions and use of the social support available to them when negative outcomes occur were influenced by their appraisal of those outcomes. They found that victims who thought the event was more likely to happen to them than to others, who blamed their own inadequacies, and who attributed the outcome to global factors, were more likely to have withdrawn socially. Brewin et al. (1989) speculated that the reason for victims' social withdrawal was to avoid the negative social reactions they expected, due to the belief that their victim status would be stigmatized by others.

Descriptive studies also support the notion that victims construct their social experiences so as to avoid negative social reactions. For example, Gottlieb (in press) has noted that many of the parents of children with cystic fibrosis and juvenile diabetes whom he interviewed reported monitoring the level of distress they displayed to their spouse in order to avoid marital conflict over their child's illness.

Meyerowitz et al. (1990, Study 2) also found that while only 13% of the cancer patients they interviewed reported no changes in their close relationships following the diagnosis of their cancer, all of these subjects had attempted to conceal their diagnosis whenever possible, and had avoided any reference to "cancer." AIDS patients also protect themselves from rejecting social experiences, but they seem to do this by avoiding contact with those whom they believe will respond negatively to their circumstances (Blasband, Dunkel-Schetter, & Herbert, 1990). Finally, victims may attempt to avoid negative social responses when they believe that the cause of the event will be perceived as arising from involvement in an activity that network members did not approve of in the first place (Gottlieb, in press; Pearlin & McCall, in press). Thus, depending on the nature of the event itself, victims may anticipate more or less criticism, hostility, and rejection from social network members, which may affect the likelihood of their engaging in interactions that acknowledge or center around their victim status.

Social Network Member Factors

In this section, characteristics of social network members that might determine whether they respond to victims in a negative fashion are discussed. The factors addressed include network members' needs to reduce feelings of vulnerability regarding the possibility that victimizing events will happen to them, attributions made by network members regarding the cause of the event, the specific affect induced in network members as a result of the victim's plight, and network members' feelings of helplessness and frustration.

Social Network Member Needs/Beliefs and Vulnerability

Early research and theory in social psychology considered reactions to victimization and suffering, and found that, generally, innocent victims are subjected to derogation and blame by others (Lerner, 1971; Walster, 1966; Wortman, 1976). Three lines of reasoning were put forth to account for these seemingly undeserved negative social reactions. First, Walster (1966) suggested that persons' assignment of blame for a negative event will be affected by their desire to avoid the frightening thought of their own victimization. Further, she proposed that derogation and blame of innocent victims would be more likely with increasing severity of the consequences of the event, and when the outcome of the event is personally threatening. There is some empirical evidence to support this assertion (Chaiken & Darley, 1973). The exception seems to be the case where a person feels highly similar to a victim, and realizes the strong possibility that the negative event could happen to them. In these cases, "defensive attributions" seem to be more likely (Shaver, 1970). That is, people appear motivated to avoid blaming and derogating victims because they would not want to be blamed or derogated if the event should happen to them.

Lerner and colleagues have offered a second account for the undeserved derogation and blaming of innocent victims (Lerner, 1971; Lerner, Miller, & Holmes, 1976). Lerner argues that people have a need to believe in a "just world" in which people "get what they deserve and deserve what they get." If we can believe that people do not suffer unless something is wrong with them or their behavior, we will feel protected from undeserved suffering ourselves, and our feelings of vulnerability to similar fates should be reduced. There is empirical evidence that supports the notion that the need to believe in a just world is related to the derogation and blaming of innocent victims (Lerner, 1971; Lerner & Matthews, 1967; Lerner & Simmons, 1966). In addition, recent evidence (Montada, this volume; Montada & Schneider, 1990) also suggests that blaming victims may be functional for preserving the belief in a just world because if victims are held responsible for their plight, the issue of justice is simply not raised.

Finally, in an attempt to integrate both Walster's (1966) and Lerner's (1971) formulations, Wortman (1976) has suggested that our needs for predictability and control are important mediators of our tendency to respond in a negative fashion to victims. Specifically, if we are able to derogate and blame innocent victims, we will feel more able to control the future occurrence of negative events in our own lives, and hence, our own suffering and distress. Moreover, if we can blame and derogate victims for the occurrence of negative events, our own assumptions about the world as a predictable and orderly place will not be threatened (Wortman, 1976).

Social Network Member Attributions About Event

Weiner and colleagues have employed an attributional framework to investigate the effects of others' attributions about the ability of victims to control the onset of the event or condition, on subsequent negative and positive reactions (see Weiner, 1985, for a review). Negative reactions in this research paradigm have been operationally defined as unwillingness to help victims, whereas positive reactions have been operationalized as willingness to give help, charity, or social support. This program of research has repeatedly replicated one particular pattern of findings. Specifically, results suggest that stigmas perceived as onset-uncontrollable elicit pity and greater willingness to help, while those perceived as onset-controllable elicit anger and less willingness to help (e.g., Betancourt, 1983; Reisenzein, 1986; Schmidt & Weiner, 1988; Weiner, 1980a, 1980b; Weiner et al., 1988). In addition, in the Schwarzer and Weiner (in press) study described earlier, individuals seen as responsible for the onset of stigmatizing conditions received less pity, were perceived as more socially disruptive, and were blamed more. Thus, if actual interaction with these victims occurred, more negative social reactions would be a likely result.

Social Network Member Affect

Attributions about the controllability of events or stigmatizing conditions also elicit particular affective reactions in others. In fact, the pattern of results in a number of studies, some employing structural equation modeling, has strongly supported Weiner's hypothesized motivational attribution-affect-helping pathway (see Weiner, 1985). Specifically, the consistent finding in studies investigating the influence of the affect elicited by victims is that controllable events give rise to anger, which in turn, evokes unwillingness to help, whereas uncontrollable events give rise to pity, which in turn, evokes help-giving (Betancourt, 1983; Reisenzein, 1986; Schmidt & Weiner, 1988; Weiner, 1980a, 1980b; Weiner et al., 1988). Moreover, when the onset of events is perceived as uncontrollable, but the alleviation of suffering is perceived as within the control of individuals (e.g., through coping efforts), anger and unwillingness to help are elicited if victims do nothing to help themselves, whereas pity and helping are elicited if victims are actively coping (Schwarzer & Weiner, in press). Thus, attributions about both the origin of the victim's problem and its solution (Brickman et al., 1982) appear to be important determinants of the affective response, and hence the negative social reactions of others.

One recent study took a slightly different slant and helps to elucidate the ways in which inconsistent (i.e., both positive and negative) reactions to victims may develop. Specifically, Sacco and Dunn (1990) investigated the ways in which others differentially explain the successes and failures of hypothetically depressed and nondepressed people, and how these attributions relate to affective and behavioral reactions following a request for help. Their results suggested that others attribute more internality, stability, globality, and controllability to depressed than nondepressed people for failures, whereas more external, unstable, specific, and uncontrollable attributions are made for successes of depressed versus nondepressed persons. As a result of these attributions, high degrees of both anger and concern were elicited by the depressed person following a request for help. Behavioral responses to the request for help were determined by the affective reactions elicited by the attributions, but depended on the specific dimension assessed. That is, no differences were found in terms of willingness to help the depressed versus nondepressed person, probably because anger and concern are conflicting emotions. However, desire for future contact was significantly less for depressed than for nondepressed targets. Therefore, a depressed person may experience confusion regarding others' true reactions: Others are willing to help a depressed person when help is requested, but are also likely to avoid future contact.

Social Network Member Feelings of Helplessness and Frustration

Wortman and colleagues (Dunkel-Schetter & Wortman, 1981, 1982; Wortman & Dunkel-Schetter, 1979; Wortman & Lehman, 1985) have discussed the importance of helplessness and frustration in network members with respect to negative social reactions to victims. In particular, they have hypothesized that if the objective characteristics of a situation or the displays of victim distress are overwhelming to potential support providers, the resulting social responses are likely to be negative. Although there is not a substantial amount of direct empirical evidence for these assertions, three studies help to illustrate the effects of network members' feelings of helplessness and frustration on negative reactions to victims.

First, in the Dunkel-Schetter et al. (1988) study described earlier, the results suggested that the more subjects perceived their telephone interaction partner to be deviant, the greater the feelings of helplessness they experienced. Feelings of helplessness, in turn, were associated with less willingness to interact with the target in the future, forming a less favorable impression of the target, and experiencing more negative feelings during the interaction.

The second study used transcripts to simulate interactions with depressed people in a two-trial design (Winer et al., 1981). On the first trial, these researchers replicated the findings that negative reactions to depressed people occur. In the second trial, Winer et al. (1981) demonstrated that this effect was enhanced by the lack of improvement in the depression displayed by the target. Specifically, if the target did not show improvement from the first to second exposure, more rejection was seen.

In the third study, Notarius and Herrick (1988) examined the association between a helper's response style and her affective reactions following a face-to-face interaction with a depressed confederate. They found that helpers who acknowledged their depressed partner's mood and relied on supportive listening techniques (e.g., expressions of empathy, encouragement), were significantly less depressed themselves after the interaction than helpers who relied on providing advice, idle conversation, or distracting the confederate from focusing on the dysphoric mood by joking. In addition, they found that the latter helpers were significantly less willing to engage in future interaction with the depressed confederate. Notarius and Herrick (1988) suggested that the depressed mood and rejection by these helpers may have arisen from a sense of helplessness at the task of alleviating another person's depressed mood, and that the unwillingness to engage in future interaction may have been a result of a desire to avoid a social situation in which they would feel helpless (Notarius & Herrick, 1988). Thus, those who were invested in alleviating their partner's distress apparently felt helpless after their failure to have an effect, and thus, more rejecting of the prospect of future interaction.

The helplessness and frustration of the potential helpers in the Notarius and Herrick (1988) study is reminiscent of the argument of Coyne et al. (1988) regarding the overinvolvement of network members. Specifically, Coyne et al. (1988) argue that when network members are highly invested in the victim's outcome, they become intrusive and demanding, and later, critical and hostile. These negative reactions occur, in part, because continued displays of distress by the victim come to be interpreted as signs that support is inadequate, leaving the network member feeling helpless and frustrated.

Mere Presence or Occurrence of Victim Status

There are a handful of studies that suggest that the victim and social network member factors we have discussed contribute to negative social reactions, but are not necessary to elicit them. For example, in those studies investigating the responses of others to depressed persons, some have found evidence of rejection in the absence of any measurable affective effects on the interaction partners (e.g., Gotlib & Robinson, 1982; Howes & Hokanson, 1979). In these studies, it appears that something about the direct exposure to depressed persons itself led to the rejection from others (Gurtman, 1986).

Other studies also suggest that the mere presence or occurrence of a victim status is sufficient to lead to negative reactions. For example, two aspects of the Silver et al. (1990) study described earlier indicated that mere exposure to cancer patients resulted in negative social reactions. First, interaction partners of cancer patients communicating no information about the distress they were experiencing over their cancer demonstrated significant behavioral avoidance and expressed little willingness to engage in future interaction with them, indicating that it was not the communication of distress per se that was solely responsible for eliciting negative reactions. Second, Silver et al. (1990) found that even when cancer patients said they were not distressed or presented a balanced picture, they elicited significantly more discomfort, distress, and avoidance in interaction partners than did confederates who portrayed a healthy person.

Meyerowitz et al. (1990, Study 1) also found that interactions with apparent cancer patients were more negative than interactions with apparently healthy individuals, but these results were more subtle. In this study, subjects had a conversation with a confederate who was described to some of them as a cancer patient. The results suggested that there were no differences on the behavioral measures or subject self-reports of reactions to the conversations (i.e., comfort, concern, liking) between the conditions. Differences did occur, however, on the confederate and observer ratings of the positivity of the conversation, which indicated that subjects who believed they were speaking with a cancer patient were more negative in tone during their interactions. What is most intriguing about these results is that neither the confederate nor observers could pinpoint the exact qualities of the interactions that had been different. On the basis of further exploratory analyses, Meyerowitz et al. (1990, Study 1) found that these subjects reported conflicting reactions around the interaction. For example, they reported being simultaneously comfortable and anxious during the conversation. Meyerowitz et al. (1990, Study 1) concluded that these conflicting reactions led to a display of subtle nonverbal differences in the interactions with cancer patients.

An exception to those studies that find that the mere presence or occurrence of a victim status is sufficient to elicit negative social reactions is Winer et al. (1981). The results of this study showed that it was the victim's depression, and not the occurrence of an event, that led to negative responses. However, the two events utilized in this study were a relationship break-up and nonadmittance to law school, which may be less likely to cause discomfort in subjects than events like depression, cancer, or AIDS. Therefore, mounting evidence suggests that in many cases the mere occurrence or presence of a victim status is sufficient to elicit negative social reactions, and that this might be due to the discomfort aroused when interacting with a victim of a negative event.

SUMMARY AND CONCLUSIONS

This chapter grew out of earlier work on the victimization perspective which suggested generally that network members often respond in unhelpful and negative ways to victims of life events. We distinguished ineffective support attempts from the negative responses of network members, and integrated several bodies of research in order to elucidate the determinants of negative social reactions. The negative reactions identified include rude or insensitive remarks, negative affective reactions, negative evaluations, victim blame and derogation, physical avoidance and rejection, and discrimination. The determinants of negative reactions, including both victim and social network member factors, were discussed, as was the possibility that the mere presence or occurrence of a victim status is sufficient to elicit negative social responses. Overall, it appears that victims who are distressed, who are not actively coping with their situation, who appear to be responsible for the occurrence of the condition, and whose situation leads to feelings of helplessness and frustration in others, are most likely to elicit negative social reactions.

Undoubtedly, other determinants of negative social reactions to victims exist, but they have yet to be addressed empirically. Two such determinants are the nature of the relationship between the victim and network member, and the type of victimization that has occurred. It was noted earlier that the likelihood of experiencing negative reactions will probably vary with the nature of the relationship between the victim and network member (Dakof & Taylor, 1990; Dunkel-Schetter & Skokan, 1990). One might argue, for example, that victims would be more likely to elicit negative reactions from strangers or acquaintances than they would from more intimate ties. This makes sense intuitively, however, some of the research that was discussed suggests that close ties may be just as likely to respond in a negative fashion. For example, Lichtman et al. (1985) found that the daughters of breast cancer patients were the people most likely to react negatively to the cancer diagnosis. In addition, Winer et al. (1981) found that rejection of depressed persons was greatest when they did not improve over time, and close ties are likely to be those who witness this lack of improvement. Moreover, close ties may be more likely to feel helpless and frustrated by an apparent lack of improvement on the part of the victim (Dunkel-Schetter & Wortman, 1982).

Gottlieb (in press) has argued that network members may sometimes respond in a negative fashion in order to serve their own emotional needs. For example, if network members experience a great deal of distress over the victimizing event themselves, negative responses such as physical avoidance may be a way to minimize their own distress. Earlier we suggested that in most cases, egoistic or self-serving motivations might underlie negative social reactions, whereas positive social reactions are probably altruistically motivated (Batson et al., 1983). Montada (this volume) suggests that altruistic motivations might be elicited when victims are perceived as suffering an undeserved fate or harm. Furthermore, Betancourt (1990) recently showed in the context of altruistically motivated behavior, that perceived controllability for specific events significantly diminished when a helper approached the situation from an empathic rather than an "objective" perspective. Thus, the degree of empathy network members have may affect the attributions they make for the cause of the event, which may determine their initial motivation to help, which may then determine their responses to victims. The conditions under which network members will be empathic, or will hold egoistic versus altruistic motivations are fascinating areas for further empirical work, as are the relationships of these variables to subsequent social responses to victims.

The type of victimizing event might also determine the extent to which network members respond in a negative fashion. One distinction that Dunkel-Schetter and colleagues have made with respect to support provision and whether support attempts are perceived as helpful or ineffective, is between threat/loss and challenge events (Dunkel-Schetter et al., in press; Dunkel-Schetter & Skokan, 1990). For example, behaviors reported to be particularly unhelpful in threat/loss situations (e.g., cancer, AIDS, bereavement) are minimization or trivialization of the event, and closing off communication about the event. In contrast, with certain challenge events (e.g., a diabetic's adherence to their strict dietary regimen), talking *too much* about the situation is often viewed as particularly unhelpful (Dunkel-Schetter et al., in press). In addition to this distinction, the specific event may be an important determinant of negative reactions because people have varying degrees of past exposure to various events (Dunkel-Schetter & Skokan, 1990).

Other authors have also distinguished between types of events (e.g., Cutrona & Russell, 1990; Weiner et al., 1988). For example, Weiner et al. (1988) have differentiated events that are "physically" versus "mentally behaviorally" based, and have found that those perceived as physically based (e.g., blindness, paraplegia, Alzheimer's disease, cancer) elicit more positive social reactions, whereas those perceived as mentally behaviorally based (e.g., obesity, drug addiction) elicit more negative social reactions.

An even more refined listing of the characteristics of events is provided by Jones et al. (1984), who discuss six characteristics of stigmas, and the different sorts of effects they may have on those interacting with them: concealability (e.g., is the stigma hidden or obvious?); course (e.g., does the course change over time and what is its ultimate outcome?); disruptiveness (in terms of social interaction and communication); aesthetic qualities (e.g., how repellent, ugly, upsetting is it?); origin (e.g., under what circumstances did it originate? Who was responsible?); and peril (e.g., what kind of danger does the stigma present, how imminent and serious is the threat?).

In light of these characteristics, the diagnosis of AIDS is an especially complex and devastating event. It combines the most unfavorable of these stigma qualities, including the fact that it is an infectious life-threatening illness that is usually associated with either a homosexual lifestyle or intravenous drug use, two dimensions to which many individuals respond negatively (Herek & Glunt, 1988). One study has found, in fact, that the association of AIDS with the homosexual lifestyle is an important predictor of negative social reactions, more important than the fear of contracting the disease (Pryor, Reeder, Vinacco, & Kott, 1989). Another study (Montada & Figura, 1990) found that the tendency to socially isolate AIDS victims was associated with the perceived risk of casual contact and the extent to which they were blamed for their victim status. These two factors, however, were highly related to social prejudices against groups at risk for AIDS. Thus, the diagnosis of AIDS carries with it a number of symbolic issues to which others might respond negatively. This might be why Weiner et al. (1988) found that the stigma of AIDS did not fit neatly into either of their physically based or mentally-behaviorally based categories.

A more general theoretical point might be made in closing. While this chapter has focused on negative social reactions to victims of life events, many of the reactions, as well as their determinants, have been discussed in terms of the stigmatized (Goffman, 1963), the deviant (Freedman & Doob, 1968), the marked (Jones et al., 1984), and those who are targets of prejudice and discrimination (see Crosby, Bromley, & Saxe, 1980). Therefore, our attempt to examine determinants of negative social reactions to victims may actually extend more broadly. A task of future research, then, is to determine the degree of overlap of victimizing negative events with these other conditions, and ideally, to find a better term than "victims" to refer to people in various kinds of unfortunate circumstances.

We are all disadvantaged in one way or another, at some time, or in some way, be it physically, emotionally, socially, or because of our history or current circumstances. Thus, most of us have been the targets of negative social reactions of some kind. It is our belief that the processes described herein are broad and far-reaching. In this sense, it is exciting to begin to explicate the specific features of negative social reactions to misfortune and their determinants.

REFERENCES

Abbey, A., Abramis, D. J., & Caplan, R. D. (1985). Effects of different sources of social support and social conflict on emotional well-being. *Basic and Applied Social Psychology, 6*(2), 111-129.

Batson, C. D., O'Quin, K., Fultz, J., Vanderplas, M., & Isen, A. M. (1983). Influence of self-reported distress and empathy on egoistic versus altruistic motivation to help. *Journal of Personality and Social Psychology, 45*, 706-718.

Betancourt, H. (1983). *Causal attributions, empathy, and emotions as determinants of helping behavior: An integrative approach.* Unpublished doctoral dissertation, University of California, Los Angeles.

Betancourt, H. (1990). An attribution-empathy model of helping behavior: Behavioral intentions and judgements of help-giving. *Personality and Social Psychology Bulletin, 16*, 573-591.

Blasband, D. E. (1989). *Social support, rejection, stress, and coping among gay men with AIDS.* Unpublished doctoral dissertation, University of California, Los Angeles.

Blasband, D. E., Dunkel-Schetter, C., & Herbert, T. B. (1990). *The social experiences of gay men with AIDS.* Unpublished manuscript.

Boswell, P. C., & Murray, E. J. (1981). Depression, schizophrenia, and social attraction. *Journal of Consulting and Clinical Psychology, 49*, 641-647.

Brewin, C. R., MacCarthy, B., & Furnham, A. (1989). Social support in the face of adversity: The role of cognitive appraisal. *Journal of Research in Personality, 23*, 354-372.

Brickman, P., Rabinowitz, V. C., Karuza, J., Coates, D., Cohn, E., & Kidder, L. (1982). Models of helping and coping. *American Psychologist, 37*, 368-384.

Chaiken, A. L., & Darley, J. M. (1973). Victim or perpetrator? Defensive attribution of responsibility and the need for order and justice. *Journal of Personality and Social Psychology, 25*, 268-275.

Coates, D., & Wortman, C. B. (1980). Depressive maintenance and interpersonal control. In A. Baum & J. Singer (Eds.), *Advances in environmental psychology* (Vol. 2, pp. 149-182). Hillsdale, NJ: Erlbaum.

Coates, D., Wortman, C. B., & Abbey, A. (1979). Reactions to victims. In I. H. Frieze, D. Bar-Tal, & J. S. Carrol (Eds.), *New approaches to social problems* (pp. 21-52). San Francisco: Jossey-Bass.

Cohen, S., & Lichtenstein, E. (1990). Partner behaviors that support quitting smoking. *Journal of Consulting and Clinical Psychology, 58*, 304-309.

Coyne, J. C. (1976a). Depression and the response of others. *Journal of Abnormal Psychology, 85*, 186-193.

Coyne, J. C. (1976b). Toward an interactional description of depression. *Psychiatry, 39*, 28-40.

Coyne, J. C., Wortman, C. B., & Lehman, D. R. (1988). The other side of support: Emotional overinvolvement and miscarried helping. In B. H. Gottlieb (Ed.), *Marshalling social support* (pp. 305-329). Newbury Park, CA: Sage.

Crosby, F., Bromley, S., & Saxe, L. (1980). Recent unobstrusive studies of black and white discrimination and prejudice: A literature review. *Psychological Bulletin, 87*, 546-563.

Cutrona, C. E., & Russell, D. W. (1990). Type of social support and specific stress: Toward a theory of optimal matching. In I. G. Sarason, B. R. Sarason, & G. R. Pierce (Eds.), *Social support: An interactional view* (pp. 319-366). New York: Wiley.

Dakof, G. A., & Taylor, S. E. (1990). Recipient perceptions of social support: What is helpful from whom? *Journal of Personality and Social Psychology, 58*, 80-89.

Dunkel-Schetter, C. (1984). Social support and cancer: Findings based on patient interviews and their implications. *Journal of Social Issues, 40*(4), 77-98.

Dunkel-Schetter, C., & Bennett, T. L. (1990). Differentiating the cognitive and behavioral aspects of social support. In I. G. Sarason, B. R. Sarason, & G. R. Pierce (Eds.), *Social support: An interactional view* (pp. 267-296). New York: Wiley.

Dunkel-Schetter, C., Blasband, D., Feinstein, L., & Herbert, T. B. (in press). Elements of supportive social interactions: When are support attempts effective? In S. Spacapan & S. Oskamp (Eds.), *Helping and being helped in the real world.* Newbury Park, CA: Sage.

Dunkel-Schetter, C., Silver, R. C., & Wortman, C. B. (1988). *Self-perceptions and negative reactions following interactions between depressed and nondepressed college students.* Unpublished manuscript.

Dunkel-Schetter, C., & Skokan, L. A. (1990). Determinants of social support provision in personal relationships. *Journal of Social and Personal Relationships, 7,* 437-450.

Dunkel-Schetter, C., & Wortman, C. B. (1981). Dilemmas of social support: Parallels between victimization and aging In S. B. Kiesler, J. N. Morgan, & V. K. Oppenheimer (Eds.), *Aging: Social change* (pp. 349-381). New York: Academic Press.

Dunkel-Schetter, C., & Wortman, C. B. (1982). The interpersonal dynamics of cancer: Problems in social relationships and their impact on the patient. In H. S. Friedman & M. R. DiMatteo (Eds.), *Interpersonal issues in health care* (pp. 69-100). New York: Academic Press.

Fiore, J., Becker, J., & Coppel, D. B. (1983). Social network interactions: A buffer or a stress. *American Journal of Community Psychology, 11,* 423-437.

Freedman, J. L., & Doob, A. N. (1968). *Deviancy: The psychology of being different.* New York: Academic Press.

Goffman, E. (1963). *Stigma.* Englewood Cliffs, NJ: Prentice-Hall.

Gotlib, I. H., & Robinson, L. A. (1982). Responses to depressed individuals: Discrepancies between self-report and observer-rated behavior. *Journal of Abnormal Psychology, 91,* 231-240.

Gottlieb, B. H. (1978). The development and application of a classification scheme of informal helping behaviors. *Canadian Journal of Behavioral Science, 10,* 105-115.

Gottlieb, B. H. (in press). Stress and support processes in close relationships. In J. Eckenrode (Ed.), *The social context of stress.* New York: Plenum.

Gurtman, M. B. (1986). Depression and the response of others: Reevaluating the reevaluation. *Journal of Abnormal Psychology, 95,* 99-101.

Hammen, C. L., & Peters, S. D. (1978). Interpersonal consequences of depression: Responses to men and women enacting a depressed role. *Journal of Abnormal Psychology, 87,* 322-332.

Heller, K. (1979). The effects of social support: Prevention and treatment implications. In A. P. Goldstein & F. H. Kanfer (Eds.), *Maximizing treatment gains: Transfer enhancement in psychotherapy* (pp. 353-382). New York: Academic Press.

Herek, G. M., & Glunt, E. K. (1988). An epidemic of stigma: Public reactions to AIDS. *American Psychologist, 43,* 886-891.

Howes, M. J., & Hokanson, J. E. (1979). Conversational and social responses to depressive interpersonal behavior. *Journal of Abnormal Psychology, 88,* 625-634.

Jones, E. G., Farina, A., Hastorf, A. H., Markus, H., Miller, D. T., & Scott, R. A. (1984). *Social stigma: The psychology of marked relationships.* New York: Freeman.

Lehman, D. R., Ellard, J. H., & Wortman, C. B. (1986). Social support for the bereaved: Recipients' and providers' perspectives on what is helpful. *Journal of Consulting and Clinical Psychology, 54,* 438-446.

Lerner, M. J. (1971). Observer's evaluation of a victim: Justice, guilt, and veridical perception. *Journal of Personality and Social Psychology, 20,* 127-135.

Lerner, M. J., & Matthews, G. (1967). Reactions to suffering of others under conditions of indirect responsibility. *Journal of Personality and Social Psychology, 5,* 319-325.

Lerner, M. J., Miller, D. T., & Holmes, J. (1976). Deserving and the emergence of forms of justice. In L. Berkowitz & E. Walster (Eds.), *Advances in experimental social psychology* (pp. 134-162). New York: Academic Press.

Lerner, M. J., & Simmons, C. H. (1966). Observer's reactions to the "innocent victim": Compassion or rejection? *Journal of Personality and Social Psychology, 4,* 203-210.

Lichtman, R. R. (1982). *Close relationships after breast cancer.* Unpublished doctoral dissertation, University of California, Los Angeles.

Lichtman, R. R., & Taylor, S. E. (1986). Close relationships and the female cancer patient. In B. L. Anderson (Ed.), *Women with cancer: Psychological perspectives* (pp. 233-256). New York: Springer.

Lichtman, R. R., Taylor, S. E., Wood, J. V., Bluming, A. Z., Dosik, G. M., & Leibowitz, R. L. (1985). Relations with children after breast cancer: The mother-daughter relationship at risk. *Journal of Psychosocial Oncology, 2*(3/4), 1-19.

Manne, S. L., & Zautra, A. J. (1989). Spouse criticism and support: Their association with coping and psychological adjustment among women with rheumatoid arthritis. *Journal of Personality and Social Psychology, 56*, 608-617.

Meyerowitz, B. E., Yarkin-Levin, K., & Harvey, J. (1990). *On the nature of cancer patients' social interactions*. Manuscript submitted for publication.

Montada, L., & Figura, E. (1988). *Some psychological factors underlying the request for social isolation of AIDS victims* (Berichte aus der Arbeitsgruppe "Verantwortung, Gerechtigkeit, Moral" Nr. 50). Trier: Universität Trier, Fachbereich Psychologie.

Montada, L., & Schneider, A. (1988). *Justice and emotional reactions to victims*. (E.S.-Bericht Nr. 7 = Berichte aus der Arbeitsgruppe "Verantwortung, Gerechtigkeit, Moral" Nr. 47). Trier: Universität Trier, Fachbereich Psychologie.

Notarius, C. I., & Herrick. L. R. (1988). Listener response strategies to a distressed other. *Journal of Social and Personal Relationships, 5*, 97-108.

Pagel, M. D., Erdly, W. W., & Becker, J. (1987). Social networks: We get by with (and in spite of) a little help from our friends. *Journal of Personality and Social Psychology, 53*, 793-804.

Pearlin, L. I., & McCall, M. E. (in press). Occupational stress and marital support: A description of microprocesses. In J. Eckenrode & S. Gore (Eds.), *Stress between work and family*. New York: Plenum.

Pryor, J. B., Reeder, G. D., Vinacco, R., & Kott, T. L. (1989). The instrumental and symbolic functions of attitudes toward persons with AIDS. *Journal of Applied Social Psychology, 19*, 377-404.

Reisenzein, R. (1986). A structural equation analysis of Weiner's attribution-affect model of helping behavior. *Journal of Personality and Social Psychology, 50*, 1123-1133.

Robbins, B. P., Strack, S., & Coyne, J. C. (1979). Willingness to provide feedback to depressed persons. *Social Behavior and Personality, 7*, 199-203.

Rook, K. S. (1984). The negative side of social interaction: Impact on psychological well-being. *Journal of Personality and Social Psychology, 46*, 1097-1108.

Sacco, W. P., & Dunn, V. K. (1990). Effect of actor depression on observer attributions: Existence and impact of negative attributions toward the depressed. *Journal of Personality and Social Psychology, 59*, 517-524.

Sandler, I. N., & Barrera, M., Jr. (1984). Toward a multimethod approach to assessing the effects of social support. *American Journal of Community Psychology, 12*, 37-52.

Schmidt, G., & Weiner, B. (1988). An attribution-affect-action theory of behavior: Replications of judgements of help-giving. *Personality and Social Psychology Bulletin, 14*, 610-621.

Schwarzer, R., & Weiner, B. (in press). Disease-related stigmas causing attributions, emotions, and social support. *Journal of Social and Personal Relationships*.

Shaver, K. G. (1970). Defensive attribution: Effects of severity and relevance on the responsibility assigned for an accident. *Journal of Personality and Social Psychology, 14*, 101-113.

Shinn, M., Lehman, S., & Wong, N. W. (1984). Social interaction and social support. *Journal of Social Issues, 40*(4), 55-76.

Shumaker, S. A., & Brownell, A. (1984). Toward a theory of social support: Closing conceptual gaps. *Journal of Social Issues, 40*(4), 11-36.

Silver, R. C., & Wortman, C. B. (1980). Coping with undesirable life events. In J. Garber & M. E. Seligman (Eds.), *Human helplessness* (pp. 279-375). New York: Academic Press.

Silver, R. C., Wortman, C. B., & Crofton, C. (1990). The role of coping in support provision: The self-presentational dilemma of victims of life crises. In I. G. Sarason, B. R. Sarason, & G. R. Pierce (Eds.), *Social support: An interactional view* (pp. 397-426). New York: Wiley.

Solomon, S. D. (1986). Mobilizing social support networks in times of disaster. In C. R. Fisley (Ed.), *Trauma and its wake. Volume II: Traumatic stress theory, research, and intervention* (pp. 232-263). New York: Brunner/Mazel.

Strack, S., & Coyne, J. C. (1983). Social confirmation of dysphoria: Shared and private reactions to depression. *Journal of Personality and Social Psychology, 44*, 798-806.

Suls, J. (1982). Social support, interpersonal relations, and health: Benefits and liabilities. In G. S. Sanders & J. Suls (Eds.), *Social psychology of health and illness* (pp. 255-277). Hillsdale, NJ: Erlbaum.

Tempelaar, R., de Haes, J. C. J. M., de Ruiter, J. H., Bakker, D., van den Heuvel, W. J. A., & van Nieuwenhuijzen, M. G. (in press). The social experiences of cancer patients under treatment: A comparative study. *Social Science and Medicine*.

Walster, E. (1966). Assignment of responsibility for an accident. *Journal of Personality and Social Psychology, 3*, 73-79.

Weiner, B. (1980a). A cognitive (attributional)-emotion-action model of motivated behavior: An analysis of judgments of help-giving. *Journal of Personality and Social Psychology, 39*, 186-200.

Weiner, B. (1980b). May I borrow your class notes? An attributional analysis of judgments of help-giving in an achievement-related context. *Journal of Educational Psychology, 72*, 676-681.

Weiner, B. (1985). An attributional theory of achievement motivation and emotion. *Psychological Review, 92*, 548-573.

Weiner, B., Perry, R. P., & Magnusson, J. (1988). An attributional analysis of reactions to stigmas. *Journal of Personality and Social Psychology, 55*, 738-748.

Winer, D. L., Bonner, T. O., Blaney, P. H., & Murray, E. J. (1981). Depression and social attraction. *Motivation and Emotion, 5*, 153-166.

Wortman, C. B. (1976). Causal attributions and personal control. In J. H. Harvey, W. J. Ickes, & R. F. Kidd (Eds.), *New directions in attribution research* (pp. 23-52). Hillsdale, NJ: Erlbaum.

Wortman, C. B., & Dunkel-Schetter, C. (1979). Interpersonal relationships and cancer: A theoretical analysis. *Journal of Social Issues, 35*(1), 120-155.

Wortman, C. B., & Lehman, D. R. (1985). Reactions to victims of life crisis: Support attempts that fail. In I. G. Sarason & B. R. Sarason (Eds.), *Social support: Theory, research, and applications* (pp. 463-489). Dordrecht: Martinus Nijhoff.

Wortman, C. B., & Silver, R. C. (1987). Coping with irrevocable loss. In G. R. VandenBos & B. K. Bryant (Eds.), *Cataclysms, crises, and catastrophes: Psychology in action* (Master Lecture Series, Vol. 6, pp. 189-235). Washington, DC: American Psychological Association.

Methodological Comment

26 Quandary: Correlation Coefficients and Contexts[1]

Robyn M. Dawes
Carnegie Mellon University, Pittsburgh

In the mid-1970s, I was asked to consult with the Board of Directors of a local counter culture drug clinic in Eugene, Oregon. A precondition of its continued funding from public sources was that it make an "evaluation" of its impact on the community. My friends who worked at this clinic were quite concerned. They felt that they were performing an important service by staying with people who had overdosed, by providing members of the counter culture with information about the introduction of contaminated drugs into the area ("bad batches"), and by serving as a clearing house for more general information about the effects of various drugs. While there was some concern within the community that the clinic was promoting illegal drug use, and preventing people with drug problems from being "cured" through standard psychiatric and psychological treatment, the clinic had general community support; there were even several local doctors who volunteered as consultants, and who were on call whenever members of the clinic staff found somebody who had experienced a medically severe drug reaction. Aside from emergency situations, the standard operating procedure of the clinic was to make sure that somebody who experienced a problem with a drug had a place to stay where he or she could be monitored by people who had experienced a similar problem in the past—and who most often wiled away the time with the person by smoking pot.

At our meeting, we assessed the problem of evaluating impact on the community. This Eugene clinic was widely known in both southern Oregon and in northern

[1] I would like to express my gratitude to Leo Montada, to Sigrun-Heide Filipp, and to Melvin J. Lerner for providing the opportunity to attend the 1st International Conference on "Crises and Loss Experiences in the Adult Years" and for their gentle urgings that I complete this comment.

California, which had no other such clinics north of San Francisco. Our conclusion was that the most probable effect of the clinic on the community was to attract "heads" from northern California, thereby increasing the local drug problem. We decided not to attempt a precise evaluation of this impact, but instead to create "baseball statistics"—i.e., extensive records of the number of clients "treated" and the length of time they were seen. This type of evaluation was quite acceptable to the funders.

My best judgment was (and is) that the clinic performed a valuable service. Why, then, would the former evaluation of impact have most probably been negative? The reason is that the area was not saturated with such clinics. Had there been many nearby, the problem of attracting "heads" from northern California would not have arisen. It is tempting to frame this seemingly paradoxical effect in terms of "selective migration," or some other term. What I want this example to show, however, is a more general principle. The effect of a particular program or procedure is often determinated by factors outside it. Here, we have an extreme example: We hypothesize a negative impact on reducing the community rate of drug problems given one set of contextual conditions (no alternative clinics) while simultaneously hypothesizing a positive impact were another set of conditions to hold (alternative clinics available). That's a rather severe example of context dependence. What I want to argue in general, however, is that when we use basically correlational techniques to evaluate the effect of a particular factor in a particular context, we are simultaneously evaluating the effects of the other factors in that context—whether we wish to do so or not. This problem in exacerbated by the fact that many of these other factors are unobserved, or even unobservable. It also makes statistical inference extremely difficult, because our standard statistical evaluations (e.g., of whether a particular correlation is "significant," or "significantly greater than another," or an assessment of its magnitude through confidence intervals) are predicated on sampling from *a* population. Contexts, however, vary in meaningful ways that are not captured by standard measures of statistical variation—most often based on assumptions about distributions in the population from which we sample. (So, at best our statistical inference is context bound.) But is that what we want?

Let me give another example of this principle. Wicker (1971) conducted a widely-cited study in the relationship between religious attitudes and religious behaviors of 152 members of the United Methodist churches in Milwaukee, Wisconsin. His measures of religious attitude correlated on the average .27 with frequency of church attendance, .16 with amount of contribution, and .11 with holding responsible positions. He concluded (p. 27) that his attitude measures had "relatively low behavioral validity" for predicting behavior. Now consider what *else* will predict church attendance. First, whether or not one is a member at all is an excellent predictor. (By simply including an arbitrarily large number of atheists, he could undoubtedly have shown that his attitude measures had relatively *high* behavior validity.) Second, the weather in Wisconsin during the winter is not benign—and people will have varying attitudes about traveling in such weather.

Contribution, in contrast, is clearly effected by income—while holding responsible positions is affected not only by talent, experience, and age, but by the flexibility of working hours. In short, these low correlations may simply reflect the importance of the factors that Wicker *isn't* studying. The generalization problem arises because these factors may well be different in Pittsburgh, PA, and in Fort Lauderdale, FL, than they are in Milwaukee, WI; thus, it is not even possible to say that these correlations represent the *relative* "behavioral validity" of the attitudinal measures in any sense that is meant to be generalizeable across contexts.[2] In fact, as I've argued previously (Dawes & Smith, 1985), the low correlations purporting to demonstrate "inconsistency" between attitude and behavior all demonstrate a remarkable consistency: They are all positive. The same observation may be made of the studies attempting to show "situational specificity" of behavior; while low correlations are taken as evidence of the absence of general personality traits related to behavior across situations, the uniformly positive value of these correlations may be taken as evidence for their presence.[3]

As can also be seen in this volume, many people present correlation coefficients or mean differences to evaluate both the magnitude and the significance of the effect of the variables they study. There is even discussion of whether one particular variable—such as "productive thinking" has a higher correlation with an outcome variable of interest than does another particular variable. But at best few contexts can be studied, and when the magnitude of a particular effect is so vitally dependent on the magnitude of effects that we *don't* study in these contexts, generalization is extraordinarily dubious. Moreover, differences between study results—often the topic of hot "theoretical" debate—may be due simply to differences in these other effects in the different contexts sampled. In fact, it is even possible to argue that any variable that indeed has an effect would have a magnitude of effect reaching the limits of predictability (which may be far from perfect; see Dawes, 1979, 1988, in press) were it not for these other factors. So what are we discovering when we evaluate "the effect" of a particular loss, or of a particular coping style? How should we modify our research procedures?

First, I have a very concrete suggestion. Consider, for example, the effect of the sudden death of an infant child, or of taking care of a spouse or a parent with Alzheimer's. If caring about and caring for the other individual were the only ongoing activity in the life of the person affected, the magnitude of the effect would be enormous. Fortunately, that's not true. It follows that the magnitude of the effect

---

[2] Even neglecting "measurement error" or "misspecification," problems that make generalization yet more problematic.

[3] Alternatively, one may *define* the similarity of two situations in terms of the degree to which the independent variable of interest has the same correlation with the dependent variable—or (in the "traits versus situation controversy") in terms of the magnitude of the positive correlation between behaviors across people. There is, after all, no alternative broad conception of context similarity. Such a definition is circular, but it may not create a "vicious circle." (I have no basis for judging at this point of time.)

may best be predicted by studying factors that have absolutely nothing to do with the focal loss or caretaking problem. To be even more specific, note that the problems addressed have a negative quality. Could not the presence or absence of positive experiences outside the focal problem be an excellent predictor of well-being? Could not even these other factors play a more important role in the reaction of the problem than does the problem itself—or the attempts to "cope" with it? For those of us for whom the absence of pleasure (good) is less tolerable than the presence of pain (bad), these other—often unstudied—factors may be of overwhelming importance.

Second, I suggest that our real goal must be cross-situational generalization: consistency in our findings, rather than a standard evaluation of their magnitude or significance within a context. That's tough. What most people do when they present differences in correlations is to use the usual population/sample framework for evaluating them. What this framework assumes is random sampling form *a* population; we infer the shape of sampling distributions of various statistics on the basis of this assumption, and then make the "backward inference" to the population after observing a result that can be located in this sampling distribution—using either a classical hypothesis test or a Bayesian update. If all we wish to do is to evaluate effects in *this here setting right now*, then this standard model is quite good. It works well if we wish to apply our findings to a context we believe to be extraordinarily similar (but of course it is difficult to justify a judgment of "similarity," and in the flux of human behavior we have less reason for hypothesizing extraordinary similarity that we do in many physical sciences). If, however, we wish to make more general statements that will be true across contexts, we are in a bind. Here, "population" refers not just to people but to the characteristics of the context (again often unobserved), and to the chronological time at which we sample.

One solution is to consider ourselves to be sampling contexts, and then each correlation or effect becomes a *single* observation. The other crucial factors could then be conceptualized as random "noise." If we were to attempt to use standard statistical techniques in this framework, however, we come to the question of exactly what we would mean by a population of contexts. Unlike people, contexts are ill-defined. We know how to evaluate a claim of randomly sampling from a population of voters; we do not know very well how to verify that we have sampled from a population of representative contexts in which people must care for a spouse or parent with Alzheimer's, or even how we would define such a population denotatively. Consequently, we cannot sample from it in *any* specifiable way—let alone randomly. (Sampling requires a definition that can lead to a listing of set elements, even if their number is infinite.)

What we are left with is an attempt at inductive generalization for which we have very little analytic rationale. As in meta-analysis, we're often "mixing apples and oranges," in an unknown proportion, a proportion that doesn't have a strong correspondence to whatever the proportion is "in nature." My point, however, is that apples and oranges induction is exactly what we want to accomplish: i.e., reach generalization about fruit that are applicable to both apples and oranges.

Let me give an example from some of my own work (Dawes, Faust, & Meehl, 1989). Studies from a wide variety of contexts involving the synthesis of incomparable factors to predict human outcomes—such as staying out of jail on parole, successfully completing graduate or medical school, or behaving violently — uniformly indicate that an actuarial synthesis is superior to one based on the "clinical judgment" of experienced experts. One problem, however, is that there is no way to define the population of prediction tasks from which researchers sampled to reach this conclusion. (In fact, most researchers do exactly what I've outlined above: Assess magnitude and significance on the basis of the standard models as if the real question of interest was to make predictions only in this here context at this here point of time.) So how can we possibly justify a *general* statement about a relative efficacy of "clinical versus actuarial prediction." Our actual rationale is well-stated by Meehl (1986, p. 373): "There's no controversy in social science that shows such a large body of qualitatively diverse studies coming out uniformly in the same direction as this one [the relative validity of actuarial versus clinical prediction]. When you're pushing 90 investigations [now closer to 140], predicting everything from the outcome of football games to the diagnosis of liver disease, and you can hardly come up with a half-dozen studies showing even a weak tendency in favor of the clinician, it is time to draw a practical conclusion." A crucial phrase in this quote is "*qualitatively diverse studies*." I wish I could present a coherent analytic model that captures this notion, so that we could then treat each of our studies as a sample from the qualitative diversity in which we're interested—and subsequently reach generalizations unhampered by bias, preconception, selective choice, or selective recall. Unfortunately, I can't. I must, therefore, end this comment on a slightly negative note. The standard statistical model doesn't do it, and many of the statistics used provide very little help in achieving our real goal, which is to obtain generalization across "qualitatively diverse" contexts. On a more positive note, I'm impressed by the consistency of many of the findings reported in this volume across such contexts.

Many researchers find the above comments disturbing. What I am arguing is that ours is a statistically—rather than deterministically—based science in which low predictability is accepted as a norm. Worse yet, I am making this argument without even accepting the standard statistical model of sampling from a well-defined population. Are my comments merely expressing despair, or a rationalization for accepting quite seriously many of the low correlation coefficients found in work in this volume and other similar work? Surely, the argument runs, if we "really" knew a great deal about human behavior we could "really" predict it with far greater certainty.

One proposal for achieving greater predictability is to eschew main effects in the interests of interaction effects. This proposal is consistent with a "clinical" approach to problems, an approach based on the implicit assumption that by understanding enough factors in the individual case—together with their "complex" interactions—we can achieve an "understanding" of at least that case.

The first problem with this proposal is that it limits generality. Even if it is successful, it precludes generalization to other cases except to the degree to which they "match" the cases studied on all the variables involved in the interactions, and generalization based on matching—a form of "representative thinking" (see Dawes, 1986)—is in general inferior to generalization based on understanding the dimensions of a problem, how they are best coded, and how they are best combined *singly*. (For a justification of this assertion, see Dawes, 1988, Chapter 10, which both summarizes the empirical findings and provides a theoretical framework in which they are unsurprising.) The second problem is that this approach is not consistent with that used in an allied field—medicine—which has had considerable success in this century. While the individual medical practitioner may "tailor" treatment to the individual client, the scientific basis for many recommendations made in recent years has been established through the use of "randomized trials." In such trials, randomly chosen experimental and control groups are treated identically except for a *single* difference—e.g., injected with the Salk vaccine or with a salt water placebo, given a lumpectomy or a mastectomy—and then are compared (as "blindly" as possible) on outcome measures. The complex interactions with other relevant variables are treated as "noise." Moreover, while it is the individual patient who receives the vaccine or drug, or one type or another type of operation, the scientific basis for the recommendation is based of a generalization *from* the group results *to* this individual, a simple-minded generalization based on a "main effect." The context problem is not as important as in behavioral science, because we can assume a greater consistency of bodies across contexts than of behaviors, attitudes, and feelings. It is, however, there—as witnessed by the recent contradictory findings about the effects of immoderate coffee drinking, which are most recently ascribed (CBS News, 10/10/90) to the different contexts in which the studies are conducted, specifically to the degree to which they include a relatively high proportion of smokers who tend to drink more coffee than others in the sample.

Further, consider what an interaction effect looks like in the absence of a main effect. The interaction must be of a crossed nature, with the negative effect of some values of the moderating variables exactly balancing the positive effect of others. (Of course, the situation is symmetric; any of the effects may be considered as moderating the others in a situation involving interactions.) Not only is such balancing implausible on an apriori basis, but theories concerning moderation usually predict, in contrast, a monotone interaction—i.e., that an effect will be enhanced or diminished at various levels of another, not that its direction will be reversed (see Dawes, 1990). Crossed interactions are easy to hypothesize but very difficult to find. There are exceptions (e.g., Revelle, 1988), but they are rare. Thus, most interactions hypothesized entail main effects; consequently, even if we are concerned primarily with establishing such interactions, we must establish these main effects as well. The effects of social support in ameliorating symptoms of stress is a well-known example (Cohen & Wills, 1985). Simplified, the basic hypothesis is that people will experience symptoms following stress to the degree to which they have little social support; i.e., high social support "buffers" people against symptoms. That implies both a main effect for stress and one for social support, as well as an interaction. An absence of either of these main effects would imply a nonsensical pattern—e.g., that people with high social support experience symptoms in the absence of stress.

When main effects are not found, the argument is often made that their absence is due to unspecified interactions. That's "arguing from a vacuum" (Dawes, 1979), because these effects are hypothesized without being identified; the implicit premise is that the situation *must* be predictable, or that the main effect studied and found wanting *must* have some influence—once again without specification. This type of arguing from a vacuum is particularly prominent in the area of psychotherapy outcome, where the hoped-for main effects of therapist training or experience are not discovered (for a discussion, see Smith & Secrest, in press). Particularly in this context, the discovery of an interaction effect without a main one would not only be bizarre, but have implications that the apologists for the lack of a main effect might not like. It would mean that under certain conditions of any moderating variables established, the greater the training or experience of the therapist the *worse* the outcome.

We are back to main effect—across contexts. I would like to end by pointing out that the presence of these effects, however weak, can have profound implications. Let me return briefly to the clinical versus statistical prediction context. Consistent with all the other findings, Carroll, Wiener, Coates, Galegher, & Alibrio (1982) discovered that in a sample of 838 parolees in Pennsylvania, predictions of successful completion of parole were better made from a few simple background variables (e.g., number of convictions and number of prison violations) than from ratings of parole officer interviewers, despite the fact these interviewers had knowledge of these variables. The correlations were not large: .22 (significant) versus .06 (chance). The parole interviewers did a slightly better than chance job of predicting the seriousness of the offenses of those who did commit them ($r = .25$, $p < .05$), but past heroin use alone predicted with an $r = .45$ ($p < .001$). These results are not only consistent with the general findings in the clinical versus statistical prediction area, but with previous results in the area of predicting criminal behavior in particular (Gottfredson, Wilkins, & Hoffman, 1978). Now consider how much suffering of victims, and even of failed parolees, would be avoided cross the entire country if the better statistical prediction were used in place of the inferior judgment of the parole interviewers. (I also believe it to be more ethical, given it is someone else in an irrelevant context.) That would yield *roughly* a 10% improvement in prediction, perhaps much more if we hypothesize that there are many crimes parolees commit for which they are not apprehended. A 5% increase versus decrease in crime is not trivial!

Or consider two of the papers in this volume. Contrary to popular belief in the "stages of mourning," positive affect soon after a substantial loss may not be pathological, but in fact predictive of a favorable outcome (Wortman & Silver, this volume). Also, contrary to popular belief, attempting to find a "reason" for being a victim ("why me?") may be negatively rather than positively related to outcome (Frey, this volume). If these findings hold up across contexts (as does the importance of productive thinking), knowing of their existence could have a positive effect on the ability of people (with or without professional help) to cope with such loss and victimization, even though the magnitude of the effect may be quite small (especially because "expert" counselors at the present time may be urging the exact opposite). Moreover, further research oriented toward understanding these results could have an even more profound effect.

REFERENCES

Carroll, J. S., Wiener, R. L., Coates, D., Galegher, J., & Alibrio, J. J. (1982). Evaluation, diagnosis, and prediction in parole decision making. *Law and Society Review, 17*, 199-228.

Cohen, S., & Wills, T. A. (1985). Stress, social support, and the buffering hypothesis. *Psychological Bulletin, 98*, 310-357.

Dawes, R. M. (1979). The robust beauty of improper linear models. *American Psychologist, 34*, 571-582.

Dawes, R. M. (1986). *Representative thinking in clinical judgment*. Clinical Psychology Review, 6, *425-441*.

Dawes, R. M. (1988). *Rational choice in an uncertain world*. San Diego, CA: Harcourt, Brace, Jovanovich.

Dawes, R. M. (1990). Monotone interactions: It's even simpler than that. *Behavioral and Brain Sciences, 13*(1), 128-129.

Dawes, R. M. (in press). Probabilistic versus causal thinking. In D. Cicchetti & W. Grove (Eds.), *Thinking clearly about psychology: Essays in honor of Paul Everett Meehl*. Minnesota: University of Minnesota Press.

Dawes, R. M., & Smith, T. E. (1985). Attitude and opinion measurement. In G. Lindzey & E. Aronson (Eds.), *Handbook of social psychology* (Vol. I, pp. 509-566). New York: Random House.

Dawes, R. M., Faust, D., & Meehl, P. E. (1989). Clinical versus actuarial judgment. *Science, 243, 1668-1674*.

Gottfredson, D., Wilkins, L. T., & Hoffman, T. B. (1978). *Guideline for parole and sentencing*. Lexington, MA: Lexington Books.

Meehl, P.E. (1986). Causes and effects of my disturbing little book. *Journal of Personality Research, 50*, 370-375.

Revelle, W. (1988). Personality, motivation, and cognitive performance. In P. Ackerman & R. Cudeck (Eds.), *Learning and individual differences: Abilities, motivation, and methodology* (pp. 297-341). New York: Freeman.

Smith, B., & Sechrest, L. (in press). The treatment of aptitude x treatment interactions. *Journal of Consulting and Clinical Psychology*.

Wicker, A. W. (1971). An examination of the "other variables" explanation of attitude-behavior inconsistency. *Journal of Personality and Social Psychology, 19*, 18-30.

Author Index

Italics indicate reference pages.

F

G

K

L

M

Y

Z

Subject Index

For Product Safety Concerns and Information please contact our EU
representative GPSR@taylorandfrancis.com
Taylor & Francis Verlag GmbH, Kaufingerstraße 24, 80331 München, Germany

www.ingramcontent.com/pod-product-compliance
Ingram Content Group UK Ltd.
Pitfield, Milton Keynes, MK11 3LW, UK
UKHW022113190926
475702UK00013B/1415

* 9 7 8 1 1 3 8 9 9 5 4 1 3 *